Stanley Gibbons

GREAT BRITAIN
CONCISE
STAMP CATALOGUE

1995 Edition

Stanley Gibbons Ltd
London and Ringwood

By Appointment to Her Majesty The Queen
Stanley Gibbons Ltd., London
Philatelists

Published by **Stanley Gibbons Publications**
Editorial, Sales Offices and Distribution Centre:
5 Parkside, Christchurch Road, Ringwood,
Hants BH24 3SH

First Edition — May 1986
Second Edition — May 1987
Third Edition — May 1988
Fourth Edition — May 1989
Fifth Edition — May 1990
Sixth Edition — May 1991
Seventh Edition — May 1992
Eighth Edition — April 1993
Ninth Edition — April1994
Tenth Edition — April 1995

© Stanley Gibbons Ltd. 1995

ISBN: 0-85259-388-0

Item No. 2887 (95)

Origination by Stanley Gibbons Ltd., Ringwood, Hampshire. Made and Printed in Great Britain by Black Bear Press Limited, Cambridge.

THE GREAT BRITAIN CONCISE CATALOGUE

1995 Edition

The *Concise Catalogue*, now in its tenth year of publication, has rapidly established itself as an essential guide for the "one-country" collector of Great Britain.

The popularity of Great Britain stamps continues to grow — the *Concise Catalogue* supplies the information to enhance your collection.

The *Concise* listings are based on the Great Britain section of our *Part 1 (British Commonwealth) Catalogue*, but there is much more additional material within its pages:

- All issues from the Penny Black of 1840 to March 1995 including Regional, Postage Due, Official and Postal Fiscal stamps.
- All different stamp designs are illustrated.
- Every basic stamp listed, including those with different watermarks or perforations and those showing graphite lines or phosphor bands.
- Unmounted mint and mounted mint prices quoted for King Edward VII and King George V issues.
- Missing colours, missing embossing, watermark errors, imperforate errors and phosphor omitted varieties from those stamps normally issued with phosphor bands.
- Gutter Pairs and "Traffic light" Gutter Pairs listed in mint sets.
- First Day Covers for all Special Issues, definitives, Sponsored Booklet definitive panes and Regionals of the present reign. All British Post Office special First Day of Issue postmarks are illustrated and priced on cover.
- Post Office Picture Cards (PHQ cards) are priced as sets, both mint and used with First Day of Issue postmarks.
- Presentation, Collector and Gift Packs, including the scarce versions with foreign inscriptions.
- Quick-reference diagrams for listed Machin decimal booklet panes.
- Design Index for Commemorative and Special Stamps after the Philatelic Information Section.
- Machin and commemorative underprints given separate catalogue numbers.
- Post Office Yearbooks.
- Royal Mail Postage Labels priced in mint or used sets and on British Post Office First Day Covers.
- Wartime issues for the Channel Islands.
- Separate section for Post Office Stamp Booklets with dated editions of King George VI listed separately.
- Helpful introductory section providing definitions and guidance for the collector and including all watermark illustrations shown together to assist identification.
- Separate section for Postmaster and U.P.U. Specimen overprints.
- Addresses for specialist philatelic societies covering Great Britain stamps.
- Recently discovered errors and varieties listed. See Nos. 201d, 316Ei, 351b, 392a, 419c, 758c, 776b, 783b, 803f, 823a, 835a, X933a, X964a, 948j, 981b, **MS**1058e, **MS**1099j, 1268a, 1293a, 1359Ea, Y1700a, Y1701a, Y1748la, 1822ab, 1843a.

id J. Aggersberg

Stanley Gibbons Holdings Plc.

STANLEY GIBBONS LTD, STANLEY GIBBONS AUCTIONS

399 STRAND, LONDON WC2R 0LX

Auction Room and Specialist Departments. Open Monday–Friday, 9.30 a.m. to 5 p.m.

Shop: Open Monday–Friday 8.30 a.m. to 6 p.m. and Saturday 10 a.m. to 4.00 p.m.
Telephone 0171 836 8444 and Fax 0171 836 7342 for all departments.

STANLEY GIBBONS PUBLICATIONS

5 PARKSIDE, CHRISTCHURCH ROAD, RINGWOOD, HANTS BH24 3SH

Telephone 01425 472363 (24 hour answerphone service) and **Fax 01425 470247**
Publications Showroom (at above address). Open Monday–Friday 9.00 a.m. to 3.00 p.m.
Publications Mail Order. FREEPHONE 0800 611622 Monday–Friday 8.30 a.m. to 5.00 p.m.

URCH HARRIS & CO.,

1 DENMARK AVENUE, BRISTOL BS1 5HD

Monday–Friday 8.30 a.m. to 5 p.m.

For the Great Britain specialist collector . . .

Stanley Gibbons Great Britain Specialised Catalogue in five volumes. Recognised as leading publications of their kind, and spanning British stamp issues from the 1840s to the 1990s.

Item 0285 Volume 1 (Queen Victoria)
Item 0286 Volume 2 (King Edward VII to King George VI)
Item 2810 Volume 3 (Queen Elizabeth II Pre-decimal issues)
Item 2820 Volume 4 (Queen Elizabeth II Decimal Definitive issues)
Item 2891 Volume 5 (Queen Elizabeth II Decimal Special issues)

Great Britain Checklist

Printed in colour, published annually, this handy size checklist provides a clear update on GB stamp prices.

Item 0289 Collect British Stamps

For details of these and other S.G. Publications write to the Ringwood address for free Mail Order catalogue.

Great Britain Philatelic Societies

The Great Britain Philatelic Society. Hon. Membership Secretary: A. G. Lajer, P.O. Box 42, Henley on Thames, Oxon., RG9 1FF.

The British Decimal Stamps Study Circle. The Secretary: S. van Kimmenade, 99 Clay Bottom, Eastville, Bristol, Avon, BS5 7HB.

The Great Britain Decimal Stamp Book Study Circle. Hon. Membership Secretary: A. J. Wilkins, 3 Buttermere Close, Brierley Hill, West Midlands, DY5 3SD.

Contents

STANLEY GIBBONS PUBLICATIONS

OVERSEAS REPRESENTATION

Stanley Gibbons Publications are represented overseas by the following sole distributors (*), distributors (**) or licensees (***)

Australia
Lighthouse Philatelic (Aust.) Pty Ltd*
PO Box 763
Strawberry Hills
New South Wales 2012
Australia

Stanley Gibbons (Australia) Pty Ltd***
PO Box 863J
Melbourne 3001
Australia

Belgium and Luxembourg**
Davo
c/o Philac
Rue du Midi 48
Bruxelles 1000
Belgium

Canada*
Lighthouse Publications (Canada) Ltd
255 Duke Street
Montreal
Quebec
Canada H3C 2M2

Denmark**
Davo
c/o Lindner Falzlos
Gl Randersvej 28
8450 Hammel
Denmark

Finland**
Davo
c/o Suomen Postimerkkeily
Ludvingkatu 5
SF-00130 Helsinki
Finland

France*
Davo France (Casteilla)
10 Rue Leon Foucault
78184 St. Quentin Yvelines Cesex
France

Germany and Austria*
Leuchtturm Albenverlag
Paul Koch KG
Am Spakenberg 45
Postfach 1340
D-2054 Geesthacht
Germany

Hong Kong**
Po-on Stamp Service
GPO Box 2498
Hong Kong

Israel**
Capital Stamps
PO Box 3769
Jerusalem 91036
Israel

Italy*
Secrian Srl
Via Pantelleria 2
1-20156 Milano
Italy

Japan**
Japan Philatelic Co Ltd
PO Box 2
Suginami-Minami
Tokyo
Japan

Netherlands*
Davo Publications
PO Box 411
7400 AK Deventer
Netherlands

New Zealand*
Stanley Gibbons (New Zealand) Ltd
PO Box 80
Wellington
New Zealand

Norway**
Davo Norge A/S
PO Box 738 Sentrum
N-01 05 Oslo
Norway

Singapore*
Stanley Gibbons (Singapore)
Pte Ltd
Raffles City
PO Box 1689
Singapore 9117

South Africa
Philatelic Holdings (Pty) Ltd***
PO Box 930
Parklands
RSA 2121

Republic Coin and Stamp
Accessories (Pty) Ltd**
PO Box 11199
Johannesburg
RSA 2000

Sweden*
Chr Winther Sorensen AB
Box 43
S-310 Knaered
Sweden

Switzerland**
Phila Service
Burgstrasse 160
CH4125 Riehen
Switzerland

USA*
Lighthouse Publications Inc.
P.O. Box 705
274 Washington Avenue
Hackensack
New Jersey 07602-0705
USA

West Indies/Caribbean**
Hugh Dunphy
PO Box 413
Kingston 10
Jamaica
West Indies

PRICES

The prices quoted in this catalogue are the estimated selling prices of Stanley Gibbons Ltd at the time of publication. They are, *unless it is specifically stated otherwise*, for examples in fine condition for the issue concerned. Superb examples are worth more; those of a lower quality considerably less.

All prices are subject to change without prior notice and Stanley Gibbons Ltd may from time to time offer stamps below catalogue price in consequence of special purchases or particular promotions.

No guarantee is given to supply all stamps priced, since it is not possible to keep every catalogued item in stock.

Quotation of prices. The prices in the left-hand column are for unused stamps and those in the right-hand column are for used.

A dagger (†) denotes that the item listed does not exist in that condition and a blank, or dash, that it exists, or may exist, but no market price is known.

Prices are expressed in pounds and pence sterling. One pound comprises 100 pence (£1 = 100p).

The method of notation is as follows: pence in numerals (e.g. 5 denotes five pence); pounds and pence up to £100, in numerals (e.g. 4·25 denotes four pounds and twenty-five pence); prices above £100 expressed in whole pounds with the "£" sign shown.

Unused and Used stamps. The prices for unused stamps of Queen Victoria are for lightly hinged examples. Unused stamps of King Edward VII and King George V are priced in both unmounted and mounted condition. Unused prices for King Edward VIII to Queen Elizabeth II issues are for unmounted mint (though when not available, mounted mint stamps are often supplied at a lower price). Prices for used stamps are for postally used examples.

Prices quoted for bisects on cover or on large piece are for those dated during the period officially authorised.

Minimum price. The minimum price quoted is ten pence. This represents a handling charge rather than a basis for valuing common stamps, for which the 10p price should not be reckoned automatically, since it covers a variation in real scarcity.

Set prices. Set prices are generally for one of each value, excluding shades and varieties, but including major colour changes. Where there are alternative shades, etc., the cheapest is usually included. The number of stamps in the set is always stated for clarity.

The mint prices for sets containing *se-tenant* pieces are based on the prices quoted for such combinations, and not on those for individual stamps. The used set price is for single stamps.

Gutter Pairs. These, and traffic light gutter pairs, are priced as complete sets.

Used on Cover prices. To assist collectors, cover prices are quoted in a third column for postage and Official stamps issued in the reign of Queen Victoria and in boxed notes for King Edward VII and King George V stamps.

The cover should be of non-philatelic origin, bearing the correct postal rate for the period and distance involved and cancelled with the markings normal to the offices

concerned. Purely philatelic items have a cover value only slightly greater than the catalogue value for the corresponding used stamps. This applies generally to those high-value stamps used philatelically rather than in the normal course of commerce.

Oversized covers, difficult to accommodate on an album page, should be reckoned as worth little more than the corresponding value of the used stamps. The condition of a cover affects its value. Except for "wreck covers", serious damage or soiling reduce the value where the postal markings and stamps are ordinary ones. Conversely, visual appeal adds to the value and this can include freshness of appearance, important addresses, old-fashioned but legible handwriting, historic town-names, etc. The prices quoted are a base on which further value would be added to take account of the cover's postal historical importance in demonstrating such things as unusual, scarce or emergency cancels, interesting routes, significant postal markings, combination usage, the development of postal rates, and so on.

First Day Cover prices. Prices are quoted for commemorative first day covers from 1924 British Empire Exhibition pair onwards. These prices are for special covers (from 1937) franked with complete sets and cancelled by ordinary operational postmarks to the end of 1962 or the various standard "First Day of Issue" markings from 1963.

The Philatelic Bureau and other special "First Day of Issue" postmarks provided by the Post Office since 1963 are listed under each issue. Prices quoted are for these postmarks used on illustrated covers (from 1964 those produced by the Post Office), franked with complete sets.

The British Post Office did not introduce special First Day of Issue postmarks for definitive issues until the first instalment of the Machin £sd series, issued 5 June 1967, although "First Day" treatment had been provided for some Regional stamps from 8 June 1964 onwards. Prices for the First Day Covers from 1952 to 1966, showing definitive stamps are for the stamps indicated, used on illustrated envelopes and postmarked with operational cancellations.

From 1967 onwards the prices quoted are for stamps as indicated, used on illustrated envelopes and postmarked with special First Day of Issue handstamps. Other definitives issued during this period were not accepted for "First Day" treatment by the British Post Office.

Guarantee

All stamps are guaranteed genuine originals in the following terms:

If not as described, and returned by the purchaser, we undertake to refund the price paid to us in the original transaction. If any stamp is certified as genuine by the Expert Committee of the Royal Philatelic Society, London, or by B.P.A. Expertising Ltd, the purchaser shall not be entitled to make any claim against us for any error, omission or mistake in such certificate.

Consumers' statutory rights are not affected by the above guarantee.

The recognised Expert Committees in this country are those of the Royal Philatelic Society, 41 Devonshire Place, London W1N 1PE, and B.P.A. Expertising Ltd, P.O. Box 137, Leatherhead, Surrey KT22 0RG. They do not undertake valuations under any circumstances and fees are payable for their services.

CONTACTING THE CATALOGUE EDITOR

The Editor is always interested in hearing from people who have new information which will improve or correct the Catalogue. As a general rule he must see and examine the actual stamps before they can be considered for listing; photographs or photocopies are insufficent evidence.

Submissions should be made in writing to the Catalogue Editor, Stanley Gibbons Publications. The cost of return postage for items submitted is appreciated, and this should include the registration fee if required.

Where information is solicited purely for the benefit of the enquirer, the editor cannot undertake to reply if the answer is already contained in these published notes or if return postage is omitted. Written communications are greatly preferred to enquiries by telephone and the editor regrets that he or his staff cannot see personal callers without a prior appointment being made. Correspondence may be subject to delay during the production period of each new edition.

Please note that the following classes of material are outside the scope of this Catalogue:
(a) Non-postal revenue or fiscal stamps.
(b) Postage stamps used fiscally.
(c) Local carriage labels and private local issues.
(d) Punctured postage stamps (perfins).
(e) Telegraph stamps.
(f) Bogus or phantom stamps.
(g) Railway or airline letter fee stamps, bus or road transport company labels.
(h) Postal stationery cut-outs.
(i) All types of non-postal labels and souvenirs.
(j) Documentary labels for the postal service, e.g. registration, recorded delivery, airmail etiquettes, etc.
(k) Privately applied embellishments to official issues and privately commissioned items generally.
(l) Stamps for training postal staff.

> We regret we do not give opinions as to the genuineness of stamps, nor do we identify stamps or number them by our Catalogue.

Stanley Gibbons Stamp Collecting Series
A well illustrated series of handbooks, packed with essential information for all collectors.

Item 2760 Stamp Collecting: How to Start — Especially for the beginner. A clear outline of the basic elements.

Item 2762 Stamp Collecting: Collecting by Theme — Sound practical advice on how to form and develop a thematic collection, including an A–Z of collecting subjects.

Item 2766 The Stanley Gibbons Guide to Stamp Collecting — Based on the classic work by Stanley Phillips, thoroughly revised and updated by John Holman. Everything you need to know about stamp collecting.

GENERAL ABBREVIATIONS

Alph	Alphabet
Anniv	Anniversary
Brt	Bright (colour)
C,c	Chalky paper
C.	Overprinted in carmine
Des	Designer; designed
Dp	Deep (colour)
Eng	Engraver; engraved
Horiz	Horizontal; horizontally
Imp, Imperf	Imperforate
Inscr	Inscribed
L	Left
Litho	Lithographed
Lt	Light (colour)
mm	Millimetres
MS	Miniature sheet
O,o	Ordinary paper
Opt(d)	Overprint(ed)
P, Perf	Perforated
Photo	Photogravure
Pl	Plate
Pr	Pair
Ptd	Printed
Ptg	Printing
PVA	Polyvinyl alcohol (gum)
R	Right
R.	Row
Recess	Recess-printed
T	Type
Typo	Typographed
Un	Unused
Us	Used
Vert	Vertical; vertically
W or wmk	Watermark
Wmk s	Watermark sideways

(†) = Does not exist.
(—) (or blank price column) = Exists, or may exist, but no market price is known.
/ between colours means "on" and the colour following is that of the paper on which the stamp is printed.

PRINTERS

B.W.	Bradbury Wilkinson & Co, Ltd.
D.L.R.	De La Rue & Co, Ltd, London, and (from 1961) Bogota, Colombia.
Enschedé	Joh. Enschedé en Zonen, Haarlem, Netherlands.
Harrison	Harrison & Sons, Ltd, High Wycombe.
J.W.	John Waddington Security Print, Ltd, Leeds.
P.B.	Perkins Bacon Ltd, London.
Questa	Questa Colour Security Printers, Ltd.
Waterlow	Waterlow & Sons, Ltd, London.
Walsall	Walsall Security Printers, Ltd.

PHILATELIC INFORMATION

Catalogue Numbers

The catalogue number appears in the extreme left column. The boldface Type numbers in the next column are merely cross-reference to illustrations. Catalogue numbers in the *Gibbons Stamp Monthly* Supplements are provisional only and may need to be altered when the lists are consolidated.

Our Catalogue numbers are universally recognised in specifying stamps and as a hallmark of status.

Inverted and other watermark varieties incorporate "Wi", etc., within the number. Other items which appear in this Catalogue but not *Part 1 (British Commonwealth) Catalogue*, incorporate "Ea", etc.

Catalogue Illustrations

Stamps and first day postmarks are illustrated at three-quarters linear size. Stamps not illustrated are the same size and format as the value shown, unless otherwise indicated. Overprints, surcharges and watermarks are normally actual size. Illustrations of varieties are often enlarged to show the detail. Illustrations of miniature sheets are half linear size and their dimensions, in millimetres, are stated with the width given first.

Designers

Designers' names are quoted where known, though space precludes naming every individual concerned in the production of a set. In particular, photographers supplying material are usually named only when they also make an active contribution in the design stage; posed photographs of reigning monarchs are, however, an exception to this rule.

Printing Errors

Errors in printing are of major interest to this Catalogue. Authenticated items meriting consideration would include: background, centre or frame inverted or omitted; centre or subject transposed; error of colour; error or omission of value; double prints and impressions; printed both sides; and so on. Designs *tête-bêche*, whether intentionally or by accident, are listable. Colours only partially omitted are not listed. However, stamps with embossing, phosphor or both omitted and stamps printed on the gummed side are included.

Printing technology has radically improved over the years, during which time photogravure and lithography have become predominant. Varieties nowadays are more in the nature of flaws which are almost always outside the scope of this book.

In no catalogue, however, do we list such items as: dry prints, kiss prints, doctor-blade flaws, colour shifts or registration flaws (unless they lead to the complete omission of a colour from an individual stamp), lithographic ring flaws, and so on. Neither do we recognise fortuitous happenings like paper creases or confetti flaws.

Paper Types

All stamps listed are deemed to be on "ordinary" paper of the wove type and white in colour; only departures from this are normally mentioned.

A coloured paper is one that is coloured right through (front and back of the stamp). In the Catalogue the colour of the paper is given in *italics*, thus:

purple/yellow = purple design on yellow paper.

Papers have been made specially white in recent years by, for example, a very heavy coating of chalk. We do not classify shades of whiteness of paper as distinct varieties.

The availability of many postage stamps for revenue purposes made necessary some safeguard against the illegitimate re-use of stamps with removable cancellations. This was at first secured by using fugitive inks and later by printing on chalky (chalk-surfaced) paper, both of which made it difficult to remove any form of obliteration without also damaging the stamp design. We have indicated the existence of the papers by the letters "**O**" (ordinary) and "**C**" (chalky) after the description of all stamps where the chalky paper may be found. Where no indication is given the paper is "ordinary".

Our chalky paper is specifically one which shows a black mark when touched with a silver wire. Stamps on chalk-surfaced paper can easily lose this coating through immersion in water.

Perforation Measurement

The gauge of a perforation is the number of holes in a length of 2 cm.

The Gibbons *Instanta* gauge is the standard for measuring perforations. The stamp is viewed against a dark background with the transparent gauge put on top of it. Though the gauge measures to decimal accuracy, perforations read from it are generally quoted in the Catalogue to the nearest half. For example:

Just over perf $12\frac{3}{4}$ to just under $13\frac{1}{4}$ = perf 13
Perf $13\frac{1}{4}$ exactly, rounded up   = perf $13\frac{1}{2}$
Just over perf $13\frac{1}{4}$ to just under $13\frac{3}{4}$ = perf $13\frac{1}{2}$
Perf $13\frac{3}{4}$ exactly, rounded up   = perf 14

However, where classification depends on it, actual quarter-perforations are quoted. Perforations are usually abbreviated (and spoken) as follows, though sometimes they may be spelt out for clarity.

P 14: perforated alike on all sides (read: "perf 14").

P 14 x 15: the first figure refers to top and bottom, the second to left and right sides (read: "perf 14 by 15"). This is a compound perforation.

Such headings as "*P* 13 x 14 (*vert*) and *P* 14 x 13 (*horiz*)" indicate which perforations apply to which stamp format—vertical or horizontal.

From 1992 onwards most definitive and greetings stamps from both sheets and booklets occur with a large elliptical (oval) hole inserted in each line of vertical perforations as a security measure. The £10 definitive, No. 1658, is unique in having two such holes in the horizontal perforations.

Elliptical Perforations

Perforation Errors

Authenticated errors, where a stamp normally perforated is accidentally issued imperforate, are listed provided no traces of perforations (blind holes or indentations) remain. They must be provided as pairs, both stamps wholly imperforate, and are only priced in that form.

Numerous part-perforated stamps have arisen from the introduction of the Jumelle Press. This has a rotary perforator with rows of pins on one drum engaging with holes on another. Engagement is only gradual when the perforating unit is started up or stopped, giving rise to perforations "fading out", a variety mentioned above as not listed.

Stamps from the Jumelle printings sometimes occur imperforate between stamp and sheet margin. Such errors are not listed in this catalogue, but are covered by the volumes of the *Great Britain Specialised Catalogue*.

Pairs described as "imperforate between" have the line of perforations between the two stamps omitted.

Imperf between (*horiz pair*): a horizontal pair of stamps with perfs all around the edges but none between the stamps.

Imperf between (*vert pair*): a vertical pair of stamps with perfs all around the edges but none between the stamps.

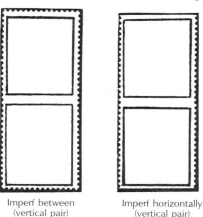

Imperf between
(vertical pair)

Imperf horizontally
(vertical pair)

Where several of the rows have escaped perforation the resulting varieties are listable. Thus:

Imperf vert (horiz pair): a horizontal pair of stamps perforated at top and bottom; all three vertical directions are imperf—the two outer edges and between the stamps.

Imperf horiz (vert pair): a vertical pair perforated at left and right edges; all three horizontal directions are imperf—the top, bottom and between the stamps.

Varieties of double, misplaced or partial perforation caused by error or machine malfunction are not listable, neither are freaks, such as perforations placed diagonally from paper folds, nor missing holes caused by broken pins.

Phosphor Issues

Machines which sort mail electronically have been introduced progressively and the British Post Office issued the first stamps specially marked for electronic sorting in 1957. This first issue had easily visible graphite lines printed on the back beneath the gum (see Nos. 561/6). They were issued in the Southampton area where the experiment was carried out.

The graphite lines were replaced by phosphor bands, activated by ultra-violet light. The bands are printed on the front of the stamps and show as a matt surface against the usual smooth or shiny appearance of the untreated surface of the paper. The bands show clearly in the top or bottom horizontal margins of the sheet.

The first phosphor issues appeared in 1959 (see Nos. 599/609) and these stamps also had graphite lines on the back. Further details will be found in the listings above No. 599 and 619. From 1962 onwards most commemoratives were issued in versions with or without bands. From 1967 all commemorative stamps had phosphor bands, but from 1972 they were replaced by "all-over" phosphor covering the entire area of the stamp.

After a considerable period of development a special paper was produced in which the phosphor had been incorporated into the coating. From 15 August 1979 phosphorised paper was accepted for use generally, this paper replacing phosphor bands on most issues for all values except the second class letter rate. Phosphorised paper can only be identified by ultra-violet light. The Stanley Gibbons Uvitec Micro ultra-violet lamp is firmly recommended for use in identifying the phosphor stamps listed in this Catalogue. *Warning*. Never stare at the lighted lamp but follow the manufacturer's instructions.

During the years 1967 to 1972, when all issues, except the high values, should have shown phosphor bands, a number of stamps appeared with them omitted in error. These varieties are listed in this Catalogue. Stamps with "all-over" phosphor omitted can only be detected by the use of an ultra-violet lamp and these varieties are listed in the Stanley Gibbons *Great Britain Specialised Catalogue*. Note that prices are for unmounted mint examples only. Varieties such as double bands, misplaced or printed on the back are not listed in this Catalogue.

Gum Description

All stamps listed are assumed to have gum of some kind and original gum (o.g.) means that which was present on the stamp as issued to the public. Deleterious climates and the presence of certain chemicals can cause gum to crack and, with early stamps, even make the paper deteriorate. Unscrupulous fakers are adept in removing it and regumming the stamp to meet the unreasoning demand often made for "full o.g." in cases where such a thing is virtually impossible.

The gum normally used on stamps has been gum arabic until the late 1960's when synthetic adhesives were introduced. Harrison and Sons Ltd for instance use *polyvinyl alcohol*, known to philatelists as PVA (see note above SG723).

Colour Identification

The 200 colours most used for stamp identification are given in the Stanley Gibbons Stamp Colour Key. The Catalogue has used the Colour Key as a standard for describing new issues for some years. The names are also introduced as lists are rewritten, though exceptions are made for those early issues where traditional names have become universally established.

In compound colour names the second is the predominant one, thus:

orange-red = a red tending towards orange.

red-orange = an orange containing more red than usual.

When comparing actual stamps with colour samples in the Colour Key, view in a good north daylight (or its best substitute: fluorescent "colour-matching" light). Sunshine is not recommended. Choose a solid portion of the stamp design; if available, marginal markings such as solid bars of colour or colour check dots are helpful. Shading lines in the design can be misleading as they appear lighter than solid colour. Furthermore, the listings refer to colours as issued: they may deteriorate into something different through the passage of time.

Shades are particularly significant when they can be linked to specific printings. In general, shades need to be quite marked to fall within the scope of this Catalogue.

Modern colour printing by lithography is prone to marked differences of shade, even within a single run, and variations can occur within the same sheet. Such shades are not listed.

Errors of Colour

Major colour errors in stamps or overprints which qualify for listing are: wrong colours; albinos (colourless impressions), where these have Expert Committee certificates; colours completely omitted, but only on unused stamps (if found on used stamps the information is usually footnoted) and with good credentials, missing colours being frequently faked.

Colours only partially omitted are not recognised. Colour shifts, however spectacular, are not listed.

Booklet Stamps

Single stamps from booklets are listed if they are distinguishable in some way (such as watermark or phosphor bands) from similar sheet stamps.

Booklet Pane with Printed Labels   *Se-tenant* Pane of Four

Booklet panes are listed where they contain stamps of different denominations *se-tenant*, where stamp-size printed labels are included, or where such panes are otherwise identifiable. Booklet panes are placed in the listing under the lowest denomination present.

In the listing of complete booklets the numbers and prefix letters are the same as used in the Stanley Gibbons *Great Britain Specialised Catalogue*.

Coil Stamps

Stamps only issued in coil form are given full listing. If stamps are issued in both sheets and coils, the coil stamps are listed separately only where there is some feature (e.g. watermark sideways or gum change) by which single stamps can be distinguished. Coil strips containing different values *se-tenant* are also listed.

Multi-value Coil Strip

Coil join pairs are generally too random and easily faked to permit listing; similarly ignored are coil stamps which have accidentally suffered an extra row of perforations from the claw mechanism in a malfunctioning vending machine.

Gutter Pairs

In 1988 the recess-printed Castle high value definitives were issued in sheets containing four panes separated by a gutter margin. All modern Great Britain commemoratives and special stamps are produced in sheets containing two panes separated by a blank horizontal or vertical margin known as a gutter. This feature first made its appearance on some supplies of the 1972 Royal Silver Wedding 3p and marked the introduction of Harrison & Sons' new "Jumelle" stamp-printing press. There are advantages for both the printer and the Post Office in such a layout which has been used for most commemorative issues since 1974.

The term "gutter pair" is used for a pair of stamps separated by part of the blank gutter margin as illustrated below.

Most printers include some form of colour check device on the sheet margins, in addition to the cylinder or plate numbers. Harrison & Sons use round "dabs", or spots of colour, resembling traffic lights. For the period from the 1972 Royal Silver Wedding until the end of 1979 these colour dabs appeared in the gutter margin. There was always one example to every double pane sheet of stamps. They can also be found in the high value Machin issue printed in photogravure. Gutter pairs showing these "traffic lights" are worth considerably more than the normal version.

Gutter Pair   Traffic Light Gutter Pair

Miniature Sheets

A miniature sheet contains a single stamp or set with wide inscribed or decorated margins. The stamps usually also exist in normal sheet format. This Catalogue lists, with **MS** prefix, complete miniature sheets which have been issued by the Post Office and which are valid for postal purposes.

Miniature Sheet containing a set of stamps

Se-tenant Combinations

Se-tenant means "joined together". Some sets include stamps of different design arranged *se-tenant* as blocks or strips and, in mint condition, these are usually collected unsevered as issued. Such *se-tenant* combinations are supplied in used condition at a premium over the used prices of the individual stamps. See also the note on Set Prices.

Specimen Stamps

Stamps of Great Britain overprinted "SPECIMEN" for circulation to postmasters and the Universal Postal Union are listed in a special section following the Postal Fiscal stamps. For other "SPECIMEN" overprints see Stanley Gibbons *Great Britain Specialised Catalogue.*

Presentation and Souvenir Packs

Special Packs comprising slip-in cards with printed commemorative inscriptions and notes on the back and with protective covering, were introduced in 1964 for the Shakespeare issue. Definitive issues first appeared in Presentation Packs in 1960. Notes will be found in the listings to describe souvenir books issued on special occasions.

Issues of 1968–1969 (British Paintings to the Prince of Wales Investiture) were also issued in packs with text in German for sale through the Post Office's German Agency and these are also included.

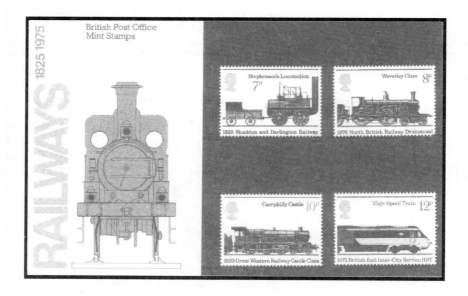

13 August 1975 Public Railways Presentation Pack

Collectors packs, first called gift packs, containing commemoratives issued in the preceding twelve months, first appeared in 1967. These are listed and priced.

Yearbooks

Special Post Office Yearbooks were first available in 1984. They contain all of the commemorative issues for one year in a hardbound book, illustrated in colour complete with slip case. These are listed and priced.

Commemorative First Day Covers

Until 1963 the Post Office did not provide any special first day of issue postmark facilities for collectors. Several philatelic organisations and stamp dealers did produce pictorial covers for the various commemorative issues and collectors serviced these to receive ordinary operational postmarks. Occasionally a special handstamp was produced which coincided with a new stamp issue, or relevant slogan postmarks, like the 1953 "Long Live the Queen" type, were in general use at the time.

On 21 March 1963 the Post Office installed special posting boxes at eleven main post offices so that collectors could obtain "uniformly high standard" impressions, from normal operational postmarks, for their first day covers. From 7 May 1963 special "First Day of Issue" slogans (Type A) were applied to mail posted in these special boxes, whose number had, by then, risen to thirty. The Philatelic Bureau accepted orders by post for such covers from the issue of 16 May 1963 onwards.

The slogan type was replaced on 23 April 1964 by "First Day of Issue" handstamps (Type B). These were, initially, of considerable size, but were later replaced by smaller versions (Type C) which remain in service today at nearly 200 principal offices. From 1970 the Bureau postmarks as Type C were inscribed "British Philatelic Bureau".

Since 1972 the Post Office has provided for virtually all issues an "alternative" pictorial "First Day of Issue" cancellation, additional to that of the Philatelic Bureau, at a town connected with the issue. Being available from the Bureau, these cancellations are illustrated and listed in this catalogue.

From time to time "First Day of Issue" postmarks, of standard or pictorial type, have been provided on a "one-off" basis for places linked to particular stamp issues, e.g. Weymouth for 1975 Sailing set. Such postmarks, which are not available from the Bureau, are footnoted.

Local pictorial "First Day of Issue" postmarks featuring Durham Cathedral, the City badge, and the Giant's Causeway with Edinburgh Castle have been provided on a regular basis at Durham, City of London EC and Glasgow since 1988, 1989 and 1993 respectively. (A similar postmark showing the Tyne Bridge was provided for Newcastle upon Tyne, 1992-94.) In addition pictorial "First Day of Issue" postmarks for "London" (no postal district shown) were introduced in 1993 with the design changing for each issue. Such postmarks are available from the appropriate Special Handstamp Centre, not the Bureau, so are not included in this catalogue.

Royal Mail established Special Handstamp Centres in 1990 where all sponsored special handstamps and many "First Day of Issue" postmarks are now applied.

Type A. First Day of Issue Slogan **Type B.** Large Handstamp **Type C.** Small Handstamp

Type D. Maltese Cross **Type E** **Type F.** £ Sign

Type G. Three Lions **Type H.** Four Castles **Type I.** Windsor Keep

PHQ Cards

From 1973 the Post Office produced sets of picture cards to accompany commemorative issues which can be sent through the post as postcards. Each card shows an enlarged colour reproduction of one stamp, initially of a single value from one set and subsequently of all values. The Post Office gives each card a "PHQ" serial number, hence the term. The cards are usually on sale shortly before the date of issue of the stamps, but there is no officially designated "first day".

PHQ Card cancelled on First Day of Issue

Cards are priced in fine mint condition for complete sets as issued. Used prices are for cards franked with the stamp affixed, on the obverse, as illustrated above, or reverse; the stamp being cancelled with an official postmark for first day of issue.

Watermark Types

Stamps are on unwatermarked paper except where the heading to the set states otherwise.

Watermarks are detected for Catalogue description by one of four methods: (1) holding stamps to the light; (2) laying stamps face down on a dark background; (3) by use of the Morley-Bright Detector, which works by revealing the thinning of the paper at the watermark; or (4) by the more complex electric watermark detectors such as the Signoscope.

The diagram below shows how watermark position is described in the Catalogue. Watermarks are usually impressed so that they read normally when looked through from the printed side. However, since philatelists customarily detect watermarks by looking at the back of the stamp, the watermark diagram also makes clear what is actually seen. Note that "G v R" is only an example and illustrations of the different watermarks employed are shown in the listings. The illustrations are actual size and shown in normal positions (from the front of the stamps).

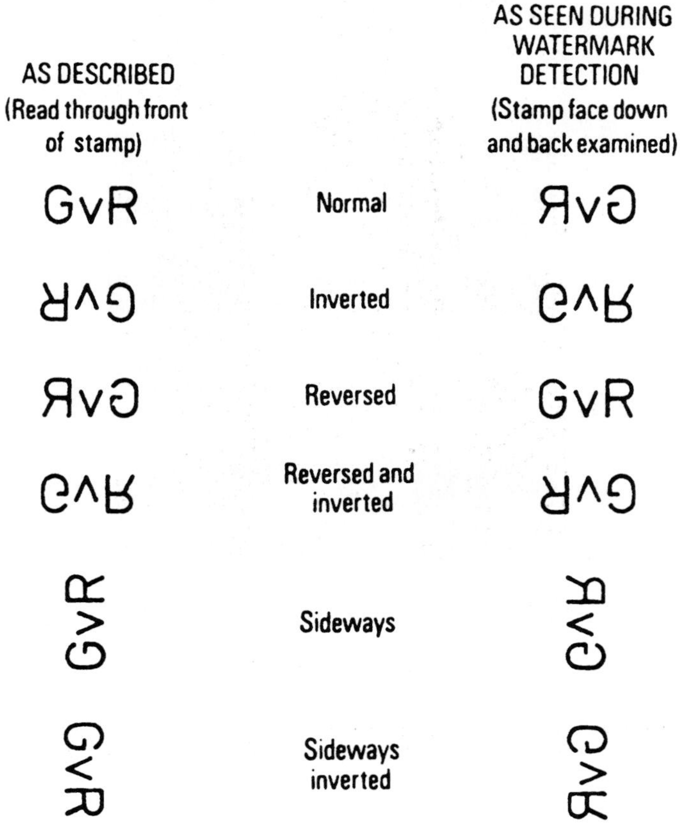

AS DESCRIBED (Read through front of stamp)		AS SEEN DURING WATERMARK DETECTION (Stamp face down and back examined)
GvR	Normal	ЯvᎮ
Яʌϱ	Inverted	ϱʌЯ
ЯvᎮ	Reversed	GvR
ϱʌЯ	Reversed and inverted	Яʌϱ
GvR (sideways)	Sideways	ϱʌЯ (sideways)
GvR (sideways)	Sideways inverted	Яvϱ (sideways)

General Types of watermark as seen through the front side of the stamp.

2 Small Crown

4 Large Crown

9 (Extends over three stamps)

13 V R

15 Small Garter

16 Medium Garter

17 Large Garter

20 Emblems

33 Spray of Rose

39 Maltese Cross

40 Large Anchor

47 Small Anchor

48 Orb

49 Imperial Crown

100 Simple Cypher

103 Multiple Cypher

110 Single Cypher

111 Block Cypher

117 PUC £1

125 E8R

127

133

153 Tudor Crown

Postal Fiscals

165 St. Edward's Crown

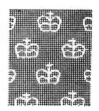

179 Multiple Crowns

F5 Double-lined Anchor

F6 Single-lined Anchor

Watermark Errors and Varieties

Watermark errors are recognised as of major importance. They comprise stamps showing the wrong watermark devices or stamps printed on paper with the wrong watermark. Stamps printed on paper showing broken or deformed bits on the dandy roll, are not listable.

Underprints

From 1982 various values appeared with underprints, printed on the reverse, in blue, over the gum. These were usually from special stamp booklets, sold at a discount by the Post Office, but in 1985 surplus stocks of such underprinted paper were used for other purposes.

In this Catalogue stamps showing underprints are priced mint only. Used examples can be obtained, but care has to be taken in floating the stamps since the ink employed to print the device is solvent in water.

Underprint Types

1 Star with central dot

2 Double-lined Star

3 Double-lined "D"

4 Multiple double-lined Stars

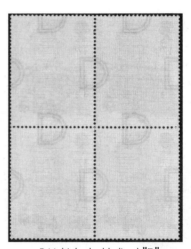

5 Multiple double-lined "D"

*(Types **4/5** are shown $\frac{3}{4}$ actual size)*

Note: Types **4/5** are arranged in a random pattern so that the stamps from the same sheet or booklet pane will show the underprint in a slightly different position to the above. Stamps, when inspected, should be placed the correct way up, face down, when comparing with the illustrations.

COMMEMORATIVE DESIGN INDEX

This index gives an easy reference to the inscriptions and designs of the Special Stamps 1953 to March 1995. Where a complete set shares an inscription or type of design, then only the catalogue number of the first stamp is given in addition to separate entries for stamps depicting popular thematic subjects. Paintings, inventions, etc., are indexed under the name of the artist or inventor, where this is shown on the stamp.

1. £.s.d. ISSUES 1953–70

Commemorative Design Index

Commemorative Design Index

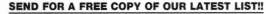

UNITED KINGDOM OF GREAT BRITAIN AND IRELAND

QUEEN VICTORIA

20 June 1837-22 January 1901

MULREADY ENVELOPES AND LETTER SHEETS, so called from the name of the designer, William Mulready, were issued concurrently with the first British adhesive stamps.

1d. black

Envelopes: . . . . . . £125 *unused*; £190 *used*.
Letter Sheets: . . . £110 *unused*; £160 *used*.

2d. blue

Envelopes: . . . . . . £200 *unused*; £600 *used*.
Letter Sheets: . . . £175 *unused*; £575 *used*.

LINE-ENGRAVED ISSUES

GENERAL NOTES

Brief notes on some aspects of the line-engraved stamps follow, but for further information and a full specialist treatment of these issues collectors are recommended to consult Volume 1 of the Stanley Gibbons *Great Britain Specialised Catalogue*.

Alphabet I   Alphabet II

Alphabet III   Alphabet IV

Typical Corner Letters of the four Alphabets

Alphabets. Four different styles were used for the corner letters on stamps prior to the issue with letters in all four corners, these being known to collectors as:
Alphabet I. Used for all plates made from 1840 to the end of 1851. Letters small.
Alphabet II. Plates from 1852 to mid-1855. Letters larger, heavier and broader..
Alphabet III. Plates from mid-1855 to end of period. Letters tall and more slender.
Alphabet IV. 1861. 1d. Die II, Plates 50 and 51 only. Letters were hand-engraved instead of being punched on the plate. They are therefore inconsistent in shape and size but generally larger and outstanding.
While the general descriptions and the illustrations of typical letters given above may be of some assistance, only long experience and published aids can enable every stamp to be allocated to its particular Alphabet without hesitation, as certain letters in each are similar to those in one of the others.

Blued Paper. The blueing of the paper of the earlier issues is believed to be due to the presence of prussiate of potash in the printing ink, or in the paper, which, under certain conditions, tended to colour the paper when the sheets were damped for printing. An alternative term is bleuté paper.

Corner Letters. The corner letters on the early British stamps were intended as a safeguard against forgery, each stamp in the sheet

having a different combination of letters. Taking the first 1d. stamp, printed in 20 horizontal rows of 12, as an example, the lettering is as follows:

Row 1.   A A, A B, A C, etc. to A L.

Row 2.   B A, B B, B C, etc. to B L.

and so on to

Row 20.   T A, T B, T C, etc. to T L.

On the stamps with four corner letters, those in the upper corners are in the reverse positions to those in the lower corners. Thus in a sheet of 240 (12 × 20) the sequence is:

Row 1.   A A B A C A   etc. to   L A
          A A A B A C   A L

Row 2.   A B B B C B   etc. to   L B
          B A B B B C   B L

and so on to

Row 20.   A T B T C T   etc. to   L T
           T A T B T C   T L

Placing letters in all four corners was not only an added precaution against forgery but was meant to deter unmarked parts of used stamps being pieced together and passed off as an unused whole.

Dies. The first die of the 1d. was used for making the original die of the 2d., both the No Lines and White Lines issues. In 1855 the 1d. Die I was amended by retouching the head and deepening the lines on a transferred impression of the original. This later version, known to collectors as Die II, was used for making the dies for the 1d. and 2d. with letters in all four corners and also for the 1½d.

The two dies are illustrated above No. 17 in the catalogue.

Double letter   Guide line in corner

Guide line through value

Double Corner Letters. These are due to the workman placing his letter-punch in the wrong position at the first attempt, when lettering the plate, and then correcting the mistake; or to a slight shifting of the punch when struck. If a wrong letter was struck in the first instance, traces of a wrong letter may appear in a corner in addition to the correct one. A typical example is illustrated.

Guide Lines and Dots. When laying down the impressions of the design on the early plates, fine vertical and horizontal guide lines were marked on the plates to assist the operative. These were usually removed from the gutter margins, but could not be removed from the stamp impression without damage to the plate, so that in such cases they appear on the printed stamps, sometimes in the corners, sometimes through "POSTAGE" or the value. Typical examples are illustrated.
Guide dots or cuts were similarly made to indicate the spacing of the guide lines. These too sometimes appear on the stamps.

Ivory Head

"Ivory Head". The so-called "ivory head" variety is one in which the Queen's Head shows white on the back of the stamp. It arises from the comparative absence of ink in the head portion of the design, with consequent absence of blueing. (See "Blued Paper", on page 1).

Line-engraving. In this context "line-engraved" is synonymous with recess-printing, in which the engraver cuts recesses in a plate and printing (the coloured areas) is from these recesses. "Line-engraved" is the traditional philatelic description for these stamps; other equivalent terms found are "engraving in *taille-douce*" (French) or "in *intaglio*" (Italian).

Plates. Until the introduction of the stamps with letters in all four corners, the number of the plate was not indicated in the design of the stamp, but was printed on the sheet margin. By long study of identifiable blocks and the minor variation in the design, coupled with the position of the corner letters, philatelists are now able to allot many of these stamps to their respective plates. Specialist collectors often endeavour to obtain examples of a given stamp printed from its different plates and our catalogue accordingly reflects this depth of detail.

Maltese Cross   Type of Town postmark

Type of Penny Post cancellation

Example of 1844 type postmark

Postmarks. The so-called "Maltese Cross" design was the first employed for obliterating British postage stamps and was in use from 1840 to 1844. Being hand-cut, the obliterating stamps varied greatly in detail and some distinctive types can be allotted to particular towns or offices. Local types, such as those used at Manchester, Norwich, Leeds, etc., are keenly sought. A red ink was first employed, but was superseded by black, after some earlier experiments, in February 1841. Maltese Cross obliterations in other colours are rare.

Obliterations of this type, numbered 1 to 12 in the centre, were used at the London Chief Office in 1843 and 1844.

Some straight-line cancellations were in use in 1840 at the Penny Post receiving offices, normally applied on the envelope, the adhesives then being obliterated at the Head Office. They are nevertheless known, with or without Maltese Cross, on the early postage stamps.

In 1842 some offices in S.W. England used dated postmarks in place of the Maltese Cross, usually on the back of the letter since they were not originally intended as obliterators. These town postmarks have likewise been found on adhesives.

In 1844 the Maltese Cross design was superseded by numbered obliterators of varied type, one of which is illustrated. They are naturally comparatively scarce on the first 1d. and 2d. stamps. Like the Maltese Cross they are found in various colours, some of which are rare.

Re-entry

"Union Jack" re-entry

Re-entries. Re-entries on the plate show as a doubling of part of the design of the stamp generally at top or bottom. Many re-entries are very slight while others are most marked. A typical one is illustrated.

The *"Union Jack"* re-entry, so-called owing to the effect of the re-entry on the appearance of the corner stars (see *illustration*) occurs on stamp L K of Plate 75 of the 1d. red, Die I.

T A (T L)   M A (M L)
Varieties of Large Crown Watermark

I   Two states of Large Crown Watermark   II

Watermarks. Two watermark varieties, as illustrated, consisting of crowns of entirely different shape, are found in sheets of the Large Crown paper and fall on stamps lettered M A and T A (or M L and T L when the paper is printed on the wrong side). Both varieties are found on the 1d. rose-red of 1857, while the M A (M L) variety comes also on some plates of the 1d. of 1864 (Nos. 43, 44) up to about Plate 96. On the 2d. the T A (T L) variety is known on plates 8 and 9, and the M A (M L) on later prints of plate 9. These varieties may exist inverted, or inverted reversed on stamps lettered A A and A L and H A and H L, and some are known.

In 1861 a minor alteration was made in the Large Crown watermark by the removal of the two vertical strokes, representing *fleurs-de-lis*, which projected upwards from the uppermost of the three horizontal curves at the base of the Crown. Hence two states are distinguishable, as illustrated.

CONDITION—IMPERFORATE LINE-ENGRAVED ISSUES

The prices quoted for the 1840 and 1841 imperforate Line-engraved issues are for "fine" examples. As condition is most important in assessing the value of a stamp, the following definitions will assist collectors in the evaluation of individual examples.

Four main factors are relevant when considering quality.

(a) **Impression.** This should be clean and the surface free of any rubbing or unnatural blurring which would detract from the appearance.

(b) **Margins.** This is perhaps the most difficult factor to evaluate. Stamps described as "fine", the standard adopted in this catalogue for pricing purposes, should have margins of the recognised width, defined as approximately one half of the distance between two adjoining unsevered stamps. Stamps described as "very fine" or "superb" should have margins which are proportionately larger than those of a "fine" stamp. Examples with close margins should not, generally, be classified as "fine".

(c) **Cancellation.** On a "fine" stamp this should be reasonably clear and not noticeably smudged. A stamp described as "superb" should have a neat cancellation, preferably centrally placed or to the right.

(d) **Appearance.** Stamps, at the prices quoted, should always be without any tears, creases, bends or thins and should not be toned on either the front or back. Stamps with such defects are worth only a proportion of the catalogue price.

Good

Fine

Very Fine

Superb

The actual size illustrations of 1840 1d. blacks show the various grades of quality. When comparing these illustrations it should be assumed that they are all from the same plate and that they are free of any hidden defects.

PRINTERS. Nos. 1/53a were recess-printed by Perkins, Bacon & Petch, known from 1852 as Perkins, Bacon & Co.

> **STAMPS ON COVER.** Prices are quoted, for those Victorian and Edwardian issues usually found used on cover. In general these prices refer to the cheapest versions of each basic stamp with other shades, plates or varieties, together with unusual frankings and postmarks, being worth more.

1

1a

2 Small Crown

(Eng Charles and Frederick Heath)

1840 (6–8 May). *Letters in lower corners. Wmk Small Crown, W **2**.
Imperf.*

			Un	Used	Used on cover
1	**1**	1d. intense black	£3500	£200	
2		1d. black	£3000	£150	£250
		Wi. Watermark inverted	£3750	£400	
3		1d. grey-black (worn plate)	£3000	£200	
4	**1a**	2d. dp full blue (8.5.40)	£7000	£400	
5		2d. blue	£5500	£300	£650
		Wi. Watermark inverted	£7000	£700	
6		2d. pale blue	£7000	£375	

The 1d. stamp in black was printed from Plates 1 to 11. Plate 1 exists in two states (known to collectors as 1a and 1b), the latter being the result of extensive repairs.

Repairs were also made to plates 2, 5, 6, 8, 9, 10 and 11, and certain impressions exist in two or more states.

The so-called "Royal reprint" of the 1d. black was made in 1864, from Plate 66, Die II, on paper with Large Crown watermark, inverted. A printing was also made in carmine, on paper with the same watermark, normal.

For 1d. black with "VR" in upper corners *see* No. V1 under Official Stamps.

The 2d. stamps were printed from Plates 1 and 2.

Plates of 1d. black

Plate	Un	Used	Used on cover
1a	£4500	£180	£300
1b	£3000	£150	£250
2	£3000	£150	£250
3	£3500	£190	£325
4	£3000	£175	£275
5	£3000	£175	£275
6	£3000	£175	£275
7	£3250	£180	£325
8	£3500	£200	£350
9	£4000	£250	£400
10	£4500	£325	£600
11	£4500	£1600	£3000

Varieties of 1d. black

		Un	Used
a.	On *bleuté* paper (Plates 1 to 8) ....*from*	—	£225
b.	Double letter in corner ....*from*	£3000	£180
bb.	Re-entry ....*from*	£3250	£200
bc.	"PB" re-entry (Plate 5, 3rd state)	—	£4000
c.	Guide line in corner	£3000	£180
cc.	Large letters in each corner (E J, I L, J C and P A) (Plate 1*b*) ....*from*	£3500	£325
d.	Guide line through value	£3000	£180
g.	Obliterated by Maltese Cross		
	In red	—	£160
	In black	—	£150
	In blue	—	£1500
	In magenta	—	£650
	In yellow	—	—
h.	Obliterated by Maltese Cross with number in centre ....*from*		
	No. 1	—	£2500
	No. 2	—	£1500
	No. 3	—	£1500
	No. 4	—	£1500
	No. 5	—	£1500
	No. 6	—	£1500
	No. 7	—	£1500
	No. 8	—	£1500
	No. 9	—	£1500
	No. 10	—	£1500
	No. 11	—	—
	No. 12	—	£1500
i.	Obliterated "Penny Post" in black ....*from*	—	£1300
j.	Obliterated by town postmark (without Maltese Cross)		
	In black ....*from*	—	£1250
	In yellow ....*from*	—	£5500
	In red ....*from*	—	£1300
k.	Obliterated by 1844 type postmark in black *from*	—	£475

Plates of 2d. blue

Plate			Un	Used	Used on cover
1	...............*Shades from*	£5500	£300	£650
2	...............*Shades from*	£6500	£375	£650

Varieties of 2d. blue

		Un	Used
a.	Double letter in corner	—	£425
aa.	Re-entry	—	£475
b.	Guide line in corner	—	£375
c.	Guide line through value	—	£375
e.	Obliterated by Maltese Cross		
	In red	—	£325
	In black	—	£300
	In blue	—	£2500
	In magenta	—	£2250
f.	Obliterated by Maltese Cross with number in centre ....*from*		
	No. 1	—	£2500
	No. 2	—	£2500
	No. 3	—	—
	No. 4	—	£2500
	No. 5	—	£2500
	No. 6	—	£2750
	No. 7	—	£2500
	No. 8	—	£2500
	No. 9	—	£3000
	No. 10	—	£2750
	No. 11	—	£2750
	No. 12	—	£2500
g.	Obliterated "Penny Post" in black ....*from*	—	£1400

			Un	Used
h.	Obliterated by town postmark (without Maltese Cross) in black ....*from*	—	£1200
i.	Obliterated by 1844 type postmark		
	In black ....*from*	—	£750
	In blue ....*from*	—	£2250

1841 (10 Feb). *Printed from "black" plates. Wmk W **2**. Paper more or less blued. Imperf.*

			Un	Used	Used on cover
7	**1**	1d. red-brown (*shades*)	£450	40·00	75·00
		a. "PB" re-entry (Plate 5, 3rd state)	—	£1200	
		Wi. Watermark inverted (Plates 1b and 8)	—	£850	

The first printings of the 1d. in red-brown were made from Plates 1*b*, 2, 5 and 8 to 11 used for the 1d. black.

1d. red-brown from "black" plates

Plate		Un	Used	Used on cover
1*b*	....	£3000	£150	£250
2	....	£1750	£100	£160
5	....	£650	50·00	95·00
8	....	£500	40·00	85·00
9	....	£450	40·00	75·00
10	....	£475	40·00	85·00
11	....	£500	40·00	75·00

1841 (late Feb). *Plate 12 onwards. Wmk W **2**. Paper more or less blued. Imperf.*

			Un	Used	Used on cover
8	**1**	1d. red-brown	£130	3·50	8·00
		Wi. Watermark inverted	£350	45·00	
8a		1d. red-brown on very blue paper	£150	3·50	
9		1d. pale red-brown (worn plates)	£200	12·00	
10		1d. deep red-brown	£150	7·00	
11		1d. lake-red	£650	£250	
12		1d. orange-brown	£300	50·00	

Error. No letter "A" in right lower corner (Stamp B (A), Plate 77)

			Un	Used
12a	**1**	1d. red-brown	—	£5000

The error "No letter A in right corner" was due to the omission to insert this letter on stamp B A of Plate 77. The error was discovered some months after the plate was registered and was then corrected.

There are innumerable variations in the colour shade of the 1d. "red" and those given in the above list represent colour groups each covering a wide range.

Varieties of 1d. red-brown, etc.

		Un	Used
b.	Re-entry ....*from*	—	22·00
c.	Double letter in corner ....*from*	—	14·00
d.	Double Star (Plate 75) "Union Jack" re-entry	—	£500
e.	Guide line in corner	—	6·00
f.	Guide line through value	—	12·00
g.	Thick outer frame to stamp	—	12·00
h.	Ivory head	£180	6·00
j.	Left corner letter "S" inverted (Plates 78, 105, 107) *from*	—	45·00
k.	P converted to R (Plates 30, 33, 83, 86) ....*from*	—	35·00
l.	Obliterated by Maltese Cross		
	In red	—	£900
	In black	—	8·00
	In blue	—	£125
m.	Obliterated by Maltese Cross with number in centre		
	No. 1	—	32·00
	No. 2	—	32·00
	No. 3	—	45·00
	No. 4	—	£110

No. 5	....	—	32·00
No. 6	....	—	28·00
No. 7	....	—	25·00
No. 8	....	—	22·00
No. 9	....	—	30·00
No. 10	....	—	45·00
No. 11	....	—	55·00
No. 12	....	—	70·00

n. Obliterated "Penny Post" in black .... — £225
o. Obliterated by town postmark (without Maltese Cross)

In black	.... *from*	—	£125
In blue	.... *from*	—	£250
In green	.... *from*	—	£400
In yellow	.... *from*	—	—
In red	.... *from*	—	£2000

p. Obliterated by 1844 type postmark

In blue	.... *from*	—	30·00
In red	.... *from*	—	£900
In green	.... *from*	—	£200
In violet	.... *from*	—	£500
In black	.... *from*	—	3·50

Stamps with thick outer frame to the design are from plates on which the frame-lines have been straightened or recut, particularly Plates 76 and 90.

For "Union Jack" re-entry *see* General Notes to Line-engraved Issues.

In "P converted to R" the corner letter "R" is formed from the "P", the distinctive long tail having been hand-cut.

KEY TO LINE-ENGRAVED ISSUES

S.G. Nos.

Nos.	Description	Date	Wmk	Perf	Die	Alpha-bet
THE IMPERFORATE ISSUES						
1/3	1d. black	6.5.40	SC	Imp	I	I
4/6	2d. no lines	8.5.40	SC	Imp	I	I
	PAPER MORE OR LESS BLUED					
7	1d. red-brown	Feb 1841	SC	Imp	I	I
8/12	1d. red-brown	Feb 1841	SC	Imp	I	I
8/12	1d. red-brown	6.2.52	SC	Imp	I	II
13/15	2d. white lines	13.3.41	SC	Imp	I	I
	THE PERFORATED ISSUES					
	ONE PENNY VALUE					
16a	1d. red-brown	1848	SC	Roul	I	I
16b	1d. red-brown	1850	SC	16	I	I
16c	1d. red-brown	1853	SC	16	I	II
16d	1d. red-brown	1854	SC	14	I	I
17/18	1d. red-brown	Feb 1854	SC	16	I	II
22	1d. red-brown	Jan 1855	SC	14	I	II
24/5	1d. red-brown	28.2.55	SC	14	II	II
21	1d. red-brown	1.3.55	SC	16	II	II
26	1d. red-brown	15.5.55	LC	16	II	II
29/33	1d. red-brown	Aug 1855	LC	14	II	III
	NEW COLOURS ON WHITE PAPER					
37/41	1d. rose-red	Nov 1856	LC	14	II	III
36	1d. rose-red	26.12.57	LC	16	II	III
42	1d. rose-red	1861	LC	14	II	IV
	TWO PENCE VALUE					
19, 20	2d. blue	1.3.54	SC	16	I	I
23	2d. blue	22.2.55	SC	14	I	I
23a	2d. blue	5.7.55	SC	14	I	II
20a	2d. blue	18.8.55	SC	16	I	II
27	2d. blue	20.7.55	LC	16	I	II
34	2d. blue	20.7.55	LC	14	I	II
35	2d. blue	2.7.57	LC	14	I	III
36a	2d. blue	1.2.58	LC	16	I	III

LETTERS IN ALL FOUR CORNERS

48/9	½d. rose-red	1.10.70	W **9**	14	—
43/4	1d. rose-red	1.4.64	LC	14	II
53a	1½d. rosy mauve	1860	LC	14	II
51/3	1½d. rose-red	1.10.70	LC	14	II
45	2d. blue	July 1858	LC	14	II
46/7	2d. thinner lines	7.7.69	LC	14	II

Watermarks: SC = Small Crown, T **2**. LC = Large Crown, T **4**.
Dies: See notes above No. 17 in the catalogue.
Alphabets: See General Notes to this section.

3 White lines added

1841 (13 Mar)–**51**. *White lines added. Wmk W* **2**. *Paper more or less blued. Imperf.*

				Un	Used	Used on cover
13	**3**	2d. pale blue	....	£1300	45·00	
14		2d. blue	....	£1000	35·00	£150
		Wi. Watermark inverted	....	£2250	£225	
15		2d. dp full blue	....	£1400	50·00	
15aa		2d. violet-blue (1851)	....	£7000	£500	

The 2d. stamp with white lines was printed from Plates 3 and 4.

No. 15aa came from Plate 4 and the quoted price is for examples on thicker, lavender tinted paper.

Plates of 2d. blue

Plate		Un	Used
3	...............Shades *from*	£1000	40·00
4	...............Shades *from*	£1300	35·00

Varieties of 2d. blue

		Un	Used
a.	Guide line in corner	—	38·00
b.	Guide line through value	£1500	38·00
bb.	Double letter in corner	—	45·00
be.	Re-entry	£1800	60·00
c.	Ivory head	£1600	40·00
e.	Obliterated by Maltese Cross		

	In red	—	£4500
	In black	—	55·00
	In blue	—	£900

f. Obliterated by Maltese Cross with number in centre

No. 1	....	—	£160
No. 2	....	—	£160
No. 3	....	—	£160
No. 4	....	—	£150
No. 5	....	—	£200
No. 6	....	—	£150
No. 7	....	—	£300
No. 8	....	—	£200
No. 9	....	—	£300
No. 10	....	—	£350
No. 11	....	—	£200
No. 12	....	—	£110

g. Obliterated by town postmark (without Maltese Cross)

In black	.... *from*	—	£400
In blue	.... *from*	—	£700

h.   Obliterated by 1844 type postmark

In black	...........*from*	—	35·00
In blue	...........*from*	—	£350
In red	...........*from*	—	£4000
In green	...........*from*	—	£600

1841 (Apr).   *Trial printing (unissued) on Dickinson silk-thread paper. Imperf.*

16   **1**   1d. red-brown (Plate 11) £1750

Eight sheets were printed on this paper, six being gummed, two ungummed, but we have only seen examples without gum.

1848.   *Wmk W **2**. Rouletted approx* 11½ *by Henry Archer.*

16a   **1**   1d. red-brown (Plates 70, 71) £4000

1850.   *Wmk W **2**. P 16 by Henry Archer.*

16b   **1**   1d. red-brown (Alph 1) (from Plates 71, 79, 90–101, 105 & 107. Also Plate 8, unused only)

	from	£500 £150
bWi. Watermark inverted	—	£300

1853.   *Wmk W **2**. Government Trial Perforations.*

16c	**1**	1d. red-brown (*p* 16) (Alph II) (*on cover*)	† £4750
16d		1d. red-brown (*p* 14) (Alph I)	£3750

SEPARATION TRIALS. Although the various trials of machines for rouletting and perforating were unofficial, Archer had the consent of the authorities in making his experiments, and sheets so experimented upon were afterwards used by the Post Office.

As Archer ended his experiments in 1850 and plates with corner letters of Alphabet II did not come into issue until 1852, perforated stamps with corner letters of Alphabet I may safely be assumed to be Archer productions, if genuine.

The Government trial perforations were done on Napier machines in 1853. As Alphabet II was by that time in use, the trials can be distinguished from the perforated stamps listed below by being dated prior to 28 January 1854, the date when the perforated stamps were officially issued.

Die I	Die II	**4** Large Crown

Die I: The features of the portrait are lightly shaded and consequently lack emphasis.

Die II (Die I retouched): The lines of the features have been deepened and appear stronger. The eye is deeply shaded and made more lifelike. The nostril and lips are more clearly defined, the latter appearing much thicker. A strong downward stroke of colour marks the corner of the mouth. There is a deep indentation of colour between lower lip and chin. The band running from the back of the ear to the chignon has a bolder horizontal line below it than in Die I.

1854–57.   *Paper more or less blued. (a) Wmk Small Crown, W **2**. P 16.*

				★ *Used on*
			Un	*Used cover*
17	**1**	1d. red-brown (Die I) (2.54)	£125	4·00 10·00
		Wi. Watermark inverted	—	30·00

18	**1**	1d. yellow-brown (Die I)	£200	12·00	
19	**3**	2d. dp blue (Plate 4) (1.3.54)	£1400	35·00	55·00
		a. Imperf three sides (horiz pair)	†	—	
		Wi. Watermark inverted	—	80·00	
20		2d. pale blue (Plate 4)	£1400	50·00	
20a		2d. blue (Plate 5) (18.8.55)	£2000	£140	£225
		aWi. Watermark inverted	£2250	£275	
21	**1**	1d. red-brown (Die II) (1.3.55)	£190	14·00	24·00
		a. Imperf (Plates 2, 14)	£425	40·00	
		Wi. Watermark inverted			

*(b) Wmk Small Crown, W **2**. P 14*

22	**1**	1d. red-brown (Die II) (1.55)	£300	20·00	38·00
		Wi. Watermark inverted	—	75·00	
23	**3**	2d. blue (Plate 4) (22.2.55)	£2000	£120	£160
		Wi. Watermark inverted	—	£225	
23a		2d. blue (Plate 5) (5.7.55)	£2000	£120	£150
		b. Imperf (Plate 5)			
		aWi. Watermark inverted	—	£225	
24	**1**	1d red-brown (Die II) (28.2.55)	£250	16·00	25·00
		Wi. Watermark inverted	£400	50·00	
24a		1d. dp red-brown (very blue paper) (Die II)	£300	20·00	
25		1d. orange-brown (Die II)	£675	45·00	

*(c) Wmk Large Crown, W **4**. P 16*

26	**1**	1d. red-brown (Die II) (15.5.55)	£500	35·00	50·00
		a. Imperf (Plate 7)			
		Wi. Watermark inverted	—	85·00	
27	**3**	2d. blue (Plate 5) (20.7.55)	£2250	£140	£225
		a. Imperf	—	£2500	
		Wi. Watermark inverted	—	£300	

*(d) Wmk Large Crown, W **4**. P 14.*

29	**1**	1d. red-brown (Die II) (18.8.55)	£110	1·00	5·50
		a. Imperf (*shades*) (Plates 22, 24, 25, 32, 43)	£975	£775	
		Wi. Watermark inverted	£400	20·00	
30		1d. brick-red (Die II)	£175	14·00	
31		1d. plum (Die II) (2.56)	£900	£300	
32		1d. brown-rose (Die II)	£190	15·00	
33		1d. orange-brown (Die II) (3.57)	£300	18·00	
34	**3**	2d. blue (Plate 5) (20.7.55)	£1100	27·00	70·00
		Wi. Watermark inverted	—	£100	
35		2d. blue (Plate 6) (2.7.57)	£1200	24·00	60·00
		a. Imperf	—	£3000	
		b. Imperf horiz (vert pair)	†	—	
		Wi. Watermark inverted	—	75·00	
★17/35a		**For well-centred, lightly used**	+125%		

1856–58.   *Paper no longer blued. (a) Wmk Large Crown, W **4**. P 16.*

36	**1**	1d. rose-red (Die II) (26.12.57)	£650	24·00	45·00
36a	**3**	2d. blue (Plate 6) (1.2.58)	£3500	£140	£225
		aWi. Watermark inverted	—	£325	

*(b) (Die II) Wmk Large Crown, W **4**. P 14*

37	**1**	1d. red-brown (11.56)	£275	60·00	
38		1d. pale red (9.4.57)	£40·00	2·00	
		a. Imperf	£500	£425	
39		1d. pale rose (3.57)	£40·00	6·00	
40		1d. rose-red (9.57)	£25·00	1·00	2·00
		a. Imperf	£550	£425	
		Wi. Watermark inverted	£45·00	25·00	
41		1d. dp rose-red (7.57)	£45·00	2·50	

1861.   *Letters engraved on plate instead of punched (Alphabet IV).*

42	**1**	1d. rose-red (Die II) (Plates 50 & 51)	£125	8·00	22·00
		a. Imperf	—	£1800	
		Wi. Watermark inverted	£190	20·00	
★36/42a		**For well-centred, lightly used**	+125%		

The original die (Die I) was used to provide roller dies for the laying down of all the line-engraved stamps from 1840 to 1855. In that year a new master die was laid down (by means of a Die I roller die) and the

impression was retouched by hand engraving by William Humphrys. This retouched die, always known to philatelists as Die II, was from that time used for preparing all new roller dies.

One Penny. The numbering of the 1d. plates recommenced at 1 on the introduction of Die II. Plates 1 to 21 were Alphabet II from which a scarce plum shade exists. Corner letters of Alphabet III appear on Plate 22 and onwards.

As an experiment, the corner letters were engraved by hand on Plates 50 and 51 in 1856, instead of being punched (Alphabet IV), but punching was again resorted to from Plate 52 onwards. Plates 50 and 51 were not put into use until 1861.

Two Pence. Unlike the 1d. the old sequence of plate numbers continued. Plates 3 and 4 of the 2d. had corner letters of Alphabet I, Plate 5 Alphabet II and Plate 6 Alphabet III. In Plate 6 the white lines are thinner than before.

In both values, varieties may be found as described in the preceding issues—ivory heads, inverted watermarks, re-entries, and double letters in corners.

The change of perforation from 16 to 14 was decided upon late in 1854 since the closer holes of the former gauge tended to cause the sheets of stamps to break up when handled, but for a time both gauges were in concurrent use. Owing to faulty alignment of the impressions on the plates and to shrinkage of the paper when dampened, badly perforated stamps are plentiful in the line-engraved issues.

5

6

Showing position of the plate number on the 1d. and 2d. values. (Plate 170 shown)

1858–79. *Letters in all four corners. Wmk Large Crown, W* **4.** *Die II (1d. and 2d.). P 14.*

		Un	Used	* Used on cover
43	**5** 1d. rose-red (1.4.64)	4·50	50	1·50
44	1d. lake-red	4·50	50	
	a. Imperf *from*	£750	£600	
	Wi. Watermark inverted	22·00	5·00	
*43/4a	**For well-centred, lightly used**	+ **125%**		

Plate	Un	Used		Plate	Un	Used
71	12·00	2·00		88	80·00	5·50
72	18·00	2·50		89	20·00	50
73	12·00	2·00		90	14·00	50
74	10·00	50		91	20·00	3·50
76	20·00	50		92	7·00	50
77	—	—		93	20·00	50
78	50·00	50		94	20·00	3·00
79	15·00	50		95	12·00	50
80	10·00	75		96	14·00	50
81	30·00	1·00		97	8·00	1·75
82	60·00	2·50		98	8·00	3·50
83	70·00	4·00		99	12·00	3·00
84	30·00	50		100	18·00	1·25
85	12·00	1·00		101	25·00	6·00
86	15·00	2·50		102	10·00	55
87	4·50	50		103	10·00	1·50

Plate	Un	Used		Plate	Un	Used
104	14·00	3·00		166	7·50	3·50
105	35·00	4·00		167	5·00	50
106	15·00	55		168	6·00	5·50
107	20·00	3·75		169	15·00	4·00
108	15·00	1·00		170	6·00	50
109	38·00	1·75		171	4·50	50
110	10·00	6·00		172	4·50	90
111	18·00	1·00		173	25·00	6·00
112	30·00	1·00		174	4·50	40
113	8·00	7·50		175	18·00	1·75
114	£175	8·00		176	3·00	90
115	50·00	1·00		177	5·00	50
116	38·00	6·00		178	7·50	2·00
117	8·00	50		179	8·00	1·00
118	12·00	50		180	8·00	3·00
119	5·00	75		181	7·50	50
120	4·50	50		182	50·00	3·00
121	20·00	6·00		183	13·00	1·50
122	4·50	50		184	4·50	75
123	6·00	75		185	7·50	1·50
124	6·00	50		186	15·00	1·00
125	8·00	1·00		187	6·00	50
127	17·00	1·00		188	10·00	7·00
129	6·00	5·00		189	18·00	4·00
130	9·00	1·00		190	7·00	3·50
131	38·00	11·00		191	4·50	4·00
132	50·00	16·00		192	13·00	50
133	45·00	6·00		193	4·50	50
134	4·50	50		194	7·50	5·00
135	50·00	20·00		195	7·50	5·00
136	50·00	15·00		196	5·00	3·00
137	8·00	90		197	8·00	6·00
138	6·00	50		198	4·50	3·50
139	16·00	11·00		199	10·00	3·50
140	6·00	50		200	10·00	50
141	75·00	6·00		201	4·50	3·00
142	25·00	18·00		202	7·50	5·00
143	15·00	10·00		203	4·50	10·00
144	50·00	15·00		204	6·00	75
145	4·50	1·00		205	6·00	2·00
146	5·00	3·50		206	6·00	6·00
147	9·00	2·00		207	6·00	6·00
148	10·00	1·50		208	6·00	10·00
149	7·50	3·50		209	7·50	6·00
150	4·50	50		210	10·00	8·00
151	13·00	6·00		211	22·00	15·00
152	9·00	3·25		212	7·50	7·50
153	35·00	6·00		213	7·50	7·50
154	7·50	50		214	13·00	13·00
155	8·00	75		215	13·00	13·00
156	7·50	50		216	13·00	13·00
157	7·50	50		217	10·00	4·00
158	4·50	50		218	6·00	5·00
159	4·50	50		219	30·00	50·00
160	4·50	50		220	4·50	3·50
161	15·00	4·00		221	15·00	10·00
162	8·00	4·00		222	25·00	25·00
163	7·50	1·50		223	30·00	40·00
164	7·50	2·00		224	35·00	35·00
165	10·00	50		225	£1100	£350

Error. Imperf. Issued at Cardiff (Plate 116)

		Un	Used
44b	**5** 1d. rose-red (18.1.70)	£2000	£1250

The following plate numbers are also known imperf and used (No. 44a); 72, 79, 80, 81, 82, 83, 84, 85, 86, 87, 88, 90, 91, 92, 93, 96, 97, 100, 101, 102, 103, 104, 105, 107, 108, 109, 112, 113, 114, 116, 117, 120, 121, 122, 136, 137, 142, 146, 148, 158, 162, 164, 166, 171, 174, 191 and 202.

The numbering of this series of 1d. red plates follows after that of the previous 1d. stamp, last printed from Plate 68.

Plates 69, 70, 75, 126 and 128 were prepared for this issue but rejected owing to defects, and stamps from these plates do not exist, so that specimens which appear to be from these plates (like many of those which optimistic collectors believe to be from Plate 77) bear other plate numbers. Owing to faulty engraving or printing it is not always easy to identify the plate number. Plate 77 was also rejected but some stamps printed from it were used. One specimen is in the Tapling Collection and six or seven others are known. Plates 226 to 228 were made but not used.

Specimens from most of the plates are known with inverted watermark. The variety of watermark described in the General Notes to this section occurs on stamp M A (or M L) on plates up to about 96 (*Prices from £110 used*).

Re-entries in this issue are few, the best being on stamps M K and T K of Plate 71 and on S L and T L, Plate 83.

			Un	* Used on cover
45 **6**	2d. blue (thick lines) (7.58)		£150	4·00	15·00
	a. Imperf (Plate 9)		—	£3000
	Wi. Watermark inverted		£250	50·00
	Plate			
	7		£400	18·00
	8		£450	14·00
	9		£150	4·00
	12		£700	40·00
46	2d. blue (thin lines) (1.7.69)		£160	8·00	16·00
	Wi. Watermark inverted		£225	50·00
47	2d. dp blue (thin lines)		£160	8·00
	a. Imperf (Plate 13)		£2000	
	Plate			
	13		£180	8·00
	14		£200	10·00
	15		£160	8·00
*45/7	**For well-centred, lightly used**			+125%

Plates 10 and 11 of the 2d. were prepared but rejected. Plates 13 to 15 were laid down from a new roller impression on which the white lines were thinner.

There are some marked re-entries and repairs, particularly on Plates 7, 8, 9 and 12.

Stamps with inverted watermark may be found and also the T A (T L) and M A (M L) watermark varieties (*see* General Notes to this section).

Though the paper is normally white, some printings showed blueing and stamps showing the "ivory head" may therefore be found.

7

Showing the plate number (9)

9

1870 (1 Oct). *Wmk W **9**, extending over three stamps. P 14.*

			Un	* Used on cover
48 **7**	½d. rose-red		45·00	6·00	24·00
49	½d. rose		45·00	6·00
	a. Imperf (Plates 1, 4, 5, 6, 8, 14) *from*	£950	£600
	Wi. Watermark inverted		—	40·00
	Wj. Watermark reversed		—	30·00

(49) | Wk. Watermark inverted & reversed .. | £120 | 25·00 |
	Plate		
	1	95·00	45·00
	3	60·00	14·00
	4	75·00	8·00
	5	55·00	6·00
	6	45·00	6·00
	8	85·00	45·00
	9	£2250	£300
	10	75·00	6·00
	11	45·00	6·00
	12	45·00	6·00
	13	45·00	6·00
	14	45·00	6·00
	15	60·00	10·00
	19	90·00	22·00
	20	95·00	35·00
*48/9a	**For well-centred, lightly used**		+200%

The ½d. was printed in sheets of 480 (24 × 20) so that the check letters run from $\begin{matrix} AA \\ AA \end{matrix}$ to $\begin{matrix} XT \\ TX \end{matrix}$

Plates 2, 7, 16, 17 and 18 were not completed while Plates 21 and 22, though made, were not used.

Owing to the method of perforating, the outer side of stamps in either the A or X row (ie the left or right side of the sheet) is imperf.

Stamps may be found with watermark inverted or reversed, or without watermark, the latter due to misplacement of the paper when printing.

8 | Position of plate number

1870 (1 Oct). *Wmk W **4**. P 14.*

			Un	* Used on cover
51 **8**	1½d. rose-red		£175	20·00	£140
52	1½d. lake-red		£175	20·00
	a. Imperf (Plates 1 & 3) ....*from*	£1900	†
	Wi. Watermark inverted		—	£120
	Plate		
	(1)	£375	30·00
	3	£175	20·00
	Error of lettering. OP–PC for CP–PC (Plate 1)		
53 **8**	1½d. rose-red		£4000	£650
*51/3	**For well-centred, lightly used**		+125%

1860. *Prepared for use but not issued; blued paper. Wmk W **4**. P 14.*

		Un Used
53a **8**	1½d. rosy mauve (Plate 1)	£2000
	b. Error of lettering, OP–PC for CP–PC	

Owing to a proposed change in the postal rates, 1½d. stamps were first printed in 1860, in rosy mauve, No. 53a, but the change was not approved and the greater part of the stock was destroyed.

In 1870 a 1½d. stamp was required and was issued in rose-red.

Plate 1 did not have the plate number in the design of the stamps, but on stamps from Plate 3 the number will be found in the frame as shown above.

Plate 2 was defective and was not used.

The error of lettering OP–PC on Plate 1 was apparently not noticed by the printer, and therefore not corrected.

EMBOSSED ISSUES

Volume 1 of the Stanley Gibbons *Great Britian Specialised Catalogue* gives further detailed information on the embossed issues.

PRICES. The prices quoted are for cut-square stamps with average to fine embossing. Stamps with exceptionally clear embossing are worth more.

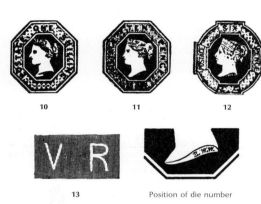

| 10 | 11 | 12 |

13   Position of die number

(Primary die engraved at the Royal Mint by William Wyon. Stamps printed at Somerset House)

1847–54. *Imperf* (For paper and wmk see footnote).

			Un	Used	Used on cover
54	**10**	1s. pale green (11.9.47)	£3000	£375	£475
55		1s. green	£3000	£425	
56		1s. dp green	£3500	£475	
		Die 1 (1847)	£3000	£375	
		Die 2 (1854)	£3500	£450	
57	**11**	10d. brown (6.11.48)	£2500	£600	£950
		Die 1 (1848)	£2750	£650	
		Die 2 (1850)	£2500	£600	
		Die 3 (1853)	£2500	£600	
		Die 4 (1854)	£2750	£650	
		Die 5	£16000		
58	**12**	6d. mauve (1.3.54)	£2750	£450	
59		6d. dull lilac	£2750	£425	£525
60		6d. purple	£2750	£425	
		Wi. Watermark inverted	—	£425	
		Wj. Watermark reversed	£2750	£450	
		Wk. Watermark inverted & reversed	£2750	£425	
61		6d. violet	£4000	£800	

The 1s. and 10d. are on "Dickinson" paper with "silk" threads. The 6d. is on paper watermarked V R in single-lined letters, W **13**, which may be found in four ways:—upright inverted, upright reversed, and inverted reversed; upright reversed being the commonest.

The die numbers are indicated on the base of the bust. Only Die 1 (1 W W) of the 6d. was used for the adhesive stamps. The 10d. is from Die 1 (W.W.1 on stamps), and Dies 2 to 5 (2W.W., 3W.W., 4W.W. and 5W.W.) but the number and letters on stamps from Die 1 are seldom clear and many specimens are known without any trace of them. Because of this stamp we previously listed as "No die number" has been deleted. That they are from Die 1 is proved by the existence of blocks showing stamps with and without the die number. The 1s. is from Dies 1 and 2 (W.W.1, W.W.2).

The normal arrangement of the "silk" threads in the paper was in pairs running down each vertical row of the sheets, the space between the threads of each pair being approximately 5 mm and between pairs of threads 20 mm. Varieties due to misplacement of the paper in printing show a single thread on the first stamp from the sheet margin and two threads 20 mm apart on the other values 20 mm apart of the row. Faulty manufacture is the cause of stamps with a single thread in the middle.

Through bad spacing of the impressions, which were handstruck, all values may be found with two impressions more or less overlapping. Owing to the small margin allowed for variation of spacing, specimens with good margins on all sides are not common.

Double impressions are known of all values.

Later printings of the 6d. had the gum tinted green to enable the printer to distinguish the gummed side of the paper.

SURFACE-PRINTED ISSUES

GENERAL NOTES

Volume 1 of the Stanley Gibbons *Great Britain Specialised Catalogue* gives further detailed information on the surface-printed issues.

"Abnormals". The majority of the great rarities in the surface-printed group of issues are the so-called "abnormals", whose existence is due to the practice of printing six sheets from every plate as soon as made, one of which was kept for record purposes at Somerset House, while the others were perforated and usually issued. If such sheets were not used for general production or if, before they came into full use, a change of watermark or colour took place, the six sheets originally printed would differ from the main issue in plate, colour or watermark and, if issued would be extremely rare.

The abnormal stamps of this class listed in this Catalogue and distinguished, where not priced, by an asterisk (*) are:

No.		
78	3d. Plate 3 (with white dots)	
152	4d. vermilion, Plate 16	
153	4d. sage-green, Plate 17	
109	6d. mauve, Plate 10	
124/a	6d. pale chestnut & 6d. chestnut, Plate 12	
145	6d. pale buff, Plate 13	
88	9d. Plate 3 (hair lines)	
98	9d. Plate 5 (see footnote to No. 98)	
113	10d. Plate 2	
91	1s. Plate 3 ("Plate 2")	
148/50	1s. green, Plate 14	
120	2s. blue, Plate 3	

Those which may have been issued, but of which no specimens are known, are 2½d. wmk Anchor, Plates 4 and 5; 3d. wmk Emblems, Plate 5; 3d. wmk Spray, Plate 21, 6d. grey, wmk Spray, Plate 18; 8d. orange, Plate 2; 1s. wmk Emblems, Plate 5; 5s. wmk Maltese Cross, Plate 4.

The 10d. Plate 1, wmk Emblems (No. 99), is sometimes reckoned among the abnormals, but was an error, due to the use of the wrong paper.

Corner Letters. With the exception of the 4d., 6d. and 1s. of 1855–57, the ½d., 1½d., 2d. and 5d. of 1880, the 1d. lilac of 1881 and the £5 (which had letters in lower corners only, and in the reverse order to the normal), all the surface-printed stamps issued prior to 1887 had letters in all four corners, as in the later line-engraved stamps. The arrangement is the same, the letters running in sequence right across and down the sheets, whether these were divided into panes or not. The corner letters existing naturally depend on the number of stamps in the sheet and their arrangement.

Imprimaturs and Imperforate Stamps. The Post Office retained in their records (now in the National Postal Museum) one imperforate sheet from each plate, known as the Imprimatur (or officially approved) sheet. Some stamps were removed from time to time for presentation purposes and have come on to the market, but these imperforates are not listed as they were not issued. Full details can be found in Volume 1 of the *Great Britain Specialised Catalogue*.

However, other imperforate stamps are known to have been issued and these are listed where it has been possible to prove that they do not come from the Imprimatur sheets. It is therefore advisable to purchase these only when accompanied by an Expert Committee certificate of genuineness.

Plate Numbers. All stamps from No. 75 to No. 163 bear in their designs either the plate number or, in one or two earlier instances, some other indication by which one plate can be distinguished from another. With the aid of these and of the corner letters it is thus possible to "reconstruct" a sheet of stamps from any plate of any issue or denomination.

Surface-printing. In this context the traditional designation "surface-printing" is synonymous with typo(graphy)—a philatelic term—or letterpress—the printers' term—as meaning printing from (the surface of) raised type. It is also called relief-printing, as the image is in relief (in French, *en épargne*), unwanted parts of the design having been cut away. Duplicate impressions can be electrotyped or stereotyped from an original die, the resulting *clichés* being locked together to form the printing plate.

Wing Margins. As the vertical gutters (spaces) between the panes, into which sheets of stamps of most values were divided until the introduction of the Imperial Crown watermark, were perforated through the centre with a single row of holes, instead of each vertical row of stamps on the inner side of the panes having its own line of perforation as is now usual, a proportion of the stamps in each sheet have what is called a "wing margin" about 5 mm wide on one or other side.

The stamps with "wing margins" are the watermark Emblems and Spray of Rose series (3d., 6d., 9d., 10d., 1s. and 2s.) with letters D, E, H or I in S.E. corner, and the watermark Garter series (4d. and 8d.) with letters F or G in S.E. corner. Knowledge of this lettering will enable collectors to guard against stamps with wing margin cut down and re-perforated, but note that wing margin stamps of Nos. 62 to 73 are also to be found re-perforated.

PRINTERS. The issues of Queen Victoria, Nos. 62/214, were typo by Thomas De La Rue & Co.

PERFORATIONS. All the surface-printed issues of Queen Victoria are perf 14, with the exception of Nos. 126/9.

1855–57. *No corner letters.*
(a) *Wmk Small Garter, W* **15**. *Highly glazed, deeply blued paper* (31 July 1855)

			Un	* Used	Used on cover
62	**14**	4d. carmine (*shades*)	£2250	£170	£275
		a. Paper slightly blued	£2500	£170	
		b. White paper	£3000	£350	
		Wi. Watermark inverted	—	£250	

(b) *Wmk Medium Garter, W* **16**

(i) *Thick, blued highly glazed paper* (25 February 1856)

63	**14**	4d. carmine (*shades*)	£2750	£170	£250
		a. White paper	£2500		
		Wi. Watermark inverted	—	£250	

(ii) *Ordinary thin white paper* (September 1856)

64	**14**	4d. pale carmine	£1800	£150	£225
		a. Stamp printed double	†		
		Wi. Watermark inverted	—	£180	

(iii) *Ordinary white paper, specially prepared ink* (1 November 1856)

65	**14**	4d. rose or dp rose	£1800	£160	£250

(c) *Wmk Large Garter, W* **17**. *Ordinary white paper* (January 1857)

66	**14**	4d. rose-carmine	£700	30·00	75·00
		a. Rose	£600	30·00	
		b. Thick glazed paper	£1700	£100	
		Wi. Watermark inverted	—	55·00	
		Wj. Watermark inverted & reversed	...		
*62/6b		**For well-centred, lightly used**		+ 125%	

18

19

20 Emblems wmk (normal)

20a Watermark error, three roses and shamrock

20b Watermark error, three roses and thistle

(d) *Wmk Emblems, W* **20**

			Un	* Used	Used on cover
69	**18**	6d. dp lilac (21.10.56)	£575	65·00	
70		6d. pale lilac	£500	40·00	75·00
		a. Azure paper	£2500	£375	
		b. Thick paper	£750	£140	
		c. Error. Watermark W **20a**			
		Wi. Watermark inverted	—	75·00	
		Wj. Watermark reversed			
		Wk. Watermark inverted & reversed	...		
71	**19**	1s. dp green (1.11.56)	£1200	£160	
72		1s. green	£650	£140	£160

14

15 Small Garter

16 Medium Garter

17 Large Garter

73 **19**	1s. pale green	....	£650	£140
	a. Azure paper	....	—	£500
	b. Thick paper	....	—	£160
	c. Imperf	....		
	Wi. Watermark inverted	....	—	£160
	Wj. Watermark reversed	....	—	£650
	Wk. Watermark inverted and reversed .			
*69/73b	**For well-centred, lightly used**			**+125**%

KEY TO SURFACE-PRINTED ISSUES 1855–83

S.G. Nos.	Description	Watermark	Date of Issue
	NO CORNER LETTERS		
62	4d. carmine	Small Garter	31.7.55
63/5	4d. carmine	Medium Garter	25.2.56
66/a	4d. carmine	Large Garter	Jan 1857
69/70	6d. lilac	Emblems	21.10.56
71/3	1s. green	Emblems	1.11.56
	SMALL WHITE CORNER LETTERS		
75/7	3d. carmine	Emblems	1.5.62
78	3d. carmine (dots)	Emblems	Aug 1862
79/82	4d. red	Large Garter	15.1.62
83/5	6d. lilac	Emblems	1.12.62
86/8	9d. bistre	Emblems	15.1.62
89/91	1s. green	Emblems	1.12.62
	LARGE WHITE CORNER LETTERS		
92	3d. rose	Emblems	1.3.65
102/3	3d. rose	Spray	July 1867
93/5	4d. vermilion	Large Garter	4.7.65
96/7	6d. lilac	Emblems	7.3.65
104/7	6d. lilac	Spray	21.6.67
108/9	6d. lilac	Spray	8.3.69
122/4	6d. chestnut	Spray	12.4.72
125	6d. grey	Spray	24.4.73
98	9d. straw	Emblems	30.10.65
110/11	9d. straw	Spray	3.10.67
99	10d. brown	Emblems	11.11.67
112/14	10d. brown	Spray	1.7.67
101	1s. green	Emblems	Feb 1865
115/17	1s. green	Spray	13.7.67
118/20b	2s. blue	Spray	1.7.67
121	2s. brown	Spray	27.2.80
126/7	5s. rose	Cross	1.7.67
128	10s. grey	Cross	26.9.78
129	£1 brown-lilac	Cross	26.9.78
130, 134	5s. rose	Anchor	25.11.82
131, 135	10s. grey-green	Anchor	Feb 1883
132, 136	£1 brown-lilac	Anchor	Dec 1882
133, 137	£5 orange	Anchor	21.3.82
	LARGE COLOURED CORNER LETTERS		
138/9	2½d. rosy mauve	Anchor	1.7.75
141	2½d. rosy mauve	Orb	1.5.76
142	2½d. blue	Orb	5.2.80
157	2½d. blue	Crown	23.3.81
143/4	3d. rose	Spray	5.7.73
158	3d. rose	Crown	Jan 1881
159	3d. on 3d. lilac	Crown	1.1.83
152	4d. vermilion	Large Garter	1.3.76
153	4d. sage-green	Large Garter	12.3.77
154	4d. brown	Large Garter	15.8.80
160	4d. brown	Crown	9.12.80
145	6d. buff	Spray	15.3.73

146/7	6d. grey	Spray	20.3.74
161	6d. grey	Crown	1.1.81
162	6d. on 6d. lilac	Crown	1.1.83
156a	8d. purple-brown	Large Garter	July 1876
156	8d. orange	Large Garter	11.9.76
148/50	1s. green	Spray	1.9.73
151	1s. brown	Spray	14.10.80
163	1s. brown	Crown	29.5.81

Watermarks:	Anchor	W **40, 47**
	Cross	W **39**
	Crown	W **49**
	Emblems	W **20**
	Large Garter	W **17**
	Medium Garter	W **16**
	Orb	W **48**
	Small Garter	W **15**
	Spray	W **33**

21 **22**

23 **24** **25** Plate 2

A. White dots added

B. Hair lines

1862–64. *A small uncoloured letter in each corner, the 4d. wmk Large Garter, W **17**, the others Emblems, W **20**.*

				★ Used on	
			Un	Used	cover
75 **21**	3d. dp carmine-rose (Plate 2) (1.5.62) ..	£1300	£140		
76	3d. brt carmine-rose	£700	£110	£225	
	Wi. Watermark inverted	—	£160		
77	3d. pale carmine-rose	£700	£100		
	b. Thick paper	—	£175		
	Wj. Watermark reversed				
78	3d. rose (with white dots, Type A, Plate 3) (8.62)		*	£2500	
	a. Imperf (Plate 3)	£2000			

79	**22**	4d. brt red (Plate 3) (15.1.62)	£750	55·00	
80		4d. pale red	£500	35·00	85·00
		Wi. Watermark inverted	—	75·00	
81		4d. brt red (Hair lines, Type B, Plate 4) (16.10.63)	£650	40·00	
82		4d. pale red (Hair lines, Type B, Plate 4)	£550	28·00	75·00
		a. Imperf (Plate 4)	£1500		
		Wi. Watermark inverted	—	50·00	
83	**23**	6d. dp lilac (Plate 3) (1.12.62)	£800	55·00	
84		6d. lilac	£650	30·00	65·00
		a. Azure paper	—	£300	
		b. Thick paper	—	70·00	
		c. Error. Watermark W **20b** (stamp TF)			
		Wi. Watermark inverted	—	50·00	
		Wj. Watermark inverted and reversed			
85		6d. lilac (Hair lines, Plate 4) (20.4.64) ..	£800	50·00	£120
		a. Imperf (watermark inverted)	£1100		
		Eb. Imperf and watermark upright			
		c. Thick paper	£1200	85·00	
		Wi. Watermark inverted	—	80·00	
		Wj. Watermark inverted and reversed			
86	**24**	9d. bistre (Plate 2) (15.1.62)	£1200	£140	£250
		Wi. Watermark inverted	—	£175	
		Wj. Watermark reversed	—	£200	
87		9d. straw	£1200	£130	
		a. On azure paper			
		b. Thick paper	£1800	£225	
88		9d. bistre (Hair lines, Plate 3) (5.62) ...	£6000	£1800	
89	**25**	1s. dp green (Plate No. 1 = Plate 2) (1.12.62)	£850	£120	
90		1s. green (Plate No. 1 = Plate 2)	£700	65·00	£130
		a. "K" in lower left corner in white circle (stamp KD)	£4500	£550	
		aa. "K" normal (stamp KD)	—	£800	
		b. On azure paper			
		c. Thick paper	—	£175	
		ca. Thick paper, "K" in circle as No. 90a	—	£1100	
		Wi. Watermark inverted	—	90·00	
		Wj. Watermark inverted and reversed			
91		1s. dp green (Plate No. 2 = Plate 3) .	£11000		
		a. Imperf	£1500		
		aWi. Watermark inverted	£1000		
*75/91		**For well-centred, lightly used**	+**125**%		

The 3d. as Type **21**, but with network background in the spandrels which is found overprinted SPECIMEN, was never issued.

The plates of this issue may be distinguished as follows:

3d. Plate 2   No white dots.
    Plate 3   White dots as Illustration A.
4d. Plate 3   No hair lines. Roman I next to lower corner letters.
    Plate 4   Hair lines in corners. (Illustration B.). Roman II.
6d. Plate 3   No hair lines.
    Plate 4   Hair lines in corners.
9d. Plate 2   No hair lines.
    Plate 3   Hair lines in corners. Beware of faked lines.
1s. Plate 2   Numbered 1 on stamps.
    Plate 3   Numbered 2 on stamps & with hair lines.

The 9d. on azure paper (No. 87a) is very rare, only one confirmed example being known.

The variety "K" in circle, No. 90a, is believed to be due to a damaged letter having been cut out and replaced. It is probable that the punch was driven in too deeply, causing the flange to penetrate the surface, producing an indentation showing as an uncoloured circle.

The watermark variety "three roses and a shamrock" illustrated in W **20a** was evidently due to the substitution of an extra rose for the thistle in a faulty watermark bit. It is found on stamp TA of Plate 4 of the 3d., Plates 1 (No. 70c), 3, 5 and 6 of the 6d., Plate 4 of the 9d. and Plate 4 of the 1s.

A similar variety, W **20b**, but showing three roses and a thistle is found on stamp T F of the 6d. (No. 84) and 9d. (No. 98).

26	27

28
(with hyphen)

28a
(without hyphen)

29	30	31

1865–67. *Large uncoloured corner letters. Wmk Large Garter (4d.); others Emblems.*

					★ Used on
			Un	Used	cover
92	**26**	3d. rose (Plate 4) (1.3.65)	£400	45·00	£100
		a. Error. Watermark W **20a**	£900	£275	
		b. Thick paper	£500	55·00	
		Wi. Watermark inverted	—	75·00	
		Wj. Watermark reversed			
		Wk. Watermark inverted and reversed			
93	**27**	4d. dull vermilion (4.7.65)	£225	15·00	35·00
94		4d. vermilion	£225	15·00	
		a. Imperf (Plates 11, 12)	£500		
		Wi. Watermark inverted	£225	18·00	
95		4d. dp vermilion	£225	20·00	
		Plate			
		7 (1865)	£300	19·00	
		8 (1866)	£250	19·00	
		9 (1867)	£250	15·00	
		10 (1868)	£300	30·00	
		11 (1869)	£250	15·00	
		12 (1870)	£225	15·00	
		13 (1872)	£250	17·00	
		14 (1873)	£300	35·00	
96	**28**	6d. dp lilac (with hyphen) (7.3.65)	£400	45·00	
97		6d. lilac (with hyphen)	£350	30·00	65·00
		a. Thick paper	£450	60·00	
		b. Stamp doubly printed (Plate 6) ..	—	£4500	
		c. Error. Watermark W **20a** (Pl 5, 6)			
			from	—	£300
		Wi. Watermark inverted	—	55·00	
		Wj. Watermark reversed			
		Plate			
		5 (1865)	£350	30·00	
		6 (1867)	£1000	60·00	
98	**29**	9d. straw (Plate 4) (30.10.65)	£700	£200	£300
		a. Thick paper	£950	£325	
		b. Error. Watermark W **20a**	—	£375	
		c. Error. Watermark W **20b** (stamp TF)			
		Wi. Watermark inverted	—	£275	

			Un	Used	
99	**30**	10d. red-brown (Plate 1) (11.11.67)		*£12000	
101	**31**	1s. green (Plate 4) (26.1.65)	£650	70·00	£110
		a. Error. Watermark W **20a**	—	£350	
		b. Thick paper	£750	£130	
		c. Imperf between (vert pair)	—	£4250	
		Wi. Watermark inverted	—	£100	
		Wj. Imperf watermark inverted			
*92/101c		**For well-centred, lightly used**		+**100**%	

From mid-1866 to about the end of 1871 4d. stamps of this issue appeared generally with watermark inverted.

Unused examples of No. 98 from Plate 5 exist, but this was never put to press and all evidence points to such stamps originating from a portion of the Imprimatur sheet which was perforated by De La Rue in 1887 for insertion in albums to be presented to members of the Stamp Committee (*Price* £10000 un).

The 10d. stamps, No. 99, were printed in *error* on paper watermarked "Emblems" instead of on "Spray of Rose".

32

33 Spray of Rose

34

1867–80. *Wmk Spray of Rose. W* **33**.

			Un	* Used	Used on cover
102	**26**	3d. dp rose (12.7.67)	£225	20·00	
103		3d. rose	£200	14·00	40·00
		a. Imperf (Plates 5, 6, 8) .....from	£700		
		Wi. Watermark inverted	£350	45·00	
		Plate			
		4 (1867)	£300	60·00	
		5 (1868)	£200	16·00	
		6 (1870)	£225	14·00	
		7 (1871)	£275	17·00	
		8 (1872)	£250	16·00	
		9 (1872)	£250	22·00	
		10 (1873)	£275	50·00	
104	**28**	6d. lilac (with hyphen) (Plate 6) (21.6.67)	£550	32·00	90·00
		a. Imperf			
		Wi. Watermark inverted	—	60·00	
105		6d. dp lilac (with hyphen) (Plate 6) .	£550	32·00	
106		6d. purple (with hyphen) (Plate 6) ..	£550	50·00	
107		6d. brt violet (with hyphen) (Plate 6) (22.7.68)	£550	35·00	
108	**28a**	6d. dull violet (without hyphen) (Plate 8) (18.3.69)	£325	25·00	
		Wi. Watermark inverted	—	60·00	
109		6d. mauve (without hyphen)	£275	25·00	55·00
		a. Imperf (Plate Nos. 8 & 9)	£750	£650	
		Wi. Watermark inverted	—	60·00	
		Plate			
		8 (1869, mauve)	£275	25·00	
		9 (1870, mauve)	£275	25·00	
		10 (1869, mauve)		*£12000	
110	**29**	9d. straw (Plate No. 4) (3.10.67)	£600	£110	£200
		Wi. Watermark inverted	—	£150	
111		9d. pale straw (Plate No. 4)	£600	£110	
		a. Imperf (Plate 4)	£1900		

			Un	Used	
112	**30**	10d. red-brown (1.7.67)	£1000	£150	£325
		Wi. Watermark inverted	—	£250	
113		10d. pale red-brown	£1000	£160	
114		10d. dp red-brown	£1200	£180	
		a. Imperf (Plate 1)	£1800		
		Plate			
		1 (1867)	£1000	£150	
		2 (1867)	£12000	£2500	
115	**31**	1s. dp green (13.7.67)	£425	12·00	
117		1s. green	£350	12·00	25·00
		a. Imperf between (horiz pair) (Pl 7) ...	£1000	£600	
		b. Imperf (Plate 4)	£1000	£600	
		Wi. Watermark inverted	£450	35·00	
		Plate			
		4 (1870)	£350	17·00	
		5 (1871)	£400	14·00	
		6 (1872)	£550	12·00	
		7 (1873)	£550	35·00	
118	**32**	2s. dull blue (1.7.67)	£1000	65·00	£325
		Wi. Watermark inverted	—	£150	
119		2s. dp blue	£1000	65·00	
		a. Imperf (Plate 1)	£1900		
120		2s. pale blue	£1500	£100	
		aa. Imperf (Plate 1)	£1800		
120a		2s. cobalt	£5000	£900	
120b		2s. milky blue	£3000	£400	
		Plate			
		1 (1867)	£1000	65·00	
		3 (1868)	*	£3000	
121		2s. brown (Plate No. 1) (27.2.80) ...	£6500	£1250	
		a. Imperf	£4000		
		b. No watermark	†	—	
		Wi. Watermark inverted			
*102/21		**For well-centred, lightly used** ...		+**75**%	

Examples of the 1s. from Plates 5 and 6 *without* watermark are postal forgeries used at the Stock Exchange Post Office in the early 1870s.

1872–73. *Uncoloured letters in corners. Wmk Spray, W* **33**.

			Un	* Used	Used on cover
122	**34**	6d. dp chestnut (Plate 11) (12.4.72) ...	£425	20·00	50·00
122a		6d. chestnut (Plate 11) (22.5.72) ...	£350	20·00	
		Wi. Watermark inverted	—	65·00	
122b		6d. pale chestnut (Plate 11) (1872) ..	£350	20·00	
123		6d. pale buff (24.10.72)	£400	40·00	£130
		Wi. Watermark inverted	—	£100	
		Plate			
		11 (1872, pale buff)	£400	40·00	
		12 (1872, pale buff)	£750	60·00	
124		6d. chestnut (Plate 12) (1872)	*	£1300	
124a		6d. pale chestnut (Plate 12) (1872) ..	*	£1300	
125		6d. grey (Plate No. 12) (24.4.73)	£650	90·00	£130
		a. Imperf	£1300		
		Wi. Watermark inverted	£800	£110	
*122/5		**For well-centred, lightly used** ...		+**50**%	

35

36

37

38

41

42

43

44

45

46

39 Maltese Cross

40 Large Anchor

47 Small Anchor

48 Orb

1867–83. *Uncoloured letters in corners.*

(a) *Wmk Maltese Cross, W* **39**. *P* $15\frac{1}{2} \times 15$

			Un	Used
126	**35**	5s. rose (1.7.67)	£2750	£275
127		5s. pale rose	£3000	£275
		a. Imperf (Plate 1)	£4250	
		Plate		
		1 (1867)	£2750	£275
		2 (1874)	£3750	£350
128	**36**	10s. greenish grey (Plate 1) (26.9.78)	£19000	£900
129	**37**	£1 brown-lilac (Plate 1) (26.9.78)	£24000	£1400

(b) *Wmk Anchor, W* **40**. *P* 14. (i) *Blued paper*

130	**35**	5s. rose (Plate 4) (25.11.82)	£5000	£900
		Wi. Watermark inverted	—	£2000
131	**36**	10s. grey-green (Plate 1) (2.83)	£22000	£1300
132	**37**	£1 brown-lilac (Plate 1) (12.82)	£30000	£2500
133	**38**	£5 orange (Plate 1) (21.3.82)	£17000	£4000

(ii) *White paper*

134	**35**	5s. rose (Plate 4)	£4500	£900
135	**36**	10s. greenish grey (Plate 1)	£24000	£1300
136	**37**	£1 brown-lilac (Plate 1)	£35000	£2250
137	**38**	£5 orange (Plate 1)	£4500	£1300
*126/37		**For well-centred, lightly used**		+**75**%

1873–80. *Large coloured letters in the corners.*

(a) *Wmk Anchor, W* **47**

				Un	Used	* Used on cover
138	**41**	2½d. rosy mauve (*blued paper*) (1.7.75)		£400	40·00	
		a. Imperf				
		Wi. Watermark inverted		£525	85·00	
139		2½d. rosy mauve (*white paper*)		£250	30·00	55·00
		Wi. Watermark inverted		£375	45·00	
		Plate				
		1 (*blued paper*) (1875)		£400	40·00	
		1 (*white paper*) (1875)		£250	30·00	
		2 (*blued paper*) (1875)		£3000	£600	
		2 (*white paper*) (1875)		£250	30·00	
		3 (*white paper*) (1875)		£425	35·00	
		3 (*blued paper*) (1875)		—	£2250	

Error of Lettering L H—F L *for* L H—H L (*Plate 2*)

140	**41**	2½d. rosy mauve	£7000	£700

(b) *Wmk Orb, W* **48**

			Un	Used	
141	**41**	2½d. rosy mauve (1.5.76)	£225	14·00	35·00
		Wi. Watermark inverted	£325	30·00	
		Plate			
		3 (1876)	£500	32·00	
		4 (1876)	£225	14·00	
		5 (1876)	£225	18·00	
		6 (1876)	£225	14·00	
		7 (1877)	£225	14·00	
		8 (1877)	£225	18·00	
		9 (1877)	£225	14·00	
		10 (1878)	£250	22·00	
		11 (1878)	£225	14·00	
		12 (1878)	£225	18·00	
		13 (1878)	£225	18·00	
		14 (1879)	£225	14·00	
		15 (1879)	£225	14·00	
		16 (1879)	£225	14·00	
		17 (1880)	£550	90·00	

142	**41**	2½d. blue (5.2.80)	£180	12·00	18·00
		Wi. Watermark inverted	£250	24·00	
		Plate			
		17 (1880)	£180	22·00	
		18 (1880)	£200	14·00	
		19 (1880)	£180	12·00	
		20 (1880)	£180	12·00	

*(c) Wmk Spray, W **33***

143	**42**	3d. rose (5.7.73)	£200	13·00	35·00
		Wi. Watermark inverted	£300	35·00	
144		3d. pale rose	£200	13·00	
		Plate			
		11 (1873)	£200	13·00	
		12 (1873)	£225	15·00	
		14 (1874)	£250	16·00	
		15 (1874)	£200	15·00	
		16 (1875)	£200	15·00	
		17 (1875)	£225	15·00	
		18 (1875)	£225	15·00	
		19 (1876)	£200	15·00	
		20 (1879)	£200	32·00	
145	**43**	6d. pale buff (Plate 13) (15.3.73)	*	£4500	
146		6d. dp grey (20.3.74)	£225	20·00	40·00
147		6d. grey	£225	20·00	
		Wi. Watermark inverted	£325	40·00	
		Plate			
		13 (1874)	£225	22·00	
		14 (1875)	£225	22·00	
		15 (1876)	£225	20·00	
		16 (1878)	£225	20·00	
		17 (1880)	£300	40·00	
148	**44**	1s. dp green (1.9.73)	£325	40·00	
150		1s. pale green	£250	30·00	50·00
		Wi. Watermark inverted	£300	48·00	
		Plate			
		8 (1873)	£325	40·00	
		9 (1874)	£325	40·00	
		10 (1874)	£300	40·00	
		11 (1875)	£300	40·00	
		12 (1875)	£250	30·00	
		13 (1876)	£250	30·00	
		14 (—)	*	£10000	
151		1s. orange-brown (Plate 13)			
		(14.10.80)	£1200	£200	£325
		Wi. Watermark inverted	£1500	£250	

*(d) Wmk Large Garter, W **17***

152	**45**	4d. vermilion (1.3.76)	£650	£140	£275
		Wi. Watermark inverted	—	£180	
		Plate			
		15 (1876)	£650	£140	
		16 (1877)	*	£10000	
153		4d. sage-green (12.3.77)	£425	£100	£190
		Wi. Watermark inverted	—	£120	
		Plate			
		15 (1877)	£475	£110	
		16 (1877)	£425	£100	
		17 (1877)	*	£6000	
154		4d. grey-brown (Plate 17) (15.8.80) ..	£600	£160	£250
		a. Imperf	£2000		
		Wi. Watermark inverted	—	£175	
156	**46**	8d. orange (Plate 1) (11.9.76)	£550	£125	£200
		Wi. Watermark inverted	—	£150	
★138/56		**For well-centred, lightly used**		**+100**%	

1876 (July). *Prepared for use but not issued.*

156a	**46**	8d. purple-brown (Plate 1)	£3000	

49 Imperial Crown

(50)

1880–83. *Wmk Imperial Crown, W **49**.*

				*	*Used on*
			Un	*Used*	*cover*
157	**41**	2½d. blue (23.3.81)	£180	8·00	20·00
		Wi. Watermark inverted	£250	18·00	
		Plate			
		21 (1881)	£225	11·00	
		22 (1881)	£180	10·00	
		23 (1881)	£180	8·00	
158	**42**	3d. rose (3.81)	£200	32·00	45·00
		Wi. Watermark inverted	£500	50·00	
		Plate			
		20 (1881)	£250	48·00	
		21 (1881)	£200	32·00	
159		3d. on 3d. lilac (T **50**) (C.) (Plate 21)			
		(1.1.83)	£225	75·00	£225
		Wi. Watermark inverted			
160	**45**	4d. grey-brown (8.12.80)	£180	25·00	70·00
		Wi. Watermark inverted	—	75·00	
		Plate			
		17 (1880)	£180	25·00	
		18 (1882)	£180	25·00	
161	**43**	6d. grey (1.1.81)	£150	25·00	45·00
		Wi. Watermark inverted	—	55·00	
		Plate			
		17 (1881)	£180	25·00	
		18 (1882)	£150	25·00	
162		6d. on 6d. lilac (as T **50**) (C.) (Plate 18)			
		(1.1.83)	£200	70·00	£140
		a. Slanting dots (various) ......*from*	£250	80·00	
		b. Opt double	—	£4000	
		Wi. Watermark inverted	£325	95·00	
163	**44**	1s. orange-brown (29.5.81)	£250	45·00	90·00
		Wi. Watermark inverted	£300	65·00	
		Plate			
		13 (1881)	£300	45·00	
		14 (1881)	£250	45·00	
★157/63		**For well-centred, lightly used**		**+75**%	

The 1s. plate 14 (line perf 14) exists in purple but was not issued in this shade (*Price £2500 unused*). Examples were included in a few of the Souvenir Albums prepared for members of the "Stamp Committee of 1884".

52

53

54    **55**    **56**

1880–81. *Wmk Imperial Crown, W* **49**.

			Un	*Used*	*★ Used on cover*
164	52	½d. dp green (14.10.80)	18·00	4·00	7·00
		a. Imperf	£650		
		b. No watermark	£2750		
		Wi. Watermark inverted	—	30·00	
165		½d. pale green	19·00	6·00	
166	53	1d. Venetian red (1.1.80)	6·00	3·00	5·00
		a. Imperf	£650		
		Wi. Watermark inverted	—	35·00	
167	54	1½d. Venetian red (14.10.80)	85·00	16·00	65·00
168	55	2d. pale rose (8.12.80)	£100	35·00	65·00
		Wi. Watermark inverted	£175	75·00	
168a		2d. dp rose	£100	35·00	
169	56	5d. indigo (15.3.81)	£350	45·00	£125
		a. Imperf	£1200	£800	
		Wi. Watermark inverted	—	£850	
★164/9		**For well-centred, lightly used**	+**75**%		

57    Die I    Die II

1881. *Wmk Imperial Crown, W* **49**. (a) 14 *dots in each corner, Die I* (12 July).

			Un	*Used*	*★ Used on cover*
170	57	1d. lilac	75·00	12·00	20·00
		Wi. Watermark inverted			
171		1d. pale lilac	75·00	12·00	
		(b) 16 *dots in each corner, Die* II (13 December)			
172	57	1d. lilac	1·00	50	1·50
		Wi. Watermark inverted	9·00	5·00	
172a		1d. bluish lilac	£180	50·00	
173		1d. dp purple	1·00	40	
		a. Printed both sides	£400	†	
		b. Frame broken at bottom	£475	£180	
		c. Printed on gummed side	£375	†	
		d. Imperf three sides (pair)	£2500	†	
		e. Printed both sides but impression on back inverted	£400	†	
		f. No watermark	£750	†	
		g. Blued paper	£1500		
174		1d. mauve	1·00	50	
		a. Imperf (pair)	£900		
★170/4		**For well-centred, lightly used**	+**50**%		

1d. stamps with the words "PEARS SOAP" printed on back in *orange, blue* or *mauve* price *from* £300, *unused*.

The variety "frame broken at bottom" (No. 173b) shows a white space just inside the bottom frame-line from between the "N" and "E" of "ONE" to below the first "N" of "PENNY", breaking the pearls and cutting into the lower part of the oval below "PEN".

KEY TO SURFACE-PRINTED ISSUES 1880–1900

S.G. Nos.	Description	Date of Issue
164/5	½d. green	14.10.80
187	½d. slate-blue	1.4.84
197/d	½d. vermilion	1.1.87
213	½d. blue-green	17.4.1900
166	1d. Venetian red	1.1.80
170/1	1d. lilac, Die I	12.7.81
172/4	1d. lilac, Die II	12.12.81
167	1½d. Venetian red	14.10.80
188	1½d. lilac	1.4.84
198	1½d. purple & green	1.1.87
168/a	2d. rose	8.12.80
189	2d. lilac	1.4.84
199/200	2d. green & red	1.1.87
190	2½d. lilac	1.4.84
201	2½d. purple on blue paper	1.1.87
191	3d. lilac	1.4.84
202/4	3d. purple on yellow paper	1.1.87
192	4d. dull green	1.4.84
205/a	4d. green & brown	1.1.87
206	4½d. green and carmine	15.9.92
169	5d. indigo	15.3.81
193	5d. dull green	1.4.84
207	5d. purple & blue, Die I	1.1.87
207a	5d. purple & blue, Die II	1888
194	6d. dull green	1.4.84
208/a	6d. purple on rose-red paper	1.1.87
195	9d. dull green	1.8.83
209	9d. purple & blue	1.1.87
210	10d. purple & carmine	24.2.90
196	1s. dull green	1.4.84
211	1s. green	1.1.87
214	1s. green & carmine	11.7.1900
175	2s. 6d. lilac on blued paper	2.7.83
178/9	2s. 6d. lilac	1884
176	5s. rose on blued paper	1.4.84
180/1	5s. rose	1884
177/a	10s. ultramarine on blued paper	1.4.84
182/3a	10s. ultramarine	1884
185	£1 brown-lilac, wmk Crowns	1.4.84
186	£1 brown-lilac, wmk Orbs	1.2.88
212	£1 green	27.1.91

Note that the £5 value used with the above series is listed as Nos. 133 and 137.

58    **59**

60

62   **63**   **64**

65   **66**

1883–84. *Coloured letters in the corners. Wmk Anchor, W* **40**.

(a) Blued paper

			Un	★ Used
175	**58**	2s. 6d. lilac (2.7.83)	£2000	£500
176	**59**	5s. rose (1.4.84)	£3500	£1000
177	**60**	10s. ultramarine (1.4.84)	£12000	£3000
177a		10s. cobalt (5.84)	£14000	£4000

(b) White paper

178	**58**	2s. 6d. lilac	£225	65·00
179		2s. 6d. dp lilac	£225	65·00
		a. Error. On blued paper	£1600	£550
		Wi. Watermark inverted	—	£2500
180	**59**	5s. rose	£425	80·00
		Wi. Watermark inverted	†	—
181		5s. crimson	£425	80·00
182	**60**	10s. cobalt	£13000	£3250
183		10s. ultramarine	£800	£250
183a		10s. pale ultramarine	£800	£250
★175/83a		**For well-centred, lightly used**		+**50**%

For No. 180 perf 12 *see* second note below No. 196.

61

Broken frames, Plate 2

1884 (1 Apr). *Wmk Three Imperial Crowns, W* **49**.

			Un	★ Used
185	**61**	£1 brown-lilac	£11000	£950
		a. Frame broken	£18000	£1500
		Wi. Watermark inverted	—	£3000

1888 (1 Feb). *Watermark Three Orbs, W* **48**.

186	**61**	£1 brown-lilac	£18000	£1500
		a. Frame broken	£25000	£2250
★185/6a		**For well-centred, lightly used**		+**50**%

The broken-frame varieties, Nos. 185a and 186a, are on Plate 2 stamps JC and TA, as illustrated. *See also* No. 212a.

1883 (1 Aug) (9d.) *or* **1884** (1 Apr) (*others*). *Wmk Imperial Crown, W* **49** (*sideways on horiz designs*).

			Un	★ Used	Used on cover
187	**52**	½d. slate-blue	10·00	2·00	6·00
		a. Imperf	£650		
		Wi. Watermark inverted	—	38·00	
188	**62**	1½d. lilac	55·00	18·00	55·00
		a. Imperf	£650		
		Wi. Watermark inverted	—	60·00	
189	**63**	2d. lilac	75·00	32·00	65·00
		a. Imperf	£700		
		Wi. Watermark sideways-inverted			
190	**64**	2½d. lilac	40·00	5·00	12·00
		a. Imperf	£700		
		Wi. Watermark sideways-inverted			
191	**65**	3d. lilac	90·00	45·00	65·00
		a. Imperf	£700		
		Wi. Watermark inverted	†	—	
192	**66**	4d. dull green	£250	95·00	£140
		a. Imperf	£750		
193	**62**	5d. dull green	£250	95·00	£130
		a. Imperf	£750		
194	**63**	6d. dull green	£275	£100	£150
		a. Imperf	£750		
		Wi. Watermark sideways-inverted			
195	**64**	9d. dull green (1.8.83)	£500	£250	£650
		Wi. Watermark sideways-inverted	£625	£375	
196	**65**	1s. dull green	£350	£130	£250
		a. Imperf	£1500		
		Wi. Watermark-inverted			
★187/96		**For well-centred, lightly used**		+**100**%	

The above prices are for stamps in the true dull green colour. Stamps which have been soaked, causing the colour to run, are virtually worthless.

Stamps of the above set and No. 180 are also found perf 12; these are official perforations, but were never issued. A second variety of the 5d. is known with a line instead of a stop under the "d" in the value; this was never issued and is therefore only known *unused* (*Price* £5500).

71   **72**   **73**

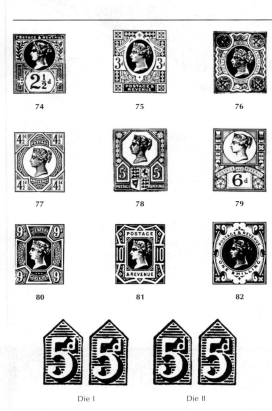

74   75   76

77   78   79

80   81   82

Die I   Die II

Die I: Square dots to right of "d".
Die II: Thin vertical lines to right of "d".

1887 (1 Jan)–**92**.   "Jubilee" issue. New types. The bicoloured stamps have the value tablets, or the frames including the value tablets, in the second colour. Wmk Imperial Crown, W **49** (Three Crowns on £1).

			Un	★ Used on Used	cover
197	**71**	½d. vermilion	1·00	50	5·00
		a. Printed on gummed side	£800	†	
		b. Printed both sides			
		c. Doubly printed	£4000		
		d. Imperf	£900		
		Wi. Watermark inverted	12·00		
197e		½d. orange-vermilion	1·00	50	
198	**72**	1½d. dull purple & pale green	10·00	4·00	18·00
		a. Purple part of design double	—	£3250	
		Wi. Watermark inverted	£350	£150	
199	**73**	2d. green & scarlet	£275	£150	
200		2d. grey-green & carmine	15·00	7·00	18·00
		Wi. Watermark inverted	£450	£160	
201	**74**	2½d. purple/blue	10·00	1·00	5·00
		a. Printed on gummed side	£2000	†	
		b. Imperf three sides	£1500		
		c. Imperf	£2000		
		Ed. Missing "d" in value	†	—	
		Wi. Watermark inverted	£450		

202	**75**	3d. purple/yellow	15·00	1·50	20·00
		a. Imperf	£3000		
		Wi. Watermark inverted	—	£180	
203		3d. dp purple/yellow	15·00	1·50	
204		3d. purple/orange (1891)	£400	£150	
205	**76**	4d. green & purple-brown	18·00	8·00	18·00
		aa. Imperf			
		Wi. Watermark inverted	£400	£140	
205a		4d. green & dp brown	18·00	8·00	
206	**77**	4½d. green & carmine (15.9.92)	5·00	20·00	55·00
		Wi. Watermark inverted			
206a		4½d. green & dp brt carmine	£450	£300	
207	**78**	5d. dull purple & blue (Die I)	£400	40·00	80·00
207a		5d. dull purple & blue (Die II) (1888)	18·00	6·00	22·00
		Wi. Watermark inverted	—	£160	
208	**79**	6d. purple/rose-red	18·00	7·50	15·00
		Wi. Watermark inverted	£475	£125	
208a		6d. dp purple/rose-red	18·00	7·50	
209	**80**	9d. dull purple & blue	40·00	25·00	50·00
		Wi. Watermark inverted	£500	£160	
210	**81**	10d. dull purple & carmine (shades) (24.2.90)	35·00	25·00	60·00
		aa. Imperf	£3750		
		Wi. Watermark inverted	£600	£300	
210a		10d. dull mauve & dp carmine	£350	£150	
210b		10d. dull purple & dull scarlet	45·00	32·00	
211	**82**	1s. dull green	£140	35·00	75·00
		Wi. Watermark inverted	£350	£160	
212	**61**	£1 green (28.1.91)	£2000	£375	
		a. Frame broken	£4500	£800	
		Wi. Watermark inverted	£18000	£2000	

★197/212a   **For well-centred, lightly used** ....   + 50%

The broken-frame varieties, No. 212a, are on Plate 2 stamps JC or TA, as illustrated above No. 185.

½d. stamps with "PEARS SOAP" printed on the back in orange, blue or mauve, price from £300 each.

1900.   Colours changed. Wmk Imperial Crown, W **49**.

			Un	★ Used on Used	cover
213	**71**	½d. blue-green (17.4)	1·00	60	5·00
		a. Printed on gummed side	—	†	
		b. Imperf	£1500		
		Wi. Watermark inverted	12·00		
214	**82**	1s. green & carmine (11.7)	45·00	80·00	£225
		Wi. Watermark inverted	£500	£150	
		Set of 14	£325	£200	

★213/14   **For well-centred, lightly used** ....   + 50%

The ½d. No. 213, in bright blue, is a colour changeling caused by a constituent of the ink used for some months in 1900.

KING EDWARD VII

22 January 1901–6 May 1910

PRINTINGS. Distinguishing De La Rue printings from the provisional printings of the same values made by Harrison & Sons Ltd. or at Somerset House may prove difficult in some cases. For very full guidance Volume 2 of the Stanley Gibbons Great Britain Specialised Catalogue should prove helpful.

Note that stamps perforated 15 × 14 must be Harrison; the 2½d., 3d. and 4d. in this perforation are useful reference material, their shades and appearance in most cases matching the Harrison perf 14 printings.

Except for the 6d. value, all stamps on chalk-surfaced paper were printed by De La Rue.

Of the stamps on ordinary paper, the De La Rue impressions are usually clearer and of a higher finish than those of the other printers. The shades are markedly different except in some printings of the 4d., 6d. and 7d. and in the 5s., 10s. and £1.

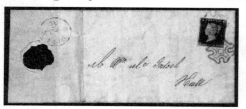

Used stamps in good, clean, unrubbed condition and with dated postmarks can form the basis of a useful reference collection, the dates often assisting in the assignment to the printers.

PRICES. For Nos. 215/456a prices are quoted for unmounted mint, mounted mint and used stamps.

USED STAMPS. For well-centred, lightly used examples of King Edward VII stamps, add the following percentages to the used prices quoted below:

De La Rue printings (Nos. 215/66)—3d. values + 35%, 4d. orange + 100%, 6d. + 75%, 7d. & 1s. + 25%, all other values + 50%.
Harrison printings (Nos 267/86)—all values and perforations + 75%.
Somerset House printings (Nos. 287/320)—1s. values + 25%, all other values + 50%.

95

96

97

(Des E. Fuchs)

1902 (1 Jan)–**10**. *Printed by De La Rue & Co. Wmk Imperial Crown W **49** (½d. to 1s. Three Crowns on £1); Anchor, W **40** (2s. 6d. to 10s.). Ordinary paper.* P 14.

83   84   85

86   87   88

89   90   91

92   93   94

			Unmtd mint	Mtd mint	Used
215	83	½d. dull blue-green (1.1.02)	1·00	50	30
		Wi. Watermark inverted	£1000	£850	£450
216		½d. blue-green	1·00	50	30
217		½d. pale yellowish green (26.11.04) ..	1·00	50	30
218		½d. yellowish green	1·00	50	30
		a. Booklet pane. Five stamps plus St. Andrew's Cross label (6.06)	£250	£175	
		b. Doubly printed (bottom row on one pane) (Control H9)	—	£10000	
		Wi. Watermark inverted	10·00	6·00	3·50
219		1d. scarlet (1.1.02)	1·00	50	30
220		1d. brt scarlet	1·00	50	30
		a. Imperf (pair)	—	£8000	
		Wi. Watermark inverted	3·00	2·00	2·00
221	84	1½d. dull purple & green (21.3.02)	28·00	12·00	6·00
222		1½d. slate-purple & green	28·00	12·00	4·75
		Wi. Watermark inverted	—	—	£300
223		1½d. pale dull purple & green (*chalk-surfaced paper*) (8.05)	30·00	18·00	5·50
224		1½d. slate-purple & bluish green (*chalk-surfaced paper*)	30·00	18·00	4·25
225	85	2d. yellowish green & carmine-red (25.3.02)	30·00	18·00	6·00
226		2d. grey-green & carmine-red (1904) .	30·00	18·00	6·00
227		2d. pale grey-green & carmine-red (*chalk-surfaced paper*) (4.06)	32·00	16·00	8·00
		Wi. Watermark inverted			
228		2d. pale grey-green & scarlet (*chalk-surfaced paper*) (1909)	32·00	16·00	7·00
229		2d. dull blue-green & carmine (*chalk-surfaced paper*) (1907)	65·00	40·00	22·00
230	86	2½d. ultramarine (1.1.02)	8·00	5·00	3·00
231		2½d. pale ultramarine	8·00	5·00	3·00
		Wi. Watermark inverted	—	—	£600
232	87	3d. dull purple/orange-yellow (20.3.02)	32·00	18·00	3·00
		Wi. Watermark inverted			
		a. Chalk-surfaced paper	£150	80·00	18·00
232b		3d. dp purple/orange-yellow	32·00	18·00	3·00
232c		3d. pale reddish purple/orange-yellow (*chalk-surfaced paper*) (3.06)	£140	75·00	15·00
233		3d. dull reddish purple/yellow (*lemon back*) (*chalk-surfaced paper*)	£150	80·00	28·00

233b	**87**	3d. pale purple/*lemon* (*chalk-surfaced paper*)	30·00	14·00	6·00
234		3d. purple/*lemon* (*chalk-surfaced paper*)	30·00	14·00	6·00
235	**88**	4d. green & grey-brown (27.3.02)	55·00	24·00	12·00
		Wi. Watermark inverted			
236		4d. green & chocolate-brown	55·00	24·00	12·00
		a. Chalk-surfaced paper (1.06)	30·00	18·00	7·00
238		4d. dp green & chocolate-brown (*chalk-surfaced paper*)	30·00	18·00	8·50
239		4d. brown-orange (1.11.09)	£140	95·00	80·00
240		4d. pale orange (12.09)	12·00	8·00	6·50
241		4d. orange-red (12.09)	12·00	8·00	7·00
242	**89**	5d. dull purple & ultramarine (14.5.02)	45·00	18·00	6·00
		a. Chalk-surfaced paper (5.06)	45·00	18·00	8·00
244		5d. slate-purple & ultramarine (*chalk-surfaced paper*)	45·00	18·00	9·00
		Wi. Watermark inverted	£650	£500	
245	**83**	6d. pale dull purple (1.1.02)	30·00	15·00	5·00
		a. Chalk-surfaced paper (1.06)	32·00	15·00	5·00
246		6d. slate-purple	30·00	15·00	5·00
248		6d. dull purple (*chalk-surfaced paper*)	30·00	15·00	5·00
		Wi. Watermark inverted			£750
249	**90**	7d. grey-black (4.5.10)	5·00	4·00	6·00
249a		7d. dp grey-black	80·00	65·00	65·00
250	**91**	9d. dull purple & ultramarine (7.4.02)	90·00	40·00	26·00
		a. Chalk-surfaced paper (6.05)	£100	40·00	32·00
		aWi. Watermark inverted	—		£750
251		9d. slate-purple & ultramarine	90·00	40·00	26·00
		a. Chalk-surfaced paper (6.05)	90·00	40·00	32·00
254	**92**	10d. dull purple & carmine (3.7.02) . . .	£100	40·00	22·00
		a. No cross on crown	£250	£180	£110
		b. Chalk-surfaced paper (9.06)	£100	40·00	24·00
255		10d. slate-purple & carmine (*chalk-surfaced paper*) (9.06)	90·00	40·00	30·00
		a. No cross on crown	£225	£150	£100
256		10d. dull purple & scarlet (*chalk-surfaced paper*) (9.10)	90·00	38·00	38·00
		a. No cross on crown	£210	£140	90·00
257	**93**	1s. dull purple & carmine (24.3.02) . . .	90·00	38·00	10·00
		a. Chalk-surfaced paper (9.05)	95·00	38·00	14·00
259		1s. dull green & scarlet (*chalk-surfaced paper*) (9.10)	95·00	38·00	20·00
260	**94**	2s. 6d. lilac (5.4.02)	£225	£110	50·00
		Wi. Watermark inverted	£950	£750	£500
261		2s. 6d. pale dull purple (*chalk-surfaced paper*) (7.10.05)	£250	£110	80·00
		Wi. Watermark inverted	£950	£750	£500
262		2s. 6d. dull purple (*chalk-surfaced paper*)	£250	£110	60·00
263	**95**	5s. brt carmine (5.4.02)	£250	£120	60·00
		Wi. Watermark inverted	—		£750
264		5s. dp brt carmine	£250	£120	60·00
265	**96**	10s. ultramarine (5.4.02)	£500	£325	£200
266	**97**	£1 dull blue-green (16.6.02)	£1200	£800	£325
		Wi. Watermark inverted	—	£15000	£5000

97a

1910 (May). *Prepared for use, but not issued.*

266a	**97**a	2d. Tyrian plum	£12000	£10000

One example of this stamp is known used, but it was never issued to the public.

1911. *Printed by Harrison & Sons. Ordinary paper. Wmk Imperial Crown, W* **49.** *(a) P* 14.

			Unmtd mint	Mtd mint	Used
267	**83**	½d. dull yellow-green (3.5.11)	2·00	1·10	40
		Wi. Watermark inverted	20·00	10·00	5·00
268		½d. dull green	2·50	1·75	40
269		½d. dp dull green	10·00	6·00	2·00
270		½d. pale bluish green	45·00	25·00	22·00
		a. Booklet pane. Five stamps plus St. Andrew's Cross label	£275	£225	
		b. Watermark sideways	†	†	£10000
		c. Imperf (pair)	—	£10000	†
271		½d. brt green (fine impression) (6.11) .	£200	£175	£110
272		1d. rose-red (3.5.11)	3·50	2·25	5·00
		Wi. Watermark inverted	15·00	8·00	6·00
		a. No wmk	40·00	35·00	35·00
273		1d. dp rose-red	4·50	3·00	5·50
274		1d. rose-carmine	45·00	30·00	12·00
275		1d. aniline pink (5.11)	£400	£275	£125
275a		1d. aniline rose	£130	85·00	80·00
276	**86**	2½d. brt blue (10.7.11)	40·00	22·00	12·00
		Wi. Watermark inverted	£450	£350	
277	**87**	3d. purple/*lemon* (12.9.11)	65·00	40·00	£120
277a		3d. grey/*lemon*	£3750	£2750	
278	**88**	4d. brt orange (13.7.11)	65·00	35·00	30·00

(b) P 15 × 14

279	**83**	½d. dull green (30.10.11)	30·00	22·00	25·00
279a		½d. dp dull green	45·00	25·00	25·00
280		1d. rose-red (5.10.11)	25·00	18·00	12·00
281		1d. rose-carmine	13·00	7·00	6·00
282		1d. pale rose-carmine	17·00	10·00	5·00
283	**86**	2½d. brt blue (14.10.11)	20·00	12·00	5·00
284		2½d. dull blue	20·00	12·00	5·00
		Wi. Watermark inverted	—		£225
285	**87**	3d. purple/*lemon* (22.9.11)	32·00	18·00	5·00
285a		3d. grey/*lemon*	£3000	£2250	
286	**88**	4d. brt orange (11.11.11)	20·00	12·00	6·00
		Set of 5	£120	70·00	40·00

USED ON COVER PRICES					
No. 215	60p	No. 217	40p	No. 219	£1·50
No. 222	£12	No. 225	£15	No. 230	£10
No. 232	£20	No. 236a	£28	No. 240	£20
No. 242	£30	No. 245	£30	No. 249	£120
No. 250	£120	No. 254	£125	No. 257	£85
No. 260	£500	No. 263	£550		

USED ON COVER PRICES					
No. 267	£3	No. 272	£7	No. 276	£20
No. 277	£400	No. 278	£110	No. 279	£65
No. 281	£18	No. 283	£15	No. 285	£18
No. 286	£45				

1911–13. *Printed at Somerset House. Ordinary paper. Wmk as 1902–10. P 14.*

287	**84**	1½d. reddish puple & brt green (13.7.11)	40·00	25·00	15·00
288		1½d. dull purple & green	20·00	12·00	10·00
289		1½d. slate-purple & green (9.12)	25·00	15·00	12·00
290	**85**	2d. dp dull green & red (8.8.11)	20·00	12·00	6·00
291		2d. dp dull green & carmine	20·00	12·00	6·00
292		2d. grey-green & brt carmine (carmine shows clearly on back) (11.3.12)	20·00	12·00	7·00
293	**89**	5d. dull reddish purple & brt blue (7.8.11)	25·00	14·00	6·00
294		5d. dp dull reddish purple & brt blue	22·00	12·00	6·00
295	**83**	6d. royal purple (31.10.11)	45·00	28·00	45·00
296		6d. brt magenta (*chalk-surfaced paper*) (31.10.11)	£2750	£1900	
297		6d. dull purple	22·00	14·00	6·00
298		6d. reddish purple (11.11)	22·00	14·00	8·00
		a. No cross on crown (*various shades*)	£275	£200	
299		6d. very deep reddish purple (11.11) .	40·00	25·00	22·00
300		6d. dark purple (3.12)	24·00	16·00	16·00
301		6d. dull purple "Dickinson" coated paper* (3.13)	£150	£110	85·00
303		6d. dp plum (*chalk-surfaced paper*) (7.13)	22·00	12·00	40·00
		a. No cross on crown	£325	£225	
305	**90**	7d. slate-grey (1.8.12)	8·00	5·00	8·50
306	**91**	9d. reddish purple & lt blue (24.7.11)	85·00	50·00	35·00
306a		9d. dp dull reddish purple & dp brt blue (9.11)	85·00	50·00	35·00
307		9d. dull reddish purple & blue (10.11)	55·00	30·00	25·00
307a		9d. dp plum & blue (7.13)	55·00	30·00	40·00
308		9d. slate-purple & cobalt-blue (3.12) .	85·00	60·00	40·00
309	**92**	10d. dull purple & scarlet (9.10.11)	75·00	45·00	30·00
310		10d. dull reddish purple & aniline pink	£250	£180	£110
311		10d. dull reddish purple & carmine (5.12)	55·00	35·00	25·00
		a. No cross on crown	£650	£450	
312	**93**	1s. dark green & scarlet (13.7.11)	95·00	55·00	25·00
313		1s. dp green & scarlet (9.10.11)	75·00	40·00	12·00
		Wi. Wmk inverted	90·00	75·00	†
314		1s. green & carmine (15.4.12)	55·00	28·00	10·00
315	**94**	2s. 6d. dull greyish purple (27.9.11) ..	£450	£300	£160
316		2s. 6d. dull reddish purple (10.11) ...	£225	£110	60·00
		Ei. Wmk inverted	†	†	—
317		2s. 6d. dark purple	£225	£110	60·00
318	**95**	5s. carmine (29.2.12)	£275	£160	60·00
319	**96**	10s. blue (14.1.12)	£550	£325	£225
320	**97**	£1 dp green (3.9.11)	£1200	£800	£350
		Set of 15 (to 1s incl. ½d. (2))	£340	£170	£100

*No. 301 was on an experimental coated paper which does not respond to the silver test.

KING GEORGE V

6 May 1910–20 January 1936

Further detailed information on the issues of King George V will be found in Volume 2 of the Stanley Gibbons *Great Britain Specialised Catalogue.*

PRINTERS. Types **98** to **102** were typographed by Harrison & Sons Ltd, with the exception of certain preliminary printings made at Somerset House and distinguishable by the controls "A.11", "B.11" or "B.12" (the Harrison printings do not have a full stop after the letter). The booklet stamps, Nos. 334/7, and 344/5 were printed by Harrison only.

WATERMARK VARIETIES. Many British stamps to 1967 exist without watermark owing to misplacement of the paper, and with either inverted, reversed, or inverted and reversed watermarks. A proportion of the low-value stamps issued in booklets have the watermark inverted in the normal course of printing.

Low values with *watermark sideways* are normally from stamp rolls used on machines with sideways delivery or, from June 1940, certain booklets.

STAMPS WITHOUT WATERMARK. Stamps found without watermark, due to misplacement of the sheet in relation to the dandy roll, are not listed here but will be found in the *Great Britain Specialised Catalogue.*

The 1½d. and 5d. 1912–22, and 2d. and 2½d., 1924–26, listed here, are from *whole* sheets completely without watermark.

98	99	100 Simple Cypher

For type difference with T **101/2** *see notes below the latter.*

Die A	Die B

Dies of Halfpenny

Die A. The three upper scales on the body of the right hand dolphin form a triangle; the centre jewel of the cross inside the crown is suggested by a comma.

Die B. The three upper scales are incomplete; the centre jewel is suggested by a crescent.

Die A	Die B

ALL ASPECTS *and* PERIODS *of* GREAT BRITAIN

1840-1951

I specialise in the more unusual and also in the finest quality material. Be it a common stamp or a world rarity.

I include postal history, colour trials, essays, proofs, and issued stamps in my stock and can usually find something for you. Your wants lists are welcome.

Buying: I am also looking to buy individual stamps and collections intact.

I look forward to hearing from you.

A n d r e w . G . L a j e r
P H I L A T E L I S T

ANDREW G. LAJER
P.O. Box 42
Henley on Thames
Oxon. RG9 1FF
Tel: 01491 579662
Fax: 01491 579148

Dies of One Penny

Die A. The second line of shading on the ribbon to the right of the crown extends right across the wreath; the line nearest to the crown on the right hand ribbon shows as a short line at the bottom of the ribbon.

Die B. The second line of shading is broken in the middle; the first line is little more than a dot.

(Des Bertram Mackennal and G. W. Eve. Head from photograph by W. and D. Downey. Die eng J.A.C. Harrison)

1911–12. *Wmk Imperial Crown, W* **49**. *P* 15 × 14.

			Unmtd mint	Mtd mint	Used
321	**98**	½d. pale green (Die A) (22.6.11)	5·00	3·00	1·00
322		½d. green (Die A) (22.6.11)	4·00	2·50	1·00
		a. Error. Perf 14 (8.11)	—	—	£250
		Wi. Watermark inverted	—	—	£550
323		½d. bluish green (Die A)	£300	£225	£130
324		½d. yellow-green (Die B)	7·50	4·00	70
325		½d. brt green (Die B)	7·50	4·00	70
		a. Watermark sideways	—	—	£1800
		Wi. Watermark inverted	9·00	6·00	3·00
326		½d. bluish green (Die B)	£175	£140	70·00
327	**99**	1d. carmine-red (Die A) (22.6.11) ...	4·50	2·50	1·00
		c. Watermark sideways	†	†	—
		Wi. Watermark inverted	£750	£500	£350
328		1d. pale carmine (Die A) (22.6.11) ...	12·00	8·00	1·25
		a. No cross on crown	£350	£250	£150
329		1d. carmine (Die B)	6·00	4·00	1·00
		Wi. Watermark inverted	8·00	6·00	2·50
330		1d. pale carmine (Die B)	6·00	4·00	1·00
		a. No cross on crown	£450	£350	£275
331		1d. rose-pink (Die B)	85·00	60·00	22·00
332		1d. scarlet (Die B) (6.12)	20·00	13·00	9·00
		Wi. Watermark inverted	20·00	13·00	7·00
333		1d. aniline scarlet (Die B)	£150	95·00	55·00

For note on the aniline scarlet No. 333 *see below* No. 343.

1912 (Aug). *Booklet stamps. Wmk Royal Cypher ("Simple"), W* **100**. *P* 15 × 14.

334	**98**	½d. pale green (Die B)	40·00	25·00	28·00
335		½d. green (Die B)	40·00	25·00	28·00
		Wi. Watermark inverted	40·00	25·00	28·00
		Wj. Watermark reversed	£325	£275	£150
		Wk. Watermark inverted and reversed	£325	£275	£150
336	**99**	1d. scarlet (Die B)	20·00	15·00	15·00
		Wi. Watermark inverted	20·00	15·00	15·00
		Wj. Watermark reversed	£300	£275	
		Wk. Watermark inverted and reversed	—	—	75·00
337		1d. brt scarlet (Die B)	20·00	15·00	15·00

101

102

103 Multiple Cypher

Type differences

½d. In T **98** the ornament above "P" of "HALFPENNY" has two thin lines of colour and the beard is undefined. In T **101** the ornament has one thick line and the beard is well defined.

1d. In T **99** the body of the lion is unshaded and in T **102** it is shaded.

1912 (1 Jan). *Wmk Imperial Crown, W* **49**. *P* 15 × 14.

338	**101**	½d. dp green	12·00	7·00	3·00
339		½d. green	6·00	3·00	50
340		½d. yellow-green	6·00	3·00	75
		a. No cross on crown	75·00	50·00	15·00
		Wi. Watermark inverted	£300	£250	£150
341	**102**	1d. brt scarlet	3·00	1·75	75
		a. No cross on crown	60·00	40·00	15·00
		b. Printed double, one albino	£125	95·00	
		Wi. Watermark inverted	£150	£125	£100
342		1d. scarlet	3·00	1·75	75
343		1d. aniline scarlet*	£140	£100	55·00
		a. No cross on crown	£750	£600	

*Our prices for the aniline scarlet 1d. stamps, Nos. 333 and 343, are for the specimens in which the colour is suffused on the surface of the stamp and shows through clearly on the back. Specimens without these characteristics but which show "aniline" reactions under the quartz lamp are relatively common.

1912 (Aug). *Wmk Royal Cypher ("Simple"), W* **100**. *P* 15 × 14.

344	**101**	½d. green	4·50	3·00	1·00
		a. No cross on crown	75·00	60·00	15·00
		Wi. Watermark inverted	75·00	50·00	15·00
		Wj. Watermark reversed	70·00	40·00	15·00
		Wk. Watermark inverted and reversed	6·50	4·50	2·50
345	**102**	1d. scarlet	5·00	4·00	75
		a. No cross on crown	65·00	50·00	15·00
		Wi. Watermark inverted	11·00	7·00	5·50
		Wj. Watermark reversed	20·00	10·00	6·00
		Wk. Watermark inverted and reversed	8·00	4·00	4·00

1912 (Sept–Oct). *Wmk Royal Cypher ("Multiple"), W* **103**. *P* 15 × 14.

346	**101**	½d. green (Oct)	7·00	6·00	4·00
		a. No cross on crown	75·00	60·00	30·00
		b. Imperf	£110	75·00	
		c. Watermark sideways	†	†	£1100
		d. Printed on gummed side	—	—	†
		Wi. Watermark inverted	8·00	5·00	4·00
		Wj. Watermark reversed	8·00	5·00	4·00
		Wk. Watermark inverted and reversed	20·00	12·00	
347		½d. yellow-green	8·00	6·00	4·50
348		½d. pale green	10·00	6·00	4·00
349	**102**	1d. brt scarlet	10·00	6·00	5·00
350		1d. scarlet	9·00	5·00	5·00
		a. No cross on crown	85·00	65·00	20·00
		b. Imperf	95·00	65·00	
		c. Watermark sideways	95·00	65·00	75·00
		d. Watermark sideways. No cross on crown	£550	£450	
		Wi. Watermark inverted	10·00	6·00	
		Wj. Watermark reversed	10·00	6·00	
		Wk. Watermark inverted and reversed	£350	£250	£150

104

105

106

107    108

No. 357ab

No. 357ac

No. 357a

Die I

Die II

Two Dies of the 2d.

Die I.— Inner frame-line at top and sides close to solid of background. *Four* complete lines of shading between top of head and oval frame-line. These four lines do *not* extend to the oval itself. White line round "TWOPENCE" thin.

Die II.—Inner frame-line further from solid of background. *Three* lines between top of head and extending to the oval. White line round "TWOPENCE" thicker.

(Des Bertram Mackennal (heads) and G.W. Eve (frames). Coinage head (½, 1½, 2, 3 and 4d.); large medal head (1d., 2½d.); intermediate medal head (5d. to 1s.); small medal head used for fiscal stamps. Dies eng J. A. C. Harrison)

(Typo by Harrison & Sons Ltd., except the 6d. printed by the Stamping Department of the Board of Inland Revenue, Somerset House. The latter also made printings of the following which can only be distinguished by the controls: ½d. B.13; 1½d. A.12; 2d. C.13; 2½d. A.12; 3d. A12, B.13, C.13; 4d. B.13; 5d. B.13; 7d. C.13; 8d. C.13; 9d. agate B.13; 10d. C.13; 1s. C.13)

1912–24. *Wmk Royal Cypher, W* **100**. *Chalk-surfaced paper* (6d.). *P* 15 × 14.

351	**105**	½d. green (1.13)	60	40	35
		a. Partial double print (half of bottom row) (Control G15)	—£13500	†	
		b. Gummed both sides			
		Wi. Watermark inverted	2·00	1·00	35
		Wj. Watermark reversed	12·00	8·00	5·00
		Wk. Watermark inverted and reversed	3·00	2·25	1·50
352	**105**	½d. brt green	60	40	35
353		½d. dp green	4·00	2·25	1·00
354		½d. yellow-green	5·00	3·50	1·25
355		½d. very yellow (Cyprus) green (1914)	£2500	£1750	†
356		½d. blue-green	32·00	20·00	12·00
357	**104**	1d. brt scarlet (10.12)	60	30	25
		a. "Q" for "O" (R.1/4) (Control E14)	£150	£125	75·00
		ab. "Q" for "O" (R.4/11) (Control T22)	£225	£175	£100
		ac. Reversed "Q" for "O" (R.15/9) (Control T22)	£300	£225	£130
		ad. Inverted "Q" for "O" (R.20/3) ..	£375	£300	£150
		b. *Tête-bêche* (pair)	—£50000	†	
		Wi. Watermark inverted	2·75	1·00	30
		Wj. Watermark reversed	12·00	8·00	5·00
		Wk. Watermark inverted and reversed	2·00	1·00	50
358		1d. vermilion	3·00	1·50	60
359		1d. pale rose-red	10·00	6·00	50
360		1d. carmine-red	7·00	4·00	2·25
361		1d. scarlet-vermilion	95·00	70·00	20·00
		a. Printed on back†	£225	£175	†
362	**105**	1½d. red-brown (10.12)	2·00	1·50	30
		a. "PENCF" (R.15/12)	£225	£180	£125
		b. Booklet pane. Four stamps plus two printed labels (2.24)	£325	£275	
		Wi. Watermark inverted	4·00	2·50	75
		Wi. Watermark reversed	12·00	8·00	3·00
		Wk. Watermark inverted and reversed	6·00	4·50	2·25
363		1½d. chocolate-brown	3·75	2·25	40
		a. No watermark	£120	90·00	
364		1½d. chestnut	2·75	1·75	30
		a. "PENCF" (R.15/12)	£125	95·00	75·00
365		1½d. yellow-brown	12·00	8·00	9·00
366	**106**	2d. orange-yellow (Die I) (8.12)	6·00	4·00	1·50
367		2d. reddish orange (Die I) (11.13) ...	2·50	1·25	50
368		2d. orange (Die I)	1·50	1·00	50
		Wi. Watermark inverted	11·00	7·50	3·00
		Wj. Watermark reversed	10·00	7·00	4·50
		Wk. Watermark inverted and reversed	7·00	5·00	2·50
369		2d. brt orange (Die I)	2·75	1·50	70
370		2d. orange (Die II) (9.21)	3·00	2·00	1·75
		Wi. Watermark inverted	15·00	10·00	5·50
		Wj. Watermark inverted and reversed	12·00	8·00	4·50
371	**104**	2½d. cobalt-blue (10.12)	9·00	5·00	1·25
371a		2½d. brt blue (1914)	9·00	5·00	1·25
372		2½d. blue	9·00	5·00	1·25
		Wi. Watermark inverted	30·00	20·00	14·00
		Wj. Watermark reversed	15·00	10·00	3·50
		Wk. Watermark inverted and reversed	15·00	10·00	4·00
373		2½d. indigo-blue* (1920)	£1100	£850	£550
373a		2d. dull Prussian blue* (1921)	£600	£475	£350
374	**106**	3d. dull reddish violet (10.12)	9·00	6·00	1·10
375		3d. violet	3·00	2·00	75
		Wi. Watermark inverted	40·00	20·00	9·00
		Wj. Watermark reversed	70·00	50·00	15·00
		Wk. Watermark inverted and reversed	12·00	8·00	6·00
376		3d. bluish violet (11.13)	5·00	2·75	90
377		3d. pale violet	6·00	4·00	90
378		4d. dp grey-green (1.13)	25·00	15·00	3·50
379		4d. grey-green	8·50	4·50	1·00
		Wi. Watermark inverted	16·00	9·00	10·00
		Wj. Watermark reversed	40·00	25·00	6·00
		Wk. Watermark inverted and reversed	25·00	18·00	4·50
380		4d. pale grey-green	15·00	10·00	2·00

381	**107**	5d. brown (6.13)	9·00	4·00	3·25
		Wi. Watermark inverted	£350	£250	£150
		Wj. Watermark inverted and reversed	£110	90·00	40·00
		Wk. Watermark reversed	†	†	—
382		5d. yellow-brown	9·00	5·00	3·25
		a. No watermark	£600	£400	
383		5d. bistre-brown	90·00	65·00	25·00
384		6d. dull purple (8.13)	20·00	12·00	4·00
385		6d. reddish purple	12·00	6·00	2·00
		a. Perf 14 (10.20)	80·00	65·00	90·00
		Wi. Watermark inverted	30·00	18·00	10·00
		Wj. Watermark reversed	£550	£400	
		Wk. Watermark inverted and reversed	30·00	18·00	7·00
386		6d. dp reddish purple	25·00	12·00	1·50
387		7d. olive (8.13)	16·00	9·00	4·50
		Wi. Watermark inverted	30·00	22·00	16·00
		Wj. Watermark inverted and reversed	£1250	£900	
		Wk. Watermark reversed	†	†	—
388		7d. bronze-green (1915)	50·00	35·00	12·00
389		7d. sage-green (1917)	50·00	35·00	6·00
390		8d. black/yellow (8.13)	28·00	18·00	7·00
		Wi. Watermark inverted	55·00	38·00	38·00
		Wj. Watermark reversed	80·00	60·00	
		Wk. Watermark inverted and reversed	£1500	£1250	
391		8d. black/yellow-buff (granite) (5.17) .	28·00	18·00	9·00
392	**108**	9d. agate (6.13)	18·00	10·00	2·75
		a. Printed double, one albino			
		Wi. Watermark inverted	50·00	32·00	20·00
		Wj. Watermark inverted and reversed	45·00	30·00	14·00
393		9d. dp agate	20·00	12·00	3·00
393a		9d. olive-green (9.22)	£130	70·00	18·00
		aWi. Watermark inverted	£500	£400	£250
		aWj. Watermark inverted and reversed	£400	£300	£250
393b		9d. pale olive-green	£150	70·00	18·00
394		10d. turquoise-blue (8.13)	16·00	10·00	12·00
		Wi. Watermark inverted	£900	£650	£225
		Wj. Watermark inverted and reversed	£110	85·00	28·00
394a		10d. dp turquoise-blue	55·00	40·00	15·00
395		1s. bistre (8.13)	28·00	16·00	1·00
		Wi. Watermark inverted	95·00	65·00	15·00
		Wj. Watermark inverted and reversed	30·00	20·00	10·00
396		1s. bistre-brown	30·00	19·00	5·00
		Set of 15	£250	£140	50·00

Imperf stamps of this issue exist but may be war-time colour trials.
† The impression of No. 361a is set sideways and is very pale.

*No. 373 comes from Control O 20 and also exists on toned paper. No. 373a comes from Control R 21 and also exists on toned paper, but both are unlike the rare Prussian blue shade of the 1935 2½d. Jubilee issue.

Examples of the 2d., T **106** which were in the hands of philatelists, are known bisected in Guernsey from 27 December 1940 to February 1941.

See also Nos. 418/29.

1913 (Aug). *Wmk Royal Cypher ("Multiple"), W* **103**. *P* 15 × 14.

397	**105**	½d. brt green	£175	80·00	£100
		Wi. Watermark inverted	£375	£250	
398	**104**	1d. dull scarlet	£275	£150	£140
		Wi. Watermark inverted	£450	£325	

Both these stamps were originally issued in rolls only. Subsequently sheets were found, so that horizontal pairs and blocks are known but are of considerable rarity.

109

A

110 Single Cypher

Major Re-entries on 2s. 6d.

Nos. 400a and 408a

No. 415b

(Des Bertram Mackennal. Dies eng J.A.C. Harrison. Recess)

High values, so-called "Sea Horses" design: T **109**. *Background around portrait consists of horizontal lines, Type A. Wmk Single Cypher, W* **110**. *P* 11 × 12.

1913 (30 June–Aug). *Printed by Waterlow Bros & Layton.*

399	**109**	2s. 6d. dp sepia-brown	£200	£125	65·00
400		2s. 6d. sepia-brown	£200	£125	60·00
		a. Re-entry (R.2/1)	£900	£650	£400
401		5s. rose-carmine (4 July)	£300	£225	£150
402		10s. indigo-blue (1 Aug)	£600	£350	£225
403		£1 green (1 Aug)	£1600	£1000	£600
404		£1 dull blue-green (1 Aug)	£1600	£1000	£650
★399/404		**For well-centred, lightly used**			+**30**%

For full information on all future British issues, collectors should write to the British Post Office Philatelic Bureau, 20 Brandon Street, Edinburgh EH3 5TT

1915 (Nov–Dec). *Printed by De la Rue & Co.*

405	**109**	2s. 6d. dp yellow-brown	£225	£150	70·00
		Wi. Watermark inverted	£450	£350	
406		2s. 6d. yellow-brown	£225	£150	65·00
		Wi. Watermark inverted	£400	£300	
		Wj. Watermark reversed	£400	£300	
		Wk. Watermark inverted and reversed	£950	£800	
407		2s. 6d. pale brown (worn plate)	£200	£125	65·00
		Wi. Watermark inverted	£400	£300	
		Wj. Watermark reversed	£450	£350	
408		2s. 6d. sepia (seal-brown)	£225	£150	70·00
		a. Re-entry (R.2/1)	£700	£550	£400
		Wi. Watermark inverted	£400	£300	
		Wj. Watermark reversed	£400	£300	
409		5s. brt carmine	£325	£225	£150
		Wi. Watermark inverted	£950	£750	
		Wj. Watermark reversed	£900	£700	
		Wk. Watermark inverted and reversed	£3000	£2500	†
410		5s. pale carmine (worn plate)	£350	£250	£150
411		10s. dp blue (12.15)	£1250	£850	£325
412		10s. blue	£1000	£650	£275
		Wi. Watermark inverted and reversed	—	—	†
413		10s. pale blue	£1000	£650	£275
★405/13		**For well-centred, lightly used**			+35%

1918 (Dec)–**19**. *Printed by Bradbury, Wilkinson & Co, Ltd.*

413a	**109**	2s. 6d. olive-brown	£100	60·00	25·00
414		2s. 6d. chocolate-brown	£100	75·00	30·00
415		2s. 6d. reddish brown	£110	80·00	30·00
415a		2s. 6d. pale brown	£100	80·00	25·00
		b. Major re-entry (R.1/2)	£600	£450	£250
416		5s. rose-red (1.19)	£200	£150	45·00
417		10s. dull grey-blue (1.19)	£325	£225	80·00
		Set of 4 (inc. no. 403)	£2000	£1300	£700
★413a/17		**For well-centred, lightly used**			+30%

DISTINGUISHING PRINTINGS. Note that the £1 value was only printed by Waterlow.

Waterlow and De La Rue stamps measure exactly 22 mm vertically. In the De La Rue printings the gum is usually patchy and yellowish, and the colour of the stamp, particularly in the 5s., tends to show through the back. The holes of the perforation are smaller than those of the other two printers, but there is a thick perforation tooth at the top of each vertical side.

In the Bradbury Wilkinson printings the height of the stamp is 22¾ or 23 mm. On most of the 22¾ mm high stamps a minute coloured guide dot appears in the margin just above the middle of the upper frame-line.

For (1934) re-engraved Waterlow printings *see* Nos. 450/2.

UNITED KINGDOM OF GREAT BRITAIN AND NORTHERN IRELAND

111	Block Cypher	**111**a

The watermark Type **111**a, as compared with Type **111**, differs as follows: Closer spacing of horizontal rows (12½ mm instead of 14½ mm). Letters shorter and rounder. Watermark thicker.

(Typo by Waterlow & Sons, Ltd (all values except 6d.) and later, 1934–35, by Harrison & Sons, Ltd (all values). Until 1934 the 6d. was printed at Somerset House where a printing of the 1½d. was also made in 1926 (identifiable only by control E.26). Printings by Harrisons in 1934–35 can be identified, when in mint condition, by the fact that the gum shows a streaky appearance vertically, the Waterlow gum being uniformly applied, but Harrisons also used up the balance of the Waterlow "smooth gum" paper)

1924 (Feb)–**26**. *Wmk Block Cypher, W* **111**. *P* 15 × 14.

418	**105**	½d. green	35	20	25
		a. Watermark sideways (5.24)	7·00	5·00	2·50
		b. Doubly printed	—	£7000	†
		Wi. Watermark inverted	3·50	1·25	60
		Wj. Watermark sideways-inverted . .			
419	**104**	1d. scarlet	40	20	25
		a. Watermark sideways	20·00	12·00	12·00
		b. Experimental paper, W **111**a (10.24)	25·00	20·00	
		c. Partial double print, one inverted			
		d. Inverted "Q" for "O" (R.20/3) . . .	£375	£275	
		Wi. Watermark inverted	4·00	1·50	75
420	**105**	1½d. red-brown	30	20	25
		a. Tête-bêche (pair)	£375	£275	£500
		b. Watermark sideways (8.24)	10·00	5·00	2·50
		c. Printed on the gummed side . . .	£400	£300	†
		d. Booklet pane. Four stamps plus two printed labels (6.24)	£125	90·00	
		e. Ditto. Watermark sideways	£3500	£3000	
		f. Experimental paper, W **111**a (10.24)	50·00	35·00	
		g. Double impression	—	£8000	†
		Wi. Watermark inverted	1·25	75	40
		Wj. Watermark sideways-inverted . .			
421	**106**	2d. orange (Die II) (9.24)	2·00	1·00	1·00
		a. No watermark	£550	£425	
		b. Watermark sideways (7.26)	90·00	55·00	60·00
		c. Partial double print	—	£13000	†
		Wi. Watermark inverted	12·00	7·00	10·00
422	**104**	2½d. blue (10.24)	5·50	3·00	1·25
		a. No watermark	£800	£600	
		b. Watermark sideways	†	†	—
		Wi. Watermark inverted	22·00	16·00	15·00
423	**106**	3d. violet (10.24)	11·00	5·00	1·00
		Wi. Watermark inverted	20·00	10·00	10·00
424		4d. grey-green (11.24)	13·00	6·50	1·00
		a. Printed on the gummed side . . .	£1300	£950	†
		Wi. Watermark inverted	55·00	35·00	10·00
425	**107**	5d. brown (11.24)	22·00	11·00	1·75
		Wi. Watermark inverted	40·00	30·00	20·00
426		6d. reddish purple (chalk-surfaced paper) (9.24)	10·00	5·00	1·50
		Wi. Watermark inverted	25·00	16·00	12·00
		Wj. Watermark inverted and reversed	£125	75·00	
426a		6d. purple (6.26)	3·50	1·75	50
		aWi. Watermark inverted	25·00	16·00	12·00
427	**108**	9d. olive-green (12.24)	22·00	6·00	2·50
		Wi. Watermark inverted	55·00	30·00	25·00
428		10d. turquoise-blue (11.24)	45·00	20·00	20·00
		Wi. Watermark inverted	£750	£525	£275
429		1s. bistre-brown (10.24)	28·00	12·00	1·50
		Wi. Watermark inverted	£250	£200	£175
		Set of 12	£140	60·00	28·00

There are numerous shades in this issue.

The 6d. on chalk-surfaced and ordinary papers was printed by both Somerset House and Harrisons. The Harrison printings have streaky gum, differ slightly in shade, and that on chalk-surfaced paper is printed in a highly fugitive ink. The prices quoted are for the commonest (Harrison) printing in each case.

112

(Des H. Nelson. Eng J. A. C. Harrison. Recess Waterlow)

1924–25. British Empire Exhibition. W 111. P 14.

(a) Dated "1924" (23.4.24)

430	**112**	1d. scarlet	....	8·00	5·00	6·00
431		1½d. brown	....	15·00	7·50	11·00
		Set of 2	....	23·00	12·00	17·00
		First Day Cover	....			£350

(b) Dated "1925" (9.5.25)

432	**112**	1d. scarlet	....	10·00	8·00	17·00
433		1½d. brown	....	40·00	25·00	50·00
		Set of 2	....	50·00	32·00	65·00
		First Day Cover	....			£1200

113   **114**   **115**

116 St. George and the Dragon

117

(Des J. Farleigh (T **113** and **115**), E. Linzell (T **114**) and H. Nelson (T **116**). Eng C. G. Lewis (T **113**), T.E. Storey (T **115**), both at the Royal Mint; J. A. C. Harrison, of Waterlow (T **114** & **116**). Typo by Waterlow from plates made at the Royal Mint, except T **116**, recess by Bradbury, Wilkinson from die and plate of their own manufacture)

1929 (10 May).   **Ninth U.P.U. Congress, London.**

(a) W **111**. P 15 × 14

434	**113**	½d. green	....	2·25	1·50	1·50
		a. Watermark sideways	....	35·00	25·00	32·00
		Wi. Watermark inverted	....	22·00	10·00	8·00
435	**114**	1d. scarlet	....	2·25	1·50	1·50
		a. Watermark sideways	....	75·00	45·00	45·00
		Wi. Watermark inverted	....	22·00	10·00	9·00
436		1½d. purple-brown	....	1·50	1·00	1·00
		a. Watermark sideways	....	45·00	25·00	21·00
		b. Booklet pane. Four stamps plus two printed labels	....	£175	£150	
		Wi. Watermark inverted	....	8·00	3·00	6·00
437	**115**	2½d. blue	....	15·00	7·50	9·00
		Wi. Watermark inverted	....	£1000	£600	£375

(b) W **117**. P 12

438	**116**	£1 black	....	£775	£550	£400
		Set of 4 (to 2½d.)	....	19·00	10·00	11·50
		First Day Cover (4 vals.)	....			£500
		First Day Cover (5 vals.)	....			£3000

PRINTERS. All subsequent issues were printed in photogravure by Harrison & Sons, Ltd, *except where otherwise stated.*

118   **119**   **120**

121   **122**

1934–36. W **111**. P 15 × 14.

439	**118**	½d. green (19.11.34)	....	25	10	25
		a. Watermark sideways	....	10·00	6·00	3·00
		b. Imperf three sides	....	£1250	£1100	
		Wi. Watermark inverted	....	15·00	4·50	1·25
		Wj. Watermark sideways-inverted	...	£175	£150	75·00
440	**119**	1d. scarlet (24.9.34)	....	35	15	25
		a. Imperf (pair)	....	£1250	£950	
		b. Printed on gummed side	....	£500	£375	†
		c. Watermark sideways	....	20·00	10·00	4·25
		d. Double impression	....	†	†	£12500
		e. Imperf between (pair)	....	£1750	£1250	
		f. Imperf (three sides) (pair)	......	£1250	£950	
		Wi. Watermark inverted	....	12·00	6·50	2·75
		Wj. Watermark sideways-inverted	...	40·00	30·00	
441	**118**	1½d. red-brown (20.8.34)	....	25	10	25
		a. Imperf (pair)	....	£350	£275	
		b. Imperf (three sides) (lower stamp in vert pair)	....	£700	£500	
		c. Imperf between (horiz pair)	......			
		d. Watermark sideways	....	6·00	5·00	3·00
		e. Booklet pane. Four stamps plus two printed labels (1.35)	....	75·00	60·00	
		Wi. Watermark inverted	....	2·00	1·00	50
		Wj. Watermark sideways-inverted	...			

442	**120**	2d. orange (21.1.35)	60	30	25
		a. Imperf (pair)	£1350	£1100	
		b. Watermark sideways	£120	60·00	50·00
443	**119**	2½d. ultramarine (18.3.35)	1·50	75	60
444	**120**	3d. violet (18.3.35)	1·75	1·00	50
		Wi. Watermark inverted	—	—	£450
445		4d. dp grey-green (2.12.35)	2·75	1·25	55
		Wi. Watermark inverted	†	†	—
446	**121**	5d. yellow-brown (17.2.36)	9·00	4·50	1·50
447	**122**	9d. dp olive-green (2.12.35)	16·00	11·00	1·60
448		10d. turquoise-blue (24.2.36)	22·00	13·00	9·00
449		1s. bistre-brown (24.2.36)	30·00	13·00	50
		a. Double impression	—	—	†
		Set of 11	75·00	40·00	13·00

Owing to the need for wider space for the perforations the size of the designs of the ½d. and 2d. were once, and the 1d. and 1½d. twice reduced from that of the first printings.

The format description, size in millimetres and S.G. catalogue number are given but further details will be found in the *Great Britain Specialised Catalogue, Volume 2.*

Description	Size	S.G. Nos.	Date of Issue
½d. intermediate format	18.4 × 22.2	—	19.11.34
½d. small format	17.9 × 21.7	439	1935
1d. large format	18.7 × 22.5	—	24.9.34
1d. intermediate format	18.4 × 22.2	—	1934
1d. small format	17.9 × 21.7	440	1935
1½d. large format	18.7 × 22.5	—	20.8.34
1½d. intermediate format	18.4 × 22.2	—	1934
1½d. small format	17.9 × 21.7	441	1935
2d. intermediate format	18.4 × 22.2	—	21.1.35
2d. small format	18.15 × 21.7	442	1935

There are also numerous minor variations, due to the photographic element in the process.

The ½d. imperf three sides, No. 439b, is known in a block of four, from a sheet, in which the bottom pair is imperf at top and sides.

Examples of 2d., T **120**, which were in the hands of philatelists are known bisected in Guernsey from 27 December 1940 to February 1941.

B	**123**

(Eng J .A .C. Harrison. Recess Waterlow)

1934 (Oct). T **109** (*re-engraved*). *Background around portrait consists of horizontal and diagonal lines, Type B, W* **110**. *P* 11 × 12.

450	**109**	2s. 6d. chocolate-brown	80·00	45·00	20·00
451		5s. brt rose-red	£225	£100	55·00
452		10s. indigo	£350	£350	55·00
		Set of 3	£575	£350	£120

There are numerous other minor differences in the design of this issue.

(Des B. Freedman)

1935 (7 May). **Silver Jubilee**. *W* **111**. *P* 15 × 14.

453	**123**	½d. green	75	25	20
		Wi. Watermark inverted	12·00	6·00	3·00
454		1d. scarlet	2·00	1·00	1·00
		Wi. Watermark inverted	12·00	6·00	4·00
455		1½d. red-brown	75	25	20
		Wi. Watermark inverted	4·00	3·00	1·00
456		2½d. blue	5·00	4·00	5·50
456a		2½d. Prussian blue	£4000	£3000	£3250
		Set of 4	7·00	5·00	6·00
		First Day Cover			£400

The 1d., 1½d. and 2½d. values differ from T **123** in the emblem in the panel at right.

Four sheets of No. 456a, printed in the wrong shade, were issued in error by the Post Office Stores Department on 25 June 1935. It is known that three of the sheets were sold at the sub-office at 134 Fore Street, Upper Edmonton, London, between that date and 4 July.

KING EDWARD VIII
20 January–10 December 1936

Further detailed information on the stamps of King Edward VIII will be found in Volume 2 of the Stanley Gibbons *Great Britain Specialised Catalogue.*

> **PRICES.** From S.G. 457 prices quoted in the first column are for stamps in unmounted mint condition.

124	 **125**

(Des H. Brown, adapted Harrison using a photo by Hugh Cecil)

1936. W **125**. *P* 15 × 14.

457	**124**	½d. green (1.9.36)	20	20	
		a. Double impression			
		Wi. Watermark inverted	7·00	1·75	
458		1d. scarlet (14.9.36)	50	25	
		Wi. Watermark inverted	6·50	1·75	
459		1½d. red-brown (1.9.36)	25	20	
		a. Booklet pane. Four stamps plus two printed labels	40·00		
		Wi. Watermark inverted	1·00	1·00	
460		2½d. brt blue (1.9.36)	25	60	
		Set of 4	1·00	1·10	

KING GEORGE VI
11 December 1936–6 February 1952

Further detailed information on the stamps of King George VI will be found in Volume 2 of the Stanley Gibbons *Great Britain Specialised Catalogue.*

126 King George VI and Queen Elizabeth

(Des E. Dulac)

1937 (13 May). **Coronation.** W **127**. *P* 15 × 14.

461	**126**	1½d. maroon	40	25	
		First Day Cover		25·00	

127

128

129

130

King George VI and National Emblems

(Des T **128/9**, E. Dulac (head) and E. Gill (frames). T **130**, E. Dulac (whole stamp))

1937–47. *W* **127**. *P* 15 × 14.

462	**128**	½d. green (10.5.37)		10	15
		a. Watermark sideways (1.38)		25	25
		ab. Booklet pane of 4		20·00	
		Wi. Watermark inverted		8·50	40
463		1d. scarlet (10.5.37)		10	15
		a. Watermark sideways (2.38)		14·00	4·00
		ab. Booklet pane of 4		45·00	
		Wi. Watermark inverted		28·00	1·75
464		1½d. red-brown (30.7.37)		20	15
		a. Watermark sideways (2.38)		60	70
		b. Booklet pane. Four stamps plus two printed labels		35·00	
		c. Imperf three sides (pair)			
		Wi. Watermark inverted		10·00	50
465		2d. orange (31.1.38)		1·00	45
		a. Watermark sideways (2.38)		55·00	25·00
		b. Bisected (on cover)		†	22·00
		Wi. Watermark inverted		48·00	3·50
466		2½d. ultramarine (10.5.37)		25	15
		a. Watermark sideways (6.40)		50·00	15·00
		b. *Tête-bêche* (horiz pair)			
		Wi. Watermark inverted		27·00	2·00
467		3d. violet (31.1.38)		3·75	60
468	**129**	4d. grey-green (21.11.38)		35	40
		a. Imperf (pair)		£1500	
		b. Imperf three sides (horiz pair)		£1750	
469		5d. brown (21.11.38)		2·50	35
		a. Imperf (pair)		£1600	
		b. Imperf three sides (horiz pair)		£1200	
470		6d. purple (30.1.39)		1·25	40
471	**130**	7d. emerald-green (27.2.39)		3·50	50
		a. Imperf three sides (horiz pair)		£1200	
472		8d. brt carmine (27.2.39)		4·00	50
473		9d. dp olive-green (1.5.39)		5·75	50
474		10d. turquoise-blue (1.5.39)		5·25	60
		aa. Imperf (pair)		£2500	
474a		11d. plum (29.12.47)		2·25	1·50
475		1s. bistre-brown (1.5.39)		6·75	40
		Set of 15		32·00	6·00

For later printings of the lower values in apparently lighter shades and different colours, see Nos. 485/90 and 503/8.

No. 465b was authorised for use in Guernsey from 27 December 1940 until February 1941.

Nos. 468b and 469b are perforated at foot only and each occurs in the same sheet as Nos. 468a and 469a.

No. 471a is also perforated at foot only, but occurs on the top row of a sheet.

131

132

133

(Des E. Dulac (T **131**) and Hon. G. R. Bellew (T **132**). Eng J. A. C. Harrison. Recess Waterlow)

1939–48. *W* **133**. *P* 14.

476	**131**	2s. 6d. brown (4.9.39)		40·00	7·00
476a		2s. 6d. yellow-green (9.3.42)		9·00	1·00
477		5s. red (21.8.39)		18·00	1·50
478	**132**	10s. dark blue (30.10.39)		£130	18·00
478a		10s. ultramarine (30.11.42)		40·00	4·50
478b		£1 brown (1.10.48)		15·00	19·00
		Set of 6		£225	45·00

134 Queen Victoria and King George VI

(Des H. L. Palmer)

1940 (6 May). **Centenary of First Adhesive Postage Stamps.** *W* **127**. *P* 14½ × 14.

479	**134**	½d. green		30	20
480		1d. scarlet		90	40
481		1½d. red-brown		30	30
482		2d. orange		50	40
		a. Bisected (on cover)		†	16·00
483		2½d. ultramarine		1·90	80
484		3d. violet		4·00	3·50
		Set of 6		7·00	5·00
		First Day Cover			35·00

No. 482a was authorised for use on Guernsey from 27 December 1940 until February 1941.

1941–42. *Head as Nos. 462/7, but lighter background.* W **127.**
P 15 × 14.
485 **128** ½d. pale green (1.9.41) 15   10
　　　a. *Tête-bêche* (horiz pair) £2750
　　　b. Imperf (pair) £1500
　　　Wi. Watermark inverted .... 3·00   20
486 　　1d. pale scarlet (11.8.41) 15   10
　　　a. Watermark sideways (10.42) .... 3·00   5·00
　　　b. Imperf (pair) £1750
　　　c. Imperf three sides (horiz pair) £1200
　　　d. Imperf between (vert pair) ....
487 　　1½d. pale red-brown (28.9.42) 75   45
488 　　2d. pale orange (6.10.41) 50   40
　　　a. Watermark sideways (6.42) .... 20·00   12·00
　　　b. *Tête-bêche* (horiz pair) £2000
　　　c. Imperf (pair) £1750
　　　d. Imperf pane* £4500
　　　Wi. Watermark inverted .... 2·50   20
489 　　2½d. light ultramarine (21.7.41) 15   10
　　　a. Watermark sideways (8.42) .... 11·00   8·00
　　　b. *Tête-bêche* (horiz pair) £1750
　　　c. Imperf (pair) £2250
　　　d. Imperf pane* £3000
　　　e. Imperf three sides (horiz pair) ....
　　　Wi. Watermark inverted .... 1·00   40
490 　　3d. pale violet (3.11.41) .... 1·50   50
　　　Set of 6 .... 2·75   1·50

The *tête-bêche* varieties are from defectively made-up stamp booklets.

Nos. 486c and 489e are perforated at foot only and occur in the same sheets as Nos. 486b and 489c.

*BOOKLET ERRORS. Those listed as "imperf panes" show one row of perforations either at the top or at the bottom of the pane of 6.

135　　　　　　**136**

(Des H. L. Palmer (T **135**) and R. Stone (T **136**))

1946 (11 June).   **Victory.** W **127.** *P* 15 × 14.
491 **135** 2½d. ultramarine 25   15
492 **136** 3d. violet 25   15
　　　Set of 2 50   30
　　　First Day Cover .... 45·00

137　　　　　　**138**
King George VI and Queen Elizabeth

(Des G. Knipe and Joan Hassall from photographs by Dorothy Wilding)

1948 (26 Apr).   **Royal Silver Wedding.** W **127.** *P* 15 × 14 (2½d.) or
14 × 15 (£1).
493 **137** 2½d. ultramarine 30   30
494 **138** £1 blue .... 32·00   32·00
　　　Set of 2 .... 32·00   32·00
　　　First Day Cover £350

1948 (10 May). Stamps of 1d. and 2½d. showing seaweed-gathering were on sale at eight Head Post Offices in Great Britain, but were primarily for use in the Channel Islands and are listed there (see Nos. C1/2, after Royal Mail Postage Labels).

139 Globe and Laurel Wreath　　**140** "Speed"

141 Olympic Symbol　　**142** Winged Victory

(Des P. Metcalfe (T **139**), A. Games (T **140**), S. D. Scott (T **141**) and E. Dulac (T **142**))

1948 (29 July).   **Olympic Games.** W **127.** *P* 15 × 14.
495 **139** 2½d. ultramarine 10   10
496 **140** 3d. violet 30   30
497 **141** 6d. brt purple 60   30
498 **142** 1s. brown .... 1·25   1·50
　　　Set of 4 .... 2·00   2·00
　　　First Day Cover .... 28·00

143 Two Hemispheres　　**144** U.P.U. Monument, Berne

145 Goddess Concordia, Globe　　**146** Posthorn and Globe
and Points of Compass

(Des Mary Adshead (T **143**), P. Metcalfe (T **144**), H. Fleury (T **145**) and
Hon. G. R. Bellew (T **146**))

1949 (10 Oct).   **75th Anniv of Universal Postal Union.** W **127.**
P 15 × 14.
499 **143** 2½d. ultramarine 10   10
500 **144** 3d. violet 30   40

501	**145**	6d. brt purple	60	75
502	**146**	1s. brown	1·25	1·50
		Set of 4	2·00	2·75
		First Day Cover		50·00

1950–52. 4d. as No. 468 and others as Nos. 485/9, but colours changed. W **127**. P 15 × 14.

503	**128**	½d. pale orange (3.5.51)	10	15
		a. Imperf (pair)		
		b. Tête-bêche (horiz pair)	£2500	
		c. Imperf pane*	£3750	
		Wi. Watermark inverted	10	30
504		1d. lt ultramarine (3.5.51)	15	15
		a. Watermark sideways (5.51)	40	45
		b. Imperf (pair)	£1300	
		c. Imperf three sides (horiz pair)	£1200	
		d. Booklet pane. Three stamps plus three printed labels (3.52)	11·00	
		e. Ditto. Partial tête-bêche pane	£2250	
		Wi. Watermark inverted	2·00	1·00
505		1½d. pale green (3.5.51)	25	30
		a. Watermark sideways (9.51)	2·00	2·50
		Wi. Watermark inverted	2·00	60
506		2d. pale red-brown (3.5.51)	25	20
		a. Watermark sideways (5.51)	80	1·10
		b. Tête-bêche (horiz pair)	£2500	
		c. Imperf three sides (horiz pair)	£1100	
		Wi. Watermark inverted	2·75	3·50
507		2½d. pale scarlet (3.5.51)	20	15
		a. Watermark sideways (5.51)	80	90
		b. Tête-bêche (horiz pair)		
		Wi. Watermark inverted	60	35
508	**129**	4d. lt ultramarine (2.10.50)	1·50	1·10
		a. Double impression	† £3000	
		Set of 6	2·25	1·75

*BOOKLET ERRORS. Those listed as "imperf panes" show one row of perforations either at the top or at the bottom of the pane of 6.

No. 504c is perforated at foot only and occurs in the same sheet as No. 504b.

No. 506c is also perforated at foot only.

147 H.M.S. Victory   **148** White Cliffs of Dover

149 St. George and the Dragon   **150** Royal Coat of Arms

(Des Mary Adshead (T **147/8**), P. Metcalfe (T **149/50**). Recess Waterlow)

1951 (3 May). W **133**. P 11 × 12.

509	**147**	2s. 6d. yellow-green	5·00	75
510	**148**	5s. red	24·00	1·50
511	**149**	10s. ultramarine	14·00	10·00
512	**150**	£1 brown	30·00	14·00
		Set of 4	65·00	22·00

151 "Commerce and Prosperity"   **152** Festival Symbol

(Des E. Dulac (T **151**), A. Games (T **152**))

1951 (3 May). **Festival of Britain.** W **127**. P 15 × 14.

513	**151**	2½d. scarlet	25	15
514	**152**	4d. ultramarine	50	45
		Set of 2	75	60
		First Day Cover		22·00

QUEEN ELIZABETH II
6 February 1952

Further detailed information on the stamps of Queen Elizabeth II will be found in Volumes 3, 4 and 5 of the Stanley Gibbons Great Britain Specialised Catalogue.

153 Tudor Crown   **154**

155   **156**   **157**

158   **159**   **160**

Queen Elizabeth II and National Emblems

I   II

Two types of the 2½d.

Type I:—In the frontal cross of the diadem, the top line is only half the width of the cross.

Type II:—The top line extends to the full width of the cross and there are signs of strengthening in other parts of the diadem.

(Des Enid Marx (T **154**), M. Farrar-Bell (T **155/6**), G. Knipe (T **157**), Mary Adshead (T **158**), E. Dulac (T **159/60**). Portrait by Dorothy Wilding)

1952–54. W **153**. P 15 × 14.

515	**154**	½d. orange-red (31.8.53)	10	15
		Wi. Watermark inverted (3.54)	30	45
516		1d. ultramarine (31.8.53)	20	20
		a. Booklet pane. Three stamps plus three printed labels	18·00	
		Wi. Watermark inverted (3.54)	3·50	1·50
517		1½d. green (5.12.52)	10	15
		a. Watermark sideways (15.10.54)	35	60
		b. Imperf pane*		
		Wi. Watermark inverted (5.53)	25	40
518		2d. red-brown (31.8.53)	20	15
		a. Watermark sideways (8.10.54)	80	1·25
		Wi. Watermark inverted (3.54)	18·00	14·00
519	**155**	2½d. carmine-red (Type I) (5.12.52)	10	15
		a. Watermark sideways (15.11.54)	7·50	7·50
		b. Type II (booklets) (5.53)	1·00	70
		bWi. Watermark inverted (5.53)	15	50
520		3d. dp lilac (18.1.54)	1·00	30
521	**156**	4d. ultramarine (2.11.53)	3·00	80
522	**157**	5d. brown (6.7.53)	90	2·00
523		6d. reddish purple (18.1.54)	3·00	60
		a. Imperf three sides (pair)		
524		7d. brt green (18.1.54)	9·00	3·50
525	**158**	8d. magenta (6.7.53)	1·00	60
526		9d. bronze-green (8.2.54)	22·00	3·00
527		10d. Prussian blue (8.2.54)	18·00	3·00
528		11d. brown-purple (8.2.54)	30·00	16·00
529	**160**	1s. bistre-brown (6.7.53)	1·00	40
530	**159**	1s. 3d. green (2.11.53)	4·50	2·00
531	**160**	1s. 6d. grey-blue (2.11.53)	11·00	2·75
		Set of 17	95·00	28·00

See also Nos. 540/56, 561/6, 570/94 and 599/618a.

*BOOKLET ERRORS.—This pane of 6 stamps is *completely* imperf (see No. 540a, etc).

Stamps with *sideways watermark* come from left-side delivery coils and stamps with *inverted watermark* are from booklets.

First Day Covers

5.12.52	1½d., 2½d. (*517, 519*)	6·00
6.7.53	5d., 8d., 1s. (*522, 525, 529*)	30·00
31.8.53	½d., 1d., 2d. (*515/16, 518*)	30·00
2.11.53	4d., 1s. 3d., 1s. 6d. (*521, 530/1*)	£120
18.1.54	3d., 6d., 7d. (*520, 523/4*)	70·00
8.2.54	9d., 10d., 11d. (*526/8*)	£125

161

162

163

164

(Des E. Fuller (2½d.), M. Goaman (4d.), E. Dulac (1s. 3d.), M. Farrar-Bell (1s. 6d.). Portrait (except 1s. 3d.) by Dorothy Wilding)

1953 (3 June). **Coronation.** W **153**. P 15 × 14.

532	**161**	2½d. carmine-red	10	25
533	**162**	4d. ultramarine	40	1·50
534	**163**	1s. 3d. dp yellow-green	3·50	2·50
535	**164**	1s. 6d. dp grey-blue	7·00	3·50
		Set of 4	10·00	7·00
		First Day Cover		32·00

165 St. Edward's Crown

166 Carrickfergus Castle

167 Caernarvon Castle

168 Edinburgh Castle

169 Windsor Castle

(Des L. Lamb. Portait by Dorothy Wilding. Recess Waterlow (until 31.12.57) and De La Rue (subsequently))

1955–58. W **165**. P 11 × 12.

536	**166**	2s. 6d. black-brown (23.9.55)	10·00	2·00
		a. De La Rue printing (17.7.58)	30·00	2·50
		Wi. Watermark inverted	†	—
537	**167**	5s. rose-carmine (23.9.55)	30·00	3·50
		a. De La Rue printing (30.4.58)	75·00	6·50
538	**168**	10s. ultramarine (1.9.55)	80·00	11·00
		a. De La Rue printing. *Dull ultramarine* (25.4.58)	£150	19·00
539	**169**	£1 black (1.9.55)	£130	28·00
		a. De La Rue printing (28.4.58)	£300	50·00
		Set of 4 (Nos. 536/9)	£225	40·00
		Set of 4 (Nos 536a/9a)	£500	70·00
		First Day Cover (538/9)		£450
		First Day Cover (536/7)		£300

See also Nos. 595/8a & 759/62.

On 1 January 1958, the contract for printing the high values, T **166** to **169**, was transferred to De La Rue & Co, Ltd.

The work of the two printers is very similar, but the following notes will be helpful to those attempting to identify Waterlow and De La Rue stamps of the W **165** issue.

The De La Rue sheets are printed in pairs and have a –| or |– shaped guide-mark at the centre of one side-margin, opposite the middle row of perforations, indicating left and right-hand sheets respectively.

The Waterlow sheets have a small circle (sometimes crossed) instead of a " |–" and this is present in both side-margins opposite the 6th row of stamps, though one is sometimes trimmed off. Short dashes are also present in the perforation gutter between the marginal stamps marking the middle of the four sides and a cross is at the centre of the sheet. The four corners of the sheet have two lines forming a right-angle as trimming marks, but some are usually trimmed off. All these gutter marks and sheet-trimming marks are absent in the De La Rue printings.

De La Rue used the Waterlow die and no alterations were made to it, so that no difference exists in the design or its size, but the making of new plates at first resulted in slight but measurable variations in the width of the gutters between stamps, particularly the horizontal, as follows:

	Waterlow	De La Rue
Horiz gutters, mm	3.8 to 4.0	3.4 to 3.8

Later D.L.R. plates were however less distinguishable in this respect.

For a short time in 1959 the D.L.R. 2s. 6d. appeared with one dot in the bottom margin below the first stamp.

It is possible to sort singles with reasonable certainty by general characteristics. The individual lines of the D.L.R. impression are cleaner and devoid of the whiskers of colour of Waterlow's, and the whole impression lighter and softer.

Owing to the closer setting of the horizontal rows the strokes of the perforating comb are closer; this results in the topmost tooth on each side of De La Rue stamps being narrower than the corresponding teeth in Waterlow's which were more than normally broad.

Shades also help. The 2s. 6d. D.L.R. is a warmer, more chocolate shade than the blackish brown of Waterlow; the 5s. a lighter red with less carmine than Waterlow's; the 10s. more blue and less ultramarine; the £1 less intense black.

The paper of D.L.R. printings is uniformly white, identical with that of Waterlow printings from February 1957 onwards, but earlier Waterlow printings are on paper which is creamy by comparison.

In this and later issues of T 166/9 the dates of issue given for changes of watermark or paper are those on which supplies were first sent by the Supplies Department to Postmasters.

1955–58. W **165.** P 15 × 14.

540	**154**	½d. orange-red (booklets 8.55, sheets 12.12.55)	10	15
		a. Part perf pane*		
		Wi. Watermark inverted (9.55)	15	25
541		1d. ultramarine (19.9.55)	25	15
		a. Booklet pane. Three stamps plus three printed labels	10·00	
		b. Tête-bêche (horiz pair)		
		Wi. Watermark inverted (9.55)	40	30
542		1½d. green (booklet 8.55, sheets 11.10.55) ...	10	15
		a. Watermark sideways (7.3.56)	15	75
		b. Tête-bêche (horiz pair)	£900	
		Wi. Watermark inverted (8.55)	20	25
543		2d. red-brown (6.9.55)	20	20
		aa. Imperf between (vert pair)	£1500	
		a. Watermark sideways (31.7.56)	20	60
		ab. Imperf between (wmk sideways) (horiz pair)	£1500	
		Wi. Watermark inverted (9.55)	10·00	6·00
543b		2d. light red-brown (17.10.56)	20	15
		ba. Tête-bêche (horiz pair)	£600	
		bb. Imperf pane*		
		bc. Part perf pane*		
		bWi. Watermark inverted (1.57)	4·00	2·00
		d. Watermark sideways (5.3.57)	9·00	5·50
544	**155**	2½d. carmine-red (Type I) (28.9.55)	20	15
		a. Watermark sideways (Type I) (23.3.56) .	1·25	1·10
		b. Type II (booklets 9.55, sheets 1957)	25	40
		ba. Tête-bêche (horiz pair)	£750	
		bb. Imperf pane*	£900	
		bc. Part perf pane*		
		bWi. Watermark inverted (9.55)	25	50
545		3d. dp lilac (17.7.56)	20	15
		aa. Tête-bêche (horiz pair)	£750	
		a. Imperf three sides (pair)	£500	
		b. Watermark sideways (22.11.57)	13·00	10·00
		Wi. Watermark inverted (1.10.57)	60	1·00

546	**156**	4d. ultramarine (14.11.55)	1·40	40
547	**157**	5d. brown (21.9.55)	5·50	3·50
548		6d. reddish purple (20.12.55)	4·00	75
		aa. Imperf three sides (pair)	£400	
		a. Deep claret (8.5.58)	3·50	80
		ab. Imperf three sides (pair)	£400	
549		7d. brt green (23.4.56)	50·00	7·50
550	**158**	8d. magenta (21.12.55)	6·00	1·00
551		9d. bronze-green (15.12.55)	23·00	2·25
552		10d. Prussian blue (22.9.55)	19·00	2·25
553		11d. brown-purple (28.10.55)	40	1·50
554	**160**	1s. bistre-brown (3.11.55)	19·00	40
555	**159**	1s. 3d. green (27.3.56)	27·00	1·50
556	**160**	1s. 6d. grey-blue (27.3.56)	19·00	1·25
		Set of 18	£150	22·00

The dates given for Nos. 540/556 are those on which they were first issued by the Supplies Dept to postmasters.

In December 1956 a completely imperforate sheet of No. 543b was noticed by clerks in a Kent post office, one of whom purchased it against P.O. regulations. In view of this irregularity we do not consider it properly issued.

Types of 2½d. In this issue, in 1957, Type II formerly only found in stamps from booklets, began to replace Type I on sheet stamps.

*BOOKLET ERRORS. Those listed as "imperf panes" show one row of perforations either at top or bottom of the booklet pane; those as "part perf panes" have one row of 3 stamps imperf on three sides.

For Nos. 542 and 553 in Presentation Pack, see after No. 586.

170 Scout Badge and "Rolling Hitch"

171 "Scouts coming to Britain"

172 Globe within a Compass

(Des Mary Adshead (2½d.), P. Keely (4d.), W. H. Brown (1s. 3d.))

1957 (1 Aug). **World Scout Jubilee Jamboree.** W 165. P 15 × 14.

557	**170**	2½d. carmine-red	15	10
558	**171**	4d. ultramarine	50	1·00
559	**172**	1s. 3d. green	5·00	4·50
		Set of 3	5·00	4·50
		First Day Cover		15·00

173

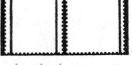

½d.to 1½d., 2½d., 3d.   2d.
Graphite-line arrangements
(Stamps viewed from back)

957 (12 Sept).   **46th Inter-Parliamentary Union Conference.** W **165**.
P 15 × 14.

50 **173**	4d. ultramarine	....	1·00	1·00
	First Day Cover	....		80·00

GRAPHITE-LINED ISSUES. These were used in connection with automatic sorting machinery, first introduced experimentally at Southampton.

The graphite lines were printed in black on the back, beneath the gum; two lines per stamp, except for the 2d.

In November 1959 phosphor bands were introduced (see notes after No. 598).

957 (19 Nov).   *Graphite-lined issue. Two graphite lines on the back, except 2d. value, which has one line.* W **165**. P 15 × 14.

51 **154**	½d. orange-red	....	20	30
52	1d. ultramarine	....	20	35
53	1½d. green	....	30	1·25
	a. Both lines at left	....	£800	£400
54	2d. light red-brown	....	2·50	1·50
	a. Line at left	....	£500	£175
55 **155**	2½d. carmine-red (Type II)	....	7·00	6·25
56	3d. dp lilac	....	30	50
	Set of 6	....	9·50	9·00
	First Day Cover	....		70·00

No. 564a results from a misplacement of the line and horizontal pairs exist showing one stamp without line. No. 563a results from a similar misplacement.

See also Nos. 587/94.

176 Welsh Dragon   **177** Flag and Games Emblem

178 Welsh Dragon

(Des R. Stone (3d.), W. H. Brown (6d.), P. Keely (1s. 3d.))

958 (18 July).   **Sixth British Empire and Commonwealth Games, Cardiff.** W **165**. P 15 × 14.

67 **176**	3d. dp lilac	....	15	10
68 **177**	6d. reddish purple	....	25	45
69 **178**	1s. 3d. green	....	2·25	2·25
	Set of 3	....	2·25	2·25
	First Day Cover	....		48·00

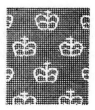

179 Multiple Crowns

1958–65.		W **179**. P 15 × 14.		
570 **154**	½d. orange-red (25.11.58)	....	10	10
	a. Watermark sideways (26.5.61)	....	10	15
	c. Part perf pane*	....	£800	
	Wi. Watermark inverted (11.58)	....	30	25
	k. Chalk-surfaced paper (15.7.63)	....	2·00	2·25
	kWi. Watermark inverted	....	2·00	2·25
	l. Booklet pane. No. 570k × 3 *se-tenant* with 574k	....	7·50	
	m. Booklet pane. No. 570a × 2 *se-tenant* with 574l × 2 (1.7.64)	....	1·25	
571	1d. ultramarine (booklets 11.58, sheets 24.3.59)	....	10	10
	aa. Imperf (vert pair from coil)	....		
	a. Watermark sideways (26.5.61)	....	60	40
	b. Part perf pane*	....		
	c. Imperf pane	....		
	Wi. Watermark inverted (11.58)	....	15	20
	l. Booklet pane. No. 571a × 2 *se-tenant* with 575a × 2† (16.8.65)	....	7·50	
572	1½d. green (booklets 12.58, sheets 30.8.60)	...	10	15
	a. Imperf three sides (horiz strip of 3)	.....		
	b. Watermark sideways (26.5.61)	....	7·50	3·50
	Wi. Watermark inverted (12.58)	....	1·00	40
573	2d. light red-brown (4.12.58)	....	10	10
	a. Watermark sideways (3.4.59)	....	25	65
	Wi. Watermark inverted (10.4.61)	....	75·00	30·00
574 **155**	2½d. carmine-red (Type II) (booklets 11.58, sheets 15.9.59)	....	10	10
	a. Imperf strip of 3	....		
	b. *Tête-bêche* (horiz pair)	....		
	c. Imperf pane*	....	£1100	
	Wi. Watermark inverted (Type II) (11.58)	....	3·00	90
	d. Watermark sideways (Type I) (10.11.60)	.	20	30
	da. Imperf strip of 6	....		
	e. Type I (wmk upright) (4.10.61)	....	15	35
	k. Chalk-surfaced paper (Type II) (15.7.63)	.	20	45
	kWi. Do. Watermark inverted (15.7.63)	....	20	60
	l. Watermark sideways (Type II) (1.7.64)	....	40	75
575	3d. dp lilac (booklets 11.58, sheets 8.12.58)	.	10	10
	a. Watermark sideways (24.10.58)	....	15	25
	b. Imperf pane*	....	£850	
	c. Part perf pane*	....		
	d. Phantom "R" (Cyl 41 no dot)	....	£250	
	Eda. Do. First retouch	....	10·00	
	Edb. Do. Second retouch	....	10·00	
	e. Phantom "R" (Cyl 37 no dot)	....	25·00	
	Eea. Do. Retouch	....	8·00	
	Wi. Watermark inverted (11.58)	....	15	20
576 **156**	4d. ultramarine (29.10.58)	....	50	20
	a. *Dp ultramarine*†† (28.4.65)	....	15	10
	ab. Watermark sideways (31.5.65)	....	45	35
	ac. Imperf pane*	....		
	ad. Part perf pane*	....	£650	
	aWi. Watermark inverted (21.6.65)	....	30	30
577	4½d. chestnut (9.2.59)	....	10	15
	Ea. Phantom frame	....	5·00	
578 **157**	5d. brown (10.11.58)	....	25	20
579	6d. dp claret (23.12.58)	....	25	15
	a. Imperf three sides (pair)	....	£450	
	b. Imperf (pair)	....	£550	
580	7d. brt green (26.11.58)	....	40	20
581 **158**	8d. magenta (24.2.60)	....	40	15
582	9d. bronze-green (24.3.59)	....	40	15
583	10d. Prussian blue (18.11.58)	....	1·00	15
584 **160**	1s. bistre-brown (30.10.58)	....	40	15
585 **159**	1s. 3d. green (17.6.59)	....	25	15
586 **160**	1s. 6d. grey-blue (16.12.58)	....	4·00	40
	Set of 17 (one of each value)	....	7·00	2·10
	First Day Cover (577)	....		£150
	*Presentation Pack****	....	80·00	

*BOOKLET ERROR. See note after No. 556.

**This was issued in 1960 and comprises Nos. 542, 553, 570/1 and 573/86. It exists in two forms: (a) inscribed "10s 6d" for sale in the U.K.; and (b) inscribed "$1.80" for sale in the U.S.A.

†Booklet pane No. 571l comes in two forms, with the 1d. stamps on the left or on the right.

††This "shade" was brought about by making more deeply etched cylinders, resulting in apparent depth of colour in parts of the design. There is no difference in the colour of the ink.

Sideways watermark. The 2d., 2½d., 3d. and 4d. come from coils and the ½d., 1d., 1½d., 2½d., 3d. and 4d. come from booklets. In coil stamps the sideways watermark shows the top of the watermark to the left *as seen from the front of the stamp*. In the *booklet* stamps it comes equally to the left or right.

Nos. 570k and 574k only come from 2s. "Holiday Resort" experimental undated booklets issued in 1963, in which one page contained 1 x 2½d. *se-tenant* with 3 x ½d. (See No. 570l).

No. 574l comes from coils, and the "Holiday Resort" experimental booklets dated "1964" comprising four panes each containing two of these 2½d. stamps *se-tenant* vertically with two ½d. No. 570a. (See No. 570m).

2½d. imperf. No. 574a comes from a booklet with watermark upright. No. 574da is from a coil with sideways watermark.

No. 574e comes from sheets bearing cylinder number 42 and is also known on vertical delivery coils.

In 1964 No. 575 was printed from cylinder number 70 no dot and dot on an experimental paper which is distinguishable by an additional watermark letter "T" lying on its side, which occurs about four times in the sheet, usually in the side margins, 48,000 sheets were issued.

Phantom "R" varieties

Nos. 575d and 615a   No. 575Eda
(Cyl 41 no dot)

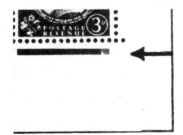

No. 575e (Cyl 37 no dot)

3d. An incomplete marginal rule revealed an "R" on cyls 37 and 41 no dot below R.20/12. It is more noticeable on cyl 41 because of the wider marginal rule. The "R" on cyl 41 was twice retouched, the first being as illustrated here (No. 575Eda) and traces of the "R" can still be seen in the second retouch.

The rare variety, No. 575d, is best collected in a block of 4 or 6 with full margins in order to be sure that it is not 615a with phosphor lines removed.

The retouch on cyl 37 is not easily identified: there is no trace of the "R" but the general appearance of that part of the marginal rule is uneven.

Phantom Frame variety

Nos. 577Ea and 616Eba

4½d. An incomplete marginal rule revealed a right-angled shaped frame-line on cyl 8 no dot below R.20/12. It occurs on ordinary and phosphor.

WHITER PAPER. On 18 May 1962 the Post Office announced that a whiter paper was being used for the current issue (including Nos. 595/8). This is beyond the scope of this catalogue, but the whiter papers are listed in Vol. 3 of the Stanley Gibbons *Great Britain Specialised Catalogue.*

1958 (24 Nov)–**61.** *Graphite-lined issue. Two graphite lines on the back, except 2d. value, which has one line.* W **179.** P 15 × 14.

587	**154**	½d. orange-red (15.6.59)		6·00	6·00
		Wi. Watermark inverted (4.8.59)		1·25	2·25
588		1d. ultramarine (18.12.58)		1·00	1·50
		a. Misplaced graphite lines (7.61)*		60	90
		Wi. Watermark inverted (4.8.59)		1·25	2·00
589		1½d. green (4.8.59)		95·00	60·00
		Wi. Watermark inverted (4.8.59)		40·00	40·00
590		2d. lt red-brown (24.11.58)		6·00	3·25
591	**155**	2½d. carmine-red (Type II) (9.6.59)		8·00	10·00
		Wi. Watermark inverted (21.8.59)		48·00	45·00
592		3d. dp lilac (24.11.58)		50	50
		a. Misplaced graphite lines (5.61)*		£375	£350
		Wi. Watermark inverted (4.8.59)		35	60
593	**156**	4d. ultramarine (29.4.59)		3·50	4·50
		a. Misplaced graphite lines (1961)*		£1500	
594		4½d. chestnut (3.6.59)		5·00	4·50
		Set of 8 (cheapest)		60·00	60·00

Nos. 587/9 were only issued in booklets or coils (587/8).

*No. 588a (in coils), and Nos. 592a and 593a (both in sheets) result from the use of a residual stock of graphite-lined paper. As the use of graphite lines had ceased, the register of the lines in relation to the stamps was of no importance and numerous misplacements occurred —two lines close together, one line only, etc. No. 588a refers to two lines at left or right; No. 592a refers to stamps with two lines only at left and both clear of the perforations and No. 593a to stamps with two lines at left (with left line down perforations) and traces of a third line down the opposite perforations.

(Recess D.L.R. (until 31.12.62), then B.W.)

1959–68. W **179.** P 11 × 12.

595	**166**	2s. 6d. black-brown (22.7.59)		10·00	75
		Wi. Watermark inverted			
		a. B.W. printing (1.7.63)		50	30
		aWi. Watermark inverted		£800	75·00
		k. Chalk-surfaced paper (30.5.68)		50	1·10

596	**167**	5s. scarlet-vermilion (15.6.59)	55·00	2·00
		Wi. Watermark inverted	—	£250
		a. B.W. ptg. *Red* (shades) (3.9.63)	1·00	60
		ab. Printed on the gummed side	£750	
		aWi. Watermark inverted	£225	50·00
597	**168**	10s. blue (21.7.59)	35·00	5·00
		a. B.W. ptg. *Bright ultramarine* (16.10.63) ...	2·50	3·00
		aWi. Watermark inverted	—	£650
598	**169**	£1 black (23.6.59)	85·00	12·00
		Wi. Watermark inverted	—	£1500
		a. B.W. printing (14.11.63)	10·00	5·00
		aWi. Watermark inverted	—	£2000
		Set of 4 (Nos. 595/8)	£150	17·00
		Set of 4 (Nos. 595a/8a)	13·00	8·00
		*Presentation Pack (1960)**	£450	

The B.W. printings have a marginal Plate Number. They are generally more deeply engraved than the D.L.R. showing more of the Diadem detail and heavier lines on Her Majesty's face. The vertical perf is 11.9 to 12 against D.L.R. 11.8.

*This exists in two forms: (a) inscribed "$6.50" for sale in the U.S.A.; and (b) without price for sale in the U.K.

See also Nos. 759/62.

PHOSPHOR BAND ISSUES. These are printed on the front and are wider than graphite lines. They are not easy to see but show as broad vertical bands at certain angles to the light.

Values representing the rate for printed papers (and when this was abolished in 1968 for second issue class mail) have one band and others two, three or four bands as stated, according to the size and format.

In the small size stamps the bands are on each side with the single band at left (*except where otherwise stated*). In the large-size commemorative stamps the single band may be at left, centre or right, varying in different designs. The bands are vertical on both horizontal and vertical designs *except where otherwise stated*.

The phosphor was originally applied typographically but later usually by photogravure and sometimes using flexography, a typographical process using rubber cylinders.

Three different types of phosphor have been used, distinguishable by the colour emitted under an ultra-violet lamp, the first being green, then blue and now violet. Different sized bands are also known. All these are fully listed in Vol. 3 of the Stanley Gibbons *Great Britain Specialised Catalogue*.

Varieties. Misplaced and missing phosphor bands are known but such varieties are beyond the scope of this Catalogue.

1959 (18 Nov). *Phosphor-Graphite issue. Two phosphor bands on front and two graphite lines on back, except 2d. value, which has one band on front and one line on back. P 15 × 14.* (a) W **165**.

599	**154**	½d. orange-red	4·00	6·00
600		1d. ultramarine	8·00	6·00
601		1½d. green	2·00	5·00

(b) W **179**

605	**154**	2d. lt red-brown (1 band)	4·50	3·75
		a. Error. W **165**	£160	£160
606	**155**	2½d. carmine-red (Type II)	20·00	11·00
607		3d. dp lilac	9·00	8·00
608	**156**	4d. ultramarine	12·00	25·00
609		4½d. chestnut	35·00	15·00
		Set of 8	80·00	70·00
		*Presentation Pack**	£200	

*This was issued in 1960 and comprises two each of Nos. 599/609. It exists in two forms: (a) inscribed "3s 8d" for sale in the U.K. and (b) inscribed "50 c" for sale in the U.S.A.

1960 (22 June)–**67**. *Phosphor issue. Two phosphor bands on front, except where otherwise stated.* W **179**. P 15 × 14.

610	**154**	½d. orange-red	10	15
		a. Watermark sideways (26.5.61)	9·00	8·00
		Wi. Watermark inverted (14.8.60)	60	60

611	**154**	1d. ultramarine	10	10
		a. Watermark sideways (14.7.61)	35	40
		Wi. Watermark inverted (14.8.60)	20	30
		l. Booklet pane. No. 611a × 2 *se-tenant* with 615d × 2† (16.8.65)	10·00	
		m. Booklet pane. No. 611a × 2 *se-tenant* with 615b × 2†† (11.67)	4·75	
612		1½d. green	10	20
		a. Watermark sideways (14.7.61)	9·00	9·00
		Wi. Watermark inverted (14.8.60)	9·00	5·00
613		2d. lt red-brown (1 band)	16·00	20·00
613a		2d. lt red-brown (2 bands) (4.10.61)	10	10
		aa. Imperf three sides***		
		ab. Watermark sideways (6.4.67)	15	60
614	**155**	2½d. carmine-red (Type II) (2 bands)*	10	40
		Wi. Watermark inverted (14.8.60)	£140	80·00
614a		2½d. carmine-red (Type II) (1 band) (4.10.61) .	40	75
		aWi. Watermark inverted (3.62)	30·00	18·00
614b		2½d. carmine-red (Type I) (1 band) (4.10.61) .	32·00	27·00
615		3d. dp lilac (2 bands)	60	45
		a. Phantom "R" (Cyl 41 no dot)	20·00	
		Wi. Watermark inverted (14.8.60)	45	70
		b. Watermark sideways (14.7.61)	1·00	90
615c		3d. dp lilac (1 band at right) (29.4.65)	35	60
		cEa. Band at left	35	60
		cWi. Watermark inverted (band at right) (2.67)	60	60
		cWia. Watermark inverted (band at left) (2.67)	16·00	12·00
		d. Watermark sideways (band at right) (16.8.65)	4·50	3·50
		dEa. Watermark sideways (band at left)	4·50	3·50
		e. One centre band (8.12.66)	25	40
		eWi. Watermark inverted (8.67)	75	80
		ea. Wmk sideways (19.6.67)	25	60
616	**156**	4d. ultramarine	3·00	2·50
		a. *Dp ultramarine* (28.4.65)	15	15
		aa. Part perf pane**		
		ab. Watermark sideways (16.8.65)	15	25
		aWi. Watermark inverted (21.6.65)	25	20
616b		4½d. chestnut (13.9.61)	15	25
		Eba. Phantom frame	10·00	
616c	**157**	5d. brown (9.6.67)	20	25
617		6d. dp claret (27.6.60)	40	20
617a		7d. brt green (15.2.67)	60	25
617b	**158**	8d. magenta (28.6.67)	20	25
617c		9d. bronze-green (29.12.66)	60	25
617d		10d. Prussian blue (30.12.66)	80	35
617e	**160**	1s. bistre-brown (28.6.67)	40	20
618	**159**	1s. 3d. green	1·75	2·50
618a	**160**	1s. 6d. grey-blue (12.12.66)	2·00	1·00
		Set of 17 (one of each value)	7·00	6·00

The automatic facing equipment was brought into use on 6 July 1960 but the phosphor stamps may have been released a few days earlier.

The stamps with watermark sideways are from booklets except Nos. 613ab and 615ea which are from coils. No. 616ab comes from both booklets and coils.

No. 615a. See footnote after No. 586.

*No. 614 with two bands on the creamy paper was originally from cylinder 50 dot and no dot. When the change in postal rates took place in 1965 it was reissued from cylinder 57 dot and no dot on the whiter paper. Some of these latter were also released in error in districts of S.E. London in September 1964. The shade of the reissue is slightly more carmine.

**Booklet error. Two stamps at bottom left imperf on three sides and the third imperf on two sides.

***This comes from the bottom row of a sheet which is imperf at bottom and both sides.

†Booklet pane No. 611l comes in two forms, with the 1d. stamps on the left or on the right. This was printed in this manner to provide for 3d. stamps with only one band.

††Booklet pane No. 611m comes from 2s. booklets of January and March 1968. The two bands on the 3d. stamp were intentional because of the technical difficulties in producing one band and two band stamps se-tenant.

The Phosphor-Graphite stamps had the phosphor applied by typography but the Phosphor issue can be divided into those with the phosphor applied typographically and others where it was applied by photogravure. Moreover the photogravure form can be further divided into those which phosphoresce green and others which phosphoresce blue under ultra-violet light. From 1965 violet phosphorescence was introduced in place of the blue. All these are fully listed in Vol. 3 of the Stanley Gibbons *Great Britain Specialised Catalogue*.

The Stanley Gibbons Uvitec Micro ultra-violet lamp will reveal these differences. See also Philatelic Information at the beginning of this Catalogue.

Unlike previous one-banded phosphor stamps, No. 615c has a broad band extending over two stamps so that alternate stamps have the band at left or right (same prices either way). No. 615cWi comes from the 10s phosphor booklet of February 1967 and No. 615eWi comes from the 10s. phosphor booklets of August 1967 and February 1968.

Varieties:

Nos. 615a (Phantom "R") and 615Eba (Phantom frame), *see* illustrations following No. 586.

180 Postboy of 1660	181 Posthorn of 1660

(Des R. Stone (3d.), Faith Jaques (1s. 3d.))

1960 (7 July).   **Tercentenary of Establishment of General Letter Office.** W **179** (*sideways on* 1s. 3d.). P 15 × 14 (3d.) or 14 × 15 (1s. 3d.).
619	180	3d. dp lilac	20	10
620	181	1s. 3d. green	3·00	3·50
		Set of 2	3·00	3·50
		First Day Cover		35·00

182 Conference Emblem

(Des R. Stone (emblem, P. Rahikainen))

1960 (19 Sept).   **First Anniversary of European Postal and Telecommunications Conference.** *Chalk-surfaced paper.* W **179**. P 15 × 14.
621	182	6d. bronze-green & purple	40	60
622		1s. 6d. brown & blue	5·50	4·50
		Set of 2	5·75	4·50
		First Day Cover		30·00

SCREENS. Up to this point all photogravure stamps were printed in a 200 screen (200 dots per linear inch), but all later commemorative stamps are a finer 250 screen. Exceptionally No. 622 has a 200 screen for the portrait and a 250 screen for the background.

184 "Growth of Savings"

183 Thrift Plant	185 Thrift Plant

(Des P. Gauld (2½d.), M. Goaman (others))

1961 (28 Aug).   **Centenary of Post Office Savings Bank.** *Chalk-surfaced paper.* W **179** (*sideways on* 2½d.) P 14 × 15 (2½d.) or 15 × 14 (*others*).
I. "TIMSON" Machine
II. "THRISSELL" Machine

			I		II	
623	183	2½d. black & red	10	10	2·00	1·75
		a. Black omitted	£6000	—		†
624	184	3d. orange-brown & violet ...	10	10	25	25
		a. Orange-brown omitted ..	£110	—	£250	—
		x. Perf through side sheet margin	26·00	23·00		†
		xa. Orange-brown omitted ..	£400	—		†
625	185	1s. 6d. red & blue	2·25	2·00		†
		Set of 3	2·25	2·00		
		First Day Cover		50·00		

2½d. TIMSON. Cyls 1E–1F. Deeply shaded portrait (brownish black).

2½d. THRISSELL. Cyls 1D–1B or 1D (dot)–1B (dot). Lighter portrait (grey-black).

3d. TIMSON. Cyls 3D–3E. Clear, well-defined portrait with deep shadows and bright highlights.

3d. THRISSELL. Cyls 3C–3B or 3C (dot)–3B (dot). Dull portrait, lacking in contrast.

Sheet marginal examples *without* single extension perf hole on the short side of the stamp are always "Timson", as are those with large punch-hole *not* coincident with printed three-sided box guide mark.

The 3d. "Timson" perforated completely through the right-hand side margin comes from a relatively small part of the printing perforated on a sheet-fed machine.

Normally the "Timsons" were perforated in the reel, with three large punch-holes in both long margins and the perforations completely through both short margins. Only one punch-hole coincides with the guide-mark.

The "Thrissells" have one large punch-hole in one long margin, coinciding with guide-mark and one short margin imperf (except sometimes for encroachments).

186 C.E.P.T. Emblem	187 Doves and Emblem

188 Doves and Emblem

(Des M. Goaman (doves T. Kurpershoek))

1961 (18 Sept). **European Postal and Telecommunications (C.E.P.T.) Conference, Torquay.** *Chalk-surfaced paper.* W **179**. P 15 × 14.

626	**186**	2d. orange, pink & brown	10	10
		a. Orange omitted		
627	**187**	4d. buff, mauve & ultramarine	20	10
628	**188**	10d. turquoise, pale green & Prussian blue ...	40	35
		a. Pale green omitted	£3000	
		b. Turquoise omitted	£1800	
		Set of 3	60	50
		First Day Cover		3·50

189 Hammer Beam Roof, Westminster Hall

190 Palace of Westminster

(Des Faith Jaques)

1961 (25 Sept). **Seventh Commonwealth Parliamentary Conference.** *Chalk-surfaced paper.* W **179** (*sideways on 1s. 3d.*). P 15 × 14 (6d.) or 14 × 15 (1s. 3d.).

629	**189**	6d. purple & gold	25	25
		a. Gold omitted	£300	
630	**190**	1s. 3d. green & blue	2·50	2·00
		a. Blue (Queen's head) omitted	£4000	
		Set of 2	2·50	2·00
		First Day Cover		26·00

191 "Units of Productivity"

192 "National Productivity"

193 "Unified Productivity"

(Des D. Gentleman)

1962 (14 Nov). **National Productivity Year.** *Chalk-surfaced paper.* W **179** (*inverted on 2½d. and 3d.*). P 15 × 14.

631	**191**	2½d. myrtle-green & carmine-red (*shades*)	20	10
		Ea. Blackish olive & carmine-red	25	15
		p. One phosphor band. *Blackish olive & carmine-red*	1·00	40
632	**192**	3d. light blue & violet (*shades*)	25	10
		a. Lt blue (Queen's head) omitted	£600	
		p. Three phosphor bands	1·00	50
633	**193**	1s. 3d. carmine, lt blue & dp green	1·75	1·60
		a. Lt blue (Queen's head) omitted	£3500	
		p. Three phosphor bands	25·00	18·00
		Set of 3 (Ordinary)	2·00	1·60
		Set of 3 (Phosphor)	25·00	18·00
		First Day Cover (Ordinary)		30·00
		First Day Cover (Phosphor)		80·00

194 Campaign Emblem and Family   **195** Children of Three Races

(Des M. Goaman)

1963 (21 Mar). **Freedom from Hunger.** *Chalk-surfaced paper.* W **179** (*inverted*). P 15 × 14.

634	**194**	2½d. crimson & pink	10	10
		p. One phosphor band	1·00	1·00
635	**195**	1s. 3d. bistre-brown & yellow	2·00	1·75
		p. Three phosphor bands	25·00	18·00
		Set of 2 (Ordinary)	2·00	1·75
		Set of 2 (Phosphor)	25·00	18·00
		First Day Cover (Ordinary)		28·00
		First Day Cover (Phosphor)		32·00

196 "Paris Conference"

(Des R. Stone)

1963 (7 May). **Paris Postal Conference Centenary.** *Chalk-surfaced paper.* W **179** (*inverted*). P 15 × 14.

636	**196**	6d. green & mauve	50	40
		a. Green omitted	£1200	
		p. Three phosphor bands	5·50	5·00
		First Day Cover (Ordinary)		12·00
		First Day Cover (Phosphor)		20·00

197 Posy of Flowers   **198** Woodland Life

(Des S. Scott (3d.), M. Goaman (4½d.))

1963 (16 May). **National Nature Week.** *Chalk-surfaced paper.* W **179.**
P 15 × 14.

637	**197**	3d. yellow, green, brown & black	25	20
		p. Three phosphor bands	50	50
638	**198**	4½d. black, blue, yellow, magenta & brown-red	40	40
		p. Three phosphor bands	2·25	2·25
		Set of 2 (Ordinary)	60	60
		Set of 2 (Phosphor)	2·50	2·50
		First Day Cover (Ordinary)		20·00
		First Day Cover (Phosphor)		26·00

Special First Day of Issue Postmark

	Ordin- ary	Phos- phor
London E.C. (Type A)	21·00	27·00

This postmark was used on first day covers serviced by the Philatelic Bureau.

199 Rescue at Sea

200 19th-century Lifeboat

201 Lifeboatmen

(Des D. Gentleman)

1963 (31 May). **Ninth International Lifeboat Conference, Edinburgh.** *Chalk-surfaced paper.* W **179.** *P* 15 × 14.

639	**199**	2½d. blue, black & red	10	10
		p. One phosphor band	40	50
640	**200**	4d. red, yellow, brown, black & blue	40	30
		p. Three phosphor bands	20	50
641	**201**	1s. 6d. sepia, yellow & grey-blue	2·50	2·50
		p. Three phosphor bands	35·00	24·00
		Set of 3 (Ordinary)	2·75	2·50
		Set of 3 (Phosphor)	35·00	24·00
		First Day Cover (Ordinary)		26·00
		First Day Cover (Phosphor)		32·00

Special First Day of Issue Postmark

	Ordin- ary	Phos- phor
London	50·00	65·00

This postmark was used on first day covers serviced by the Philatelic Bureau.

202 Red Cross

203

204

(Des H. Bartram)

1963 (15 Aug). **Red Cross Centenary Congress.** *Chalk-surfaced paper.* W **179.** *P* 15 × 14.

642	**202**	3d. red & dp lilac	10	10
		a. Red omitted	£1750	
		p. Three phosphor bands	60	60
		pa. Red omitted	£5500	
643	**203**	1s. 3d. red, blue & grey	2·75	2·50
		p. Three phosphor bands	40·00	30·00
644	**204**	1s. 6d. red, blue & bistre	2·50	2·50
		p. Three phosphor bands	30·00	30·00
		Set of 3 (Ordinary)	5·00	4·50
		Set of 3 (Phosphor)	65·00	45·00
		First Day Cover (Ordinary)		26·00
		First Day Cover (Phosphor)		55·00

Special First Day of Issue Postmark

	Ordin- ary	Phos- phor
London E.C.	65·00	90·00

This postmark was used on first day covers serviced by the Philatelic Bureau.

205 Commonwealth Cable

(Des P. Gauld)

1963 (3 Dec). **Opening of COMPAC (Trans-Pacific Telephone Cable).** *Chalk-surfaced paper.* W **179.** *P* 15 × 14.

645	**205**	1s. 6d. blue & black	2·25	2·25
		a. Black omitted	£2250	
		p. Three phosphor bands	14·00	13·50
		First Day Cover (Ordinary)		22·00
		First Day Cover (Phosphor)		26·00

Special First Day of Issue Postmark

	Ordin- ary	Phos- phor
Philatelic Bureau, London E.C.1 (Type A)	30·00	38·00

PRESENTATION PACKS. Special Packs comprising slip-in cards with printed commemorative inscriptions and descriptive notes on the back and with protective covering, were introduced in 1964 with the Shakespeare issue. These are listed and priced.

Issues of 1968–69 (British Paintings to the Prince of Wales Investiture) were also issued in packs with text in German for sale through the Post Office's German Agency and these are also quoted. Subsequently, however, the packs sold in Germany were identical with the normal English version with the addition of a separate printed insert card with German text. These, as also English packs with Japanese and Dutch printed cards for sale in Japan and the Netherlands respectively, are listed in Vols. 3 and 5 of the Stanley Gibbons *Great Britain Specialised Catalogue*.

206 Puck and Bottom *(A Midsummer Night's Dream)*   **207** Feste *(Twelfth Night)*

208 Balcony Scene *(Romeo and*   **209** "Eve of Agincourt" *(Henry V)* *Juliet)*

210 Hamlet contemplating Yorick's Skull *(Hamlet)* and Queen Elizabeth II

(Des D. Gentleman. Photo Harrison & Sons (3d., 6d., 1s. 3d., 1s. 6d.). Des C. and R. Ironside. Recess B.W. (2s. 6d.))

1964 (23 Apr). **Shakespeare Festival.** *Chalk-surfaced paper.* W **179**. *P* 11 × 12 (2s. 6d.) *or* 15 × 14 (*others*).

646	**206**	3d. yellow-bistre, black & dp violet-blue		
		(shades)	10	10
		p. Three phosphor bands	20	30
647	**207**	6d. yellow, orange, black & yellow-olive		
		(shades)	20	30
		p. Three phosphor bands	60	70
648	**208**	1s. 3d. cerise, blue-green, black & sepia		
		(shades)	90	1·00
		Wi. Watermark inverted		
		p. Three phosphor bands	5·75	5·50
		pWi. Watermark inverted	£100	
649	**209**	1s. 6d. violet, turquoise, black & blue		
		(shades)	1·25	1·00
		Wi. Watermark inverted		
		p. Three phosphor bands	9·00	5·75
650	**210**	2s. 6d. dp slate-purple (shades)	2·00	2·00
		Wi. Watermark inverted	£300	
		Set of 5 (Ordinary)	4·00	4·00
		Set of 4 (Phosphor)	13·00	11·00
		First Day Cover (Ordinary)		10·00
		First Day Cover (Phosphor)		11·00
		Presentation Pack (Ordinary)	10·00	

The 3d. is known with yellow-bistre missing in the top two-thirds of the figures of Puck and Bottom. This occured in the top row only of a sheet.

Special First Day of Issue Postmark

	Ordin-ary	Phos-phor
Stratford-upon-Avon, Warwicks	13·00	15·00

This postmark was used on first day covers serviced by the Philatelic Bureau, as well as on covers posted at Stratford P.O.

211 Flats near Richmond Park   **212** Shipbuilding Yards, Belfast ("Urban Development")   ("Industrial Activity")

213 Beddgelert Forest Park,   **214** Nuclear Reactor, Dounreay Snowdonia ("Forestry")   ("Technological Development")

(Des D. Bailey)

1964 (1 July). **20th International Geographical Congress, London.** *Chalk-surfaced paper.* *P* 15 × 14.

651	**211**	2½d. black, olive-yellow, olive-grey &		
		turquoise-blue	10	10
		p. One phosphor band	50	40
652	**212**	4d. orange-brown, red-brown, rose, black &		
		violet	25	25
		a. Violet omitted	£150	
		c. Violet and red-brown omitted	£150	
		Wi. Watermark inverted	£500	
		p. Three phosphor bands	75	70
653	**213**	8d. yellow-brown, emerald, green & black ..	60	50
		a. Green (lawn) omitted	£3750	
		Wi. Watermark inverted	£250	
		p. Three phosphor bands	1·75	1·50
654	**214**	1s. 6d. yellow-brown, pale pink, black, &		
		brown	3·25	3·25
		Wi. Watermark inverted	19·00	
		p. Three phosphor bands	21·00	18·00
		Set of 4 (Ordinary)	4·00	4·00
		Set of 4 (Phosphor)	21·00	18·00
		First Day Cover (Ordinary)		18·00
		First Day Cover (Phosphor)		27·00
		Presentation Pack (Ordinary)	90·00	

A used example of the 4d. is known with the red-brown omitted.

Special First Day of Issue Postmark

	Ordinary	Phosphor
G.P.O. Philatelic Bureau, London E.C.1 (Type B)	25·00	35·00

215 Spring Gentian

216 Dog Rose

217 Honeysuckle   **218** Fringed Water Lily

(Des M. and Sylvia Goaman)

1964 (5 Aug). **Tenth International Botanical Congress, Edinburgh.** *Chalk-surfaced paper.* W **179**. *P* 15 × 14.

			Ordinary	Phosphor
655	215	3d. violet, blue & sage-green	10	10
		a. Blue omitted	£3500	
		p. Three phosphor bands	20	20
656	216	6d. apple-green, rose, scarlet & green	20	20
		Wi. Watermark inverted		
		p. Three phosphor bands	1·50	1·00
657	217	9d. lemon, green, lake & rose-red	1·60	2·00
		a. Green (leaves) omitted	£3500	
		Wi. Watermark inverted	32·00	
		p. Three phosphor bands	4·50	3·00
658	218	1s. 3d. yellow, emerald, reddish violet & grey-green	2·50	1·90
		a. Yellow (flowers) omitted	£7500	
		Wi. Watermark inverted	£225	
		p. Three phosphor bands	20·00	16·00
		Set of 4 (Ordinary)	4·00	4·00
		Set of 4 (Phosphor)	24·00	18·00
		First Day Cover (Ordinary)		22·00
		First Day Cover (Phosphor)		30·00
		Presentation Pack (Ordinary)	85·00	

Special First Day of Issue Postmark

	Ordinary	Phosphor
G.P.O. Philatelic Bureau, London E.C.1 (Type B)	25·00	32·00

219 Forth Road Bridge

220 Forth Road and Railway Bridges

(Des A. Restall)

1964 (4 Sept). **Opening of Forth Road Bridge.** *Chalk-surfaced paper.* W **179**. *P* 15 × 14.

			Ordinary	Phosphor
659	219	3d. black, blue & reddish violet	15	10
		p. Three phosphor bands	50	50
660	220	6d. black, lt blue & carmine-red	45	40
		a. Lt blue omitted	£1500	£1500
		Wi. Watermark inverted	1·50	
		p. Three phosphor bands	4·50	4·50
		pWi. Watermark inverted	55·00	
		Set of 2 (Ordinary)	60	50
		Set of 2 (Phosphor)	5·00	5·00
		First Day Cover (Ordinary)		6·00
		First Day Cover (Phosphor)		10·00
		Presentation Pack (Ordinary)	£200	

Special First Day of Issue Postmarks

	Ordinary	Phosphor
G.P.O. Philatelic Bureau, London E.C.1 (Type B)	10·00	15·00
North Queensferry, Fife	22·00	95·00
South Queensferry, West Lothian	17·00	70·00

The Queensferry postmarks were applied to first day covers sent to a temporary Philatelic Bureau at Edinburgh.

221 Sir Winston Churchill

(Des D. Gentleman and Rosalind Dease, from photograph by Karsh)

1965 (8 July). **Churchill Commemoration.** *Chalk-surfaced paper.* W **179**. *P* 15 × 14.

I. "REMBRANDT" Machine

			Ordinary	Phosphor
661	221	4d. black & olive-brown	15	10
		Wi. Watermark inverted	1·75	
		p. Three phosphor bands	30	30

II. "TIMSON" Machine

			Ordinary	Phosphor
661a	221	4d. black & olive-brown	25	25

III. "L. & M. 4" Machine

			Ordinary	Phosphor
662	—	1s. 3d. black & grey	45	30
		Wi. Watermark inverted	65·00	
		p. Three phosphor bands	3·00	3·25
		Set of 2 (Ordinary)	60	40
		Set of 2 (Phosphor)	3·00	3·25
		First Day Cover (Ordinary)		3·00
		First Day Cover (Phosphor)		6·50
		Presentation Pack (Ordinary)	13·00	

The 1s. 3d. shows a closer view of Churchill's head.

Two examples of the 4d. value exist with the Queen's head omitted, one due to something adhering to the cylinder and the other due to a paper fold. The stamp also exists with Churchill's head omitted, also due to a paper fold.

4d. REMBRANDT, Cyls 1A-1B dot and no dot. Lack of shading detail on Churchill's portrait. Queen's portrait appears dull and coarse. This is a rotary machine which is sheet-fed.

4d. TIMSON. Cyls 5A-6B no dot. More detail on Churchill's portrait—furrow on forehead, his left eyebrow fully drawn and more shading on cheek. Queen's portrait lighter and sharper. This is a reel-fed two-colour 12-in. wide rotary machine and the differences in impressions are due to the greater pressure applied by this machine.

1s. 3d. Cyls 1A-1B no dot. The "Linotype and Machinery No. 4" machine is an ordinary sheet-fed rotary press machine. Besides being used for printing the 1s. 3d. stamps it was also employed for overprinting the phosphor bands on both values.

Special First Day of Issue Postmark

	Ordinary	Phosphor
G.P.O. Philatelic Bureau, London E.C.1 (Type B)	9·00	12·00

A First Day of Issue handstamp was provided at Bladon, Oxford, for this issue.

222 Simon de Montfort's Seal

223 Parliament Buildings
(after engraving by Hollar, 1647)

(Des S. Black (6d.), R. Guyatt (2s. 6d.))

1965 (19 July). **700th Anniversary of Simon de Montfort's Parliament.** *Chalk-surfaced paper.* W **179**. *P* 15 × 14.

663	222	6d. olive-green	10	10
		p. Three phosphor bands	40	40
664	223	2s. 6d. black, grey & pale drab	1·25	1·25
		Wi. Watermark inverted	12·00	
		Set of 2 (Ordinary)	1·25	1·25
		First Day Cover (Ordinary)		10·00
		First Day Cover (Phosphor)		11·00
		Presentation Pack (Ordinary)	35·00	

Special First Day of Issue Postmark

	Ordinary
G.P.O. Philatelic Bureau, London E.C.1 (Type B)	12·00

A First Day of Issue handstamp was provided at Evesham, Worcs, for this issue.

224 Bandsmen and Banner

225 Three Salvationists

(Des M. Farrar-Bell (3d.), G. Trenaman (1s. 6d.))

1965 (9 Aug). **Salvation Army Centenary.** *Chalk-surfaced paper.* W **179**. *P* 15 × 14.

665	224	3d. indigo, grey-blue, cerise, yellow & brown	10	10
		p. One phosphor band	40	40
666	225	1s. 6d. red, blue, yellow & brown	1·00	1·00
		p. Three phosphor bands	2·75	3·25
		Set of 2 (Ordinary)	1·10	1·10
		Set of 2 (Phosphor)	3·00	3·50
		First Day Cover (Ordinary)		20·00
		First Day Cover (Phosphor)		25·00

The Philatelic Bureau did not provide first day cover services for Nos. 665/70.

226 Lister's Carbolic Spray   **227** Lister and Chemical Symbols

(Des P. Gauld (4d.), F. Ariss (1s.))

1965 (1 Sept). **Centenary of Joseph Lister's Discovery of Antiseptic Surgery.** *Chalk-surfaced paper.* W **179**. *P* 15 × 14.

667	226	4d. indigo, brown-red & grey-black	10	10
		a. Brown-red (tube) omitted	£150	75·00
		b. Indigo omitted	£1600	
		p. Three phosphor bands	15	20
		pa. Brown-red (tube) omitted	£1250	
668	227	1s. black, purple & new blue	1·00	1·25
		Wi. Watermark inverted	£140	
		p. Three phosphor bands	2·40	2·40
		pWi. Watermark inverted	£140	
		Set of 2 (Ordinary)	1·10	1·25
		Set of 2 (Phosphor)	2·50	2·50
		First Day Cover (Ordinary)		9·50
		First Day Cover (Phosphor)		11·00

228 Trinidad Carnival Dancers   **229** Canadian Folk-dancers

(Des D. Gentleman and Rosalind Dease)

1965 (1 Sept). **Commonwealth Arts Festival.** *Chalk-surfaced paper.* W **179**. *P* 15 × 14.

669	228	6d. black & orange	10	10
		p. Three phosphor bands	30	30
670	229	1s. 6d. black & lt reddish violet	1·25	1·50
		p. Three phosphor bands	2·25	2·25
		Set of 2 (Ordinary)	1·25	1·50
		Set of 2 (Phosphor)	2·50	2·50
		First Day Cover (Ordinary)		12·00
		First Day Cover (Phosphor)		16·00

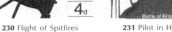

230 Flight of Spitfires   **231** Pilot in Hurricane

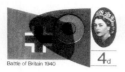

232 Wing-tips of Spitfire and
Messerschmitt "ME-109"

233 Spitfires attacking Heinkel
"HE-111" Bomber

234 Spitfire attacking Stuka
Dive-bomber

235 Hurricanes over Wreck of
Dornier "DO-17z2" Bomber

236 Anti-aircraft Artillery in Action

237 Air-battle over St. Paul's
Cathedral

(Des D. Gentleman and Rosalind Dease (4d. × 6 and 1s. 3d.), A. Restall
(9d.))

1965 (13 Sept). **25th Anniv of Battle of Britain.** *Chalk-surfaced paper.*
W **179**. *P* 15 × 14.

671	**230**	4d. yellow-olive & black	30	35
		a. Block of 6. Nos. 671/6	5·50	5·50
		p. Three phosphor bands	40	50
		pa. Block of 6. Nos. 671p/6p	10·50	9·00
672	**231**	4d. yellow-olive, olive-grey & black	30	35
		p. Three phosphor bands	40	50
673	**232**	4d. red, new blue, yellow-olive, olive-grey & black	30	35
		p. Three phosphor bands	40	50
674	**233**	4d. olive-grey, yellow-olive & black	30	35
		p. Three phosphor bands	40	50
675	**234**	4d. olive-grey, yellow-olive & black	30	35
		p. Three phosphor bands	40	50
676	**235**	4d. olive-grey, yellow-olive, new blue & black	30	35
		a. New blue omitted	†	£3000
		p. Three phosphor bands	40	50
677	**236**	9d. bluish violet, orange & slate-purple	1·25	1·25
		Wi. Watermark inverted	25·00	
		p. Three phosphor bands	1·25	80
678	**237**	1s. 3d. lt grey, dp grey, black, lt blue & brt blue	1·25	1·25
		Wi. Watermark inverted	18·00	
		p. Three phosphor bands	1·25	80
		pWi. Watermark inverted	3·00	
		Set of 8 (Ordinary)	6·50	4·25
		Set of 8 (Phosphor)	12·00	4·25
		First Day Cover (Ordinary)		16·00
		First Day Cover (Phosphor)		16·00
		Presentation Pack (Ordinary)	45·00	

Nos. 671/6 were issued together *se-tenant* in blocks of 6 (3 × 2)
within the sheet.

No. 676a is only known commercially used on cover from Truro.

Special First Day of Issue Postmark

	Ordinary	Phosphor
G.P.O. Philatelic Bureau, London E.C.1 (Type C)	17·00	18·00

238 Tower and Georgian
Buildings

239 Tower and "Nash" Terrace,
Regent's Park

(Des C. Abbott)

1965 (8 Oct). **Opening of Post Office Tower.** *Chalk-surfaced paper.*
W **179** (*sideways on* 3d.). *P* 14 × 15 (3d.) *or* 15 × 14 (1s. 3d.).

679	**238**	3d. olive-yellow, new blue & bronze-green .	10	10
		a. Olive-yellow (Tower) omitted	£500	
		p. One phosphor band at right	10	10
		pEa. Band at left	10	10
680	**239**	1s. 3d. bronze-green, yellow-green & blue ..	65	75
		Wi. Watermark inverted	38·00	
		p. Three phosphor bands	50	50
		pWi. Watermark inverted	35·00	
		Set of 2 (Ordinary)	75	85
		Set of 2 (Phosphor)	60	60
		First Day Cover (Ordinary)		6·00
		First Day Cover (Phosphor)		8·00
		Presentation Pack (Ordinary)	3·00	
		Presentation Pack (Phosphor)	3·00	

The one phosphor band on No. 679p was produced by printing
broad phosphor bands across alternate vertical perforations. Individual
stamps show the band at right or left.

Special First Day of Issue Postmark

	Ordinary	Phosphor
G.P.O. Philatelic Bureau, London E.C.1 (Type C)	6·50	8·50

The Philatelic Bureau did not provide first day cover services for Nos.
681/4.

240 U.N. Emblem

241 I.C.Y. Emblem

(Des J. Matthews)

1965 (25 Oct). **20th Anniv of U.N.O. and International Co-operation
Year.** *Chalk-surfaced paper. W* **179.** *P* 15 × 14.

681	**240**	3d. black, yellow-orange & lt blue	15	20
		p. One phosphor band	25	25
682	**241**	1s. 6d. black, brt purple & lt blue	1·10	90
		Wi. Watermark inverted		
		p. Three phosphor bands	2·75	2·50
		Set of 2 (Ordinary)	1·25	1·10
		Set of 2 (Phosphor)	2·75	2·75
		First Day Cover (Ordinary)		10·00
		First Day Cover (Phosphor)		12·00

242 Telecommunications
Network

243 Radio Waves and
Switchboard

(Des A. Restall)

1965 (15 Nov). **I.T.U. Centenary.** *Chalk-surfaced paper.* W **179**.
P 15 × 14.

683	**242**	9d. red, ultramarine, dp slate, violet, black & pink	20	20
		Wi. Watermark inverted	12·00	
		p. Three phosphor bands	60	50
		pWi. Watermark inverted	60·00	
684	**243**	1s. 6d. red, greenish blue, indigo, black & lt pink	1·40	1·10
		a. Lt pink omitted	£850	
		Wi. Watermark inverted	45·00	
		p. Three phosphor bands	4·50	4·50
		Set of 2 (Ordinary)	1·50	1·25
		Set of 2 (Phosphor)	5·00	5·00
		First Day Cover (Ordinary)		11·50
		First Day Cover (Phosphor)		13·00

Originally scheduled for issue on 17 May 1965, supplies from the
Philatelic Bureau were sent in error to reach a dealer on that date and
another dealer received his supply on 27 May.

244 Robert Burns (after Skirving
chalk drawing)

245 Robert Burns (after Nasmyth
portrait)

(Des G. Huntly)

1966 (25 Jan). **Burns Commemoration.** *Chalk-surfaced paper.* W **179**.
P 15 × 14.

685	**244**	4d. black, dp violet-blue & new blue	15	15
		p. Three phosphor bands	25	25
686	**245**	1s. 3d. black, slate-blue & yellow-orange..	70	70
		p. Three phosphor bands	1·00	1·00
		Set of 2 (Ordinary)	85	85
		Set of 2 (Phosphor)	1·25	1·25
		First Day Cover (Ordinary)	3·00	
		First Day Cover (Phosphor)		3·75
		Presentation Pack (Ordinary)	35·00	

Special First Day of Issue Postmarks
(35 mm diameter)

	Ordin-ary	Phos-phor
Alloway, Ayrshire	5·00	5·00
Ayr	9·00	9·00
Dumfries	7·00	7·00
Edinburgh	7·00	7·00
Glasgow	7·00	7·00
Kilmarnock, Ayrshire	9·00	9·00

A special Philatelic Bureau was set up in Edinburgh to deal with first
day covers of this issue. The Bureau serviced covers to receive the
above postmarks, and other versions were applied locally. The locally
applied handstamps were 38–39mm in diameter, the Bureau postmarks, applied by machine, 35mm. The Ayr, Edinburgh, Glasgow and
Kilmarnock postmarks are similar in design to that for Alloway. Similar
handstamps were also provided at Greenock and Mauchline, but the
Bureau did not provide a service for these.

246 Westminster Abbey

247 Fan Vaulting, Henry VII Chapel

(Des Sheila Robinson. Photo Harrison (3d.). Des and eng Bradbury,
Wilkinson. Recess (2s. 6d.))

1966 (28 Feb). **900th Anniversary of Westminster Abbey.** *Chalk-
surfaced paper* (3d.). W **179**. P 15 × 14 (3d.) or 11 × 12 (2s. 6d.).

687	**246**	3d. black, red-brown & new blue	15	10
		p. One phosphor band	30	30
688	**247**	2s. 6d. black	85	90
		Set of 2	1·00	1·00
		First Day Cover (Ordinary)		5·00
		First Day Cover (Phosphor)		9·50
		Presentation Pack (Ordinary)	15·00	

Special First Day of Issue Postmark

	Ordin-ary
G.P.O. Philatelic Bureau, London E.C.1 (Type B)	6·00

The Bureau did not provide a first day cover service for the 3d.
phosphor stamp.

248 View near Hassocks, Sussex

249 Antrim, Northern Ireland

250 Harlech Castle, Wales

251 Cairngorm Mountains,
Scotland

(Des L. Rosoman. Queen's portrait, adapted by D. Gentleman from coinage)

1966 (2 May). **Landscapes.** *Chalk-surfaced paper.* W **179**. P 15×14.

689	**248**	4d. black, yellow-green & new blue		15	15
		p. Three phosphor bands		15	15
690	**249**	6d. black, emerald & new blue		15	15
		Wi. Watermark inverted		4·50	
		p. Three phosphor bands		25	25
		pWi. Watermark inverted		25·00	
691	**250**	1s. 3d. black, greenish yellow & greenish blue		35	35
		p. Three phosphor bands		35	35
692	**251**	1s. 6d. black, orange & Prussian blue		50	50
		Wi. Watermark inverted		8·00	
		p. Three phosphor bands		50	50
		Set of 4 (*Ordinary*)		1·00	1·00
		Set of 4 (*Phosphor*)		1·00	1·00
		First Day Cover (*Ordinary*)		6·00	
		First Day Cover (*Phosphor*)		7·00	

Special First Day of Issue Postmark

	Ordin-ary	Phos-phor
G.P.O. Philatelic Bureau, London E.C.1 (Type B)	10·00	11·00

First Day of Issue handstamps were provided at Lewes, Sussex; Coleraine, Co. Londonderry; Harlech, Merioneth and Grantown-on-Spey, Morayshire, for this issue.

252 Players with Ball

253 Goalmouth Mêlée

254 Goalkeeper saving Goal

(Des D. Gentleman (4d.), W. Kempster (6d.), D. Caplan (1s. 3d.). Queen's portrait adapted by D. Gentleman from coinage)

1966 (1 June). **World Cup Football Competition.** *Chalk-surfaced paper.* W **179** (*sideways on 4d.*). P 14×15 (4d.) *or* 15×14 (*others*).

693	**252**	4d. red, reddish purple, brt blue, flesh & black		15	10
		p. Two phosphor bands		15	10
694	**253**	6d. black, sepia, red, apple-green & blue		20	20
		a. Black omitted		85·00	
		b. Apple-green omitted		£1900	
		c. Red omitted		£1900	
		Wi. Watermark inverted		1·25	
		p. Three phosphor bands		20	20
		pa. Black omitted		£300	

695	**254**	1s. 3d. black, blue, yellow, red & lt yellow-olive		50	50
		a. Blue omitted		£150	
		Wi. Watermark inverted		60·00	
		p. Three phosphor bands		50	50
		pWi. Watermark inverted		1·25	
		Set of 3 (*Ordinary*)		75	75
		Set of 3 (*Phosphor*)		75	75
		First Day Cover (*Ordinary*)		7·50	
		First Day Cover (*Phosphor*)		7·50	
		Presentation Pack (*Ordinary*)		12·00	

Special First Day of Issue Postmark

	Ordin-ary	Phos-phor
G.P.O. Philatelic Bureau, London E.C.1 (Type C)	9·00	10·00

A First Day of Issue handstamp was provided at Wembley, Middx, for this issue.

255 Black-headed Gull

256 Blue Tit

257 European Robin

258 Blackbird

(Des J. Norris Wood)

1966 (8 Aug). **British Birds.** *Chalk-surfaced paper.* W **179**. P 15×14.

696	**255**	4d. grey, black, red, emerald-green, brt blue, greenish yellow & bistre		10	15
		Wi. Watermark inverted		3·00	
		a. Block of 4. Nos. 696/9		1·00	1·00
		ab. Black (value), etc. omitted * (*block of four*)		£4000	
		ac. Black only omitted*		£2500	
		aWi. Watermark inverted (*block of four*)		12·00	
		p. Three phosphor bands		10	15
		pWi. Watermark inverted		14·00	
		pa. Block of 4. Nos. 696p/9p		1·00	1·00
		paWi. Watermark inverted (*block of four*)		60·00	
697	**256**	4d. black, greenish yellow, grey, emerald-green, brt blue & bistre		10	15
		Wi. Watermark inverted		3·00	
		p. Three phosphor bands		10	15
		pWi. Watermark inverted		14·00	
698	**257**	4d. red, greenish yellow, black, grey, bistre, reddish brown & emerald-green		10	15
		Wi. Watermark inverted		3·00	
		p. Three phosphor bands		10	15
		pWi. Watermark inverted		14·00	

699 **258** 4d. black, reddish brown, greenish yellow,
grey & bistre** 10 15
Wi. Watermark inverted .... 3·00
p. Three phosphor bands 10 15
pWi. Watermark inverted .... 14·00
Set of 4 (Ordinary) .... 1·00 50
Set of 4 (Phosphor) .... 1·00 50
First Day Cover (Ordinary) .... 7·00
First Day Cover (Phosphor) .... 7·50
Presentation Pack (Ordinary) .... 7·00

Nos. 696/9 were issued together *se-tenant* in blocks of four within
the sheet.

*In No. 696ab the blue, bistre and reddish brown are also omitted
but in No. 696ac only the black is omitted.

**In No. 699 the black was printed over the bistre.
Other colours omitted, and the stamps affected:

d.	Greenish yellow (Nos. 696/9)	£400
e.	Red (Nos. 696 and 698)	£400
f.	Emerald-green (Nos. 696/8)	75·00
pf.	Emerald-green (Nos. 696p/8p)	75·00
g.	Brt blue (Nos. 696/7)	£250
pg.	Brt blue (Nos. 696p and 697p)	£800
h.	Bistre (Nos. 696/9)	90·00
ph.	Bistre (Nos. 696p/9p)	90·00
j.	Reddish brown (Nos. 698/9)	80·00
pj.	Reddish brown (Nos. 698p and 699p)	80·00

The prices quoted are for each stamp.

Special First Day of Issue Postmark

	Ordin-ary	Phos-phor
G.P.O. Philatelic Bureau, London E.C.1 (Type C)	8·00	11·00

259 Cup Winners

1966 (18 Aug). **England's World Cup Football Victory.** *Chalk-surfaced
paper.* W **179** *(sideways).* P 14 × 15.
700 **259** 4d. red, reddish purple, brt blue, flesh &
black 20 20
First Day Cover .... 2·00

These stamps were only put on sale at post offices in England, the
Channel Islands and the Isle of Man, and at the Philatelic Bureau in
London and also, on 22 August, in Edinburgh on the occasion of the
opening of the Edinburgh Festival as well as at Army post offices at
home and abroad.

The Philatelic Bureau did not service first day covers for this stamp,
but a First Day of Issue handstamp was provided inscribed "Harrow &
Wembley" to replace the "Wembley, Middx" postmark of the initial
issue.

For full information on all future British issues, collectors
should write to the British Post Office Philatelic Bureau, 20
Brandon Street, Edinburgh EH3 5TT

260 Jodrell Bank Radio Telescope

261 British Motor-cars

262 "SRN 6" Hovercraft

263 Windscale Reactor

(Des D. and A. Gillespie (4d., 6d.), A. Restall (others))

1966 (19 Sept). **British Technology.** *Chalk-surfaced paper.* W **179**.
P 15 × 14.
701 **260** 4d. black & lemon 15 15
p. Three phosphor bands 15 15
702 **261** 6d. red, dp blue & orange 15 15
a. Red (Mini-cars) omitted £4000
b. Dp blue (Jaguar & inscr) omitted £2500
p. Three phosphor bands 15 15
703 **262** 1s. 3d. black, orange-red, slate & lt greenish
blue 30 40
p. Three phosphor bands 45 50
704 **263** 1s. 6d. black, yellow-green, bronze-green,
lilac & dp blue 50 45
p. Three phosphor bands 65 60
Set of 4 (Ordinary) .... 1·00 1·00
Set of 4 (Phosphor) .... 1·25 1·25
First Day Cover (Ordinary) .... 4·00
First Day Cover (Phosphor) .... 4·50
Presentation Pack (Ordinary) .... 7·00

Special First Day of Issue Postmark

	Ordin-ary	Phos-phor
G.P.O. Philatelic Bureau, Edinburgh 1 (Type C)	5·00	6·00

264

265

266

267

268   **269**

All the above show battle scenes and they were issued together *se-tenant* in horizontal strips of six within the sheet.

270 Norman Ship

271 Norman Horsemen attacking Harold's Troops

(All the above are scenes from the Bayeux Tapestry)

(Des D. Gentleman. Photo. Queen's head die-stamped (6d., 1s. 3d.))

1966 (14 Oct). **900th Anniv of Battle of Hastings.** *Chalk-surfaced paper.* W **179** (*sideways on* 1s. 3d.). P 15 × 14.

705	**264**	4d. black, olive-green, bistre, dp blue, orange, green, blue & grey …	10	15
		a. Strip of 6. Nos. 705/10 …………	2·00	2·00
		aWi. Strip of 6. Watermark inverted ………	35·00	
		Wi. Watermark inverted ………………	5·00	
		p. Three phosphor bands ……………	10	25
		pa. Strip of 6. Nos. 705p/10p …………	2·00	2·00
		paWi. Strip of 6. Watermark inverted ………	15·00	
		pWi. Watermark inverted ………………	2·00	
706	**265**	4d. black, olive-green, bistre, dp blue, orange, magenta, green, blue & grey …	10	15
		Wi. Watermark inverted ………………	5·00	
		p. Three phosphor bands ……………	10	25
		pWi. Watermark inverted ………………	2·00	
707	**266**	4d. black, olive-green, bistre, dp blue, orange, magenta, green, blue & grey …	10	15
		Wi. Watermark inverted ………………	5·00	
		p. Three phosphor bands ……………	10	25
		pWi. Watermark inverted ………………	2·00	
708	**267**	4d. black, olive-green, bistre, dp blue, magenta, green, blue & grey …………	10	15
		Wi. Watermark inverted ………………	5·00	
		p. Three phosphor bands ……………	10	25
		pWi. Watermark inverted ………………	2·00	
709	**268**	4d. black, olive-green, bistre, dp blue, orange, magenta, green, blue & grey …	10	15
		Wi. Watermark inverted ………………	5·00	
		p. Three phosphor bands ……………	10	25
		pWi. Watermark inverted ………………	2·00	
710	**269**	4d. black, olive-green, bistre, dp blue, orange, magenta, green, blue & grey …	10	15
		Wi. Watermark inverted ………………	5·00	
		p. Three phosphor bands ……………	10	25
		pWi. Watermark inverted ………………	2·00	

711	**270**	6d. black, olive-green, violet, blue, green & gold ……………………………	10	10
		Wi. Watermark inverted ………………	35·00	
		p. Three phosphor bands ……………	10	10
		pWi. Watermark inverted ………………	45·00	
712	**271**	1s. 3d. black, lilac, bronze-green, rosine bistre-brown & gold ………………	20	20
		a. Lilac omitted ………………………	£450	
		Wi. Watermark sideways inverted (top of crown pointing to right)* …………	30·00	
		p. Four phosphor bands ……………	20	20
		pa. Lilac omitted ……………………	£650	
		pWi. Watermark sideways inverted (top of crown pointing to right)* …………	11·00	
		Set of 8 (Ordinary) …………………	2·25	1·50
		Set of 8 (Phosphor) …………………	2·25	1·90
		First Day Cover (Ordinary) …………		3·00
		First Day Cover (Phosphor) …………		3·00
		Presentation Pack (Ordinary) ………	7·00	

*The normal sideways watermark shows the tops of the Crowns pointing to the left, *as seen from the back of the stamp.*

Other colours omitted in the 4d. values and the stamps affected:

b.	Olive-green (Nos. 705/10) ………………	25·00
pb.	Olive-green (Nos. 705p/10p) ……………	25·00
c.	Bistre (Nos. 705/10) ……………………	25·00
pc.	Bistre (Nos. 705p/10p) …………………	30·00
d.	Dp blue (Nos. 705/10) …………………	35·00
pd.	Dp blue (Nos. 705p/10p) ………………	35·00
e.	Orange (Nos. 705/7 and 709/10) ………	25·00
pe.	Orange (Nos. 705p/7p and 709p/10p) …	20·00
f.	Magenta (Nos. 705/10) …………………	30·00
pf.	Magenta (Nos. 705p/10p) ………………	30·00
g.	Green (Nos. 705/10) ……………………	25·00
pg.	Green (Nos. 705p/10p) …………………	25·00
h.	Blue (Nos. 705/10) ……………………	20·00
ph.	Blue (Nos. 705p/10p) …………………	35·00
j.	Grey (Nos. 705/10) ……………………	20·00
pj.	Grey (Nos. 705p/10p) …………………	20·00
pk.	Magenta & green (Nos. 705p/10p) ………	

The prices quoted are for each stamp.

Nos. 705 and 709, with grey and blue omitted, have been seen commercially used, posted from Middleton-in-Teesdale.

The 6d. phosphor is known in a yellowish gold as well as the reddish gold as used in the 1s. 3d.

Three examples of No. 712 in a right-hand top corner block of 10 (2 × 5) are known with the Queen's head omitted as a result of a double paper fold prior to die-stamping. The perforation is normal. Of the other seven stamps, four have the Queen's head misplaced and three are normal.

MISSING GOLD HEADS. The 6d. and 1s. 3d. were also issued with the die-stamped gold head omitted but as these can also be removed by chemical means we are not prepared to list them unless a way is found of distinguishing the genuine stamps from the fakes which will satisfy the Expert Committees.

The same remarks apply to Nos. 713/14.

Special First Day of Issue Postmark

	Ordinary	Phosphor
G.P.O. Philatelic Bureau, Edinburgh 1 (Type C) ……………………………	5·00	6·00

A First Day of Issue handstamp was provided at Battle, Sussex, for this issue.

NEW INFORMATION

The editor is always interested to correspond with people who have new information that will improve or correct the Catalogue.

272 King of the Orient   **273** Snowman

(Des Tasveer Shemza (3d.), J. Berry (1s. 6d.) (winners of children's design competition). Photo, Queen's head die-stamped)

1966 (1 Dec). **Christmas.** *Chalk-surfaced paper.* W **179** (*sideways on 3d.*). P 14 × 15.

713	**272**	3d. black, blue, green, yellow, red & gold ...	10	10
		a. Queen's head double		
		b. Green omitted	—	£150
		p. One phosphor band at right	10	10
		pEa. Band at left	10	10
714	**273**	1s. 6d. blue, red, pink, black & gold	35	35
		a. Pink (hat) omitted	£750	
		Wi. Watermark inverted	9·00	
		p. Two phosphor bands	35	35
		pWi. Watermark inverted	38·00	
		Set of 2 (Ordinary)	45	45
		Set of 2 (Phosphor)	45	45
		First Day Cover (Ordinary)		1·50
		First Day Cover (Phosphor)		1·50
		Presentation Pack (Ordinary)	7·00	

Special First Day of Issue Postmarks

	Ordinary	Phosphor
G.P.O. Philatelic Bureau, Edinburgh 1 (Type C)	1·50	1·50
Bethlehem, Llandeilo, Carms (Type C)	2·50	2·50

274 Sea Freight   **275** Air Freight

(Des C. Abbott)

1967 (20 Feb). **European Free Trade Association (EFTA).** *Chalk-surfaced paper.* W **179**. P 15 × 14.

715	**274**	9d. dp blue, red, lilac, green. brown, new blue, yellow & black	15	15
		a. Black (Queen's head, etc.), brown, new blue & yellow omitted	£650	
		b. Lilac omitted	60·00	
		c. Green omitted	40·00	
		d. Brown omitted	45·00	
		e. New blue omitted	42·00	
		f. Yellow omitted	42·00	
		Wi. Watermark inverted	20·00	
		p. Three phosphor bands	15	15
		pb. Lilac omitted	75·00	
		pc. Green omitted	45·00	
		pd. Brown omitted	45·00	
		pe. New blue omitted	75·00	
		pf. Yellow omitted	75·00	
		pWi. Watermark inverted	10·00	

716	**275**	1s. 6d. violet, red, dp blue, brown, green, blue-grey, new blue, yellow & black	30	30
		a. Red omitted		
		b. Dp blue omitted	£225	
		c. Brown omitted	45·00	
		d. Blue-grey omitted	45·00	
		e. New blue omitted	45·00	
		f. Yellow omitted	45·00	
		p. Three phosphor bands	30	30
		pa. Red omitted		
		pb. Dp blue omitted	£200	
		pc. Brown omitted	45·00	
		pd. Blue-grey omitted	45·00	
		pf. New blue omitted	45·00	
		pWi. Watermark inverted	22·00	
		Set of 2 (Ordinary)	40	40
		Set of 2 (Phosphor)	40	40
		First Day Cover (Ordinary)		2·00
		First Day Cover (Phosphor)		2·50
		Presentation Pack (Ordinary)	1·50	

Special First Day of Issue Postmark

	Ordinary	Phosphor
G.P.O. Philatelic Bureau, Edinburgh 1 (Type C)	4·00	5·00

276 Hawthorn and Bramble   **277** Larger Bindweed and Viper's Bugloss

278 Ox-eye Daisy, Coltsfoot and Buttercup   **279** Bluebell, Red Campion and Wood Anemone

T 276/9 were issued together *se-tenant* in blocks of four within the sheet.

280 Dog Violet   **281** Primroses

(Des Rev. W. Keble Martin (T **276**/9), Mary Grierson (others))

1967 (24 Apr). **British Wild Flowers.** *Chalk-surfaced paper.* W **179**. P 15 × 14.

717 **276**	4d.	grey, lemon, myrtle-green, red, agate & slate-purple	15	10
	a.	Block of 4. Nos. 717/20	1·25	1·25
	aWi.	Block of 4. Watermark inverted	7·50	
	b.	Grey double*		
	c.	Red omitted	£1750	
	f.	Slate-purple omitted		
	Wi.	Watermark inverted	1·50	
	p.	Three phosphor bands	10	10
	pa.	Block of 4. Nos. 717p/20p	1·00	1·00
	paWi.	Block of 4. Watermark inverted	7·50	
	pd.	Agate omitted	£900	
	pf.	Slate-purple omitted	£150	
	pWi.	Watermark inverted	1·50	
718 **277**	4d.	grey, lemon, myrtle-green, red, agate & violet	15	10
	b.	Grey double*		
	Wi.	Watermark inverted	1·50	
	p.	Three phosphor bands	10	10
	pd.	Agate omitted	£450	
	pe.	Violet omitted	£1250	
	pWi.	Watermark inverted	1·50	
719 **278**	4d.	grey, lemon, myrtle-green, red & agate .	15	10
	b.	Grey double*		
	Wi.	Watermark inverted	1·50	
	p.	Three phosphor bands	10	10
	pd.	Agate omitted	£450	
	pWi.	Watermark inverted	1·50	
720 **279**	4d.	grey, lemon, myrtle-green, reddish purple, agate & violet	15	10
	b.	Grey double*		
	c.	Reddish purple omitted	£950	
	Wi.	Watermark inverted	1·50	
	p.	Three phosphor bands	10	10
	pd.	Agate omitted	£450	
	pe.	Violet omitted	£1250	
	pWi.	Watermark inverted	1·50	
721 **280**	9d.	lavender-grey, green, reddish violet & orange-yellow	15	10
	Wi.	Watermark inverted	75	
	p.	Three phosphor bands	10	10
722 **281**	1s.	9d. lavender-grey, green, greenish yellow & orange	20	20
	p.	Three phosphor bands	30	20
		Set of 6 (*Ordinary*)	1·40	65
		Set of 6 (*Phosphor*)	1·25	65
		First Day Cover (*Ordinary*)		3·00
		First Day Cover (*Phosphor*)		3·50
		Presentation Pack (*Ordinary*)	3·00	
		Presentation Pack (*Phosphor*)	3·00	

*The double impression of the grey printing affects the Queen's head, value and inscription.

Special First Day of Issue Postmark

	Ordinary	Phosphor
G.P.O. Philatelic Bureau, Edinburgh 1 (Type C)	5·00	5·50

PHOSPHOR BANDS. Issues from No. 723 are normally with phosphor bands only, except for the high values but most stamps have appeared with the phosphor bands omitted in error. Such varieties are listed under "Ey" numbers and are priced unused only. See also further notes after 1971–95 Decimal Machin issue.

PHOSPHORISED PAPER. Following the adoption of phosphor bands the Post Office started a series of experiments involving the addition of the phosphor to the paper coating before the stamps were printed. No. 743c was the first of these experiments to be issued for normal postal use. See also notes after 1971–95 Decimal Machin issue.

PVA GUM. Polyvinyl alcohol was introduced by Harrisons in place of gum arabic in 1968. It is almost invisible except that a small amount of pale yellowish colouring matter was introduced to make it possible to see that the stamps had been gummed. Although this can be distinguished from gum arabic in unused stamps there is, of course, no means of detecting it in used examples. Where the two forms of gum exist on the same stamps, the PVA type are listed under "Ev" numbers, except in the case of the 1d. and 4d. (vermilion), both one centre band, which later appeared with gum arabic and these have "Eg" numbers. "Ev" and "Eg" numbers are priced unused only. All stamps printed from No. 763 onwards were issued with PVA gum only *except where otherwise stated*.

It should be further noted that gum arabic is shiny in appearance, and that, normally, PVA gum has a matt appearance. However, depending upon the qualities of the paper ingredients and the resultant absorption of the gum, occasionally, PVA gum has a shiny appearance. In such cases, especially in stamps from booklets, it is sometimes impossible to be absolutely sure which gum has been used except by testing the stamps chemically which destroys them. Therefore, whilst all gum arabic is shiny it does not follow that all shiny gum is gum arabic.

282	282a

Two types of the 2d.

I. Value spaced away from left side of stamp (cylinders 1 no dot and dot).

II. Value close to left side from new multipositive used for cylinders 5 no dot and dot onwards. The portrait appears in the centre, thus conforming to the other values.

Three types of the Machin head, known as Head A, B or C, are distinguished by specialists. These are illustrated in Vol. 3 of the *Great Britain Specialised Catalogue*.

(Des after plaster cast by Arnold Machin)

1967 (5 June)–**70**. *Chalk-surfaced paper. Two phosphor bands except where otherwise stated. No wmk. PVA gum except Nos. 725m, 728, 729, 731, 731Ea, 740, 742/Ea, 743/a and 744/Ea.*

723 **282**	½d.	orange-brown (5.2.68)	10	20
	Ey.	Phosphor omitted	30·00	
724	1d.	lt olive (*shades*) (2 bands) (5.2.68)	10	10
	a.	Imperf (coil strip)†	£750	
	b.	Part perf pane*		
	c.	Imperf pane*	£3750	
	d.	Uncoated paper (1970)**	65·00	
	Ey.	Phosphor omitted	1·00	

(724)	**282**	l. Booklet pane. No. 724 × 2 se-tenant with 730 × 2 (6.4.68)	2·75		
		lEy. Booklet pane. Phosphor omitted	75·00		
		m. Booklet pane. No. 724 × 4 se-tenant with 734 × 2 (6.1.69)	3·25		
		mEy. Booklet pane. Phosphor omitted	£100		
		n. Booklet pane. No. 724 × 6, 734 × 3, 734Eb × 3 & 735 × 3 se-tenant (1.12.69)	8·50		
		na. Booklet pane. Uncoated paper**	£900		
		nEy. Booklet pane. Phosphor omitted	£150		
725		1d. yellowish olive (1 centre band) (16.9.68)	25	30	
		Eg. Gum arabic (27.8.69)	25		
		l. Booklet pane. No. 725 × 4 se-tenant with 732 × 2	3·75		
		lEy. Booklet pane. Phosphor omitted	30·00		
		m. Coil strip. No. 728 × 2 se-tenant with 729, 725Eg & 733Eg (27.8.69)	1·25		
726		2d. lake-brown (Type I) (2 bands) (5.2.68)	10	15	
		Ey. Phosphor omitted	25·00		
727		2d. lake-brown (Type II) (2 bands) (1969)	15	15	
		Ey. Phosphor omitted	1·00		
728		2d. lake-brown (Type II) (1 centre band) (27.8.69)	40	50	
729		3d. violet (shades) (1 centre band) (8.8.67)	10	10	
		a. Imperf (pair)	£550		
		Ey. Phosphor omitted	1·25		
		Ev. PVA gum (shades) (12.3.68)	10		
		Evy. Phosphor omitted	1·25		
730		3d. violet (2 bands) (6.4.68)	30	30	
		a. Uncoated paper**	£900		
731		4d. dp sepia (shades) (2 bands)	10	10	
		Ey. Phosphor omitted	1·00		
		Ea. Dp olive-brown	10	15	
		Eay. Phosphor omitted	2·00		
		b. Part perf pane*	£650		
		Ev. PVA gum (shades) (22.1.68)	10		
		Evy. Phosphor omitted	2·00		
732		4d. dp olive-brown (shades) (1 centre band) (16.9.68)	10	10	
		a. Part perf pane*	£750		
		l. Booklet pane. Two stamps plus two printed labels	75		
		lEy. Booklet pane. Phosphor omitted	45·00		
733		4d. brt vermilion (1 centre band) (6.1.69)	10	10	
		a. Tête-bêche (horiz pair)	£2500		
		b. Uncoated paper**	6·00		
		Ey. Phosphor omitted	1·25		
		Eg. Gum arabic (27.8.69)	10		
		Egy. Phosphor omitted	£800		
		l. Booklet pane. Two stamps plus two printed labels (3.3.69)	80		
		lEy. Booklet pane. Phosphor omitted	70·00		
734		4d. brt vermilion (1 band at left) (6.1.69)	1·40	1·60	
		a. Uncoated paper**	£175		
		Eb. One band at right (1.12.69)	2·00	3·00	
		Eba. Ditto. Uncoated paper**	£175		
735		5d. royal blue (shades) (1.7.68)	10	10	
		a. Imperf pane*	£550		
		b. Part perf pane*	£500		
		c. Imperf (pair)††	£200		
		d. Uncoated paper**	15·00		
		Ey. Phosphor omitted	2·00		
		Ee. Dp blue	10	15	
		Eey. Phosphor omitted	3·00		
736		6d. brt reddish purple (shades) (5.2.68)	20	20	
		Ey. Phosphor omitted	6·50		
		Ea. Brt magenta	3·00	50	
		Eb. Claret	50	40	
		Eby. Phosphor omitted	10·00		

737	**282a**	7d. brt emerald (1.7.68)	40	30	
		Ey. Phosphor omitted	45·00		
738		8d. brt vermilion (1.7.68)	15	30	
		Ey. Phosphor omitted	£400		
739		8d. lt turquoise-blue (6.1.69)	45	50	
		Ey. Phosphor omitted	50·00		
740		9d. myrtle-green (8.8.67)	50	30	
		Ey. Phosphor omitted	20·00		
		Ev. PVA gum (29.11.68)	50		
		Evy. Phosphor omitted	20·00		
741	**282**	10d. drab (1.7.68)	45	50	
		a. Uncoated paper**	23·00		
		Ey. Phosphor omitted	40·00		
742		1s. lt bluish violet (shades)	40	30	
		Ey. Phosphor omitted	70·00		
		Ea. Pale bluish violet	60	30	
		Ev. Ditto. PVA gum (26.4.68)	50		
		Evy. Phosphor omitted	3·50		
743		1s. 6d. greenish blue & deep blue (shades) (8.8.67)	50	30	
		a. Greenish blue omitted	£125		
		Ey. Phosphor omitted	6·00		
		Ev. PVA gum (28.8.68)	60		
		Eva. Greenish blue omitted	80·00		
		Evy. Phosphor omitted	14·00		
		Evb. Prussian blue & indigo	1·50	75	
		Evby. Phosphor omitted	11·00		
		c. Phosphorised paper (Prussian blue & indigo) (10.12.69)	75	90	
		ca. Prussian blue omitted	£400		
744		1s. 9d. dull orange & black (shades)	40	30	
		Ey. Phosphor omitted	30·00		
		Ea. Brt orange & black	1·50	50	
		Ev. PVA gum (brt orange & black) (16.11.70)	40		
		Set of 16 (one of each value & colour)	3·00	3·25	
		Presentation Pack (one of each value)	6·00		
		Presentation Pack (German)	45·00		

*BOOKLET ERRORS. See note after No. 556.

** Uncoated paper. This does not respond to the chalky test, and may be further distinguished from the normal chalk-surfaced paper by the fibres which clearly show on the surface, resulting in the printing impression being rougher, and by the screening dots which are not so evident. The 1d., 4d. and 5d. come from the £1 "Stamps for Cooks" Booklet (1970); the 3d. and 10d. from sheets (1969). The 20p. and 50p. high values (Nos. 830/1) exist with similar errors.

†No. 724a occurs in a vertical strip of four, top stamp perforated on three sides, bottom stamp imperf three sides and the two middle stamps completely imperf.

††No. 735c comes from the original state of cylinder 15 which is identifiable by the screening dots which extend through the gutters of the stamps and into the margins of the sheet. This must not be confused with imperforate stamps from cylinder 10, a large quantity of which was stolen from the printers early in 1970.

The 1d. with centre band and PVA gum (725) only came in the September 1968 10s. booklet (No. XP6). The 1d., 2d. and 4d. with centre band and gum arabic (725Eg, 728 and 733Eg respectively) only came in the coil strip (725m). The 3d. (No. 730) appeared in booklets on 6.4.68, from coils during Dec 68 and from sheets in Jan 1969. The 4d. with one side band at left (734) came from 10s. and £1 booklet se-tenant panes, and the 4d. with one side band at right (734Eb) came from the £1 booklet se-tenant panes only.

The 4d. (731) in shades of washed-out grey are colour changelings which we understand are caused by the concentrated solvents used in modern dry cleaning methods.

For decimal issue, see Nos. X841, etc.

First Day Covers

5.6.67	4d., 1s., 1s. 9d. (731, 742, 744)	1·00
8.8.67	3d., 9d., 1s. 6d. (729, 740, 743)	1·00
5.2.68	½d., 1d., 2d., 6d. (723/4, 726, 736)	1·00
1.7.68	5d., 7d., 8d., 10d. (735, 737/8, 741)	1·00

283 "Master Lambton"
(Sir Thomas Lawrence)

284 "Mares and Foals in a Landscape"
(George Stubbs)

285 "Children Coming Out of School"
(L. S. Lowry)

(Des S. Rose)

1967 (10 July). **British Paintings.** *Chalk-surfaced paper. Two phosphor bands. No wmk. P 14 × 15 (4d.) or 15 × 14 (others).*

748	**283**	4d. rose-red, lemon, brown, black, new blue & gold	10	10
		a. Gold (value & Queen's head) omitted ...	£180	
		b. New blue omitted	£2500	
		Ey. Phosphor omitted	5·00	
749	**284**	9d. Venetian red, ochre, grey-black, new blue, greenish yellow & black	20	20
		a. Black (Queen's head & value) omitted ..	£400	
		b. Greenish yellow omitted	£1200	
		Ey. Phosphor omitted	£450	
750	**285**	1s. 6d. greenish yellow, grey, rose, new blue, grey-black & gold	35	25
		a. Gold (Queen's head) omitted	£750	
		b. New blue omitted	£140	
		c. Grey omitted	85·00	
		Ey. Phosphor omitted	£300	
		Set of 3	50	50
		First Day Cover		2·50
		Presentation Pack	4·25	

Special First Day of Issue Postmark
G.P.O. Philatelic Bureau, Edinburgh 1 (Type C) .... 4·00
A First Day of Issue handstamp was provided at Bishop Auckland, Co. Durham, for this issue.

286 *Gypsy Moth IV*

(Des M. and Sylvia Goaman)

1967 (24 July). **Sir Francis Chichester's World Voyage.** *Chalk-surfaced paper. Three phosphor bands. No wmk. P 15 × 14.*

751	**286**	1s. 9d. black, brown-red, lt emerald & blue	25	25
		First Day Cover		1·00

Special First Day of Issue Postmarks

G.P.O. Philatelic Bureau, Edinburgh 1	2·00
Greenwich, London SE10	3·00
Plymouth, Devon	3·00

The Philatelic Bureau and Greenwich postmarks are similar in design to that for Plymouth. A First Day of Issue handstamp was provided at Chichester, Sussex for this issue.

287 Radar Screen

288 *Penicillium notatum*

289 "VC-10" Jet Engines

290 Television Equipment

(Des C. Abbott (4d., 1s.), Negus-Sharland team (others))

1967 (19 Sept). **British Discovery and Invention.** *Chalk-surfaced paper. Three phosphor bands (4d.) or two phosphor bands (others). W 179 (sideways on 1s. 9d.). P 14 × 15 (1s. 9d.) or 15 × 14 (others).*

752	**287**	4d. greenish yellow, black & vermilion	10	10
		Ey. Phosphor omitted	1·25	
753	**288**	1s. blue-green, lt greenish blue, slate-purple & bluish violet	10	10
		Wi. Watermark inverted	10·00	
		Ey. Phosphor omitted	7·00	
754	**289**	1s. 6d. black, grey, royal blue, ochre & turquoise-blue	25	15
		Wi. Watermark inverted	30·00	
		Ey. Phosphor omitted	£500	
755	**290**	1s. 9d. black, grey-blue, pale olive-grey, violet & orange	30	20
		a. Grey-blue omitted	£500	
		Ey. Phosphor omitted	£500	
		Set of 4	60	50
		First Day Cover		1·50
		Presentation Pack	2·00	

Special First of Issue Postmark
G.P.O. Philatelic Bureau, Edinburgh (Type C) .... 3·00

WATERMARK. All issues from this date are on unwatermarked paper.

291 "The Adoration of the Shepherds" (School of Seville)

292 "Madonna and Child" (Murillo)

293 "The Adoration of the Shepherds" (Louis le Nain)

(Des S. Rose)

1967. Christmas. *Chalk-surfaced paper. One phosphor band (3d.) or two phosphor bands (others). P 15 × 14 (1s. 6d.) or 14 × 15 (others).*

756	291	3d. olive-yellow, rose, blue, black & gold (27.11)	10	10
		a. Gold (value & Queen's head) omitted	60·00	
		b. Printed on the gummed side	£300	
		c. Rose omitted		
		Ey. Phosphor omitted	50	
757	292	4d. brt purple, greenish yellow, new blue, grey-black & gold (18.10)	10	10
		a. Gold (value & Queen's head) omitted	60·00	
		b. Greenish yellow (Child, robe & Madonna's face) omitted		
		Ey. Phosphor omitted	£100	
758	293	1s. 6d. brt purple, bistre, lemon, black, orange-red, ultramarine & gold (27.11)	35	35
		a. Gold (value & Queen's head) omitted	£2000	
		b. Ultramarine omitted	£300	
		c. Lemon omitted		
		Ey. Phosphor omitted	10·00	
		Set of 3	50	50
		First Day Covers (2)	2·00	

Distinct shades exist of the 4d. value but are not listable as there are intermediate shades. Stamps emanating from one machine show a darker background and give the appearance of the yellow colour being omitted but this is not so and these should not be confused with the true missing yellow No. 757b.

Special First Day of Issue Postmarks

G.P.O. Philatelic Bureau, Edinburgh 1 (4d.) (18 Oct.) (Type C)	2·00
G.P.O. Philatelic Bureau, Edinburgh 1 (3d., 1s. 6d.) (27 Nov.) (Type C)	3·00
Bethlehem, Llandeilo, Carms (4d.) (18 Oct.) (Type C) . .	3·00
Bethlehem, Llandeilo, Carms (3d., 1s. 6d.) (27 Nov.) (Type C)	4·00

Gift Pack 1967

1967 (27 Nov.) *Comprises Nos. 715p/22p and 748/58.*

GP758c	Gift Pack	2·50

(Recess Bradbury, Wilkinson)

1967–68. *No wmk. White paper. P 11 × 12.*

759	166	2s. 6d. black-brown (1.7.68)	40	50
760	167	5s. red (10.4.68)	1·00	1·00
761	168	10s. brt ultramarine (10.4.68)	5·00	5·50
762	169	£1 black (4.12.67)	4·00	4·00
		Set of 4	9·00	10·00

PVA GUM. All the following issues from this date have PVA gum *except where footnotes state otherwise.*

294 Tarr Steps, Exmoor

295 Aberfeldy Bridge

296 Menai Bridge

297 M4 Viaduct

(Des A. Restall (9d.), L. Rosoman (1s. 6d.), J. Matthews (others))

1968 (29 Apr). **British Bridges.** *Chalk-surfaced paper. Two phosphor bands. P 15 × 14.*

763	294	4d. black, bluish violet, turquoise-blue & gold	10	10
		a. Printed on gummed side	25·00	
		Ey. Phosphor omitted	1·25	
764	295	9d. red-brown, myrtle-green, ultramarine, olive-brown, black & gold	10	10
		a. Gold (Queen's head) omitted	£100	
		b. Ultramarine omitted	† £3250	
		Ey. Phosphor omitted	13·00	
765	296	1s. 6d. olive-brown, red-orange, brt green, turquoise-green & gold	20	15
		a. Gold (Queen's head) omitted	£100	
		b. Red-orange omitted	£150	
		Ey. Phosphor omitted	40·00	
766	297	1s. 9d. olive-brown, greenish yellow, dull green, dp ultramarine & gold	25	30
		a. Gold (Queen's head) omitted	£150	
		Ey. Phosphor omitted	7·00	
		Eya. Gold (Queen's head) & phosphor omitted	£300	
		Set of 4	60	60
		First Day Cover		2·00
		Presentation Pack	2·00	

No 764b is only known on first day covers posted from Canterbury, Kent, or the Philatelic Bureau, Edinburgh.

Special First Day of Issue Postmarks

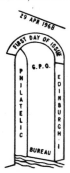

Special First Day of Issue Postmarks

G.P.O. Philatelic Bureau, Edinburgh 1 .... 4·00
Bridge, Canterbury, Kent .... 4·00
Aberfeldy, Perthshire (Type A) (9d. value only) .... 20·00
Menai Bridge, Anglesey (Type A) (1s. 6d. value only) . 20·00
The Bridge, Canterbury, postmark is similar in design to that for the Philatelic Bureau.

G.P.O. Philatelic Bureau, Edinburgh 1 (Type C) .... 4·00
Manchester (4d. value only) .... 2·00
Aldeburgh, Suffolk (9d. value only) .... 3·00
Hendon, London NW4 (1s. value only) .... 3·00
Whitby, Yorkshire (1s. 9d. value only) .... 3·00
The Philatelic Bureau postmark was used on sets of four, but the other postmarks were only available on single stamps.

298 "TUC" and Trades Unionists

299 Mrs. Emmeline Pankhurst (statue)

302 "Queen Elizabeth I" (unknown artist)

303 "Pinkie" (Lawrence)

300 Sopwith "Camel" and "Lightning" Fighters

301 Captain Cook's *Endeavour* and Signature

(Des D. Gentleman (4d.), C. Abbott (others))

1968 (29 May). **British Anniversaries.** *Events described on stamps. Chalk-surfaced paper. Two phosphor bands. P 15 × 14.*

767	**298**	4d. emerald, olive, blue & black	10	10
		Ey. Phosphor omitted	10·00	
768	**299**	9d. reddish violet, bluish grey & black	10	10
		Ey. Phosphor omitted	5·50	
769	**300**	1s. olive-brown, blue, red, slate-blue & black	20	20
		Ey. Phosphor omitted	8·00	
770	**301**	1s. 9d. yellow-ochre & blackish brown	25	25
		Ey. Phosphor omitted	£140	
		Set of 4	60	60
		First Day Cover		4·00
		Presentation Pack	3·00	

304 "Ruins of St. Mary Le Port" (Piper)

305 "The Hay Wain" (Constable)

(Des S. Rose)

1968 (12 Aug). **British Paintings.** *Queen's head embossed. Chalk-surfaced paper. Two phosphor bands. P 15 × 14 (1s. 9d.) or 14 × 15 (others).*

771	**302**	4d. black, vermilion, greenish yellow, grey & gold	10	10
		a. Gold (value & Queen's head) omitted ...	£100	
		b. Vermilion omitted*	£200	
		Ec. Embossing omitted	80·00	
		Ey. Phosphor omitted	1·00	
		Eya. Gold (value & Queen's head) & phosphor omitted	£180	

772	**303**	1s. mauve, new blue, greenish yellow, black, magenta & gold		15	15
		a. Gold (value & Queen's head) omitted ...	£180		
		Eb. Gold (value & Queen's head), embossing & phosphor omitted	£200		
		Ec. Embossing omitted			
		Ey. Phosphor omitted	6·00		
773	**304**	1s. 6d. slate, orange, black, mauve, greenish yellow, ultramarine & gold		20	20
		a. Gold (value & Queen's head) omitted ...	£100		
		Eb. Embossing omitted			
		Ey. Phosphor omitted	6·00		
774	**305**	1s. 9d. greenish yellow, black, new blue, red & gold		25	25
		a. Gold (value & Queen's head) & embossing omitted	£450		
		b. Red omitted			
		Ec. Embossing omitted			
		Ey. Phosphor omitted	17·00		
		Set of 4	60	60	
		First Day Cover		1·50	
		Presentation Pack	2·00		
		Presentation Pack (German)	6·00		

No. 774a is only known with the phosphor also omitted.
*The effect of this is to leave the face and hands white and there is more yellow and olive in the costume.

The 4d. also exists with the value only omitted resulting from a colour shift.

Special First Day of Issue Postmark
G.P.O. Philatelic Bureau, Edinburgh 1 (Type C) .... 4·00

Gift Pack 1968

1968 (16 Sept). *Comprises Nos. 763/74.*
GP774c   Gift Pack .... 6·00
GP774d   Gift Pack (German) .... 24·00

Collectors Pack 1968

1968 (16 Sept). *Comprises Nos. 752/8 and 763/74.*
CP774e   Collectors Pack .... 6·00

306 Boy and Girl with Rocking Horse

307 Girl with Doll's House

308 Boy with Train Set

(Des Rosalind Dease. Head printed in gold and then embossed)

1968 (25 Nov).   **Christmas.** *Chalk-surfaced paper. One centre phosphor band* (4d.) *or two phosphor bands* (others). *P* 15 × 14 (4d.) *or* 14 × 15 (others).

775	**306**	4d. black, orange, vermilion, ultramarine, bistre & gold		10	10
		a. Gold omitted	£1500		
		b. Vermilion omitted*	£200		
		c. Ultramarine omitted	£150		
		Ed. Embossing omitted	5·00		
		Ey. Phosphor omitted	1·25		
776	**307**	9d. yellow-olive, black, brown, yellow, magenta, orange, turquoise-green & gold ..		15	15
		a. Yellow omitted	50·00		
		b. Turquoise-green (dress) omitted			
		Ec. Embossing omitted	5·00		
		Ey. Phosphor omitted	8·00		
		Eya. Embossing & phosphor omitted	7·50		
777	**308**	1s. 6d. ultramarine, yellow-orange, brt purple, blue-green, black & gold		25	25
		Ea. Embossing omitted			
		Ey. Phosphor omitted	13·00		
		Set of 3	40	40	
		First Day Cover		1·00	
		Presentation Pack	2·00		
		Presentation Pack (German)	5·00		

*The effect of the missing vermilion is shown on the rocking horse, saddle and faces which appear orange instead of red.

A single used example of the 4d. exists with the bistre omitted.

No. 775c is only known with phosphor also omitted.

Two machines were used for printing for the 4d. value:
Stamps from cylinders 1A–1B–2C–1D–1E in combination with 1F, 2F or 3F (gold) were printed entirely on the Rembrandt sheet-fed machine. They invariably have the Queen's head level with the top of the boy's head and the sheets are perforated through the left side margin.

Stamps from cylinders 2A–2B–3C–2D–2E in combination with 1F, 2F, 3F or 4F (gold) were printed on the reel-fed Thrissell machine in five colours (its maximum colour capacity) and subsequently sheet-fed on the Rembrandt machine for the Queen's head and the embossing. The position of the Queen's head is generally lower than on the stamps printed at one operation but it varies in different parts of the sheet and is not, therefore, a sure indication for identifying single stamps. Another small difference is that the boy's grey pullover is noticeably "moth-eaten" in the Thrissell printings and is normal on the Rembrandt. The Thrissell printings are perforated through the top margin.

Special First Day of Issue Postmarks
G.P.O. Philatelic Bureau, Edinburgh 1 (Type C) .... 3·00
Bethlehem, Llandeilo, Carms (Type C) .... 4·50

309 *Queen Elizabeth 2*

310 Elizabethan Galleon

311 East Indiaman

312 *Cutty Sark*

315 "Concorde" in Flight

316 Plan and Elevation Views

313 *Great Britain*

317 "Concorde's" Nose and Tail

(Des M. and Sylvia Goaman (4d.), D. Gentleman (9d., 1s. 6d.))

1969 (3 Mar). **First Flight of "Concorde".** *Chalk-surfaced paper. Two phosphor bands.* P 15 × 14.

784	**315**	4d. yellow-orange, violet, greenish blue, blue-green & pale green		10	10
		a. Violet (value etc.) omitted	£200		
		b. Yellow-orange omitted	90·00		
		Ey. Phosphor omitted	75		
		Eya. Yellow-orange & phosphor omitted	£100		
785	**316**	9d. ultramarine, emerald, red & grey-blue		20	20
		Ey. Phosphor omitted	£100		
786	**317**	1s. 6d. deep blue, silver-grey & lt blue		30	30
		a. Silver-grey omitted	£275		
		Ey. Phosphor omitted	7·00		
		Set of 3		50	50
		First Day Cover			2·00
		Presentation Pack	2·50		
		Presentation Pack (German)	18·00		

No. 786a affects the Queen's head which appears in the light blue colour.

314 *Mauretania I*

(Des D. Gentleman)

1969 (15 Jan). **British Ships.** *Chalk-surfaced paper. Two vertical phosphor bands at right* (1s.), *one horizontal phosphor band* (5d.) *or two phosphor bands* (9d.). P 15 × 14.

778	**309**	5d. black, grey, red & turquoise		10	10
		a. Black (Queen's head, value, hull and inscr) omitted	£600		
		b. Grey (decks, etc.) omitted	90·00		
		c. Red omitted	50·00		
		Ey. Phosphor omitted	1·50		
		Eya. Red & phosphor omitted	80·00		
779	**310**	9d. red, blue, ochre, brown, black & grey		10	15
		a. Strip of 3. Nos. 779/81	1·00		1·00
		ab. Red & blue omitted	£900		
		ac. Blue omitted	£1000		
		Ey. Phosphor omitted	10·00		
		Eya. Strip of 3. Nos. 779/81. Phosphor omitted	35·00		
780	**311**	9d. ochre, brown, black & grey		10	15
		Ey. Phosphor omitted	10·00		
781	**312**	9d. ochre, brown, black & grey		10	15
		Ey. Phosphor omitted	10·00		
782	**313**	1s. brown, black, grey, green & greenish yellow		25	25
		a. Pair. Nos. 782/3	90		85
		ab. Greenish yellow omitted	£2000		
		Ey. Phosphor omitted	25·00		
		Eya. Pair. Nos. 782/3. Phosphor omitted	60·00		
783	**314**	1s. red, black, brown, carmine & grey		25	25
		a. Carmine (hull overlay) omitted	£7500		
		b. Red (funnels) omitted			
		Ey. Phosphor omitted	25·00		
		Set of 6	1·75		90
		First Day Cover			4·00
		Presentation Pack	3·00		
		Presentation Pack (German)	22·00		

The 9d. and 1s. values were arranged in horizontal strips of three and pairs respectively throughout the sheet.

No. 779ab is known only with the phosphor also omitted.

Special First Day of Issue Postmark
G.P.O. Philatelic Bureau, Edinburgh 1 (Type C) .... 5·00

Special First Day of Issue Postmarks
G.P.O. Philatelic Bureau, Edinburgh (Type C) .... 3·50
Filton, Bristol (Type C) .... 4·00

318 Queen Elizabeth II. (See also Type **357**)

(Des after plaster cast by Arnold Machin. Recess Bradbury, Wilkinson)

1969 (5 Mar). P 12.

787	**318**	2s. 6d. brown	50	30
788		5s. crimson-lake	2·25	60
789		10s. dp ultramarine	7·00	6·00
790		£1 bluish black	3·00	1·60
		Set of 4	11·50	7·50
		First Day Cover		7·50
		Presentation Pack	18·00	
		Presentation Pack (German)	45·00	

Special First Day of Issue Postmarks
G.P.O. Philatelic Bureau (Type C) .... 8·00
Windsor, Berks (Type C) .... 15·00

For decimal issue, see Nos. 829/31b and notes after No. 831b.

319 Page from *Daily Mail*, and Vickers "Vimy" Aircraft

320 Europa and CEPT Emblems

321 ILO Emblem

322 Flags of NATO Countries

323 Vickers "Vimy" Aircraft and Globe showing Flight

(Des P. Sharland (5d., 1s., 1s. 6d.), M. and Sylvia Goaman (9d., 1s. 9d.))

1969 (2 Apr). **Anniversaries.** *Events described on stamps. Chalk-surfaced paper. Two phosphor bands.* P 15 × 14.

791	**319**	5d. black, pale sage-green, chestnut & new blue	10	10
		Ey. Phosphor omitted		
792	**320**	9d. pale turquoise, dp blue, lt emerald-green & black	20	20
		Ey. Phosphor omitted	16·00	
793	**321**	1s. brt purple, dp blue & lilac	20	20
		Ey. Phosphor omitted	5·00	
794	**322**	1s. 6d. red, royal blue, yellow-green, black, lemon & new blue	20	20
		e. Black omitted	60·00	
		f. Yellow-green omitted	48·00	
		Ey. Phosphor omitted	7·00	
		Eya. Yellow-green & phosphor omitted	55·00	
795	**323**	1s. 9d. yellow-olive, greenish yellow & pale turquoise-green	25	25
		a. Uncoated paper*	£200	
		Ey. Phosphor omitted	4·00	
		Set of 5	85	85
		First Day Cover		2·50
		Presentation Pack	2·50	
		Presentation Pack (German)	40·00	

*Uncoated paper. The second note after No. 744 also applies here.

Special First Day of Issue Postmark
G.P.O. Philatelic Bureau, Edinburgh (Type C) .... 6·00

324 Durham Cathedral

325 York Minster

326 St. Giles' Cathedral, Edinburgh

327 Canterbury Cathedral

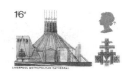

328 St. Paul's Cathedral

329 Liverpool Metropolitan Cathedral

(Des P. Gauld)

1969 (28 May). **British Architecture. Cathedrals.** *Chalk-surfaced paper. Two phosphor bands.* P 15 × 14.

796	**324**	5d. grey-black, orange, pale bluish violet & black	10	10
		a. Block of 4. Nos. 796/9	85	1·00
		ab. Block of 4. Uncoated paper†		
		b. Pale bluish violet omitted	£1750	
797	**325**	5d. grey-black, pale bluish violet, new blue & black	10	10
		b. Pale bluish violet omitted	£1750	
798	**326**	5d. grey-black, purple, green & black	10	10₉
		c. Green omitted*	40·00	
799	**327**	5d. grey-black, green, new blue & black	10	10
800	**328**	9d. grey-black, ochre, pale drab, violet & black	15	15
		a. Black (value) omitted	£100	
		Ey. Phosphor omitted	40·00	
801	**329**	1s. 6d. grey-black, pale turquoise, pale reddish violet, pale yellow-olive & black	15	15
		a. Black (value) omitted	£1850	
		b. Black (value) double		
		Ey. Phosphor omitted	18·00	
		Set of 6	1·00	55
		First Day Cover		3·00
		Presentation Pack	3·00	
		Presentation Pack (German)	22·00	

*The missing green on the roof top is known on R.2/5, R.8/5 and R.10/5 but all are from different sheets and it only occured in part of the printing, being "probably caused by a batter on the impression cylinder". Examples are also known with the green partly omitted.

†Uncoated paper. The second note after No. 744 also applies here. The 5d. values were issued together *se-tenant* in blocks of four throughout the sheet.

Special First Day of Issue Postmark
G.P.O. Philatelic Bureau, Edinburgh (Type C) .... 5·00

330 The King's Gate, Caernarvon Castle

331 The Eagle Tower, Caernarvon Castle

332 Queen Eleanor's Gate, Caernarvon Castle

333 Celtic Cross, Margam Abbey

334 H.R.H. The Prince of Wales
(after photo by G. Argent)

(Des D. Gentleman)

1969 (1 July). **Investiture of H.R.H. The Prince of Wales.** *Chalk-surfaced paper. Two phosphor bands. P 14 × 15.*

802 **330**	5d. dp olive-grey, lt olive-grey, dp grey, lt grey, red, pale turquoise-green, black & silver	10	10
	a. Strip of 3. Nos. 802/4	70	75
	b. Black (value & inscr) omitted	£150	
	c. Red omitted*	£250	
	d. Dp grey omitted**	90·00	
	e. Pale turquoise-green omitted	£250	
	Ey. Phosphor omitted	3·00	
	Eya. Strip of 3. Nos. 802/4. Phosphor omitted	10·00	
803 **331**	5d. dp olive-grey, lt olive-grey, dp grey, lt grey, red, pale turquoise-green, black & silver	10	10
	b. Black (value and inscr) omitted	£150	
	c. Red omitted*	£250	
	d. Dp grey omitted**	90·00	
	e. Pale turquoise-green omitted	£250	
	f. Light grey (marks on walls, window frames, etc) omitted	†	—
	Ey. Phosphor omitted	3·00	

804 **332**	5d. dp olive-grey, lt olive-grey, dp grey, lt grey, red, pale turquoise-green, black & silver	10	10
	b. Black (value & inscr) omitted	£150	
	c. Red omitted*	£250	
	d. Dp grey omitted**	90·00	
	e. Pale turquoise-green omitted	£250	
	Ey. Phosphor omitted	3·00	
805 **333**	9d. dp grey, lt grey, black & gold	20	10
	Ey. Phosphor omitted	20·00	
806 **334**	1s. blackish yellow-olive & gold	20	10
	Ey. Phosphor omitted	11·00	
	Set of 5	1·00	45
	First Day Cover		1·00
	Presentation Pack†	2·00	
	Presentation Pack (German)	16·00	

The 5d. values were issued together *se-tenant* in strips of three throughout the sheet.

*The 5d. value is also known with the red misplaced downwards and where this occurs the red printing does not take very well on the silver background and in some cases is so faint it could be mistaken for a missing red. However, the red can be seen under a magnifying glass and caution should therefore be exercised when purchasing copies of Nos. 802/4c.

**The deep grey affects the dark portions of the windows and doors.

†In addition to the generally issued Presentation Pack a further pack in different colours and with all texts printed in both English and Welsh was made available exclusively through Education Authorities for free distribution to all schoolchildren in Wales and Monmouthshire (*Price £4*).

No. 803f is only known commercially used on cover.

Special First Day of Issue Postmarks

G.P.O. Philatelic Bureau, Edinburgh 1 (Type C)	4·50
Day of Investiture, Caernarvon	2·50

335 Mahatma Gandhi

(Des B. Mullick)

1969 (13 Aug). **Gandhi Centenary Year.** *Chalk-surfaced paper. Two phosphor bands. P 15 × 14.*

807 **335**	1s. 6d. black, green, red-orange & grey	30	30
	a. Printed on the gummed side	£300	
	Ey. Phosphor omitted	3·00	
	First Day Cover		1·25

Special First Day of Issue Postmark
G.P.O. Philatelic Bureau, Edinburgh (Type C) .... 2·00

Collectors Pack 1969

1969 (15 Sept). *Comprises Nos. 775/86 and 791/807.*
CP807*b* Collectors Pack .... 20·00

336 National Giro "G" Symbol

337 Telecommunications—
International Subscriber Dialling

338 Telecommunications—
Pulse Code Modulation

339 Postal Mechanisation—
Automatic Sorting

(Des D. Gentleman. Litho De La Rue)

1969 (1 Oct). **Post Office Technology Commemoration.** *Chalk-surfaced paper. Two phosphor bands.* P $13\frac{1}{2} \times 14$.

808	**336**	5d. new blue, greenish blue, lavender & black		10	10
		Ey. Phosphor omitted		4·00	
809	**337**	9d. emerald, violet-blue & black		15	15
810	**338**	1s. emerald, lavender & black		15	15
		Ey. Phosphor omitted		£300	
811	**339**	1s. 6d. brt purple, lt blue, grey-blue & black		40	40
		Set of 4		70	70
		First Day Cover			1·00
		Presentation Pack		2·25	

Special First Day of Issue Postmark
G.P.O. Philatelic Bureau, Edinburgh (Type C) .... 2·00

340 Herald Angel

341 The Three Shepherds

342 The Three Kings

(Des F. Wegner. Queen's head (and stars 4d., 5d. and scroll-work 1s. 6d.) printed in gold and then embossed)

1969 (26 Nov). **Christmas.** *Chalk-surfaced paper. Two phosphor bands* (5d., 1s. 6d.) *or one centre band* (4d.). P 15 × 14.

812	**340**	4d. vermilion, new blue, orange, brt purple, lt green, bluish violet, blackish brown & gold		10	10
		a. Gold (Queen's head etc.) omitted		£2000	
		Eb. Centre band $3\frac{1}{2}$ mm		25	15

813	**341**	5d. magenta, lt blue, royal blue, olive-brown, green, greenish yellow, red & gold		10	10
		a. Lt blue (sheep, etc.) omitted		60·00	
		b. Red omitted*		£500	
		c. Gold (Queen's head) omitted		£400	
		d. Green omitted		£200	
		e. Olive-brown, red & gold omitted			
		Ef. Embossing omitted		20·00	
		Ey. Phosphor omitted		1·00	
814	**342**	1s. 6d. greenish yellow, brt purple, bluish violet, dp slate, orange, green, new blue & gold		30	30
		a. Gold (Queen's head etc.) omitted		80·00	
		b. Dp slate (value) omitted		£250	
		c. Greenish yellow omitted		£130	
		d. Bluish violet omitted		£300	
		e. New blue omitted		50·00	
		Ef. Embossing omitted		8·00	
		Ey. Phosphor omitted		5·00	
		Eya. Embossing and phosphor omitted		8·00	
		Set of 3		45	45
		First Day Cover			1·00
		Presentation Pack		2·25	

*The effect of the missing red is shown on the hat, leggings and purse which appear as dull orange.

No. 812 has one centre band 8 mm. wide but this was of no practical use in the automatic facing machines and after about three-quarters of the stamps had been printed the remainder were printed with a $3\frac{1}{2}$mm. band (No. 812Eb).

No. 813e was caused by a paper fold.

Used copies of the 5d. have been seen with the olive-brown or greenish yellow omitted.

Special First Day of Issue Postmarks
P.O. Philatelic Bureau, Edinburgh (Type C) .... 2·00
Bethlehem, Llandeilo, Carms (Type C) .... 2·25

343 Fife Harling

344 Cotswold Limestone

345 Welsh Stucco

346 Ulster Thatch

(Des D. Gentleman (5d., 9d.), Sheila Robinson (1s., 1s. 6d.))

1970 (11 Feb). **British Rural Architecture.** *Chalk-surfaced paper. Two phosphor bands.* P 15 × 14.

815	**343**	5d. grey, grey-black, black, lemon, greenish blue, orange-brown, ultramarine & green		10	10
		a. Lemon omitted		50·00	
		b. Grey (Queen's head & cottage shading) omitted		£4000	
		Ey. Phosphor omitted		1·50	

816 **344** 9d. orange-brown, olive-yellow, brt green, black, grey-black & grey 20 20
Ey. Phosphor omitted .... 6·00
817 **345** 1s. dp blue, reddish lilac, drab & new blue . 20 20
a. New blue omitted .... 45·00
Ey. Phosphor omitted .... 12·00
818 **346** 1s. 6d. greenish yellow, black, turquoise-blue & lilac 35 35
a. Turquoise-blue omitted £3500
Ey. Phosphor omitted .... 2·25
Set of 4 75 75
First Day Cover .... 1·25
Presentation Pack .... 3·00

Used examples of the 5d. have been seen with the greenish blue colour omitted.

Special First Day of Issue Postmark
British Philatelic Bureau, Edinburgh (Type C) .... 2·00

347 Signing the Declaration of Arbroath

348 Florence Nightingale attending Patients

349 Signing of International Co-operative Alliance

350 Pilgrims and *Mayflower*

351 Sir William Herschel, Francis Baily, Sir John Herschel and Telescope

(Des F. Wegner (5d., 9d., and 1s. 6d.), Marjorie Saynor (1s., 1s. 9d.). Queen's head printed in gold and then embossed)

1970 (1 Apr). **Anniversaries.** *Events described on stamps. Chalk-surfaced paper. Two phosphor bands.* P 15 × 14.
819 **347** 5d. black, yellow-olive, blue, emerald, green-ish yellow, rose-red, gold & orange-red . 10 10
a. Gold (Queen's head) omitted £400
b. Emerald omitted .... 50·00
Ey. Phosphor omitted £300
820 **348** 9d. ochre, dp blue, carmine, black, blue-green, yellow-olive, gold & blue 15 15
a. Ochre omitted £150
Eb. Embossing omitted .... 10·00
Ey. Phosphor omitted .... 2·25
821 **349** 1s. green, greenish yellow, brown, black, cerise, gold & lt blue 25 15
a. Gold (Queen's head) omitted .... 50·00
Eb. Green & embossing omitted .... 75·00
c. Green omitted .... 75·00
d. Brown omitted £100
Ee. Embossing omitted .... 10·00

(821) Ey. Phosphor omitted .... 4·00
Eya. Brown & phosphor omitted £110
Eyb. Embossing & phosphor omitted .... 20·00
822 **350** 1s. 6d. greenish yellow, carmine, dp yellow-olive, emerald, black, blue, gold & sage-green 30 30
a. Gold (Queen's head) omitted .... 75·00
b. Emerald omitted .... 40·00
Ec. Embossing omitted .... 5·00
Ey. Phosphor omitted .... 2·50
823 **351** 1s. 9d. black, slate, lemon, gold & brt purple 30 30
a. Lemon (trousers and document) omitted † —
Ey. Phosphor omitted .... 2·50
Set of 5 1·00 90
First Day Cover .... 2·00
Presentation Pack .... 3·00
No. 823a is only known used on first day cover postmarked London WC.

Special First Day of Issue Postmark
British Philatelic Bureau, Edinburgh (Type C) .... 2·50
First Day of Issue handstamps were provided at Billericay, Essex; Boston, Lincs and Rochdale, Lancs for this issue.

352 "Mr. Pickwick and Sam" (*Pickwick Papers*)

353 "Mr. and Mrs. Micawber" (*David Copperfield*)

354 "David Copperfield and Betsy Trotwood" (*David Copperfield*)

355 "Oliver asking for more" (*Oliver Twist*)

356 "Grasmere" (from engraving by J. Farrington, R.A.)

T **352/5** were issued together *se-tenant* in blocks of four throughout the sheet.

(Des Rosalind Dease. Queen's head printed in gold and then embossed)

1970 (3 June). **Literary Anniversaries. Death Centenary of Charles Dickens (novelist)** (5d. × 4) **and Birth Bicentenary of William Wordsworth (poet)** (1s. 6d.). *Chalk-surfaced paper. Two phosphor bands.* P 14 × 15.
824 **352** 5d. black, orange, silver, gold & magenta ... 10 10
a. Block of 4. Nos. 824/7 .... 90 90
ab. Imperf (block of four) £600
825 **353** 5d. black, magenta, silver, gold & orange ... 10 10

826 **354**	5d.	black, lt greenish blue, silver, gold &		
		yellow-bistre	10	10
	b.	Yellow-bistre (value) omitted	£1200	
827 **355**	5d.	black, yellow-bistre, silver, gold & lt		
		greenish blue	10	10
	b.	Yellow-bistre (background) omitted	£3000	
	c.	Lt greenish blue (value) omitted*	£450	
828 **356**	1s.	6d. yellow-olive, black, silver, gold &		
		bright blue	20	20
	a.	Gold (Queen's head) omitted	£225	
	b.	Silver ("Grasmere") omitted	60·00	
	Ec.	Embossing omitted	5·00	
	Ey.	Phosphor omitted	4·00	
	Eya.	Embossing & phosphor omitted	20·00	
		Set of 5	1·00	55
		First Day Cover		2·50
		Presentation Pack	3·00	

*No. 827c (unlike No. 826b) comes from a sheet on which the colour was only partially omitted so that, although No. 827 was completely without the light greenish blue colour, it was still partially present on No. 826.

Special First Day of Issue Postmarks

British Philatelic Bureau, Edinburgh (Type C) .... 3·50
Cockermouth, Cumberland (Type C) (No. 828 only) .. 3·00
Rochester, Kent (Type C) (Nos. 824/7) .... 3·00
A First Day of Issue handstamp was provided at Broadstairs, Kent, for this issue.

357 (Value redrawn)

(Des after plaster cast by Arnold Machin. Recess B.W.)

1970 (17 June)–**72**. *Decimal Currency. Chalk-surfaced paper or phosphorised paper* (10p.). *P* 12.

829	**357**	10p. cerise	1·00	75
830		20p. olive-green	70	15
	Ea.	Thinner uncoated paper*	*	
831		50p. dp ultramarine	1·50	40
	Ea.	Thinner uncoated paper*	22·00	
831b		£1 bluish black (6.12.72)	3·50	75
		Set of 4	6·00	1·75
		First Day Cover (829/31)		2·00
		First Day Cover (831b)		2·50
		Presentation Pack (829/31)	7·00	
		Presentation Pack (790 (or 831b), 830/1)	8·00	

*These are not as apparent as uncoated photogravure issues where there is normally a higher degree of chalk-surfacing. The 20p. is known only as a block of four with Plate No. 5. The 50p. comes from Plate No. 9.

The 10p. on phosphorised paper continued the experiments which started with the Machin 1s. 6d. When the experiment had ended a quantity of the 50p. value was printed on the phosphorised paper to use up the stock. These stamps were issued on 1 February 1973, but they cannot be distinguished from No. 831 by the naked eye. (*Price £2*).

A £1 was also issued in 1970, but it is difficult to distinguish it from the earlier No. 790. In common with the other 1970 values it was issued in sheets of 100.

A whiter paper was introduced in 1973. The £1 appeared on 27 Sept. 1973, the 20p. on 30 Nov. 1973 and the 50p. on 20 Feb. 1974.

Special First Day of Issue Postmarks

British Philatelic Bureau, Edinburgh (Type C) (Nos. 829/31) .... 2·50
Windsor, Berks (Type C) (Nos. 829/31) .... 6·00
Philatelic Bureau, Edinburgh (Type E) (No. 831b) ...... 5·00
Windsor, Berks (Type E) (No 831b) .... 8·50

358 Runners   **359** Swimmers

360 Cyclists

(Des A. Restall. Litho D.L.R.)

1970 (15 July). **Ninth British Commonwealth Games.** *Chalk-surfaced paper. Two phosphor bands. P* $13\frac{1}{2} \times 14$.

832 **358**	5d.	pink, emerald, greenish yellow & dp yellow-green	10	10
	a.	Greenish yellow omitted	£4000	
	Ey.	Phosphor omitted	£200	
833 **359**	1s.	6d. lt greenish blue, lilac, bistre-brown & Prussian blue	50	50
	Ey.	Phosphor omitted	60·00	
834 **360**	1s.	9d. yellow-orange, lilac, salmon & dp red-brown	50	50
		Set of 3	1·00	1·00
		First Day Cover		1·25
		Presentation Pack	2·50	

Special First Day of Issue Postmark

British Philatelic Bureau, Edinburgh (Type C) .... 2·00

Collectors Pack 1970

1970 (14 Sept). *Comprises Nos. 808/28 and 832/4.*
CP834a   Collectors Pack .... 24·00

1840 first engraved issue   1847 first embossed issue

361 1d. Black (1840)   **362** 1s. Green (1847)

363 4d. Carmine (1855)

(Des D. Gentleman)

1970 (18 Sept). **"Philympia 70" Stamp Exhibition.** *Chalk-surfaced paper. Two phosphor bands.* P 14 × 14½.

835	**361**	5d. grey-black, brownish bistre, black & dull purple	10	10
		a. Grey-black (Queen's head) omitted		
		Ey. Phosphor omitted	2·75	
836	**362**	9d. lt drab, bluish green, stone, black & dull purple	35	35
		Ey. Phosphor omitted	9·00	
837	**363**	1s. 6d. carmine, lt drab, black & dull purple	40	40
		Ey. Phosphor omitted	3·00	
		Set of 3	75	75
		First Day Cover		1·25
		Presentation Pack	2·50	

Special First Day of Issue Postmark
British Post Office Philatelic Bureau, Edinburgh
(Type D) .... 2·00

364 Shepherds and Apparition
of the Angel

365 Mary, Joseph, and Christ
in the Manger

(Des Sally Stiff after De Lisle Psalter. Queen's head printed in gold and then embossed)

1970 (25 Nov). **Christmas.** *Chalk-surfaced paper. One centre phosphor band (4d.) or two phosphor bands (others).* P 14 × 15.

838	**364**	4d. brown-red, turquoise-green, pale chestnut, brown, grey-black, gold & vermilion	10	10
		Ea. Embossing omitted	40·00	
		Ey. Phosphor omitted	55·00	
839	**365**	5d. emerald, gold, blue, brown-red, ochre, grey-black & violet	10	10
		a. Gold (Queen's head) omitted	†	£2500
		b. Emerald omitted	60·00	
		c. Imperf (pair)	£250	
		Ed. Embossing omitted	12·00	
		Ey. Phosphor omitted	2·25	
840	**366**	1s. 6d. gold, grey-black, pale turquoise-green, salmon, ultramarine, ochre & yellow-green	35	35
		a. Salmon omitted	80·00	
		b. Ochre omitted	50·00	
		Ec. Embossing omitted	30·00	
		Ey. Phosphor omitted	3·50	
		Eya. Embossing and phosphor omitted		
		Set of 3	50	50
		First Day Cover		1·00
		Presentation Pack	2·50	

Special First Day of Issue Postmarks

British Post Office Philatelic Bureau, Edinburgh
(Type D) .... 1·50
Bethlehem, Llandeilo, Carms .... 2·00

366 The Wise Men bearing gifts

(New Currency. 100 new pence = £1)

"X" NUMBERS. The following definitive series has been allocated "X" prefixes to the catalogue numbers to avoid re-numbering all subsequent issues.

NO VALUE INDICATED. Stamps as Types **367**/a inscribed "2nd" or "1st" are listed as Nos. 1445/52, 1511/16 and 1663a/6.

ELLIPTICAL PERFORATIONS. These were introduced in 1993 and stamps showing them will be found listed as Nos. Y1667 etc.

367   **367**a

Printing differences

Litho   **Photo**
(Illustrations enlarged × 6)

Litho. Clear outlines to value and frame of stamp.
Photo. Uneven lines to value and frame formed by edges of screen.

Two types of the 3p, 10p and 26p (Nos. X930/c, X886/b and X971/a)

Figures of face value as I (all ptgs of 3p. brt magenta except the multi-value coil No. 930cl and sheets from 21.1.92 onwards, 10p. orange-brown except 1984 "Christmas Heritage" £4 booklet and 26p rosine except 1987 £1.04 barcode booklet.

Figures of face value narrower as in II (from coil No. X930cl and in sheets from 21.1.92 (3p.), 1984 "Christian Heritage" £4 booklet (10p.) or 1987 £1.04 barcode booklet (26p.).

This catalogue includes changes of figure styles on these stamps where there is no other listable difference. Similar changes have also taken place on other values, but only in conjuction with listed colour, paper or perforation changes.

1971 (15 Feb)–**95.** *Decimal Currency.* T *367. Chalk-surfaced paper.*

(a) Photo Harrison (except for some printings of Nos. X879 and X913 in sheets produced by Enschedé in 1979 (8p.) and 1991 (18p.)). With phosphor bands. P 15 × 14.

X841	½p. turquoise-blue (2 bands)	10	10
	a. Imperf (pair)†	£900	
	l. Booklet pane. No. X841 × 2 se-tenant vert with X849 × 2	5·00	
	lEy. Booklet pane. Phosphor omitted	£150	
	la. Booklet pane. No. X841 × 2 se-tenant horiz with X849 × 2 (14.7.71)	80	
	laEy. Booklet pane. Phosphor omitted	£350	
	m. Booklet pane. No. X841 × 5 plus label ...	5·00	
	mEy. Booklet pane. Phosphor omitted	90·00	
	n. Coil strip. No. X849Eg, X841Eg × 2 and X844Eg × 2	2·00	
	nEy. Coil strip. Phosphor omitted	30·00	
	nEv. Coil strip. PVA gum. No. X849, X841 × 2 and X844 × 2 (4.74)	35	
	nEvy. Coil strip. Phosphor omitted	9·00	
	o. Booklet pane. No. X841, X851, X852, X852Ea, each × 3 (24.5.72)	12·00	
	oEy. Booklet pane. Phosphor omitted	£1500	
	p. Booklet pane. No. X841 × 3, X842 and X852 × 2 (24.5.72)	70·00	
	pEy. Booklet pane. Phosphor omitted		
	q. Coil strip. No. X870, X849, X844 and X841 × 2 (3.12.75)	80	
	r. Booklet pane. No. X841 × 2, X844 × 3 and X870 (10.3.76)	70	
	s. Booklet pane. No. X841 × 2, X844 × 2, X873 × 2 and X881 × 4 (8½p. values at right) (26.1.77)	2·50	
	sa. Ditto, but No. X873Ea and 8½p. values at left	2·50	
	t. Booklet pane. No. X841, X844, X894 × 3 and X902 (14p. value at right) (26.1.81) ..	2·00	
	tEy. Booklet pane. Phosphor omitted	35·00	
	ta. Booklet pane. No. X841, X844, X894Ea × 3 and X902 (14p. value at left)	2·00	
	taEy. Booklet pane. Phosphor omitted	35·00	
	u. Booklet pane. No. X841, X857 × 4 and X899 × 3 (12½p. values at left) (1.2.82)	2·50	
	ua. Ditto, but No. X899Ea and 12½p. values at right	2·50	
	Eg. Gum arabic (from coil strip, and on 22.9.72 from sheets)	40	
	Egy. Phosphor omitted	50·00	
X842	½p. turquoise-blue (1 side band at left) (24.5.72)	60·00	25·00
X843	½p. turquoise-blue (1 centre band) (14.12.77)	30	20
	l. Coil strip. No. X843 × 2, X875 and X845 × 2 (14.12.77)	55	
	m. Booklet pane. No. X843 × 2, X845 × 2 and X875 plus label (8.2.78)	75	
	mEy. Booklet pane. Phosphor omitted	25·00	
X844	1p. crimson (2 bands)	10	10
	a. Imperf (vert coil)		
	b. Pair, one imperf 3 sides (vert coil)		
	c. Imperf (pair)		
	l. Booklet pane. No. X844 × 2 se-tenant vert with X848 × 2	5·00	
	m. Ditto, but se-tenant horiz (14.7.71)	80	
	mEy. Booklet pane. Phosphor omitted	80·00	
	n. Booklet pane. No. X844 × 2, X876 × 3 and X883 × 3 (9p. values at right) (13.6.77) ...	4·00	
	na. Ditto, but No. X876Ea and 9p. values at left	2·50	
	Eg. Gum arabic (from coil strip)	40	
	Egy. Phosphor omitted	45·00	

X845	1p. crimson (1 centre band) (14.12.77)	20	20
	l. Booklet pane. No. X879 and X845 × 2 plus label (17.10.79)	50	
	m. Coil strip. No. X879 and X845 × 2 plus 2 labels (16.1.80)	45	
	n. Booklet pane. No. X845 × 2, X860 and X898 each × 3 (5.4.83)	5·00	
	nEy. Booklet pane. Phosphor omitted	16·00	
	p. Booklet pane. No. X845 × 3, X863 × 2 and X900 × 3 (3.9.84)	3·50	
	pEy. Booklet pane. Phosphor omitted	£180	
	q. Booklet pane. No. X845 × 2 and X896 × 4 (29.7.86)	8·00	
	s. Booklet pane. No. X845, X867 × 2 and X900 × 3 (20.10.86)	3·00	
	sa. Ditto, but with vertical edges of pane imperf (29.9.87)	3·00	
	saEy. Booklet pane. Phosphor omitted	£150	
X846	1p. crimson ("all-over") (10.10.79)	20	20
X847	1p. crimson (1 side band at left) (20.10.86) ..	1·00	1·00
	Ea. Band at right (3.3.87)	3·50	2·75
	l. Booklet pane. No. X847, X901 and X912 × 2 (20.10.86)	3·00	
	lEy. Booklet pane. Phosphor omitted	90·00	
	m. Booklet pane. No. X847Ea, X901 × 2, X912 × 5 and X918 with margins all round (3.3.87)	11·50	
X848	1½p. black (2 bands)	20	15
	a. Uncoated paper*	£110	
	b. Imperf (pair)		
	c. Imperf 3 sides (horiz pair)		
	Ey. Phosphor omitted	10·00	
X849	2p. myrtle-green (2 bands)	20	10
	a. Imperf (horiz pair)	£1250	
	l. Booklet pane. No. X849 × 2, X880 × 2 and X886 × 3 plus label (10p. values at right) (28.8.79)	2·50	
	la. Ditto, but No. X880Ea and 10p. values at left	2·00	
	m. Booklet pane. No. X849 × 3, X889 × 2 and X895 × 2 plus label (12p. values at right) (4.2.80)	2·00	
	mEy. Booklet pane. Phosphor omitted	40·00	
	ma. Booklet pane. No. X849 × 3, X889Ea × 2 and X895 × 2 plus label (12p. values at left)	2·00	
	maEy. Booklet pane. Phosphor omitted	40·00	
	n. Booklet pane. No. X849, X888 × 3, X889Ea and X895 × 4 with margins all round (16.4.80)	3·75	
	nEy. Booklet pane. Phosphor omitted	50·00	
	o. Booklet pane. No. X849 × 6 with margins all round (16.4.80)	80	
	oEy. Booklet pane. Phosphor omitted	50·00	
	p. Booklet pane. No. X849, X857, X898, X899 × 3 and X899Ea × 3 with margins all round (19.5.82)	6·00	
	pEy. Booklet pane. Phosphor omitted	£100	
	Eg. Gum arabic (from coil strip)	2·25	
	Egy. Phosphor omitted	£175	
X850	2p. myrtle-green ("all-over") (10.10.79)	20	15
X851	2½p. magenta (1 centre band)	15	10
	a. Imperf (pair)†	£250	
	Ey. Phosphor omitted	6·50	
	l. Booklet pane. No. X851 × 5 plus label ...	3·00	
	lEy. Booklet pane. Phosphor omitted	35·00	
	m. Booklet pane. No. X851 × 4 plus two labels	4·00	
	mEy. Booklet pane. Phosphor omitted	75·00	

(X851)	n. Booklet pane. No. X851 × 3, X852Ea × 3 and X855 × 6 (24.5.72)	7·00	
	nEy. Booklet pane. Phosphor omitted		
	Eg. Gum arabic (13.9.72)	15	
X852	2½p. magenta (1 band at left)	1·25	1·75
	l. Booklet pane. No. X852 × 2 and X855 × 4	5·00	
	lEy. Booklet pane. Phosphor omitted	90·00	
	Ea. Band at right (24.5.72)	1·25	2·25
X853	2½p. magenta (2 bands) (21.5.75)	30	75
X854	2½p. rose-red (2 bands) (26.8.81)	50	75
	l. Booklet pane. No. X854 × 3, X862 × 2 and X894 × 3, (11½p. values at left)	5·00	
	la. Ditto, but No. X894Ea and 11½p. values at right	6·50	
X855	3p. ultramarine (2 bands)	20	10
	a. Imperf (coil strip of 5)	£1000	
	b. Imperf (pair)†	£250	
	c. Uncoated paper*	40·00	
	Ey. Phosphor omitted	2·00	
	l. Booklet pane. No. X855 × 5 plus label	2·00	
	lEy. Booklet pane. Phosphor omitted	£250	
	Eg. Gum arabic (23.8.72)	75	
	Egy. Phosphor omitted	7·00	
X856	3p. ultramarine (1 centre band) (10.9.73)	20	25
	a. Imperf (pair)†	£250	
	b. Imperf between (vert pair)†	£375	
	c. Imperf horiz (vert pair)†	£200	
	Eg. Gum arabic	30	
	Egy. Phosphor omitted	75·00	
X857	3p. brt magenta (Type I) (2 bands) (1.2.82) ...	30	25
X858	3½p. olive-grey (2 bands) (shades)	30	30
	a. Imperf (pair)	£350	
	Ey. Phosphor omitted	4·50	
	Eb. Bronze-green (18.7.73)	60	50
	Eby. Phosphor omitted	8·00	
X859	3½p. olive-grey (1 centre band) (24.6.74)	30	15
X860	3½p. purple-brown (1 centre band) (5.4.83) ...	1·25	1·25
X861	4p. ochre-brown (2 bands)	20	20
	a. Imperf (pair)†	£950	
	Ey. Phosphor omitted	30·00	
	Eg. Gum arabic (1.11.72)	20	
X862	4p. greenish blue (2 bands) (26.8.81)	1·25	1·50
X863	4p. greenish blue (1 centre band) (3.9.84) ...	1·00	1·00
X864	4p. greenish blue (1 band at right) (8.1.85) ...	1·50	2·00
	Ea. Band at left	1·50	2·00
	l. Booklet pane. No. X864, X864Ea, X901 × 2, X901Ea × 2, X909 × 2 and X920 with margins all round (8.1.85)	11·50	
	lEy. Booklet pane. Phosphor omitted	£1000	
X865	4½p. grey-blue (2 bands) (24.10.73)	20	25
	a. Imperf (pair)	£300	
	Ey. Phosphor omitted	5·00	
X866	5p. pale violet (2 bands)	20	10
X867	5p. claret (1 centre band) (20.10.86)	1·60	1·60
	Ey. Phosphor omitted	70·00	
X868	5½p. violet (2 bands) (24.10.73)	25	25
X869	5½p. violet (1 centre band) (17.3.75)	20	20
	a. Uncoated paper*	£375	
	Ey. Phosphor omitted	15·00	
X870	6p. lt emerald (2 bands)	30	15
	a. Uncoated paper*	15·00	
	Ey. Phosphor omitted	65·00	
	Eg. Gum arabic (6.6.73)	1·50	
X871	6½p. greenish blue (2 bands) (4.9.74)	45	45
X872	6½p. greenish blue (1 centre band) (24.9.75) ...	30	15
	a. Imperf (vert pair)	£300	
	b. Uncoated paper*	£160	
	Ey. Phosphor omitted	11·00	
X873	6½p. greenish blue (1 band at right) (26.1.77) ...	60	55
	Ea. Band at left	60	75

X874	7p. purple-brown (2 bands) (15.1.75)	35	25
	a. Imperf (pair)	£250	
	Ey. Phosphor omitted	1·25	
X875	7p. purple-brown (1 centre band) (13.6.77) ..	35	20
	a. Imperf (pair)	£100	
	l. Booklet pane. No. X875 and X883,		
	each × 10 (15.11.78)	4·50	
X876	7p. purple-brown (1 band at right) (13.6.77) .	60	75
	Ea. Band at left	60	75
X877	7½p. pale chestnut (2 bands)	30	25
	Ey. Phosphor omitted	15·00	
X878	8p. rosine (2 bands) (24.10.73)	25	20
	a. Uncoated paper*	10·00	
X879	8p. rosine (1 centre band) (20.8.79)	25	15
	a. Uncoated paper*	£600	
	b. Imperf (pair)	£600	
	Ey. Phosphor omitted	£275	
	l. Booklet pane. No. X879 and X886,		
	each × 10 (14.11.79)	5·00	
X880	8p. rosine (1 band at right) (28.8.79)	60	60
	Ea. Band at left	60	60
X881	8½p. lt yellowish green (2 bands) (shades)		
	(24.9.75)	35	20
	a. Imperf (pair)	£750	
	Eb. Yellowish green (24.3.76)	30	35
X882	9p. yellow-orange and black (2 bands)	60	30
	Ey. Phosphor omitted	75·00	
X883	9p. dp violet (2 bands) (25.2.76)	45	25
	a. Imperf (pair)	£200	
	Ey. Phosphor omitted	2·50	
X884	9½p. purple (2 bands) (25.2.76)	45	30
	Ey. Phosphor omitted	17·50	
X885	10p. orange-brown & chestnut (2 bands)		
	(11.8.71)	40	30
	a. Orange-brown omitted	£150	
	b. Imperf (horiz pair)	£2000	
	Ey. Phosphor omitted	7·50	
X886	10p. orange-brown (Type I) (2 bands) (25.2.76)	40	20
	a. Imperf (pair)	£250	
	b. Type II (4.9.84)	12·00	12·00
	bl. Booklet pane. No. X886b, X901Ea and		
	X909 × 7 with margins all round	12·50	
	blEy. Booklet pane. Phosphor omitted		
X887	10p. orange-brown (Type I) ("all-over")		
	(3.10.79)	30	45
X888	10p. orange-brown (Type I) (1 centre band)		
	(4.2.80)	30	20
	a. Imperf (pair)	£275	
	l. Booklet pane. No. X888 × 9 with margins		
	all round (16.4.80)	2·75	
	lEy. Booklet pane. Phosphor omitted	45·00	
	m. Booklet pane. No. X888 and X895,		
	each × 10 (12.11.80)	6·00	
X889	10p. orange-brown (Type I) (1 band at right)		
	(4.2.80)	75	75
	Ea. Band at left	60	60
X890	10½p. yellow (2 bands) (25.2.76)	40	30
X891	10½p. dp dull blue (2 bands) (26.4.78)	60	45
X892	11p. brown-red (2 bands) (25.2.76)	60	25
	a. Imperf (pair)	£1750	
X893	11½p. drab (1 centre band) (14.1.81)	45	30
	a. Imperf (pair)	£225	
	Ey. Phosphor omitted	5·50	
	l. Booklet pane. No. X893 and X902,		
	each × 10 (11.11.81)	7·00	
X894	11½p. drab (1 band at right) (26.1.81)	60	60
	Ea. Band at left	60	60
	l. Booklet pane. No. X894/Ea, each × 2 &		
	X902 × 6 (6.5.81)	4·00	

X895	12p. yellowish green (2 bands) (4.2.80)	60	40
	l. Booklet pane. No. X895 × 9 with margins		
	all round (16.4.80)	3·00	
	lEy. Booklet pane. Phosphor omitted	40·00	
X896	12p. brt emerald (1 centre band) (29.10.85) ..	60	40
	Eu. Underprint Type 4 (29.10.85)	60	
	Ey. Phosphor omitted	8·00	
	l. Booklet pane. No. X896 × 9 with margins		
	all round (18.3.86)	3·00	
	lEy. Booklet pane. Phosphor omitted	£175	
X897	12p. brt emerald (1 band at right) (14.1.86) ..	75	75
	Ea. Band at left	75	75
	l. Booklet pane. No. X897/Ea, each × 2 and		
	X909 × 6 (12p. values at left) (14.1.86) ...	6·00	
	la. Ditto, but 12p. values at right	6·00	
	m. Booklet pane. No. X897/Ea, each × 3,		
	X909 × 2 and X919 with margins all		
	round (18.3.86)	9·00	
	mEy. Booklet pane. Phosphor omitted	£1250	
X898	12½p. lt emerald (1 centre band) (27.1.82)	45	25
	a. Imperf (pair)	£100	
	Eu. Underprint Type 1 (10.11.82)	45	
	Eua. Underprint Type 2 (9.11.83)	45	
	Ey. Phosphor omitted	5·50	
	l. Booklet pane. No. X898Eu and X907Eu,		
	each × 10 (10.11.82)	9·00	
X899	12½p. lt emerald (1 band at right) (1.2.82)	60	60
	Ea. Band at left	60	60
	l. Booklet pane. No. X899/Ea, each × 2 and		
	X907 × 6 (1.2.82)††	5·00	
	m. Booklet pane. No. X899/Ea, each × 3,		
	margins all round (19.5.82)	2·50	
	mEy. Booklet pane. Phosphor omitted	35·00	
	n. Booklet pane. No. X899/Ea, each × 2,		
	X908 × 6 (12½p. values at left) (5.4.83)	8·00	
	na. Ditto, but 12½p. values at right	8·00	
X900	13p. pale chestnut (1 centre band) (28.8.84) ..	45	35
	a. Imperf (pair)	£500	
	Eu. Underprint Type 2 (2.12.86)	45	
	Ey. Phosphor omitted	5·50	
	l. Booklet pane. No. X900 × 9 with margins		
	all round (8.1.85)	3·25	
	lEy. Booklet pane. Phosphor omitted	£350	
	m. Booklet pane. No. X900 × 6 with margins		
	all round (3.3.87)	2·50	
	n. Booklet pane. No. X900 × 4 with margins		
	all round (4.8.87)	2·50	
	o. Booklet pane. No. X900 × 10 with margins		
	all round (4.8.87)	4·50	
X901	13p. pale chestnut (1 band at right) (3.9.84) ..	60	60
	Ea. Band at left	60	60
	l. Booklet pane. No. X901/Ea, each × 2, and		
	X909 × 6 (13p. values at left)††	7·00	
	la. Ditto, but 13p. values at right	7·00	
	m. Booklet pane. No. X901/Ea, each × 3 with		
	margins all round (4.9.84)	2·50	
	mEy. Booklet pane. Phosphor omitted	£300	
	n. Booklet pane. No. X901Ea and X912 × 5		
	(20.10.86)	5·00	
	na. Ditto, but with vertical edges of pane		
	imperf (29.9.87)	5·00	
X902	14p. grey-blue (2 bands) (26.1.81)	1·00	45
X903	14p. dp blue (1 centre band) (23.8.88)	60	40
	a. Imperf (pair)	£275	
	Ey. Phosphor omitted	7·00	
	l. Booklet pane. No. X903 × 4 with margins		
	all round	5·00	
	lEy. Booklet pane. Phosphor omitted	40·00	
	m. Booklet pane. No. X903 × 10 with margins		
	all round	7·00	

(X903)	n. Booklet pane. No. X903 × 4 with horizontal edges of pane imperf (11.10.88)	5·00		
	p. Booklet pane. No. X903 × 10 with horizontal edges of pane imperf (11.10.88)	7·00		
	pEy. Booklet pane. Phosphor omitted	£125		
	q. Booklet pane. No. X903 × 4 with three edges of pane imperf (24.1.89)	16·00		
	qEy. Booklet pane. Phosphor omitted	16·00		
X904	14p. dp blue (1 band at right) (5.9.88)	1·75	1·75	
	l. Booklet pane. No. X904 and X914 × 2 plus label	3·00		
	lEy. Booklet pane. Phosphor omitted	10·00		
	m. Booklet pane. No. X904 × 2 and X914 × 4 with vertical edges of pane imperf	6·00		
X905	15p. brt blue (1 centre band) (26.9.89)	25	20	
	a. Imperf (pair)	£325		
	Ey. Phosphor omitted	7·00		
X906	15p. brt blue (1 band at left) (2.10.89)	2·00	1·75	
	Ea. Band at right (20.3.90)	2·00	1·75	
	l. Booklet pane. No. X906 × 2 and X916 plus label	5·00		
	lEy. Booklet pane. Phosphor omitted			
	m. Booklet pane. No. X906Ea, X916, X922, 1446, 1448, 1468Ea, 1470 and 1472 plus label with margins all round (20.3.90)	14·00		
X907	15½p. pale violet (2 bands) (1.2.82)	45	45	
	Eu. Underprint Type 1 (10.11.82)	45		
	l. Booklet pane. No. X907 × 6 with margins all round (19.5.82)	3·00		
	lEy. Booklet pane. Phosphor omitted	75·00		
	m. Booklet pane. No. X907 × 9 with margins all round (19.5.82)	4·00		
	mEy. Booklet pane. Phosphor omitted	40·00		
X908	16p. olive-drab (2 bands) (5.4.83)	1·50	1·25	
X909	17p. grey-blue (2 bands) (3.9.84)	75	75	
	Eu. Underprint Type 4 (4.11.85)	75		
	l. Booklet pane. No. X909Eu × 3 plus label (4.11.85)	3·00		
	Ela. Booklet pane. No. X909 × 3 plus label (12.8.86)	3·75		
	lEy. Booklet pane. Phosphor omitted	50·00		
X910	17p. dp blue (1 centre band) (4.9.90)	50	50	
	a. Imperf (pair)			
	Ey. Phosphor omitted	6·00		
X911	17p. dp blue (1 band at right) (4.9.90)	1·00	1·00	
	Ea. Band at left	70	70	
	l. Booklet pane. No. X911 and X911Ea × 2 plus label	3·00		
	lEy. Booklet pane. Phosphor omitted	30·00		
	m. Booklet pane. No. X911 × 2 and X917 × 3 plus three labels with vertical edges of pane imperf	4·00		
X912	18p. dp olive-grey (2 bands) (20.10.86)	75	75	
X913	18p. brt green (1 centre band) (10.9.91)	30	35	
	a. Imperf (pair)	£375		
X914	19p. brt orange-red (2 bands) (5.9.88)	1·25	1·25	
X915	20p. dull purple (2 bands) (25.2.76)	90	40	
X916	20p. brownish black (2 bands) (2.10.89)	2·50	1·00	
X917	22p. brt orange-red (2 bands) (4.9.90)	1·00	1·00	
X918	26p. rosine (Type I) (2 bands) (3.3.87)	7·00	6·00	
X919	31p. purple (2 bands) (18.3.86)	8·00	8·00	
X920	34p. ochre-brown (2 bands) (8.1.85)	7·00	7·00	
X921	50p. ochre-brown (2 bands) (2.2.77)	1·75	40	
X922	50p. ochre (2 bands) (20.3.90)	3·00	3·00	
	(b) Photo Harrison. On phosphorised paper. P 15 × 14			
X924	½p. turquoise-blue (10.12.80)	10	10	
	a. Imperf (pair)	£130		
	l. Coil strip. No. X924 and X932 × 3 (30.12.81)	45		

X925	1p. crimson (12.12.79)	10	10	
	a. Imperf (pair)	£750		
	l. Coil strip. No. X925 and X932Ea × 3 (14.8.84)	60		
	m. Booklet pane. No. X925 and X969, each × 2 (10.9.91)	75		
X926	2p. myrtle-green (face value as T **367**) (12.12.79)	10	10	
	a. Imperf (pair)	£900		
X927	2p. dp green (face value as T **367**a) (26.7.88)	10	10	
	l. Booklet pane. No. X927 × 2 and X969 × 4 plus 2 labels with vert edges of pane imperf (10.9.91)	1·50		
X928	2p. myrtle-green (face value as T **367**a) (5.9.88)	1·00	75	
	l. Coil strip. No. X928 and X932Ea × 3	1·00		
X929	2½p. rose-red (14.1.81)	20	20	
	l. Coil strip. No. X929 and X930 × 3 (6.81)	75		
X930	3p. brt magenta (Type I) (22.10.80)	20	20	
	a. Imperf (horiz pair)	£1000		
	b. Booklet pane. No. X930, X931 × 2 and X949 × 6 with margins all round (14.9.83)	6·00		
	c. Type II (10.10.89)	1·00	50	
	cl. Coil strip. No. X930c and X933 × 3	2·75		
X931	3½p. purple-brown (30.3.83)	45	45	
X932	4p. greenish blue (30.12.81)	25	20	
	Ea. Pale greenish blue (14.8.84)	25	25	
X933	4p. new blue (26.7.88)	10	10	
	a. Imperf (pair)			
	l. Coil strip. No. X933 × 3 and X935 (27.11.90)	1·00		
	m. Coil strip. No. X933 and X935, each × 2 (1.10.91)	30		
	n. Coil strip. No. X933 and X935 × 3 (31.1.95)	30		
X934	5p. pale violet (10.10.79)	30	25	
X935	5p. dull red-brown (26.7.88)	10	10	
	a. Imperf (pair)			
X936	6p. olive-yellow (10.9.91)	10	15	
X937	7p. brownish red (29.10.85)	2·00	2·00	
X938	8½p. yellowish green (24.3.76)	30	55	
X939	10p. orange-brown (Type I) (11.79)	30	20	
X940	10p. dull orange (Type II) (4.9.90)	15	15	
X941	11p. brown-red (27.8.80)	75	75	
X942	11½p. ochre-brown (15.8.79)	50	45	
X943	12p. yellowish green (30.1.80)	45	40	
X944	13p. olive-grey (15.8.79)	60	45	
X945	13½p. purple-brown (30.1.80)	65	60	
X946	14p. grey-blue (14.1.81)	50	40	
X947	15p. ultramarine (15.8.79)	50	40	
X948	15½p. pale violet (14.1.81)	50	40	
	a. Imperf (pair)	£200		
X949	16p. olive-drab (30.3.83)	60	30	
	a. Imperf (pair)	£130		
	Eu. Underprint Type 3 (10.8.83)	75		
	l. Booklet pane. No. X949 × 9 with margins all round (14.9.83)	3·75		
X950	16½p. pale chestnut (27.1.82)	85	75	
X951	17p. lt emerald (30.1.80)	70	40	
X952	17p. grey-blue (30.3.83)	50	40	
	a. Imperf (pair)	£275		
	Eu. Underprint Type 3 (5.3.85)	80		
	l. Booklet pane. No. X952 × 6 with margins all round (4.9.84)	3·00		
	m. Booklet pane. No. X952 × 9 with margins all round (8.1.85)	4·50		
X953	17½p. pale chestnut (30.1.80)	80	80	
X954	18p. dp violet (14.1.81)	70	75	
X955	18p. dp olive-grey (28.8.84)	70	60	
	a. Imperf (pair)	£130		

(X955)	l. Booklet pane. No. X955 × 9 with margins all round (3.3.87)	4·50	
	m. Booklet pane. No. X955 × 4 with margins all round (4.8.87)	3·00	
	n. Booklet pane. No. X955 × 10 with margins all round (4.8.87)	5·50	
X956	19p. brt orange-red (23.8.88)	60	40
	a. Imperf (pair)	£325	
	l. Booklet pane. No. X956 × 4 with margins all round	6·00	
	m. Booklet pane. No. X956 × 10 with margins all round	9·00	
	n. Booklet pane. No. X956 × 4 with horizontal edges of pane imperf (11.10.88)	6·00	
	o. Booklet pane. No. X956 × 10 with horizontal edges of pane imperf (11.10.88)	19·00	
	q. Booklet pane. No. X956 × 4 with three edges of pane imperf (24.1.89)	16·00	
X957	19½p. olive-grey (27.1.82)	1·50	1·50
X958	20p. dull purple (10.10.79)	90	20
X959	20p. turquoise-green (23.8.88)	80	35
X960	20p. brownish black (26.9.89)	70	40
	a. Imperf (pair)	£650	
	l. Booklet pane. No. X960 × 5 plus label with vertical edges of pane imperf (2.10.89)	7·00	
X961	20½p. ultramarine (30.3.83)	1·50	1·00
	a. Imperf (pair)	£1100	
X962	22p. blue (22.10.80)	60	45
	a. Imperf (pair)	£200	
X963	22p. yellow-green (28.8.84)	60	55
	a. Imperf (horiz pair)	£900	
X964	22p. brt orange-red (4.9.90)	60	50
	a. Imperf (pair)	£650	
X965	23p. brown-red (30.3.83)	1·00	60
	a. Imperf (horiz pair)	£900	
X966	23p. brt green (23.8.88)	80	40
X967	24p. violet (28.8.84)	1·10	85
X968	24p. Indian red (26.9.89)	1·25	85
	a. Imperf (horiz pair)	£2250	
X969	24p. chestnut (10.9.91)	60	45
	a. Imperf (pair)	£200	
X970	25p. purple (14.1.81)	90	90
X971	26p. rosine (Type I) (27.1.82)	90	30
	a. Type II (4.8.87)	3·50	3·75
	al. Booklet pane. No. X971a × 4 with margins all round	14·00	
X972	26p. drab (Type II) (4.9.90)	80	70
	a. Imperf (horiz pair)	£1000	
X973	27p. chestnut (23.8.88)	1·00	85
	l. Booklet pane. No. X973 × 4 with margins all round	7·00	
	m. Booklet pane. No. X973 × 4 with horizontal edges of pane imperf (11.10.88)	22·00	
X974	27p. violet (4.9.90)	90	75
X975	28p. dp violet (30.3.83)	90	90
	a. Imperf (pair)	£1000	
X976	28p. ochre (23.8.88)	90	75
X977	28p. dp bluish grey (10.9.91)	80	50
	a. Imperf (pair)	£1500	
X978	29p. ochre-brown (27.1.82)	1·50	1·00
X979	29p. dp mauve (26.9.89)	1·50	75
X980	30p. dp olive-grey (26.9.89)	80	50
X981	31p. purple (30.3.83)	1·00	1·25
	a. Imperf (pair)	£1000	
X982	31p. ultramarine (4.9.90)	1·00	90
X983	32p. greenish blue (23.8.88)	1·00	1·00
	a. Imperf (pair)	£1000	
X984	33p. lt emerald (4.9.90)	90	80
X985	34p. ochre-brown (28.8.84)	1·25	80
X986	34p. dp bluish grey (26.9.89)	1·00	90
X987	34p. dp mauve (10.9.91)	90	60

X988	35p. sepia (23.8.88)	1·25	75
	a. Imperf (pair)		
X989	35p. yellow (10.9.91)	90	60
X990	37p. rosine (26.9.89)	1·00	85
X991	39p. bright mauve (10.9.91)	1·00	65
	(c) *Photo Harrison. On ordinary paper. P* 15 × 14		
X992	50p. ochre-brown (21.5.80)	1·25	80
	a. Imperf (pair)	£600	
X993	75p. grey-black (face value as T **367**a) (26.7.88)	1·75	1·25
	(d) *Photo Harrison. On ordinary or phosphorised paper. P* 15 × 14		
X994	50p. ochre (13.3.90)	1·50	45
	a. Imperf (pair)	£850	
	(e) *Litho J.W. P* 14		
X996	4p. greenish blue (2 bands) (30.1.80)	20	25
X997	4p. greenish blue (phosphorised paper) (11.81)	35	20
X998	20p. dull purple (2 bands) (21.5.80)	1·00	40
X999	20p. dull purple (phosphorised paper) (11.81) .	1·25	40
	(f) *Litho Questa. P* 14 (*Nos.* X1000, X1003/4 *and* X1023) *or* 15 × 14 (*others*)		
X1000	2p. emerald-green (face value as T **367**) (phosphorised paper) (21.5.80)	20	20
	a. Perf 15 × 14 (10.7.84)	30	20
X1001	2p. brt green and dp green (face value as T **367**a) (phosphorised paper) (23.2.88)	1·00	60
X1002	4p. greenish blue (phosphorised paper) (13.5.86)	50	50
X1003	5p. lt violet (phosphorised paper) (9.2.88) ..	40	20
X1004	5p. claret (phosphorised paper) (27.1.82)	50	20
	a. Perf 15 × 14 (21.2.84)	50	25
X1005	13p. pale chestnut (1 centre band) (9.2.88)	70	70
	l. Booklet pane. No. X1005 × 6 with margins all round	3·00	
X1006	13p. pale chestnut (1 side band at right) (9.2.88)	80	80
	Ea. Band at left	60	60
	l. Booklet pane. No. X1006/Ea each × 3, X1010, X1015 and X1021 with margins all round	14·00	
	lEa. Grey-green (on 18p.) ptg double	£1000	
X1007	14p. dp blue (1 centre band) (11.10.88)	1·40	1·00
X1008	17p. dp blue (1 centre band) (19.3.91)	75	75
	Ey. Phosphor omitted	£175	
	l. Booklet pane. No. X1008 × 6 with margins all round	3·50	
	lEy. Booklet pane. Phosphor omitted	£750	
X1009	18p. dp olive-grey (phosphorised paper) (9.2.88)	75	75
	l. Booklet pane. No. X1009 × 9 with margins all round	4·50	
	m. Booklet pane. No. X1009 × 6 with margins all round	3·00	
X1010	18p. dp olive-grey (2 bands) (9.2.88)	4·50	4·50
X1011	18p. brt green (1 centre band) (27.10.92)	75	75
	l. Booklet pane. No. X1011 × 6 with margins all round	1·60	
X1012	18p. brt green (1 side band at right) (27.10.92)	1·00	1·00
	Ea. Band at left (10.8.93)	2·00	2·00
	l. Booklet pane. No. X1012 × 2, X1018 × 2, X1022 × 2, 1451a, 1514a and centre label with margins all round	10·00	
	m. Booklet pane. No. X1012Ea, X1020, X1022 and 1451aEb, each × 2, with centre label and margins all round (10.8.93)	10·00	
X1013	19p. brt orange-red (phosphorised paper) (11.10.88)	1·50	1·50
X1014	20p. dull purple (phosphorised paper) (13.5.86)	1·25	1·25
X1015	22p. yellow-green (2 bands) (9.2.88)	5·50	5·50

X1016	22p. brt orange-red (phosphorised paper) (19.3.91)	1·00	1·00
	l. Booklet pane. No. X1016 × 9 with margins all round	5·50	
	m. Booklet pane. No. X1016 × 6, X1019 × 2 and centre label with margins all round	7·00	
X1017	24p. chestnut (phosphorised paper) (27.10.92)	80	60
	l. Booklet pane. No. X1017 × 6 with margins all round	2·10	
X1018	24p. chestnut (2 bands) (27.10.92)	1·10	1·10
X1019	33p. lt emerald (phosphorised paper) (19.3.91)	1·50	1·50
X1020	33p. lt emerald (2 bands) (25.2.92)	1·25	1·25
X1021	34p. ochre-brown (2 bands) (9.2.88)	5·50	5·50
X1022	39p. brt mauve (2 bands) (27.10.92)	1·75	1·75
X1023	75p. black (face value as T **367**) (ordinary paper) (30.1.80)	3·00	1·50
	a. Perf 15 × 14 (21.2.84)	3·00	3·00
X1024	75p. brownish grey and black (face value as T **367**a) (ordinary paper) (23.2.88)	10·00	6·50

(g) Litho Walsall. P 14

X1050	2p. dp green (phosphorised paper) (9.2.93)	50	50
	l. Booklet pane. No. X1050 × 2 and X1053 × 4 plus 2 labels with vert edges of pane imperf	1·50	
X1051	14p. dp blue (1 side band at right) (25.4.89)	3·50	3·50
	Ey. Phosphor omitted	£200	
	l. Booklet pane. No. X1051 × 2 and X1052 × 4 with vertical edges of pane imperf	8·00	
	lEy. Booklet pane. Phosphor omitted	£950	
X1052	19p. brt orange-red (2 bands) (25.4.89)	1·25	1·25
	Ey. Phosphor omitted	£150	
X1053	24p. chestnut (phosphorised paper) (9.2.93)	70	50
X1054	29p. dp mauve (2 bands) (2.10.89)	3·00	3·00
	l. Booklet pane. No. X1054 × 4 with three edges of pane imperf	12·00	
X1055	29p. dp mauve (phosphorised paper) (17.4.90)	3·50	3·50
	l. Booklet pane. No. X1055 × 4 with three edges of pane imperf	14·00	
X1056	31p. ultramarine (phosphorised paper) (17.9.90)	1·25	1·25
	l. Booklet pane. No. X1056 × 4 with horizontal edges of pane imperf	4·50	
X1057	33p. light emerald (phosphorised paper) (16.9.91)	1·00	75
	l. Booklet pane. No. X1057 × 4 with horiz edges of pane imperf	3·50	
X1058	39p. brt mauve (phosphorised paper) (16.9.91)	1·00	75
	l. Booklet pane. No. X1058 × 4 with horiz edges of pane imperf	3·50	

*See footnote after No. 744.

†These come from sheets with gum arabic.

††Examples of Booklet panes Nos. X899l, X901l and X901la are known on which the phosphor bands were printed on the wrong values in error with the result that the side bands appear on the 15½p. or 17p. and the two bands on the 12½p. or 13p. Similarly examples of the 1p. with phosphor band at right, instead of left, exist from 50p. booklet pane No. X847l.

Nos. X844a/b come from a strip of eight of the vertical coil. It comprises two normals, one imperforate at sides and bottom, one completely imperforate, one imperforate at top, left and bottom and partly perforated at right due to the bottom three stamps being perforated twice. No. X844b is also known from another strip having one stamp imperforate at sides and bottom.

Nos. X848b/c come from the same sheet, the latter having perforations at the foot of the stamps only.

Multi-value coil strips Nos. X924l, X925l, X928l, X929l, X930cl and X933l/n were produced by the Post Office for use by a large direct mail marketing firm. From 2 September 1981 No. X929l was available

from the Philatelic Bureau, Edinburgh, and, subsequently from a number of other Post Office counters. Later multi-value coil strips were sold at the Philatelic Bureau and Post Office philatelic counters.

No. X1020 comes from the *se-tenant* pane in the Wales £6 booklet. This pane is listed under No. W49a in the Wales Regional section.

PANES OF SIX FROM STITCHED BOOKLETS. Nos. X841m, X851l/m and X855l include one or two printed labels showing commercial advertisements. These were originally perforated on all four sides, but from the August 1971 editions of the 25p. and 30p. booklets (Nos. DH42, DQ59) and December 1971 edition of the 50p. (No. DT4) the line of perforations between the label and the binding margin was omitted. Similar panes, with the line of perforations omitted, exist for the 3p., 3½p. and 4½p. values (Nos. X856, X858 and X865), but these are outside the scope of this listing as the labels are blank.

PART-PERFORATED SHEETS. Since the introduction of the "Jumelle" press in 1972 a number of part perforated sheets, both definitives and commemoratives, have been discovered. It is believed that these occur when the operation of the press in interrupted. Such sheets invariably show a number of "blind" perforations, where the pins have failed to cut the paper. Our listings of imperforate errors from these sheets are for pairs showing no traces whatsoever of the perforations. Examples showing "blind" perforations are outside the scope of this catalogue.

In cases where perforation varieties affect *se-tenant* stamps, fuller descriptions will be found in Vols. 4 and 5 of the *G.B. Specialised Catalogue*.

WHITE PAPER. From 1972 printings appeared on fluorescent white paper giving a stronger chalk reaction than the original ordinary cream paper.

PHOSPHOR OMITTED ERRORS. These are listed for those stamps or booklet panes which were not subsequently issued on phosphorised paper. The following phosphor omitted errors also exist, but can only be identified by the use of an ultra-violet lamp. Prices quoted are for mint examples:

½p. X841 (£1)	8½p. X881 (£1·75)	17p. X909 (£125)
1p. X844 (£2)	10p. X886 (£1)	18p. X912 (£27)
2p. X849 (£5)	11p. X892 (£2·25)	19p. X914 (£2·25)
3p. X857 (£60)	12p. X895 (£5)	20p. X916
3½p. X860 (£5·50)	14p. X902 (£28)	31p. X919 (£650)
4p. X863 (£85)	15½p. X907 (£4)	33p. X1020
5p. X866 (£200)	16p. X908 (£100)	34p. X920 (£750)

No. X909Eu with underprint Type 4 also exists without phosphor (*price* £11).

"ALL-OVER" PHOSPHOR. To improve mechanised handling most commemoratives from the 1972 Royal Silver Wedding 3p. value to the 1979 Rowland Hill Death Centenary set had the phosphor applied by printing cylinder across the entire surface of the stamp, giving a matt effect. Printings of the 1, 2 and 10p. definitives, released in October 1979, also had "all-over" phosphor, but these were purely a temporary expedient pending the adoption of phosphorised paper. Nos. X883, X890 and X921 have been discovered with "all-over" phosphor in addition to the normal phosphor bands. These errors are outside the scope of this catalogue.

PHOSPHORISED PAPER. Following the experiments on Nos. 743c and 829 a printing of the 4½p. definitive was issued on 13 November 1974, which had, in addition to the normal phosphor bands, phosphor included in the paper coating. Because of difficulties in identifying this phosphorised paper with the naked eye this printing is not listed separately in this catalogue.

No. X938 was the first value printed on phosphorised paper without phosphor bands and was a further experimental issue to test the efficacy of this system. From 15 August 1979 phosphorised paper was accepted for use generally, this paper replacing phosphor bands on values other than those required for the second-class rate.

Stamps on phosphorised paper show a shiny surface instead of the matt areas of those printed with phosphor bands.

DEXTRIN GUM. From 1973 printings in photogravure appeared with PVA gum to which dextrin had been added. Because this is virtually colourless a bluish green colouring matter was added to distinguish it from the earlier pure PVA.

The 4p., 5p. (light violet), 20p. and 75p. printed in lithography exist with PVA and PVAD gum. From 1988 Questa printings were with PVAD gum, but did not show the bluish green additive.

VARNISH COATING. Nos. X841 and X883 exist with and without a varnish coating. This cannot easily be detected without the use of an ultra-violet lamp as it merely reduces the fluorescent paper reaction.

POSTAL FORGERIES. In mid-1993 a number of postal forgeries of the 24p. chestnut were detected in the London area. These forgeries, produced by lithography, can be identified by the lack of phosphor in the paper, screening dots across the face value and by the perforations which were applied by a line machine gauging 11.

First Day Covers

15.2.71	$\frac{1}{2}$p., 1p., 1$\frac{1}{2}$p., 2p., 2$\frac{1}{2}$p., 3p., 3$\frac{1}{2}$p., 4p., 5p., 6p., 7$\frac{1}{2}$p., 9p. (X841, X844, X848/9, X851, X855, X858, X861, X866, X870, X877, X882) (Covers carry "POSTING DELAYED BY THE POST OFFICE STRIKE 1971" cachet) .	2·00
11.8.71	10p. (X885)	1·00
24.5.72	Wedgwood se-tenant pane $\frac{1}{2}$p., 2$\frac{1}{2}$p. (X841p)	20·00
24.10.73	4$\frac{1}{2}$p., 5$\frac{1}{2}$p., 8p. (X865, X868, X878)	1·00
4.9.74	6$\frac{1}{2}$p. (X871)	1·00
15.1.75	7p. (X874)	1·00
24.9.75	8$\frac{1}{2}$p. (X881)	1·00
25.2.76	9p., 9$\frac{1}{2}$p., 10p., 10$\frac{1}{2}$p., 11p., 20p. (X883/4, X886, X890, X892, X915)	2·00
2.2.77	50p. (X921)	1·00
26.4.78	10$\frac{1}{2}$p. (X891)	1·00
15.8.79	11$\frac{1}{2}$p., 13p., 15p. (X942, X944, X947)	1·00
30.1.80	4p., 12p., 13$\frac{1}{2}$p., 17p., 17$\frac{1}{2}$p., 75p. (X996, X943, X945, X951, X953, X1023)	2·00
16.4.80	Wedgwood se-tenant pane 2p., 10p., 12p. (X849n)	3·00
22.10.80	3p., 22p. (X930, X962)	1·00
14.1.81	2$\frac{1}{2}$p., 11$\frac{1}{2}$p., 14p., 15$\frac{1}{2}$p., 18p., 25p. (X929, X893, X946, X948, X954, X970)	1·00
27.1.82	5p., 12$\frac{1}{2}$p., 16$\frac{1}{2}$p., 19$\frac{1}{2}$p., 26p., 29p. (X1004, X898, X950, X957, X971, X978)	2·00
19.5.82	Stanley Gibbons se-tenant pane 2p., 3p., 12$\frac{1}{2}$p. (X849p)	2·50
30.3.83	3$\frac{1}{2}$p., 16p., 17p., 20$\frac{1}{2}$p., 23p., 28p., 31p. (X931, X949, X952, X961, X965, X975, X981)	3·00
14.9.83	Royal Mint se-tenant pane 3p., 3$\frac{1}{2}$p., 16p. (X930b)	3·50
28.8.84	13p., 18p., 22p., 24p., 34p. (X900, X955, X963, X967, X985)	3·00
4.9.84	Christian Heritage se-tenant pane 10p., 13p., 17p. (X886bl)	8·00
8.1.85	The Times se-tenant pane 4p., 13p., 17p., 34p. (X864l)	8·50
29.10.85	7p., 12p. (X937, X896)	2·00

18.3.86	British Rail se-tenant pane 12p., 17p., 31p. (X897m)	9·00
3.3.87	P & O se-tenant pane 1p., 13p., 18p., 26p. (X847m)	7·50
9.2.88	Financial Times se-tenant pane 13p., 18p., 22p., 34p. (X1006l)	8·00
23.8.88	14p., 19p., 20p., 23p., 27p., 28p., 32p., 35p. (X903, X956, X959, X966, X973, X976 X983, X988)	3·75
26.9.89	15p., 20p., 24p., 29p., 30p., 34p., 37p. (X905, X960, X968, X979/80, X986, X990)	4·00
20.3.90	London Life se-tenant pane 15p., (2nd), 20p., (1st), 15p., 20p., 29p. (X906m)	7·50
4.9.90	10p., 17p., 22p., 26p., 27p., 31p., 33p. (X910, X940, X964, X972, X974, X982, X984)	3·50
19.3.91	Alias Agatha Christie se-tenant pane 22p., 33p. (X1016m)	8·00
10.9.91	6p., 18p., 24p., 28p., 34p., 35p., 39p. (X936, X913, X969, X977, X987, X989, X991)	4·00
27.10.92	Tolkien se-tenant pane. 18p., (2nd), 24p., (1st), 39p. (X1012l)	4·25
10.8.93	Beatrix Potter se-tenant pane 18p., (2nd), 33p., 39p. (X1012m)	8·50

Post Office Presentation Packs

15.2.71	P.O. Pack No. 26. $\frac{1}{2}$p. (2 bands), 1p. (2 bands), 1$\frac{1}{2}$p. (2 bands), 2p. (2 bands), 2$\frac{1}{2}$p. magenta (1 centre band), 3p. ultramarine (2 bands), 3$\frac{1}{2}$p. olive-grey (2 bands), 4p. ochre-brown (2 bands), 5p. pale violet (2 bands), 6p. (2 bands), 7$\frac{1}{2}$p. (2 bands), 9p. yellow-orange and black (2 bands). (Nos. X841, X844, X848/9, X851, X855, X858, X861, X866, X870, X877, X882)	4·00
15.4.71**	"Scandinavia 71". Contents as above	32·00
25.11.71	P.O. Pack No. 37. $\frac{1}{2}$p. (2 bands), 1p. (2 bands), 1$\frac{1}{2}$p., (2 bands), 2p. (2 bands), 2$\frac{1}{2}$p. magenta (1 centre band), 3p. ultramarine (2 bands) or (1 centre band), 3$\frac{1}{2}$p. olive-grey (2 bands) or (1 centre band). 4p. ochre-brown (2 bands), 4$\frac{1}{2}$p. (2 bands), 5p. pale violet (2 bands), 5$\frac{1}{2}$p. (2 bands) or (1 centre band), 6p. (2 bands), 6$\frac{1}{2}$p. (2 bands) or (1 centre band), 7p. (2 bands), 7$\frac{1}{2}$p. (2 bands), 8p. (2 bands), 9p. yellow-orange and black (2 bands), 10p. orange-brown and chestnut (2 bands). (Nos. X841, X844, X848/9, X851, X855 or X856, X858 or X859, X861, X865/6, X868 or X869, X870, X871 or X872, X874, X877/8, X882, X885)	4·00
2.2.77	P.O. Pack No. 90. $\frac{1}{2}$p. (2 bands), 1p. (2 bands), 1$\frac{1}{2}$p. (2 bands), 2p. (2 bands), 2$\frac{1}{2}$p. magenta (1 centre band), 3p. ultramarine (1 centre band), 5p. pale violet (2 bands), 6$\frac{1}{2}$p. (1 centre band), 7p. (2 bands) or (1 centre band), 7$\frac{1}{2}$p. (2 bands), 8p. (2 bands), 8$\frac{1}{2}$p. (2 bands), 9p. deep violet (2 bands), 9$\frac{1}{2}$p. (2 bands), 10p. orange-brown (2 bands), 10$\frac{1}{2}$p. yellow (2 bands), 11p. (2 bands), 20p. dull purple (2 bands), 50p. ochre-brown (2 bands). (Nos. X841, X844, X848/9, X851, X856, X866, X872, X874 or X875, X877/8, X881, X883/4, X886, X890, X892, X915, X921)	5·00

28.10.81   P.O. Pack No. 129a. 10$\frac{1}{2}$p. deep dull blue (2 bands), 11$\frac{1}{2}$p. (1 centre band), 2$\frac{1}{2}$p. (phos paper), 3p. (phos paper), 11$\frac{1}{2}$p. (phos paper), 12p. (phos paper), 13p. (phos paper), 13$\frac{1}{2}$p. (phos paper), 14p. (phos paper), 15p. (phos paper), 15$\frac{1}{2}$p. (phos paper), 17p. light emerald (phos paper), 17$\frac{1}{2}$p. (phos paper), 18p. deep violet (phos paper), 22p. blue (phos paper), 25p. (phos paper), 4p. greenish blue (litho, 2 bands), 75p. (litho). (*Nos.* X891, X893, X929/30, X942/8, X951, X953/4, X970, X996, X1023)   16·00

3.8.83   P.O. Pack No. 1. 10p. orange-brown (1 centre band), 12$\frac{1}{2}$p. (1 centre band), $\frac{1}{2}$p. (phos paper), 1p. (phos paper), 3p. (phos paper), 3$\frac{1}{2}$p. (phos paper), 16p. (phos paper), 16$\frac{1}{2}$p. (phos paper), 17p. grey-blue (phos paper), 20$\frac{1}{2}$p. (phos paper), 23p. brown-red (phos paper), 26p. rosine (phos paper), 28p. deep violet (phos paper), 31p. purple (phos paper), 50p. (ord paper), 2p. (litho phos paper), 4p. (litho phos paper), 5p. claret (litho phos paper), 20p. (litho phos paper), 75p. (litho). (*Nos.* X888, X898, X924/5, X930/1, X949/50, X952, X961, X965, X971, X975, X981, X992, X997, X999, X1000, X1004, X1023)   22·00

23.10.84   P.O. Pack No. 5. 13p. (1 centre band), $\frac{1}{2}$p. (phos paper), 1p. (phos paper), 3p. (phos paper), 10p. orange-brown (phos paper), 16p. (phos paper), 17p. grey-blue (phos paper), 18p. dp olive-grey (phos paper), 22p. bright green (phos paper), 24p. violet (phos paper), 26p. rosine (phos paper), 28p. deep violet (phos paper), 31p. purple (phos paper), 34p. ochre-brown (phos paper), 50p. (ord paper), 2p. (litho phos paper), 4p. (litho phos paper), 5p. claret (litho phos paper), 20p. (litho phos paper), 75p. (litho). (*Nos.* X900, X924/5, X930, X939, X949, X952, X955, X963, X967, X971, X975, X981, X985, X992, X1000a, X997, X999, X1004a, X1023a)   20·00

3.3.87   P.O. Pack No. 9. 12p. (1 centre band), 13p. (1 centre band), 1p. (phos paper), 3p. (phos paper), 7p. (phos paper), 10p. orange-brown (phos paper), 17p. grey-blue (phos paper), 18p. dp olive-grey (phos paper), 22p. bright green (phos paper), 24p. violet (phos paper), 26p. rosine (phos paper), 28p. deep violet (phos paper), 31p. purple (phos paper), 34p. ochre-brown (phos paper), 50p. (ord paper), 2p. (litho phos paper), 4p. (litho phos paper), 5p. claret (litho phos paper), 20p. (litho phos paper), 75p. (litho). (*Nos.* X896, X900, X925, X930, X937, X939, X952, X955, X963, X967, X971, X975, X981, X985, X992, X997, X999, X1000a, X1004a, X1023a)   16·00

23.8.88   P.O. Pack No. 15. 14p. (1 centre band), 19p. (phos paper), 20p. turquoise-green (phos paper), 23p. bright green (phos paper), 27p. chestnut (phos paper), 28p. ochre (phos paper), 32p. (phos paper), 35p. sepia (phos paper). (*Nos.* X903, X956, X959, X966, X973, X976, X983, X988)   9·00

26.9.89   P.O. Pack No. 19. 15p. (centre band), 20p. brownish black (phos paper), 24p. Indian red (phos paper), 29p. deep mauve (phos paper), 30p. (phos paper), 34p. deep bluish grey (phos paper), 37p. (phos paper). (*Nos.* X905, X960, X968, X979/80, X986, X990)   7·00

4.9.90   P.O. Pack No. 22. 10p. dull orange (phos paper), 17p. (centre band), 22p. bright orange-red (phos paper), 26p. drab (phos paper), 27p. violet (phos paper), 31p. ultramarine (phos paper), 33p. (phos paper). (*Nos.* X910, X940, X964, X972, X974, X982, X984)   6·00

14.5.91   P.O. Pack No. 24. 1p. (phos paper), 2p. (phos paper), 3p. (phos paper), 4p. new blue (phos paper), 5p. dull red-brown (phos paper), 10p. dull orange (phos paper), 17p. (centre band), 20p. turquoise-green (phos paper), 22p. bright orange-red (phos paper), 26p. drab (phos paper), 27p. violet (phos paper), 30p. (phos paper), 31p. ultramarine (phos paper), 32p. (phos paper), 33p. (phos paper), 37p. (phos paper), 50p. (ord paper), 75p. (ord paper). (*Nos.* X910, X925, X927, X930, X933, X935, X940, X959, X964, X972, X974, X980, X990, X993/4)   9·00

10.9.91   P.O. Pack No. 25. 6p. (phos paper), 18p. (centre band), 24p. chestnut (phos paper), 28p. deep bluish grey (phos paper), 34p. deep mauve (phos paper), 35p. yellow (phos paper), 39p. (phos paper). (*Nos.* X913, X936, X969, X977, X987, X989, X991)   4·50

**The "Scandinavia 71" was a special pack produced for sale during a visit to six cities in Denmark, Sweden and Norway by a mobile display unit between 15 April and 20 May 1971. The pack gives details of this tour and also lists the other stamps which were due to be issued in 1971, the text being in English. A separate insert gives translations in Danish, Swedish and Norwegian. The pack was also available at the Philatelic Bureau, Edinburgh.

DECIMAL MACHIN INDEX

Those booklet stamps shown below with an * after the catalogue number do not exist with perforations on all four sides, but show one or two sides imperforate.

Val.	Process	Colour	Phosphor	Cat. No.	Source
$\frac{1}{2}$p.	photo	turquoise-blue	2 bands	X841/Eg	(a) with P.V.A. gum—sheets, 5p. m/v coil (X841nEv), 10p. m/v coil (X841q), 10p. booklets (DN46/75, FA1/3), 25p. booklets (DH39/52), 50p. booklets (DT1/12, FB1, FB14/16, FB19/23), £1 Wedgwood booklet (DX1) (b) with gum arabic—sheets, 5p. m/v coil (X841n)
$\frac{1}{2}$p.	photo	turquoise-blue	1 band at left	X842	£1 Wedgwood booklet (DX1)
$\frac{1}{2}$p.	photo	turquoise-blue	1 centre band	X843	10p. m/v coil (X843l), 10p. booklets (FA4/9)
$\frac{1}{2}$p.	photo	turquoise-blue	phos paper	X924	sheets, 12$\frac{1}{2}$p. m/v coil (X924l)
1p.	photo	crimson	2 bands	X844/Eg	(a) with P.V.A. gum—sheets, coils, 5p. m/v coil (X841nEv), 10p. m/v coil (X841q), 10p. booklets (DN46/75, FA1/3), 50p. booklets (FB1/8, FB14/16) (b) with gum arabic—coils, 5p. m/v coil (X841n)
1p.	photo	crimson	1 centre band	X845	10p. m/v coils (X843l, X845m), 10p. booklets (FA4/11), 50p. booklets (FB24/30, 34/36, 43/6, 48, 50)
1p.	photo	crimson	"all-over"	X846	sheets
1p.	photo	crimson	phos paper	X925	sheets, coils, 13p. m/v coil (X925l), 50p. booklet (FB59/66)
1p.	photo	crimson	1 band at left	X847	50p. booklets (FB37/42, 47, 49)
1p.	photo	crimson	1 band at right	X847Ea	£5 P. & O. booklet (DX8)
1$\frac{1}{2}$p.	photo	black	2 bands	X848	sheets, 10p. booklets (DN46/75)
2p.	photo	myrtle-green	2 bands	X849/Eg	(a) with P.V.A. gum—sheets, 5p. m/v coil (X841nEv), 10p. m/v coil (X841q), 10p. booklets (DN46/75), 50p. booklets (FB9/13), £3 Wedgwood booklet (DX2), £4 SG booklet (DX3) (b) with gum arabic—5p. m/v coil (X841n)
2p.	photo	myrtle-green	"all-over"	X850	sheets
2p.	photo	myrtle-green	phos paper	X926	sheets
2p.	photo	myrtle-green	phos paper	X928	14p. m/v coil (X928l)
2p.	litho	emerald-green	phos paper	X1000/a	sheets
2p.	litho	brt grn & dp grn	phos paper	X1001	sheets
2p.	photo	dp green	phos paper	X927	sheets, £1 booklets (FH23/7)
2p.	litho	dp green	phos paper	X1050*	£1 booklets (FH28/30)
2$\frac{1}{2}$p.	photo	magenta	1 centre band	X851/Eg	(a) with P.V.A. gum—sheets, coils, 25p. booklets (DH39/52), 50p. booklets (DT1/12), £1 Wedgwood booklet (DX1) (b) with gum arabic—sheets, coils
2$\frac{1}{2}$p.	photo	magenta	1 side band	X852/Ea	(a) band at left—50p. booklets (DT1/12), £1 Wedgwood booklet (DX1) (b) band at right—£1 Wedgwood booklet (DX1)
2$\frac{1}{2}$p.	photo	magenta	2 bands	X853	sheets
2$\frac{1}{2}$p.	photo	rose-red	phos paper	X929	sheets, 11$\frac{1}{2}$p. m/v coil (X929l)
2$\frac{1}{2}$p.	photo	rose-red	2 bands	X854	50p. booklets (FB17/18)
3p.	photo	ultramarine	2 bands	X855/Eg	(a) with P.V.A. gum—sheets, coils, 30p. booklets (DQ56/72), 50p. booklets (DT1/12), £1 Wedgwood booklet (DX1) (b) with gum arabic—sheets, coils
3p.	photo	ultramarine	1 centre band	X856/Eg	(a) with P.V.A. gum—sheets, coils, 30p. booklets (DQ73/4), 50p. booklets (DT13/14) (b) with gum arabic—sheets
3p.	photo	brt magenta	phos paper	X930	Type I. sheets, 11$\frac{1}{2}$p. m/v coil (X929l), £4 Royal Mint booklet (DX4)
3p.	photo	brt magenta	phos paper	X930c	Type II. sheets (from 21.1.92), 15p. m/v coil (X930cl)
3p.	photo	brt magenta	2 bands	X857	Type I. 50p. booklets (FB19/23), £4 SG booklet (DX3)
3$\frac{1}{2}$p.	photo	olive-grey	2 bands	X858/Eb	sheets, coils, 35p. booklets (DP1/3), 50p. booklets (DT13/14)
3$\frac{1}{2}$p.	photo	olive-grey	1 centre band	X859	sheets, coils, 35p. booklet (DP4), 85p. booklet (DW1)
3$\frac{1}{2}$p.	photo	purple-brown	phos paper	X931	sheets, £4 Royal Mint booklet (DX4)
3$\frac{1}{2}$p.	photo	purple-brown	1 centre band	X860	50p. booklets (FB24/6)

Val.	Process	Colour	Phosphor	Cat. No.	Source
4p.	photo	ochre-brown	2 bands	X861/Eg	(a) with P.V.A. gum—sheets. (b) with gum arabic—sheets
4p.	litho	greenish blue	2 bands	X996	sheets
4p.	photo	greenish blue	2 bands	X862	50p. booklets (FB17/18)
4p.	litho	greenish blue	phos paper	X997 X1002	sheets J.W. ptg. sheets Questa ptg.
4p.	photo	greenish blue	phos paper	X932 X932Ea	$12\frac{1}{2}$p. m/v coil (X924l) 13p. m/v coil (X925l), 14p. m/v coil (X928l)
4p.	photo	greenish blue	1 centre band	X863	50p. booklets (FB27/30)
4p.	photo	greenish blue	1 side band	X864/Ea	(a) band at right—£5 Times booklet (DX6) (b) band at left—£5 Times booklet (DX6)
4p.	photo	new blue	phos paper	X933	sheets, 15p. m/v coil (X930cl), 17p. m/v coil (X933l), 18p. m/v coil (X933m), 19p m/v coil (X933n)
$4\frac{1}{2}$p.	photo	grey-blue	2 bands	X865	sheets, coils, 45p. booklets (DS1/2), 85p. booklet (DW1)
5p.	photo	pale violet	2 bands	X866	sheets
5p.	photo	pale violet	phos paper	X934	sheets
5p.	litho	lt violet	phos paper	X1003	sheets
5p.	litho	claret	phos paper	X1004/a	sheets
5p.	photo	claret	1 centre band	X867	50p. booklets (FB35/36, 43/6, 48, 50)
5p.	photo	dull red-brown	phos paper	X935	sheets, 17p. m/v coil (X933l), 18p. m/v coil (X933m), 19p m/v coil (X933n)
$5\frac{1}{2}$p.	photo	violet	2 bands	X868	sheets
$5\frac{1}{2}$p.	photo	violet	1 centre band	X869	sheets
6p.	photo	lt emerald	2 bands	X870/Eg	(a) with P.V.A. gum—sheets, 10p. m/v coil (X841q), 10p. booklets (FA1/3) (b) with gum arabic—sheets
6p.	photo	olive-yellow	phos paper	X936	sheets
$6\frac{1}{2}$p.	photo	greenish blue	2 bands	X871	sheets
$6\frac{1}{2}$p.	photo	greenish blue	1 centre band	X872	sheets, coils, 65p. booklet (FC1)
$6\frac{1}{2}$p.	photo	greenish blue	1 side band	X873/Ea	(a) band at right—50p. booklet (FB1A). (b) band at left—50p. booklet (FB1B)
7p.	photo	purple-brown	2 bands	X874	sheets
7p.	photo	purple-brown	1 centre band	X875	sheets, coils, 10p. m/v coil (X843l), 10p. booklets (FA4/9), 70p. booklets (FD1/7), £1.60 Christmas booklet (FX1)
7p.	photo	purple-brown	1 side band	X876/Ea	(a) band at right—50p. booklets (FB2A/8A) (b) band at left—50p. booklets (FB2B/8B)
7p.	photo	brownish red	phos paper	X937	sheets
$7\frac{1}{2}$p.	photo	pale chestnut	2 bands	X877	sheets
8p.	photo	rosine	2 bands	X878	sheets
8p.	photo	rosine	1 centre band	X879	sheets, coils, 10p. m/v coil (X845m), 10p. booklets (FA10/11), 80p. booklet (FE1), £1.80 Christmas booklet (FX2)
8p.	photo	rosine	1 side band	X880/Ea	(a) band at right—50p. booklets (FB9A/10A) (b) band at left—50p. booklets (FB9B/10B)
$8\frac{1}{2}$p.	photo	lt yellowish green	2 bands	X881	sheets, coils, 50p. booklet (FB1), 85p. booklet (FF1)
$8\frac{1}{2}$p.	photo	yellowish green	phos paper	X938	sheets
9p.	photo	yellow-orange & black	2 bands	X882	sheets
9p.	photo	dp violet	2 bands	X883	sheets, coils, 50p. booklet (FB2/8), 90p. booklets (FG1/8), £1.60 Christmas booklet (FX1)
$9\frac{1}{2}$p.	photo	purple	2 bands	X884	sheets
10p.	recess	cerise	phos paper	829	sheets
10p.	photo	orange-brown & chestnut	2 bands	X885	sheets
10p.	photo	orange-brown	2 bands	X886	Type I. sheets, 50p. booklets (FB9/10), £1.80 Christmas booklet (FX2)
10p.	photo	orange-brown	2 bands	X886b	Type II. £4 Christian Heritage booklet (DX5)
10p.	photo	orange-brown	"all-over"	X887	Type I. sheets, coils, £1 booklet (FH1)
10p.	photo	orange-brown	phos paper	X939	Type I. sheets

Decimal Machin Index (continued)

Val.	Process	Colour	Phosphor	Cat. No.	Source
10p.	photo	orange-brown	1 centre band	X888	Type I. sheets, coils, £1 booklets (FH2/4), £2.20 Christmas booklet (FX3), £3 Wedgwood booklet (DX2)
10p.	photo	orange-brown	1 side band	X889/Ea	Type I. (a) band at right—50p. booklets (FB11A/13A) (b) band at left—50p. booklets (FB11B/13B), £3 Wedgwood booklet (DX2)
10p.	photo	dull orange	phos paper	X940	sheets
10½p.	photo	yellow	2 bands	X890	sheets
10½p.	photo	dp dull blue	2 bands	X891	sheets
11p.	photo	brown-red	2 bands	X892	sheets
11p.	photo	brown-red	phos paper	X941	sheets
11½p.	photo	ochre-brown	phos paper	X942	sheets
11½p.	photo	drab	1 centre band	X893	sheets, coils, £1.15 booklets (F1/4), £2.55 Christmas booklet (FX4)
11½p.	photo	drab	1 side band	X894/Ea	(a) band at right—50p. booklets (FB14A/18A), £1.30 booklets (FL1/2) (b) band at left—50p. booklets (FB14B/18B), £1.30 booklets (FL1/2)
12p.	photo	yellowish green	phos paper	X943	sheets, coils, £1.20 booklets (FJ1/3)
12p.	photo	yellowish green	2 bands	X895	50p. booklets (FB11/13), £2.20 Christmas booklet (FX3), £3 Wedgwood booklet (DX2)
12p.	photo	brt emerald	1 centre band	X896	sheets, coils, 50p. booklet (FB34), £1.20 booklets (FJ4/6), £5 British Rail booklet (DX7)
12p.	photo	brt emerald	1 side band	X897/Ea	(a) band at right—£1.50 booklets (FP1/2), £5 British Rail booklet (DX7) (b) band at left—£1.50 booklets (FP1/2), £5 British Rail booklet (DX7)
12p.	photo	brt emerald	1 centre band Underprint T.4	X896Eu	sheets
12½p.	photo	lt emerald	1 centre band	X898	sheets, coils, 50p. booklets (FB24/6), £1.25 booklets (FK1/8), £4 SG booklet (DX3)
12½p.	photo	lt emerald	1 centre band Underprint T.1	X898Eu	£2.80 Christmas booklet (FX5)
12½p.	photo	lt emerald	1 centre band Underprint T.2	X898Eua	£2.50 Christmas booklet (FX6)
12½p.	photo	lt emerald	1 side band	X899/Ea	(a) band at right—50p. booklets (FB19A/23A), £1.43 booklets (FN1/6), £1.46 booklets (FO1/3), £4 SG booklet (DX3), £4 Royal Mint booklet (DX4) (b) band at left—50p. booklets (FB19B/23B), £1.43 booklets (FN1/6), £1.46 booklets (FO1/3), £4 SG booklet (DX3), £4 Royal Mint booklet (DX4)
13p.	photo	olive-grey	phos paper	X944	sheets
13p.	photo	pale chestnut	1 centre band	X900	sheets, coils, 50p. booklets (FB27/30, 35/6, 43/6, 48, 50), 52p. booklet (GA1), £1.30 booklets (FL3/14, GI1), £5 Times booklet (DX6), £5 P & O booklet (DX8)
13p.	photo	pale chestnut	1 centre band Underprint T.2	X900Eu	£1.30 Christmas booklet (FX9)
13p.	photo	pale chestnut	1 side band	X901/Ea	(a) band at right—50p. booklets (FB37/42, 47, 49), £1.54 booklets (FQ1/4), £4 Christian Heritage booklet (DX5), £5 Times booklet (DX6), £5 P & O booklet (DX8) (b) band at left—£1 booklets (FH6/13), £1.54 booklets (FQ1/4), £4 Christian Heritage booklet (DX5), £5 Times booklet (DX6)
13p.	litho	pale chestnut	1 centre band	X1005	£5 Financial Times booklet (DX9)
13p.	litho	pale chestnut	1 side band	X1006/Ea	£5 Financial Times booklet (DX9)
13½p.	photo	purple-brown	phos paper	X945	sheets
14p.	photo	grey-blue	phos paper	X946	sheets, coils, £1.40 booklets (FM1/4)
14p.	photo	grey-blue	2 bands	X902	50p. booklets (FB14/16), £1.30 booklets (FL1/2), £2.55 Christmas booklet (FX4)
14p.	photo	dp blue	1 centre band	X903	sheets, coils, 56p. booklets (GB1/4), £1.40 booklets (FM5/6, GK1, 3)
14p.	photo	dp blue	1 band at right	X904	50p. booklets (FB51/4), £1 booklets (FH14/15)
14p.	litho	dp blue	1 centre band	X1007	£1.40 booklets (GK2, 4)
14p.	litho	dp blue	1 band at right	X1051*	£1 booklet (FH16)
15p.	photo	ultramarine	phos paper	X947	sheets
15p.	photo	brt blue	1 centre band	X905	sheets, coils

Val.	Process	Colour	Phosphor	Cat. No.	Source
15p.	photo	brt blue	1 side band	X906/Ea	(a) band at left—50p. booklet (FB55)
					(b) band at right—£5 London Life booklet (DX11)
$15\frac{1}{2}$p.	photo	pale violet	phos paper	X948	sheets, coils, £1.55 booklets (FR1/6)
$15\frac{1}{2}$p.	photo	pale violet	2 bands	X907	£1.43 booklets (FN1/6), £4 SG booklet (DX3)
$15\frac{1}{2}$p.	photo	pale violet	2 bands Underprint T.1	X907/Eu	£2.80 Christmas booklet (FX5)
16p.	photo	olive-drab	phos paper	X949	sheets, coils, £1.60 booklets (FS1, 3/4), £4 Royal Mint booklet (DX4)
16p.	photo	olive-drab	phos paper Underprint T.3	X949Eu	£1.60 booklet (FS2)
16p.	photo	olive-drab	2 bands	X908	£1.46 booklets (FO1/3)
$16\frac{1}{2}$p.	photo	pale chestnut	phos paper	X950	sheets
17p.	photo	lt emerald	phos paper	X951	sheets
17p.	photo	grey-blue	phos paper	X952	sheets, coils, £1 booklet (FH5), £1.70 booklets (FT1, 3 & 5/7), £4 Christian Heritage booklet (DX5), £5 Times booklet (DX6), £5 British Rail booklet (DX7)
17p.	photo	grey-blue	phos paper Underprint T.3	X952Eu	£1.70 booklet (FT2)
17p.	photo	grey-blue	2 bands	X909	50p. booklet (FB33), £1.50 booklets (FP1/3), £1.54 booklets (FQ1/4), £4 Christian Heritage booklet (DX5), £5 Times booklet (DX6), £5 British Rail booklet (DX7)
17p.	photo	grey-blue	2 bands Underprint T.4	X909Eu	50p. booklets (FB31/3)
17p.	photo	dp blue	1 centre band	X910	sheets, coils
17p.	photo	dp blue	1 side band	X911/Ea	(a) band at right—50p. booklet (FB57/8), £1 booklet (FH21/2)
					(b) band at left—50p. booklet (FB57/8)
17p.	litho	dp blue	1 centre band	X1008	£6 Alias Agatha Christie booklet (DX12)
$17\frac{1}{2}$p.	photo	pale chestnut	phos paper	X953	sheets
18p.	photo	dp violet	phos paper	X954	sheets
18p.	photo	dp olive-grey	phos paper	X955	sheets, coils, 72p. booklet (GC1), £1.80 booklets (FU1/8, GM1), £5 P & O booklet (DX8)
18p.	photo	dp olive-grey	2 bands	X912	50p. booklets (FB37/42, 47, 49), £1 booklet (FH6/13), £5 P & O booklet (DX8)
18p.	litho	dp olive-grey	phos paper	X1009	£5 Financial Times booklet (DX9)
18p.	litho	dp olive-grey	2 bands	X1010	£5 Financial Times booklet (DX9)
18p.	photo	brt green	1 centre band	X913	sheets, coils
18p.	litho	brt green	1 centre band	X1011	£6 Tolkien booklet (DX14)
18p.	litho	brt green	1 side band	X1012	(a) band at right—£6 Tolkien booklet (DX14).
					(b) band at left—£6 (£5.64 Beatrix Potter booklet (DX15)).
19p.	photo	brt orange-red	2 bands	X914	50p. booklets (FB51/4), £1 booklets (FH14/15, 17)
19p.	photo	brt orange-red	phos paper	X956	sheets, coils, 76p. booklets (GD1/4), £1.90 booklets (FV1/2, GN1, 3)
19p.	litho	brt orange-red	phos paper	X1013	£1.90 booklets (GN2, 4)
19p.	litho	brt orange-red	2 bands	X1052*	£1 booklet (FH16)
$19\frac{1}{2}$p.	photo	olive-grey	phos paper	X957	sheets
20p.	recess	olive-green	none	830	sheets
20p.	photo	dull purple	2 bands	X915	sheets
20p.	photo	dull purple	phos paper	X958	sheets
20p.	litho	dull purple	2 bands	X998	sheets
20p.	litho	dull purple	phos paper	X999	sheets J.W. ptg.
				X1014	sheets Questa ptg.
20p.	photo	turquoise-green	phos paper	X959	sheets
20p.	photo	brownish black	2 bands	X916	50p. booklet (FB55), £5 London Life booklet (DX11)
20p.	photo	brownish black	phos paper	X960	sheets, coils, £1 booklet (FH18)
$20\frac{1}{2}$p.	photo	ultramarine	phos paper	X961	sheets
22p.	photo	blue	phos paper	X962	sheets
22p.	photo	yellow-green	phos paper	X963	sheets

Val.	Process	Colour	Phosphor	Cat. No.	Source
22p.	litho	yellow-green	2 bands	X1015	£5 Financial Times booklet (DX9)
22p.	litho	brt orange-red	2 bands	X917*	£1 booklet (FH21/2)
22p.	photo	brt orange-red	phos paper	X964	sheets, coils
22p.	litho	brt orange-red	phos paper	X1016	£6 Alias Agatha Christie booklet (DX12)
23p.	photo	brown-red	phos paper	X965	sheets
23p.	photo	brt green	phos paper	X966	sheets
24p.	photo	violet	phos paper	X967	sheets
24p.	photo	Indian red	phos paper	X968	sheets
24p.	photo	chestnut	phos paper	X969	sheets, coils, 50p. booklets (FB59/66), £1 booklets (FH23/7)
24p.	litho	chestnut	phos paper	X1017	£6 Tolkien booklet (DX14) (Questa ptg)
				X1053*	£1 booklet (FH28/30) Walsall ptg
24p.	litho	chestnut	2 bands	X1018	£6 Tolkien booklet (DX14)
25p.	photo	purple	phos paper	X970	sheets
26p.	photo	rosine	2 bands	X918	Type I. £5 P & O booklet (DX8)
26p.	photo	rosine	phos paper	X971	Type I. sheets
26p.	photo	rosine	phos paper	X971a	Type II. £1.04 booklet (GE1)
26p.	photo	drab	phos paper	X972	sheets
27p.	photo	chestnut	phos paper	X973	sheets, £1.08 booklets (GF1/2)
27p.	photo	violet	phos paper	X974	sheets
28p.	photo	dp violet	phos paper	X975	sheets
28p.	photo	ochre	phos paper	X976	sheets
28p.	photo	dp bluish grey	phos paper	X977	sheets
29p.	photo	ochre-brown	phos paper	X978	sheets
29p.	photo	dp mauve	phos paper	X979	sheets
29p.	litho	dp mauve	2 bands	X1054*	£1.16 booklet (GG1)
29p.	litho	dp mauve	phos paper	X1055*	£1.16 booklet (GG2)
30p.	photo	dp olive-grey	phos paper	X980	sheets
31p.	photo	purple	2 bands	X919	£5 British Rail booklet (DX7)
31p.	photo	purple	phos paper	X981	sheets
31p.	photo	ultramarine	phos paper	X982	sheets
31p.	litho	ultramarine	phos paper	X1056*	£1.24 booklet (GH1)
32p.	photo	greenish blue	phos paper	X983	sheets
33p.	photo	lt emerald	phos paper	X984	sheets, coils
33p.	litho	lt emerald	phos paper	X1019	£6 Alias Agatha Christie booklet (DX12)
33p.	litho	emerald	phos paper	X1057*	£1.32 booklet (GJ1)
33p.	litho	lt emerald	2 bands	X1020	£6 Wales booklet (DX13), £6 (£5.64) Beatrix Potter booklet (DX15)
34p.	photo	ochre-brown	2 bands	X920	£5 Times booklet (DX6)
34p.	photo	ochre-brown	phos paper	X985	sheets
34p.	litho	ochre-brown	2 bands	X1021	£5 Financial Times booklet (DX9)
34p.	photo	dp bluish grey	phos paper	X986	sheets
34p.	photo	dp mauve	phos paper	X987	sheets
35p.	photo	sepia	phos paper	X988	sheets
35p.	photo	yellow	phos paper	X989	sheets
37p.	photo	rosine	phos paper	X990	sheets
39p.	photo	brt mauve	phos paper	X991	sheets, coils
39p.	litho	brt mauve	phos paper	X1058*	78p. booklet (GD4a), £1.56 booklet (G L1)
39p.	litho	brt mauve	2 bands	X1022	£6 Tolkien booklet (DX14), £6 (£5.64) Beatrix Potter booklet (DX15)
50p.	recess	dp ultramarine	none or phos paper	831/Ea	sheets

Val.	Process	Colour	Phosphor	Cat. No.	Source
50p.	photo	ochre-brown	2 bands	X921	sheets
50p.	photo	ochre-brown	none	X992	sheets
50p.	photo	ochre	2 bands	X922	£5 London Life (DX11)
50p.	photo	ochre	none or phos paper	X994	sheets
75p.	litho	black	none	X1023/a	sheets
75p.	litho	brownish grey & black	none	X1024	sheets
75p.	photo	grey-black	none	X993	sheets
£1	recess	bluish black	none	831b	sheets
£1	photo	brt yellow-green & blackish olive	none	1026	sheets
£1.30	photo	drab & dp greenish blue	none	1026b	sheets
£1.33	photo	pale mauve & grey-black	none	1026c	sheets
£1.41	photo	drab & dp greenish blue	none	1026d	sheets
£1.50	photo	pale mauve & grey-black	none	1026e	sheets
£1.60	photo	pale drab & dp greenish blue	none	1026f	sheets
£2	photo	lt emerald & purple-brown	none	1027	sheets
£5	photo	salmon & chalky blue	none	1028	sheets

For 1st and 2nd class no value indicated (NVI) stamps, see Nos. 1445/52 and 1511/16.
For table covering Machin stamps with elliptical perforations see after Nos. Y1667, etc, in 1993.

Decimal Machin Booklet Pane Guide

Abbreviations used in the diagrams: 2B = 2 bands, CB = centre band, LB = left band and RB = right band. The shaded squares represent printed labels. Panes completed by unprinted white labels are outside the scope of this catalogue.

Unless otherwise stated the panes were printed in photogravure. Some panes exist in photogravure and lithography and these are separately identified and listed. **Imperforate or straight edges.** These are described under the appropriate illustration and listed as complete panes.

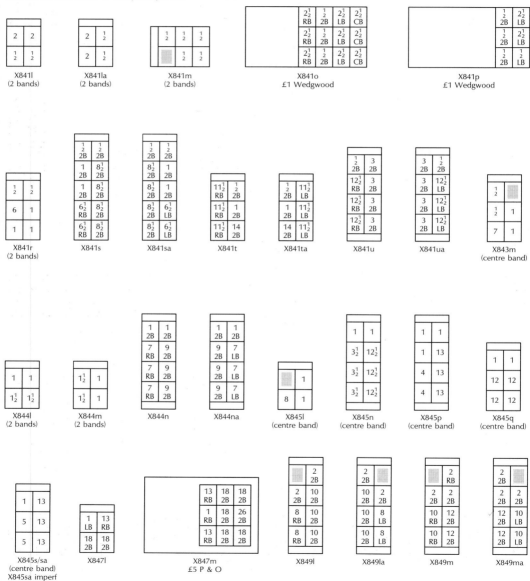

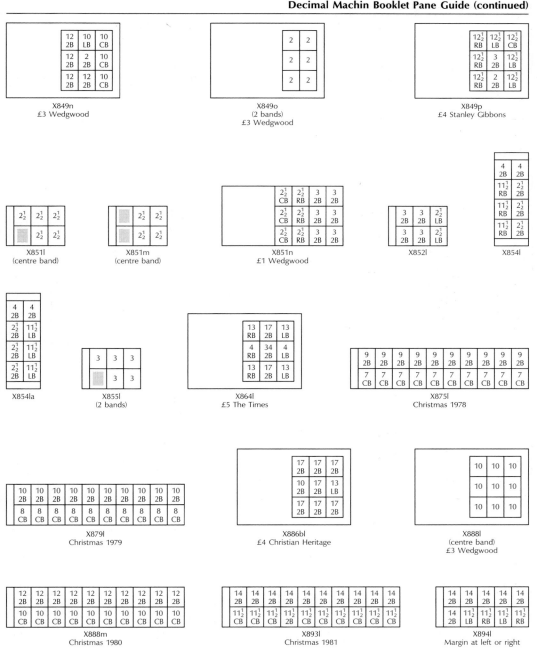

X849n
£3 Wedgwood

X849o
(2 bands)
£3 Wedgwood

X849p
£4 Stanley Gibbons

X851l
(centre band)

X851m
(centre band)

X851n
£1 Wedgwood

X852l

X854l

X854la

X855l
(2 bands)

X864l
£5 The Times

X875l
Christmas 1978

X879l
Christmas 1979

X886bl
£4 Christian Heritage

X888l
(centre band)
£3 Wedgwood

X888m
Christmas 1980

X893l
Christmas 1981

X894l
Margin at left or right

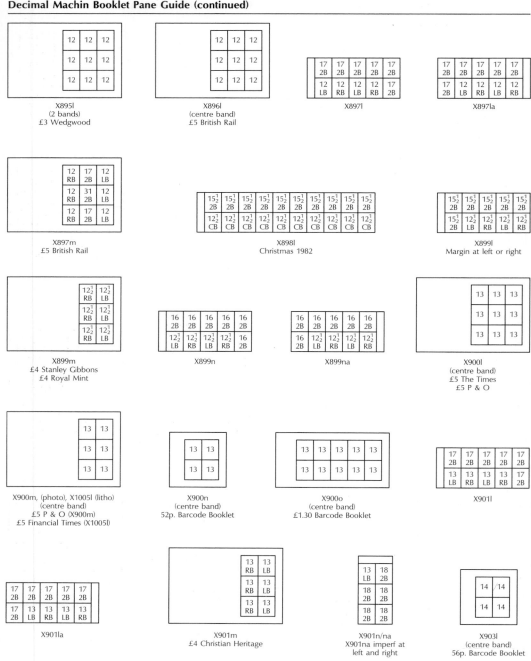

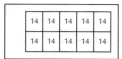

X903m
(centre band)
£1.40 Barcode Booklet

X903n, X903q
(centre band)
56p. Barcode Booklet
X903n imperf at top
and bottom
X903q imperf 3 sides

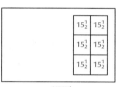

X903p
(centre band)
£1.40 Barcode Booklet
Imperf at top
and bottom

X904l

14 RB	19 2B
14 RB	19 2B
19 2B	19 2B

X904m, (photo)
X1051l (litho)
imperf at left
and right

X906l

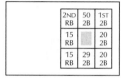

X906m
£5 London Life
The stamps in the bottom row are
Penny Black Anniversary definitives
(Nos. 1468Ea, 1470 and 1472)

$15\frac{1}{2}$	$15\frac{1}{2}$
$15\frac{1}{2}$	$15\frac{1}{2}$
$15\frac{1}{2}$	$15\frac{1}{2}$

X907l
(2 bands)
£4 Stanley Gibbons

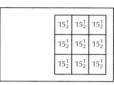

X907m
(2 bands)
£4 Stanley Gibbons

	17
17	17

X909l
(2 bands)
and underprint
X909 Ela (as X909l
but without
underprint)

X911l

X911m
Imperf at left
and right

1	1
24	24

X925m
(phosphorised paper)

X927l (photo)
X1050l (litho)
(phosphorised paper)
Imperf at left and
right

16	16	16
$3\frac{1}{2}$	3	$3\frac{1}{2}$
16	16	16

X930b
(phosphorised paper)
£4 Royal Mint

16	16	16
16	16	16
16	16	16

X949l
(phosphorised paper)
£4 Royal Mint

17	17
17	17
17	17

X925l
(phosphorised paper)
£4 Christian Heritage
£5 The Times
£5 British Rail
X1008l
(centre band)
£6 Agatha Christie

17	17	17
17	17	17
17	17	17

X952m
(phosphorised paper)
£5 The Times
£5 British Rail

18	18	18
18	18	18
18	18	18

X955l (photo), X1009l (litho)
(phosphorised paper)
£5 P & O (X955l)
£5 Financial Times (X1009l)

Decimal Machin Booklet pane Guide (continued)

18	18
18	18

X955m
(phosphorised paper)
72p. Barcode Booklet

18	18	18	18	18
18	18	18	18	18

X955n
(phosphorised paper)
£1.80 Barcode Booklet

19	19
19	19

X956l
(phosphorised paper)
76p. Barcode Booklet

19	19	19	19	19
19	19	19	19	19

X956m
(phosphorised paper)
£1.90 Barcode Booklet

19	19
19	19

X956n, X956q
(phosphorised paper)
76p. Barcode Booklet
X956n imperf at top and bottom
X956q imperf on three sides

19	19	19	19	19
19	19	19	19	19

X956o
(phosphorised paper)
£1.90 Barcode Booklet
Imperf at top and bottom

	20
20	20
20	20

X960l
(phosphorised paper)
Imperf at left and
right

26	26
26	26

X971al
(phosphorised paper)
£1.04 Barcode Booklet

27	27
27	27

X937l
(phosphorised paper)
£1.08 Barcode Booklet

27	27
27	27

X973m
(phosphorised paper)
£1.08 Barcode Booklet
imperf at top and
bottom

13 RB	22 2B	13 LB
13 RB	34 2B	13 LB
13 RB	18 2B	13 LB

X1006l (litho)
£5 Financial Times

18	18
18	18
18	18

X1009m (litho)
(phosphorised paper)
£5 Financial Times
X1011l (litho)
(centre band)
£6 Tolkien

18 RB	39 2B	24 2B
1ST 2B		2ND RB
18 RB	39 2B	24 2B

X1012l (litho)
£6 Tolkien

33 2B	18 LB	39 2B
2ND LB		2ND LB
33 2B	18 LB	39 2B

X1012m (litho)
£6 (£5.64) Beatrix Potter

22	22	22
22	22	22
22	22	22

X1016l (litho)
(phosphorised paper)
£6 Agatha Christie

22	33	22
22		22
22	33	22

X1016m (litho)
(phosphorised paper)
£6 Agatha Christie

24	24
24	24
24	24

X1017l (litho)
(phosphorised paper)
£6 Tolkien

29	29
29	29

X1054l (litho), X1055l (litho)
(X1054l 2 bands)
(X1055l phosphorised paper)
£1.16 Barcode Booklet
Imperf on three sides

31	31
31	31

X1056l (litho)
(phosphorised paper)
£1.24 Barcode Booklet
Imperf at top and
bottom

33	33
33	33

X1057l
(phosphorised paper)
£1.32 Barcode Booklet
Imperf top and bottom

39	39
39	39

X1058l
(phosphorised paper)
£1.56 Barcode Booklet
Imperf top and
bottom

368 "A Mountain Road"
(T. P. Flanagan)

369 "Deer's Meadow"
(Tom Carr)

371 John Keats
(150th Death Anniv)

372 Thomas Gray
(Death Bicentenary)

373 Sir Walter Scott (Birth Bicentenary)

(Des Rosalind Dease. Queen's head printed in gold and then embossed)

1971 (28 July). **Literary Anniversaries.** *Chalk-surfaced paper. Two phosphor bands.* P 15 × 14.

884	371	3p. black, gold & greyish blue	....	10	10
		a. Gold (Queen's head) omitted	....	75·00	
		Ey. Phosphor omitted	....	2·00	
885	372	5p. black, gold & yellow-olive	....	50	50
		a. Gold (Queen's head) omitted	....	£160	
		Ey. Phosphor omitted	....	20·00	
886	373	7½p. black, gold & yellow-brown	......	50	50
		Eb. Embossing omitted	....	25·00	
		Ey. Phosphor omitted	....	13·00	
		Set of 3	....	1·00	1·00
		First Day Cover	....		1·75
		Presentation Pack	....	5·00	

Special First Day of Issue Postmarks

British Post Office Philatelic Bureau, Edinburgh
(Type D, see Introduction) .... 4·00
London EC .... 4·50

374 Servicemen and Nurse of 1921

375 Roman Centurion

---

368 (Ulster '71 Paintings)

370 "Slieve na brock"
(Colin Middleton)

1971 (16 June). **"Ulster 1971" Paintings.** *Chalk-surfaced paper. Two phosphor bands.* P 15 × 14.

881	368	3p. yellow-buff, pale yellow, Venetian red, black, blue & drab	....	10	10
		Ey. Phosphor omitted	....	2·00	
882	369	7½p. olive-brown, brownish grey, pale olive-grey, dp blue, cobalt & grey-blue	....	50	50
		a. Pale olive-grey omitted*	....	60·00	
		Ey. Phosphor omitted	....	12·00	
883	370	9p. greenish yellow, orange, grey, lavender-grey, bistre, black, pale ochre-brown & ochre-brown	....	50	50
		a. Orange omitted	....	£650	
		Ey. Phosphor omitted	....	13·00	
		Set of 3	....	1·00	1·00
		First Day Cover	....		1·75
		Presentation Pack	....	5·00	

A used example of the 3p. has been seen with the Venetian red omitted.

*This only affects the boulder in the foreground, which appears whitish and it only applied to some stamps in the sheet.

Special First Day of Issue Postmarks

**FIRST DAY OF ISSUE
16 JUNE 1971
BELFAST**

British Post Office Philatelic Bureau, Edinburgh
(Type D, see Introduction) .... 2·50
Belfast .... 4·50
First Day of Issue handstamps, in the same design as that for Belfast, were provided at Armagh, Ballymena, Coleraine, Cookstown, Enniskillen, Londonderry, Newry, Omagh and Portadown for this issue.

HAVE YOU READ THE NOTES AT THE BEGINNING OF THIS CATALOGUE?
These often provide answers to the enquiries we receive.

376 Rugby Football, 1871

(Des F. Wegner)

1971 (25 Aug). **British Anniversaries.** *Events described on stamps. Chalk-surfaced paper. Two phosphor bands. P 15 × 14.*

887	**374**	3p. red-orange, grey, dp blue, olive-green, olive-brown, black, rosine & violet-blue .	10	10
		a. Dp blue omitted*	£600	
		b. Red-orange (nurse's cloak) omitted	£275	
		c. Olive-brown (faces, etc.) omitted	£160	
		d. Black omitted	£10000	
		Ey. Phosphor omitted	1·25	
888	**375**	7½p. grey, yellow-brown, vermilion, mauve, grey-black, black, silver, gold & ochre ..	50	50
		a. Grey omitted	75·00	
		Ey. Phosphor omitted	6·00	
889	**376**	9p. new blue, myrtle-green, grey-black, lemon, olive-brown, magenta & yellow-olive	50	50
		a. Olive-brown omitted	£110	
		b. New blue omitted	£2000	
		c. Myrtle-green omitted	£2000	
		Ey. Phosphor omitted	£400	
		Set of 3	1·00	1·00
		First Day Cover		1·75
		Presentation Pack	5·00	

*The effect of the missing deep blue is shown on the sailor's uniform, which appears as grey.

Used examples have been seen of the 3p. with grey omitted and of the 9p. with the lemon (jerseys) omitted.

Special First Day of Issue Postmarks

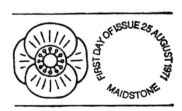

377 Physical Sciences Building, University College of Wales, Aberystwyth

378 Faraday Building, Southampton University

379 Engineering Department, Leicester University

380 Hexagon Restaurant, Essex University

(Des N. Jenkins)

1971 (22 Sept). **British Architecture. Modern University Buildings.** *Chalk-surfaced paper. Two phosphor bands. P 15 × 14.*

890	**377**	3p. olive-brown, ochre, lemon, black & yellow-olive	10	10
		a. Lemon omitted		
		b. Black (windows) omitted	£5500	
		Ey. Phosphor omitted	3·75	
891	**378**	5p. rose, black, chestnut & lilac	20	20
		Ey. Phosphor omitted	50·00	
892	**379**	7½p. ochre, black & purple-brown	50	50
		Ey. Phosphor omitted	7·00	
893	**380**	9p. pale lilac, black, sepia-brown & dp blue	90	90
		Ey. Phosphor omitted	10·00	
		Set of 4	1·50	1·50
		First Day Cover		1·75
		Presentation Pack	5·00	

Mint examples of the 5p. exist with a larger "P" following the face value

Special First Day of Issue Postmarks

British Post Office Philatelic Bureau, Edinburgh
(Type D, see Introduction) .... 4·00
Aberystwyth .... 13·50
Colchester .... 13·50
Leicester .... 13·50
Southampton .... 13·50

Collectors Pack 1971

1971 (29 Sept). *Comprises Nos. 835/40 and 881/93.*
CP893a   Collectors Pack .... 28·00

381 "Dream of the Wise Men"   **382** "Adoration of the Magi"

383 "Ride of the Magi"

HAVE YOU READ THE NOTES AT THE BEGINNING OF THIS CATALOGUE?
These often provide answers to the enquiries we receive.

(Des Clarke-Clements-Hughes design team, from stained-glass windows, Canterbury Cathedral. Queen's head printed in gold and then embossed)

1971 (13 Oct).   **Christmas.** *Ordinary paper. One centre phosphor band ($2\frac{1}{2}$p.) or two phosphor bands (others). P 15 × 14.*

894	**381**	$2\frac{1}{2}$p. new blue, black, lemon, emerald, reddish violet, carmine-red, carmine-rose & gold	10	10
		a. Imperf (pair)	£450	
		Eb. Embossing omitted		
895	**382**	3p. black, reddish violet, lemon, new blue, carmine-rose, emerald, ultramarine & gold	10	10
		a. Gold (Queen's head) omitted	£350	
		b. Carmine-rose omitted	£1750	
		c. Lemon omitted	60·00	
		d. New blue omitted	†	—
		Ee. Embossing omitted	5·00	
		Ey. Phosphor omitted	1·75	
		Eya. Embossing and phosphor omitted	50·00	
896	**383**	$7\frac{1}{2}$p. black, lilac, lemon, emerald, new blue, rose, green & gold	90	90
		a. Gold (Queen's head) omitted	90·00	
		b. Lilac omitted	£400	
		c. Emerald omitted	£200	
		Ed. Embossing omitted	30·00	
		Ee. Embossing double	30·00	
		Ey. Phosphor omitted	6·00	
		Eya. Embossing and phosphor omitted	20·00	
		Set of 3	1·00	1·00
		First Day Cover		1·50
		Presentation Pack	4·00	

The 3p. is known with reddish violet and embossing omitted, used in Llandudno and with lemon and carmine-rose both omitted used in Falkirk. The $7\frac{1}{2}$p. is known in used condition showing the lemon omitted.

Special First Day of Issue Postmarks

British Post Office Philatelic Bureau, Edinburgh
(Type D, see Introduction) .... 4·00
Bethlehem, Llandeilo, Carms .... 7·00
Canterbury .... 7·00

WHITE CHALK-SURFACED PAPER. From No. 897 all issues, with the exception of Nos. 940/8, were printed on fluorescent white paper, giving a stronger chalk reaction than the original cream paper.

Special First Day of Issue Postmarks

Philatelic Bureau, Edinburgh .... 6·00
London WC .... 7·50

384 Sir James Clark Ross

385 Sir Martin Frobisher

388 Statuette of Tutankhamun

389 19th-century Coastguard

386 Henry Hudson

387 Capt. Scott

390 Ralph Vaughan Williams and Score

(Des Rosalind Dease (3p.), F. Wegner (7½p.), C. Abbott (9p.). Queen's head printed in gold and then embossed (7½p., 9p.))

(Des Marjorie Saynor. Queen's head printed in gold and then embossed)

1972 (16 Feb). **British Polar Explorers.** *Two phosphor bands.* P 14 × 15.
897 384 3p. yellow-brown, indigo, slate-black, flesh,
          lemon, rose, brt blue & gold 10   10
        a. Gold (Queen's head) omitted .... 60·00
        b. Slate-black (hair, etc.) omitted £2250
        c. Lemon omitted ....
       Ed. Embossing omitted .... 25·00
       Ee. Gold (Queen's head) & embossing
            omitted .... 75·00
       Ey. Phosphor omitted ....   1·25
      Eya. Embossing and phosphor omitted ...... 20·00
898 385 5p. salmon, flesh, purple-brown, ochre, black
            & gold 20   20
        a. Gold (Queen's head) omitted .... 90·00
       Eb. Embossing omitted .... 12·00
       Ey. Phosphor omitted ....   7·00
      Eya. Gold and phosphor omitted £110
      Eyb. Embossing and phosphor omitted ......
899 386 7½p. reddish violet, blue, dp slate, yellow-
            brown, buff, black & gold 50   50
        a. Gold (Queen's head) omitted £200
       Ey. Phosphor omitted .... 14·00
900 387 9p. dull blue, ultramarine, black, greenish
            yellow, pale pink, rose-red & gold 90   90
       Ey. Phosphor omitted £275
            Set of 4 .... 1·50   1·50
            First Day Cover ....   2·00
            Presentation Pack .... 4·50
An example of the 3p. is known used on piece with the flesh colour omitted.

1972 (26 Apr). **General Anniversaries.** *Events described on stamps. Two phosphor bands.* P 15 × 14.
901 388 3p. black, grey, gold, dull bistre-brown,
            blackish brown, pale stone & lt brown .. 10   10
902 389 7½p. pale yellow, new blue, slate-blue, violet-
            blue, slate & gold 50   50
       Ea. Embossing omitted ....
       Ey. Phosphor omitted £250
903 390 9p. bistre-brown, black, sage-green, dp slate,
            yellow-ochre, brown & gold 50   50
        a. Gold (Queen's head) omitted £1250
        b. Brown (facial features) omitted £750
        c. Deep slate omitted £7500
       Ed. Embossing omitted ....
       Ey. Phosphor omitted .... 22·00
            Set of 3 .... 1·00   1·00
            First Day Cover ....   1·75
            Presentation Pack .... 4·00

Special First Day of Issue Postmarks

Philatelic Bureau, Edinburgh .... 3·00
London EC .... 4·00

391 St. Andrew's, Greensted-juxta-Ongar, Essex

392 All Saints, Earls Barton, Northants

393 St. Andrew's, Letheringsett, Norfolk

394 St. Andrew's, Helpringham, Lincs

395 St. Mary the Virgin, Huish Episcopi, Somerset

(Des R. Maddox. Queen's head printed in gold and then embossed)

1972 (21 June). **British Architecture. Village Churches.** *Ordinary paper. Two phosphor bands. P* 14 × 15.

904	**391**	3p. violet-blue, black, lt yellow-olive, emerald-green, orange-vermilion & gold	10	10
		a. Gold (Queen's head) omitted	75·00	
		Eb. Embossing omitted	20·00	
		Ey. Phosphor omitted	2·00	
		Eya. Gold (Queen's head) & phosphor omitted	£110	
		Eyb. Embossing & phosphor omitted	10·00	
905	**392**	4p. dp yellow-olive, black, emerald, violet-blue, orange-vermilion and gold	20	20
		a. Gold (Queen's head) omitted	£2000	
		b. Violet-blue omitted	£110	
		Ec. Embossing omitted	6·00	
		Ey. Phosphor omitted ....:......	10·00	
906	**393**	5p. dp emerald, black, royal blue, lt yellow-olive, orange-vermilion & gold	20	25
		a. Gold (Queen's head) omitted	£150	
		Eb. Embossing omitted	25·00	
		Ey. Phosphor omitted	15·00	

907	**394**	7½p. orange-red, black, dp yellow-olive, royal blue, lt emerald & gold	70	80
		Ey. Phosphor omitted	8·00	
908	**395**	9p. new blue, black, emerald-green, dp yellow-olive, orange-vermilion & gold ...	75	90
		Ea. Embossing omitted	12·00	
		Ey. Phosphor omitted	14·00	
		Set of 5	1·75	2·00
		First Day Cover		2·75
		Presentation Pack	5·00	

Nos. 905a and 906a only exist with the phosphor omitted.
An example of the 3p. is known used on piece with the orange-vermilion omitted.

Special First Day of Issue Postmarks

Philatelic Bureau, Edinburgh .... 5·00
Canterbury .... 6·25

"Belgica '72" Souvenir Pack

1972 (24 June). *Comprises Nos.* 894/6 *and* 904/8.
CP908*b* Souvenir Pack .... 8·00
This pack was specially produced for sale at the "Belgica '72" Stamp Exhibition, held in Brussels between 24 June and 9 July. It contains information on British stamps with a religious theme with text in English, French and Flemish, and was put on sale at Philatelic Bureaux in Britain on 26 June.

396 Microphones, 1924–69

387 Horn Loudspeaker

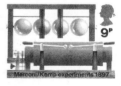

398 T.V. Camera, 1972

399 Oscillator and Spark Transmitter, 1897

(Des D. Gentleman)

1972 (13 Sept). **Broadcasting Anniversaries. 75th Anniv of Marconi and Kemp's Radio Experiments** (9*p*.), **and 50th Anniv of Daily Broadcasting by the B.B.C.** (*others*). *Two phosphor bands. P* 15 × 14.

909	**396**	3p. pale brown, black, grey, greenish yellow & brownish slate	10	10
		a. Greenish yellow (terminals) omitted	£1750	

910	**397**	5p. brownish slate, lake-brown, salmon, lt brown, black & red-brown	15	20
		Ey. Phosphor omitted	2·75	
		Eya. Phosphor on back but omitted on front	30·00	
911	**398**	7½p. lt grey, slate, brownish slate, magenta & black	60	60
		a. Brownish slate (Queen's head) omitted .	†	—
		Ey. Phosphor omitted	5·00	
912	**399**	9p. lemon, brown, brownish slate, dp brownish slate, bluish slate & black	60	60
		a. Brownish slate (Queen's head) omitted .	£1500	
		Ey. Phosphor omitted	10·00	
		Set of 4	1·25	1·25
		First Day Cover		2·00
		Presentation Pack	3·50	

In addition to the generally issued Presentation Pack a further pack exists inscribed "1922–1972". This pack of stamps commemorating the 50th Anniversary of the B.B.C. was specially produced as a memento of the occasion for the B.B.C. staff. It was sent with the good wishes of the Chairman and Board of Governors, the Director-General and Board of Management. The pack contains Nos. 909/11 only (*Price* £35).

No. 911a is only found in first day covers posted from the Philatelic Bureau in Edinburgh.

Special First Day of Issue Postmarks

Philatelic Bureau, Edinburgh .... 4·00
London W1 .... 7·50

400 Angel holding Trumpet   **401** Angel playing Lute

402 Angel playing Harp

(Des Sally Stiff. Photo and embossing)

1972 (18 Oct). **Christmas.** *One centre phosphor band (2½p.) or two phosphor bands (others).* P 14 × 15.

913	**400**	2½p. cerise, pale reddish brown, yellow-orange, orange-vermilion, lilac, gold, red-brown & dp grey	10	15
		a. Gold omitted	£250	
		Eb. Embossing omitted	7·00	
		c. Dp grey omitted		
		Ey. Phosphor omitted	5·00	
914	**401**	3p. ultramarine, lavender, lt turquoise-blue, brt green, gold, red-brown & bluish violet	10	15
		a. Red-brown omitted	£500	
		b. Brt green omitted	70·00	
		c. Bluish violet omitted	75·00	
		Ed. Embossing omitted	3·50	
		Ey. Phosphor omitted	2·50	
		Eya. Embossing and phosphor omitted	6·00	
915	**402**	7½p. dp brown, pale lilac, lt cinnamon, ochre, gold, red-brown & blackish violet	90	80
		a. Ochre omitted	55·00	
		Eb. Embossing omitted	7·50	
		Ey. Phosphor omitted	5·00	
		Eya. Embossing and phosphor omitted	16·00	
		Set of 3	1·00	1·00
		First Day Cover		1·25
		Presentation Pack	2·75	

The gold printing on the 3p. is from two cylinders: 1E and 1F. Examples have been seen with the gold of the 1F cylinder omitted, but these are difficult to detect on single stamps.

Special First Day of Issue Postmarks

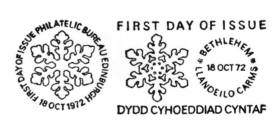

Philatelic Bureau, Edinburgh .... 3·00
Bethlehem, Llandeilo, Carms .... 5·00

403 Queen Elizabeth and Duke of Edinburgh   **404** "Europe"

(Des J. Matthews from photo by N. Parkinson)

1972 (20 Nov). **Royal Silver Wedding.** *"All-over" phosphor* (3p.) *or without phosphor* (20p.) *P* 14 × 15.

I. "REMBRANDT" Machine

916	**403**	3p. brownish black, dp blue & silver	20	20
		a. Silver omitted	£300	
917		20p. brownish black, reddish purple & silver .	80	80

II. "JUMELLE" Machine

918	**403**	3p. brownish black, dp blue & silver	20	25
		Set of 2	1·00	1·00
		Gutter Pair (No. 918)	1·00	
		Traffic Light Gutter Pair	15·00	
		First Day Cover		1·25
		Presentation Pack	2·25	
		Presentation Pack (Japanese)	3·50	
		Souvenir Book	3·00	

The souvenir book is a twelve-page booklet containing photographs of the Royal Wedding and other historic events of the royal family and accompanying information.

The 3p. "JUMELLE" has a lighter shade of the brownish black than the 3p. "REMBRANDT". It also has the brown cylinders less deeply etched, which can be distinguished in the Duke's face which is slightly lighter, and in the Queen's hair where the highlights are sharper.

3p. "REMBRANDT". Cyls. 3A–1B–11C no dot. Sheets of 100 (10 x 10).
3p. "JUMELLE". Cyls. 1A–1B–3C dot and no dot. Sheets of 100 (two panes 5 x 10, separated by gutter margin).

Special First Day of Issue Postmarks

Philatelic Bureau, Edinburgh	....	2·25
Windsor, Berks	....	5·00

Collectors Pack 1972

1972 (20 Nov). *Comprises Nos. 897/917.*

CP918a	Collectors Pack	28·00

(Des P. Murdoch)

1973 (3 Jan). **Britain's Entry into European Communities.** *Two phosphor bands. P* 14 × 15.

919	**404**	3p. dull orange, brt rose-red, ultramarine, lt lilac & black	10	10
920		5p. new blue, brt rose-red, ultramarine, cobalt-blue & black	25	35
		a. Pair. Nos. 920/1	1·10	1·25
921		5p. lt emerald-green, brt rose-red, ultramarine, cobalt-blue & black	25	35
		Set of 3	1·50	70
		First Day Cover		1·50
		Presentation Pack	2·25	

Nos. 920/1 were printed horizontally *se-tenant* throughout the sheet.

Special First Day of Issue Postmark

Philatelic Bureau, Edinburgh	....	3·50

405 Oak Tree

(Des D. Gentleman)

1973 (28 Feb). **Tree Planting Year. British Trees (1st issue).** *Two phosphor bands. P* 15 × 14.

922	**405**	9p. brownish black, apple-green, dp olive, sepia, blackish green & brownish grey ..	50	50
		a. Brownish black (value & inscr) omitted .	£400	
		b. Brownish grey (Queen's head) omitted ..	£250	
		Ey. Phosphor omitted	80·00	
		First Day Cover		1·00
		Presentation Pack	2·25	

See also No. 949.

Special First Day of Issue Postmark

Philatelic Bureau, Edinburgh	....	2·75

CHALK-SURFACED PAPER. The following issues are printed on chalk-surfaced paper but where "all-over" phosphor has been applied there is no chalk reaction except in the sheet margins outside the phosphor area.

406 David Livingstone   **407** H. M. Stanley

T **406/7** were printed together, horizontally *se-tenant* within the sheet

408 Sir Francis Drake   **409** Walter Raleigh

410 Charles Sturt

(Des Marjorie Saynor. Queen's head printed in gold and then embossed)

1973 (18 Apr).   **British Explorers.** *"All-over"* phosphor. P 14 × 15.

923	**406**	3p.	orange-yellow, lt orange-brown, grey-black, lt turquoise-blue, turquoise-blue & gold	25	20
		a.	Pair. Nos. 923/4	1·00	1·75
		b.	Gold (Queen's head) omitted	32·00	
		c.	Turquoise-blue (background & inscr) omitted	£350	
		d.	Lt orange-brown omitted	£300	
		Ee.	Embossing omitted	20·00	
924	**407**	3p.	orange-yellow, lt orange-brown, grey-black, lt turquoise-blue, turquoise-blue & gold	25	20
		b.	Gold (Queen's head) omitted	32·00	
		c.	Turquoise-blue (background & inscr) omitted	£350	
		d.	Lt orange-brown omitted	£300	
		Ee.	Embossing omitted	20·00	

925	**408**	5p.	lt flesh, chrome-yellow, orange-yellow, sepia, brownish grey, grey-black, violet-blue & gold	20	30
		a.	Gold (Queen's head) omitted	90·00	
		b.	Grey-black omitted	£500	
		c.	Sepia omitted	£350	
		Ed.	Embossing omitted	6·50	
926	**409**	7½p.	lt flesh, reddish brown, sepia, ultramarine, grey-black, brt lilac & gold	20	30
		a.	Gold (Queen's head) omitted	£1750	
		b.	Ultramarine (eyes) omitted	£1400	
927	**410**	9p.	flesh, pale stone, grey-blue, grey-black, brown-grey, Venetian red, brown-red & gold	25	40
		a.	Gold (Queen's head) omitted	90·00	
		b.	Brown-grey printing double ....*from*	£800	
		c.	Grey-black omitted	£1000	
		Ed.	Embossing omitted	22·00	
			Set of 5	1·50	1·25
			First Day Cover		2·00
			Presentation Pack	3·50	

Caution is needed when buying missing gold heads in this issue as they can be removed by using a hard eraser, etc., but this invariably affects the "all-over" phosphor. Genuine examples have the phosphor intact. Used examples off cover cannot be distinguished as much of the phosphor is lost in the course of floating.

In the 5p. value the missing grey-black affects the doublet, which appears as brownish grey, and the lace ruff, which is entirely missing. The missing sepia affects only Drake's hair, which appears much lighter.

The double printing of the brown-grey (cylinder 1F) on the 9p., is a most unusual type of error to occur in a multicoloured photogravure issue. Two sheets are known and it is believed that they stuck to the cylinder and went through a second time. This would result in the following two sheets missing the colour but at the time of going to press this error has not been reported. The second print is slightly askew and more prominent in the top half of the sheets. Examples from the upper part of the sheet showing a clear double impression of the facial features are worth a substantial premium over the price quoted.

Special First Day of Issue Postmark

Philatelic Bureau, Edinburgh .... 4·75

First Day of Issue handstamps were provided at Blantyre, Glasgow, and Denbigh for this issue.

411   **412**

413

416 "Nelly O'Brien"
(Reynolds)

417 "Rev. R. Walker
(The Skater)" (Raeburn)

(T **411**/13 show sketches of W.G. Grace by Harry Furniss)

(Des S. Rose. Queen's head printed in gold and then embossed)

(Des E. Ripley. Queen's head printed in gold and then embossed)

1973 (16 May). **County Cricket 1873–1973.** *"All-over" phosphor.* P 14 × 15.

928	**411**	3p. black, ochre & gold	10	10
		a. Gold (Queen's head) omitted	£1750	
		Eb. Embossing omitted	7·00	
929	**412**	7½p. black, light sage-green & gold	70	70
		Eb. Embossing omitted	16·00	
930	**413**	9p. black, cobalt & gold	90	90
		Eb. Embossing omitted	50·00	
		Set of 3	1·50	1·50
		First Day Cover		2·00
		Presentation Pack	3·50	
		Souvenir Book	6·25	
		P.H.Q. Card (No. 928)	60·00	£140

The souvenir book is a 24-page illustrated booklet containing a history of County Cricket with text by John Arlott.

The P.H.Q. card did not become available until mid-July. The used price quoted is for an example used in July or August 1973.

1973 (4 July). **British Paintings. 250th Birth Anniv of Sir Joshua Reynolds and 150th Death Anniv of Sir Henry Raeburn.** *"All-over" phosphor.* P 14 × 15.

931	**414**	3p. rose, new blue, jet-black, magenta, greenish yellow, black, ochre & gold	10	10
		a. Gold (Queen's head) omitted	60·00	
		Ec. Gold (Queen's head) & embossing omitted	65·00	
932	**415**	5p. cinnamon, greenish yellow, new blue, lt magenta, black, yellow-olive & gold	20	25
		a. Gold (Queen's head) omitted	75·00	
		b. Greenish yellow omitted	£350	
		Ec. Embossing omitted	15·00	
933	**416**	7½p. greenish yellow, new blue, lt magenta, black, cinnamon & gold	45	40
		a. Gold (Queen's head) omitted	75·00	
		b. Cinnamon omitted	£3500	
		Ec. Embossing omitted	12·00	
934	**417**	9p. brownish rose, black, dull rose, pale yellow, brownish grey, pale blue & gold	50	50
		b. Brownish rose omitted	30·00	
		Ec. Embossing omitted	£100	
		Set of 4	1·10	1·10
		First Day Cover		1·75
		Presentation Pack	2·75	

Special First Day of Issue Postmarks

Philatelic Bureau, Edinburgh .... 4·00
Lords, London NW .... 6·50

Special First Day of Issue Postmark

Philatelic Bureau, Edinburgh .... 4·00

414 "Self-portrait"
(Reynolds)

415 "Self-portrait"
(Raeburn)

418 Court Masque Costumes

419 St. Paul's Church, Covent Garden

420 Prince's Lodging, Newmarket **421** Court Masque Stage Scene

T **418/19** and T **420/1** were printed horizontally *se-tenant* within the sheet.

(Des Rosalind Dease. Litho and typo B.W.)

1973 (15 Aug). **400th Birth Anniv of Inigo Jones (architect and designer).** *"All-over"* phosphor. *P* 15 × 14.

935	**418**	3p. dp mauve, black & gold	....	10	15
		a. Pair. Nos. 935/6	....	35	40
		Eb. 9 mm. phosphor band*	....	12·00	
936	**419**	3p. dp brown, black & gold	....	10	15
937	**420**	5p. blue, black & gold	....	40	45
		a. Pair. Nos. 937/8	....	1·50	1·50
		Eb. 9 mm. phosphor band*	....	15·00	
938	**421**	5p. grey-olive, black & gold	....	40	45
		Set of 4	....	1·60	1·10
		First Day Cover	....		1·50
		Presentation Pack	....	3·50	
		P.H.Q. Card (No. 936)	....	£140	60·00

*On part of the printings for both values the "all-over" phosphor band missed the first vertical row and a 9 mm. phosphor band was applied to correct this.

Special First Day of Issue Postmark

Philatelic Bureau, Edinburgh .... 3·50

422 Palace of Westminster **423** Palace of Westminster
seen from Whitehall seen from Millbank

(Des R. Downer. Recess and typo B.W.)

1973 (12 Sept). **19th Commonwealth Parliamentary Conference.** *"All-over"* phosphor. *P* 15 × 14.

939	**422**	8p. black, brownish grey & stone	....	50	60
940	**423**	10p. gold & black	....	50	40
		Set of 2	....	1·00	1·00
		First Day Cover	....		1·25
		Presentation Pack	....	2·00	
		Souvenir Book	....	5·00	
		P.H.Q. Card (No. 939)	....	45·00	£100

The souvenir book is a twelve-page booklet containing a history of the Palace of Westminster.

Special First Day of Issue Postmark

Philatelic Bureau, Edinburgh .... 2·50

424 Princess Anne and Capt. Mark Phillips

(Des C. Clements and E. Hughes from photo by Lord Litchfield)

1973 (14 Nov). **Royal Wedding.** *"All-over"* phosphor. *P* 15 × 14.

941	**424**	3½p. dull violet & silver	....	10	10
		a. Imperf (horiz pair)	....	£900	
942		20p. dp brown & silver	....	90	90
		a. Silver omitted	....	£900	
		Set of 2	....	1·00	1·00
		Set of 2 Gutter Pairs	....	4·00	
		Set of 2 Traffic Light Gutter Pairs	....	90·00	
		First Day Cover	....		1·25
		Presentation Pack	....	2·00	
		P.H.Q. Card (No. 941)	....	8·00	22·00

Special First Day of Issue Postmarks

Philatelic Bureau, Edinburgh .... 2·50
Westminster Abbey, London SW1 .... 4·75
Windsor, Berks .... 5·00

425   426

427   428

429

T **425/9** depict the carol "Good King Wenceslas" and were printed horizontally *se-tenant* within the sheet.

430 Good King Wenceslas, the Page and Peasant

(Des D. Gentleman)

1973 (28 Nov). **Christmas.** *One centre phosphor band* (3p.) *or "all-over" phosphor* ($3\frac{1}{2}$p.). *P* 15 × 14.

943	**425**	3p. grey-black, blue, brownish grey, lt brown, brt rose-red, turquoise-green, salmon-pink & gold	15	15
		a. Strip of 5. Nos. 943/7	2·75	2·50
		b. Imperf (horiz strip of 5)	£1000	
		Eg. Gum arabic	20	
		Ega. Strip of 5. Nos. 943Eg/7Eg	2·75	
		Egb. Imperf (strip of 5. Nos. 943Eg/7Eg)		
944	**426**	3p. grey-black, violet-blue, slate, brown, rose-red, rosy mauve, turquoise-green, salmon-pink & gold	15	15
		a. Rosy mauve omitted	£625	
		Eg. Gum arabic	20	
945	**427**	3p. grey-black, violet-blue, slate, brown, rose-red, rosy mauve, turquoise-green, salmon-pink & gold	15	15
		a. Rosy mauve omitted	£625	
		Eg. Gum arabic	20	

946	**428**	3p. grey-black, violet-blue, slate, brown, rose-red, rosy mauve, turquoise-green, salmon-pink & gold	15	15
		a. Rosy mauve omitted	£625	
		Eg. Gum arabic	20	
947	**429**	3p. grey-black, violet-blue, slate, brown, rose-red, rosy mauve, turquoise-green, salmon-pink & gold	15	15
		a. Rosy mauve omitted	£625	
		Eg. Gum arabic	20	
948	**430**	$3\frac{1}{2}$p. salmon-pink, grey-black, red-brown, blue, turquoise-green, brt rose-red, rosy mauve, lavender-grey & gold	15	15
		a. Imperf (pair)	£450	
		b. Grey-black (value, inscr, etc.) omitted	75·00	
		c. Salmon-pink omitted	70·00	
		d. Blue (leg, robes) omitted	£130	
		e. Rosy mauve (robe at right) omitted	80·00	
		f. Blue and rosy mauve omitted	£250	
		g. Brt rose-red (King's robe) omitted	75·00	
		h. Red-brown (logs, basket, etc.) omitted		
		i. Turquoise-green (leg, robe, etc.) omitted	£2000	—
		j. Gold (background) omitted	†	
		Set of 6	2·75	80
		First Day Cover		2·00
		Presentation Pack	3·25	

Examples of No. 948j are only known used on covers from Gloucester. The $3\frac{1}{2}$p. has also been seen with the lavender-grey omitted used on piece.

The 3p. and $3\frac{1}{2}$p. are normally with PVA gum with added dextrin, but the $3\frac{1}{2}$p. also exists with normal PVA gum.

Special First Day of Issue Postmarks

Philatelic Bureau, Edinburgh	2·25
Bethlehem, Llandeilo, Carms	4·50

Collectors Pack 1973

1973 (28 Nov). *Comprises Nos. 919/48.*

CP948*k*	Collectors Pack	26·00

431 Horse Chestnut

(Des D. Gentleman)

1974 (27 Feb). **British Trees (2nd issue).** *"All-over" phosphor.* P 15 × 14.

949	431	10p. lt emerald, brt green, greenish yellow, brown-olive, black & brownish grey		50	50
		Gutter Pair		3·00	
		Traffic Light Gutter Pair		55·00	
		First Day Cover			1·00
		Presentation Pack		2·25	
		P.H.Q. Card	£140		60·00

Special First Day of Issue Postmark

Philatelic Bureau, Edinburgh .... 2·50

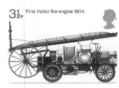

432 First Motor Fire-engine, 1904

433 Prize-winning Fire-engine, 1863

434 First Steam Fire-engine, 1830

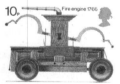

435 Fire-engine, 1766

(Des D. Gentleman)

1974 (24 Apr). **Bicentenary of the Fire Prevention (Metropolis) Act.** *"All-over" phosphor.* P 15 × 14.

950	432	3½p. grey-black, orange-yellow, greenish yellow, dull rose, ochre & grey		10	10
		a. Imperf (pair)	£850		
951	433	5½p. greenish yellow, dp rosy magenta, orange-yellow, lt emerald, grey-black & grey		25	25
952	434	8p. greenish yellow, lt blue-green, lt greenish blue, lt chestnut, grey-black & grey		35	35
953	435	10p. grey-black, pale reddish brown, lt brown, orange-yellow & grey		40	40
		Set of 4		1·00	1·10
		Set of 4 Gutter Pairs		4·00	
		Set of 4 Traffic Light Gutter Pairs		55·00	
		First Day Cover			2·50
		Presentation Pack		2·50	
		P.H.Q. Card (No. 950)	£150		50·00

The 3½p. exists with ordinary PVA gum.

Special First Day of Issue Postmark

Philatelic Bureau, Edinburgh .... 3·75

436 P & O Packet, *Peninsular,* 1888

437 Farman Biplane, 1911

438 Airmail-blue Van and Postbox, 1930

439 Imperial Airways "C" Class Flying Boat, 1937

(Des Rosalind Dease)

1974 (12 June). **Centenary of Universal Postal Union.** *"All-over" phosphor.* P 15 × 14.

954	436	3½p. dp brownish grey, brt mauve, grey-black & gold		10	10
955	437	5½p. pale orange, lt emerald, grey-black & gold		20	25
956	438	8p. cobalt, brown, grey-black & gold		30	35
957	439	10p. dp brownish grey, orange, grey-black & gold		50	40
		Set of 4		1·00	1·00
		Set of 4 Gutter Pairs		4·00	
		Set of 4 Traffic Light Gutter Pairs	40·00		
		First Day Cover			1·25
		Presentation Pack		2·00	

Special First Day of Issue Postmark

Philatelic Bureau, Edinburgh .... 3·25

440 Robert the Bruce

441 Owain Glyndwr

442 Henry the Fifth

443 The Black Prince

(Des F. Wegner)

1974 (10 July). **Medieval Warriors.** *"All-over"* phosphor. *P* 15 × 14.

958	**440**	4½p.	greenish yellow, vermilion, slate-blue, red-brown, reddish brown, lilac-grey & gold	10	10
959	**441**	5½p.	lemon, vermilion, slate-blue, red-brown, reddish brown, olive-drab & gold	20	20
960	**442**	8p.	dp grey, vermilion, greenish yellow, new blue, red-brown, dp cinnamon & gold	40	40
961	**443**	10p.	vermilion, greenish yellow, new blue, red-brown, reddish brown, lt blue & gold	40	40

Set of 4	1·00	1·00
Set of 4 Gutter Pairs	6·00	
Set of 4 Traffic Light Gutter Pairs	65·00	
First Day Cover		2·50
Presentation Pack	3·50	
P.H.Q. Cards (set of 4)	30·00	25·00

Special First Day of Issue Postmark

Philatelic Bureau, Edinburgh . . . . 3·50

444 Churchill in Royal Yacht Squadron Uniform

445 Prime Minister, 1940

446 Secretary for War and Air, 1919

447 War Correspondent, South Africa, 1899

(Des C. Clements and E. Hughes)

1974 (9 Oct). **Birth Centenary of Sir Winston Churchill.** *"All-over"* phosphor. *P* 14 × 15.

962	**444**	4½p.	Prussian blue, pale turquoise-green & silver	15	15
963	**445**	5½p.	sepia, brownish grey & silver	20	25
964	**446**	8p.	crimson, lt claret & silver	50	50
965	**447**	10p.	lt brown, stone & silver	55	50

Set of 4	1·25	1·25
Set of 4 Gutter Pairs	4·00	
Set of 4 Traffic Light Gutter Pairs	40·00	
First Day Cover		1·60
Presentation Pack	1·75	
Souvenir Book	2·50	
P.H.Q. Card (No. 963)	6·00	12·00

The souvenir book consists of an illustrated folder containing a biography of Sir Winston.

Nos. 962/5 come with PVA gum containing added dextrin, but the 8p. also exists with normal PVA.

Special First Day of Issue Postmarks

Philatelic Bureau, Edinburgh	3·50
Blenheim, Woodstock, Oxford	4·50
House of Commons, London SW	4·50

448 "Adoration of the Magi"
(York Minster, *circa* 1355)

449 "The Nativity" (St. Helen's
Church, Norwich, *circa* 1480)

450 "Virgin and Child" (Ottery
St. Mary Church, *circa* 1350)

451 "Virgin and Child"
(Worcester Cathedral, *circa* 1224)

(Des Peter Hatch Partnership)

1974 (27 Nov). **Christmas. Church Roof Bosses.** *One phosphor band*
($3\frac{1}{2}$p.) *or "all-over" phosphor (others). P 15 × 14.*

966	**448**	$3\frac{1}{2}$p. gold, lt new blue, lt brown, grey-black & lt stone	10	10
		a. Lt stone (background shading) omitted .	£8000	
		Ey. Phosphor omitted	7·00	
967	**449**	$4\frac{1}{2}$p. gold, yellow-orange, rose-red, lt brown, grey-black & lt new blue	10	10
968	**450**	8p. blue, gold, lt brown, rose-red, dull green & grey-black	45	45
969	**451**	10p. gold, dull rose, grey-black, lt new blue, pale cinnamon & lt brown	50	50
		Set of 4	1·00	1·00
		Set of 4 Gutter Pairs	4·00	
		Set of 4 Traffic Light Gutter Pairs	40·00	
		First Day Cover		1·50
		Presentation Pack	1·75	

The phosphor band on the $3\frac{1}{2}$p. was first applied down the centre of the stamp but during the printing this was deliberately placed to the right between the roof boss and the value; however, intermediate positions, due to shifts, are known.

Two used examples of the $3\frac{1}{2}$p. have been reported with the light brown colour omitted.

Special First Day of Issue Postmarks

Philatelic Bureau, Edinburgh	2·75
Bethlehem, Llandeilo, Carms	5·00

Collectors Pack 1974

1974 (27 Nov). *Comprises Nos. 949/69.*

CP969a	Collectors Pack	8·50

452 Invalid in Wheelchair

(Des P. Sharland)

1975 (22 Jan). **Health and Handicap Funds.** *"All-over" phosphor. P 15 × 14.*

970	**452**	$4\frac{1}{2}$p. + $1\frac{1}{2}$p. azure & grey-blue	25	25
		Gutter Pair	50	
		Traffic Light Gutter Pair	1·00	
		First Day Cover		1·00

Special First Day of Issue Postmark

Philatelic Bureau, Edinburgh	2·25

453 "Peace—Burial at Sea"

454 "Snowstorm—Steamer off a
Harbour's Mouth"

455 "The Arsenal, Venice"

456 "St. Laurent"

(Des S. Rose)

1975 (19 Feb). **Birth Bicentenary of J. M. W. Turner (painter).** *"All-over" phosphor. P 15 × 14.*

971	**453**	$4\frac{1}{2}$p. grey-black, salmon, stone, blue & grey .	10	10
972	**454**	$5\frac{1}{2}$p. cobalt, greenish yellow, lt yellow-brown, grey-black & rose	15	15
973	**455**	8p. pale yellow-orange, greenish yellow, rose, cobalt & grey-black	40	40

974 **456** 10p. dp blue, lt yellow-ochre, lt brown, dp
cobalt & grey-black 45   45
    Set of 4 .... 1·00   1·00
    Set of 4 Gutter Pairs .... 2·50
    Set of 4 Traffic Light Gutter Pairs .... 5·00
    First Day Cover ....   1·50
    Presentation Pack .... 2·50
    P.H.Q. Card (No. 972) .... 35·00   11·00

Special First Day of Issue Postmarks

Philatelic Bureau, Edinburgh .... 3·25
London WC .... 4·50

457 Charlotte Square, Edinburgh   **458** The Rows, Chester

T **457/8** were printed horizontally *se-tenant* within the sheet.

459 Royal Observatory,   **460** St. George's Chapel,
Greenwich   Windsor

461 National Theatre, London

(Des P. Gauld)

1975 (23 Apr). **European Architectural Heritage Year.** *"All-over"*
phosphor. P 15 × 14.
975 **457** 7p. greenish yellow, brt orange, grey-black,
red-brown, new blue, lavender & gold .. 30   30
    a. Pair. Nos. 975/6 80   90
976 **458** 7p. grey-black, greenish yellow, new blue,
brt orange, red-brown & gold 30   30

977 **459** 8p. magenta, dp slate, pale magenta, lt
yellow-olive, grey-black & gold 20   25
978 **460** 10p. bistre-brown, greenish yellow, dp slate,
emerald-green, grey-black & gold 20   25
979 **461** 12p. grey-black, new blue, pale magenta &
gold 20   35
    Set of 5 .... 1·25   1·25
    Set of 5 Gutter Pairs .... 4·00
    Set of 5 Traffic Light Gutter Pairs .... 22·00
    First Day Cover ....   2·00
    Presentation Pack .... 3·00
    P.H.Q. Cards (Nos. 975/7) .... 8·00   11·00

Special First Day of Issue Postmark

Philatelic Bureau, Edinburgh .... 4·00

462 Sailing Dinghies   **463** Racing Keel Yachts

464 Cruising Yachts   **465** Multihulls

(Des A. Restall. Recess and photo)

1975 (11 June). **Sailing.** *"All-over" phosphor. P* 15 × 14.
980 **462** 7p. black, bluish violet, scarlet, orange-
vermilion, orange & gold 20   20
981 **463** 8p. black, orange-vermilion, orange, lavender, brt mauve, brt blue, dp ultramarine
& gold 30   30
    a. Black omitted .... 55·00
    b. Gold (Queen's head) omitted ....
982 **464** 10p. black, orange, bluish emerald, lt olive-
drab, chocolate & gold 30   30
983 **465** 12p. black, ultramarine, turquoise-blue, rose,
grey, steel-blue & gold 35   35
    Set of 4 .... 1·00   1·00
    Set of 4 Gutter Pairs .... 2·50
    Set of 4 Traffic Light Gutter Pairs .... 20·00
    First Day Cover ....   1·50
    Presentation Pack .... 1·50
    P.H.Q. Card (No. 981) .... 4·50   10·00
On No. 981a the recess-printed black colour is completely omitted.

Special First Day of Issue Postmark

Philatelic Bureau, Edinburgh .... 2·50
A First Day of Issue handstamp was provided at Weymouth for this issue.

Special First Day of Issue Postmarks

466 Stephenson's *Locomotion*, 1825

467 *Abbotsford*, 1876

Philatelic Bureau, Edinburgh .... 3·50
Darlington, Co. Durham .... 5·00
Shildon, Co. Durham .... 5·00
Stockton-on-Tees, Cleveland .... 5·00

1825 Stockton and Darlington Railway

1876 North British Railway Drummond

470 Palace of Westminster

1923 Great Western Railway Castle Class

1975 British Rail Inter-City Service HST

468 *Caerphilly Castle*, 1923

469 High Speed Train, 1975

(Des B. Craker)

1975 (13 Aug). **150th Anniv of Public Railways.** "All-over" phosphor. P 15 × 14.

984	**466**	7p.	red-brown, grey-black, greenish yellow, grey & silver	20	20
985	**467**	8p.	brown, orange-yellow, vermilion, grey-black, grey & silver	25	25
986	**468**	10p.	emerald-green, grey-black, yellow-orange, vermilion, grey & silver	30	30
987	**469**	12p.	grey-black, pale lemon, vermilion, blue, grey & silver	35	35
			Set of 4	1·00	1·00
			Set of 4 Gutter Pairs	3·00	
			Set of 4 Traffic Light Gutter Pairs	9·00	
			First Day Cover		2·50
			Presentation Pack	2·25	
			Souvenir Book	3·00	
			P.H.Q. Cards (set of 4)	65·00	25·00

The souvenir book is an eight-page booklet containing a history of the railways.

(Des R. Downer)

1975 (3 Sept). **62nd Inter-Parliamentary Union Conference.** "All-over" phosphor. P 15 × 14.

988	**470**	12p.	lt new blue, black, brownish grey & gold	50	50
			Gutter Pair	1·00	
			Traffic Light Gutter Pair	2·00	
			First Day Cover		1·00
			Presentation Pack	1·25	

Special First Day of Issue Postmark

Philatelic Bureau, Edinburgh .... 1·75

GIBBONS STAMP MONTHLY
– finest and most informative magazine for all collectors. Obtainable from your newsagent or by postal subscription – details on request.

471 Emma and Mr. Woodhouse (*Emma*)

472 Catherine Morland (*Northanger Abbey*)

473 Mr. Darcy (*Pride and Prejudice*)

474 Mary and Henry Crawford (*Mansfield Park*)

(Des Barbara Brown)

1975 (22 Oct). **Birth Bicentenary of Jane Austen (novelist).** *"All-over"* phosphor. P 14 × 15.

989	471	8½p.	blue, slate, rose-red, lt yellow, dull green, grey-black & gold	20	20
990	472	10p.	slate, brt magenta, grey, lt yellow, grey-black & gold	25	25
991	473	11p.	dull blue, pink, olive-sepia, slate, pale greenish yellow, grey-black & gold	30	30
992	474	13p.	brt magenta, lt new blue, slate, buff, dull blue-green, grey-black & gold	35	35
			Set of 4	1·00	1·00
			Set of 4 Gutter Pairs	2·50	
			Set of 4 Traffic Light Gutter Pairs	7·00	
			First Day Cover		1·25
			Presentation Pack	2·00	
			P.H.Q. Cards (set of 4)	16·00	15·00

Special First Day of Issue Postmark

Philatelic Bureau, Edinburgh	2·50
Steventon, Basingstoke, Hants	3·00

475 Angels with Harp and Lute   **476** Angel with Mandolin

477 Angel with Horn   **478** Angel with Trumpet

(Des R. Downer)

1975 (26 Nov). **Christmas.** *One phosphor band (6½p.), phosphor-inked background (8½p.), "all-over" phosphor (others).* P 15 × 14.

993	475	6½p.	bluish violet, brt reddish violet, light lavender & gold	20	15
994	476	8½p.	turquoise-green, brt emerald-green, slate, lt turquoise-green & gold	20	20
995	477	11p.	vermilion, cerise, pink & gold	30	35
996	478	13p.	drab, brown, brt orange, buff & gold ...	40	40
			Set of 4	1·00	1·00
			Set of 4 Gutter Pairs	2·50	
			Set of 4 Traffic Light Gutter Pairs	7·00	
			First Day Cover		1·25
			Presentation Pack	2·00	

The 6½p. exists with both ordinary PVA gum and PVA containing added dextrin.

Special First Day of Issue Postmarks

Philatelic Bureau, Edinburgh	2·25
Bethlehem, Llandeilo, Dyfed	3·25

Collectors Pack 1975

1975 (26 Nov). *Comprises Nos. 970/96.*

CP996a	Collectors Pack	7·50

479 Housewife   **480** Policeman

481 District Nurse   **482** Industrialist

(Des P. Sharland)

1976 (10 Mar). **Telephone Centenary.** *"All-over" phosphor.* P 15 × 14.

997	479	8½p.	greenish blue, dp rose, black & blue ...	20	20
		a.	Dp rose (vase and picture frame) omitted	£2000	
998	480	10p.	greenish blue, black & yellow-olive	25	25
999	481	11p.	greenish blue, dp rose, black & brt mauve	30	30
1000	482	13p.	olive-brown, dp rose, black & orange-red	35	35
			Set of 4	1·00	1·00
			Set of 4 Gutter Pairs	2·50	
			Set of 4 Traffic Light Gutter Pairs	7·00	
			First Day Cover		1·25
			Presentation Pack	2·00	

Special First Day of Issue Postmark

Philatelic Bureau, Edinburgh .... 2·50

483 Hewing Coal   **484** Machinery (Robert Owen)
(Thomas Hepburn)

485 Chimney Cleaning   **486** Hands clutching Prison Bars
(Lord Shaftesbury)   (Elizabeth Fry)

(Des D. Gentleman)

1976 (28 Apr). **Social Reformers.** *"All-over" phosphor.* P 15 × 14.

1001	483	8½p.	lavender-grey, grey-black, black & slate-grey	20	20
1002	484	10p.	lavender-grey, grey-black, grey & slate-violet	25	25
1003	485	11p.	black, slate-grey & drab	30	30
1004	486	13p.	slate-grey, black & dp dull green	35	35
			Set of 4	1·00	1·00
			Set of 4 Gutter Pairs	2·50	
			Set of 4 Traffic Light Gutter Pairs	7·00	
			First Day Cover		1·25
			Presentation Pack	2·00	
			P.H.Q. Card (No. 1001)	5·00	7·50

Special First Day of Issue Postmark

Philatelic Bureau, Edinburgh .... 2·50

487 Benjamin Franklin
(bust by Jean-Jacques Caffieri)

(Des P. Sharland)

1976 (2 June). **Bicentenary of American Revolution.** *"All-over" phosphor.* P 14 × 15.

1005	487	11p.	pale bistre, slate-violet, pale blue-green, black & gold	50	50
			Gutter Pair	1·00	
			Traffic Light Gutter Pair	2·00	
			First Day Cover		1·00
			Presentation Pack	1·25	
			P.H.Q. Card	2·50	8·50

Special First Day of Issue Postmark

Philatelic Bureau, Edinburgh .... 2·00

488 "Elizabeth of Glamis"

489 "Grandpa Dickson"

492 Archdruid

493 Morris Dancing

490 "Rosa Mundi"

491 "Sweet Briar"

494 Scots Piper

495 Welsh Harpist

(Des Kristin Rosenberg)

1976 (30 June). **Centenary of Royal National Rose Society.** *"All-over"*
phosphor. P 14 × 15.

1006	488	8½p. brt rose-red, greenish yellow, emerald, grey-black & gold	20	20
1007	489	10p. greenish yellow, brt green, reddish brown, grey-black & gold	30	30
1008	490	11p. brt magenta, greenish yellow, emerald, grey-blue, grey-black & gold	45	50
1009	491	13p. rose-pink, lake-brown, yellow-green, pale greenish yellow, grey-black & gold	45	40
		a. Value omitted*	£20000	
		Set of 4	1·25	1·25
		Set of 4 Gutter Pairs	2·50	
		Set of 4 Traffic Light Gutter Pairs	8·00	
		First Day Cover		1·75
		Presentation Pack	2·25	
		P.H.Q. Cards (set of 4)	26·00	14·00

*During repairs to the cylinder the face value on R.1/9 was
temporarily covered with copper. This covering was inadvertently
left in place during printing, but the error was discovered before issue
and most examples were removed from the sheets. Two mint and one
used examples have so far been reported, but only one of the mint
remains in private hands.

Special First Day of Issue Postmark

Philatelic Bureau, Edinburgh .... 2·50

(Des Marjorie Saynor)

1976 (4 Aug). **British Cultural Traditions.** *"All-over" phosphor. P* 14 × 15.

1010	492	8½p. yellow, sepia, brt rose, dull ultramarine, black & gold	20	20
1011	493	10p. dull ultramarine, brt rose-red, sepia, greenish yellow, black & gold	25	25
1012	494	11p. bluish green, yellow-brown, yellow-orange, black, brt rose-red & gold	30	30
1013	495	13p. dull violet-blue, yellow-orange, yellow, black, bluish green & gold	35	35
		Set of 4	1·00	1·00
		Set of 4 Gutter Pairs	2·50	
		Set of 4 Traffic Light Gutter Pairs	8·50	
		First Day Cover		1·25
		Presentation Pack	2·00	
		P.H.Q. Cards (set of 4)	18·00	10·00

The 8½p. and 13p. commemorate the 800th anniversary of the Royal
National Eisteddfod.

Special First Day of Issue Postmarks

Philatelic Bureau, Edinburgh .... 2·50
Cardigan, Dyfed .... 3·50

496 Woodcut from
The Canterbury Tales

497 Extract from
The Tretyse of Love

498 Woodcut from
The Game and Playe of Chesse

499 Early Printing Press

(Des R. Gay. Queen's head printed in gold and then embossed)

1976 (29 Sept). **500th Anniv of British Printing.** *"All-over" phosphor.*
P 14 × 15.

1014	**496**	8½p. black, lt new blue & gold	20	20
1015	**497**	10p. black, olive-green & gold	25	25
1016	**498**	11p. black, brownish grey & gold	30	30
1017	**499**	13p. chocolate, pale ochre & gold	35	35
		Set of 4	1·00	1·00
		Set of 4 Gutter Pairs	2·50	
		Set of 4 Traffic Light Gutter Pairs	8·50	
		First Day Cover		1·25
		Presentation Pack	2·50	
		P.H.Q. Cards (set of 4)	14·00	10·00

Special First Day of Issue Postmarks

Philatelic Bureau, Edinburgh .... 2·75
London SW1 .... 3·50

500 Virgin and Child   **501** Angel with Crown

502 Angel appearing to   **503** The Three Kings
Shepherds

(Des Enid Marx)

1976 (24 Nov). **Christmas. English Medieval Embroidery.** *One
phosphor band (6½p.) or "all-over" phosphor (others). P 15 × 14.*

1018	**500**	6½p. blue, bistre-yellow, brown & orange	15	15
		a. Imperf (pair)	£450	
1019	**501**	8½p. sage-green, yellow, brown-ochre, chest-nut & olive-black	20	20
1020	**502**	11p. dp magenta, brown-orange, new blue, black & cinnamon	35	35
		a. Uncoated paper*	60·00	30·00
1021	**503**	13p. bright purple, new blue, cinnamon, bronze-green & olive-grey	40	40
		Set of 4	1·00	1·00
		Set of 4 Gutter Pairs	2·50	
		Set of 4 Traffic Light Gutter Pairs	6·50	
		First Day Cover		1·25
		Presentation Pack	2·00	
		P.H.Q. Cards (set of 4)	4·00	8·00

*See footnote after No. 744.

Special First Day of Issue Postmarks

Philatelic Bureau, Edinburgh .... 2·75
Bethlehem, Llandeilo, Dyfed .... 2·75

Collectors Pack 1976

1976 (24 Nov). *Comprises Nos. 997/1021.*
CP1021a   Collectors Pack .... 10·00

504 Lawn Tennis   **505** Table Tennis

506 Squash **507** Badminton

(Des A. Restall)

1977 (12 Jan). **Racket Sports.** *Phosphorised paper.* P 15 × 14.

1022	504	8½p. emerald-green, black, grey & bluish green	20	20
		a. Imperf (horiz pair)	£850	
1023	505	10p. myrtle-green, black, grey-black & dp blue-green	25	25
1024	506	11p. orange, pale yellow, black, slate-black & grey	30	30
1025	507	13p. brown, grey-black, grey & brt reddish violet	35	35
		Set of 4	1·00	1·00
		Set of 4 Gutter Pairs	2·50	
		Set of 4 Traffic Light Gutter Pairs	6·00	
		First Day Cover		1·50
		Presentation Pack	2·00	
		P.H.Q. Cards (set of 4)	6·00	9·50

Special First Day of Issue Postmark

Philatelic Bureau, Edinburgh .... 2·75

508

1977 (2 Feb)**–87.** *P 14 × 15.*

1026	508	£1 brt yellow-green & blackish olive	3·00	20
		a. Imperf (pair)	£650	
1026b		£1.30 pale drab & dp greenish blue (3.8.83)	6·50	6·00
1026c		£1.33 pale mauve & grey-black (28.8.84) ..	6·50	6·00
1026d		£1.41 pale drab & dp greenish blue (17.9.85)	7·00	6·00
1026e		£1.50 pale mauve & grey-black (2.9.86) ...	6·00	4·00

1026f	508	£1.60 pale drab & dp greenish blue (15.9.87)	6·00	6·00
1027		£2 light emerald & purple-brown	5·50	75
1028		£5 salmon & chalky blue	13·00	2·00
		a. Imperf (vert pair)	£2750	
		Set of 8	48·00	27·00
		Set of 8 Gutter Pairs	£100	
		Set of 8 Traffic Light Gutter Pairs	£130	
		First Day Cover (1026, 1027/8)		8·00
		First Day Cover (1026b)		5·50
		First Day Cover (1026c)		5·00
		First Day Cover (1026d)		5·50
		First Day Cover (1026e)		4·00
		First Day Cover (1026f)		4·50
		Presentation Pack (1026, 1027/8)	22·00	
		Presentation Pack (1026f)	12·00	

Special First Day of Issue Postmarks
(for illustrations see Introduction)

Philatelic Bureau, Edinburgh (Type F) (£1, £2, £5) ..	8·00
Windsor, Berks (Type F) (£1, £2, £5)	16·00
Philatelic Bureau, Edinburgh (Type F) (£1.30)	5·50
Windsor, Berks (Type F) (£1.30)	8·00
British Philatelic Bureau, Edinburgh (Type F) (£1.33)	5·00
Windsor, Berks (Type F) (£1.33)	7·00
British Philatelic Bureau, Edinburgh (Type G) (£1.41)	5·50
Windsor, Berks (Type G) (£1.41)	7·00
British Philatelic Bureau, Edinburgh (Type G) (£1.50)	5·00
Windsor, Berks (Type G) (£1.50)	7·00
British Philatelic Bureau, Edinburgh (Type G) (£1.60)	4·50
Windsor, Berks (Type G) (£1.60)	6·00

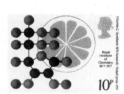

509 Steroids—Conformational **510** Vitamin C—Synthesis
Analysis

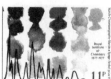
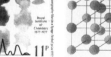

511 Starch—Chromatography **512** Salt—Crystallography

(Des J. Karo)

1977 (2 Mar). **Royal Institute of Chemistry Centenary.** *"All-over" phosphor.* P 15 × 14.

1029	509	8½p. rosine, new blue, olive-yellow, brt mauve, yellow-brown, black & gold ...	20	20
		a. Imperf (horiz pair)	£850	
1030	510	10p. brt orange, rosine, new blue, brt blue, black & gold	30	30

1031	**511**	11p. rosine, greenish yellow, new blue, dp violet, black & gold	30	30
1032	**512**	13p. new blue, brt green, black & gold	30	30
		Set of 4	1·00	1·00
		Set of 4 Gutter Pairs	2·50	
		Set of 4 Traffic Light Gutter Pairs	6·00	
		First Day Cover		1·10
		Presentation Pack	2·25	
		P.H.Q. Cards (set of 4)	7·00	10·00

Special First Day of Issue Postmark

Philatelic Bureau, Edinburgh .... 3·00

513   **514**

515   **516**

T **513/16** differ in the decorations of "ER".

(Des R. Guyatt)

1977 (11 May–15 June). **Silver Jubilee.** "All-over" phosphor. P 15 × 14.

1033	**513**	8½p. blackish green, black, silver, olive-grey & pale turquoise-green	20	20
		a. Imperf (pair)	£750	
1034		9p. maroon, black, silver, olive-grey & lavender (15 June)	25	25
1035	**514**	10p. blackish blue, black, silver, olive-grey & ochre	25	25
		a. Imperf (horiz pair)		

1036	**515**	11p. brown-purple, black, silver, olive-grey & rose-pink	30	30
		a. Imperf (horiz pair)	£1300	
1037	**516**	13p. sepia, black, silver, olive-grey & bistre-yellow	40	40
		a. Imperf (pair)	£1300	
		Set of 5	1·25	1·25
		Set of 5 Gutter Pairs	2·75	
		Set of 5 Traffic Light Gutter Pairs	4·50	
		First Day Covers (2)		1·50
		Presentation Pack (Nos. 1033, 1035/7)	2·00	
		Souvenir Book	4·00	
		P.H.Q. Cards (set of 5)	12·00	10·00

The souvenir book is a 16-page booklet containing a history of the Queen's reign.

Special First Day of Issue Postmarks

Philatelic Bureau, Edinburgh (1033, 1035/7) (11 May)	2·50
Philatelic Bureau, Edinburgh (1034) (15 June)	1·50
Windsor, Berks (1033, 1035/7) (11 May)	3·00
Windsor, Berks (1034) (15 June)	1·50

517 "Gathering of Nations"

(Des P. Murdoch. Recess and photo)

1977 (8 June). **Commonwealth Heads of Government Meeting, London.** "All-over" phosphor. P 14 × 15.

1038	**517**	13p. black, blackish green, rose-carmine & silver	50	50
		Gutter Pair	1·00	
		Traffic Light Gutter Pair	1·25	
		First Day Cover		1·00
		Presentation Pack	1·00	
		P.H.Q. Card	2·25	6·00

Special First Day of Issue Postmarks

Philatelic Bureau, Edinburgh .... 1·75
London SW .... 1·75

518 Hedgehog

519 Brown Hare

520 Red Squirrel

521 Otter

522 Badger

T **518/22** were printed horizontally *se-tenant* within the sheet.

(Des P. Oxenham)

1977 (5 Oct). **British Wildlife.** *"All-over"* phosphor. P 14 × 15.

1039	518	9p. reddish brown, grey-black, pale lemon, brt turquoise-blue, brt magenta & gold	25	20
		a. Horiz strip of 5. Nos. 1039/43	1·50	1·50
		b. Imperf (vert pair)		
		c. Imperf (horiz pair. Nos. 1039/40)		

1040	519	9p. reddish brown, grey-black, pale lemon, brt turquoise-blue, brt magenta & gold	25	20
1041	520	9p. reddish brown, grey-black, pale lemon, brt turquoise-blue, brt magenta & gold	25	20
1042	521	9p. reddish brown, grey-black, pale lemon, brt turquoise-blue, brt magenta & gold	25	20
1043	522	9p. grey-black, reddish brown, pale lemon, brt turquoise-blue, brt magenta & gold	25	20
		Set of 5	1·50	90
		Gutter Strip of 10	3·75	
		Traffic Light Gutter Strip of 10	4·00	
		First Day Cover		2·25
		Presentation Pack	2·25	
		P.H.Q. Cards (set of 5)	4·00	5·00

Special First Day of Issue Postmark

Philatelic Bureau, Edinburgh .... 2·75

523 "Three French Hens, Two Turtle Doves and a Partridge in a Pear Tree"

524 "Six Geese-a-laying, Five Gold Rings, Four Colly Birds"

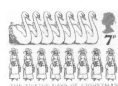

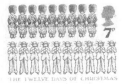

525 "Eight Maids-a-milking, Seven Swans a-swimming"

526 "Ten Pipers piping, Nine Drummers drumming"

527 "Twelve Lords a-leaping, Eleven Ladies dancing"

T **523/7** depict the card "The Twelve Days of Christmas" and were printed horizontally *se-tenant* within the sheet.

528 "A Partridge in a Pear Tree"

(Des D. Gentleman)

1977 (23 Nov). **Christmas.** *One centre phosphor band (7p.) or "all-over" phosphor (9p.). P* 15 × 14.

1044	**523**	7p. slate, grey, brt yellow-green, new blue, rose-red & gold	15	15
		a. Horiz strip of 5. Nos. 1044/8	90	1·00
		ab. Imperf (strip of 5. Nos. 1044/8)	£1100	
1045	**524**	7p. slate, brt yellow-green, new blue & gold	15	15
1046	**525**	7p. slate, grey, brt yellow-green, new blue, rose-red & gold	15	15
1047	**526**	7p. slate, grey, brt yellow-green, new blue, rose-red & gold	15	15
1048	**527**	7p. slate, grey, brt yellow-green, new blue, rose-red & gold	15	15
1049	**528**	9p. pale brown, pale orange, brt emerald, pale greenish yellow, slate-black & gold	20	20
		a. Imperf (pair)	£850	
		Set of 6	1·00	85
		Set of 6 Gutter Pairs	2·50	
		Traffic Light Gutter Pairs	4·50	
		First Day Cover		1·10
		Presentation Pack	2·00	
		P.H.Q. Cards (set of 6)	3·25	4·00

Special First Day of Issue Postmarks

Philatelic Bureau, Edinburgh . . . . 2·75
Bethlehem, Llandeilo, Dyfed . . . . 2·75

Collectors Pack 1977

1977 (23 Nov). *Comprises Nos. 1022/5 and 1029/49.*
CP1049*b* Collectors Pack . . . . 7·00

529 Oil—North Sea Production Platform   **530** Coal—Modern Pithead

531 Natural Gas—Flame Rising from Sea

532 Electricity—Nuclear Power Station and Uranium Atom

(Des P. Murdoch)

1978 (25 Jan). **Energy Resources.** *"All-over" phosphor. P* 14 × 15.

1050	**529**	9p. dp brown, orange-vermilion, grey-black, greenish yellow, rose-pink, new blue & silver	25	20
1051	**530**	10½p. lt emerald-green, grey-black, red-brown, slate-grey, pale apple-green & silver	25	30
1052	**531**	11p. greenish blue, brt violet, violet-blue, blackish brown, grey-black & silver	30	30
1053	**532**	13p. orange-vermilion, grey-black, dp brown, greenish yellow, lt brown, lt blue & silver	30	30
		Set of 4	1·00	1·00
		Set of 4 Gutter Pairs	2·50	
		Set of 4 Traffic Light Gutter Pairs	4·00	
		First Day Cover		1·25
		Presentation Pack	2·00	
		P.H.Q. Cards (set of 4)	4·00	4·00

Special First Day of Issue Postmark

Philatelic Bureau, Edinburgh . . . . 4·25

533 The Tower of London   **534** Holyroodhouse

535 Caernarvon Castle   **536** Hampton Court Palace

(Des R. Maddox (stamps), J. Matthews (miniature sheet))

1978 (1 Mar). **British Architecture. Historic Buildings.** *"All-over" phosphor.* P 15 × 14.

1054	**533**	9p. black, olive-brown, new blue, brt green, lt yellow-olive & rose-red	25	20
1055	**534**	10½p. black, brown-olive, orange-yellow, brt green, lt yellow-olive & violet-blue	25	30
1056	**535**	11p. black, brown-olive, violet-blue, brt green, lt yellow-olive & dull blue	30	30
1057	**536**	13p. black, orange-yellow, lake-brown, brt green & lt yellow-olive	30	30
		Set of 4	1·00	1·00
		Set of 4 Gutter Pairs	2·50	
		Set of 4 Traffic Light Gutter Pairs	4·00	
		First Day Cover		1·25
		Presentation Pack	2·00	
		P.H.Q. Cards (set of 4)	4·00	4·00
MS1058	121 × 89 mm. Nos. 1054/7 (sold at 53½p.)		1·25	1·50
		a. Imperforate	£4000	
		b. Lt yellow-olive (Queen's head) omitted	£3000	
		c. Rose-red (Union Jack on 9p.) omitted ..	£1750	
		d. Orange-yellow omitted	£1750	
		e. New blue (Union Jack on 9p.) omitted .		
		First Day Cover		2·00

The premium on No. **MS**1058 was used to support the London 1980 International Stamp Exhibition.

No. **MS**1058d is most noticeable on the 10½p. (spheres absent on towers) and around the roadway and arch on the 13p.

539 The Sovereign's Orb   540 Imperial State Crown

(Des J. Matthews)

1978 (31 May). **25th Anniv of Coronation.** *"All-over" phosphor.* P 14 × 15.

1059	**537**	9p. gold & royal blue	20	20
1060	**538**	10½p. gold & brown-lake	25	30
1061	**539**	11p. gold & dp dull green	30	30
1062	**540**	13p. gold & reddish violet	35	30
		Set of 4	1·00	1·00
		Set of 4 Gutter Pairs	2·50	
		Set of 4 Traffic Light Gutter Pairs	4·00	
		First Day Cover		1·25
		Presentation Pack	2·00	
		Souvenir Book	4·00	
		P.H.Q. Cards (set of 4)	2·50	4·00

The souvenir book is a 16-page booklet illustrated with scenes from the Coronation.

Special First Day of Issue Postmarks

Philatelic Bureau, Edinburgh (stamps)	2·00
Philatelic Bureau, Edinburgh (miniature sheet)	3·25
London EC (stamps)	2·00
London EC (miniature sheet)	3·25

Special First Day of Issue Postmarks

Philatelic Bureau, Edinburgh	2·50
London SW1	2·50

541 Shire Horse   542 Shetland Pony

537 State Coach   538 St. Edward's Crown

543 Welsh Pony   544 Thoroughbred

HAVE YOU READ THE NOTES AT THE BEGINNING OF THIS CATALOGUE?
These often provide answers to the enquiries we receive.

(Des P. Oxenham)

1978 (5 July).   **Horses.** *"All-over" phosphor.* P 15 × 14.

1063	**541**	9p.	black, pale reddish brown, grey-black, greenish yellow, lt blue, vermilion & gold	20	20
1064	**542**	10½p.	pale chestnut, magenta, brownish grey, greenish yellow, greenish blue, grey-black & gold	25	25
1065	**543**	11p.	reddish brown, black, lt green, greenish yellow, bistre, grey-black & gold	30	30
1066	**544**	13p.	reddish brown, pale reddish brown, emerald, greenish yellow, grey-black & gold	35	35
			Set of 4	1·00	1·00
			Set of 4 Gutter Pairs	2·50	
			Set of 4 Traffic Light Gutter Pairs	4·00	
			First Day Cover		1·50
			Presentation Pack	2·00	
			P.H.Q. Cards (set of 4)	2·50	5·00

Special First Day of Issue Postmarks

Philatelic Bureau, Edinburgh .... 2·75
Peterborough .... 2·75

545 "Penny-farthing" and 1884 Safety Bicycle

546 1920 Touring Bicycles

547 Modern Small-wheel Bicycles

548 1978 Road-racers

(Des F. Wegner)

1978 (2 Aug).   **Centenaries of Cyclists Touring Club and British Cycling Federation.** *"All-over" phosphor.* P 15 × 14.

1067	**545**	9p.	brown, dp dull blue, rose-pink, pale olive, grey-black & gold	20	20
			a. Imperf (pair)	£350	
1068	**546**	10½p.	olive, pale yellow-orange, orange-vermilion, rose-red, lt brown, grey-black & gold	25	25

1069	**547**	11p.	orange-vermilion, greenish blue, lt brown, pale greenish yellow, dp grey, grey-black & gold	30	30
1070	**548**	13p.	new blue, orange-vermilion, lt brown, olive-grey, grey-black & gold	35	35
			a. Imperf (pair)	£750	
			Set of 4	1·00	1·00
			Set of 4 Gutter Pairs	2·50	
			Set of 4 Traffic Light Gutter Pairs	4·00	
			First Day Cover		1·25
			Presentation Pack	2·00	
			P.H.Q. Cards (set of 4)	1·50	3·25

Special First Day of Issue Postmarks

Philatelic Bureau, Edinburgh .... 2·75
Harrogate, North Yorkshire .... 2·75

549 Singing Carols round the Christmas Tree

550 The Waits

551 18th-century Carol Singers

552 "The Boar's Head Carol"

(Des Faith Jaques)

1978 (22 Nov).   **Christmas.** *One centre phosphor band* (7p.) *or "all-over" phosphor* (others). P 15 × 14.

1071	**549**	7p.	brt green, greenish yellow, magenta, new blue, black & gold	20	20
			a. Imperf (vert pair)	£350	
1072	**550**	9p.	magenta, greenish yellow, new blue, sage-green, black & gold	25	25
			a. Imperf (pair)		
1073	**551**	11p.	magenta, new blue, greenish yellow, yellow-brown, black & gold	30	30
			a. Imperf (horiz pair)		

1074 **552**	13p. salmon-pink, new blue, greenish yellow, magenta, black & gold	35	35
	Set of 4	1·00	1·00
	Set of 4 Gutter Pairs	2·50	
	Set of 4 Traffic Light Gutter Pairs	3·00	
	First Day Cover		1·25
	Presentation Pack	1·75	
	P.H.Q. Cards (set of 4)	1·50	4·00

Special First Day of Issue Postmarks

Philatelic Bureau, Edinburgh	1·75
Bethlehem, Llandeilo, Dyfed	1·75

Collectors Pack 1978

1978 (22 Nov). *Comprises Nos. 1050/7 and 1059/74.*
CP1074a   Collectors Pack .... 7·00

553 Old English Sheepdog   **554** Welsh Springer Spaniel

555 West Highland Terrier   **556** Irish Setter

(Des P. Barrett)

1979 (7 Feb).   **Dogs.** *"All-over" phosphor. P 15 × 14.*

1075 **553**	9p. grey-black, sepia, turquoise-green, pale greenish yellow, pale greenish blue & grey	20	20
1076 **554**	10½p. grey-black, lake-brown, apple-green, pale greenish yellow, pale greenish blue & grey	30	30
1077 **555**	11p. grey-black, claret, yellowish green, greenish yellow, cobalt & grey	30	30
	a. Imperf (horiz pair)	£850	
1078 **556**	13p. grey-black, lake-brown, green, greenish yellow & dp turquoise-blue ...	30	30
	Set of 4	1·00	1·00
	Set of 4 Gutter Pairs	2·50	
	Set of 4 Traffic Light Gutter Pairs	3·75	
	First Day Cover		1·50
	Presentation Pack	2·00	
	P.H.Q. Cards (set of 4)	3·00	5·00

Special First Day of Issue Postmarks

Philatelic Bureau, Edinburgh	2·00
London SW	2·00

557 Primrose   **558** Daffodil

559 Bluebell   **560** Snowdrop

(Des P. Newcombe)

1979 (21 Mar).   **Spring Wild Flowers.** *"All-over" phosphor. P 14 × 15.*

1079 **557**	9p. slate-black, dp brown, pale greenish yellow, dp olive, pale new blue & silver	20	20
	a. Imperf (pair)	£400	
1080 **558**	10½p. greenish yellow, grey-green, steel-blue, slate-black, new blue & silver	30	30
	a. Imperf (vert pair)	£1500	
1081 **559**	11p. slate-black, dp brown, ultramarine, lt greenish blue, pale greenish yellow & silver	30	30
	a. Imperf (horiz pair)	£1200	
1082 **560**	13p. slate-black, indigo, grey-green, sepia, ochre & silver	30	30
	a. Imperf (horiz pair)	£750	
	Set of 4	1·00	1·00
	Set of 4 Gutter Pairs	2·50	
	Set of 4 Traffic Light Gutter Pairs	3·75	
	First Day Cover		1·50
	Presentation Pack	2·00	
	P.H.Q. Cards (set of 4)	2·00	4·00

Special First Day of Issue Postmark

Philatelic Bureau, Edinburgh .... 2·00

Special First Day of Issue Postmarks

Philatelic Bureau, Edinburgh .... 2·50
London SW .... 2·50

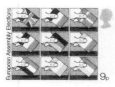 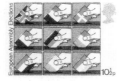

561   **562**

 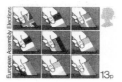

563   **564**

T **561/4** show Hands placing National Flags in Ballot Boxes.

(Des S. Cliff)

1979 (9 May). **First Direct Elections to European Assembly.** *Phosphorised paper.* P 15 × 14.

1083	**561**	9p. grey-black, vermilion, cinnamon, pale greenish yellow, pale turquoise-green & dull ultramarine	20	20
1084	**562**	10½p. grey-black, vermilion, cinnamon, pale greenish yellow, dull ultramarine, pale turquoise-green & chestnut	30	30
1085	**563**	11p. grey-black, vermilion, cinnamon, pale greenish yellow, dull ultramarine, pale turquoise-green & grey-green	30	30
1086	**564**	13p. grey-black, vermilion, cinnamon, pale greenish yellow, dull ultramarine, pale turquoise-green & brown	30	30
		Set of 4	1·00	1·00
		Set of 4 Gutter Pairs	2·50	
		Set of 4 Traffic Light Gutter Pairs	3·75	
		First Day Cover		1·25
		Presentation Pack	2·00	
		P.H.Q. Cards (set of 4)	1·50	3·50

565 "Saddling 'Mahmoud' for the Derby, 1936" (Sir Alfred Munnings)

566 "The Liverpool Great National Steeple Chase, 1839" (aquatint by F. C. Turner)

567 "The First Spring Meeting, Newmarket, 1793" (J. N. Sartorius)

568 "Racing at Dorsett Ferry, Windsor, 1684" (Francis Barlow)

(Des S. Rose)

1979 (6 June). **Horseracing Paintings. Bicentenary of the Derby (9p.).** *"All-over" phosphor.* P 15 × 14.

1087	**565**	9p. lt blue, red-brown, rose-pink, pale greenish yellow, grey-black & gold	25	25
1088	**566**	10½p. bistre-yellow, slate-blue, salmon-pink, lt blue, grey-black & gold	30	30
1089	**567**	11p. rose, vermilion, pale greenish yellow, new blue, grey-black & gold	30	30
1090	**568**	13p. bistre-yellow, rose, turquoise, grey-black & gold	30	30
		Set of 4	1·10	1·10
		Set of 4 Gutter Pairs	2·50	
		Set of 4 Traffic Light Gutter Pairs	3·75	
		First Day Cover		1·50
		Presentation Pack	2·00	
		P.H.Q. Cards (set of 4)	1·50	3·00

Special First Day of Issue Postmarks

Philatelic Bureau, Edinburgh .... 2·50
Epsom, Surrey .... 2·50

Special First Day of Issue Postmark

Philatelic Bureau, Edinburgh .... 2·00
First Day of Issue handstamps were provided at Hartfield, East
Sussex and Stourbridge, West Midlands for this issue.

569 *The Tale of Peter Rabbit*
(Beatrix Potter)

570 *The Wind in the*
Willows (Kenneth Grahame)

573 Sir Rowland Hill

574 *Postman, circa* 1839

572 *Winnie-the-Pooh*
(A. A. Milne)

572 *Alice's Adventures in*
Wonderland (Lewis Carroll)

(Des E. Hughes)

575 London Postman,
circa 1839

576 Woman and Young Girl
with Letters, 1840

(Des E. Stemp)

1979 (11 July). **International Year of the Child. Children's Book
Illustrations.** *"All-over" phosphor. P* 14 × 15.

1091 **569** 9p. dp bluish green, grey-black, bistre-
brown, brt rose, greenish yellow & silver ... 35 ... 20
1092 **570** 10½p. dull ultramarine, grey-black, olive-
brown, brt rose, yellow-orange, pale
greenish yellow & silver .... 40 ... 35
1093 **571** 11p. drab, grey-black, greenish yellow, new
blue, yellow-orange, agate & silver .... 45 ... 40
1094 **572** 13p. pale greenish yellow, grey-black, brt
rose, dp bluish green, olive-brown,
new blue & silver .... 50 ... 55
Set of 4 .... 1·50 ... 1·40
Set of 4 Gutter Pairs .... 4·00
Set of 4 Traffic Light Gutter Pairs .... 4·75
First Day Cover .... 2·00
Presentation Pack .... 2·25
P.H.Q. Cards (set of 4) .... 2·50 ... 3·00

1979 (22 Aug–24 Oct). **Death Centenary of Sir Rowland Hill.** *"All-
over" phosphor. P* 14 × 15.

1095 **573** 10p. grey-black, brown-ochre, myrtle-green,
pale greenish yellow, rosine, brt blue &
gold .... 25 ... 25
1096 **574** 11½p. grey-black, brown-ochre, brt blue, rosine,
bistre-brown, pale greenish yellow &
gold .... 30 ... 35
1097 **575** 13p. grey-black, brown-ochre, brt blue, rosine, bistre-brown, pale greenish yellow
& gold .... 35 ... 40
1098 **576** 15p. grey-black, brown-ochre, myrtle-green,
bistre-brown, rosine, pale greenish yel-
low & gold .... 50 ... 40
Set of 4 .... 1·25 ... 1·25
Set of 4 Gutter Pairs .... 2·50
Set of 4 Traffic Light Gutter Pairs .... 3·75
First Day Cover .... 1·25
Presentation Pack .... 2·00
P.H.Q. Cards (set of 4) .... 1·50 ... 3·00

MS1099 89 × 121 mm. Nos. 1095/8 (*sold at* 59½p.) (24 Oct) 1·25 1·25
    a. Imperforate £1100
    b. Brown-ochre (15p. background, etc.)
       omitted £750
    c. Gold (Queen's head) omitted £150
    d. Brown-ochre, myrtle-green & gold
       omitted £3000
    e. Brt blue (13p. background, etc.) omitted £950
    f. Myrtle-green (10p. (background), 15p.)
       omitted £1300
    g. Pale greenish yellow omitted £160
    h. Rosine omitted £600
    i. Bistre-brown omitted £750
    j. Grey-black and pale greenish yellow
       omitted
      First Day Cover .... 1·25

The premium on No. **MS**1099 was used to support the London 1980 International Stamp Exhibition.

Special First Day of Issue Postmarks

Philatelic Bureau, Edinburgh (stamps) (22 Aug) ..... 1·75
Philatelic Bureau, Edinburgh (miniature sheet) (24 Oct) 1·75
London EC (stamps) (22 Aug) .... 1·75
London EC (miniature sheet) (24 Oct) .... 1·75

First Day of Issue handstamps were provided at Kidderminster, Worcs on 22 August (pictorial) and 24 October (Type C) and at Sanquhar, Dumfriesshire on 22 August and 24 October (both Type C).

577 Policeman on the Beat   578 Policeman directing Traffic

579 Mounted Policewoman   580 River Patrol Boat

(Des B. Sanders)

1979 (26 Sept). **150th Anniv of Metropolitan Police.** *Phosphorised paper.* P 15 × 14.

1100	577	10p. grey-black, red-brown, emerald, greenish yellow, brt blue & magenta	25	25
1101	578	11½p. grey-black, brt orange, purple-brown, ultramarine, greenish yellow & dp bluish green	30	35
1102	579	13p. grey-black, red-brown, magenta, olive-green, greenish yellow & dp dull blue .	35	40
1103	580	15p. grey-black, magenta, brown, slate-blue, dp brown & greenish black	50	40
		Set of 4	1·25	1·25
		Set of 4 Gutter Pairs	2·50	
		Set of 4 Traffic Light Gutter Pairs	3·75	
		First Day Cover		1·25
		Presentation Pack	2·00	
		PHQ Cards (set of 4)	1·50	3·00

Special First Day of Issue Postmarks

Philatelic Bureau, Edinburgh .... 1·75
London SW .... 1·75

581 The Three Kings   582 Angel appearing to the Shepherds

583 The Nativity   584 Mary and Joseph travelling to Bethlehem

585 The Annunciation

(Des F. Wegner)

1979 (21 Nov). **Christmas.** *One centre phosphor band (8p.) or phosphorised paper (others).* P 15 × 14.

1104	**581**	8p.	blue, grey-black, ochre, slate-violet & gold	20	20
		a.	Imperf (pair)	£550	
1105	**582**	10p.	brt rose-red, grey-black, chestnut, chrome-yellow, dp violet & gold	25	25
		a.	Imperf between (vert pair)	£450	
		b.	Imperf (pair)	£600	
1106	**583**	11½p.	orange-vermilion, steel-blue, drab, grey-black, dp blue-green & gold	30	35
1107	**584**	13p.	brt blue, orange-vermilion, bistre, grey-black & gold	40	40
1108	**585**	15p.	orange-vermilion, blue, bistre, grey-black, green & gold	50	45
			Set of 5	1·50	1·50
			Set of 5 Gutter Pairs	3·00	
			Set of 5 Traffic Light Gutter Pairs	3·75	
			First Day Cover		1·50
			Presentation Pack	2·25	
			P.H.Q. Cards (set of 5)	1·50	3·50

Special First Day of Issue Postmarks

Philatelic Bureau, Edinburgh	2·00
Bethlehem, Llandeilo, Dyfed	2·00

Collectors Pack 1979

1979 (21 Nov). *Comprises Nos. 1075/98 and 1100/8.*

CP1108a	Collectors Pack	9·00

586 Common Kingfisher

587 Dipper

588 Moorhen

589 Yellow Wagtails

(Des M. Warren)

1980 (16 Jan). **Centenary of Wild Bird Protection Act.** *Phosphorised paper.* P 14 × 15.

1109	**586**	10p.	brt blue, brt yellow-green, vermilion, pale greenish yellow, grey-black & gold	25	25
1110	**587**	11½p.	sepia, grey-black, dull ultramarine, vermilion, grey-green, pale greenish yellow & gold	30	35
1111	**588**	13p.	emerald-green, grey-black, brt blue, vermilion, pale greenish yellow & gold	40	40
1112	**589**	15p.	greenish yellow, brown, lt green, slate-blue, grey-black & gold	45	45
			Set of 4	1·25	1·25
			Set of 4 Gutter Pairs	2·50	
			First Day Cover		1·40
			Presentation Pack	2·00	
			P.H.Q. Cards (set of 4)	1·50	3·00

Special First Day of Issue Postmarks

Philatelic Bureau, Edinburgh	2·00
Sandy, Beds	2·00

590 *Rocket* approaching Moorish Arch, Liverpool

591 First and Second Class Carriages passing through Olive Mount Cutting

592 Third Class Carriage and Cattle Truck crossing Chat Moss

593 Horsebox and Carriage Truck near Bridgewater Canal

594 Goods Truck and Mail-Coach at Manchester

T **590/4** were printed together, *se-tenant*, in horizontal strips of 5 throughout the sheet.

(Des D. Gentleman)

1980 (12 Mar). **150th Anniv of Liverpool and Manchester Railway.** *Phosphorised paper.* P 15 x 14.

1113	590	12p. lemon, lt brown, rose-red, pale blue & grey-black	25	25
		a. Strip of 5. Nos. 1113/17	1·50	1·60
		ab. Imperf (horiz strip of 5. Nos. 1113/17) ..	£1200	
		ac. Lemon omitted (horiz strip of 5. Nos. 1113/17)		
1114	591	12p. rose-red, lt brown, lemon, pale blue & grey-black	25	25
1115	592	12p. pale blue, rose-red, lemon, lt brown & grey-black	25	25
1116	593	12p. lt brown, lemon, rose-red, pale blue & grey-black	25	25
1117	594	12p. lt brown, rose-red, pale blue, lemon & grey-black	25	25
		Set of 5	1·50	1·10
		Gutter Block of 10	3·25	
		First Day Cover		1·60
		Presentation Pack	2·50	
		P.H.Q. Cards (set of 5)	1·50	3·75

Special First Day of Issue Postmarks

Philatelic Bureau, Edinburgh .... 2·00
Liverpool .... 2·00
Manchester .... 2·00

595 Montage of London Buildings

During the printing of No. 1118 the die was re-cut resulting in the following two types:

Type I (original). Top and bottom lines of shading in portrait oval broken. Hatched shading below left arm of Tower Bridge and hull of ship below right arm. Other points: Hatched shading on flag on Westminster Abbey, bottom right of Post Office Tower and archway of entrance to Westminster Abbey.

Type II (re-engraved). Lines in oval unbroken. Solid shading on bridge and ship. Also solid shading on flag, Post Office Tower and archway.

(Des J. Matthews. Recess)

1980 (9 Apr–7 May). **"London 1980" International Stamp Exhibition.** *Phosphorised paper. P* 14½ × 14.

1118	**595**	50p. agate (I)	....	1·50	1·50
	Ea.	Type II	....	1·50	1·50
		Gutter Pair	....	3·00	
		First Day Cover	....		1·50
		Presentation Pack	....	2·00	
		P.H.Q. Card	....	50	1·75
MS1119		90 × 123 mm. No. 1118 (*sold at 75p.*) (7 May) ..		1·50	1·50
		a. Error. Imperf	....	£700	
		First Day Cover	....		1·50

Examples of No 1118 are known in various shades of green. Such shades result from problems with the drying of the printed sheets on the press, but are not listed as similar colours can be easily faked.

Special First Day of Issue Postmarks

Philatelic Bureau, Edinburgh (stamp) (9 Apr.)	2·00
Philatelic Bureau, Edinburgh (miniature sheet) (7 May)	2·00
London SW (stamp) (9 Apr.)	2·00
London SW (miniature sheet) (7 May)	2·00

596 Buckingham Palace

597 The Albert Memorial

598 Royal Opera House

599 Hampton Court

600 Kensington Palace

(Des Sir Hugh Casson)

1980 (7 May). **London Landmarks.** *Phosphorised paper. P* 14 × 15.

1120	**596**	10½p.	grey, pale blue, rosine, pale greenish yellow, yellowish green & silver	25	25
1121	**597**	12p.	grey-black, bistre, rosine, yellowish green, pale greenish yellow & silver ...	30	30
			a. Imperf (vert pair)	£550	
1122	**598**	13½p.	grey-black, pale salmon, pale olive-green, slate-blue & silver	35	35
			a. Imperf (pair)	£550	
1123	**599**	15p.	grey-black, pale salmon, slate-blue, dull yellowish green, olive-yellow & silver ..	40	40
1124	**600**	17½p.	grey, slate-blue, red-brown, sepia, yellowish green, pale greenish yellow & silver .	40	40
			a. Silver (Queen's head) omitted	£175	
			Set of 5	1·50	1·50
			Set of 5 Gutter Pairs	3·00	
			First Day Cover		1·75
			Presentation Pack	2·50	
			P.H.Q. Cards (set of 5)	1·50	3·00

No. 1124a shows the Queen's head in pale greenish yellow, this colour being printed beneath the silver for technical reasons.

Special First Day of Issue Postmarks

Philatelic Bureau, Edinburgh	2·25
Kingston-upon-Thames	2·00

601 Charlotte Brontë
(*Jane Eyre*)

602 George Eliot
(*The Mill on the Floss*)

603 Emily Brontë
(*Wuthering Heights*)

604 Mrs. Gaskell
(*North and South*)

T **601/4** show authoresses and scenes from their novels. T **601/2** also include the "Europa" C.E.P.T. emblem.

(Des Barbara Brown)

1980 (9 July).   **Famous Authoresses.** *Phosphorised paper. P* 15 × 14.

1125	**601**	12p.	red-brown, brt rose, brt blue, greenish yellow, grey & gold	30	30
		Ea.	Missing "p" in value (R.4/6)	25·00	
1126	**602**	13½p.	red-brown, dull vermilion, pale blue, pale greenish yellow, grey & gold	35	35
		a.	Pale blue omitted	£1500	
1127	**603**	15p.	red-brown, vermilion, blue, lemon, grey & gold	40	45
1128	**604**	17½p.	dull vermilion, slate-blue, ultramarine, pale greenish yellow, grey & gold	60	60
		a.	Imperf and slate-blue omitted (pair) ...	£700	
			Set of 4	1·50	1·50
			Set of 4 Gutter Pairs	3·00	
			First Day Cover		1·50
			Presentation Pack	2·50	
			P.H.Q. Cards (set of 4)	1·50	3·00

Special First Day of Issue Postmarks

Philatelic Bureau, Edinburgh .... 1·75
Haworth, Keighley, W. Yorks .... 1·75

605 Queen Elizabeth the Queen Mother

(Des J. Matthews from photograph by N. Parkinson)

1980 (4 Aug).   **80th Birthday of Queen Elizabeth the Queen Mother.** *Phosphorised paper. P* 14 × 15.

1129	**605**	12p.	brt rose, greenish yellow, new blue, grey & silver	50	50
		a.	Imperf (horiz pair)	£1200	
			Gutter Pair	1·00	
			First Day Cover		60
			P.H.Q. Card	50	1·25

Special First Day of Issue Postmarks

Philatelic Bureau, Edinburgh .... 1·75
Glamis Castle, Forfar .... 1·75

606 Sir Henry Wood

607 Sir Thomas Beecham

608 Sir Malcolm Sargent

609 Sir John Barbirolli

(Des P. Gauld)

1980 (10 Sept).   **British Conductors.** *Phosphorised paper. P* 14 × 15.

1130	**606**	12p.	slate, rose-red, greenish yellow, bistre & gold	30	30
1131	**607**	13½p.	grey-black, vermilion, greenish yellow, pale carmine-rose & gold	35	40
1132	**608**	15p.	grey-black, brt rose-red, greenish yellow, turquoise-green & gold	45	45
1133	**609**	17½p.	black, brt rose-red, greenish yellow, dull violet-blue & gold	55	50
			Set of 4	1·50	1·50
			Set of 4 Gutter Pairs	3·00	
			First Day Cover		1·50
			Presentation Pack	2·00	
			P.H.Q. cards (set of 4)	1·50	2·50

Special First Day of Issue Postmarks

Philatelic Bureau, Edinburgh .... 2·00
London SW .... 2·00

Special First Day of Issue Postmarks

Philatelic Bureau, Edinburgh .... 2·00
Cardiff .... 2·00

610 Running   **611** Rugby

612 Boxing   **613** Cricket

614 Christmas Tree   **615** Candles

616 Apples and Mistletoe   **617** Crown, Chains and Bell

618 Holly

(Des R. Goldsmith. Litho Questa)

1980 (10 Oct). **Sport Centenaries.** *Phosphorised paper.* P 14 × 14½.

1134	**610**	12p.	pale new blue, greenish yellow, magenta, lt brown, reddish purple & gold	30	30
		a.	Gold (Queen's head) omitted	£9000	
1135	**611**	13½p.	pale new blue, olive-yellow, brt purple, orange-vermilion, blackish lilac & gold .	35	40
1136	**612**	15p.	pale new blue, greenish yellow, brt purple, chalky blue & gold	40	40
		a.	Gold (Queen's head) omitted		
1137	**613**	17½p.	pale new blue, greenish yellow, magenta, dp olive, grey-brown & gold	60	55
			Set of 4	1·50	1·50
			Set of 4 Gutter Pairs	3·00	
			First Day Cover		1·50
			Presentation Pack	2·00	
			P.H.Q. Cards (set of 4)	1·50	2·50

Centenaries:—12p. Amateur Athletics Association; 13½p. Welsh Rugby Union; 15p. Amateur Boxing Association; 17½p. First England–Australia Test Match.

Nos. 1134a and 1136a were caused by paper folds.

(Des J. Matthews)

1980 (19 Nov). **Christmas.** *One centre phosphor band (10p.) or phosphorised paper (others).* P 15 × 14.

1138	**614**	10p.	black, turquoise-green, greenish yellow, vermilion & blue	25	25
		a.	Imperf (horiz pair)		
1139	**615**	12p.	grey, magenta, rose-red, greenish grey & pale orange	30	35
1140	**616**	13½p.	grey-black, dull yellow-green, brown, greenish yellow & pale olive-bistre	35	40
1141	**617**	15p.	grey-black, bistre-yellow, brt orange, magenta & new blue	40	40

1142 **618** 17½p. black, vermilion, dull yellowish green & greenish yellow 40 40
  Set of 5 .... 1·50 1·60
  Set of 5 Gutter Pairs .... 3·00
  First Day Cover .... 1·60
  Presentation Pack .... 2·25
  P.H.Q. Cards (set of 5) .... 1·50 2·50

Special First Day of Issue Postmarks

Philatelic Bureau, Edinburgh .... 2·00
Bethlehem, Llandeilo, Dyfed .... 2·00

Collectors Pack 1980

1980 (19 Nov). *Comprises Nos. 1109/18 and 1120/42.*
CP1142a Collectors Pack .... 12·00

619 St. Valentine's Day

620 Morris Dancers

621 Lammastide

622 Medieval Mummers

T **619/20** also include the "Europa" C.E.P.T. emblem.

(Des F. Wegner)

1981 (6 Feb). **Folklore.** *Phosphorised paper.* P 15 × 14.
1143 **619** 14p. cerise, green, yellow-orange, salmon-pink, black & gold 35 35
1144 **620** 18p. dull ultramarine, lemon, lake-brown, brt green, black & gold 45 50
1145 **621** 22p. chrome-yellow, rosine, brown, new blue, black & gold 60 60
1146 **622** 25p. brt blue, red-brown, brt rose-red, greenish yellow, black & gold 75 70
  Set of 4 .... 2·00 2·00
  Set of 4 Gutter Pairs .... 4·00
  First Day Cover .... 2·00
  Presentation Pack .... 2·50
  P.H.Q. Cards (set of 4) .... 1·50 2·50

Special First Day of Issue Postmarks

Philatelic Bureau, Edinburgh .... 2·00
London WC .... 2·00

623 Blind Man with Guide Dog

624 Hands spelling "Deaf" in Sign Language

625 Disabled Man in Wheelchair

626 Disabled Artist painting with Foot

(Des J. Gibbs)

1981 (25 Mar). **International Year of the Disabled.** *Phosphorised paper.* P 15 × 14.
1147 **623** 14p. drab, greenish yellow, brt rose-red, dull purple & silver 35 35
  a. Imperf (pair) £750
1148 **624** 18p. dp blue-green, brt orange, dull vermilion, grey-black & silver 45 50
1149 **625** 22p. brown-ochre, rosine, purple-brown, greenish blue, black & silver 60 60
1150 **626** 25p. vermilion, lemon, pale salmon, olive-brown, new blue, black & silver 75 70
  Set of 4 .... 2·00 2·00
  Set of 4 Gutter Pairs .... 4·00
  First Day Cover .... 2·00
  Presentation Pack .... 2·50
  P.H.Q. Cards (set of 4) .... 1·50 2·75
All known examples of No. 1147a are creased.

GIBBONS STAMP MONTHLY
– finest and most informative magazine for all collectors. Obtainable from your newsagent or by postal subscription – details on request.

Special First Day of Issue Postmarks

Special First Day of Issue Postmarks

Philatelic Bureau, Edinburgh .... 2·00
Windsor .... 2·00

Philatelic Bureau, Edinburgh .... 2·50
London SW .... 2·25

631 Glenfinnan, Scotland **632** Derwentwater, England

627 *Aglais urticae* **628** *Maculinea arion*

633 Stackpole Head, Wales **634** Giant's Causeway, Northern Ireland

629 *Inachis io* **630** *Carterocephalus palaemon*

635 St. Kilda, Scotland

(Des G. Beningfield)

1981 (13 May). **Butterflies.** *Phosphorised paper.* P 14 × 15.

1151	**627**	14p. greenish yellow, yellow-green, brt rose, brt blue, emerald & gold	35	35
		a. Imperf (pair)	£950	
1152	**628**	18p. black, greenish yellow, dull yellowish green, brt mauve, brt blue, brt green & gold	50	50
1153	**629**	22p. black, greenish yellow, bronze-green, rosine, ultramarine, lt green & gold	60	65
1154	**630**	25p. black, greenish yellow, bronze-green, brt rose-red, ultramarine, brt emerald & gold	70	75
		Set of 4	2·00	2·00
		Set of 4 Gutter Pairs	4·00	
		First Day Cover		2·00
		Presentation Pack	2·50	
		P.H.Q. Cards (set of 4)	2·00	3·00

(Des M. Fairclough)

1981 (24 June). **50th Anniv of National Trust for Scotland. British Landscapes.** *Phosphorised paper.* P 15 × 14.

1155	**631**	14p. lilac, dull blue, reddish brown, bistre-yellow, black & gold	30	30
1156	**632**	18p. bottle green, brt blue, brown, bistre-yellow, black & gold	40	40
1157	**633**	20p. dp turquoise-blue, dull blue, greenish yellow, reddish brown, black & gold ...	50	50
1158	**634**	22p. chrome-yellow, reddish brown, new blue, yellow-brown, black & gold	60	60
1159	**635**	25p. ultramarine, new blue, olive-green, olive-grey & gold	70	70
		Set of 5	2·25	2·25
		Set of 5 Gutter Pairs	4·50	
		First Day Cover		2·25
		Presentation Pack	2·75	
		P.H.Q. Cards (set of 5)	2·00	2·75

Special First Day of Issue Postmarks

Special First Day of Issue Postmarks

Philatelic Bureau, Edinburgh	2·75
Glenfinnan	3·50
Keswick	3·50

Philatelic Bureau, Edinburgh	2·25
Caernarfon, Gwynedd	2·50
London EC	2·50

636 Prince Charles and Lady Diana Spencer

(Des J. Matthews from photograph by Lord Snowdon)

1981 (22 July). **Royal Wedding.** *Phosphorised paper.* P 14 × 15.

1160	**636**	14p. grey-black, greenish yellow, brt rose-red, ultramarine, pale blue, blue & silver	25	25
1161		25p. drab, greenish yellow, brt rose-red, ultramarine, grey-brown, grey-black & silver	75	75
		Set of 2	1·00	1·00
		Set of 2 Gutter Pairs	2·00	
		First Day Cover		2·00
		Presentation Pack	2·00	
		Souvenir Book	4·00	
		P.H.Q. Cards (set of 2)	1·00	2·75

The souvenir book is a 12-page illustrated booklet with a set of mint stamps in a sachet attached to the front cover.

HAVE YOU READ THE NOTES AT THE BEGINNING OF THIS CATALOGUE?

These often provide answers to the enquiries we receive.

637 "Expeditions"

638 "Skills"

639 "Service"

640 "Recreation"

(Des P. Sharland. Litho J.W.)

1981 (12 Aug). **25th Anniv of Duke of Edinburgh Award Scheme.** *Phosphorised paper.* P 14.

1162	**637**	14p. greenish yellow, magenta, pale new blue, black, emerald & silver	35	35
1163	**638**	18p. greenish yellow, magenta, pale new blue, black, cobalt & gold	50	50
1164	**639**	22p. greenish yellow, magenta, pale new blue, black, red-orange & gold	60	60
1165	**640**	25p. brt orange, mauve, pale new blue, black, flesh & bronze	70	70
		Set of 4	2·00	2·00
		Set of 4 Gutter Pairs	4·00	
		First Day Cover		2·00
		Presentation Pack	2·50	
		P.H.Q. Cards (set of 4)	1·60	2·25

Special First Day of Issue Postmarks

Special First Day of Issue Postmarks

Philatelic Bureau, Edinburgh	2·50
London W2	2·75

Philatelic Bureau, Edinburgh	2·50
Hull	2·75

641 Cockle-dredging from *Linsey II*   **642** Hauling in Trawl Net

645 Father Christmas   **646** Jesus Christ

643 Lobster Potting   **644** Hoisting Seine Net

647 Flying Angel   **648** Joseph and Mary arriving at Bethlehem

(Des B. Sanders)

1981 (23 Sept). **Fishing Industry.** *Phosphorised paper.* P 15 × 14.

1166	**641**	14p. slate, greenish yellow, magenta, new blue, orange-brown, olive-grey & bronze-green	35	35
1167	**642**	18p. slate, greenish yellow, brt crimson, ultramarine, black & greenish slate	50	50
1168	**643**	22p. grey, greenish yellow, brt rose, dull ultramarine, reddish lilac & black	60	60
1169	**644**	25p. grey, greenish yellow, brt rose, cobalt & black	70	65
		Set of 4	2·00	2·00
		Set of 4 Gutter Pairs	4·00	
		First Day Cover		2·00
		Presentation Pack	2·50	
		P.H.Q. Cards (set of 4)	2·00	2·50

Nos. 1166/9 were issued on the occasion of the centenary of the Royal National Mission to Deep Sea Fishermen.

649 Three Kings approaching Bethlehem

(Des Samantha Brown (11½p.), Tracy Jenkins (14p.), Lucinda Blackmore (18p.), Stephen Moore (22p.), Sophie Sharp (25p.))

1981 (18 Nov). **Christmas. Children's Pictures.** One phosphor band (11½p.) or phosphorised paper (others). P 15 × 14.

1170	**645**	11½p. ultramarine, black, red, olive-bistre, brt green & gold	30	30
1171	**646**	14p. bistre-yellow, brt magenta, blue, greenish blue, brt green, black & gold	40	40
1172	**647**	18p. pale blue-green, bistre-yellow, brt magenta, ultramarine, black & gold	50	50
1173	**648**	22p. dp turquoise-blue, lemon, magenta, black & gold	60	60

1174 **649** 25p. royal blue, lemon, brt magenta, black &
gold 70 70
Set of 5 .... 2·25 2·25
Set of 5 Gutter Pairs .... 4·50
First Day Cover .... 2·25
Presentation Pack .... 2·75
P.H.Q. Cards (set of 5) .... 2·00 3·50

Special First Day of Issue Postmarks

Philatelic Bureau, Edinburgh .... 2·50
Bethlehem, Llandeilo, Dyfed .... 2·75

Collectors Pack 1981

1981 (18 Nov). *Comprises Nos. 1143/74.*
CP1174a Collectors Pack .... 18·00

650 Charles Darwin and   **651** Darwin and Marine Iguanas
Giant Tortoises

 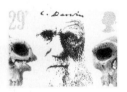

652 Darwin, Cactus Ground   **653** Darwin and Prehistoric Skulls
Finch and Large Ground Finch

(Des D. Gentleman)

1982 (10 Feb). **Death Centenary of Charles Darwin.** *Phosphorised paper.* P 15 × 14.
1175 **650** 15½p. dull purple, drab, bistre, black & grey-
black 35 35
1176 **651** 19½p. violet-grey, bistre-yellow, slate-black,
red-brown, grey-black & black 60 60
1177 **652** 26p. sage green, bistre-yellow, orange,
chalky blue, grey-black, red-brown &
black 70 70
1178 **653** 29p. grey-brown, yellow-brown, brown-
ochre, black & grey-black 75 75
Set of 4 .... 2·25 2·25
Set of 4 Gutter Pairs .... 4·50
First Day Cover .... 2·25
Presentation Pack .... 3·00
P.H.Q. Cards (set of 4) .... 2·50 6·50

Special First Day of Issue Postmarks

Philatelic Bureau, Edinburgh .... 2·25
Shrewsbury .... 2·25

654 Boys' Brigade   **655** Girls' Brigade

656 Boy Scout Movement   **657** Girl Guide Movement

(Des B. Sanders)

1982 (24 Mar). **Youth Organizations.** *Phosphorised paper.* P 15 × 14.
1179 **654** 15½p. gold, greenish yellow, pale orange,
mauve, dull blue & grey-black 35 35
1180 **655** 19½p. gold, greenish yellow, pale orange, brt
rose, dp ultramarine, olive-bistre &
grey-black 60 50
1181 **656** 26p. gold, greenish yellow, olive-sepia, rosine, dp blue, dp dull green & grey-black 85 75
1182 **657** 29p. gold, yellow, dull orange, cerise, dull
ultramarine, chestnut & grey-black .... 1·00 90
Set of 4 .... 2·50 2·25
Set of 4 Gutter Pairs .... 5·00
First Day Cover .... 2·25
Presentation Pack .... 3·50
P.H.Q. Cards (set of 4) .... 2·50 6·50

Nos. 1179/82 were issued on the occasion of the 75th anniversary of
the Boy Scout Movement; the 125th birth anniversary of Lord Baden-
Powell and the centenary of the Boys' Brigade (1983).

Special First Day of Issue Postmarks

Edinburgh Philatelic Bureau .... 2·25
Glasgow .... 2·25
London SW .... 2·25

15½P

658 Ballerina

19½P

659 Harlequin

26P

660 Hamlet

29P

661 Opera Singer

(Des A. George)

1982 (28 Apr). **Europa. British Theatre.** *Phosphorised paper.* P 15 × 14.
1183 **658** 15½p. carmine-lake, greenish blue, greenish
yellow, grey-black, bottle green & silver   35   35
1184 **659** 19½p. rosine, new blue, greenish yellow, black,
ultramarine & silver   60   50
1185 **660** 26p. carmine-red, brt rose-red, greenish
yellow, black, dull ultramarine, lake-
brown & silver   90   75

1186 **661** 29p. rose-red, greenish yellow, brt blue, grey-
black & silver ....   1·25   90
      Set of 4 ....   2·75   2·25
      Set of 4 Gutter Pairs ....   5·50
      First Day Cover ....   2·25
      Presentation Pack ....   3·25
      P.H.Q. Cards (set of 4) ....   2·50   6·50

Special First Day of Issue Postmarks

Philatelic Bureau, Edinburgh .... 2·25
Stratford-upon-Avon .... 2·25

15½P
HENRY VIII/MARY ROSE

662 Henry VIII and *Mary Rose*

19½P
ADMIRAL BLAKE/TRIUMPH

663 Admiral Blake and *Triumph*

24P
LORD NELSON/HMS VICTORY

664 Lord Nelson and
H.M.S. *Victory*

26P
LORD FISHER/HMS DREADNOUGHT

665 Lord Fisher and H.M.S.
Dreadnought

29P
VISCOUNT CUNNINGHAM/HMS WARSPITE

666 Viscount Cunningham and H.M.S. *Warspite*

(Des Marjorie Saynor. Eng C. Slania. Recess and photo)

1982 (16 June). **Maritime Heritage.** *Phosphorised paper.* P 15 × 14.
1187 **662** 15½p. black, lemon, brt rose, pale orange,
ultramarine & grey   35   35
      a. Imperf (pair) £750
1188 **663** 19½p. black, greenish yellow, brt rose-red, pale
orange, ultramarine & grey   60   60
1189 **664** 24p. black, orange-yellow, brt rose-red, lake-
brown, dp ultramarine & grey   70   70

1190 **665** 26p. black, orange-yellow, brt rose, lemon,
ultramarine & grey 80 80
    a. Imperf (pair) ....
1191 **666** 29p. black, olive-yellow, brt rose, orange-
yellow, ultramarine & grey 90 90
    Set of 5 .... 3·00 3·00
    Set of 5 Gutter Pairs .... 6·00
    First Day Cover .... 3·00
    Presentation Pack .... 3·50
    P.H.Q. Cards (set of 5) .... 3·00 6·50

Nos. 1187/91 were issued on the occasion of Maritime England Year, the Bicentenary of the Livery Grant by the City of London to the Worshipful Company of Shipwrights and the raising of the *Mary Rose* from Portsmouth Harbour.

Several used examples of the 15½p. have been seen with the black recess (ship and waves) omitted.

Special First Day of Issue Postmarks

Philatelic Bureau, Edinburgh .... 3·50
Portsmouth .... 3·25

667 "Strawberry Thief"
(William Morris)

668 Untitled (Steiner and Co)

669 "Cherry Orchard"
(Paul Nash)

670 "Chevron"
(Andrew Foster)

(Des Peter Hatch Partnership)

1982 (23 July). **British Textiles.** *Phosphorised paper.* P 14 × 15.
1192 **667** 15½p. blue, olive-yellow, rosine, dp blue-
green, bistre & Prussian blue 35 35
    a. Imperf (horiz pair) £950
1193 **668** 19½p. olive-grey, greenish yellow, brt magenta, dull green, yellow-brown & black .. 55 55
    a. Imperf (vert pair) £1500
1194 **669** 26p. brt scarlet, dull mauve, dull ultramarine
& brt carmine 70 70
1195 **670** 29p. bronze-green, orange-yellow, turquoise-
green, stone, chestnut & sage-green ... 90 90
    Set of 4 .... 2·25 2·25
    Set of 4 Gutter Pairs .... 4·50
    First Day Cover .... 2·50
    Presentation Pack .... 3·25
    P.H.Q. Cards (set of 4) .... 3·00 6·50

Nos. 1192/5 were issued on the occasion of the 250th birth anniversary of Sir Richard Arkwright (inventor of spinning machine).

Special First Day of Issue Postmarks

Philatelic Bureau, Edinburgh .... 3·00
Rochdale .... 3·00

671 Development of Communications

672 Modern Technological Aids

(Des Delaney and Ireland)

1982 (8 Sept). **Information Technology.** *Phosphorised paper.* P 14 × 15.
1196 **671** 15½p. black, greenish yellow, brt rose-red,
bistre-brown, new blue & lt ochre 45 50
    a. Imperf (pair) £250
1197 **672** 26p. black, greenish yellow, brt rose-red,
olive-bistre, new blue & lt olive-grey ... 80 85
    a. Imperf (pair) £1300
    Set of 2 .... 1·25 1·25
    Set of 2 Gutter Pairs .... 2·50
    First Day Cover .... 1·50
    Presentation Pack .... 2·00
    P.H.Q. cards (set of 2) .... 1·50 4·50

Special First Day of Issue Postmarks

Philatelic Bureau, Edinburgh .... 2·00
London WC .... 2·00

673 Austin "Seven" and "Metro" **674** Ford "Model T" and "Escort"

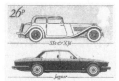
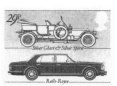

675 Jaguar "SS 1" and "XJ6" **676** Rolls-Royce "Silver Ghost" and
                                        "Silver Spirit"

(Des S. Paine. Litho Questa)

1982 (13 Oct). **British Motor Cars.** *Phosphorised paper.* P 14½ × 14.
1198 **673** 15½p. slate, orange-vermilion, brt orange,
           drab, yellow-green, olive-yellow, bluish
           grey & black 50 50
1199 **674** 19½p. slate, brt orange, olive-grey, rose-red,
           dull vermilion, grey & black 70 70
       Ea. Rose-red, grey and black ptgs double ..
1200 **675** 26p. slate, red-brown, brt orange, turquoise-
           green, myrtle-green, dull blue-green,
           grey & olive 85 90
1201 **676** 29p. slate, brt orange, carmine-red, reddish
           purple, grey & black .... 1·00 1·25
       Ea. Black ptg quadruple £350
       Eb. Brt orange, carmine-red, grey and black
           ptgs double ....
       Set of 4 .... 2·75 3·00
       Set of 4 Gutter Pairs .... 5·50
       First Day Cover .... 3·00
       Presentation Pack .... 3·75
       P.H.Q. cards (set of 4) .... 3·00 7·00

WHEN YOU BUY AN ALBUM LOOK
FOR THE NAME 'STANLEY GIBBONS'
It means Quality combined with Value for Money.

Special First Day of Issue Postmarks

Philatelic Bureau, Edinburgh .... 3·50
Birmingham .... 3·50
Crewe .... 3·50

677 "While Shepherds Watched" **678** "The Holly and the Ivy"

679 "I Saw Three Ships" **680** "We Three Kings"

681 "Good King Wenceslas"

(Des Barbara Brown)

1982 (17 Nov). **Christmas. Carols.** *One phosphor band* (12½p.) or
phosphorised paper (others). P 15 × 14.
1202 **677** 12½p. black, greenish yellow, brt scarlet, steel
           blue, red-brown & gold 30 30
1203 **678** 15½p. black, bistre-yellow, brt rose-red, brt
           blue, brt green & gold 40 40
       a. Imperf (pair) ....

1204 **679** 19½p. black, bistre-yellow, brt rose-red, dull
blue, dp brown & gold 60 60
   a. Imperf (pair) £1300
1205 **680** 26p. black, bistre-yellow, brt magenta, brt
blue, chocolate, gold & orange-red . 70 70
1206 **681** 29p. black, bistre-yellow, magenta, brt blue,
chestnut, gold & brt magenta 80 80
   Set of 5 .... 2·50 2·50
   Set of 5 Gutter Pairs .... 5·00
   First Day Cover .... 2·50
   Presentation Pack .... 3·00
   P.H.Q. cards (set of 5) .... 3·00 7·00

Special Day of Issue Postmarks

Philatelic Bureau, Edinburgh .... 3·00
Bethlehem, Llandeilo, Dyfed .... 3·25

Collectors Pack 1982

1982 (17 Nov). *Comprises Nos. 1175/1206.*
CP1206a Collectors Pack .... 24·00

682 Salmon

683 Pike

684 Trout

685 Perch

(Des A. Jardine)

1983 (26 Jan). **British River Fishes.** *Phosphorised paper.* P 15 × 14.
1207 **682** 15½p. grey-black, bistre-yellow, brt purple,
new blue & silver 35 35
   a. Imperf (pair) £1300
1208 **683** 19½p. black, bistre-yellow, olive-bistre, dp
claret, silver & dp bluish green 55 55
1209 **684** 26p. grey-black, bistre-yellow, chrome-yellow,
magenta, silver & pale blue 70 70
   a. Imperf (pair) £850

1210 **685** 29p. black, greenish yellow, brt carmine, new
blue & silver 90 90
   Set of 4 .... 2·25 2·25
   Set of 4 Gutter Pairs .... 4·50
   First Day Cover .... 2·50
   Presentation Pack .... 3·00
   P.H.Q. Cards (set of 4) .... 3·00 6·50
All known examples of No. 1209a are creased.

Special First Day of Issue Postmarks

Philatelic Bureau, Edinburgh .... 2·50
Peterborough .... 2·50

686 Tropical Island   **687** Desert

688 Temperate Farmland   **689** Mountain Range

(Des D. Fraser)

1983 (9 Mar). **Commonwealth Day. Geographical Regions.** *Phosphorised paper.* P 14 × 15.
1211 **686** 15½p. greenish blue, greenish yellow, brt rose,
lt brown, grey-black, dp claret & silver 35 35
1212 **687** 19½p. brt lilac, greenish yellow, magenta, dull
blue, grey-black, dp dull blue & silver . 55 55
1213 **688** 26p. lt blue, greenish yellow, brt magenta,
new blue, grey-black, violet & silver ... 70 70
1214 **689** 29p. dull violet-blue, reddish violet, slate-
lilac, new blue, myrtle-green, black &
silver 90 90
   Set of 4 .... 2·25 2·25
   Set of 4 Gutter Pairs .... 4·50
   First Day Cover .... 2·50
   Presentation Pack .... 3·25
   P.H.Q. Cards (set of 4) .... 3·00 6·50

Special First Day of Issue Postmarks

Philatelic Bureau, Edinburgh .... 2·50
London SW .... 2·50

690 Humber Bridge   **691** Thames Flood Barrier

692 *Iolair* (oilfield emergency support vessel)

(Des M. Taylor)

1983 (25 May). **Europa. Engineering Achievements.** *Phosphorised paper.* P 15 × 14.
1215 **690** 16p. silver, orange-yellow, ultramarine, black
    & grey 45   45
1216 **691** 20½p. silver, greenish yellow, brt purple, blue,
    grey-black & grey 95   1·10
1217 **692** 28p. silver, lemon, brt rose-red, chestnut,
    dull ultramarine, black & grey .... 1·10   1·25
    Set of 3 .... 2·25   2·50
    Set of 3 Gutter Pairs .... 4·50
    First Day Cover ....   2·50
    Presentation Pack .... 3·50
    P.H.Q. Cards (set of 3) .... 2·50   6·00

Special First Day of Issue Postmarks

Philatelic Bureau, Edinburgh .... 2·50
Hull .... 2·50

693 Musketeer and Pikeman,
The Royal Scots (1633)

694 Fusilier and Ensign,
The Royal Welch Fusiliers
(mid-18th century)

695 Riflemen, 95th Rifles (The
Royal Green Jackets) (1805)

695 Sergeant (khaki service)
and Guardsman (full dress),
The Irish Guards (1900)

697 Paratroopers, The Parachute Regiment (1983)

(Des E. Stemp)

1983 (6 July). **British Army Uniforms.** *Phosphorised paper.* P 14 × 15.
1218 **693** 16p. black, buff, dp brown, slate-black, rose-
    red, gold & new blue 40   40
1219 **694** 20½p. black, buff, greenish yellow, slate-black,
    brown-rose, gold & brt blue 70   70
1220 **695** 26p. black, buff, slate-purple, green, bistre &
    gold 85   85
    a. Imperf (pair) £1300
1221 **696** 28p. black, buff, lt brown, grey, dull rose,
    gold & new blue 85   85
1222 **697** 31p. black, buff, olive-yellow, grey, dp ma-
    genta, gold & new blue .... 1·10   1·10
    Set of 5 .... 3·50   3·50
    Set of 5 Gutter Pairs .... 7·00
    First Day Cover ....   3·25
    Presentation Pack .... 4·25
    P.H.Q. Cards (set of 5) .... 3·00   6·00

Nos. 1218/22 were issued on the occasion of the 350th anniversary
of the Royal Scots, the senior line regiment of the British Army.

Special First Day of Issue Postmarks

Philatelic Bureau, Edinburgh .... 3·50
Aldershot .... 4·00

Special First Day of Issue Postmarks

Philatelic Bureau, Edinburgh .... 3·50
Oxford .... 3·50

SISSINGHURST   BIDDULPH GRANGE

698 20th-century Garden,   **699** 19th-century Garden,
Sissinghurst   Biddulph Grange

702 Merry-go-round   **703** Big Wheel, Helter-skelter and
Performing Animals

  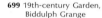

BLENHEIM   PITMEDDEN

700 18th-century Garden,   **701** 17th-century Garden,
Blenheim   Pitmedden

(Des Liz Butler. Litho J.W.)

1983 (24 Aug). **British Gardens.** *Phosphorised paper.* P 14.
1223 **698** 16p. greenish yellow, brt purple, new blue,
        black, brt green & silver 40   40
1224 **699** 20½p. greenish yellow, brt purple, new blue,
        black, brt green & silver 50   50
1225 **700** 28p. greenish yellow, brt purple, new blue,
        black, brt green & silver 70   90
1226 **701** 31p. greenish yellow, brt purple, new blue,
        black, brt green & silver 90   1·00
        Set of 4 .... 2·25   2·50
        Set of 4 Gutter Pairs .... 4·50
        First Day Cover ....   2·75
        Presentation Pack .... 3·50
        P.H.Q. Cards (set of 4) .... 3·00   6·00
    Nos. 1223/6 were issued on the occasion of the death bicentenary of
"Capability" Brown (landscape gardener).

704 Side Shows   **705** Early Produce Fair

(Des A. Restall)

1983 (5 Oct). **British Fairs.** *Phosphorised paper.* P 15 × 14.
1227 **702** 16p. grey-black, greenish yellow, orange-red,
        ochre & turquoise-blue 40   40
1228 **703** 20½p. grey-black, yellow-ochre, yellow-orange,
        brt magenta, violet & black 65   65
1229 **704** 28p. grey-black, bistre-yellow, orange-red,
        violet & yellow-brown 85   85
1230 **705** 31p. grey-black, greenish yellow, red, dp
        turquoise-green, slate-violet & brown .. 90   90
        Set of 4 .... 2·50   2·50
        Set of 4 Gutter Pairs .... 5·00
        First Day Cover ....   2·75
        Presentation Pack .... 3·50
        P.H.Q. Cards (set of 4) .... 3·00   6·00

Special First Day of Issue Postmarks

Philatelic Bureau, Edinburgh .... 3·50
Nottingham .... 3·50

For full information on all future British issues, collectors
should write to the British Post Office Philatelic Bureau, 20
Brandon Street, Edinburgh EH3 5TT

706 "Christmas Post" (pillar-box)   **707** "The Three Kings" (chimney-pots)

708 "World at Peace" (Dove and Blackbird)   **709** "Light of Christmas" (street lamp)

710 "Christmas Dove" (hedge sculpture)

(Des T. Meeuwissen)

1983 (16 Nov). **Christmas.** One phosphor band (12½p.) or phosphorised paper (others). P 15 × 14.

1231	**706**	12½p. black, greenish yellow, brt rose-red, brt blue, gold & grey-black	30	30
		a. Imperf (horiz pair)	£750	
1232	**707**	16p. black, greenish yellow, brt rose, pale new blue, gold & brown-purple	35	35
		a. Imperf (pair)	£850	
1233	**708**	20½p. black, greenish yellow, brt rose, new blue, gold & blue	60	60
1234	**709**	28p. black, lemon, brt carmine, bluish violet, gold, dp turquoise-green & purple	70	80
1235	**710**	31p. black, greenish yellow, brt rose, new blue, gold, green & brown-olive	85	1·00
		Set of 5	2·50	2·75
		Set of 5 Gutter Pairs	5·00	
		First Day Cover		2·75
		Presentation Pack	3·50	
		P.H.Q. Cards (set of 5)	3·00	6·00

Special First Day of Issue Postmarks

Philatelic Bureau, Edinburgh . . . . 3·00
Bethlehem, Llandeilo, Dyfed . . . . 3·00

Collectors Pack 1983

1983 (16 Nov). Comprises Nos. 1207/35.
CP1235a Collectors Pack . . . . 40·00

711 Arms of the College of Arms   **712** Arms of King Richard III (founder)

713 Arms of the Earl Marshal   **714** Arms of the City of London of England

(Des J. Matthews)

1984 (17 Jan). **500th Anniv of College of Arms.** Phosphorised paper. P 14½.

1236	**711**	16p. black, chrome-yellow, reddish brown, scarlet-vermilion, brt blue & grey-black	40	40
1237	**712**	20½p. black, chrome-yellow, rosine, brt blue & grey-black	60	60
1238	**713**	28p. black, chrome-yellow, rosine, brt blue, dull green & grey-black	85	85
1239	**714**	31p. black, chrome-yellow, rosine, brt blue & grey-black	95	95
		a. Imperf (horiz pair)	£1800	
		Set of 4	2·50	2·50
		Set of 4 Gutter Pairs	5·00	
		First Day Cover		2·50
		Presentation Pack	3·50	
		P.H.Q. Cards	3·00	6·00

Special First Day of Issue Postmarks

Philatelic Bureau, Edinburgh . . . . 3·00
London EC . . . . 3·50

715 Highland Cow

716 Chillingham Wild Bull

720 Garden Festival Hall, Liverpool

721 Milburngate Centre, Durham

717 Hereford Bull

718 Welsh Black Bull

722 Bush House, Bristol

723 Commercial Street Development, Perth

719 Irish Moiled Cow

(Des B. Driscoll)

1984 (6 Mar). **British Cattle.** *Phosphorised paper. P* 15 × 14.

1240	**715**	16p.	grey-black, bistre-yellow, rosine, yellow-orange, new blue & pale drab	40	40
1241	**716**	20½p.	grey-black, greenish yellow, magenta, bistre, dull blue-green, pale drab & lt green	65	65
1242	**717**	26p.	black, chrome-yellow, rosine, reddish brown, new blue & pale drab	70	70
1243	**718**	28p.	black, greenish yellow, brt carmine, orange-brown, dp dull blue & pale drab	70	70
1244	**719**	31p.	grey-black, bistre-yellow, rosine, red-brown, lt blue & pale drab	90	90
			Set of 5	3·00	3·00
			Set of 5 Gutter Pairs	6·00	
			First Day Cover		3·00
			Presentation Pack	4·25	
			P.H.Q. Cards (set of 5)	3·00	6·00

Nos. 1240/4 were issued on the occasion of the centenary of the Highland Cattle Society and the bicentenary of the Royal Highland and Agricultural Society of Scotland.

(Des R. Maddox and Trickett and Webb Ltd)

1984 (10 Apr). **Urban Renewal.** *Phosphorised paper. P* 15 × 14.

1245	**720**	16p.	brt emerald, greenish yellow, cerise, steel-blue, black, silver & flesh	40	40
1246	**721**	20½p.	brt orange, greenish yellow, dp dull blue, yellowish green, azure, black & silver	60	60
			a. Imperf (horiz pair)	£1000	
1247	**722**	28p.	rosine, greenish yellow, Prussian blue, pale blue-green, black & silver	90	90
1248	**723**	31p.	blue, greenish yellow, cerise, grey-blue, brt green, black & silver	90	90
			a. Imperf (pair)	£1000	
			Set of 4	2·50	2·50
			Set of 4 Gutter Pairs	5·00	
			First Day Cover		3·00
			Presentation Pack	3·50	
			P.H.Q. Cards (set of 4)	3·00	6·00

Nos. 1245/8 were issued on the occasion of 150th anniversaries of the Royal Institute of British Architects and the Chartered Institute of Building, and to commemorate the first International Gardens Festival, Liverpool.

Special First Day of Issue Postmarks

Philatelic Bureau, Edinburgh .... 3·75
Oban, Argyll .... 3·75

Special First Day of Issue Postmarks

Philatelic Bureau, Edinburgh .... 3·50
Liverpool .... 3·75

724 C.E.P.T. 25th Anniversary Logo   **725** Abduction of Europa

(Des J. Larrivière (T **724**), F. Wegner (T **725**))

1984 (15 May). **25th Anniv of C.E.P.T. ("Europa") (T 724) and Second Elections to European Parliament** (T **725**). *Phosphorised paper.* P 15 × 14.

1249	**724**	16p. greenish slate, dp blue & gold	90	90
		a. Horiz pair. Nos. 1249/50	1·75	1·75
		ab. Imperf (horiz pair)	£1300	
1250	**725**	16p. greenish slate, dp blue, black & gold ..	90	90
1251	**724**	20½p. Venetian red, dp magenta & gold	1·50	1·50
		a. Horiz pair. Nos. 1251/2	3·00	3·00
		ab. Imperf (horiz pair)		
1252	**725**	20½p. Venetian red, dp magenta, black & gold	1·50	1·50
		Set of 4	4·25	4·25
		Set of 2 Gutter Blocks of 4	8·50	
		First Day Cover		4·25
		Presentation Pack	5·00	
		P.H.Q. Cards (set of 4)	3·00	6·00

Nos. 1249/50 and 1251/2 were each printed together, *se-tenant*, in horizontal pairs throughout the sheets.

Special First Day of Issue Postmarks

Philatelic Bureau, Edinburgh .... 4·25
London SW .... 4·25

726 Lancaster House

(Des P. Hogarth)

1984 (5 June). **London Economic Summit Conference.** *Phosphorised paper.* P 14 × 15.

1253	**726**	31p. silver, bistre-yellow, brown-ochre, black, rosine, brt blue & reddish lilac ..	1·00	1·00
		Gutter Pair	2·00	
		First Day Cover		2·00
		P.H.Q. Card	1·00	2·75

Special First Day of Issue Postmarks

Philatelic Bureau, Edinburgh .... 2·50
London SW .... 2·50

727 View of Earth from "Apollo 11"   **728** Navigational Chart of English Channel

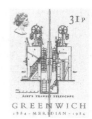

729 Greenwich Observatory   **730** Sir George Airy's Transit Telescope

(Des H. Waller. Litho Questa)

1984 (26 June). **Centenary of the Greenwich Meridian.** *Phosphorised paper. P* 14 × 14½.

1254	**727**	16p. new blue, greenish yellow, magenta, black, scarlet & blue-black	40	40
1255	**728**	20½p. olive-sepia, lt brown, pale buff, black & scarlet	65	65
1256	**729**	28p. new blue, greenish yellow, scarlet, black & brt purple	85	90
1257	**730**	31p. dp blue, cobalt, scarlet & black	90	1·10
		Set of 4	2·50	2·75
		Set of 4 Gutter Pairs	5·00	
		First Day Cover		2·75
		Presentation Pack	3·75	
		P.H.Q. Cards (set of 4)	3·00	6·00

On Nos. 1254/7 the Meridian is represented by a scarlet line.

Special First Day of Issue Postmarks

Philatelic Bureau, Edinburgh .... 3·50
London SE10 .... 3·50

731 Bath Mail Coach, 1784   **732** Attack on Exeter Mail, 1816

733 Norwich Mail in Thunderstorm, 1827   **734** Holyhead and Liverpool Mails leaving London, 1828

735 Edinburgh Mail Snowbound, 1831

(Des K. Bassford and S. Paine. Eng C. Slania. Recess and photo)

1984 (31 July). **Bicentenary of First Mail Coach Run, Bath and Bristol to London.** *Phosphorised paper. P* 15 × 14.

1258	**731**	16p. pale stone, black, grey-black & brt scarlet	60	60
		a. Horiz strip of 5. Nos. 1258/62	2·75	2·75
1259	**732**	16p. pale stone, black, grey-black & brt scarlet	60	60
1260	**733**	16p. pale stone, black, grey-black & brt scarlet	60	60
1261	**734**	16p. pale stone, black, grey-black & brt scarlet	60	60
1262	**735**	16p. pale stone, black, grey-black & brt scarlet	60	60
		Set of 5	2·75	2·75
		Gutter Block of 10	5·50	
		First Day Cover		2·75
		Presentation Pack	3·75	
		Souvenir Book	6·00	
		P.H.Q. Cards (set of 5)	3·00	6·50

Nos. 1258/62 were printed together, *se-tenant*, in horizontal strips of 5 throughout the sheet.

The souvenir book is a 24-page illustrated booklet with a set of mint stamps in a sachet attached to the front cover.

Special First Day of Issue Postmarks

Philatelic Bureau, Edinburgh .... 3·25
Bristol .... 3·50

736 Nigerian Clinic   **737** Violinist and Acropolis, Athens

738 Building Project, Sri Lanka   **739** British Council Library, Middle East

(Des F. Newell and J. Sorrell)

1984 (25 Sept). **50th Anniv of the British Council.** *Phosphorised paper.*
P 15 × 14.

1263	736	17p. grey-green, greenish yellow, brt purple, dull blue, black, pale green & yellow-green	50	50
1264	737	22p. crimson, greenish yellow, brt rose-red, dull green, black, pale drab & slate-purple	65	65
1265	738	31p. sepia, olive-bistre, red, black, pale stone & olive-brown	90	90
1266	739	34p. steel blue, yellow, rose-red, new blue, black, azure & pale blue	1·00	1·00
		Set of 4	2·75	2·75
		Set of 4 Gutter Pairs	5·50	
		First Day Cover		2·75
		Presentation Pack	3·50	
		P.H.Q. Cards (set of 4)	3·00	6·00

Special First Day of Issue Postmarks

Philatelic Bureau, Edinburgh	....	3·25
London SW	....	3·50

740 The Holy Family **741** Arrival in Bethlehem

742 Shepherd and Lamb **743** Virgin and Child

744 Offering of Frankincense

(Des Yvonne Gilbert)

1984 (20 Nov). **Christmas.** *One phosphor band (13p.) or phosphorised paper (others).* P 15 × 14.

1267	740	13p. pale cream, grey-black, bistre-yellow, magenta, red-brown & lake-brown	30	30
		Eu. Underprint Type 4	45	
1268	741	17p. pale cream, grey-black, yellow, magenta, dull blue & dp dull blue	50	50
		a. Imperf (pair)		
1269	742	22p. pale cream, grey-black, olive-yellow, brt magenta, brt blue & brownish grey	60	60
1270	743	31p. pale cream, grey-black, bistre-yellow, magenta, dull blue & lt brown	95	95
1271	744	34p. pale cream, olive-grey, bistre-yellow, magenta, turquoise-green & brown-olive	1·00	1·00
		Set of 5	3·00	3·00
		Set of 5 Gutter Pairs	6·00	
		First Day Cover		3·00
		Presentation Pack	3·75	
		P.H.Q. Cards (set of 5)	3·00	6·00

Examples of No. 1267Eu from the 1984 Christmas booklet (No. FX7) show a random pattern of blue double-lined stars printed on the reverse over the gum.

Special First Day of Issue Postmarks

Philatelic Bureau, Edinburgh	....	3·75
Bethlehem, Llandeilo, Dyfed	....	3·75

Collectors Pack 1984

1984 (20 Nov). *Comprises Nos. 1236/71.*
CP1271a Collectors Pack .... 40·00

Post Office Yearbook

1984. *Comprises Nos. 1236/71 in 24-page hardbound book with slip case, illustrated in colour* .... 75·00

745 "The Flying Scotsman" **746** "The Golden Arrow"

747 "The Cheltenham Flyer" **748** "The Royal Scot"

749 "The Cornish Riviera"

(Des T. Cuneo)

1985 (22 Jan). **Famous Trains.** *Phosphorised paper. P* 15 × 14.

1272	**745**	17p. black, lemon, magenta, dull blue, grey-black & gold	50	50
		a. Imperf (pair)	£1800	
1273	**746**	22p. black, greenish yellow, brt rose, dp dull blue, grey-black & gold	70	70
1274	**747**	29p. black, greenish yellow, magenta, blue, grey-black & gold	90	90
1275	**748**	31p. black, bistre-yellow, brt magenta, new blue, slate-black & gold	1·00	1·00
1276	**749**	34p. black, greenish yellow, brt rose, blue, slate-black & gold	1·10	1·10
		Set of 5	4·00	4·00
		Set of 5 Gutter Pairs	8·00	
		First Day Cover		5·00
		Presentation Pack	4·50	
		P.H.Q. Cards (set of 5)	4·00	11·00

Nos. 1272/6 were issued on the occasion of the 150th anniversary of the Great Western Railway Company.

Special First Day of Issue Postmarks

Philatelic Bureau, Edinburgh	6·00
Bristol	6·25

750 *Bombus terrestris* (bee)   **751** *Coccinella septempunctata* (ladybird)

752 *Decticus verrucivorus* (bush-cricket)   **753** *Lucanus cervus* (stag beetle)

754 *Anax imperator* (dragonfly)

(Des G. Beningfield)

1985 (12 Mar). **Insects.** *Phosphorised paper. P* 14 × 15.

1277	**750**	17p. black, greenish yellow, magenta, blue, azure, gold & slate-black	40	40
1278	**751**	22p. black, greenish yellow, brt rose-red, dull blue-green, slate-black & gold	60	60
1279	**752**	29p. black, greenish yellow, brt rose, greenish blue, grey-black, gold & bistre-yellow	80	80
1280	**753**	31p. black, greenish yellow, rose, pale new blue & gold	90	90
1281	**754**	34p. black, greenish yellow, magenta, greenish blue, grey-black & gold	90	90
		Set of 5	3·25	3·25
		Set of 5 Gutter Pairs	6·50	
		First Day Cover		3·50
		Presentation Pack	4·00	
		P.H.Q. Cards (set of 5)	3·00	6·50

Nos. 1277/81 were issued on the occasion of the centenaries of the Royal Entomological Society of London's Royal Charter, and of the Selborne Society.

Special First Day of Issue Postmarks

Philatelic Bureau, Edinburgh	4·50
London SW	4·50

SEVENTEEN·PENCE

WATER·MUSIC
George Frideric Handel

755 "Water Music"
(George Frederick Handel)

TWENTY·TWO·PENCE

THE·PLANETS·SUITE
Gustav Holst

756 "The Planets Suite"
(Gustav Holst)

THIRTY·ONE·PENCE

THE·FIRST·CUCKOO
Frederick Delius

757 "The First Cuckoo"
(Frederick Delius)

THIRTY·FOUR·PENCE

SEA·PICTURES
Edward Elgar

758 "Sea Pictures" (Edward
Elgar)

(Des W. McLean)

1985 (14 May). **Europa. European Music Year. British Composers.**
Phosphorised paper. P 14 × 14½.

1282 **755** 17p. black, brt yellow-green, dp magenta, new blue, grey & gold	65	65
a. Imperf (vert pair)		
1283 **756** 22p. black, greenish yellow, brt magenta, new blue, grey-black & gold	90	90
a. Imperf (pair)	£1300	
1284 **757** 31p. black, greenish yellow, magenta, greenish blue, grey-black & gold	1·40	1·40
1285 **758** 34p. black, olive-yellow, bistre, turquoise-blue, slate & gold	1·50	1·50
Set of 4	4·00	4·00
Set of 4 Gutter Pairs	8·00	
First Day Cover		4·00
Presentation Pack	4·50	
P.H.Q. Cards (set of 4)	3·00	6·00

Nos. 1282/5 were issued on the occasion of the 300th birth anniversary of Handel.

Special First Day of Issue Postmarks

Philatelic Bureau, Edinburgh .... 4·00
Worcester .... 4·00

759 R.N.L.I. Lifeboat and
Signal Flags

760 Beachy Head Lighthouse
and Chart

761 "Marecs A"
Communications Satellite and
Dish Aerials

762 Buoys

(Des F. Newell and J. Sorrell. Litho J.W.)

1985 (18 June). **Safety at Sea.** *Phosphorised paper. P* 14.

1286 **759** 17p. black, azure, emerald, ultramarine, orange-yellow, vermilion, brt blue & chrome-yellow	50	50
1287 **760** 22p. black, azure, emerald, ultramarine, orange-yellow, vermilion, brt blue & chrome-yellow	65	65
1288 **761** 31p. black, azure, emerald, ultramarine, orange-yellow, vermilion & brt blue	1·10	1·10
1289 **762** 34p. black, azure, emerald, ultramarine, orange-yellow, vermilion, brt blue & chrome-yellow	1·10	1·10
Set of 4	3·00	3·00
Set of 4 Gutter Pairs	6·00	
First Day Cover		3·50
Presentation Pack	4·25	
P.H.Q. Cards (set of 4)	3·00	6·00

Nos. 1286/9 were issued on the occasion of the bicentenary of the unimmersible lifeboat and the 50th anniversary of radar.

Special First Day of Issue Postmarks

Philatelic Bureau, Edinburgh .... 3·50
Eastbourne .... 3·50

HAVE YOU READ THE NOTES AT THE BEGINNING OF THIS CATALOGUE?

These often provide answers to the enquiries we receive.

763 Datapost Motorcyclist, City of London

764 Rural Postbus

765 Parcel Delivery in Winter   766 Town Letter Delivery

(Des P. Hogarth)

1985 (30 July). **350 Years of Royal Mail Public Postal Service.** *Phosphorised paper. P* 14 × 15.

1290	763	17p. black, greenish yellow, brt carmine, greenish blue, yellow-brown, grey-black & silver	50	50
		a. Imperf on 3 sides (vert pair) £1300		
		Eu. Underprint Type 5	70	
1291	764	22p. black, greenish yellow, cerise, steel-blue, lt green, grey-black & silver	65	65
1292	765	31p. black, greenish yellow, brt carmine, dull blue, drab, grey-black & silver	1·10	1·10
		a. Imperf (vert pair) £1300		
1293	766	34p. black, greenish yellow, cerise, ultramarine, lt brown, grey-black & silver	1·10	1·10
		a. Imperf between (vert pair)		
		Set of 4	3·00	3·00
		Set of 4 Gutter Pairs	6·00	
		First Day Cover		3·25
		Presentation Pack	4·25	
		P.H.Q. Cards (set of 4)	3·00	6·00

No. 1290a shows perforation indentations at right, but is imperforate at top, bottom and on the left-hand side.

Examples of No. 1290Eu from the 1985 £1.70 booklet (sold at £1.53) (No. FT4) show a blue double-lined D in a random pattern, on the reverse over the gum.

Special First Day of Issue Postmarks

Philatelic Bureau, Edinburgh .... 3·50
Bagshot, Surrey .... 3·50

767 King Arthur and Merlin   768 Lady of the Lake

769 Queen Guinevere and Sir Lancelot   770 Sir Galahad

(Des Yvonne Gilbert)

1985 (3 Sept). **Arthurian Legends.** *Phosphorised paper. P* 15 × 14.

1294	767	17p. grey-black, lemon, brown-lilac, ultramarine, grey-black & silver	50	50
		a. Imperf (pair) £1800		
1295	768	22p. black, lemon, brown-lilac, pale blue, grey-black, silver & grey-black	65	75
1296	769	31p. black, lemon, magenta, turquoise-blue, grey-black, silver & grey-black	1·10	1·10
1297	770	34p. grey, lemon, magenta, new blue, grey-black, silver & grey-black	1·10	1·25
		Set of 4	3·00	3·25
		Set of 4 Gutter Pairs	6·00	
		First Day Cover		3·50
		Presentation Pack	4·75	
		P.H.Q. Cards (set of 4)	3·00	6·00

Nos. 1294/7 were issued on the occasion of the 500th anniversary of the printing of Sir Thomas Malory's *Morte d'Arthur*.

Special First Day of Issue Postmarks

Philatelic Bureau, Edinburgh .... 3·50
Tintagel, Cornwall .... 3·50

771 Peter Sellers (from photo by Bill Brandt)

772 David Niven (from photo by Cornell Lucas)

773 Charlie Chaplin (from photo by Lord Snowdon)

774 Vivien Leigh (from photo by Angus McBean)

775 Alfred Hitchcock (from photo by Howard Coster)

(Des K. Bassford)

1985 (8 Oct). **British Film Year.** *Phosphorised paper.* P 14½.

1298	**771**	17p. grey-black, olive-grey, gold & silver	50	50
1299	**772**	22p. black, brown, gold & silver	75	75
1300	**773**	29p. black, lavender, gold & silver	1·10	1·10
1301	**774**	31p. black, pink, gold & silver	1·25	1·25
1302	**775**	34p. black, greenish blue, gold & silver	1·40	1·40
		Set of 5	4·50	4·50
		Set of 5 Gutter Pairs	9·00	
		First Day Cover		4·75
		Presentation Pack	6·00	
		Souvenir Book	7·00	
		P.H.Q. Cards (set of 5)	3·00	6·00

The souvenir book is a 24-page illustrated booklet with a set of mint stamps in a sachet attached to the front cover.

Special First Day of Issue Postmarks

Philatelic Bureau, Edinburgh .... 5·00
London WC .... 5·00

776 Principal Boy   **777** Genie

778 Dame   **779** Good Fairy

780 Pantomime Cat

(Des A. George)

1985 (19 Nov). **Christmas. Pantomine Characters.** *One phosphor band (12p.) or phosphorised paper (others). P* 15 × 14.

1303	**776**	12p. new blue, greenish yellow, brt rose, gold, grey-black & silver	35	30
		a. Imperf (pair)	£1300	
		Eu. Underprint Type 4	40	
1304	**777**	17p. emerald, greenish yellow, brt rose, new blue, black, gold & silver	45	40
		a. Imperf (pair)	£1800	
1305	**778**	22p. brt carmine, greenish yellow, pale new blue, grey, gold & silver	70	80
1306	**779**	31p. brt orange, lemon, rose, slate-purple, silver & gold	95	1·00
1307	**780**	34p. brt reddish violet, brt blue, brt rose, black, grey-brown, gold & silver	1·00	1·10
		Set of 5	3·00	3·25
		Set of 5 Gutter Pairs	6·00	
		First Day Cover		3·75
		Presentation Pack	4·50	
		P.H.Q. Cards (set of 5)	3·00	6·00
		Christmas Folder (contains No. *1303 × 50)*	20·00	

Examples of No. 1303Eu from the 1985 Christmas booklet (No. FX8) show a random pattern of blue double-lined stars printed on the reverse over the gum.

Special First Day of Issue Postmarks

Special First Day of Issue Postmarks

Philatelic Bureau, Edinburgh	4·00
Bethlehem, Llandeilo, Dyfed	4·00

Philatelic Bureau, Edinburgh	3·50
Birmingham	3·50

Collectors Pack 1985

1985 (19 Nov). *Comprises Nos. 1272/1307.*
CP1307a Collectors Pack .... 40·00

Post Office Yearbook

1985. *Comprises Nos. 1272/1307 in 32-page hardbound book with slip case, illustrated in colour* .... 75·00

785 Dr. Edmond Halley as Comet

786 *Giotto* Spacecraft approaching Comet

781 Light Bulb and North Sea Oil Drilling Rig (Energy)

782 Thermometer and Pharmaceutical Laboratory (Health)

787 "Maybe Twice in a Lifetime"

788 Comet orbiting Sun and Planets

783 Garden Hoe and Steelworks (Steel)

784 Loaf of Bread and Cornfield (Agriculture)

(Des K. Bassford. Litho Questa)

1986 (14 Jan). **Industry Year.** *Phosphorised paper.* P $14\frac{1}{2} \times 14$.

1308	**781**	17p.	gold, black, magenta, greenish yellow & new blue	45	45
1309	**782**	22p.	gold, pale turquoise-green, black, magenta, greenish yellow & blue	60	60
1310	**783**	31p.	gold, black, magenta, greenish yellow & new blue	90	90
1311	**784**	34p.	gold, black, magenta, greenish yellow & new blue	1·10	1·10
			Set of 4	2·75	2·75
			Set of 4 Gutter Pairs	5·50	
			First Day Cover		3·25
			Presentation Pack	4·00	
			P.H.Q. Cards (set of 4)	3·00	6·00

(Des R. Steadman)

1986 (18 Feb). **Appearance of Halley's Comet.** *Phosphorised paper.* P 15×14.

1312	**785**	17p.	black, bistre, rosine, blue, grey-black, gold & dp brown	45	45
1313	**786**	22p.	orange-vermilion, greenish yellow, brt purple, new blue, black & gold	70	70
1314	**787**	31p.	black, greenish yellow, brt purple, dp turquoise-blue, grey-black & gold	1·10	1·10
1315	**788**	34p.	blue, greenish yellow, magenta, dp turquoise-blue, black & gold	1·10	1·10
			Set of 4	3·00	3·00
			Set of 4 Gutter Pairs	6·00	
			First Day Cover		4·00
			Presentation Pack	4·50	
			P.H.Q. Cards (set of 4)	4·00	6·00

Special First Day of Issue Postmarks

Philatelic Bureau, Edinburgh . . . . 4·25
London SE10 . . . . 4·25

789 Queen Elizabeth in 1928, 1942 and 1952

790 Queen Elizabeth in 1958, 1973 and 1982

T **789/90** were printed horizontally *se-tenant* within the sheet

791 Barn Owl

792 Pine Marten

793 Wild Cat

794 Natterjack Toad

(Des J. Matthews)

1986 (21 Apr). **60th Birthday of Queen Elizabeth II.** *Phosphorised paper.* P 15 × 14.

1316 **789**	17p. grey-black, turquoise-green, brt green, green & dull blue	70	70
	a. Pair. Nos. 1316/17	1·40	1·40
1317 **790**	17p. grey-black, dull blue, greenish blue & indigo	70	70
1318 **789**	34p. grey-black, dp dull purple, yellow-orange & red	1·25	1·25
	a. Pair. Nos. 1318/19	2·50	2·50
1319 **790**	34p. grey-black, olive-brown, yellow-brown, olive-grey & red	1·25	1·25
	Set of 4	3·50	3·50
	Set of 2 Gutter Blocks of 4	7·00	
	First Day Cover		4·00
	Presentation Pack	5·00	
	Souvenir Book	7·00	
	P.H.Q. Cards (set of 4)	3·00	6·00

The souvenir book is a special booklet, fully illustrated and containing a mint set of stamps.

(Des K. Lilly)

1986 (20 May). **Europa. Nature Conservation – Endangered Species.** *Phosphorised paper.* P 14½ × 14.

1320 **791**	17p. gold, greenish yellow, rose, yellow-brown, olive-grey, new blue & black . . .	50	50
1321 **792**	22p. gold, greenish yellow, reddish brown, olive-yellow, turquoise-blue, grey-black & black	75	75
1322 **793**	31p. gold, brt yellow-green, magenta, lt brown, ultramarine, olive-brown & black	1·10	1·10
1323 **794**	34p. gold, greenish yellow, brt rose-red, brt green, grey-black & black	1·25	1·25
	Set of 4	3·25	3·25
	Set of 4 Gutter Pairs	6·50	
	First Day Cover		4·00
	Presentation Pack	4·50	
	P.H.Q. Cards (set of 4)	3·00	6·00

Special First Day of Issue Postmarks

Philatelic Bureau, Edinburgh . . . . 4·25
Windsor . . . . 4·25

Special First Day of Issue Postmarks

Philatelic Bureau, Edinburgh . . . . 4·25
Lincoln . . . . 4·25

795 Peasants working in Fields

796 Freemen working at Town Trades

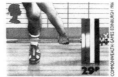

801 Weightlifting

802 Rifle Shooting

797 Knight and Retainers

798 Lord at Banquet

803 Hockey

(Des Tayburn Design Consultancy)

1986 (17 Jun). **900th Anniv of Domesday Book.** *Phosphorised paper.* P 15 × 14.

1324	**795**	17p.	yellow-brown, vermilion, lemon, brt emerald, orange-brown, grey & brownish grey	50 50
1325	**796**	22p.	yellow-ochre, red, greenish blue, chestnut, grey-black & brownish grey	75 75
1326	**797**	31p.	yellow-brown, vermilion, green, Indian red, grey-black & brownish grey	1·10 1·10
1327	**798**	34p.	yellow-ochre, bright scarlet, grey-brown, new blue, lake-brown, grey-black & grey	1·25 1·25
			Set of 4	3·25 3·25
			Set of 4 Gutter Pairs	6·50
			First Day Cover	4·00
			Presentation Pack	4·50
			P.H.Q. Cards (set of 4)	3·00 6·00

Special First Day of Issue Postmarks

 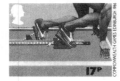

Philatelic Bureau, Edinburgh .... 4·25
Gloucester .... 4·25

(Des N. Cudworth)

1986 (15 July). **Thirteenth Commonwealth Games, Edinburgh and World Hockey Cup for Men, London** (34p.). *Phosphorised paper.* P 15 × 14.

1328	**799**	17p.	black, greenish yellow, orange-vermilion, ultramarine, chestnut & emerald	50 50
1329	**800**	22p.	black, lemon, scarlet, new blue, royal blue, chestnut & dp ultramarine	70 70
1330	**801**	29p.	grey-black, greenish yellow, scarlet, new blue, brown-ochre, brown-rose & pale chestnut	90 90
1331	**802**	31p.	black, greenish yellow, rose, blue, dull yellow-green, chestnut & yellow-green	1·10 1·10
1332	**803**	34p.	black, lemon, scarlet, brt blue, brt emerald, red-brown & vermilion	1·25 1·25
		a.	Imperf (pair)	£1300
			Set of 5	4·00 4·00
			Set of 5 Gutter Pairs	8·00
			First Day Cover	4·25
			Presentation Pack	5·25
			P.H.Q. Cards (set of 5)	4·00 6·00

No. 1332 also commemorates the centenary of the Hockey Association.

Special First Day of Issue Postmarks

Philatelic Bureau, Edinburgh .... 4·50
Head Post Office, Edinburgh .... 4·50

For full information on all future British issues, collectors should write to the British Post Office Philatelic Bureau, 20 Brandon Street, Edinburgh EH3 5TT

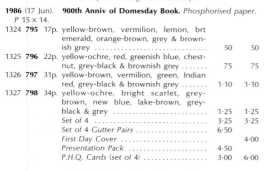

799 Athletics

800 Rowing

804　　　　　　**805**

Prince Andrew and Miss Sarah Ferguson (from photo by Gene Nocon)

(Des J. Matthews)

1986 (22 July). **Royal Wedding.** *One phosphor band* (12p.) *or phosphorised paper* (17p.). *P* 14 × 15.

1333 **804** 12p. lake, greenish yellow, cerise, ultramarine, black & silver	60	60
1334 **805** 17p. steel blue, greenish yellow, cerise, ultramarine, black & gold	90	90
a. Imperf (pair)	£850	
Set of 2	1·25	1·25
Set of 2 Gutter Pairs	2·50	
First Day Cover		2·50
Presentation Pack	2·00	
P.H.Q. Cards (set of 2)	1·50	5·00

Special First Day of Issue Postmarks

Philatelic Bureau, Edinburgh .... 2·75
London, SW1 .... 2·75

806 Stylised Cross on Ballot Paper

(Des J. Gibbs. Litho Questa)

1986 (19 Aug). **32nd Commonwealth Parliamentary Association Conference.** *Phosphorised paper. P* 14 × 14½.

1335 **806** 34p. pale grey-lilac, black, vermilion, yellow & ultramarine	1·25	1·25
Gutter Pair	2·50	
First Day Cover		2·00
P.H.Q. Card	1·00	2·50

Special First Day of Issue Postmarks

Philatelic Bureau, Edinburgh .... 2·25
London, SW1 .... 2·25

807 Lord Dowding and　　**808** Lord Tedder and Hawker
Hawker Hurricane　　　　　　　Typhoon

809 Lord Trenchard and　　**810** Sir Arthur Harris and
De Havilland DH9A　　　　　　Avro Lancaster

811 Lord Portal and De Havilland
Mosquito

(Des B. Sanders)

1986 (16 Sept). **History of the Royal Air Force.** *Phosphorised paper. P* 14½.

1336 **807** 17p. pale blue, greenish yellow, brt rose, blue, black & grey-black	50	40
a. Imperf (pair)	£950	
1337 **808** 22p. pale turquoise-green, greenish yellow, magenta, new blue, black & grey-black	70	85
a. Face value omitted*	£400	
b. Queen's head omitted*	£400	

145

1338 **809** 29p. pale drab, olive-yellow, magenta, blue,
grey-black & black .... 90 1·00
1339 **810** 31p. pale flesh, greenish yellow, magenta,
ultramarine, black & grey-black .... 1·10 1·10
1340 **811** 34p. buff, greenish yellow, magenta, blue,
grey-black & black .... 1·25 1·25
Set of 5 .... 4·00 4·25
Set of 5 Gutter Pairs .... 8·00
First Day Cover .... 5·00
Presentation Pack .... 6·00
P.H.Q. Cards (set of 5) .... 4·00 6·50

Nos. 1336/40 were issued to celebrate the 50th anniversary of the
first R.A.F. Commands.

*Nos. 1337a/b come from three consecutive sheets on which the
stamps in the first vertical row are without the face value and those in
the second vertical row the Queen's head.

Special First Day of Issue Postmarks

Philatelic Bureau, Edinburgh .... 5·25
Farnborough .... 5·25

812 The Glastonbury Thorn   **813** The Tanad Valley Plygain

814 The Hebrides Tribute   **815** The Dewsbury Church Knell

816 The Hereford Boy Bishop

(Des Lynda Gray)

1986 (18 Nov–2 Dec). **Christmas. Folk Customs.** *One phosphor band
(12p., 13p.) or phosphorised paper (others). P* 15 × 14.
1341 **812** 12p. gold, greenish yellow, vermilion, dp
brown, emerald & dp blue (2.12) 50 50
a. Imperf (pair) ....
1342 13p. dp blue, greenish yellow, vermilion, dp
brown, emerald & gold 30 30
Eu. Underprint Type 4 (2.12) 50
1343 **813** 18p. myrtle-green, yellow, vermilion, dp blue,
black, reddish brown & gold 45 45
1344 **814** 22p. vermilion, olive-bistre, dull blue, dp
brown, dp green & gold 65 65
1345 **815** 31p. dp brown, yellow, vermilion, violet, dp
dull green, black & gold 80 80
1346 **816** 34p. violet, lemon, vermilion, dp dull blue,
reddish brown & gold 90 90
Set of 6 .... 3·25 3·25
Set of 6 Gutter Pairs .... 6·50
First Day Covers (2) .... 5·25
Presentation Pack (Nos. 1342/6) .... 5·00
P.H.Q. Cards (Nos. 1342/6) (Set of 5) .... 3·00 6·00
*Christmas Folder (contains No.
1342Eu × 36)* .... 17·00

No. 1341 represented a discount of 1p., available between 2 and 24
December 1986, on the current second class postage rate.

Special First Day of Issue Postmarks

Philatelic Bureau, Edinburgh (Nos. 1342/6) (18 Nov)   4·50
Bethlehem, Llandeilo, Dyfed (Nos. 1342/6) (18 Nov)   4·50
Philatelic Bureau, Edinburgh (No. 1341) (2 Dec) ....   1·50

Collectors Pack 1986

1986 (18 Nov). *Comprises Nos. 1308/40 and 1342/6.*
CP1346a Collectors Pack .... 40·00

Post Office Yearbook

1986 (18 Nov). *Comprises Nos. 1308/46 in 32-page hardbound book
with slip case, illustrated in colour* .... 70·00

817 North American
Blanket Flower

818 Globe Thistle

821 *The Principia
Mathematica*

822 *Motion of Bodies
in Ellipses*

819 *Echeveria*

820 Autumn Crocus

823 *Optick Treatise*

824 *The System of the World*

(Adapted J. Matthews)

1987 (20 Jan). **Flower Photographs by Alfred Lammer.** *Phosphorised
paper. P $14\frac{1}{2} \times 14$.*

1347	**817**	18p. silver, greenish yellow, rosine, dp green & black	50	50
1348	**818**	22p. silver, greenish yellow, new blue, greenish blue & black	70	70
1349	**819**	31p. silver, greenish yellow, scarlet, bluegreen, dp green & black	1·10	1·10
		a. Imperf (pair)	£1600	
1350	**820**	34p. silver, greenish yellow, magenta, dull blue, dp green & black	1·25	1·25
		Set of 4	3·25	3·25
		Set of 4 Gutter Pairs	6·50	
		First Day Cover		4·25
		Presentation Pack	4·50	
		P.H.Q. Cards (set of 4)	3·00	6·00

(Des Sarah Godwin)

1987 (24 Mar). **300th Anniv of "The Principia Mathematica" by Sir
Isaac Newton.** *Phosphorised paper. P 14 × 15.*

1351	**821**	18p. black, greenish yellow, cerise, bluegreen, grey-black & silver	50	50
1352	**822**	22p. black, greenish yellow, brt orange, blue, brt emerald, silver & bluish violet	70	70
1353	**823**	31p. black, greenish yellow, scarlet, new blue, bronze-green, silver & slate-green	1·10	1·10
1354	**824**	34p. black, greenish yellow, red, brt blue, grey-black & silver	1·25	1·25
		Set of 4	3·25	3·25
		Set of 4 Gutter Pairs	6·50	
		First Day Cover		3·50
		Presentation Pack	4·50	
		P.H.Q. Cards (set of 4)	3·00	6·00

Special First Day of Issue Postmarks

Philatelic Bureau, Edinburgh	4·75
Richmond, Surrey	4·75

Special First Day of Issue Postmarks

Philatelic Bureau, Edinburgh	4·00
Woolsthorpe, Lincs	4·00

825 Willis Faber and Dumas
Building, Ipswich

826 Pompidou Centre, Paris

827 Staatsgalerie, Stuttgart

828 European Investment Bank,
Luxembourg

(Des B. Tattersfield)

1987 (12 May). **Europa. British Architects in Europe.** *Phosphorised paper. P 15 × 14.*

1355	**825**	18p. black, bistre-yellow, cerise, brt blue, dp grey & grey-black	50	50
1356	**826**	22p. black, greenish yellow, carmine, brt blue, dp grey & grey-black	70	70
1357	**827**	31p. grey-black, bistre-yellow, cerise, brt blue, brt green, black & dull violet	1·10	1·10
		a. Imperf (horiz pair)	£1000	
1358	**828**	34p. black, greenish yellow, cerise, brt blue, grey-black & dp grey	1·25	1·25
		Set of 4	3·25	3·25
		Set of 4 Gutter Pairs	6·50	
		First Day Cover		3·50
		Presentation Pack	4·50	
		P.H.Q. Cards (set of 4)	3·00	6·00

Special First Day of Issue Postmarks

Philatelic Bureau, Edinburgh .... 4·00
Ipswich .... 4·00

HAVE YOU READ THE NOTES AT THE BEGINNING OF THIS CATALOGUE?
These often provide answers to the enquiries we receive.

829 Brigade Members with
Ashford Litter, 1887

830 Bandaging Blitz
Victim, 1940

831 Volunteer with
fainting Girl, 1965

832 Transport of Transplant
Organ by Air Wing, 1987

(Des Debbie Cook. Litho Questa)

1987 (16 June). **Centenary of St. John Ambulance Brigade.** *Phosphorised paper. P 14 × 14½.*

1359	**829**	18p. new blue, greenish yellow, magenta, black, silver & pink	50	50
		Ea. Black ptg double	†	—
		Eb. Black ptg triple	†	—
1360	**830**	22p. new blue, greenish yellow, magenta, black, silver & cobalt	65	65
1361	**831**	31p. new blue, greenish yellow, magenta, black, silver & bistre-brown	1·10	1·10
1362	**832**	34p. new blue, greenish yellow, magenta, black, silver & greenish grey	1·10	1·10
		Set of 4	3·00	3·00
		Set of 4 Gutter Pairs	6·00	
		First Day Cover		3·50
		Presentation Pack	4·50	
		P.H.Q. Cards (set of 4)	3·00	6·00

Special First Day of Issue Postmarks

Philatelic Bureau, Edinburgh .... 4·00
London, EC1 .... 4·00

833 Arms of the Lord Lyon King of Arms

834 Scottish Heraldic Banner of Prince Charles

837 Crystal Palace, "Monarch of the Glen" (Landseer) and Grace Darling

838 Great Eastern, Beeton's Book of Household Management and Prince Albert

835 Arms of Royal Scottish Academy of Painting, Sculpture and Architecture

836 Arms of Royal Society of Edinburgh

839 Albert Memorial, Ballot Box and Disraeli

840 Diamond Jubilee Emblem, Newspaper Placard for Relief of Mafeking and Morse Key

(Des J. Matthews)

1987 (21 July). **300th Anniv of Revival of Order of the Thistle.** *Phosphorised paper.* P 14½.

1363	**833**	18p. black, lemon, scarlet, blue, dp green, slate & brown	50	50
1364	**834**	22p. black, greenish yellow, carmine, new blue, dp green, grey & lake-brown	65	65
1365	**835**	31p. black, greenish yellow, scarlet, new blue, dull green, grey & grey-black	1·10	1·10
1366	**836**	34p. black, greenish yellow, scarlet, dp ultramarine, dull green, grey & yellow-brown	1·10	1·10
		Set of 4	3·00	3·00
		Set of 4 Gutter Pairs	6·00	
		First Day Cover		4·25
		Presentation Pack	4·50	
		P.H.Q. Cards (set of 4)	3·00	6·00

(Des M. Dempsey. Eng C. Slania. Recess and photo)

1987 (8 Sept). **150th Anniv of Queen Victoria's Accession.** *Phosphorised paper.* P 15 × 14.

1367	**837**	18p. pale stone, dp blue, lemon, rose, greenish blue, brown-ochre & grey-black	50	50
1368	**838**	22p. pale stone, dp brown, lemon, rose, grey-black & brown-ochre	65	65
1369	**839**	31p. pale stone, dp lilac, lemon, cerise, brown-ochre, greenish blue & grey-black	1·10	1·10
1370	**840**	34p. pale stone, myrtle-green, yellow-ochre, reddish brown & brown-ochre	1·10	1·10
		Set of 4	3·00	3·00
		Set of 4 Gutter Pairs	6·00	
		First Day Cover		4·25
		Presentation Pack	4·50	
		P.H.Q. Cards (set of 4)	3·00	6·00

Special First Day of Issue Postmarks

Philatelic Bureau, Edinburgh	4·75
Rothesay, Isle of Bute	4·75

Special First Day of Issue Postmarks

Philatelic Bureau, Edinburgh	4·75
Newport, Isle of Wight	4·75

841 Pot by Bernard Leach   **842** Pot by Elizabeth Fritsch

843 Pot by Lucie Rie   **844** Pot by Hans Coper

(Des T. Evans)

1987 (13 Oct).   **Studio Pottery.** *Phosphorised paper.* P $14\frac{1}{2} \times 14$.

1371	**841**	18p.	gold, lemon, lt red-brown, chestnut, lt grey & black	50	50
1372	**842**	26p.	blue over silver, yellow-orange, brt purple, lavender, bluish violet, grey-brown & black	70	70
1373	**843**	31p.	rose-lilac over silver, greenish yellow, cerise, new blue, grey-lilac & black	1·10	1·10
1374	**844**	34p.	copper, yellow-brown, reddish brown, grey-lilac & black	1·25	1·25
			Set of 4	3·25	3·25
			Set of 4 Gutter Pairs	6·50	
			First Day Cover		3·50
			Presentation Pack	4·50	
			P.H.Q. Cards (set of 4)	3·00	6·00

Special First Day of Issue Postmarks

Philatelic Bureau, Edinburgh .... 4·00
St. Ives, Cornwall .... 4·00

845 Decorating the   **846** Waiting for Father
Christmas Tree   Christmas

847 Sleeping Child and   **848** Child reading
Father Christmas in Sleigh

849 Child playing Recorder
and Snowman

(Des M. Foreman)

1987 (17 Nov).   **Christmas.** *One phosphor band (13p.) or phosphorised paper (others).* P 15 × 14.

1375	**845**	13p.	gold, greenish yellow, rose, greenish blue & black	30	30
			Eu. Underprint Type 4	50	
1376	**846**	18p.	gold, greenish yellow, brt purple, greenish blue, brt blue & black	50	50
1377	**847**	26p.	gold, greenish yellow, brt purple, new blue, brt blue & black	75	75
1378	**848**	31p.	gold, greenish yellow, scarlet, brt magenta, dull rose, greenish blue & black	95	1·10
1379	**849**	34p.	gold, greenish yellow, dull rose, greenish blue, brt blue & black	1·10	1·25
			Set of 5	3·25	3·50
			Set of 5 Gutter Pairs	6·50	
			First Day Cover		4·25
			Presentation Pack	4·50	
			P.H.Q. Cards (set of 5)	3·00	6·00
			Christmas Folder (contains No. 1375Eu × 36)	15·00	

Special First Day of Issue Postmarks

Philatelic Bureau, Edinburgh .... 4·75
Bethlehem, Llandeilo, Dyfed .... 4·75

Collectors Pack 1987

1987 (17 Nov). *Comprises Nos. 1347/79.*
CP1379a Collectors Pack .... 32·00

Post Office Yearbook

1987 (17 Nov). *Comprises Nos. 1347/79 in 32-page hardbound book with slip case, illustrated in colour* .... 45·00

850 Bull-rout (Jonathan Couch)

851 Yellow Waterlily (Major Joshua Swatkin)

852 Whistling ("Bewick's") Swan (Edward Lear)

853 *Morchella esculenta* (James Sowerby)

854 Revd William Morgan (Bible translator, 1588)

855 William Salesbury (New Testament translator, 1567)

856 Bishop Richard Davies (New Testament translator, 1567)

857 Bishop Richard Parry (editor of Revised Welsh Bible, 1620)

(Des. E. Hughes)

1988 (19 Jan). **Bicentenary of Linnean Society. Archive Illustrations.** *Phosphorised paper. P* 15 × 14.

1380	850	18p. grey-black, stone, orange-yellow, brt purple, olive-bistre & gold	45	45
1381	851	26p. black, stone, bistre-yellow, dull orange, greenish blue, gold & pale bistre	70	70
1382	852	31p. black, stone, greenish yellow, rose-red, dp blue, gold & olive-bistre	1·10	1·10
		a. Imperf (horiz pair)	£1300	
1383	853	34p. black, stone, yellow, pale bistre, olive-grey, gold & olive-bistre	1·10	1·10
		Set of 4	3·00	3·00
		Set of 4 Gutter Pairs	6·00	
		First Day Cover		3·50
		Presentation Pack	4·50	
		P.H.Q. Cards (set of 4)	3·00	6·00

(Des K. Bowen)

1988 (1 Mar). **400th Anniv of Welsh Bible.** *Phosphorised paper. P* 14½ × 14.

1384	854	18p. grey-black, greenish yellow, cerise, blue, black & emerald	45	45
		a. Imperf (pair)	£1300	
1385	855	26p. grey-black, yellow, brt rose-red, turquoise-blue, black & orange	70	70
1386	856	31p. black, chrome-yellow, carmine, new blue, grey-black & blue	1·10	1·10
1387	857	34p. grey-black, greenish yellow, cerise, turquoise-green, black & brt violet	1·10	1·10
		Set of 4	3·00	3·00
		Set of 4 Gutter Pairs	6·00	
		First Day Cover		4·00
		Presentation Pack	4·50	
		P.H.Q. Cards (set of 4)	3·00	6·00

Special First Day of Issue Postmarks

Special First Day of Issue Postmarks

Philatelic Bureau, Edinburgh .... 4·00
London, W1 .... 4·00

Philatelic Bureau, Edinburgh .... 4·75
Ty Mawr, Wybrnant, Gwynedd .... 4·75

858 Gymnastics (Centenary of British Amateur Gymnastics Association)

859 Downhill Skiing (Ski Club of Great Britain)

860 Tennis (Centenary of Lawn Tennis Association)

861 Football (Centenary of Football League)

(Des. J. Sutton)

1988 (22 Mar). **Sports Organizations.** *Phosphorised paper. P* 14½.

1388 **858** 18p. violet-blue, greenish yellow, rosine, brt rose, new blue & silver 45 45
1389 **859** 26p. violet-blue, greenish yellow, vermilion, carmine, yellow-orange & silver 70 70
1390 **860** 31p. violet-blue, greenish yellow, rose, blue, pale greenish blue, silver & brt orange . 1·10 1·10
1391 **861** 34p. violet-blue, greenish yellow, vermilion, blue, brt emerald, silver & pink . . . . 1·10 1·10
    Set of 4 . . . . 3·00 3·00
    Set of 4 Gutter Pairs . . . . 6·00
    First Day Cover . . . . 4·00
    Presentation Pack . . . . 4·50
    P.H.Q. Cards (set of 2) . . . . 2·25 5·00

Special First Day of Issue Postmarks

Philatelic Bureau, Edinburgh . . . . 4·50
Wembley . . . . 4·50

GIBBONS STAMP MONTHLY
– finest and most informative magazine for all collectors. Obtainable from your newsagent or by postal subscription – details on request.

862 *Mallard* and Mailbags on Pick-up Arms

863 Loading Transatlantic Mail on Liner *Queen Elizabeth*

864 Glasgow Tram No. 1173 and Pillar Box

865 Imperial Airways Handley Page HP 42 and Airmail Van

(Des M. Dempsey)

1988 (10 May). **Europa. Transport and Mail Services in 1930s.** *Phosphorised paper. P* 15 × 14.

1392 **862** 18p. brown, yellow, rose-red, dull blue, dp brown, reddish violet & black 50 50
1393 **863** 26p. brown, yellow, orange-vermilion, dull blue, violet-blue, brt emerald & black . 80 80
1394 **864** 31p. brown, yellow-orange, carmine, dull purple, violet-blue, brt green & black . . 1·10 1·10
1395 **865** 34p. brown, orange-yellow, carmine-rose, bluish violet, brt blue, sepia & black . . . 1·25 1·25
    Set of 4 . . . . 3·25 3·25
    Set of 4 Gutter Pairs . . . . 6·50
    First Day Cover . . . . 3·50
    Presentation Pack . . . . 4·50
    P.H.Q. Cards (set of 4) . . . . 2·00 5·00

Special First Day of Issue Postmarks

Philatelic Bureau, Edinburgh . . . . 4·00
Glasgow . . . . 4·00

866 Early Settler and Sailing Clipper

867 Queen Elizabeth II with British and Australian Parliament Buildings

868 W.G. Grace (cricketer) and Tennis Racquet

868 Shakespeare, John Lennon (entertainer) and Sydney Opera House

872 Engagement off Isle of Wight

873 Attack of English Fire-ships, Calais

874 Armada in Storm, North Sea

(Des G. Emery. Litho Questa)

1988 (21 June).   **Bicentenary of Australian Settlement.** *Phosphorised paper.* P 14½.

1396	**866**	18p. dp ultramarine, orange-yellow, scarlet, black, bluish grey & emerald	60	60
		a. Horiz pair. Nos. 1396/7	1·25	1·25
1397	**867**	18p. dp ultramarine, orange-yellow, black, bluish grey & emerald	60	60
1398	**868**	34p. dp ultramarine, orange-yellow, scarlet, black, bluish grey & emerald	1·10	1·10
		a. Horiz pair. Nos. 1398/9	2·40	2·40
1399	**869**	34p. dp ultramarine, orange-yellow, black, bluish grey & emerald	1·10	1·10
		Set of 4	3·25	3·25
		Set of 2 Gutter Blocks of 4	6·50	
		First Day Cover		3·50
		Presentation Pack	4·50	
		Souvenir Book	6·00	
		P.H.Q. Cards (set of 4)	2·00	5·00

Nos. 1396/7 and 1398/9 were each printed together, *se-tenant*, in horizontal pairs throughout the sheets, each pair showing a background design of the Australian flag.

The 40 page souvenir book contains the British and Australian sets which were issued on the same day in similar designs.

Special First Day of Issue Postmarks

Philatelic Bureau, Edinburgh .... 4·00
Portsmouth .... 4·00

870 Spanish Galeasse off The Lizard

871 English Fleet leaving Plymouth

(Des G. Everndon)

1988 (19 July).   **400th Anniv of Spanish Armada.** *Phosphorised paper.* P 15 × 14.

1400	**870**	18p. slate-black, yellow-orange, brt carmine, brt blue, turquoise-blue, yellow-green & gold	65	65
		a. Horiz strip of 5. Nos. 1400/4	2·75	2·75
1401	**871**	18p. slate-black, yellow-orange, brt carmine, brt blue, turquoise-blue, yellow-green & gold	65	65
1402	**872**	18p. slate-black, yellow-orange, brt carmine, brt blue, turquoise-blue, yellow-green & gold	65	65
1403	**873**	18p. slate-black, yellow-orange, brt carmine, brt blue, turquoise-blue, yellow-green & gold	65	65
1404	**874**	18p. slate-black, yellow-orange, brt carmine, brt blue, turquoise-blue, yellow-green & gold	65	65
		Set of 5	2·75	2·75
		Gutter block of 10	5·50	
		First Day Cover		3·25
		Presentation Pack	4·00	
		P.H.Q. Cards (set of 5)	2·50	5·50

Nos. 1400/4 were printed together, *se-tenant*, in horizontal strips of 5 throughout the sheet, forming a composite design.

Special First Day of Issue Postmarks

Philatelic Bureau, Edinburgh .... 3·50
Plymouth .... 3·50

875 "The Owl and the Pussy-cat"

876 "Edward Lear as a Bird"
(self-portrait)

CARRICKFERGUS CASTLE

879 Carrickfergus Castle

CAERNARFON CASTLE

880 Caernarfon Castle

877 "Cat" (from alphabet book)

878 "There was a Young Lady
whose Bonnet . . ." (limerick)

EDINBURGH CASTLE

881 Edinburgh Castle

WINDSOR CASTLE

882 Windsor Castle

(Des M. Swatridge and S. Dew)

1988 (6–27 Sept). **Death Centenary of Edward Lear (artist and author).** *Phosphorised paper.* P 15 × 14.

1405	875	19p. black, pale cream & carmine	50	50
1406	876	27p. black, pale cream & yellow	65	80
1407	877	32p. black, pale cream & emerald	1·10	1·10
1408	878	35p. black, pale cream & blue	1·10	1·25
		Set of 4	3·00	3·25
		Set of 4 Gutter Pairs	6·00	
		First Day Cover		4·00
		Presentation Pack	4·50	
		P.H.Q. Cards (set of 4)	2·00	5·00
MS1409	22 × 90 mm. Nos. 1405/8 *(sold at £1.35)* (27 Sept)		8·00	7·00
		First Day Cover		7·00

The premium on No. **MS**1409 was used to support the "Stamp World London 90" International Stamp Exhibition.

(Des from photos by Prince Andrew, Duke of York. Eng C. Matthews. Recess Harrison)

1988 (18 Oct). *Ordinary paper.* P 15 × 14.

1410	879	£1 dp green	2·50	50
1411	880	£1.50 maroon	3·50	1·00
1412	881	£2 indigo	5·00	1·50
1413	882	£5 dp brown	12·00	3·00
		Set of 4	21·00	5·50
		Set of 4 Gutter Pairs	42·00	
		First Day Cover		45·00
		Presentation Pack	22·00	

For similar designs, but with silhouette of Queen's head see Nos. 1611/14.

Special First Day of Issue Postmarks
(For illustrations see Introduction)

Philatelic Bureau, Edinburgh (Type H) .... 50·00
Windsor, Berkshire (Type I) .... 50·00

Special First Day of Issue Postmarks

Philatelic Bureau, Edinburgh (stamps) (6 Sept) ..... 4·50
Philatelic Bureau, Edinburgh (miniature sheet) (27 Sept) 7·50
London N7 (stamps) (6 Sept) .... 4·50
London N22 (miniature sheet) (27 Sept) .... 7·50

883 Journey to Bethlehem

884 Shepherds and Star

885 Three Wise Men

886 Nativity

887 The Annunciation

888 Atlantic Puffin

889 Avocet

(Des L. Trickett)

1988 (15 Nov). **Christmas. Christmas Cards.** *One phosphor band (14p.) or phosphorised paper (others). P 15 × 14.*

1414	**883**	14p. gold, orange-yellow, brt mauve, bluish violet, brt blue & grey-black	35	35
		a. Error. "13p" instead of "14p"	£5000
		b. Imperf (pair)	£750
1415	**884**	19p. gold, yellow-orange, brt violet, ultramarine, rose-red, grey-black & brt blue	40	45
		a. Imperf (pair)	£600
1416	**885**	27p. gold, red, dp lavender, dp lilac, emerald, grey-black & brt blue	70	70
1417	**886**	32p. gold, orange-yellow, brt mauve, violet, grey-black & brt blue	90	1·00
1418	**887**	35p. gold, green, reddish violet, brt blue, brt purple & grey-black	1·00	1·10
		Set of 5	3·00	3·25
		Set of 5 Gutter Pairs	6·00
		First Day Cover		4·25
		Presentation Pack	4·25
		P.H.Q. Cards (set of 5)	2·50	5·25

Examples of No. 1414a were found in some 1988 Post Office Yearbooks.

Special First Day of Issue Postmarks

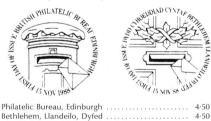

Philatelic Bureau, Edinburgh .... 4·50
Bethlehem, Llandeilo, Dyfed .... 4·50

Collectors Pack 1988

1988 (15 Nov). *Comprises Nos. 1380/1408, 1414/18.*
CP1418a Collectors Pack .... 32·00

Post Office Yearbook

1988 (15 Nov). *Comprises Nos. 1380/1404, **MS**1409, 1414/18 in 32-page hardbound book with slip case, illustrated in colour . 40·00*

890 Oystercatcher

891 Northern Gannet

(Des D. Cordery)

1989 (17 Jan). **Centenary of Royal Society for the Protection of Birds.** *Phosphorised paper. P 14 × 15.*

1419	**888**	19p. grey, orange-yellow, orange-red, dull ultramarine, grey-black & silver	45	45
1420	**889**	27p. grey, bistre, rose, steel-blue, lavender, silver & grey-black	1·10	1·10
1421	**890**	32p. grey, bistre, scarlet, orange-red, lavender, silver & black	1·10	1·10
1422	**891**	35p. grey, lemon, rose-carmine, green, new blue, silver & black	1·25	1·25
		Set of 4	3·50	3·50
		Set of 4 Gutter Pairs	7·00
		First Day Cover		4·50
		Presentation Pack	4·50
		P.H.Q. Cards (set of 4)	2·50	5·00

Special First Day of Issue Postmarks

Philatelic Bureau, Edinburgh .... 4·75
Sandy, Bedfordshire .... 4·75

892 Rose

893 Cupid

FOOD AND FARMING YEAR 1989

897 Fruit and Vegetables

FOOD AND FARMING YEAR 1989

898 Meat Products

894 Yachts

895 Fruit

FOOD AND FARMING YEAR 1989

899 Dairy Products

FOOD AND FARMING YEAR 1989

900 Cereal Products

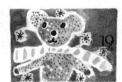

896 Teddy Bear

(Des Sedley Place Ltd)

1989 (7 Mar). **Food and Farming Year.** *Phosphorised paper. P* 14 × 14½.

1428	**897**	19p. brownish grey, greenish yellow, rose, new blue, black, pale grey & emerald .	50	50
1429	**898**	27p. brownish grey, greenish yellow, brt carmine, new blue, black, pale grey & brt orange	80	80
1430	**899**	32p. brownish grey, greenish yellow, rose-red, new blue, black, pale grey & bistre-yellow	1·10	1·10
1431	**900**	35p. brownish grey, greenish yellow, brt carmine, new blue, black, pale grey & brown-red	1·25	1·25
		Set of 4	3·25	3·25
		Set of 4 Gutter Pairs	6·50	
		First Day Cover		4·25
		Presentation Pack	4·50	
		P.H.Q. Cards (set of 4)	2·00	5·00

(Des P. Sutton)

1989 (31 Jan). **Greetings Stamps.** *Phosphorised paper. P* 15 × 14.

1423	**892**	19p. black, greenish yellow, brt rose, red, new blue, lt green & gold	2·75	2·25
		a. Booklet pane. Nos. 1423/7 × 2 plus 12 half stamp-size labels	24·00	
1424	**893**	19p. black, greenish yellow, brt rose, red, new blue, lt green & gold	2·75	2·25
1425	**894**	19p. black, greenish yellow, brt rose, red, new blue, lt green & gold	2·75	2·25
1426	**895**	19p. black, greenish yellow, brt rose, red, new blue, lt green & gold	2·75	2·25
1427	**896**	19p. black, greenish yellow, brt rose, red, new blue, lt green & gold	2·75	2·25
		Set of 5	12·00	10·00
		First Day Cover		10·00

Nos. 1423/7 were only issued in £1.90 booklets.

Special First Day of Issue Postmarks

Philatelic Bureau, Edinburgh	12·00
Lover, Salisbury, Wilts	12·00

Special First Day of Issue Postmarks

Philatelic Bureau, Edinburgh	4·50
Stoneleigh, Kenilworth, Warwicks	4·50

For full information on all future British issues, collectors should write to the British Post Office Philatelic Bureau, 20 Brandon Street, Edinburgh EH3 5TT

901 Mortar Board
(150th Anniv of Public
Education in England)

902 Cross on Ballot
Paper (3rd Direct
Elections to European
Parliament)

905 Toy Train and
Airplane

906 Building Bricks

903 Posthorn (26th
Postal, Telegraph and
Telephone International
Congress, Brighton)

904 Globe (Inter-
Parliamentary Union
Centenary Conference,
London)

907 Dice and Board
Games

908 Toy Robot, Boat
and Doll's House

(Des Lewis Moberly from firework set-pieces. Litho Questa)

1989 (11 Apr). **Anniversaries.** *Phosphorised paper.* P 14 × 14½.

1432	**901**	19p. new blue, greenish yellow, magenta & black	1·25	1·25
		a. Horiz pair. Nos. 1432/3	2·50	2·50
1433	**902**	19p. new blue, greenish yellow, magenta & black	1·25	1·25
1434	**903**	35p. new blue, greenish yellow, magenta & black	1·75	1·75
		a. Horiz pair. Nos. 1434/5	3·50	3·50
1435	**904**	35p. new blue, greenish yellow, magenta & black	1·75	1·75
		Set of 4	5·50	5·50
		Set of 2 Gutter Strips of 4	11·00	
		First Day Cover		5·50
		Presentation Pack	6·00	
		P.H.Q. Cards (set of 4)	2·00	7·00

Nos. 1432/3 and 1434/5 were each printed together, *se-tenant*, in horizontal pairs throughout the sheets.

(Des D. Fern)

1989 (16 May). **Europa. Games and Toys.** *Phosphorised paper.* P 14 × 15.

1436	**905**	19p. black, greenish yellow, vermilion, blue-green, blue, gold & pale ochre	50	50
1437	**906**	27p. black, greenish yellow, reddish orange, blue-green, blue & gold	90	90
1438	**907**	32p. black, greenish yellow, orange-red, blue-green, blue, gold & pale ochre	1·25	1·25
1439	**908**	35p. black, greenish yellow, reddish orange, blue-green, blue, gold & stone	1·40	1·40
		Set of 4	3·50	3·50
		Set of 4 Gutter Pairs	7·00	
		First Day Cover		4·25
		Presentation Pack	4·50	
		P.H.Q. Cards (set of 4)	2·00	5·00

Special First Day of Issue Postmarks

Philatelic Bureau, Edinburgh		6·00
London SW		6·00

Special First Day of Issue Postmarks

Philatelic Bureau, Edinburgh		4·50
Leeds		4·50

909 Ironbridge, Shropshire

910 Tin Mine, St. Agnes Head, Cornwall

911 Cotton Mills, New Lanark, Strathclyde

912 Pontcysyllte Aqueduct, Clwyd

1442	**911**	32p. black, yellow-orange, apple-green, yellow, dull blue, grey-black & dp reddish violet	1·00	1·00
1443	**912**	35p. black, yellow, brt rose, apple-green, dull blue, grey-black & vermilion	1·10	1·10
		Set of 4	3·00	3·00
		Set of 4 Gutter Pairs	6·50	
		First Day Cover		4·25
		Presentation Pack	4·50	
		P.H.Q. Cards (set of 4)	2·00	5·00
MS1444	**912a**	122 × 90 mm. As Nos. 1440/3, but horizontal. Each black, olive-yellow, brt rose-red, dull blue, apple-green, grey-black & vermilion (sold at £1.40) (25 July)	6·00	5·00
		First Day Cover		5·00

The premium on No. **MS**1444 was used to support the "Stamp World London 90" International Stamp Exhibition.

Special First Day of Issue Postmarks

Philatelic Bureau, Edinburgh (stamps) (4 July)	4·50
Philatelic Bureau, Edinburgh (miniature sheet) (25 July)	5·50
Telford (stamps) (4 July)	4·50
New Lanark (miniature sheet) (25 July)	5·50

INDUSTRIAL ARCHAEOLOGY

£1.40

Stamp World London 90

912a Horizontal versions of T **909/12**

913

914

1989 (22 Aug)–**93**. *Booklet Stamps.*

(a) *Photo Harrison.* P 15 x 14.

1445	**913**	(2nd) brt blue (1 centre band)	60	35
		a. Booklet pane. No. 1445 × 10 with horizontal edges of pane imperf	3·00	
		b. Booklet pane. No. 1445 × 4 with three edges of pane imperf (28.11.89)	3·00	
1446		(2nd) brt blue (1 band at right) (20.3.90)	2·25	2·25

(Des R. Maddox)

1989 (4–25 July). **Industrial Archaeology.** *Phosphorised paper.* P 14 × 15.

1440	**909**	19p. black, bistre-yellow, rose-red, apple-green, lt blue, grey-black & emerald ...	50	50
1441	**910**	27p. black, bistre-yellow, rose-red, apple-green, lt blue, grey-black & dull blue ..	80	80

1447	**914**	(1st) brownish black (phosphorised paper) ..	1·00	50
		a. Booklet pane. No. 1447 × 10 with horizontal edges of pane imperf	8·00	
		b. Booklet pane. No. 1447 × 4 with three edges of pane imperf (5.12.89)	4·00	
1448		(1st) brownish black (2 phosphor bands) (20.3.90)	2·25	2·25
		First Day Cover (Nos. 1445, 1447)		3·50

(b) Litho Walsall. P 14

1449	**913**	(2nd) brt blue (1 centre band)	90	35
		a. Imperf between (vert pair)		
		b. Booklet pane. No. 1449 × 4 with three edges of pane imperf	3·00	
		c. Booklet pane. No. 1449 × 4 with horiz edges of pane imperf (6.8.91)	1·25	
		d. Booklet pane. No. 1449 × 10 with horiz edges of pane imperf (6.8.91)	3·00	
1450	**914**	(1st) blackish brown (phosphorised paper) ...	2·00	1·75
		a. Booklet pane. No. 1450 × 4 with three edges of pane imperf	7·50	
		Ey. Phosphor omitted		

(c) Litho Questa. P 15 × 14.

1451	**913**	(2nd) brt blue (1 centre band) (19.9.89)	70	35
1451a		(2nd) brt blue (1 band at right) (25.2.92)	1·00	1·00
		aEb. Band at left (10.8.93)	1·00	1·00
		aEy. Phosphor omitted		
		al. Booklet pane. Nos. 1451aEb and 1514a, each × 3, with margins all round (10.8.93)	8·00	
1452	**914**	(1st) brownish black (phosphorised paper) (19.9.89)	1·10	1·10

Nos. 1445, 1447 and 1449/52 were initially sold at 14p. (2nd) and 19p. (1st), but these prices were later increased to reflect new postage rates.

Nos. 1446 and 1448 come from the *se-tenant* pane in the London Life £5 Booklet. This pane is listed under No. X906m in the Decimal Machin section.

No. 1451a comes from the *se-tenant* panes in the Wales and Tolkien £6 booklet. These panes are listed under Nos. X1012l and W49a (Wales Regionals). No. 1451aEb comes from the £6 (£5.64) Beatrix Potter booklet.

Nos. 1445, 1447 and 1449/50 do not exist perforated on all four sides, but come with either one or two adjacent sides imperforate.

No. 1450Ey comes from a pane in which one stamp was without phosphor bands due to a dry print.

For illustrations showing the differences between photogravure and lithography see above Type **367**.

For similar designs, but in changed colours, see Nos. 1511/16 and for those with elliptical perforations, Nos. 1663a/6.

Special First Day of Issue Postmarks
(for illustrations see Introduction)

Philatelic Bureau, Edinburgh (Type G) (in red) ...... 3·75
Windsor, Berks (Type G) (in red) .... 3·75

915 Snowflake (× 10) **916** *Calliphora erythrocephala* (× 5) (fly)

917 Blood Cells (× 500) **918** Microchip (× 600)

(Des K. Bassford. Litho Questa)

1989 (5 Sept). **150th Anniv of Royal Microscopical Society**
Phosphorised paper. P 14½ × 14.

1453	**915**	19p. gold, lemon, pale blue, grey, black & grey-black	50	50
1454	**916**	27p. gold, lemon, drab, black & grey-black .	85	85
1455	**917**	32p. gold, lemon, orange-vermilion, flesh, black & grey-black	1·25	1·25
1456	**918**	35p. gold, lemon, black, brt green & grey-black	1·40	1·40
		Set of 4	3·50	3·50
		Set of 4 Gutter Pairs	7·00	
		First Day Cover		4·25
		Presentation Pack	4·00	
		P.H.Q. Cards (set of 4)	2·00	5·00

Special First Day of Issue Postmarks

Philatelic Bureau, Edinburgh .... 4·50
Oxford .... 4·50

919 Royal Mail Coach **920** Escort of Blues and Royals

HAVE YOU READ THE NOTES AT THE BEGINNING OF THIS CATALOGUE?
These often provide answers to the enquiries we receive.

921 Lord Mayor's Coach

922 Passing St. Paul's

924 14th-century Peasants from Stained-glass Window

925 Arches and Roundels, West Front

923 Blues and Royals Drum Horse

926 Octagon Tower

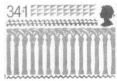
927 Arcade from West Transept

928 Triple Arch from West Front

(Des P. Cox)

1989 (17 Oct). **Lord Mayor's Show, London.** *Phosphorised paper.* P 14 × 15.

1457	**919**	20p. gold, lemon, rose, orange, pale blue & black	60	60
		a. Horiz strip of 5. Nos. 1457/61	3·25	3·25
		ab. Imperf (horiz strip of 5. Nos. 1457/61)		
		ac. Imperf (horiz strip of 4. Nos. 1457/60)		
		ad. Imperf (horiz strip of 3. Nos. 1457/9)		
1458	**920**	20p. gold, lemon, rose, orange, pale blue & black	60	60
1459	**921**	20p. gold, lemon, rose, orange, pale blue & black	60	60
1460	**922**	20p. gold, lemon, rose, orange, pale blue & black	60	60
1461	**923**	20p. gold, lemon, rose, orange, pale blue & black	60	60
		Set of 5	3·25	3·25
		Gutter Strip of 10	6·50	
		First Day Cover		3·75
		Presentation Pack	4·50	
		P.H.Q. Cards (set of 5)	2·50	5·00

Nos. 1457/61 were printed together, *se-tenant*, in horizontal strips of 5 throughout the sheet. This issue commemorates the 800th anniversary of the installation of the first Lord Mayor of London. Nos. 1457ab/ad come from a sheet partly imperf at left.

(Des D. Gentleman)

1989 (14 Nov). **Christmas. 800th Anniv of Ely Cathedral.** *One phosphor band (15p., 15p. + 1p.) or phosphorised paper (others).* P 15 × 14.

1462	**924**	15p. gold, silver & blue	35	35
1463	**925**	15p. + 1p. gold, silver & blue	50	40
		a. Imperf (pair)	£1300	
1464	**926**	20p. + 1p. gold, silver & rosine	60	50
		a. Imperf (pair)	£1300	
1465	**927**	34p. + 1p. gold, silver & emerald	1·25	1·40
1466	**928**	37p. + 1p. gold, silver & yellow-olive	1·25	1·40
		Set of 5	3·50	3·50
		Set of 5 Gutter Pairs	7·00	
		First Day Cover		4·00
		Presentation Pack	4·50	
		P.H.Q. Cards (set of 5)	2·50	5·00

Special First Day of Issue Postmarks

Philatelic Bureau, Edinburgh	4·50
Bethlehem, Llandeilo, Dyfed	4·50
Ely, Cambs	4·50

Collectors Pack 1989

1989 (14 Nov). *Comprises Nos. 1419/22, 1428/43 and 1453/66.*
CP1466a Collectors Pack .... 32·00

Special First Day of Issue Postmarks

Philatelic Bureau, Edinburgh	4·00
London, EC4	4·00

Post Office Yearbook

1989 (14 Nov). *Comprises Nos. 1419/22, 1428/44 and 1453/66 in hardbound book with slip case, illustrated in colour* . 45·00

929 Queen Victoria and Queen Elizabeth II

(Des J. Matthews (after Wyon and Machin))

1990 (10 Jan–12 June). **150th Anniv of the Penny Black.**

(a) Photo Harrison. P 15 × 14.

1467	**929**	15p. brt blue (1 centre band)	50	50
		a. Imperf (pair)	£1250	
		l. Booklet pane. No. 1467 × 10 with horizontal edges of pane imperf (30.1.90) . .	5·00	
1468		15p. brt blue (1 side band at left) (30.1.90)	1·50	1·50
		Ea. Band at right (20.3.90)	1·50	1·50
		l. Booklet pane. No. 1468 × 2 and 1470 plus label	5·00	
1469		20p. brownish black & cream (phosphorised paper)	75	75
		a. Imperf (pair)	£900	
		l. Booklet pane. No. 1469 × 5 plus label with vertical edges of pane imperf (30.1.90)	7·00	
		m. Booklet pane. No. 1469 × 10 with horizontal edges of pane imperf (30.1.90) . .	7·00	
		n. Booklet pane. No. 1469 × 6 with margins all round (20.3.90)	2·50	
		r. Booklet pane. No. 1469 × 4 with three edges of pane imperf (17.4.90)	4·50	
1470		20p. brownish black & cream (2 bands) (30.1.90)	1·50	1·50
1471		29p. dp mauve (phosphorised paper)	1·00	1·00
1472		29p. dp mauve (2 bands) (20.3.90)	5·00	5·00
1473		34p. dp bluish grey (phosphorised paper) . . .	1·25	1·25
1474		37p. rosine (phosphorised paper)	1·40	1·40

(b) Litho Walsall. P 14 (from booklets)

1475	**929**	15p. brt blue (1 centre band) (30.1.90)	80	60
		l. Booklet pane. No. 1475 × 4 with three edges of pane imperf	3·75	
		m. Booklet pane. No. 1475 × 10 with three edges of pane imperf (12.6.90)	6·00	
1476		20p. brownish black & cream (phosphorised paper) (30.1.90)	1·25	80
		l. Booklet pane. No. 1476 × 5 plus label with vertical edges of pane imperf	6·00	
		m. Booklet pane. No. 1476 × 4 with three edges of pane imperf	5·00	
		n. Booklet pane. No. 1476 × 10 with three edges of pane imperf (12.6.90)	8·00	

(c) Litho Questa. P 15 × 14

1477	**929**	15p. brt blue (1 centre band) (17.4.90)	1·25	1·25
1478		20p. brownish black (phosphorised paper) (17.4.90)	1·25	1·25
		Set of 5 (*Nos. 1467, 1469, 1471, 1473/4*)	4·50	4·50
		First Day Cover (*Nos. 1467, 1469, 1471, 1473/4*)		5·00
		Presentation Pack (*Nos. 1467, 1469, 1471, 1473/4*)	5·75	

Nos. 1475/6 do not exist perforated on all four sides, but come with either one or two adjacent sides imperforate.

Nos. 1468, 1468Ea, 1470, 1472 and 1475/8 come from booklets. Nos. 1468Ea, 1470 and 1472 occur in the *se-tenant* pane from the 1990 London Life £5 booklet. This pane is listed as No. X906m.

For illustrations showing the difference between photogravure and lithography see beneath Type **367**.

For No. 1469 in miniature sheet see No. **MS**1501.

Special First Day of Issue Postmark

Philatelic Bureau, Edinburgh (in red) . . . . 5·00
Windsor, Berks (Type G, see Introduction) (in red) . 5·00

930 Kitten   **931** Rabbit

932 Duckling   **933** Puppy

(Des T. Evans. Litho Questa)

1990 (23 Jan). **150th Anniv of Royal Society for Prevention of Cruelty to Animals.** *Phosphorised paper. P 14 × 14½.*

1479	**930**	20p. new blue, greenish yellow, brt magenta, black & silver	65	50
		a. Silver (Queen's head and face value) omitted	£150	
1480	**931**	29p. new blue, greenish yellow, brt magenta, black & silver	1·00	80
		a. Imperf (horiz pair)		
1481	**932**	34p. new blue, greenish yellow, brt magenta, black & silver	1·40	1·10
		a. Silver (Queen's head and face value) omitted	£350	
1482	**933**	37p. new blue, greenish yellow, brt magenta, black & silver	1·40	1·10
		Set of 4	4·00	3·25
		Set of 4 Gutter Pairs	8·00	
		First Day Cover		4·25
		Presentation Pack	5·00	
		P.H.Q. Cards (set of 4)	2·50	5·50

Special First Day of Issue Postmarks

Philatelic Bureau, Edinburgh .... 4·50
Horsham .... 4·50

934 Teddy Bear

935 Dennis the Menace

936 Punch

937 Cheshire Cat

938 The Man in the Moon

939 The Laughing Policeman

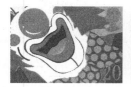

940 Clown

941 Mona Lisa

942 Queen of Hearts

943 Stan Laurel (comedian)

(Des Michael Peters and Partners Ltd)

1990 (6 Feb).   **Greetings Stamps. "Smiles".** *Two phosphor bands. P* 15 × 14.
1483 **934** 20p. gold, greenish yellow, brt rose-red, new
blue & grey-black .... 2·25   1·25
  a. Booklet pane. Nos. 1483/92 with margins all round .... 20·00
1484 **935** 20p. gold, greenish yellow, brt rose-red, new
blue, dp blue & grey-black .... 2·25   1·25
1485 **936** 20p. gold, greenish yellow, brt rose-red, new
blue, dp blue & grey-black .... 2·25   1·25
1486 **937** 20p. gold, greenish yellow, brt rose-red, new
blue & grey-black .... 2·25   1·25
1487 **938** 20p. gold, greenish yellow, brt rose-red, new
blue & grey-black .... 2·25   1·25
1488 **939** 20p. gold, greenish yellow, brt rose-red, new
blue & grey-black .... 2·25   1·25
1489 **940** 20p. gold, greenish yellow, brt rose-red, new
blue & grey-black .... 2·25   1·25
1490 **941** 20p. gold, greenish yellow, brt rose-red, new
blue & grey-black .... 2·25   1·25
1491 **942** 20p. gold, greenish yellow, brt rose-red, new
blue & grey-black .... 2·25   1·25
1492 **943** 20p. gold & grey-black .... 2·25   1·25
    Set of 10 .... 20·00 11·00
    First Day Cover .... 12·00
Nos. 1483/92 were only issued in £2 booklets. The design of Nos.
1483, 1485/7, 1489 and 1492 extend onto the pane margin.
For Types **934/43** inscribed (1st), see Nos. 1550/59.

Special First Day of Issue Postmarks

Philatelic Bureau, Edinburgh .... 12·00
Giggleswick, North Yorkshire .... 12·00

944 Alexandra Palace
("Stamp World London 90"
Exhibition)

945 Glasgow School of
Art

946 British Philatelic
Bureau, Edinburgh

947 Templeton Carpet
Factory, Glasgow

(Des P. Hogarth)

1990 (6–20 Mar). **Europa** (*Nos. 1493 and 1495*) **and "Glasgow 1990 European City of Culture"** (*Nos. 1494 and 1496*). *Phosphorised paper.* P 14 × 15.

1493	**944**	20p. silver, lemon, flesh, grey-brown, blue, grey-black & black	50	50
		a. Booklet pane. No. 1493 × 4 with margins all round (20 Mar)	2·75	
1494	**945**	20p. silver, greenish yellow, dull orange, blue, grey-black & black	50	50
1495	**946**	29p. silver, stone, orange, olive-sepia, grey-blue, grey-black & black	1·10	1·10
1496	**947**	37p. silver, greenish-yellow, brt emerald, salmon, olive-sepia, brt blue & black ..	1·25	1·25
		Set of 4	3·00	3·00
		Set of 4 Gutter Pairs	6·00	
		First Day Cover		4·25
		Presentation Pack	4·00	
		P.H.Q. Cards (set of 4)	2·50	5·25

Special First Day of Issue Postmarks

Philatelic Bureau, Edinburgh .... 4·50
Glasgow .... 4·50

948 Export Achievement
Award

949 Technological Achievement
Award

(Des S. Broom. Litho Questa)

1990 (10 Apr). **25th Anniv of Queen's Awards for Export and Technology.** *P* 14 × 14½.

1497	**948**	20p. new blue, greenish yellow, magenta, black & silver	70	70
		a. Horiz pair. Nos. 1497/8	1·40	1·40
1498	**949**	20p. new blue, greenish yellow, magenta, black & silver	70	70
1499	**948**	37p. new blue, greenish yellow, magenta, black & silver	1·25	1·25
		a. Horiz pair. Nos. 1499/500	2·50	2·50
1500	**949**	37p. new blue, greenish yellow, magenta, black & silver	1·25	1·25
		Set of 4	3·50	3·50
		Set of 2 Gutter Strips of 4	7·00	
		First Day Cover		4·50
		Presentation Pack	4·00	
		P.H.Q. Cards (set of 4)	2·50	5·25

Nos. 1497/8 and 1499/1500 were each printed together, *se-tenant*, in horizontal pairs throughout the sheets.

Special First Day of Issue Postmarks

Philatelic Bureau, Edinburgh .... 4·75
London, SW .... 4·75

949a

(Des Sedley Place Design Ltd. Eng C. Matthews. Recess and photo Harrison)

1990 (3 May). **"Stamp World 90" International Stamp Exhibition.** *Sheet* 122 × 89 *mm containing No. 1469. Phosphorised paper.* P 15 × 14.

MS1501	**949**a 20p. brownish black & cream (*sold at £1*)	4·00	4·00
	a. Error. Imperf	£6500	
	b. Black (recess-printing) omitted	£7500	
	c. Black (recess-printing) inverted	£7500	
	First Day Cover		4·50
	Souvenir Book (*Nos. 1467, 1469, 1471, 1473/4 and* **MS**1501)	12·00	

The premium on No. **MS**1501 was used to support the "Stamp World London '90" International Stamp Exhibition. In No. **MS**1501 only the example of the 20p. is perforated.

No. **MS**1501b shows an albino impression on the reverse. The 1d. black and Seahorse background are omitted due to one sheet becoming attached to the underside of another prior to recess-printing.

No. **MS**1501c shows the recess part of the design inverted in relation to the photogravure of Type **929**.

Special First Day of Issue Postmarks

Philatelic Bureau, Edinburgh (in red) .... 5·00
City of London (in red) .... 5·00
A First Day of Issue handstamp as Type B was provided at Alexandra Palace; London N22 for this issue.

950 Cycad and Sir Joseph Banks Building

951 Stone Pine and Princess of Wales Conservatory

952 Willow Tree and Palm House

953 Cedar Tree and Pagoda

(Des P. Leith)

1990 (5 June). **150th Anniv of Kew Gardens.** *Phosphorised paper.* P 14 × 15.
1502 **950** 20p. black, brt emerald, pale turquoise-green, lt brown & lavender 50 50
1503 **951** 29p. black, brt emerald, turquoise-green, reddish orange & grey-black 80 80
1504 **952** 34p. Venetian red, brt green, cobalt, dull purple, turquoise-green & yellow-green 1·10 1·25
1505 **953** 37p. pale violet-blue, brt emerald, red-brown, steel-blue & brown-rose .... 1·25 1·40
　　　　　Set of 4 .... 3·25 3·50
　　　　　Set of 4 Gutter Pairs .... 6·50
　　　　　First Day Cover .... 4·50
　　　　　Presentation Pack .... 4·00
　　　　　P.H.Q. Cards (set of 4) .... 2·50 5·00

Special First Day of Issue Postmarks

Philatelic Bureau, Edinburgh .... 4·75
Kew, Richmond .... 4·75

954 Thomas Hardy and Clyffe Clump, Dorset

(Des J. Gibbs)

1990 (10 July). **150th Birth Anniv of Thomas Hardy (author).** *Phosphorised paper.* P 14 × 15.
1506 **954** 20p. vermilion, greenish yellow, pale lake-brown, dp brown, lt red-brown & black 60 70
　　　　　a. *Imperf (pair)* £950
　　　　　Gutter Pair .... 1·25
　　　　　First Day Cover .... 2·00
　　　　　Presentation Pack .... 1·75
　　　　　P.H.Q. Card .... 75 2·00

Special First Day of Issue Postmarks

Philatelic Bureau, Edinburgh .... 2·25
Dorchester .... 2·25

955 Queen Elizabeth the Queen Mother　　　　**956** Queen Elizabeth

957 Elizabeth, Duchess of York **958** Lady Elizabeth Bowes-Lyon

(Des J. Gorham from photographs by N. Parkinson (20p.), Dorothy Wilding (29p.), B. Park (34p.), Rita Martin (37p.))

1990 (2 Aug). **90th Birthday of Queen Elizabeth the Queen Mother.** *Phosphorised paper.* P 14 × 15.

1507	**955**	20p. silver, greenish yellow, magenta, turquoise-blue & grey-black	50	50
1508	**956**	29p. silver, indigo & grey-blue	80	80
1509	**957**	34p. silver, lemon, red, new blue & grey-black	1·10	1·25
1510	**958**	37p. silver, sepia & stone	1·25	1·40
		Set of 4	3·25	3·50
		Set of 4 Gutter Pairs	6·50	
		First Day Cover		4·50
		Presentation Pack	4·50	
		P.H.Q. Cards (set of 4)	2·50	5·50

Special First Day of Issue Postmarks

Philatelic Bureau, Edinburgh	4·75
Westminster, SW1	4·75

1990 (7 Aug)–**92.** *Booklet stamps. As T 913/14, but colours changed.*

(a) *Photo Harrison.* P 15 × 14

1511	**913**	(2nd) dp blue (1 centre band)	60	50
		a. Booklet pane. No. 1511 × 10 with horiz edges of pane imperf	6·00	
1512	**914**	(1st) brt orange-red (phosphorised paper) ..	60	50
		a. Booklet pane. No. 1512 × 10 with horiz edges of pane imperf	4·00	

(b) *Litho Questa.* P 15 × 14

1513	**913**	(2nd) dp blue (1 centre band)	1·25	1·25
1514	**914**	(1st) brt orange-red (phosphorised paper) ..	60	60
1514a		(1st) brt orange-red (2 bands) (25.2.92)	1·00	1·00

(c) *Litho Walsall.* P 14

1515	**913**	(2nd) dp blue (1 centre band)	60	60
		a. Booklet pane. No. 1515 × 4 with horiz edges of pane imperf	2·50	
		b. Booklet pane. No. 1515 × 10 with horiz edges of pane imperf	6·00	

1516	**914**	(1st) brt orange-red (phosphorised paper)	60	60
		a. Booklet pane. No. 1516 × 4 with horiz edges of pane imperf	1·60	
		b. Booklet pane. No. 1516 × 10 with horiz edges of pane imperf	4·00	
		c. Perf 13	2·50	2·00
		ca. Booklet pane. No. 1516c × 4 with horiz edges of pane imperf	10·00	
		First Day Cover (Nos. 1515/16)		3·00

Nos. 1511/14 and 1515/16 were initially sold at 15p. (2nd) and 20p. (1st), but these prices were later increased to reflect new postage rates.

No. 1514a comes from the *se-tenant* panes in the Wales and Tolkien £6 booklet. These panes are listed under Nos. X1012l and W49a (Wales Regionals).

No. 1516c was caused by the use of an incorrect perforation comb.

Nos. 1511/12 and 1515/16 do not exist with perforations on all four sides, but come with either the top or the bottom edge imperforate. For similar stamps with elliptical perforations see Nos. 1663a/6.

Special First Day of Issue Postmarks
(For illustration see Introduction)

Philatelic Bureau, Edinburgh (Type G)	3·25
Windsor, Berks (Type G)	3·25

959 Victoria Cross **960** George Cross

961 Distinguished Service Cross and Distinguished Service Medal

962 Military Cross and Military Medal

963 Distinguished Flying Cross and Distinguished Flying Medal

(Des J. Gibbs and J. Harwood)

1990 (11 Sept). **Gallantry Awards.** *Phosphorised paper.* P 14 × 15 (vert) or 15 × 14 (horiz).

1517	**959**	20p. grey-black, pale stone, stone, bistre-brown & brt carmine	65	65
1518	**960**	20p. grey-black, pale stone, flesh, grey & ultramarine	65	65
1519	**961**	20p. grey-black, pale stone, flesh, pale blue & ultramarine	65	65
		a. Imperf (pair)		
1520	**962**	20p. grey-black, pale stone, ochre, pale blue, ultramarine, scarlet & violet	65	65
1521	**963**	20p. grey-black, pale stone, yellow-brown, bluish grey & purple	65	65
		Set of 5	3·00	3·00
		Set of 5 Gutter Pairs	6·00	
		First Day Cover		3·75
		Presentation Pack	4·00	
		P.H.Q. Cards (set of 5)	3·00	5·50

(Des J. Fisher. Litho Questa)

1990 (16 Oct). **Astronomy.** *Phosphorised paper.* P 14 × 14½.

1522	**964**	22p. cream, grey, dull blue-green, slate-blue, blue-green, orange-red, gold & black ..	50	40
		a. Gold (Queen's head) omitted	£350	
1523	**965**	26p. black, yellow, dull purple, pale cream, brown-rose, new blue, greenish yellow, vermilion & gold	80	90
1524	**966**	31p. black, cream, pale cream, yellow-orange, salmon, lemon, vermilion & gold	1·00	1·00
1525	**967**	37p. black, pale buff, olive-bistre, pale cream, pale flesh, flesh, grey, rose-red & gold	1·10	1·10
		Set of 4	3·00	3·00
		Set of 4 Gutter Pairs	6·00	
		First Day Cover		4·25
		Presentation Pack	4·00	
		P.H.Q. Cards (set of 4)	2·50	5·50

Special First Day of Issue Postmarks

Philatelic Bureau, Edinburgh .... 4·25
Westminster, SW1 .... 4·25

Special First Day of Issue Postmarks

Philatelic Bureau, Edinburgh .... 4·25
Armagh .... 4·25

968 Building a Snowman   **969** Fetching the Christmas Tree

964 Armagh Observatory, Jodrell Bank Radio Telescope and La Palma Telescope

965 Newton's Moon and Tides Diagram and Early Telescopes

970 Carol Singing   **971** Tobogganing

966 Greenwich Old Observatory and Early Astronomical Equipment

967 Stonehenge, Gyroscope and Navigation by Stars

972 Ice-skating

(Des J. Gorham and A. Davidson)

1990 (13 Nov). **Christmas.** *One phosphor band* (17p.) *or phosphorised paper* (others). *P* 15 × 14.

1526	**968**	17p.	gold, greenish yellow, rose, new blue & grey-black	45	35
		a.	Booklet pane of 20	9·00	
1527	**969**	22p.	gold, greenish yellow, magenta, new blue & black	55	65
		a.	Imperf (horiz pair)	£450	
1528	**970**	26p.	gold, olive-yellow, pale magenta, agate, new blue, dull violet-blue & black	80	80
1529	**971**	31p.	gold, greenish yellow, brt rose-red, dull mauve, new blue, turquoise-blue & grey-black	1·00	1·00
1530	**972**	37p.	gold, greenish yellow, rose, new blue & slate-green	1·10	1·10
			Set of 5	3·50	3·50
			Set of 5 Gutter Pairs	7·00	
			First Day Cover		4·50
			Presentation Pack	4·25	
			P.H.Q. Cards (set of 5)	3·25	6·00

Booklet pane No. 1526a has the horizontal edges of the pane imperforate.

Special First Day of Issue Postmarks

Philatelic Bureau, Edinburgh	4·50
Bethlehem, Llandeilo, Dyfed	4·50

Collectors Pack 1990

1990 (13 Nov). *Comprises Nos.* 1479/82, 1493/1510 *and* 1517/30.
CP1530a Collectors Pack .... 28·00

Post Office Yearbook

1990 (13 Nov). *Comprises Nos.* 1479/82, 1493/1500, 1502/10, 1517/30 *in hardbound book with slip case, illustrated in colour* . 40·00

973 "King Charles Spaniel"   **974** "A Pointer"

975 "Two Hounds in a   **976** "A Rough Dog"
Landscape"

977 "Fino and Tiny"

(Des Carroll, Dempsey and Thirkell Ltd)

1991 (8 Jan). **Dogs. Paintings by George Stubbs.** *Phosphorised paper.* *P* 14 × 14½.

1531	**973**	22p.	gold, greenish yellow, magenta, new blue, black & drab	75	75
		a.	Imperf (pair)	£400	
1532	**974**	26p.	gold, greenish yellow, magenta, new blue, black & drab	80	80
1533	**975**	31p.	gold, greenish yellow, magenta, new blue, black & drab	85	85
		a.	Imperf (pair)	£950	
1534	**976**	33p.	gold, greenish yellow, magenta, new blue, black & drab	95	95
1535	**977**	37p.	gold, greenish yellow, magenta, new blue, black & drab	1·10	1·10
			Set of 5	4·00	4·00
			Set of 5 Gutter Pairs	8·00	
			First Day Cover		4·25
			Presentation Pack	5·00	
			P.H.Q. Cards (set of 5)	3·25	6·00

Special First Day of Issue Postmarks

Philatelic Bureau, Edinburgh	4·50
Birmingham	4·50

HAVE YOU READ THE NOTES AT THE BEGINNING OF THIS CATALOGUE?
These often provide answers to the enquiries we receive.

978 Thrush's Nest

979 Shooting Star
and Rainbow

980 Magpies and
Charm Bracelet

981 Black Cat

982 Common Kingfisher
with Key

983 Mallard and Frog

984 Four-leaf Clover
in Boot and Match Box

985 Pot of Gold at
End of Rainbow

986 Heart-shaped Butterflies

987 Wishing Well and Sixpence

(Des T. Meeuwissen)

1991 (5 Feb). **Greetings Stamps. "Good Luck".** *Two phosphor bands.*
P 15 × 14.

1536	**978**	(1st) silver, greenish yellow, magenta, new blue, olive-brown & black	85	90
		a. Booklet pane. Nos. 1536/45 plus 12 half stamp-size labels with margins on 3 sides	8·00	

1537	**979**	(1st) silver, greenish yellow, magenta, new blue, olive-brown & black	85	90
1538	**980**	(1st) silver, greenish yellow, magenta, new blue, olive-brown & black	85	90
1539	**981**	(1st) silver, greenish yellow, magenta, new blue, olive-brown & black	85	90
1540	**982**	(1st) silver, greenish yellow, magenta, new blue, olive-brown & black	85	90
1541	**983**	(1st) silver, greenish yellow, magenta, new blue, olive-brown & black	85	90
1542	**984**	(1st) silver, greenish yellow, magenta, new blue, olive-brown & black	85	90
1543	**985**	(1st) silver, greenish yellow, magenta, new blue, olive-brown & black	85	90
1544	**986**	(1st) silver, greenish yellow, magenta, new blue, olive-brown & black	85	90
1545	**987**	(1st) silver, greenish yellow, magenta, new blue, olive-brown & black	85	90
		Set of 10	8·00	8·00
		First Day Cover		8·50

Nos. 1536/45 were ony issued in £2.20 booklets (sold at £2.40 from 16 September 1991). The backgrounds of the stamps form a composite design.

Special First Day of Issue Postmarks

Philatelic Bureau, Edinburgh .... 8·50
Greetwell, Lincs .... 8·50

988 Michael Faraday
(inventor of electric motor)
(Birth Bicentenary)

989 Charles Babbage
(computer science pioneer)
(Birth Bicentenary)

990 Radar Sweep of East
Anglia (50th Anniv of
Operational Radar Network)

991 Gloster E28/39 Airplane
over East Anglia (50th Anniv
of First Flight of Sir Frank
Whittle's Jet Engine)

(Des P. Till (Nos. 1546/7), J. Harwood (Nos. 1548/9))

1991 (5 Mar). **Scientific Achievements.** *Phosphorised paper.* P 14 × 15.

1546	**988**	22p. silver, olive-brown, greenish yellow, magenta, slate-blue, grey & black	65	65
		a. Imperf (pair)	£325	
1547	**989**	22p. silver, chrome-yellow, red, grey-black, brownish grey & sepia	65	65
1548	**990**	31p. silver, dp turquoise-green, violet-blue, steel-blue & dp dull blue	95	95
1549	**991**	37p. silver, olive-bistre, rose-red, turquoise-blue, new blue & grey-black	1·10	1·10
		Set of 4	3·00	3·00
		Set of 4 Gutter Pairs	6·00	
		First Day Cover		4·00
		Presentation Pack	3·75	
		P.H.Q. Cards (set of 4)	3·00	5·50

Special First Day of Issue Postmarks

Philatelic Bureau, Edinburgh .... 4·25
South Kensington, London, SW7 .... 4·25

992 Teddy Bear

1991 (26 Mar). **Greeting Stamps.** *As Nos. 1483/92, but inscribed "1st" as T* **992.** *Two phosphor bands.* P 15 × 14.

1550	**992**	(1st) gold, greenish yellow, brt rose-red, new blue & grey-black	40	45
		a. Booklet pane. Nos. 1550/9 plus 12 half stamp-size labels with margins on 3 sides	3·50	
1551	**935**	(1st) gold, greenish yellow, brt rose-red, new blue, dp blue & grey-black	40	45
1552	**936**	(1st) gold, greenish yellow, brt rose-red, new blue, dp blue & grey-black	40	45
1553	**937**	(1st) gold, greenish yellow, bright rose-red, new blue & grey-black	40	45
1554	**938**	(1st) gold, greenish yellow, brt rose-red, new blue & grey-black	40	45
1555	**939**	(1st) gold, greenish yellow, brt rose-red, new blue & grey-black	40	45
1556	**940**	(1st) gold, greenish yellow, brt rose-red, new blue & grey-black	40	45
1557	**941**	(1st) gold, greenish yellow, brt rose-red, new blue & grey-black	40	45
1558	**942**	(1st) gold, greenish yellow, brt rose-red, new blue & grey-black	40	45
1559	**943**	(1st) gold & grey-black	40	45
		Set of 10	3·50	4·00
		First Day Cover		7·50

Nos. 1550/9 were only issued in £2.20 booklets (sold at £2.40 from 16 September 1991 and at £2.50 from 1 November 1993). The designs of Nos. 1550, 1552/4, 1556 and 1559 extend onto the pane margin.

Special First Day of Issue Postmarks

Philatelic Bureau, Edinburgh .... 7·75
Laugherton, Lincs .... 7·75

993	**994**

Man Looking at Space

995	**996**

Space Looking at Man

(Des J.-M. Folon)

1991 (23 Apr). **Europa. Europe in Space.** *Phosphorised paper.* P 14 × 15.

1560	**993**	22p. silver-mauve, greenish yellow, scarlet, violet-blue, brt blue, brt green & black	55	55
		a. Horiz pair. Nos. 1560/1	1·10	1·10
1561	**994**	22p. silver-mauve, greenish yellow, scarlet, violet-blue, brt blue & black	55	55
1562	**995**	37p. silver-mauve, bistre-yellow, dull vermilion, blue & black	1·10	1·10
		a. Horiz pair. Nos. 1562/3	2·25	2·25
1563	**996**	37p. silver-mauve, bistre-yellow, dull vermilion, blue & black	1·10	1·10
		Set of 4	3·00	3·00
		Set of 2 Gutter Strips of 4	6·00	
		First Day Cover		4·00
		Presentation Pack	4·00	
		P.H.Q. Cards (set of 4)	3·00	5·50

Nos. 1560/1 and 1562/3 were each printed together, *se-tenant,* in horizontal pairs throughout the sheets, each pair forming a composite design.

Special First Day of Issue Postmarks

Philatelic Bureau, Edinburgh .... 4·50
Cambridge .... 4·50

1001 "Silver Jubilee"

1002 "Mme Alfred Carrière"

997 Fencing

998 Hurdling

1003 *Rosa moyesii*

1004 "Harvest Fayre"

999 Diving

1000 Rugby

1005 "Mutabilis"

(Des Yvonne Skargon. Litho Questa)

(Des Huntley Muir Partners)

1991 (11 June). **World Student Games, Sheffield** (*Nos.* 1564/6) **and World Cup Rugby Championship, London** (*No.* 1567). *Phosphorised paper.* P 14½ × 14.

1564	**997**	22p. black, greenish yellow, vermilion, brt orange, ultramarine & grey	50	50
1565	**998**	26p. pale blue, greenish yellow, red, brt blue & black	80	80
1566	**999**	31p. brt blue, bistre-yellow, rose, vermilion, new blue & black	95	95
1567	**1000**	37p. yellow-orange, greenish yellow, rose, brt blue, emerald & black	1·10	1·10
		Set of 4	3·00	3·00
		Set of 4 Gutter Pairs	6·00	
		First Day Cover		4·00
		Presentation Pack	4·00	
		P.H.Q. Cards (set of 4)	3·00	5·50

1991 (16 July). **9th World Congress of Roses, Belfast.** *Phosphorised paper.* P 14½ × 14.

1568	**1001**	22p. new blue, greenish yellow, magenta, black & silver	75	50
		a. Silver (Queen's head) omitted	£750	
		Eb. Black printing double		
1569	**1002**	26p. new blue, greenish yellow, magenta, black & silver	80	80
1570	**1003**	31p. new blue, greenish yellow, magenta, black & silver	85	85
1571	**1004**	33p. new blue, greenish yellow, magenta, black & silver	95	95
1572	**1005**	37p. new blue, greenish yellow, magenta, black & silver	1·10	1·25
		Set of 5	4·00	4·00
		Set of 5 Gutter Pairs	8·00	
		First Day Cover		4·50
		Presentation Pack	4·50	
		P.H.Q. Cards (set of 5)	3·25	6·50

Special First Day of Issue Postmarks

Philatelic Bureau, Edinburgh .... 4·50
Sheffield .... 4·50

Special First Day of Issue Postmarks

Philatelic Bureau, Edinburgh .... 5·00
Belfast .... 5·00

1006 Iguanodon

1007 Stegosaurus

1008 Tyrannosaurus

1009 Protoceratops

1010 Triceratops

(Des B. Kneale)

1991 (20 Aug). **150th Anniversary of Dinosaurs' Identification by Owen.** *Phosphorised paper.* P 14½ × 14

1573	**1006**	22p. grey, pale blue, magenta, brt blue, dull violet & grey-black	75	50
		a. Imperf (pair)	£1000	
1574	**1007**	26p. grey, greenish yellow, pale emerald, brt blue-green, pale brt blue, grey-black & black	90	1·00
1575	**1008**	31p. grey, lt blue, magenta, brt blue, pale blue, brown & grey-black	1·00	1·10
1576	**1009**	33p. grey, dull rose, pale brt blue, brt rose-red, yellow-orange, grey-black & black	1·10	1·10
1577	**1010**	37p. grey, greenish yellow, turquoise-blue, dull violet, yellow-brown & black	1·25	1·25
		Set of 5	4·50	4·50
		Set of 5 Gutter Pairs	9·00	
		First Day Cover		5·00
		Presentation Pack	5·50	
		P.H.Q. Cards (set of 5)	3·25	6·00

ALBUM LISTS
Write for our latest list of albums and accessories.
These will be sent on request.

Special First Day of Issue Postmarks

Philatelic Bureau, Edinburgh	6·00
Plymouth	6·00

1011 Map of 1816

1012 Map of 1906

1013 Map of 1959

1014 Map of 1991

(Des H. Brown. Recess and litho Harrison (24d.), litho Harrison (28p.), Questa (33p., 39p.))

1991 (17 Sept). **Bicentenary of Ordnance Survey. Maps of Hamstreet, Kent.** *Phosphorised paper.* P 14½ × 14.

1578	**1011**	24p. black, magenta & cream	50	50
		Ea. Black (litho) printing treble & magenta printing double	£950	
1579	**1012**	28p. black, brt yellow-green, new blue, reddish orange, magenta, olive-sepia & cream	80	85
1580	**1013**	33p. dull blue-green, orange-brown, magenta, olive-grey, greenish yellow, vermilion, greenish grey, pale blue, blue, dull orange, apple green & black	95	1·00
1581	**1014**	39p. black, magenta, greenish yellow & new blue	1·10	1·25
		Set of 4	3·00	3·25
		Set of 4 Gutter Pairs	6·00	
		First Day Cover		4·25
		Presentation Pack	4·00	
		P.H.Q. Cards (set of 4)	3·00	6·00

Mint examples of Type **1012** exist with a face value of 26p.

Special First Day of Issue Postmarks

Philatelic Bureau, Edinburgh .... 4·50
Southampton .... 4·50

1015 Adoration of the Magi

1016 Mary and Jesus in the Stable

1017 The Holy Family and Angel

1018 The Annunciation

1017 The Flight into Egypt

(Des D. Driver)

1991 (12 Nov). **Christmas. Illuminated Letters from "Acts of Mary and Jesus" Manuscript in Bodleian Library, Oxford.** *One phosphor band* (18p.) *or phosphorised paper* (*others*). P 15 × 14.
1582 **1015** 18p. steel-blue, greenish yellow, rose-red, orange-red, black & gold 70 40
    a. Imperf (pair) £1500
    b. Booklet pane of 20 .... 8·25
1583 **1016** 24p. brt rose-red, greenish yellow, vermilion, slate-blue, yellow-green, grey-black & gold 80 50
1584 **1017*** 28p. reddish brown, bistre-yellow, orange-vermilion, orange-red, dp dull blue, grey-black & gold .... 85 1·00
1585 **1018** 33p. green, greenish yellow, red, orange-red, blue, grey & gold .... 95 1·10

1586 **1019** 39p. orange-red, greenish yellow, orange-vermilion, dp dull blue, olive-sepia, black & gold .... 1·10 1·40
    Set of 5 .... 4·00 4·00
    Set of 5 Gutter Pairs .... 8·00
    First Day Cover .... 4·50
    Presentation Pack .... 4·25
    P.H.Q. Cards (set of 5) .... 3·00 6·00
Booklet pane No. 1582b has margins at left, top and bottom.

Special First Day of Issue Postmarks

Philatelic Bureau, Edinburgh .... 5·00
Bethlehem, Landeilo, Dyfed .... 5·00

Collectors Pack 1991

1991 (12 Nov). *Comprises Nos. 1531/5, 1546/9 and 1560/86.*
CP1586a Collectors Pack .... 28·00

Post Office Yearbook

1991 (13 Nov). *Comprises Nos. 1531/5, 1546/9 and 1560/86 in hardbound book with slip case, illustrated in colour .* 50·00

1020 Fallow Deer in Scottish Forest

1021 Hare on North Yorkshire Moors

1022 Fox in the Fens

1023 Redwing and Home Counties Village

1024 Welsh Mountain Sheep in Snowdonia

(Des J. Gorham and K. Bowen)

1992 (14 Jan-25 Feb). **The Four Seasons. Wintertime.** *One phosphor band* (18p.) *or phosphorised paper* (others). *P* 15 × 14.

1587	**1020**	18p. silver, greenish yellow, grey, dull rose, new blue & black	45	50
1588	**1021**	24p. silver, lemon, rose, blue & grey-black .	60	65
		a. Imperf (pair)	£300	
1589	**1022**	28p. silver, greenish yellow, bright rose, steel-blue & grey-black	70	75
1590	**1023**	33p. silver, greenish yellow, brt orange, brt purple, greenish blue & grey	85	90
1591	**1024**	39p. silver, yellow, yellow-orange, grey, vermilion, new blue & black	1·00	1·10
		a. Booklet pane. No. 1591 × 4 with margins all round (25 Feb)	3·25	
		Set of 5	3·25	3·50
		Set of 5 Gutter Pairs	6·50	
		First Day Cover		3·75
		Presentation Pack	4·25	
		P.H.Q. Cards (set of 5)	3·00	6·50

Booklet pane No. 1591a comes from the £6 "Cymru–Wales" Booklet.

Special First Day of Issue Postmarks

Philatelic Bureau, Edinburgh .... 4·25
Brecon .... 4·25

1025 Flower Spray   **1026** Double Locket

1027 Key

1028 Model Car and Cigarette Cards

1029 Compass and Map   **1030** Pocket Watch

1031 1854 1d. Red Stamp and Pen   **1032** Pearl Necklace

1033 Marbles   **1034** Bucket, Spade and Starfish

(Des Trickett and Webb Ltd)

1992 (28 Jan). **Greetings Stamps. "Memories".** *Two phosphor bands. P* 15 × 14.

1592	**1025**	(1st) gold, greenish yellow, magenta, ochre, lt blue & grey-black, ...	40	45
		a. Booklet pane. Nos. 1592/1601 plus 12 half stamp-size labels with margins on 3 sides	3·50	
1593	**1026**	(1st) gold, greenish yellow, magenta, ochre, lt blue & grey-black	40	45
1594	**1027**	(1st) gold, greenish yellow, magenta, ochre, lt blue & grey-black	40	45
1595	**1028**	(1st) gold, greenish yellow, magenta, ochre, lt blue & grey-black	40	45
1596	**1029**	(1st) gold, greenish yellow, magenta, ochre, lt blue & grey-black	40	45
1597	**1030**	(1st) gold, greenish yellow, magenta, ochre, lt blue & grey-black	40	45
1598	**1031**	(1st) gold, greenish yellow, magenta, ochre, lt blue & grey-black	40	45
1599	**1032**	(1st) gold, greenish yellow, magenta, ochre, lt blue & grey-black	40	45
1600	**1033**	(1st) gold, greenish yellow, magenta, ochre, lt blue & grey-black	40	45
1601	**1034**	(1st) gold, greenish yellow, magenta, ochre, lt blue & grey-black	40	45
		Set of 10	3·50	4·00
		First Day Cover		7·50
		Presentation Pack	4·00	

Nos. 1592/1601 were only issued in £2.40 booklets (sold at £2.50 from 1 November 1993). The backgrounds of the stamps form a composite design.

Special First Day of Issue Postmarks

Philatelic Bureau, Edinburgh .... 8·00
Whimsey, Gloucestershire .... 8·00

1035 Queen Elizabeth in Coronation Robes and Parliamentary Emblem

1036 Queen Elizabeth in Garter Robes and Archiepiscopal Arms

1037 Queen Elizabeth with Baby Prince Andrew and Royal Arms **1038** Queen Elizabeth at Trooping the Colour and Service Emblems

1039 Queen Elizabeth and Commonwealth Emblem

(Des Why Not Associates. Litho Questa)

1992 (6 Feb). **40th Anniv of Accession.** *Two phosphor bands. P* 14½ × 14.

1602	**1035**	24p. new blue, greenish yellow, magenta, black, silver & gold	90	75
		a. Horiz strip of 5. Nos. 1602/6	4·00	3·50
1603	**1036**	24p. new blue, greenish yellow, magenta, black, silver & gold	90	75
1604	**1037**	24p. new blue, greenish yellow, magenta, black & silver	90	75
1605	**1038**	24p. new blue, greenish yellow, magenta, black, silver & gold	90	75
1606	**1039**	24p. new blue, greenish yellow, magenta, black, silver & gold	90	75
		Set of 5	4·00	3·50
		Gutter Block of 10	8·00	
		First Day Cover		3·75
		Presentation Pack	4·25	
		P.H.Q. Cards (set of 5)	3·00	5·00

Nos. 1602/6 were printed together, *se-tenant,* in horizontal strips of five throughout the sheet.

Special First Day of Issue Postmarks

Philatelic Bureau, Edinburgh	4·50
Buckingham Palace, London SW1	4·50

1040 Tennyson in 1888 and "The Beguiling of Merlin" (Sir Edward Burne-Jones)

1041 Tennyson in 1864 and "I am Sick of the Shadows" (John Waterhouse)

1042 Tennyson in 1856 and "April Love" (Arthur Hughes)

1043 Tennyson as a Young Man and "Mariana" (Dante Gabriel Rossetti)

(Des Irene von Treskow)

1992 (10 Mar). **Death Centenary of Alfred, Lord Tennyson (poet).** *Phosphorised paper. P* 14½ × 14.

1607	**1040**	24p. gold, greenish yellow, magenta, new blue & black	50	50
1608	**1041**	28p. gold, greenish yellow, magenta, new blue & black	65	65
1609	**1042**	33p. gold, greenish yellow, magenta, new blue & black	1·10	1·10
1610	**1043**	39p. gold, greenish yellow, magenta, new blue, bistre & black	1·10	1·10
		Set of 4	3·00	3·00
		Set of 4 Gutter Pairs	6·00	
		First Day Cover		3·50
		Presentation Pack	3·75	
		P.H.Q. Cards (set of 4)	2·50	5·00

Special First Day of Issue Postmarks

Philatelic Bureau, Edinburgh	3·75
Isle of Wight	3·75

For full information on all future British issues, collectors should write to the British Post Office Philatelic Bureau, 20 Brandon Street, Edinburgh EH3 5TT

CARRICKFERGUS CASTLE

1044 Carrickfergus Castle

Elliptical hole in vertical perforations

(Des from photos by Prince Andrew, Duke of York. Eng C. Matthews. Recess Harrison)

1992 (24 Mar).   *Designs as Nos. 1410/13, but showing Queen's head in silhouette as T* **1044**. *P 15 × 14 (with one elliptical hole on each vertical side).*

1611	**1044**	£1 bottle green & gold†	1·50	1·50
1612	**880**	£1.50 maroon & gold†	2·25	2·25
1613	**881**	£2 indigo & gold†	3·00	3·00
1614	**882**	£5 dp brown & gold†	7·50	7·50
		a. Gold† (Queen's head) omitted	£250	
		Set of 4	13·00	13·00
		Set of 4 Gutter Pairs	27·00	
		First Day Cover		30·00
		Presentation Pack	14·50	
		P.H.Q. Cards†† (set of 4)	1·40	

†The Queen's head on these stamps is printed in optically variable ink which changes colour from gold to green when viewed from different angles.

††The P.H.Q. cards for this issue did not appear until 16 February 1993. They do not exist used on the first day of issue of Nos. 1611/14.

Special First Day of Issue Postmarks
(for illustrations see Introduction)

Philatelic Bureau, Edinburgh (Type H) .... 32·00
Windsor, Berkshire (Type I) .... 32·00

1045 British Olympic Association Logo (Olympic Games, Barcelona)

1046 British Paralympic Association Symbol (Paralympics '92, Barcelona)

LANDFALL IN THE AMERICAS 1492
CHRISTOPHER COLUMBUS

GRAND REGATTA COLUMBUS 1992
OPERATION RALEIGH

1047 *Santa Maria* (500th Anniv of Discovery of America by Columbus)

1048 *Kaisei* (Japanese cadet brigantine) (Grand Regatta Columbus, 1992)

1049 British Pavilion, "EXPO '92", Seville

(Des K. Bassford (Nos. 1615/16, 1619), K. Bassford and S. Paine. Eng C. Matthews (Nos. 1617/18). Litho Questa (Nos. 1615/16, 1619) or recess and litho Harrison (Nos. 1617/18))

1992 (7 Apr).   **Europa. International Events.** *Phosphorised paper.* P 14 × 14½.

1615	**1045**	24p. new blue, lemon, magenta & black ...	65	65
		a. Horiz pair. Nos. 1615/16	1·25	1·25
1616	**1046**	24p. new blue, lemon, magenta & black ...	65	65
1617	**1047**	24p. black, grey, carmine, cream & gold ...	65	65
1618	**1048**	39p. black, grey, carmine, cream & gold ...	1·00	1·10
1619	**1049**	39p. new blue, lemon, magenta & black ...	1·10	1·10
		Set of 5	3·75	3·75
		Set of 3 Gutter Pairs and a Gutter Strip of 4	7·50	
		First Day Cover		4·50
		Presentation Pack	4·25	
		P.H.Q. Cards (set of 5)	3·00	6·00

Nos. 1615/16 were printed together, *se-tenant*, throughout the sheet.

No. 1617 is known with the cream omitted used from Cornwall in September 1992.

Special First Day of Issue Postmarks

Philatelic Bureau, Edinburgh .... 4·75
Liverpool .... 4·75

THE CIVIL WAR 1642-51
fought between the forces of KING
& PARLIAMENT: *Pikeman* ♣♣♣♣

1050 Pikeman

THE CIVIL WAR 1642-51
fought between the forces of KING
& PARLIAMENT: *Drummer* ♣♣♣

1051 Drummer

THE CIVIL WAR 1642-51
fought between the forces of KING
& PARLIAMENT: *Musketeer* ♣♣♣

1052 Musketeer

THE CIVIL WAR 1642-51
fought between the forces of KING
& PARLIAMENT: *Standard Bearer*

1053 Standard Bearer

(Des J. Sancha)

1992 (16 June). **350th Anniv of the Civil War.** *Phosphorised paper.*
P 14½ × 14.

1620	**1050**	24p. black, stone, bistre, scarlet, indigo, grey-green & yellow-ochre	55	55
1621	**1051**	28p. black, yellow-ochre, rose-pink, blue, dull yellow-green & slate-lilac	70	70
1622	**1052**	33p. black, ochre, pale orange, lemon, reddish orange, new blue & olive-green	1·00	1·00
1623	**1053**	39p. black, yellow-ochre, yellow, greenish yellow, vermilion, indigo & orange-brown	1·10	1·10
		Set of 4	3·00	3·00
		Set of 4 Gutter Pairs	6·00	
		First Day Cover		4·00
		Presentation Pack	3·75	
		P.H.Q. Cards (set of 4)	2·00	5·00

Special First Day of Issue Postmarks

Philatelic Bureau, Edinburgh	4·25
Banbury, Oxfordshire	4·25

HAVE YOU READ THE NOTES AT THE BEGINNING OF THIS CATALOGUE?

These often provide answers to the enquiries we receive.

GILBERT & SULLIVAN
The Yeomen of the Guard

1054 *The Yeomen of the Guard*

GILBERT & SULLIVAN
The Gondoliers

1055 *The Gondoliers*

GILBERT & SULLIVAN
The Mikado

1056 *The Mikado*

GILBERT & SULLIVAN
The Pirates of Penzance

1057 *The Pirates of Penzance*

GILBERT & SULLIVAN
Iolanthe

1058 *Iolanthe*

(Des Lynda Gray)

1992 (21 July). **150th Birth Anniv of Sir Arthur Sullivan (composer). Gilbert and Sullivan Operas.** *One phosphor band* (18p.) *or phosphorised paper* (others). P 14½ × 14.

1624	**1054**	18p. bluish violet, bistre-yellow, scarlet, stone, blue & grey-black	40	45
1625	**1055**	24p. purple-brown, lemon, scarlet, stone, blue, olive-bistre & black	55	55
		a. Imperf (pair)	£250	
1626	**1056**	28p. rose-red, lemon, stone, new blue, bluish violet, brt emerald & black	70	70
1627	**1057**	33p. blue-green, orange-yellow, scarlet, olive-bistre, blue, brown-purple & black	1·10	1·10
1628	**1058**	39p. dp blue, lemon, scarlet, stone, lavender, olive-bistre & lake-brown	1·25	1·25
		Set of 5	3·50	3·50
		Set of 5 Gutter Pairs	7·00	
		First Day Cover		4·75
		Presentation Pack	4·00	
		P.H.Q. Cards (set of 5)	2·25	6·00

Philatelic Bureau, Edinburgh .... 5·00
Birmingham .... 5·00

Philatelic Bureau, Edinburgh (in green) .... 4·00
Torridon (in green) .... 4·00

1063 European Star

(Des D. Hockney)

1992 (13 Oct).   **Single European Market.** *Phosphorised paper. P 15 × 14.*
1633 **1063** 24p. gold, greenish yellow, brt magenta, dull
ultramarine & black 60   60
Gutter Pair .... 1·25
First Day Cover .... 1·50
Presentation Pack .... 1·40
P.H.Q. Card 60   1·60

Philatelic Bureau, Edinburgh .... 1·75
Westminster .... 1·75

1059 "Acid Rain Kills"   **1060** "Ozone Layer"

1061 "Greenhouse Effect"   **1062** "Bird of Hope"

(Des Christopher Hall (24p.), Lewis Fowler (28p.), Sarah Warren (33p.),
Alice Newton-Mold (39p.). Adapted Trickett and Webb Ltd)

1992 (15 Sept).   **Protection of the Environment. Children's Paintings.**
Phosphorised paper. P 14 × 14½.
1629 **1059** 24p. emerald, greenish yellow, pale olive-
yellow, brt carmine & black 60   45
1630 **1060** 28p. vermilion, lemon, brt blue, new blue,
brt green, ultramarine & black 85   90
1631 **1061** 33p. greenish blue, greenish yellow, brt
rose-red, brt green, emerald, blue &
black 90   1·00
1632 **1062** 39p. emerald, greenish yellow, brt magenta,
brt orange, brt blue & black .... 1·00   1·00
Set of 4 .... 3·00   3·00
Set of 4 Gutter Pairs .... 6·00
First Day Cover .... 3·75
Presentation Pack .... 3·50
P.H.Q. Cards (set of 4) .... 2·00   5·50

1064 "Angel Gabriel",   **1065** "Madonna and Child",
St. James's, Pangbourne   St. Mary's, Bilbury

1066 "King with Gold", Our Lady and St. Peter, Leatherhead

1067 "Shepherds", All Saints, Porthcawl

1068 "Kings with Frankincense and Myrrh", Our Lady and St. Peter, Leatherhead

(Des Carroll, Dempsey and Thirkell Ltd from windows by Karl Parsons (18, 24, 33p.) and Paul Woodroffe (28p. 39p.))

1992. (10 Nov). **Christmas. Stained Glass Windows.** *One centre band (18p.) or phosphorised paper (others). P 15 × 14.*

1634	**1064**	18p. black, greenish yellow, mauve, ultramarine, brt emerald & gold	40	40
		a. Booklet pane of 20	7·50	
1635	**1065**	24p. black, greenish yellow, brt purple, ultramarine, new blue, brt greenish yellow & gold	65	65
1636	**1066**	28p. black, lemon, rosine, ultramarine, reddish lilac, red-orange & gold	80	80
1637	**1067**	33p. brt ultramarine, greenish yellow, rosine, brown, yellow-orange, black & gold	95	95
1638	**1068**	39p. black, lemon, rosine, brt blue, dp violet, yellow-orange & gold	1·10	1·10
		Set of 5	3·50	3·50
		Set of 5 Gutter Pairs	7·00	
		First Day Cover		4·25
		Presentation Pack	4·00	
		P.H.Q. Cards (set of 5)	2·25	5·50

Booklet pane No. 1634a comes from a special £3.60 Christmas booklet and has margins at left, top and bottom.

Special First Day of Issue Postmarks

Philatelic Bureau, Edinburgh	4·50
Bethlehem, Llandeilo, Dyfed	4·50
Pangbourne	4·50

Collectors Pack 1992

1992 (10 Nov). *Comprises Nos. 1587/91, 1602/10 and 1615/38.*
CP1638a Collectors Pack .... 24·00

Post Office Yearbook

1992 (11 Nov). *Comprises Nos. 1587/91, 1602/10 and 1615/38 in hardbound book with slip case, illustrated in colour .* 40·00

1069 Mute Swan Cob and St. Catherine's Chapel, Abbotsbury

1070 Cygnet and Decoy

1071 Swans and Cygnet

1072 Eggs in Nest and Tithe Barn, Abbotsbury

1073 Young Swan and the Fleet

(Des D. Gentleman)

1993 (19 Jan). **600th Anniv of Abbotsbury Swannery.** *One phosphor band (18p.) or phosphorised paper (others). P 14 × 15.*

1639	**1069**	18p. gold, greenish yellow, bistre, green, vermilion & black	40	40
1640	**1070**	24p. gold, cream, brt green, grey-brown, dull blue & grey-black	65	65
1641	**1071**	28p. gold, greenish grey, yellow-brown, myrtle-green, brown, vermilion & black	90	90

1642	**1072**	33p. gold, ochre, apple-green, olive-brown,		
		brt orange & grey-black	1·00	1·00
1643	**1073**	39p. gold, cream, brt green, cobalt, lt brown		
		& black	1·25	1·25
		Set of 5	3·75	3·75
		Set of 5 Gutter Pairs	7·50	
		First Day Cover		4·50
		Presentation Pack	4·50	
		P.H.Q. Cards (set of 5)	2·25	5·00

Special First Day of Issue Postmarks

Philatelic Bureau, Edinburgh .... 4·50
Abbotsbury, Dorset .... 4·50

1080 Snowman and Father Christmas (*The Snowman*)

1081 The Big Friendly Giant and Sophie (*The BFG*)

1082 Bill Badger and Rupert Bear

1083 Aladdin and the Genie

(Des Newell and Sorell)

1993 (2 Feb–10 Aug). **Greetings Stamps. "Gift Giving".** *Two phosphor bands. P 15 × 14 (with one elliptical hole in each horizontal side).*

1644	**1074**	(1st) gold, greenish yellow, magenta, pale brown, lt blue & black	40	45
		a. Booklet pane. Nos. 1644/53	3·75	
1645	**1075**	(1st) gold, cream & black	40	45
1646	**1076**	(1st) gold, greenish yellow, magenta, cream, new blue & black	40	45
1647	**1077**	(1st) gold, greenish yellow, magenta, cream, new blue & black	40	45
1648	**1078**	(1st) gold, greenish yellow, magenta, cream, new blue & black	40	45
1649	**1079**	(1st) gold, greenish yellow, magenta, cream, new blue & black	40	45
		a. Booklet pane. No. 1649 × 4 with margins all round (10 Aug)	2·50	
1650	**1080**	(1st) gold, greenish yellow, magenta, cream, new blue & black	40	45
1651	**1081**	(1st) gold, greenish yellow, magenta, cream, new blue & black	40	45
1652	**1082**	(1st) gold, greenish yellow, magenta, cream, new blue & black	40	45
1653	**1083**	(1st) gold, greenish yellow, magenta, cream, new blue & black	40	45
		Set of 10	3·75	4·00
		First Day Cover		7·50
		Presentation Pack	4·00	
		P.H.Q. Cards (set of 10)	3·00	7·75

Nos. 1644/53 were issued in £2.40 booklets (sold at £2.50 from 1 November 1993), together with a pane of 20 half stamp-sized labels. The stamps and labels were affixed to the booklet cover by a common gutter margin.

Booklet pane No. 1649a comes from the £6 (£5.64) Beatrix Potter booklet.

1074 Long John Silver and Parrot (*Treasure Island*)

1075 Tweedledum and Tweedledee (*Alice Through the Looking-Glass*)

1076 William (*William* books)

1077 Mole and Toad (*The Wind in the Willows*)

1078 Teacher and Wilfrid ("The Bash Street Kids")

1079 Peter Rabbit and Mrs. Rabbit (*The Tale of Peter Rabbit*)

Special First Day of Issue Postmarks

Philatelic Bureau, Edinburgh (No. 1644a) (2 Feb) ... 8·00
Greetland (No. 1644a) (2 Feb) .... 8·00
Philatelic Bureau, Edinburgh (No. 1649a) (10 Aug) .. 5·00
Keswick (No. 1649a) (10 Aug) .... 5·00

Philatelic Bureau, Edinburgh .... 4·00
Greenwich .... 4·00

1084 Decorated Enamel
Dial

1085 Escapement,
Remontoire and Fusée

1088 Britannia

(Des B. Craddock, adapted Roundel Design Group. Litho (silver die-stamped, Braille symbol for "10" embossed) Questa)

1993 (2 Mar). *Granite paper.* P $14 \times 14\frac{1}{2}$ *(with two elliptical holes on each horizontal side).*

1658 **1088** £10 greenish grey, rosine, yellow, new blue,
reddish violet, vermilion, violet, brt
green & silver .... 15·00 10·00
First Day Cover .... 22·00
Presentation Pack .... 15·00
P.H.Q. Card .... 35 22·00

The paper used for No. 1658 contains fluorescent coloured fibres which, together with the ink used on the shield, react under U.V. light.

1086 Balance, Spring and
Temperature
Compensator

1087 Back of Movement

(Des H. Brown and D. Penny. Litho Questa)

1993 (16 Feb). **300th Birth Anniv of John Harrison (inventor of the marine chronometer). Details of "H4" Clock.** *Phosphorised paper.* P $14\frac{1}{2} \times 14$.

1654 **1084** 24p. new blue, greenish yellow, magenta,
black, grey-black & pale cream 50 50
1655 **1085** 28p. new blue, greenish yellow, magenta,
black, grey-black & pale cream 80 80
1656 **1086** 33p. new blue, greenish yellow, magenta,
black, grey-black & pale cream 95 95
1657 **1087** 39p. new blue, greenish yellow, magenta,
black, grey-black & pale cream .... 1·10 1·10
Set of 4 .... 3·00 3·00
Set of 4 Gutter Pairs .... 6·00
First Day Cover .... 4·00
Presentation Pack .... 4·00
P.H.Q. Cards (set of 4) .... 2·00 4·50

Philatelic Bureau, Edinburgh .... 24·00
Windsor .... 24·00

1089 Dendrobium
hellwigianum

1090 Paphiopedilum Maudiae
"Magnificum"

28

1091 *Cymbidium lowianum*

33

1092 *Vanda* Rothschildiana

39

1093 *Dendrobium vexillarius*
var *albiviride*

(Des Pandora Sellars)

1993 (16 Mar). **14th World Orchid Conference, Glasgow.** One
phosphor band (18p.) *or phosphorised paper* (others). P 15 × 14.

1659	**1089**	18p. green, greenish yellow, magenta, pale blue, apple-green & slate	40	40
		a. Imperf (pair)		
1660	**1090**	24p. green, greenish yellow, brt green & grey-black	65	65
1661	**1091**	28p. green, greenish yellow, red, brt turquoise-blue & drab	90	90
1662	**1092**	33p. green, greenish yellow, pale magenta, brt violet, brt green & grey	1·00	1·00
1663	**1093**	39p. green, greenish yellow, red, pale olive-yellow, brt green, violet & grey-black .	1·25	1·25
		Set of 5	3·50	3·50
		Set of 5 Gutter Pairs	7·00	
		First Day Cover		4·50
		Presentation Pack	4·00	
		P.H.Q. Cards (set of 5)	2·25	5·00

Special First Day of Issue Postmarks

Philatelic Bureau, Edinburgh	4·50
Glasgow	4·50

1993 (6 Apr)–**94** *Booklet Stamps. As T* **913/14,** *but P* 15 × 14 *(with one elliptical hole on each vertical side).*

(a) Photo Harrison

1663a	**913**	(2nd) brt blue (1 centre band) (7.9.93)	30	35
1664	**914**	1st brt orange-red (phosphorised paper) ..	40	45

(b) Litho Questa or Walsall

1665	**913**	2ndbrt blue (1 centre band)	30	35
		Ey. Phosphor omitted		
1666	**914**	1st brt orange-red (2 phosphor bands)	40	45
		Ey. Phosphor omitted		

(1666)		l. Booklet pane. No. 1666 × 4 plus commemorative label (27.7.94)	1·50
		m. Pane. No. 1666 with margins all round (17.8.94)	40

Nos. 1663a/6 were issued in booklet panes showing perforations on all four edges.

On 6 September 1993 Nos. 1665/6 printed in lithography by Questa were made available in sheets from post offices in Birmingham, Coventry, Falkirk and Milton Keynes. These sheet stamps became available nationally on 5 October 1993.

Nos. 1663a/6 occur from the following Barcode booklets:

No. 1663a – No. HA7; No. 1664 – Nos. HB5, HD9; No. 1665 – Nos. HA6 (Walsall), HC11 (Questa), HC12 (Walsall); No. 1666 – Nos. HB6 (Walsall), HD10 (Walsall), HD11 (Walsall), HD12/19 (Walsall); No. 1666l – No. HB7 (Questa) (includes commemorative label for 300th anniv of Bank of England)

No. 1666m, printed by Questa, was provided by the Royal Mail for inclusion in single pre-packed greetings cards sold by Boots. The pane shows large margins at top and sides with lines of roulette stretching from the bottom corners to the mid point of the top edge. Examples included with greetings cards show the top two corners of the pane folded over. Unfolded examples were available from the British Philatelic Bureau and from other Post Office philatelic outlets.

In mid-1994 a number of postal forgeries of the 2nd bright blue printed in lithography were detected. These show the Queen's head in bright greenish blue, have a fluorescent, rather than a phosphor, band and show matt, colourless gum on the reverse. The forgeries come from booklets of ten which also have forged covers.

1993 (27 Apr)–**94** *As Nos. X841, etc, but P* 15 × 14 *(with one elliptical hole on each vertical side).*

(a) Photo Enschedé. Two phosphor bands

Y1667	**367**	1p. crimson (8.6.93)	10	10
Y1669		4p. new blue (14.12.93)	10	10
Y1670		5p. dull red-brown (8.6.93)	10	10
Y1671		6p. yellow-olive	10	15
Y1672		10p. dull orange (8.6.93)	15	20
Y1673		20p. turquoise-green (14.12.93)	30	35
Y1674		29p. grey (26.10.93)	45	50
Y1675		30p. dp olive-grey (27.7.93)	45	50
Y1676		35p. yellow (17.8.93)	55	60
Y1677		36p. brt ultramarine (26.10.93)	55	60
Y1678		38p. rosine (26.10.93)	60	65
Y1679		41p. grey-brown (26.10.93)	65	70
Y1680		50p. ochre (14.12.93)	75	80

(b) Photo Harrison

Y1700	**367**	19p. bistre (1 centre band) (26.10.93)	30	35
		a. Imperf (pair)		
Y1701		25p. rose-red (phosphorised paper) (26.10.93)	40	45
		a. Imperf (pair)		
		l. Booklet pane. No. Y1701 × 2 plus 2 labels (1.11.93)	75	
Y1702		25p. rose-red (2 bands) (20.12.94)	40	45
Y1703		35p. yellow (phosphorised paper) (1.11.93) .	55	60
Y1704		41p. drab (phosphorised paper) (1.11.93) ...	65	70

(c) Litho Questa (6p., 19p.), *Questa or Walsall* (25p.), *or Walsall* (others)

Y1748	**367**	6p. yellow-olive (2 bands) (26.7.94)	2.00	2.00
		l. Booklet pane. Nos. Y1748/9 and Y1750 × 4 with margins all round	1·90	
		la. 6p. value misplaced		
Y1749		19p. bistre (1 band at left) (26.7.94)	2·00	2·00
Y1750		25p. red (2 bands) (1.11.93)	40	45
Y1751		35p. yellow (2 bands) (1.11.93)	55	60
Y1752		41p. drab (2 bands) (1.11.93)	65	70
Y1753		60p. dull blue-grey (2 bands) (9.8.94)	90	95
		First Day Cover (Nos. Y1674, Y1677/9, Y1700/1)		4·25
		First Day Cover (No. Y1753)		1·75
		Presentation Pack (Nos. Y1674, Y1677/9, Y1700/1)	3·25	

No. 1748la shows the 6p. value printed 22mm to the left so that its position on the booklet pane is completely blank except for the phosphor bands. Other more minor misplacements exist.

DECIMAL MACHIN WITH ELLIPTICAL PERFORATIONS INDEX

Val.	Process and Printer	Colour	Phosphor	Cat No.	Source
1p.	photo Enschedé	crimson	2 bands	Y1667	sheets
4p.	photo Enschedé	new blue	2 bands	Y1669	sheets
5p.	photo Enschedé	dull red-brown	2 bands	Y1670	sheets
6p.	photo Enschedé	yellow-olive	2 bands	Y1671	sheets
6p.	litho Questa	yellow-olive	2 bands	Y1748	£6.04 Northern Ireland booklet (DX16)
10p.	photo Enschedé	dull orange	2 bands	Y1672	sheets
19p.	photo Harrison	bistre	1 centre band	Y1700	sheets, coils
19p.	litho Questa	bistre	1 side band	Y1749	£6.04 Northern Ireland booklet (DX16)
20p.	photo Enschedé	turquoise-green	2 bands	Y1673	sheets
25p.	photo Harrison	rose-red	phos paper	Y1701	sheets, coils, 50p booklets (FB67/71), £1 booklets (FH33/5), £2 booklets (FW1/3)
25p.	litho Walsall or Questa	red	2 bands	Y1750	£1 booklet (FH31/2) (Walsall), £6.04 booklet (DX16) (Questa)
25p.	photo Harrison	rose-red	2 bands	Y1702	sheets
29p.	photo Enschedé	grey	2 bands	Y1674	sheets
30p.	photo Enschedé	dp olive-grey	2 bands	Y1675	sheets
35p.	photo Enschedé	yellow	2 bands	Y1676	sheets
35p.	photo Harrison	yellow	2 bands	Y1703	coils
35p.	litho Walsall	yellow	2 bands	Y1751	£1.40 booklet (GK5)
36p.	photo Enschedé	brt ultramarine	2 bands	Y1677	sheets
38p.	photo Enschedé	rosine	2 bands	Y1678	sheets
41p.	photo Enschedé	grey-brown	2 bands	Y1679	sheets
41p.	photo Harrison	drab	phos paper	Y1704	coils
41p.	litho Walsall	drab	2 bands	Y1752	£1.64 booklet (GM1)
50p.	photo Enschedé	ochre	2 bands	Y1680	sheets
60p	litho Walsall	dull blue-grey	2 bands	Y1753	£2.40 booklets (GP1/2)

1094 "Family Group"
(bronze sculpture)
(Henry Moore)

1095 "Kew Gardens"
(lithograph)
(Edward Bawden)

1098 Emperor Claudius
(from gold coin)

1099 Emperor Hadrian
(bronze head)

1096 "St. Francis and the Birds"
(Stanley Spencer)

1097 "Still Life: Odyssey I"
(Ben Nicholson)

1100 Goddess Roma
(from gemstone)

1101 Christ
(Hinton St. Mary mosaic)

(Des J. Gibbs)

1993 (15 June). **Roman Britain.** *Phosphorised paper with two phosphor bands. P* 14 × 14.

1771	**1098**	24p. black, pale orange, lt brown & silver ..	50	50
1772	**1099**	28p. black, greenish yellow, brt rose-red, silver, brt blue & grey-black	80	80
1773	**1100**	33p. black, greenish yellow, brt rose-red, silver & grey	95	95
1774	**1101**	39p. black, greenish yellow, rosine, silver, pale violet & grey	1·10	1·10
		Set of 4	3·00	3·00
		Set of 4 Gutter Pairs	6·00	
		First Day Cover		4·00
		Presentation Pack	3·50	
		PHQ Cards (set of 4)	1·40	4·00

Special First Day of Issue Postmarks

British Philatelic Bureau, Edinburgh .... 4·00
Caerllion .... 4·00

(Des. A. Dastor)

1993 (11 May). **Europa. Contemporary Art.** *Phosphorised paper.* P 14 × 14½.

1767	**1094**	24p. brownish grey, lemon, magenta, turquoise-blue & grey-black	50	50
1768	**1095**	28p. brownish grey, buff, lt green, yellow-brown, brt orange, new blue & grey-black	80	80
1769	**1096**	33p. brownish grey, cream, greenish yellow, magenta, new blue & grey-black	95	95
1770	**1097**	39p. brownish grey, cream, yellow-ochre, rose-lilac, red, lt blue & grey-black ...	1·10	1·10
		Set of 4	3·00	3·00
		Set of 4 Gutter Pairs	6·00	
		First Day Cover		4·00
		Presentation Pack	2·40	
		PHQ Cards (set of 4)	2·00	4·50

Special First Day of Issue Postmarks

British Philatelic Bureau, Edinburgh .... 4·00
London SW .... 4·00

1102 *Midland Maid* and
other Narrow Boats,
Grand Junction Canal

1103 *Yorkshire Lass* and
other Humber Keels,
Stainforth and Keadby Canal

1104 *Valley Princess* and other Horse-drawn Barges, Brecknock and Abergavenny Canal

1105 Steam Barges, including *Pride of Scotland,* and Fishing Boats, Crinan Canal

1110 Pear

(Des Charlotte Knox)

(Des T. Lewery. Litho Questa)

1993 (20 July). **Inland Waterways.** *Two phosphor bands.* P 14½ × 14.

1775	**1102**	24p.	new blue, greenish yellow, brt magenta, black, blue, vermilion, brownish grey & sage-green	50	50
1776	**1103**	28p.	new blue, greenish yellow, brt magenta, black, blue, bluish grey, vermilion & sage-green	80	80
1777	**1104**	33p.	new blue, greenish yellow, brt magenta, black, blue, vermilion, greenish grey & sage-green	95	95
1778	**1105**	39p.	new blue, greenish yellow, brt magenta, black, blue, vermilion, sage-green & dull mauve	1·10	1·10
			Set of 4	3·00	3·00
			Set of 4 Gutter Pairs	6·00	
			First Day Cover		4·00
			Presentation Pack	3·50	
			PHQ Cards (set of 4)	1·40	4·50

Nos. 1775/8 commemorate the bicentenary of the Acts of Parliament authorising the canals depicted.

Special First Day of Issue Postmarks

British Philatelic Bureau, Edinburgh .... 4·00
Gloucester .... 4·00

1993 (14 Sept). **The Four Seasons. Autumn. Fruits and Leaves.** *One phosphor band* (18p.) *or phosphorised paper (others).* P 15 × 14.

1779	**1106**	18p.	black, greenish yellow, cerise, brt green, gold & chestnut	40	40
1780	**1107**	24p.	black, lemon, cerise, myrtle-green, gold, brt green & brown	65	65
1781	**1108**	28p.	black, lemon, emerald, lake-brown & gold	80	80
1782	**1109**	33p.	grey-black, greenish yellow, rosine, lt green, gold & brown	95	95
1783	**1110**	39p.	myrtle-green, greenish yellow, rosine, olive-sepia, gold, apple-green & dp myrtle-green	1·10	1·10
			Set of 5	3·50	3·50
			Set of 5 Gutter Pairs	7·00	
			First Day Cover		4·50
			Presentation Pack	4·00	
			PHQ Cards (set of 5)	1·50	5·00

Special First Day of Issue Postmarks

British Philatelic Bureau, Edinburgh .... 4·00
Taunton .... 4·00

1106 Horse Chestnut

1107 Blackberry

1108 Hazel

1109 Rowan

1111 *The Reigate Squire*

1112 *The Hound of the Baskervilles*

1113 *The Six Napoleons*

SHERLOCK HOLMES & LESTRADE "THE SIX NAPOLEONS"

1114 *The Greek Interpreter*

SHERLOCK HOLMES & MYCROFT "THE GREEK INTERPRETER"

SHERLOCK HOLMES & MORIARTY "THE FINAL PROBLEM"

1115 *The Final Problem*

(Des A. Davidson. Litho Questa)

1993 (12 Oct). **Sherlock Holmes. Centenary of the Publication of "The Final Problem"** *Phosphorised paper.* P 14 × 14½.

1784	**1111**	24p. new blue, greenish yellow, magenta, black & gold 65	65
		a. Horiz strip of 5. Nos. 1784/8 .... 3·00	3·00
1785	**1112**	24p. new blue, greenish yellow, magenta, black & gold 65	65
1786	**1113**	24p. new blue, greenish yellow, magenta, black & gold 65	65
1787	**1114**	24p. new blue, greenish yellow, magenta, black & gold 65	65
1788	**1115**	24p. new blue, greenish yellow, magenta, black & gold 65	65
		Set of 5 .... 3·00	3·00
		Gutter strip of 10 .... 6·00	
		First Day Cover	4·50
		Presentation Pack .... 3·50	
		PHQ Cards (set of 5) .... 1·50	1·50

Nos. 1785/8 were printed together, *se-tenant*, in horizontal strips of 5 throughout the sheet.

Special First Day of Issue Postmarks

FIRST DAY OF ISSUE BRITISH PHILATELIC BUREAU EDINBURGH 12 OCTOBER 1993

221B BAKER ST. FIRST DAY OF ISSUE LONDON NW1 12 OCTOBER 1993

British Philatelic Bureau, Edinburgh .... 4·00
London NW1 .... 4·00

A First Day of Issue handstamp was provided at Autumn Stampex, London SW1, for this issue.

1ST

1116

(Des J. Matthews. Litho Walsall)

1993 (19 Oct) *Self-adhesive Booklet Stamp. Two phosphor bands. Die-cut P 14 × 15* (*with one elliptical hole on each vertical side*).

1789	**1116**	(1st) orange-red 60	60
		a. Booklet pane. No. 1789 × 20 .... 8·00	
		First Day Cover (No. 1789)	1·75
		Presentation Pack (No. 1789a) .... 10·00	
		PHQ Card 30	2·00

No. 1789 was initially sold at 24p. which was increased to 25p. from November 1993. It was only issued in booklets containing 20 stamps, each surrounded by die-cut perforations.

Special First Day of Issue Postmarks

British Philatelic Bureau, Edinburgh .... 1·50
Newcastle upon Tyne .... 1·50

1117 Bob Cratchit and Tiny Tim

1118 Mr. and Mrs. Fezziwig

1119 Scrooge

1120 The Prize Turkey

1121 Mr. Scrooge's Nephew

(Des Q. Blake)

1993 (9 Nov). **Christmas. 150th Anniv of Publication of "A Christmas Carol" by Charles Dickens.** *One phosphor band* (19p.) *or phosphorised paper* (others). P 15 × 14.

1790	**1117**	19p. new blue, yellow, magenta, salmon, brt emerald & grey-black	30	35
		a. Imperf (pair)		
1791	**1118**	25p. yellow-orange, brown-lilac, steel-blue, lake-brown, lt green, grey-black & black	40	45
1792	**1119**	30p. cerise, bistre-yellow, dull blue, brown-rose, pale green, grey-black & black ..	45	50
1793	**1120**	35p. dp turquoise-green, lemon, vermilion, dull ultramarine, Indian red, bluish grey & black	55	60
1794	**1121**	41p. reddish purple, lemon, purple, lt blue, salmon, brt green & black	65	70
		Set of 5	2·10	2·25
		Set of 5 Gutter Pairs	4·50	
		First Day Cover		4·50
		Presentation Pack	2·75	
		PHQ Cards (set of 5)	1·90	5·25

Special First Day of Issue Postmarks

British Philatelic Bureau, Edinburgh .... 4·00
Bethlehem, Llandeilo .... 4·00
A First Day of Issue handstamp (pictorial) was provided at the City of London for this issue.

Collectors Pack 1993

1993 (9 Nov). *Comprises Nos. 1639/43, 1654/7, 1659/63, 1767/88 and 1790/4.*
CP1794a Collectors Pack .... 19·00

Post Office Yearbook

1993 (9 Nov). *Comprises Nos. 1639/43, 1654/7, 1659/63, 1767/88 and 1790/4 in hardbound book with slip case, illustrated in colour* .... 32·00

1122 Class "5" No. 44957 and Class "B1" No. 61342 on West Highland Line

1123 Class "A1" No. 60149 *Amadis* at Kings Cross

1124 Class "4" No. 43000 on Turntable at Blyth North

1125 Class "4" No. 42455 near Wigan Central

1126 Class "Castle" No. 7002 *Devizes Castle* on Bridge crossing Worcester and Birmingham Canal

(Des B. Delaney)

1994 (18 Jan). **The Age of Steam. Railway Photographs by Colin Gifford.** *One phosphor band* (19p.) *or phosphorised paper with two bands* (others). P 14½.

1795	**1122**	19p. dp blue-green, grey-black & black	30	35
1796	**1123**	25p. slate-lilac, grey-black & black	40	45
1797	**1124**	30p. lake-brwon, grey-black & black	45	50
1798	**1125**	35p. dp claret, grey-black & black	55	60
1799	**1126**	41p. indigo, grey-black & black	65	70
		Set of 5	2·10	2·40
		Set of 5 Gutter Pairs	4·50	
		First Day Cover		4·50
		Presentation Pack	2·75	
		PHQ Cards (set of 5)	1·90	5·25

Nos. 1796/9 are on phosphorised paper and also show two phosphor bands.

Special First Day of Issue Postmarks

British Philatelic Bureau, Edinburgh .... 2·50
York .... 2·50
A First Day of Issue handstamp (pictorial) was provided at Bridge of Orchy for this issue.

1127 Dan Dare and the Mekon

1128 The Three Bears

1129 Rupert Bear

1130 Alice (Alice in Wonderland)

1131 Noggin and the Ice Dragon

1132 Peter Rabbit posting Letter

1133 Red Riding Hood and Wolf

1134 Orlando the Marmalade Cat

1135 Biggles

1136 Paddington Bear on Station

(Des Newell and Sorrell)

1994 (1 Feb). **Greetings Stamps. "Messages".** *Two phosphor bands.*
P 15 × 14 (with one elliptical hole on each vertical side).

1800	**1127**	(1st)	gold, greenish yellow, brt purple, bistre-yellow, new blue & black	40	45
			a. Booklet pane. Nos. 1800/9	4·00	
1801	**1128**	(1st)	gold, greenish yellow, brt purple, bistre-yellow, new blue & black	40	45
1802	**1129**	(1st)	gold, greenish yellow, brt purple, bistre-yellow, new blue & black	40	45
1803	**1130**	(1st)	gold, bistre-yellow & black	40	45
1804	**1131**	(1st)	gold, greenish yellow, brt purple, bistre-yellow, new blue & black	40	45
1805	**1132**	(1st)	gold, greenish yellow, brt purple, bistre-yellow, new blue & black	40	45
1806	**1133**	(1st)	gold, greenish yellow, brt purple, bistre-yellow, new blue & black	40	45
1807	**1134**	(1st)	gold, greenish yellow, brt purple, bistre-yellow, new blue & black	40	45
1808	**1135**	(1st)	gold, greenish yellow, brt purple, bistre-yellow, new blue & black	40	45
1809	**1136**	(1st)	gold, greenish yellow, brt purple, bistre-yellow, new blue & black	40	45
			Set of 10	4·00	4·50
			First Day Cover		5·50
			Presentation Pack	4·25	
			PHQ Cards (set of 10)	3·75	9·25

Nos. 1800/9 were issued in £.2.50 stamp booklets, together with a pane of 20 half stamp-sized labels. The stamps and labels were attached to the booklet cover by a common gutter margin.

Special First Day of Issue Postmarks

British Philatelic Bureau, Edinburgh .... 5·75
Penn, Wolverhampton .... 5·75

1137 Castell Y Waun (Chirk Castle), Clwyd, Wales

1138 BenArkle, Sutherland, Scotland

1139 Mourne Mountains, Country Down, Northern Ireland

1140 Dersingham, Norfolk. England

1141 Dolwyddelan, Gwynedd, Wales

1994 (1 Mar–26 July). **25th Anniv of Investiture of the Prince of Wales. Paintings by Prince Charles.** *One phosphor band (19p.) or phosphorised paper (others). P 15 × 14.*

1810	**1137**	19p. grey-black, greenish yellow, magenta, new blue, black & silver	30	35
1811	**1138**	25p. grey-black, orange-yellow, brt magenta, new blue, silver & black	40	45

1812 **1139** 30p. grey-black, greenish yellow, magenta,
new blue, silver & black 45 50
     a. Booklet pane. No. 1812 × 4 with
       margins all round (26 July) .... 1·75
1813 **1140** 35p. grey-black, greenish yellow, magenta,
new blue, silver & black 55 60
1814 **1141** 41p. grey-black, lemon, magenta, new blue,
silver & black 65 70
     Set of 5 .... 2·10 2·40
     Set of 5 Gutter Pairs .... 4·50
     First Day Cover .... 3·25
     Presentation Pack .... 2·75
     PHQ Cards (set of 5) .... 1·90 5·25

Booklet pane No. 1812a comes from the £6.04 "Northern Ireland" booklet.

Special First Day of Issue Postmarks

British Philatelic Bureau, Edinburgh .... 3·50
Caernarfon .... 3·50

1142 Bather at Blackpool

1143 "Where's my Little Lad?"

1144 "Wish You
were Here!"

1145 Punch and Judy
Show

1146 "The Tower Crane" Machine

(Des M. Dempsey and B. Dare. Litho Questa)

1994 (12 Apr). **Centenary of Picture Postcards.** *One side band* (19p.) or *two phosphor bands* (others). P 14 × 14½

1815 **1142** 19p. new blue, greenish yellow, magenta &
black 30 35
1816 **1143** 25p. new blue, greenish yellow, magenta &
black 40 45
1817 **1144** 30p. new blue, greenish yellow, magenta &
black 45 50
1818 **1145** 35p. new blue, greenish yellow, magenta &
black 55 60
1819 **1146** 41p. new blue, greenish yellow, magenta &
black 65 70
     Set of 5 .... 2·10 2·40
     Set of 5 Gutter Pairs .... 4·50
     First Day Cover .... 3·25
     Presentation Pack .... 2·75
     PHQ Cards (set of 5) .... 1·90 5·25

Special First Day of Issue Postmarks

British Philatelic Bureau, Edinburgh .... 3·50
Blackpool .... 3·50

1147 British Lion and French Cockerel
over Tunnel

1148 Symbolic Hands over Train

(Des G. Hardie (T **1147**), J.-P. Cousin (T **1148**))

1994 (3 May)   **Opening of Channel Tunnel.** *Phosphorised paper.* P 14 × 14½.

1820	**1147**	25p. ultramarine, brt orange, scarlet, new blue, emerald, turquoise-blue & silver	40	45
		a. Horiz pair. Nos. 1820/1	80	90
1821	**1148**	25p. ultramarine, scarlet, new blue, emerald & silver	40	45
1822	**1147**	41p. new blue, brt orange, scarlet, turquoise-blue, emerald, ultramarine & silver	65	70
		a. Horiz pair. Nos. 1822/3	1·25	1·40
		ab. Imperf (horiz pair)		
1823	**1148**	41p. ultramarine, scarlet, new blue, emerald & silver	65	70
		Set of 4	2·10	2·25
		First Day Cover		3·00
		Presentation Pack	2·50	
		PHQ Cards (set of 4)	1·50	4·50

Nos. 1820/1 and 1822/3 were printed together, *se-tenant*, in horizontal pairs throughout the sheets.

Special First Day of Issue Postmarks

British Philatelic Bureau, Edinburgh .... 3·25
Folkestone .... 3·25

1149 Groundcrew replacing Smoke Canisters on Douglas Boston of 88 Sqn

1150 H.M.S. *Warspite* (battleship) shelling Enemy Positions

1151 Commandos landing on Gold Beach

1152 Infantry regrouping on Sword Beach

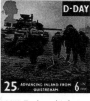

1153 Tank and Infantry advancing, Ouistreham

(Des K. Bassford from contemporary photographs. Litho Questa)

1994 (6 June).   **50th Anniv of D-Day.** Y *Two phosphor bands.* P 14½ × 14.

1824	**1149**	25p. pink, greenish yellow, blackish lilac, slate-black, brt scarlet & silver-grey ..	40	45
		a. Horiz strip of 5. Nos. 1824/8	2·00	2·25
1825	**1150**	25p. pink, greenish yellow, blackish lilac, slate-black, brt scarlet & silver-grey ..	40	45
1826	**1151**	25p. pink, greenish yellow, blackish lilac, slate-black, brt scarlet & silver-grey ..	40	45
1827	**1152**	25p. pink, greenish yellow, blackish lilac, slate-black, brt scarlet & silver-grey ..	40	45
1828	**1153**	25p. pink, greenish yellow, blackish lilac, slate-black, brt scarlet & silver-grey ..	40	45
		Set of 5	2·00	2·25
		Gutter block of 10	4·00	
		First Day Cover		2·75
		Presentation Pack	2·40	
		PHQ Cards (set of 5)	1·90	4·75

Nos. 1824/8 were printed together, *se-tenant*, in horizontal strips of 5 throughout the sheet.

Special First Day of Issue Postmarks

British Philatelic Bureau, Edinburgh .... 3·00
Portsmouth .... 3·00

1154 The Old Course, St. Andrews

1155 The 18th Hole, Muirfield

1156 The 15th Hole
("Luckyslap"),
Carnoustie

1157 The 8th Hole
("The Postage Stamp"),
Royal Troon

1158 The 9th Hole,
Turnberry

1159 Royal Welsh Show,
Llanelwedd

1160 All England Tennis
Championships, Wimbledon

1161 Cowes Week

1162 Test Match, Lord's

1163 Braemar Gathering

(Des M. Cook)

1994 (2 Aug). **The Four Seasons. Summertime.** *One phosphor band (19p.) or phosphorised paper (others). P 15 × 14.*

1834	**1159**	19p. black, greenish yellow, brt magenta, brown, yellow-brown & new blue	30	35
1835	**1160**	25p. black, greenish yellow, magenta, reddish violet, yellow-green, myrtle-green & new blue	40	45
1836	**1161**	30p. black, greenish yellow, brt magenta, yellow-ochre, dp slate-blue, blue-green & blue	45	50
1837	**1162**	35p. black, greenish yellow, magenta, slate-lilac, yellow-green, dp bluish green & brt blue	55	60
1838	**1163**	41p. black, greenish yellow, brt magenta, dp claret, lt brown, myrtle-green & brt blue	65	70
		Set of 5	2·25	2·50
		Set of 5 Gutter Pairs	4·50	
		First Day Cover		3·25
		Presentation Pack	2·75	
		PHQ Cards (set of 5)	1·90	5·25

(Des P. Hogarth)

1994 (5 July). **Scottish Golf Courses.** *One phosphor band (19p.) or phosphorised paper (others). P 14½ × 14.*

1829	**1154**	19p. yellow-green, olive-grey, orange-vermilion, apple-green, blue & grey-black	30	35
1830	**1155**	25p. yellow-green, lemon, brt orange, apple-green, blue, magenta & grey-black	40	45
1831	**1156**	30p. yellow-green, yellow, rosine, emerald, blue-green, new blue & grey-black ...	45	50
1832	**1157**	35p. yellow-green, yellow, rosine, apple-green, new blue, dull blue & grey-black	55	60
1833	**1158**	41p. yellow-green, lemon, magenta, apple-green, dull blue, new blue & grey-black	65	70
		Set of 5	2·25	2·50
		Set of 5 Gutter Pairs	4·50	
		First Day Cover		3·25
		Presentation Pack	2·75	
		PHQ Cards (set of 5)	1·90	5·25

Nos. 1829/33 commemorate the 250th anniversary of golf's first set of rules produced by the Honourable Company of Edinburgh Golfers.

Special First Day of Issue Postmarks

British Philatelic Bureau, Edinburgh .... 3·50
Turnberry .... 3·50

Special First Day of Issue Postmarks

British Philatelic Bureau, Edinburgh .... 3·50
Wimbledon .... 3·50

1164 Ultrasonic Imaging

1165 Scanning Electron Microscopy

1170 Mary with Doll

1171 Shepherds

1166 Magnetic Resonance Imaging

1167 Computed Tomography

1172 Angels

(Des Yvonne Gilbert)

(Des P. Vermier and J.-P. Tibbles. Photo Enschedé)

1994 (27 Sept). **Europa. Medical Discoveries.** *Phosphorised paper.*
P 14 × 14½.

1839	**1164**	25p. greenish yellow, brt magenta, new blue, black & silver	40	45
1840	**1165**	30p. greenish yellow, brt magenta, new blue, black & silver	45	50
1841	**1166**	35p. greenish yellow, brt magenta, new blue, black & silver	55	60
1842	**1167**	41p. greenish yellow, brt magenta, new blue, black & silver	65	70
		Set of 4	2·00	2·25
		Set of 4 Gutter Pairs	4·00	
		First Day Cover		3·00
		Presentation Pack	2·40	
		PHQ Cards (set of 4)	1·50	3·50

Special First Day of Issue Postmarks

British Philatelic Bureau, Edinburgh .... 3·25
Cambridge .... 3·25

1168 Mary and Joseph

1169 Three Wise Men

1994 (1 Nov). **Christmas. Children's Nativity Plays.** *One phosphor band* (19p.) *or phosphorised paper* (others). *P* 15 × 14.

1843	**1168**	19p. turquoise-green, greenish yellow, brt magenta, new blue, dull blue & grey-black	30	35
		a. Imperf (pair)	£225	
1844	**1169**	25p. orange-brown, greenish yellow, brt magenta, new blue, lt blue, bistre & grey-black	40	45
1845	**1170**	30p. lt brown, greenish yellow, brt magenta, blue, turquoise-blue, new blue & brownish grey	45	50
1846	**1171**	35p. dp grey-brown, greenish yellow, brt magenta, turquoise-blue, dull violet-blue, ochre & brown	55	60
1847	**1172**	41p. blue, greenish yellow, brt magenta, turquoise-blue, lt blue & dp grey	65	70
		Set of 5	2·25	2·50
		Set of 5 Gutter Pairs	4·50	
		First Day Cover		3·25
		Presentation Pack	3·50	
		PHQ Cards (set of 5)	1·90	5·25

Special First Day of Issue Postmarks

British Philatelic Bureau, Edinburgh .... 3·50
Bethlehem, Llandeilo .... 3·50

Collectors Pack 1994

1994 (14 Nov). *Comprises Nos. 1795/1847*
CP1847a Collectors Pack .... 24·00

Post Office Yearbook

1994 (14 Nov). *Comprises Nos. 1795/9 and 1810/47 in hardbound book with slip case, illustrated in colour* .... 35·00

1173 Sophie (black cat)

1174 Puskas (Siamese) and Tigger (tabby)

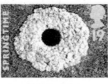

1178 Dandelions

1179 Chestnut Leaves

1175 Chloe (ginger cat)

1176 Kikko (tortoiseshell) and Rosie (Abyssinian)

1180 Garlic Leaves

1181 Hazel Leaves

1177 Fred (black and white cat)

1182 Spring Grass

(Des Elizabeth Blackadder. Litho Questa)

1995 (17 Jan). **Cats.** One phosphor band (19p.) or two phosphor bands (others). P $14\frac{1}{2} \times 14$.

1848	**1173**	19p. new blue, greenish yellow, magenta, black & brown-red	30	35
1849	**1174**	25p. new blue, greenish yellow, magenta, black & dull yellow-green	40	45
1850	**1175**	30p. new blue, greenish yellow, magenta, black & yellow-brown	45	50
1851	**1176**	35p. new blue, greenish yellow, magenta, black & yellow	55	60
1852	**1177**	41p. new blue, greenish yellow, magenta, black & reddish orange	65	70
		Set of 5	2·25	2·50
		Set of 5 Gutter Pairs	4·50	
		First Day Cover		3·25
		Presentation Pack	2·75	
		PHQ Cards (set of 5)	1·90	5·25

1995 (14 Mar). **The Four Seasons. Springtime. Plant Sculptures by Andy Goldsworthy.** One phosphor band (19p.) or two phosphor bands (others). P 15 × 14.

1853	**1178**	19p. silver, greenish yellow, magenta, green & grey-black	30	35
1854	**1179**	25p. silver, greenish yellow, magenta, new blue & black	40	45
1855	**1180**	30p. silver, greenish yellow, magenta, new blue & black	45	50
1856	**1181**	35p. silver, greenish yellow, magenta, new blue & black	55	60
1857	**1182**	41p. silver, greenish yellow, magenta, new blue, blue-green & black	65	70
		Set of 5	2·25	2·50
		Set of 5 Gutter Pairs	4·50	
		First Day Cover		3·25
		Presentation Pack	2·75	
		PHQ Cards (set of 5)	1·90	5·25

Special First Day of Issue Postmarks

British Philatelic Bureau, Edinburgh .... 3·50
Kitts Green .... 3·50

Special First Day of Issue Postmarks

British Philatelic Bureau, Edinburgh .... 3·50
Springfield .... 3·50

ROYAL MAIL POSTAGE LABELS

These imperforate labels were issued as an experiment by the Post Office. Special microprocessor controlled machines were installed at post offices in Cambridge, London, Shirley (Southampton) and Windsor to provide an after-hours sales service to the public. The machines printed and dispensed the labels according to the coins inserted and the buttons operated by the customer. Values were initially available in $\frac{1}{2}$p. steps to 16p. and in addition, the labels were sold at philatelic counters in two packs containing either 3 values ($3\frac{1}{2}$, $12\frac{1}{2}$, 16p.) or 32 values ($\frac{1}{2}$p. to 16p.).

From 28 August 1984 the machines were adjusted to provide values up to 17p. After 31 December 1984 labels including $\frac{1}{2}$p. values were withdrawn. The machines were taken out of service on 30 April 1985.

Machine postage-paid impression in red on phosphorised paper with grey-green background design. No watermark. Imperforate.

1984 (1 May–28 Aug.)

Set of 32 ($\frac{1}{2}$p. to 16p.)	....	20·00	30·00
Set of 3 ($3\frac{1}{2}$p., $12\frac{1}{2}$p., 16p.)	....	4·00	4·50
Set of 3 on *First Day Cover* (1.5.84)	....		6·50
Set of 2 ($16\frac{1}{2}$p., 17p.) (28.8.84)	....	6·00	6·00

REGIONAL ISSUES

I. CHANNEL ISLANDS

C **1** Gathering Vraic   C **2** Islanders gathering Vraic

(Des J. R. R. Stobie (1d.) or from drawing by E. Blampied ($2\frac{1}{2}$d.). Photo Harrison)

1948 (10 May). *Third Anniv of Liberation. W* **127** *of Great Britain. P* 15 × 14.

C1	C **1**	1d. scarlet	....	20	20
C2	C **2**	$2\frac{1}{2}$d. ultramarine	....	30	30
		First Day Cover	....		18·00

PRINTERS (£.s.d. stamps of all regions):—Photo Harrison & Sons. Portrait by Dorothy Wilding Ltd.

DATES OF ISSUE. Conflicting dates of issue have been announced for some of the regional issues, partly explained by the stamps being released on different dates by the Philatelic Bureau in Edinburgh or the Philatelic Counter in London and in the regions. We have adopted the practice of giving the earliest known dates, since once released the stamps could have been used anywhere in the U.K.

II. NORTHERN IRELAND

N **1**   N **2**   N **3**

(Des W. Hollywood (3d., 4d., 5d.), L. Pilton (6d., 9d.), T. Collins (1s. 3d., 1s. 6d.))

1958–67. *W* **179**. *P* 15 × 14.

NI1	N **1**	3d. deep lilac (18.8.58)	....	20	10
		p. One centre phosphor band (9.6.67)	.....	20	15
NI2		4d. ultramarine (7.2.66)	....	20	15
		p. Two phosphor bands (10.67)	....	20	15
NI3	N **2**	6d. deep claret (29.9.58)	....	20	20
NI4		9d. bronze-green (2 phosphor bands) (1.3.67)		30	50
NI5	N **3**	1s. 3d. green (29.9.58)	....	30	50
NI6		1s. 6d. grey-blue (2 phosphor bands) (1.3.67)		30	50
		Ey. Phosphor omitted	....	£200	

First Day Covers

18.8.58	3d. (*NI1*)	....	20·00
29.9.58	6d., 1s. 3d. (*NI3, NI5*)	....	25·00
7.2.66	4d. (*NI2*)	....	5·00
1.3.67	9d., 1s. 6d. (*NI4, NI6*)	....	2·00

For Nos. NI1, NI3 and NI5 in Presentation Pack, see below Wales No. W6.

1968–69. *No watermark. Chalk-surfaced paper. One centre phosphor band (Nos. NI8/9) or two phosphor bands (others). Gum arabic (No. NI7) or PVA gum (others). P* 15 × 14.

NI 7	N **1**	4d. dp brt blue (27.6.68)	....	20	15
		Ev. PVA gum* (23.10.68)	....	7·00	
NI 8		4d. olive-sepia (4.9.68)	....	20	15
		Ey. Phosphor omitted	....		
NI 9		4d. brt vermilion (26.2.69)	....	20	20
		Ey. Phosphor omitted	....	4·50	
NI10		5d. royal blue (4.9.68)	....	20	20
		Ey. Phosphor omitted	....	25·00	
NI11	N **3**	1s. 6d. grey-blue (20.5.69)	....	2·50	3·00
		Ey. Phosphor omitted	....		

4.9.68	*First Day Cover (NI8, NI10)*	....	1·00
	Presentation Pack (containing Nos. NI1p, NI4/6, NI8/10) (9.12.70)	....	3·00

*No. NI7Ev was never issued in Northern Ireland. After No. NI7 (gum arabic) had been withdrawn from Northern Ireland but whilst still on sale at the philatelic counters elsewhere, about fifty sheets with PVA gum were sold over the London Philatelic counter on 23 October, 1968, and some were also on sale at the British Philatelic Exhibition Post Office.

For full information on all future British issues, collectors should write to the British Post Office Philatelic Bureau, 20 Brandon Street, Edinburgh EH3 5TT

N **4**

I   II

Redrawn design of Type N 4 (litho ptgs.)

Two Types of Crown

Type I:—Crown with all pearls individually drawn.

Type II:—Crown with clear outlines, large pearls and strong white line below them. First 3 pearls at left are joined, except on Nos. NI39 and NI49.

The following stamps printed in lithography show a screened background behind and to the left of the emblem: 11½p., 12½p., 14p. (No. NI38), 15½p., 16p., 18p. (No. NI45), 19½p., 22p. (No. NI53) and 28p. (No. NI62). The 13p. and 17p. (No. NI43) also showed screened backgrounds in Type I, but changed to solid backgrounds for Type II. The 31p. had a solid background in Type I, but changed to a screened background for Type II. All other values printed in lithography have solid backgrounds.

(Des J. Matthews after plaster cast by Arnold Machin)

1971 (7 July)–**93.** *Decimal Currency. Chalk-surfaced paper. Type* N **4.**

(a) *Photo Harrison. With phosphor bands.* P 15 × 14.

NI12	2½p. brt magenta (1 centre band)	80	25
NI13	3p. ultramarine (2 bands)	40	15
	Ey. Phosphor omitted	20·00	
NI14	3p. ultramarine (1 centre band) (23.1.74)	20	15
NI15	3½p. olive-grey (2 bands) (23.1.74)	20	20
NI16	3½p. olive-grey (1 centre band) (6.11.74)	20	20
NI17	4½p. grey-blue (2 bands) (6.11.74)	25	25
NI18	5p. reddish violet (2 bands)	1·25	1·25
NI19	5½p. violet (2 bands) (23.1.74)	20	20
	Ey. Phosphor omitted	£225	
NI20	5½p. violet (1 centre band) (21.5.75)	20	20
NI21	6½p. greenish blue (1 centre band) (14.1.76).	20	20
NI22	7p. purple-brown (1 centre band) (18.1.78)	35	25
NI23	7½p. chestnut (2 bands)	2·00	2·00
	Ey. Phosphor omitted	55·00	
NI24	8p. rosine (2 bands) (23.1.74)	30	30
	Ey. Phosphor omitted	45·00	
NI25	8½p. yellow-green (2 bands) (14.1.76)	30	30
NI26	9p. dp violet (2 bands) (18.1.78)	30	30
	Ey. Phosphor omitted	25·00	
NI27	10p. orange-brown (2 bands) (20.10.76)	35	35
NI28	10p. orange-brown (1 centre band) (23.7.80)	35	35
NI29	10½p. steel-blue (2 bands) (18.1.78)	40	40
NI30	11p. scarlet (2 bands) (20.10.76)	40	40
	Ey. Phosphor omitted	4·50	

(b) *Photo Harrison. On phosphorised paper.* P 15 × 14.

NI31	12p. yellowish green (23.7.80)	50	45
NI32	13½p. purple-brown (23.7.80)	60	70
NI33	15p. ultramarine (23.7.80)	60	50

(c) *Litho Questa (Type II, unless otherwise stated).* P 14 (11½p., 12½p., 14p. (No. NI38), 15½p., 16p., 18p. (No. NI45), 19½p., 20½p., 22p. (No. NI53), 26p. (No. NI60), 28p. (No. NI62)) *or* 15 × 14 (*others*)

NI34	11½p. drab (Type I) (1 side band) (8.4.81)	70	60
NI35	12p. brt emerald (1 side band) (7.1.86)	70	50
NI36	12½p. lt emerald (Type I) (1 side band) (24.2.82) ...	50	40
	a. Perf 15 × 14 (28.2.84)	4·00	4·00
NI37	13p. pale chestnut (Type I) (1 side band) (23.10.84)	1·25	35
	Ea. Type II (28.11.86)	1·00	30
	Ey. Phosphor omitted (Type I)		
NI38	14p. grey-blue (Type I) (phosphorised paper) (8.4.81)	70	50
NI39	14p. dp blue (1 centre band) (8.11.88)	55	35
NI40	15p. brt blue (1 centre band) (28.11.89)	60	30
NI41	15½p. pale violet (Type I) (phosphorised paper) (24.2.82)	80	65
NI42	16p. drab (Type I) (phosphorised paper) (27.4.83) .	90	1·00
	a. Perf 15 × 14 (28.2.84)	8·00	5·00
NI43	17p. grey-blue (Type I) (phosphorised paper) (23.10.84)	1·00	40
	Ea. Type II (9.9.86)	50·00	22·00
NI44	17p. dp blue (1 centre band) (4.12.90)	50	40
NI45	18p. dp violet (Type I) (phosphorised paper) (8.4.81)	80	80
NI46	18p. dp olive-grey (phosphorised paper) (6.1.87) .	80	70
NI47	18p. brt green (1 centre band) (3.12.91)	50	50
	a. Perf 14 (31.12.92*)	90	75
NI48	18p. brt green (1 side band) (10.8.93)	2·00	2·00
	I. Booklet pane. Nos. NI48, NI59, S61, S71, W49Eb and W60 with margins all round ...	10·00	
NI49	19p. brt orange-red (phosphorised paper) (8.11.88)	70	60
NI50	19½p. olive-grey (Type I) (phosphorised paper) (24.2.82)	1·75	1·75
NI51	20p. brownish black (phosphorised paper) (28.11.89)	60	50
NI52	20½p. ultramarine (Type I) (phosphorised paper) (27.4.83)	4·00	4·00
NI53	22p. blue (Type I) (phosphorised paper) (8.4.81) ..	90	1·10
NI54	22p. yellow-green (Type I) (phosphorised paper) (23.10.84)	85	1·10
NI55	22p. brt orange-red (phosphorised paper) (4.12.90)	85	40
NI56	22p. brt green (phosphorised paper) (8.11.88)	80	1·10
NI57	24p. Indian red (phosphorised paper) (28.11.89) ...	70	1·10
NI58	24p. chestnut (phosphorised paper) (3.12.91)	60	50
NI59	24p. chestnut (2 bands) (10.8.93)	2·00	2·00
NI60	26p. rosine (Type I) (phosphorised paper) (24.2.82)	90	1·25
	a. Perf 15 × 14 (Type II) (27.1.87)	2·50	2·50
NI61	26p. drab (phosphorised paper) (4.12.90)	80	60
NI62	28p. dp violet-blue (Type I) (phosphorised paper) (27.4.83)	1·00	1·00
	a. Perf 15 × 14 (Type II) (27.1.87)	90	90
NI63	28p. dp bluish grey (phosphorised paper) (3.12.91)	90	75
NI64	31p. brt purple (Type I) (phosphorised paper) (23.10.84)	1·25	1·10
	Ea. Type II (14.4.87)	1·50	1·25
NI65	32p. greenish blue (phosphorised paper) (8.11.88)	1·10	1·10
NI66	34p. dp bluish grey (phosphorised paper) (28.11.89)	1·00	1·00
NI67	37p. rosine (phosphorised paper) (4.12.90)	1·00	1·10
NI68	39p. brt mauve (phosphorised paper) (3.12.91) ...	1·00	1·00

*Earliest known date of use.

No. NI47a was caused by the use of a reserve perforating machine for some printings in the second half of 1992.

Nos. NI48 and NI59 come from booklets.

From 1972 printing were made on fluorescent white paper and from 1973 most printings had dextrin added to the PVA gum (see notes after 1971 Decimal Machin issue).

First Day Covers

7.7.71	2½p., 3p., 5p., 7½p. (NI12/13, NI18, NI23) .	2·50
23.1.74	3p., 3½p., 5½p., 8p. (NI14/15, NI19, NI24) .	1·50
6.11.74	4½p. (NI17)	1·00
14.1.76	6½p., 8½p. (NI21, NI25)	70
20.10.76	10p., 11p. (NI27, NI30)	1·00
18.1.78	7p., 9p., 10½p. (NI22, NI26, NI29)	1·25
23.7.80	12p., 13½p., 15p. (NI31/3)	2·00
8.4.81	11½p., 14p., 18p., 22p. (NI34, NI38, NI45, NI53)	2·00
24.2.82	12½p., 15½p., 19½p., 26p. (NI36, NI41, NI50, NI60)	2·50
27.4.83	16p., 20½p., 28p. (NI42, NI52, NI62)	3·50
23.10.84	13p., 17p., 22p., 31p. (NI37, NI43, NI54, NI64)	2·50
7.1.86	12p. (NI35)	1·25
6.1.87	18p. (NI46)	1·25
8.11.88	14p., 19p., 23p., 32p. (NI39, NI49, NI56, NI65)	1·75
28.11.89	15p., 20p., 24p., 34p. (NI40, NI51, NI57, NI66)	2·25
4.12.90	17p., 22p., 26p., 37p. (NI44, NI55, NI61, NI67)	3·25
3.12.91	18p., 24p., 28p., 39p. (NI47, NI58, NI63, NI68)	3·25

Presentation Packs

7.7.71	2½p., 3p. (2 bands), 5p., 7½p. (Nos. NI12/13, NI18, NI23)	4·00
29.5.74	3p. (1 centre band), 3½p. (2 bands) or (1 centre band), 5½p. (2 bands) or (1 centre band), 8p. (Nos. NI14, NI15 or NI16, NI19 or NI20, NI24). The 4½p. (No. NI17) was added later	2·25
20.10.76	6½p., 8½p., 10p. (2 bands), 11p. (Nos. NI21, NI25, NI27, NI30)	1·75
28.10.81	7p., 9p., 10½p., 12p. (photo), 13½p., 15p. (photo), 11½p., 14p. grey-blue, 18p. dp violet, 22p. blue (Nos. NI22, NI26, NI29, NI31/4, NI38, NI45, NI53)	7·00
3.8.83	10p. (1 centre band), 12½p., 16p., 20½p., 26p. rosine, 28p. dp violet-blue (Nos. NI28, NI36, NI42, NI52, NI60, NI62)	7·00
23.10.84	10p. (1 centre band) 13p., 16p., 17p. grey-blue, 22p. yellow-green, 26p. rosine, 28p. dp violet-blue, 31p. (Nos. NI28, NI37, NI42a, NI43, NI54, NI60, NI62, NI64)	10·00
3.3.87	12p. (litho), 13p., 17p. grey-blue, 18p. dp olive-grey, 22p. yellow-green, 26p. rosine, 28p. dp violet-blue, 31p. (Nos. NI35, NI37, NI43, NI46, NI54, NI60a, NI62a, NI64)	9·00

Presentation Packs for Northern Ireland, Scotland and Wales

8.11.88	14p. dp blue, 19p., 23p., 32p. (Nos. NI39, NI49, NI56, NI65), 14p. (1 centre band), 19p. (phosphorised paper), 23p. (phosphorised paper), 32p. (Nos. S54, S62, S67, S77), 14p. dp blue, 19p., 23p., 32p. (Nos. W40, W50, W57, W66)	8·00
28.11.89	15p. (litho), 20p., 24p. Indian red, 34p. (Nos. NI40, NI51, NI57, NI66), 15p. (litho), 20p., 24p. Indian red, 34p. (Nos. S56, S64, S69, S78), 15p. (litho), 20p., 24p. Indian red, 34p. (Nos. W41, W52, W58, W67) .	7·50

4.12.90	17p. dp blue, 22p. brt orange-red, 26p. drab, 37p., (Nos. NI44, NI55, NI61, NI67), 17p. dp blue, 22p. brt orange-red, 26p. drab, 37p. (Nos. S58, S66, S73, S79), 17p. dp blue, 22p. brt orange-red, 26p. drab, 37p. (Nos. W45, W56, W62, W68)	8·50
3.12.91	18p. brt green, 24p. chestnut, 28p. dp bluish grey, 39p. (Nos. NI47, NI58, NI63, NI68), 18p. brt green, 24p. chestnut, 28p. dp bluish grey, 39p. (Nos. S60, S70, S75, S80), 18p. brt green, 24p. chestnut, 28p. dp bluish grey, 39p. (Nos. W8, W59, W64, W69)	5·50

(Des J. Matthews after plaster cast by Arnold Machin. Litho Questa)

1993 (7 Dec)–**94**.   *Chalk-surfaced paper. P 15 × 14 (with one elliptical hole on each vertical side).*

NI69	N **4**	19p. bistre (1 centre band)	30	35
NI70		19p. bistre (1 band at left) (26.7.94)	2·00	2·00
		l. Booklet pane. Nos. NI70 × 2, NI71 × 4 and NI72/3 with margins all round	3·00	
		m. Booklet pane. Nos. NI70/3 with margins all round	1·75	
NI71		25p. red (2 bands)	40	45
NI72		30p. dp olive-grey (2 bands)	45	50
NI73		41p. grey-brown (2 bands)	65	70

First Day Cover

7.12.93	19p., 25p., 30p., 41p. (NI69, NI71/3)	2·50

Presentation Packs for Northern Ireland, Scotland and Wales

7.12.93	19p., 25p., 30p., 41p., each × 3 (Nos. NI69, NI71/3, S81/4, W70/3)	6·00

III. SCOTLAND

S 1

S 2

S 3

S 4

(Des. G. Huntly (3d., 4d., 5d.), J. Fleming (6d., 9d.), A. Imrie (1s., 3d., 1s. 6d.))

1958–67. *W* **179.** *P* 15 × 14.

S1	S **1**	3d. dp lilac (18.8.58)	20	15
		p. Two phosphor bands (29.1.63)	12·00	1·00
		pa. One side phosphor band (30.4.65)	20	25
		pb. One centre phosphor band (9.11.67)	20	15
S2		4d. ultramarine (7.2.66)	20	10
		p. Two phosphor bands	20	20
S3	S **2**	6d. dp claret (29.9.58)	20	15
		p. Two phosphor bands (29.1.63)	20	25
S4		9d. bronze-green (2 phosphor bands) (1.3.67)	30	30
S5	S **3**	1s. 3d. green (29.9.58)	30	30
		p. Two phosphor bands (29.1.63)	30	30
S6		1s. 6d. grey-blue (2 phosphor bands) (1.3.67)	35	30

First Day Covers

18.8.58	3d. (*S1*)	7·50
29.9.58	6d., 1s. 3d. (*S3, S5*)	15·00
7.2.66	4d. (*S2*)	6·00
1.3.67	9d., 1s. 6d. (*S4, S6*)	2·00

The one phosphor band on No. S1pa was produced by printing broad phosphor bands across alternate vertical perforations. Individual stamps show the band at right or left (same prices either way).

For Nos. S1, S3 and S5 in Presentation Pack, see below Wales No. W6.

1967–70. *No watermark. Chalk-surfaced paper. One centre phosphor band (S7, S9/10) or two phosphor bands (others). Gum arabic (Nos. S7, S8) or PVA gum (others). P* 15 × 14.

S 7	S **1**	3d. dp lilac (16.5.68)	10	15
		Ey. Phosphor omitted	5·50	
		Ev. PVA gum	10	
		Eya. Phosphor omitted (No. S7Ev)	2·50	
S 8		4d. dp brt blue (28.11.67)	10	15
		Ey. Phosphor omitted	7·00	
		Ev. PVA gum (25.7.68)	10	
S 9		4d. olive-sepia (4.9.68)	10	10
		Ey. Phosphor omitted	1·75	
S10		4d. brt vermilion (26.2.69)	10	10
		Ey. Phosphor omitted	1·75	
S11		5d. royal blue (4.9.68)	20	10
		Ey. Phosphor omitted	42·00	
S12	S **2**	9d. bronze-green (28.9.70)	5·00	5·50
		Ey. Phosphor omitted	£140	
S13	S **3**	1s. 6d. grey-blue (12.12.68)	1·40	1·00
		Ey. Phosphor omitted	£110	

4.9.68	*First Day Cover (S9, S11)*	1·00
	Presentation Pack (containing Nos. S3, S5p., S7, S9/13) (9.12.70)	13·00

I   II

Redrawn design of Type S 4 (litho ptgs.)

The introduction of the redrawn lion took place in 1983 when Waddington's had the contract and therefore the 13, 17, 22 and 31p. exist in both types and perforated 14. The Questa printings, perforated 15 × 14, are all Type II.

The Types of Lion.

Type I:—The eye and jaw appear larger and there is no line across the bridge of the nose.

Type II:—The tongue is thick at the point of entry to the mouth and the eye is linked to the background by a solid line.

The following stamps printed in lithography show a screened background behind and to the left of the emblem: 12½p., 15½p., 16p., 19½p., 28p. (Nos. S50 and S74) and 31p. (Nos. S51 and S76). The 13p. and 17p. (No. S43) also showed screened backgrounds for both Type I and II of the John Waddington printings, but changed to solid backgrounds for the Questa Type II. All other values printed in lithography have solid backgrounds.

(Des J. Matthews after plaster cast by Arnold Machin)

1971 (7 July)**–93.** *Decimal Currency. Chalk-surfaced paper. Type S **4.***

(a) Photo Harrison. With phosphor bands. P 15 × 14.

S14	2½p. brt magenta (1 centre band)	25	15
	Ey. Phosphor omitted	3·50	
	Eg. Gum arabic (22.9.72)	20	
S15	3p. ultramarine (2 bands)	30	15
	Ey. Phosphor omitted	5·50	
	Eg. Gum arabic (14.12.72)	30	
	Ega. Imperf (pair)	£400	
S16	3p. ultramarine (1 centre band) (23.1.74)	15	15
S17	3½p. olive-grey (2 bands) (23.1.74)	20	20
	Ey. Phosphor omitted	20·00	
S18	3½p. olive-grey (1 centre band) (6.11.74)	20	20
S19	4½p. grey-blue (2 bands) (6.11.74)	25	20
S20	5p. reddish violet (2 bands)	1·25	1·25
S21	5½p. violet (2 bands) (23.1.74)	20	20
S22	5½p. violet (1 centre band) (21.5.75)	20	20
	a. Imperf (pair)	£350	
S23	6½p. greenish blue (1 centre band) (14.1.76)	20	20
S24	7p. purple-brown (1 centre band) (18.1.78)	25	25
S25	7½p. chestnut (2 bands)	1·50	1·50
	Ey. Phosphor omitted	4·50	
S26	8p. rosine (2 bands) (23.1.74)	30	40
S27	8½p. yellow-green (2 bands) (14.1.76)	30	30
S28	9p. dp violet (2 bands) (18.1.78)	30	30
S29	10p. orange-brown (2 bands) (20.10.76)	35	30

S30	10p. orange-brown (1 centre band) (23.7.80)	35	35
S31	10½p. steel-blue (2 bands) (18.1.78)	45	35
S32	11p. scarlet (2 bands) (20.10.76)	45	35
	Ey. Phosphor omitted	1·75	

(b) Photo Harrison. On phosphorised paper. P 15 × 14

S33	12p. yellowish green (23.7.80)	50	30
S34	13½p. purple-brown (23.7.80)	60	65
S35	15p. ultramarine (23.7.80)	60	45

(c) Litho J.W. (Type I unless otherwise stated). One side phosphor band (11½p., 12p., 12½p., 13p.) or phosphorised paper (others). P 14

S36	11½p. drab (8.4.81)	80	60
S37	12p. brt emerald (Type II) (7.1.86)	1·50	1·00
S38	12½p. lt emerald (24.2.82)	60	40
S39	13p. pale chestnut (Type I) (23.10.84)	70	30
	Ea. Type II (1.85)	2·50	50
S40	14p. grey-blue (8.4.81)	60	50
S41	15½p. pale violet (24.2.82)	70	65
S42	16p. drab (Type II) (27.4.83)	70	45
S43	17p. grey-blue (Type I) (23.10.84)	3·25	2·00
	Ea. Type II (1.85)	1·25	1·00
S44	18p. dp violet (8.4.81)	80	80
S45	19½p. olive-grey (24.2.82)	1·75	1·75
S46	20½p. ultramarine (Type II) (27.4.83)	4·00	4·00
S47	22p. blue (8.4.81)	80	1·10
S48	22p. yellow-green (Type I) (23.10.84)	2·00	1·50
	Ea. Type II (1.86)	7·50	2·50
S49	26p. rosine (24.2.82)	1·00	1·10
S50	28p. dp violet-blue (Type II) (27.4.83)	1·00	80
S51	31p. brt purple (Type I) (23.10.84)	1·75	1·50
	Ea. Type II (11.85*)	95·00	60·00

(d) Litho Questa (Type II). P 15 × 14

S52	12p. brt emerald (1 side band) (29.4.86)	1·75	1·25
S53	13p. pale chestnut (1 side band) (4.11.86)	70	30
S54	14p. dp blue (1 centre band) (8.11.88)	40	30
	l. Booklet pane. No. S54 × 6 with margins all round (21.3.89)	2·50	
S55	14p. dp blue (1 side band) (21.3.89)	60	1·00
	l. Booklet pane. No. S55 × 5, S63 × 2, S68 and centre label with margins all round	14·00	
	la. Error. Booklet pane imperf		
S56	15p. brt blue (1 centre band) (28.11.89)	50	30
	a. Imperf (three sides) (block of four)		
S57	17p. grey-blue (phosphorised paper) (29.4.86)	4·00	2·00
S58	17p. dp blue (1 centre band) (4.12.90)	50	35
S59	18p. dp olive-grey (phosphorised paper) (6.1.87)	80	80
S60	18p. brt green (1 centre band) (3.12.91)	50	45
	a. Perf 14 (26.9.92*)	50	50
S61	18p. brt green (1 side band) (10.8.93)	2·00	2·00
S62	19p. brt orange-red (phosphorised paper) (8.11.88)	60	45
	l. Booklet pane. No. S62 × 9 with margins all round (21.3.89)	5·00	
	m. Booklet pane. No. S62 × 6 with margins all round (21.3.89)	3·00	
S63	19p. brt orange-red (2 bands) (21.3.89)	1·50	1·50
S64	20p. brownish black (phosphorised paper) (28.11.89)	60	30
S65	22p. yellow-green (phosphorised paper) (27.1.87)	70	80
S66	22p. brt orange-red (phosphorised paper) (4.12.90)	90	40
S67	23p. brt green (phosphorised paper) (8.11.88)	90	1·10
S68	23p. brt green (2 bands) (21.3.89)	10·00	10·00
S69	24p. Indian red (phosphorised paper) (28.11.89)	70	70
S70	24p. chestnut (phosphorised paper) (3.12.91)	40	45
	a. Perf 14 (10.92*)	1·25	1·00
S71	24p. chestnut (2 bands) (10.8.93)	2·75	2·75
S72	26p. rosine (phosphorised paper) (27.1.87)	1·90	1·90
S73	26p. drab (phosphorised paper) (4.12.90)	70	70
S74	28p. dp violet-blue (phosphorised paper) (27.1.87)	85	75
S75	28p. dp bluish grey (phosphorised paper) (3.12.91)	70	70
	a. Perf 14 (18.2.93*)	1·25	1·00
S76	31p. brt purple (phosphorised paper) (29.4.86)	1·50	1·50
S77	32p. greenish blue (phosphorised paper) (8.11.88)	1·10	1·00
S78	34p. dp bluish grey (phosphorised paper) (28.11.89)	1·00	1·00
S79	37p. rosine (phosphorised paper) (4.12.90)	1·00	1·00
S80	39p. brt mauve (phosphorised paper) (3.12.91)	1·00	1·00
	a. Perf 14 (11.92)	2·00	1·75

*Earliest known date of use.

Nos. S55, S61, S63, S68 and S71 come from booklets.

No. S56a occured in the second vertical row of two sheets. It is best collected as a block of four including the left-hand vertical pair imperforate on three sides.

Nos. S60a, S70a, S75a and S80a were caused by the use of a reserve perforating machine for some printings in the second half of 1992.

From 1972 printings were on fluorescent white paper. From 1973 most printings had dextrin added to the PVA gum (see notes after the 1971 Decimal Machin issue).

First Day Covers

7.7.71	2½p., 3p., 5p., 7½p. (*S14/15, S20, S25*)	2·50
23.1.74	3p., 3½p., 5½p., 8p. (*S16/17, S21, S26*)	1·50
6.11.74	4½p. (*S19*)	1·00
14.1.76	6½p., 8½p. (*S23, S27*)	70
20.10.76	10p., 11p. (*S29, S32*)	1·00
18.1.78	7p., 9p., 10½p. (*S24, S28, S31*)	1·25
23.7.80	12p., 13½p., 15p. (*S33/5*)	2·00
8.4.81	11½p., 14p., 18p., 22p. (*S36, S40, S44, S47*)	2·00
24.2.82	12½p., 15½p., 19½p., 26p. (*S38, S41, S45, S49*)	2·50
27.4.83	16p., 20½p., 28p. (*S42, S46, S50*)	3·50
23.10.84	13p., 17p., 22p., 31p. (*S39, S43, S48, S51*)	2·50
7.1.86	12p. (*S37*)	1·25
6.1.87	18p. (*S59*)	1·25
8.11.88	14p., 19p., 23p., 32p. (*S54, S62, S67, S77*)	1·75
21.3.89	Scots Connection *se-tenant* pane 14p., 19p., 23p. (*S55l*)	8·00
28.11.89	15p., 20p., 24p., 34p. (*S56, S64, S69, S78*)	2·25
4.12.90	17p., 22p., 26p., 37p. (*S58, S66, S73, S79*)	3·25
3.12.91	18p., 24p., 28p., 39p. (*S60, S70, S75, S80*)	3·25

Presentation Packs

7.7.71	2½p., 3p. (2 bands), 5p., 7½p. (*Nos.* S14/15, S20, S25)	4·00
29.5.74	3p. (1 centre band), 3½p. (2 bands) *or* (1 centre band), 5½p. (2 bands) *or* (1 centre band), 8p. (*Nos.* S16, S17 *or* S18, S21 *or* S22, S26). The 4½p. (No. S19) was added later	2·25
20.10.76	6½p., 8½p., 10p. (2 bands), 11p. (*Nos.* S23, S27, S29, S32)	1·75
28.10.81	7p., 9p., 10½p., 12p. (photo), 13½p., 15p. (photo), 11½p., 14p. grey-blue, 18p. dp violet, 22p. blue (*Nos.* S24, S28, S31, S33/6, S40, S44, S47)	7·00
3.8.83	10p. (1 centre band), 12½p., 16p., 20½p., 26p. (J.W.), 28p. (J.W.), (*Nos.* S30, S38, S42, S46, S49/50)	7·00
23.10.84	10p. (1 centre band), 13p. (J.W.), 16p., 17p. (J.W.), 22p. yellow-green, 26p. (J.W.), 28p. (J.W.), 31p. (J.W.) (*Nos.* S30, S39, S42/3, S48/51)	9·50
3.3.87	12p. (litho), 13p. (Questa), 17p. grey-blue (Questa), 18p. dp olive-grey, 22p. yellow-green, 26p. rosine (Questa), 28p. dp violet-blue (Questa), 31p. (Questa) (*Nos.* S52/3, S57, S59, S65, S72, S74, S76)	9·00

Presentation Packs containing stamps of Northern Ireland, Scotland and Wales are listed after those for Northern Ireland.

1977–78 EXPERIMENTAL MACHINE PACKETS. These are small cartons containing loose stamps for sale in vending machines. The experiment was confined to the Scottish Postal Board area, where six vending machines were installed, the first becoming operational in Dundee about February 1977.

The cartons carry labels inscribed "ROYAL MAIL STAMPS", their total face value (30p. or 60p.) and their contents.

At first the 30p. packet contained two 6½p. and two 8½p. Scottish Regional stamps and the 60p. packet had four of each. The stamps could be in pairs or blocks, but also in strips or singles.

With the change in postal rates on 13 June 1977 these packets were withdrawn on 11 June and on 13 June the contents were changed, giving three 7p. and one 9p. for the 30p. packet and double this for the 60p. packet. However, this time ordinary British Machin stamps were used. Moreover the Edinburgh machine, situated in an automatic sorting area, was supplied with 7p. stamps with two phosphor bands instead of the new centre band 7p. stamps, despite instructions having been given to withdraw the two band stamps. However, the demand for these packets was too great to be filled and by 27 June the machine was closed down. It was brought back into use on 16 August 1977, supplying 7p. stamps with the centre band.

The 6½p. and 8½p. Scottish Regional packets were put on sale at the Edinburgh Philatelic Bureau in June 1977 and withdrawn in April 1978. The packets with the 7p. and 9p. Machin stamps were put on sale at the Bureau in June 1977 and withdrawn in December 1978.

Such machine packets are outside the scope of this catalogue.

(Des J. Matthews after plaster cast by Arnold Machin. Litho Questa)

1993 (7 Dec). *Chalk-surfaced paper. One centre phosphor band* (19p.) *or two phosphor bands* (others). *P 15 × 14 (with one elliptical hole on each vertical side).*

S81	**S 4** 19p. bistre	....	30	35
S82	25p. red	....	40	45
S83	30p. dp olive-grey	....	45	50
S84	41p. grey-brown	....	65	70

First Day Cover

7.12.93	19p., 25p., 30p., 41p. (S81/4)	....	2·50

For Presentation Pack containing stamps of Northern Ireland, Scotland and Wales see after No. NI73 of Northern Ireland.

IV. WALES

From the inception of the Regional stamps, the Welsh versions were tendered to members of the public at all Post Offices within the former County of Monmouthshire but the English alternatives were available on request. Offices with a Monnmouthshire postal address but situated outside the County, namely Beachley, Brockweir, Redbrook, Sedbury, Tutshill, Welsh Newton and Woodcroft, were not supplied with the Welsh Regional stamps.

With the re-formation of Counties, Monmouthshire became known as Gwent and was also declared to be part of Wales. From 1 July 1974, therefore, except for the offices mentioned above, only Welsh Regional stamps were available at the offices under the jurisdiction of Newport, Gwent.

W 4

| I | II |

Redrawn design of Type W 4 (litho ptgs.)

W 1    W 2    W 3

(Des R. Stone)

1958–67.   *W* **179**. *P* 15 × 14.

W1	W **1**	3d. dp lilac (18.8.58)	20	10
		p. One centre phosphor band (16.5.67) ...	20	15
W2		4d. ultramarine (7.2.66)	20	15
		p. Two phosphor bands (10.67)	20	15
W3	W **2**	6d. dp claret (29.9.58)	40	20
W4		9d. bronze-green (2 phosphor bands) (1.3.67)	30	35
		Ey. Phosphor omitted	£300	
W5	W **3**	1s. 3d. green (29.9.58)	30	30
W6		1s. 6d. grey-blue (2 phosphor bands) (1.3.67)	35	30
		Ey. Phosphor omitted	40·00	

First Day Covers

18.8.58	3d. (*W1*)	7·50
29.9.58	6d., 1s. 3d. (*W3, W5*)	15·00
7.2.66	4d. (*W2*)	5·00
1.3.67	9d., 1s. 6d. (*W4, W6*)	1·75
	Presentation Pack*	90·00

*This was issued in 1960 and comprises Guernsey No. 7, Jersey No. 10, Isle of Man No. 2, Northern Ireland Nos. NI1, NI3 and NI5, Scotland Nos. S1, S3 and S5 and Wales Nos. W1, W3 and W5 together with a 6-page printed leaflet describing the stamps. There exist two forms: (a) inscribed "7s.3d." for sale in the U.K.; and (b) inscribed "$1.20" for sale in the U.S.A.

1967–69.   *No wmk. Chalk-surfaced paper. One centre phosphor band* (W7, W9/10) *or two phosphor bands* (others). *Gum arabic* (3d.) *or PVA gum* (others). *P* 15 × 14.

W 7	W **1**	3d. dp lilac (6.12.67)	20	10
		Ey. Phosphor omitted	40·00	
W 8		4d. ultramarine (21.6.68)	20	10
W 9		4d. olive-sepia (4.9.68)	20	10
W10		4d. brt vermilion (26.2.69)	20	20
		Ey. Phosphor omitted	1·75	
W11		5d. royal blue (4.9.68)	20	10
		Ey. Phosphor omitted	2·25	
W12	W **3**	1s. 6d. grey-blue (1.8.69)	3·00	3·00

4.9.68	*First Day Cover* (W9, W11)	1·00
	Presentation Pack (containing Nos. W4, W6/7, W9/11) (9.12.70)	2·50

Two Types of Dragon

Type I:–The eye is complete with white dot in the centre. Wing-tips, tail and tongue are thin.

Type II:–The eye is joined to the nose by a solid line. Tail, wing-tips, claws and tongue are wider than in Type I.

The following stamps printed in lithography show a screened background behind and to the left of the emblem: 11½p., 12½p., 14p. (No. W39), 15½p., 16p., 18p. (No. W46), 19½p., 22p. (No. W54) and 28p. (No. W63). The 13p. and 17p. (No. W44) also show screened backgrounds in Type I, but changed to solid backgrounds for Type II. All other values printed in lithography have solid backgrounds.

(Des J. Matthews after plaster cast by Arnold Machin)

1971 (7 July)–**93**.   *Decimal Currency. Chalk-surfaced paper. Type W* **4**.

(a) Photo Harrison. With phosphor bands. P 15 × 14.

W13	2½p. brt magenta (1 centre band)		20	15
	Ey. Phosphor omitted		5·50	
	Eg. Gum arabic (22.9.72)		20	
	Ega. Imperf (pair)		£350	
W14	3p. ultramarine (2 bands)		25	15
	Ey. Phosphor omitted		15·00	
	Eg. Gum arabic (6.6.73)		30	
	Eya. Phosphor omitted (No. W14Eg)		3·50	
W15	3p. ultramarine (1 centre band) (23.1.74)		20	20
W16	3½p. olive-grey (2 bands) (23.1.74)		20	25
W17	3½p. olive-grey (1 centre band) (6.11.74)		20	25
W18	4½p. grey-blue (2 bands) (6.11.74)		25	20
W19	5p. reddish violet (2 bands)		1·25	1·00
	Ey. Phosphor omitted		11·00	
W20	5½p. violet (2 bands) (23.1.74)		20	25
	Ey. Phosphor omitted		£160	
W21	5½p. violet (1 centre band) (21.5.75)		20	25
	a. Imperf (pair)		£400	
W22	6½p. greenish blue (1 centre band) (14.1.76).		20	20
W23	7p. purple-brown (1 centre band) (18.1.78)		25	25
W24	7½p. chestnut (2 bands)		1·75	1·90
	Ey. Phosphor omitted		75·00	
W25	8p. rosine (2 bands) (23.1.74)		30	30
	Ey. Phosphor omitted		£450	
W26	8½p. yellow-green (2 bands) (14.1.76)		30	30
W27	9p. dp violet (2 bands) (18.1.78)		30	30
W28	10p. orange-brown (2 bands) (20.10.76)		35	30
W29	10p. orange-brown (1 centre band) (23.7.80)		35	30
W30	10½p. steel-blue (2 bands) (18.1.78)		40	35
W31	11p. scarlet (2 bands) (20.10.76)		40	45

(b) *Photo Harrison. On phosphorised paper.* P 15 × 14

W32	12p. yellowish green (23.7.80)	50	45
W33	13½p. purple-brown (23.7.80)	60	70
W34	15p. ultramarine (23.7.80)	60	50

(c) *Litho Questa (Type II unless otherwise stated).* P 14 (11½p., 12½p., 14p. (No. W39), 15½p., 16p., 18p. (No. W46), 19½p., 20½p., 22p. (No. W54), 26p. (No. W61), 28p. (No. W63)) or 15 × 14 (others)

W35	11½p. drab (Type I) (1 side band) (8.4.81)	85	60
W36	12p. brt emerald (1 side band) (7.1.86)	1·25	1·10
W37	12½p. lt emerald (Type I) (1 side band) (24.2.82) ...	80	60
	a. Perf 15 × 14 (10.1.84)	6·00	6·00
W38	13p. pale chestnut (Type I) (1 side band) (23.10.84)	50	35
	Ea. Type II (1.87)	1·50	1·00
W39	14p. grey-blue (Type I) (phosphorised paper) (8.4.81)	65	50
W40	14p. dp blue (1 centre band) (8.11.88)	55	30
W41	15p. brt blue (1 centre band) (28.11.89)	40	30
	Ey. Phosphor omitted		
W42	15½p. pale violet (Type I) (phosphorised paper) (24.2.82)	80	65
W43	16p. drab (Type I) (phosphorised paper) (27.4.83) .	1·50	1·25
	a. Perf 15 × 14 (10.1.84)	1·60	1·25
W44	17p. grey-blue (Type I) (phosphorised paper) (23.10.84)	80	55
	Ea. Type II (18.8.86)	15·00	8·00
W45	17p. dp blue (1 centre band) (4.12.90)	50	35
	Ey. Phosphor omitted		
W46	18p. dp violet (Type I) (8.4.81)	80	75
W47	18p. dp olive-grey (phosphorised paper) (6.1.87) .	80	60
W48	18p. brt green (1 centre band) (3.12.91)	45	45
	Ey. Phosphor omitted		
	a. Booklet pane. No. W48 × 6 with margins all round (25.2.92)	2·25	
	aEy. Phosphor omitted		
	b. Perf 14 (12.1.93*)	1·00	60
W49	18p. brt green (1 side band at right) (25.2.92)	2·00	2·00
	a. Booklet pane. No. X1020 × 2, 1451a, 1514a, W49 × 2, W60 × 2 and centre label with margins all round	10·00	
	aEy. Phosphor omitted		
	Eb. Band at left (10.8.93)	2·00	2·00
W50	19p. brt orange-red (phosphorised paper) (8.11.88)	60	45
W51	19½p. olive-grey (Type I) (phosphorised paper) (24.2.82)	2·00	2·00
W52	20p. brownish black (phosphorised paper) (28.11.89)	30	30
W53	20½p. ultramarine (Type I) (phosphorised paper) (27.4.83)	4·00	4·00
W54	22p. blue (Type I) (phosphorised paper) (8.4.81) ..	1·00	1·00
W55	22p. yellow-green (Type I) (phosphorised paper) (23.10.84)	80	1·10
W56	22p. brt orange-red (phosphorised paper) (4.12.90)	60	50
W57	23p. brt green (phosphorised paper) (8.11.88)	80	1·10
W58	24p. Indian red (phosphorised paper) (28.11.89) ..	70	1·10
W59	24p. chestnut (phosphorised paper) (3.12.91)	40	45
	a. Booklet pane. No. W59 × 6 with margins all round (25.2.92)	2·50	
	b. Perf 14 (14.9.92*)	1·00	45
W60	24p. chestnut (2 bands) (25.2.92)	1·10	85
W61	26p. rosine (Type I) (phosphorised paper) (24.2.82)	90	1·10
	a. Perf 15 × 14 (Type II) (27.1.87)	4·50	4·50
W62	26p. drab (phosphorised paper) (4.12.90)	70	70
W63	28p. dp violet-blue (Type I) (phosphorised paper) (27.4.83)	1·00	1·10
	a. Perf 15 × 14 (Type II) (27.1.87)	80	65
W64	28p. dp bluish grey (phosphorised paper) (3.12.91)	70	70
W65	31p. brt purple (Type I) (phosphorised paper) (23.10.84)	1·10	1·10
W66	32p. greenish blue (phosphorised paper) (8.11.88)	1·10	1·10

W67	34p. dp bluish grey (phosphorised paper) (28.11.89)	1·00	1·00
W68	37p. rosine (phosphorised paper) (4.12.90)	1·00	1·00
W69	39p. brt mauve (phosphorised paper) (3.12.91) ...	1·00	1·00

*Earliest known date of use.

Nos. W48b and W59b were caused by the use of a reserve perforating machine for some printings in the second half of 1992.

Nos. W49, W49Eb and W60 come from booklets.

From 1972 printings were on fluorescent white paper. From 1973 most printings had dextrin added to the PVA gum (see notes after 1971 Decimal Machin issue).

First Day Covers

7.7.71	2½p., 3p., 5p., 7½p., (W13/14, W19, W24)	2·50
23.1.74	3p., 3½p., 5½p., 8p. (W15/16, W20, W25)	1·50
6.11.74	4½p. (W18)	1·00
14.1.76	6½p., 8½p. (W22, W26)	70
20.10.76	10p., 11p. (W28, W31)	1·00
18.1.78	7p., 9p., 10½p (W23, W27, W30)	1·25
23.7.80	12p., 13½p., 15p. (W32/4)	2·00
8.4.81	11½p., 14p., 18p., 22p. (W35, W39, W46, W54)	2·00
24.2.82	12½p., 15½p., 19½p., 26p. (W37, W42, W51, W61)	2·50
27.4.83	16p., 20½p., 28p. (W43, W53, W63)	3·50
23.10.84	13p., 17p., 22p., 31p. (W38, W44, W55, W65)	2·50
7.1.86	12p. (W36)	1·25
6.1.87	18p. (W47)	1·25
8.11.88	14p., 19p., 23p., 32p. (W40, W50, W57, W66)	1·75
28.11.89	15p., 20p., 24p., 34p. (W41, W52, W58, W67)	2·25
4.12.90	17p., 22p., 26p., 37p (W45, W56, W62, W68)	3·25
3.12.91	18p., 24p., 28p., 39p. (W48, W59, W64, W69)	3·25
25.2.92	Cymru–Wales *se-tenant* pane 18p., (2nd), 24p., (1st), 33p. (W49a)	9·00

Presentation Packs

7.7.71	2½p., 3p. (2 bands), 5p., 7½p., (Nos. W13/ 14, W19, W24)	4·00
29.5.74	3p. (1 centre band), 3½p. (2 bands) or (1 centre band), 5½p. (2 bands) or (1 centre band), 8p. (Nos. W15, W16 or W17, W20 or W21, W25). The 4½p. (No. W18) was added later	2·25
20.10.76	6½p., 8½p., 10p. (2 bands), 11p. (Nos. W22, W26, W28, W31)	1·75
28.10.81	7p., 9p., 10½p., 12p. (litho), 13½p., 15p. (photo), 11½p., 14p. grey-blue, 18p. dp violet, 22p. blue (Nos. W23, W27, W30, W32/5, W39, W46, W54)	7·00
3.8.83	10p. (1 centre band), 12½p., 16p., 20½p., 26p. rosine, 28p. dp violet-blue (Nos. W29, W37, W43, W53, W61, W63)	7·00
23.10.84	10p. (1 centre band), 13p., 16p., 17p. grey-blue, 22p. yellow-green, 26p. rosine, 28p. dp violet-blue, 31p. (Nos. W29, W38, W43a, W44, W55, W61, W63, W65)	9·50
3.3.87	12p. (litho), 13p., 17p., 18p. dp olive-grey, 22p. yellow-green, 26p. rosine, 28p. dp violet-blue, 31p. (Nos. W29, W38, W44, W47, W55, W61a, W63a, W65)	9·50

Presentation Packs containing stamps of Northern Ireland, Scotland and Wales are listed after those for Northern Ireland.

(Des J. Matthews after plaster cast by Arnold Machin. Litho Questa)

1993 (7 Dec).   *Chalk-surfaced paper. One centre phosphor band (19p.)
or two phosphor bands (others). P 15 × 14 (with one elliptical hole on
each vertical side).*

W70	W **4** 19p. bistre	....	30	35
W71	25p. red	....	40	45
W72	30p. dp olive-grey	....	45	50
W73	41p. grey-brown	....	65	70

First Day Cover

7.12.93   19p., 25p., 30p., 41p. (W70/3) ....   2·50

For Presentation Pack containing stamps of Northern Ireland,
Scotland and Wales see after No. NI72 of Northern Ireland.

V. GUERNSEY

War Occupation Issues

BISECTS. On 24 December 1940 authority was given, by Post Office notice, that prepayment of penny postage could be effected by using half a British 2d. stamp, diagonally bisected. Such stamps were first used on 27 December 1940.

The 2d. stamps generally available were those of the Postal Centenary issue, 1940 (S.G. 482) and the first colour of the King George VI issue (S.G. 465). These are listed under Nos. 482a and 465b. A number of the 2d. King George V, 1912–22, and of the King George V photogravure stamp (S.G. 442) which were in the hands of philatelists, were also bisected and used.

1

1a Loops (half actual size)

(Des E. W. Vaudin. Typo Guernsey Press Co Ltd)

1941–44. *Rouletted.* (a) *White paper. No wmk.*
1	**1**	½d. light green (7.4.41)	3·00	2·75
		a. Emerald-green (6.41)	3·00	2·75
		b. Bluish green (11.41)	48·00	28·00
		c. Brt green (2.42)	24·00	12·00
		d. Dull green (9.42)	5·00	3·50
		e. Olive-green (2.43)	32·00	18·00
		f. Pale yellowish green (7.43 and later) (shades)	2·50	2·75
		g. Imperf (pair)	£150	
		h. Imperf between (horiz pair)	£600	
		i. Imperf between (vert pair)	£700	
2		1d. scarlet (18.2.41)	2·50	1·25
		a. Pale vermilion (7.43)	2·50	2·00
		b. Carmine (1943)	4·00	3·50
		c. Imperf (pair)	£150	75·00
		d. Imperf between (horiz pair)	£600	
		da. Imperf vert (centre stamp of horiz strip of 3)	£700	
		e. Imperf between (vert pair)	£700	
		f. Printed double (scarlet shade)	75·00	
3		2½d. ultramarine (12.4.44)	5·50	5·50
		a. Pale ultramarine (7.44)	5·50	5·50
		b. Imperf (pair)	£350	
		c. Imperf between (horiz pair)	£800	
		Set of 3	9·00	7·50

First Day Covers
7.4.41	½d.	6·00	
18.2.41	1d.	6·00	
12.4.44	2½d.	7·50	

(b) *Bluish French bank-note paper. W* **1**a *(sideways)*
4	**1**	½d. bright green (11.3.42)	20·00	20·00
5		1d. scarlet (9.4.42)	9·00	25·00
		Set of 2	27·00	45·00

First Day Covers
11.3.42	½d.	75·00	
9.4.42	1d.	40·00	

The dates given for the shades of Nos. 1/3 are the months in which they were printed as indicated on the printer's imprints. Others are issue dates.

Regional Issues

2   **3**

(Des E. A. Piprell. Portrait by Dorothy Wilding Ltd. Photo Harrison & Sons)

1958 (18 Aug)–**67**. *W* **179** *of Great Britain. P* 15 × 14.
6	**2**	2½d. rose-red (8.6.64)	35	40
7	**3**	3d. dp lilac	35	30
		p. One centre phosphor band (24.5.67)	20	20
8		4d. ultramarine (7.2.66)	25	30
		p. Two phosphor bands (24.10.67)	20	20
		Set of 3 (cheapest)	70	75

First Day Covers
18.8.58	3d.	10·00	
8.6.64	2½d.	17·00	
7.2.66	4d.	7·00	

For No. 7 in Presentation Pack, see Regional Issues below Wales No. W6.

1968–69. *No wmk. Chalk-surfaced paper. PVA gum*. One centre phosphor band (Nos. 10/11) or two phosphor bands (others). P* 15 × 14.
9	**3**	4d. pale ultramarine (16.4.68)	10	25
		Ey. Phosphor omitted	40·00	
10		4d. olive-sepia (4.9.68)	15	20
		Ey. Phosphor omitted	40·00	
11		4d. brt vermilion (26.2.69)	15	30
12		5d. royal blue (4.9.68)	15	30
		Set of 4	40	95

First Day Cover
4.9.68	4d., 5d.	1·00	

No. 9 was not issued in Guernsey until 22 April.

*PVA Gum. See note after No. 722 of Great Britain.

VI. ISLE OF MAN

Although specifically issued for use in the Isle of Man, these issues were also valid for use throughout Great Britain.

DATES OF ISSUE. The note at the beginning of Northern Ireland also applies here.

Nos. 8/11 and current stamps of Great Britain were withdrawn from sale on the island from 5 July 1973 when the independent postal administration was established but remained valid for use there for a time. They also remained on sale at the Philatelic Sales counters in the United Kingdom until 4 July 1974.

1   **2**

(Des J. Nicholson. Portrait by Dorothy Wilding Ltd. Photo Harrison)

1958 (18 Aug)–**68.** W **179**. P 15 × 14.
1	**1**	2½d. carmine-red (8.6.64)		45	80
2	**2**	3d. dp lilac		20	10
		a. Chalk-surfaced paper (17.5.63)		12·00	9·00
		p. One centre phosphor band (27.6.68)		20	30
3		4d. ultramarine (7.2.66)		1·50	1·10
		p. Two phosphor bands (5.7.67)		20	15
		Set of 3 (cheapest)		75	90

First Day Covers
18.8.58	3d.		20·00
8.6.64	2½d.		20·00
7.2.66	4d.		7·00

No. 2a was released in London sometime after 17 May 1963, this being the date of issue in Douglas.

For No. 2 in Presentation Pack, see Regional Issues below Wales No. W6.

1968–69. *No wmk. Chalk-surfaced paper. PVA gum. One centre phosphor band (Nos. 5/6) or two phosphor bands (others). P 15 × 14.*
4	**2**	4d. blue (24.6.68)		20	25
5		4d. olive-sepia (4.9.68)		20	30
		Ey. Phosphor omitted		20·00	
6		4d. brt vermilion (26.2.69)		45	60
7		5d. royal blue (4.9.68)		45	50
		Ey. Phosphor omitted		£150	
		Set of 4		1·00	1·60

First Day Cover
4.9.68	4d., 5d.		2·00

3

(Des J. Matthews. Portrait after plaster cast by Arnold Machin. Photo Harrison)

1971 (7 July). *Decimal Currency. Chalk-surfaced paper. One centre phosphor band (2½p.) or two phosphor bands (others). P 15 × 14.*
8	**3**	2½p. brt magenta		20	15
		Ey. Phosphor omitted		£900	

9		3p. ultramarine		20	15
10	**3**	5p. reddish violet		40	50
		Ey. Phosphor omitted		£200	
11		7½p. chestnut		40	65
		Set of 4		1·10	1·25
		Presentation Pack		2·00	

First Day Cover
7.7.71	2½p., 3p., 5p., 7½p.		2·50

All values exist with PVA gum on ordinary cream paper and the 2½p. and 3p. also on fluorescent white paper.

VII. JERSEY

War Occupation Issues

(Des Major N. V. L. Rybot. Typo *Evening Post*, Jersey)

1941–43. *White paper (thin to thick). No wmk. P 11.*
1	**1**	½d. brt green (29.1.42)		3·75	2·50
		a. Imperf between (vert pair)		£650	
		b. Imperf between (horiz pair)		£550	
		c. Imperf (pair)		£180	
		d. On greyish paper (1.43)		5·00	6·50
2		1d. scarlet (1.4.41)		4·00	2·50
		a. Imperf between (vert pair)		£650	
		b. Imperf between (horiz pair)		£550	
		c. Imperf (pair)		£200	
		d. On chalk-surfaced paper		40·00	35·00
		e. On greyish paper (1.43)		5·00	6·50

First Day Covers
29.1.42	½d.		4·50
1.4.41	1d.		4·50

2 Old Jersey Farm   **3** Portelet Bay

4 Corbière Lighthouse   **5** Elizabeth Castle

6 Mont Orgueil Castle   **7** Gathering Vraic (seaweed)

(Des E. Blampied. Eng H. Cortot. Typo French Govt Ptg Works, Paris)

1943–44. *No wmk. P 13½.*

3	**2**	½d. green (1 June)		7·00	5·50
		a. Rough, grey paper (6.10.43)		8·50	8·00
4	**3**	1d. scarlet (1 June)		1·50	50
		a. On newsprint (28.2.44)		2·00	2·00
5	**4**	1½d. brown (8 June)		2·50	3·00
6	**5**	2d. orange-yellow (8 June)		4·00	2·25
7	**6**	2½d. blue (29 June)		1·50	1·50
		a. On newsprint (25.2.44)		1·00	1·25
		ba. Thin paper*		£180	
8	**7**	3d. violet (29 June)		1·00	2·75
		Set of 6		15·00	12·50
		First Day Covers (3)			18·00

*On No. 7ba the design shows clearly through the back of the stamp.

Regional Issues

8   **9**

(Des. E. Blampied (T **8**), W. Gardner (T **9**). Potrait by Dorothy Wilding Ltd. Photo Harrison & Sons)

1958 (18 Aug)–**67.** *W 179 of Great Britain. P 15 × 14.*

9	**8**	2½d. carmine-red (8.6.64)		35	50
		a. Imperf three sides (pair)		£1800	
10	**9**	3d. dp lilac		35	30
		p. One centre phosphor band (9.6.67)		20	20
11		4d. ultramarine (7.2.66)		25	30
		p. Two phosphor bands (5.9.67)		20	25
		Set of 3 (cheapest)		60	85

First Day Covers

18.8.58	3d.		10·00
8.6.64	2½d.		17·00
7.2.66	4d.		7·00

For No.10 in Presentation Pack, see Regional Issues below Wales No. W6.

1968–69. *No wmk. Chalk-surfaced paper. PVA gum*. One centre phosphor band (4d. values) or two phosphor bands (5d.). P 15 × 14.*

12	**9**	4d. olive-sepia (4.9.68)		20	25
		Ey. Phosphor omitted		£750	
13		4d. brt vermilion (26.2.69)		20	30
14		5d. royal blue (4.9.68)		20	40
		Set of 3		50	85

First Day Cover

4.9.68	4d., 5d.		1·25

*PVA Gum. See note after No. 722 of Great Britain.

POSTAGE DUE STAMPS

PERFORATIONS. All postage due stamps are perf 14 × 15.

WATERMARK. The watermark always appears sideways and this is the "normal" listed in this Catalogue for Nos. D1/D68. Varieties occur as follows. The point of identification is which way the top of the crown points, but (where they occur) the disposition of the letters needs to be noted also.

The meaning of the terms is given below: (1) as described and illustrated in the Catalogue, i.e. as read through the front of the stamp, and (2) what is seen during watermark detection when the stamp is face down and the back is under examination.

Watermark	Crown pointing	Letters reading
	(1) As described	
Sideways	left	upwards
Sideways-inverted	right	downwards
Sideways and reversed	left	downwards, back to front
Sideways-inverted and reversed	right	upwards, back to front
	(2) As detected (stamp face down)	
Sideways	right	upwards, back to front
Sideways-inverted	left	downwards, back to front
Sideways and reversed	right	downwards
Sideways-inverted and reversed	left	upwards

D 1   **D 2**

(Des G. Eve. Typo Somerset House (early trial printings of ½d., 1d., 2d. and 5d.; all printings of 1s.) or Harrison (later printings of all values except 1s.))

1914 (20 Apr)–**22.** *W 100 (Simple Cypher) sideways-inverted on 1½d., 4d. and 1s. and sideways on others.*

			Unmtd mint	Mtd mint	Used
D1	D **1**	½d. emerald	1·00	50	50
		Wi. Watermark sideways-inverted	1·50	75	75
		Wj. Watermark sideways and reversed	15·00	10·00	12·00
		Wk. Watermark sideways-inverted and reversed			
D2		1d. carmine	1·50	50	50
		a. Pale carmine	1·50	75	75
		Wi. Watermark sideways-inverted	1·50	75	75
		Wj. Watermark sideways-inverted and reversed	12·00	10·00	10·00
D3		1½d. chestnut (1922)	95·00	40·00	15·00
		Wi. Watermark sideways	95·00	40·00	12·00
D4		2d. agate	1·50	50	40
		Wi. Watermark sideways-inverted	2·25	1·50	1·50
		Wj. Watermark sideways-inverted and reversed	8·00	5·00	5·00
D5		3d. violet (1918)	20·00	2·00	1·00
		a. Bluish violet	20·00	3·50	3·50
		Wi. Watermark sideways-inverted	20·00	7·50	2·00
		Wj. Watermark sideways-inverted and reversed			
D6		4d. dull grey-green (12.20)	80·00	25·00	3·00
		Wi. Watermark sideways	80·00	10·00	15·00
D7		5d. brownish cinnamon	10·00	5·00	2·00
		Wi. Watermark sideways-inverted	30·00	15·00	15·00
D8		1s. brt blue (1915)	80·00	25·00	2·50
		a. Dp brt blue	80·00	25·00	3·00
		Wi. Watermark sideways	70·00	20·00	20·00
		Wj. Watermark sideways-inverted and reversed			
		Set of 8	£250	90·00	22·00

The 1d. is known bisected and used to make up a 1½d. rate on understamped letters from Ceylon (1921) and to pay ½d. on a returned printed paper matter envelope at Kilburn, London (1923). The 2d. was bisected and used as 1d. at Christchurch, Malvern, Streatham and West Kensington all in 1921.

1924. *As 1914–23, but on thick chalk-surfaced paper.*

D9	D **1**	1d. carmine	7·50	2·25	3·50

(Typo Waterlow and (from 1934) Harrison)

1924–31. W **111** (*Block Cypher*) *sideways.*

D10	D **1**	½d. emerald (6.25)	2·50	50	60
		Wi. Watermark sideways-inverted	5·00	2·50	1·25
D11		1d. carmine (4.25)	2·50	50	40
		Wi. Watermark sideways-inverted	—	—	10·00
D12		1½d. chestnut (10.24)	80·00	35·00	16·00
		Wi. Watermark sideways-inverted	—	—	30·00
D13		2d. agate (7.24)	8·00	1·00	40
		Wi. Watermark sideways-inverted	—	—	10·00
D14		3d. dull violet (10.24)	9·00	1·50	40
		a. Printed on gummed side	£100	60·00	†
		b. Experimental paper W **111a**	50·00	35·00	30·00
		Wi. Watermark sideways-inverted	9·00	4·00	1·50
D15		4d. dull grey-green (10.24)	30·00	10·00	2·25
		Wi. Watermark sideways-inverted	35·00	15·00	25·00
D16		5d. brownish cinnamon (1.31)	60·00	24·00	20·00
D17		1s. dp blue (9.24)	15·00	6·00	75
		Wi. Watermark sideways-inverted			
D18	D **2**	2s. 6d. purple/*yellow* (10.24)	£160	30·00	1·75
		Wi. Watermark sideways-inverted			
		Set of 9	£325	95·00	45·00

The 2d. is known bisected to make up the 2½d. rate at Perranwell Station, Cornwall, in 1932.

			Unmtd mint	Used

1936–37. W **125** (E 8 R) *sideways.*

D19	D **1**	½d. emerald (6.37)	7·50	6·00
D20		1d. carmine (5.37)	1·50	1·60
D21		2d. agate (5.37)	7·00	7·00
D22		3d. dull violet (3.37)	1·50	1·60
D23		4d. dull grey-green (12.36)	23·00	20·00
D24		5d. brownish cinnamon (11.36)	40·00	22·00
		a. *Yellow-brown* (1937)	15·00	18·00
D25		1s. dp blue (12.36)	11·00	5·25
D26	D **2**	2s. 6d. purple/*yellow* (5.37)	£250	8·50
		Set of 8	£300	65·00

The 1d. is known bisected (Solihull, 3 July 1937).

1937–38. W **127** (G VI R) *sideways.*

D27	D **1**	½d. emerald (5.38)	8·00	3·50
D28		1d. carmine (5.38)	2·50	40
		Wi. Watermark sideways-inverted		
D29		2d. agate (6.38)	2·50	40
		Wi. Watermark sideways-inverted	10·00	
D30		3d. violet (12.37)	10·00	40
		Wi. Watermark sideways-inverted	25·00	
D31		4d. dull grey-green (9.37)	60·00	9·00
		Wi. Watermark sideways-inverted		
D32		5d. yellow-brown (11.38)	10·00	1·00
		Wi. Watermark sideways-inverted	35·00	
D33		1s. dp blue (10.37)	55·00	1·00
		Wi. Watermark sideways-inverted	55·00	
D34	D **2**	2s. 6d. purple/*yellow* (9.38)	55·00	3·00
		Set of 8	£180	16·00

The 2d. is known bisected in June 1951 (Harpenden and St. Albans) and on 30 October 1954 (Harpenden).

DATES OF ISSUE. The dates for Nos. D35/68 are those on which stamps were first issued by the Supplies Department to postmasters.

1951–52. *Colours changed and new value* (1½d.). W **127** (G VI R) *sideways.*

D35	D **1**	½d. orange (18.9.51)	1·50	2·25
D36		1d. violet-blue (6.6.51)	1·00	75
		Wi. Watermark sideways-inverted		
D37		1½d. green (11.2.52)	1·50	1·75
		Wi. Watermark sideways-inverted	8·50	
D38		4d. blue (14.8.51)	29·00	11·00
D39		1s. ochre (6.12.51)	27·00	4·00
		Wi. Watermark sideways-inverted		
		Set of 5	55·00	18·00

The 1d. is known bisected (Dorking, 1952, and Camberley, 6 April 1954).

1954–55. W **153** (*Mult Tudor Crown and* E 2 R) *sideways.*

D40	D **1**	½d. orange (8.6.55)	4·00	2·50
		Wi. Watermark sideways-inverted	10·00	
D41		2d. agate (28.7.55)	2·00	2·00
		Wi. Watermark sideways-inverted		
D42		3d. violet (4.5.55)	42·00	27·00
D43		4d. blue (14.7.55)	15·00	16·00
		a. Imperf (pair)	£225	
D44		5d. yellow-brown (19.5.55)	20·00	6·50
D45	D **2**	2s. 6d. purple/*yellow* (11.54)	£110	3·00
		Wi. Watermark sideways-inverted		
		Set of 6	£170	50·00

1955–57. W **165** (*Mult St. Edward's Crown and* E 2 R) *sideways.*

D46	D **1**	½d. orange (16.7.56)	1·50	2·50
		Wi. Watermark sideways-inverted	10·00	
D47		1d. violet-blue (7.6.56)	4·00	1·25
D48		1½d. green (13.2.56)	3·75	3·75
		Wi. Watermark sideways-inverted	12·00	
D49		2d. agate (22.5.56)	35·00	3·00
D50		3d. violet (5.3.56)	4·50	1·25
		Wi. Watermark sideways-inverted	25·00	
D51		4d. blue (24.4.56)	18·00	3·00
		Wi. Watermark sideways-inverted	30·00	
D52		5d. brown-ochre (23.3.56)	27·00	2·00
D53		1s. ochre (22.11.55)	65·00	1·25
		Wi. Watermark sideways-inverted		
D54	D **2**	2s. 6d. purple/*yellow* (28.6.57)	£160	7·50
		Wi. Watermark sideways-inverted		
D55		5s. scarlet/*yellow* (25.11.55)	90·00	19·00
		Wi. Watermark sideways-inverted		
		Set of 10	£375	40·00

The 2d. is known bisected (June 1956), and also the 4d. (Poplar, London, April 1959).

1959–63. W **179** (*Mult St. Edward's Crown*) *sideways.*

D56	D **1**	½d. orange (18.10.61)	10	60
		Wi. Watermark sideways-inverted	1·50	
D57		1d. violet-blue (9.5.60)	10	15
		Wi. Watermark sideways-inverted	5·00	
D58		1½d. green (5.10.60)	90	2·00
D59		2d. agate (14.9.59)	1·25	30
		Wi. Watermark sideways-inverted	15·00	
D60		3d. violet (24.3.59)	40	15
		Wi. Watermark sideways-inverted	3·50	
D61		4d. blue (17.12.59)	40	20
		Wi. Watermark sideways-inverted	10·00	
D62		5d. yellow-brown (6.11.61)	45	45
		Wi. Watermark sideways-inverted	5·00	
D63		6d. purple (29.3.62)	60	30
		Wi. Watermark sideways-inverted	12·00	

D64	D **1**	1s. ochre (11.4.60)	1·40	25
		Wi. Watermark sideways-inverted	5·00	
D65	D **2**	2s. 6d. purple/*yellow* (11.5.61)	4·00	45
		Wi. Watermark sideways-inverted	7·50	
D66		5s. scarlet/*yellow* (8.5.61)	7·50	80
		Wi. Watermark sideways-inverted	12·00	
D67		10s. blue/*yellow* (2.9.63)	9·00	4·00
		Wi. Watermark sideways-inverted	30·00	
D68		£1 black/*yellow* (2.9.63)	40·00	7·50
		Set of 13	55·00	15·00

Whiter paper. The note after No. 586 also applies to Postage Due stamps.

The 1d. is known bisected (Newbury, Dec. 1962).

1968–69. *Typo. No wmk. Chalk-surfaced paper.*

D69	D **1**	2d. agate (11.4.68)	20	40
		Ev. PVA gum (26.11.68)	75	
D70		3d. violet (9.9.68)	25	40
D71		4d. blue (6.5.68)	25	40
		Ev. PVA gum		
D72		5d. orange-brown (3.1.69)	4·50	5·25
D73		6d. purple (9.9.68)	60	60
D74		1s. ochre (19.11.68)	2·00	1·00
		Set of 6	7·00	7·00

The 2d. and 4d. exist with gum arabic and PVA gum; the remainder with PVA gum only.

1968–69. *Photo. No wmk. Chalk-surfaced paper. PVA gum. P 14 × 15.*

D75	D **1**	4d. blue (12.6.69)	5·00	5·00
D76		8d. red (3.10.68)	75	75

Nos. D75/6 are smaller, $21\frac{1}{2} \times 17\frac{1}{2}$mm.

D **3**   D **4**

(Des J. Matthews. Photo Harrison)

1970 (17 June)–**75**. *Decimal Currency. Chalk-surfaced paper. P 14 × 15.*

D77	D **3**	$\frac{1}{2}$p. turquoise-blue (15.2.71)	10	20
D78		1p. dp reddish purple (15.2.71)	10	15
D79		2p. myrtle-green (15.2.71)	10	15
D80		3p. ultramarine (15.2.71)	15	15
D81		4p. yellow-brown (15.2.71)	15	15
D82		5p. violet (15.2.71)	20	20
D83		7p. red-brown (21.8.74)	35	45
D84	D **4**	10p. carmine	30	20
D85		11p. slate-green (18.6.75)	50	60
D86		20p. olive-brown	60	50
D87		50p. ultramarine	1·50	40
D88		£1 black	2·75	60
D89		£5 orange-yellow and black (2.4.73)	30·00	2·00
		Set of 13	35·00	
		Presentation Pack (Nos. D77/82, D84, D86/8, (3.11.71)	10·00	
		Presentation Pack (Nos. D77/88) (30.3.77)	6·00	

Later printings were on fluorescent white paper, some with dextrin added to the PVA gum (see notes after X1058).

D **5**   D **6**

(Des Sedley Place Design Ltd. Photo Harrison)

1982 (9 June). *Chalk-surfaced paper. P 14 × 15.*

D 90	D **5**	1p. lake	10	10
D 91		2p. brt blue	10	10
D 92		3p. dp mauve	10	15
D 93		4p. dp blue	10	20
D 94		5p. sepia	10	20
D 95	D **6**	10p. lt brown	20	25
D 96		20p. olive-green	40	30
D 97		25p. dp greenish blue	50	70
D 98		50p. grey-black	1·00	50
D 99		£1 red	2·00	50
D100		£2 turquoise-blue	4·00	50
D101		£5 dull orange	10·00	50
		Set of 12	17·00	3·75
		Set of 12 Gutter Pairs	30·00	
		Presentation Pack	17·00	

D **7**

(Des Sedley Place Design Ltd. Litho Questa)

1994 (15 Feb). *P 15 × 14 (with one elliptical hole on each vertical side).*

D102	D **7**	1p. red, yellow & black	10	10
D103		2p. magenta, purple & black	10	10
D104		5p. yellow, red-brown & black	10	10
D105		10p. yellow, emerald & black	15	20
D106		20p. blue-green, violet & black	30	35
D107		25p. cerise, rosine & black	40	45
D108		£1 violet, magenta & black	1·50	1·60
D109		£1.20, greenish blue, blue-green & black .	1·75	1·90
D110		£5 greenish black, blue-green & black	7·50	7·75
		Set of 9	10·50	11·50
		First Day Cover		12·00
		Presentation Pack	12·50	

Special First Day of Issue Postmark

London EC3 .... 16·00

OFFICIAL STAMPS

In 1840 the 1d. black (Type **1**), with "V R" in the upper corners, was prepared for official use, but was never issued for postal purposes. Obliterated specimens are those which were used for experimental trials of obliterating inks, or those that passed through the post by oversight.

V **1**

1840. *Prepared for use but not issued; "V" "R" in upper corners. Imperf.*

			Un	Used	Used on cover
V1	V **1**	1d. black	£6000	£6000	£15000

The following Official stamps would be more correctly termed Departmental stamps as they were exclusively for the use of certain government departments. Until 1882 official mail used ordinary postage stamps purchased at post offices, the cash being refunded once a quarter. Later the government departments obtained Official stamps by requisition.

Official stamps were on sale to the public for a short time at Somerset House but they were not sold from post offices. The system of only supplying the Government departments with stamps was open to abuse so that all official stamps were withdrawn on 13 May 1904.

OVERPRINTS, PERFORATIONS, WATERMARKS. All official stamps were overprinted by Thomas De La Rue & Co. and are perf 14. Except for the 5s., and 10s. on Anchor, they are on Crown watermarked paper unless otherwise stated.

INLAND REVENUE

These stamps were used by revenue officials in the provinces, mail to and from Head Office passing without a stamp. The London Office used these stamps only for foreign mail.

I.R.

OFFICIAL

(O **1**)

I. R.

OFFICIAL

(O **2**)

Optd with Types O **1** (½d. to 1s.) *or* O **2** (*others*)

1882–1901. *Stamps of Queen Victoria.* (a) *Issues of 1880–81.*

			Un	Used	* Used on cover
O1	½d.	dp green (1.11.82)	12·00	3·00	40·00
O2	½d.	pale green	12·00	3·00	
O3	1d.	lilac (Die II) (1.10.82)	1·50	65	10·00
	a.	Optd in blue-black	60·00	35·00	
	b.	"OFFICIAL" omitted	—	£2250	
	Wi.	Watermark inverted	—	£600	
O4	6d.	grey (Plate 18) (3.11.82)	75·00	20·00	

No. O3 with the lines of the overprint transposed is an essay.

(b) Issues of 1884–88.

O 5	½d.	slate-blue (8.5.85)	25·00	15·00	75·00
O 6	2½d.	lilac (12.3.85)	£110	35·00	£500
O 7	1s.	dull green (12.3.85)	£2500	£450	
O 8	5s.	rose (*blued paper*) (12.3.85)	£2750	£475	
O 9	5s.	rose (3.90)	£1300	£400	
	a.	Raised stop after "R"	£1600	£400	
	b.	Optd in blue-black	£2000	£450	
O 9c	10s.	cobalt (*blued paper*) (12.3.85)	£5000	£800	
O 9d	10s.	ultramarine (*blued paper*) (12.3.85)	£5000	£1600	
O10	10s.	ultramarine (3.90)	£2500	£525	
	a.	Raised stop after "R"	£3250	£550	
	b.	Optd in blue-black	£3500	£700	
O11	£1	brown-lilac (watermark Crowns) (12.3.85)	£20000		
	a.	Frame broken	£25000		
O12	£1	brown-lilac (watermark Orbs) (3.90)	£27500		
	a.	Frame broken	£30000		

(c) Issues of 1887–92.

O13	½d.	vermilion (15.5.88)	1·50	50	20·00
	a.	Without "I.R."	£2000		
	b.	Imperf	£1200		
	c.	Opt double (imperf)	£1500		
O14	2½d.	purple/*blue* (2.92)	50·00	4·00	£150
O15	1s.	dull green (9.89)	£200	20·00	£1000
O16	£1	green (6.92)	£3750	£500	
	a.	No stop after "R"	—	£850	
	b.	Frame broken	£6000	£1000	

Nos. O3, O13, O15 and O16 may be found with two varieties of overprint, *thin letters,* and from 1894 printings, *thicker* letters.

(d) Issues of 1887 and 1900.

O17	½d.	blue-green (4.01)	4·00	3·00	85·00
O18	6d.	purple/*rose-red* (1.7.01)	£100	22·00	
O19	1s.	green and carmine (12.01)	£700	£150	
★O1/19		**For well-centred, lightly used**		+ 35%	

1902–04. *Stamps of King Edward VII. Ordinary paper.*

O20	½d.	blue-green (4.2.02)	17·00	1·50	80·00
O21	1d.	scarlet (4.2.02)	10·00	70	40·00
O22	2½d.	ultramarine (19.2.02)	£400	80·00	
O23	6d.	pale dull purple (14.3.04)	£85000	£65000	
O24	1s.	dull green & carmine (29.4.02)	£500	85·00	
O25	5s.	brt carmine (29.4.02)	£4000	£1500	
	a.	Raised stop after "R"	£4750	£1600	
O26	10s.	ultramarine (29.4.02)	£15000	£9500	
	a.	Raised stop after "R"	£18000	£12000	
O27	£1	blue-green (29.4.02)	£12000	£7000	

OFFICE OF WORKS

These were issued to Head and Branch (local) offices in London and to Branch (local) offices at Birmingham, Bristol, Edinburgh, Glasgow, Leeds, Liverpool, Manchester and Southampton. The overprints on stamps of value 2d. and upwards were created later in 1902, the 2d. for registration fees and the rest for overseas mail.

O. W.

OFFICIAL

(O **3**)

Optd with Type O 3

1896 (24 Mar)–**02.** *Stamps of Queen Victoria.*

		★ Used on
	Un	Used	cover
O31	½d. vermilion	90·00	40·00	£180
O32	½d. blue-green (2.02)	£150	75·00
O33	1d. lilac (Die II)	£150	40·00	£200
O34	5d. dull purple & blue (II) (29.4.02) ...	£750	£150
O35	10d. dull purple & carmine (28.5.02)	£1300	£250

1902 (11 Feb)–**03.** *Stamps of King Edward VII. Ordinary paper.*

O36	½d. blue-green (8.02)	£350	80·00	£850
O37	1d. scarlet	£350	80·00	£150
O38	2d. yellowish green & carmine-red (29.4.02)	£600	75·00	£1100
O39	2½d. ultramarine (29.4.02)	£7000	£1500
O40	10d. dull purple & carmine (28.5.03)	£5000	£1500
★O31/40	**For well-centred, lightly used**	+ 25%

ARMY

Letters to and from the War Office in London passed without postage. The overprinted stamps were distributed to District and Station Paymasters nationwide, including Cox and Co., the Army Agents, who were paymasters to the Household Division.

ARMY **ARMY** **ARMY**

OFFICIAL **OFFICIAL** **OFFICIAL**

(O **4**) (O **5**) (O **6**)

1896 (1 Sept)–**01.** *Stamps of Queen Victoria optd with Type O 4 (½d., 1d.) or O 5 (2½d., 6d.).*

O41	½d. vermilion	1·50	75	20·00
	a. "OFFICIAl" (R.13/7)	35·00	16·00
	b. Lines of opt transposed	£1000
	Wi. Watermark inverted	£170	75·00
O42	½d. blue-green (6.00)	1·75	4·00
	Wi. Watermark inverted	£130	60·00
O43	1d. lilac (Die II)	1·50	75	30·00
	a. "OFFICAl" (R.13/7)	35·00	20·00
O44	2½d. purple/*blue*	4·00	3·00	£250
O45	6d. purple/*rose-red* (20.9.01)	16·00	10·00	£450

Nos. O41a and O43a occur in sheets overprinted by Forme 1.

1902-03. *Stamps of King Edward VII optd with Type O 4 (Nos. O48/50) or Type O 6 (O52). Ordinary paper.*

O48	½d. blue-green (11.2.02)	2·00	65	50·00
O49	1d. scarlet (11.2.02)	1·50	55	50·00
	a. "ARMY" omitted	†	—
O50	6d. pale dull purple (23.8.02)	70·00	32·00
O52	6d. pale dull purple (12.03)	£850	£300

GOVERNMENT PARCELS

These stamps were issued to all departments, including Head Office, for use on parcels weighing over 3 lb. Below this weight government parcels were sent by letter post to avoid the 55% of the postage paid from accruing to the railway companies, as laid down by parcel-post regulations. Most government parcels stamps suffered heavy postmarks in use.

GOVᵀ PARCELS

(O **7**)

Optd as Type O 7

1883 (1 Aug)–**86.** *Stamps of Queen Victoria.*

		★
	Un	Used
O61	1½d. lilac (1.5.86)	£100	25·00
	a. No dot under "T"	£130	28·00
	b. Dot to left of "T"	£100	28·00
O62	6d. dull green (1.5.86)	£800	£275
O63	9d. dull green	£650	£180
O64	1s. orange-brown (watermark Crown, Pl 13) ...	£425	70·00
	a. No dot under "T"	£475	80·00
	b. Dot to left of "T"	£475	80·00
O64c	1s. orange-brown (Pl 14)	£750	£110
	ca. No dot under "T"	£825	£100
	cb. Dot to left of "T"	

1887–90. *Stamps of Queen Victoria.*

O65	1½d. dull purple & pale green (29.10.87)	14·00	2·00
	a. No dot under "T"	18·00	6·00
	b. Dot to right of "T"	16·00	5·00
	c. Dot to left of "T"	16·00	5·00
O66	6d. purple/*rose-red* (19.12.87)	28·00	10·00
	a. No dot under "T"	30·00	12·00
	b. Dot to right of "T"	30·00	12·00
	c. Dot to left of "T"	30·00	11·00
O67	9d. dull purple & blue (21.8.88)	55·00	15·00
O68	1s. dull green (25.3.90)	£120	70·00
	a. No dot under "T"	£140	75·00
	b. Dot to right of "T"	£140	75·00
	c. Dot to left of "T"	£160	80·00
	d. Optd in blue-black	

1891–1900 *Stamps of Queen Victoria.*

O69	1d. lilac (Die II) (18.6.97)	28·00	8·00
	a. No dot under "T"	30·00	20·00
	b. Dot to left of "T"	30·00	20·00
	c. Opt inverted	£1000	£850
	d. Ditto. Dot to left of "T"	£900	£500
	Wi. Watermark inverted	—	75·00
O70	2d. grey-green & carmine (24.10.91) ...	45·00	7·00
	a. No dot under "T"	50·00	8·00
	b. Dot to left of "T"	50·00	9·00
O71	4½d. green & carmine (29.9.92)	£100	75·00
	b. Dot to right of "T"	
	Wi. Watermark inverted	
O72	1s. green & carmine (11.00)	£160	50·00
	a. Opt inverted	—	£4000
★O61/72	**For well-centred lightly used**	+ 100%

1902. *Stamps of King Edward VII. Ordinary paper.*

O74	1d. scarlet (30.10.02)	17·00	6·00
O75	2d. yellowish green & carmine-red (29.4.02)	65·00	18·00
O76	6d. pale dull purple (19.2.02)	£100	18·00
	a. Opt double, one albino	£4500
O77	9d. dull purple & ultramarine (28.8.02)	£225	50·00
O78	1s. dull green & carmine (17.12.02)	£350	85·00

The "no dot under T" variety occured on R.12/3 and 20/2. The "dot to left of T" comes four times in the sheet on R.2/7, 6/7, 7/9 and 12/9. The best example of the "dot to right of T" is on R.20/1. All three varieties were corrected around 1897.

For full information on all future British issues, collectors should write to the British Post Office Philatelic Bureau, 20 Brandon Street, Edinburgh EH3 5TT

BOARD OF EDUCATION

BOARD

OF

EDUCATION

(O **8**)

Optd with Type O **8**

1902 (19 Feb). *Stamps of Queen Victoria.*

		Un	Used	Used on cover
O81	5d. dull purple & blue (II)	£525	£100	
O82	1s. green & carmine	£950	£375	

1902 (19 Feb)**–04** *Stamps of King Edward VII. Ordinary paper.*

O83	½d. blue-green	18·00	6·00	£200
O84	1d. scarlet	18·00	5·00	£125
O85	2½d. ultramarine	£500	50·00	
O86	5d. dull purple & ultramarine (6.2.04)	£2000	£950	
O87	1s. dull green & carmine (23.12.02)	£40000	£30000	

ROYAL HOUSEHOLD

R.H.

OFFICIAL

(O **9**)

1902. *Stamps of King Edward VII optd with Type O **9**. Ordinary paper.*

O91	½d. blue-green (29.4.02)	£150	95·00	£500
O92	1d. scarlet (19.2.02)	£130	85·00	£300

ADMIRALTY

ADMIRALTY

OFFICIAL

(O **10**)

ADMIRALTY

OFFICIAL

(O **11**)

1903 (1 Apr). *Stamps of King Edward VII optd with Type O **10**. Ordinary paper.*

O101	½d. blue-green	10·00	4·00	
O102	1d. scarlet	5·00	2·50	£150
O103	1½d. dull purple & green	60·00	45·00	
O104	2d. yellowish green & carmine-red	£100	50·00	
O105	2½d. ultramarine	£120	40·00	
O106	3d. purple/yellow	£100	38·00	

1903–04. *Stamps of King Edward VII optd with Type O **11**. Ordinary paper.*

O107	½d. blue-green (9.03)	9·00	5·00	£250
O108	1d. scarlet (12.03)	8·00	4·50	50·00
O109	1½d. dull purple & green (2.04)	£200	75·00	
O110	2d. yellowish green & carmine-red (3.04)	£425	£120	
O111	2½d. ultramarine (3.04)	£550	£300	
O112	3d. dull purple/orange-yellow (12.03)	£375	95·00	

Stamps of various issues perforated with a Crown and initials ("H.M.O.W.", "O.W.", "B.T." or "S.O.") or with initials only ("H.M.S.O." or "D.S.I.R.") have also been used for official purposes, but these are outside the scope of this catalogue.

POSTAL FISCAL STAMPS

PRICES. Prices in the used column are for stamps with genuine postal cancellations dated from the time when they were authorised for use as postage stamps. Beware of stamps with fiscal cancellations removed and fraudulent postmarks applied.

VALIDITY. The 1d. surface-printed stamps were authorised for postal use from 1 June 1881 and at the same time the 1d. postage issue, No. 166, was declared valid for fiscal purposes. The 3d. and 6d. values together with the embossed issues were declared valid for postal purposes by another Act effective from 1 January 1883.

SURFACE-PRINTED ISSUES

(Typo Thomas De La Rue & Co.)

F **1** Rectangular Buckle

F **2**

F **3** Octagonal Buckle

F **4**

F **5** Double-lined Anchor

F **6** Single-lined Anchor

1853–57. P 15½ × 15.   (a) Wmk F **5** (inverted) (1853–55).

			Un	Used	Used on cover
F1	F **1**	1d. lt blue (10.10.53)	13·00	16·00	75·00
F2	F **2**	1d. ochre (10.53)	55·00	35·00	£150
		a. Tête-bêche (in block of four)	£8000		
F3	F **3**	1d. pale turquoise-blue (1854)	18·00	15·00	£130
		Wi. Watermark upright	50·00	35·00	
F4		1d. lt blue/blue (1854)	35·00	22·00	£150
		Wi. Watermark upright	80·00	80·00	

F5	F **4**	1d. reddish lilac/blue glazed paper (25.3.55)	50·00	11·00	£100
		Wi. Watermark upright	85·00	25·00	

Only one example is known of No. F2a outside the National Postal Museum and the Royal Collection.

(b) Wmk F **6** (1856–57)

F6	F **4**	1d. reddish lilac (shades)	5·50	4·00	80·00
F7		1d. reddish lilac/bluish (shades) (1857) .	5·50	4·00	80·00

(F **7**)

1860 (3 Apr).   No. F7 optd with Type F **7**, in red.

F8	F **4**	1d. dull reddish lilac/blue	£375	£300	£500
		Wj. Wmk reversed			

BLUE PAPER. In the following issues we no longer distinguish between bluish and white paper. There is a range of papers from white or greyish to bluish.

F **8**

F **9**

F **10**

1860–67.   Bluish to white paper. P 15½ × 15. (a) Wmk F **6** (1860).

F 9	F **8**	1d. reddish lilac (May)	6·00	6·00	80·00
F10	F **9**	3d. reddish lilac (June)	£225	80·00	£150
F11	F **10**	6d. reddish lilac (Oct)	90·00	65·00	£180
		Wi. Watermark inverted	£130	85·00	
		Wj. Watermark reversed	£120	85·00	

(b) W **40**. (Anchor 16mm high) (1864)

F12	F **8**	1d. pale reddish lilac (Nov)	4·75	4·75	65·00
F13	F **9**	3d. pale reddish lilac	80·00	60·00	
F14	F **10**	6d. pale reddish lilac	80·00	60·00	£150
		Wi. Watermark inverted	£150		

(c) W **40** (Anchor 18mm high) (1867)

F15	F **8**	1d. reddish lilac	13·00	6·00	£130
F16	F **9**	3d. reddish lilac	65·00	60·00	£160
F17	F **10**	6d. reddish lilac	75·00	40·00	£150

For stamps perf 14, see Nos. F24/7.

F **11**   F **12**

Four Dies of Type F 12

Die 1. Corner ornaments small and either joined or broken; heavy shading under chin

Die 2. Ornaments small and always broken; clear line of shading under chin

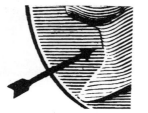

Die 3. Ornaments larger and joined; line of shading under chin extended half way down neck

Die 4. Ornaments much larger; straight line of shading continued to bottom of neck

1867–81. *White to bluish paper. P* 14. *(a) W* **47** *(Small Anchor).*

F18	F **11**	1d. purple (1.9.67)	8·00	5·00	60·00
		Wi. Watermark inverted			
F19	F **12**	1d. purple (Die I) (6.68)	1·75	1·50	40·00
		Wi. Watermark inverted	50·00		
F20		1d. purple (Die 2) (6.76)	10·00	10·00	£180
F21		1d. purple (Die 3) (3.77)	4·00	4·00	75·00
F22		1d. purple (Die 4) (7.78)	3·00	2·50	65·00

(b) W **48** *(Orb)*

F23	F **12**	1d. purple (Die 4) (1.81)	2·00	1·50	40·00
		Wi. Watermark inverted	50·00		

1881. *White to bluish paper. P* 14.

(a) W **40** *(Anchor 18mm high) (Jan)*

F24	F **9**	3d. reddish lilac	£325	£200	£325
F25	F **10**	6d. reddish lilac	£170	55·00	£150

(b) W **40** *(Anchor 20mm high) (May)*

F26	F **9**	3d. reddish lilac	£250	55·00	£150
F27	F **10**	6d. reddish lilac	£120	80·00	£250

ISSUES EMBOSSED IN COLOUR

(Made at Somerset House)

The embossed stamps were struck from dies not appropriated to any special purpose on paper which had the words "INLAND REVENUE" previously printed, and thus became available for payment of any duties for which no special stamps had been provided.

The die letters are included in the embossed designs and holes were drilled for the insertion of plugs showing figures indicating dates of striking.

F **13**   F **14**

INLAND
REVENUE

(F **15**)

INLAND
REVENUE

(F **16**)

1860 (3 Apr)–**71.** *Types F* **13/14** *and similar types embossed on bluish paper. Underprint Type F* **15**. *No wmk. Imperf.*

			Un	Used
F28	2d. pink (Die A) (1.1.71)		£120	£120
F29	3d. pink (Die C)		90·00	85·00
	a. Tête-bêche (vert pair)		£1000	
F30	3d. pink (Die D)		£325	
F31	6d. pink (Die T)		£650	

F32	6d. pink (Die U)	95·00	85·00
	a. Tête-bêche (vert pair)	£1200	
F33	9d. pink (Die C) (1.1.71)	£225	
F34	1s. pink (Die E) (28.6.61)	£325	£140
F35	1s. pink (Die F) (28.6.61)	£110	95·00
	a. Tête-bêche (vert pair)	£500	
F36	2s. pink (Die K) (6.8.61)	£250	£160
F37	2s. 6d. pink (Die N) (28.6.61)	£750	
F38	2s. 6d. pink (Die O) (28.6.61)	75·00	75·00

1861–71. *As last but perf* 12½.

F39	2d. pink (Die A) (8.71)	£225	£120
F40	3d. pink (Die C)		
F41	3d. pink (Die D)		
F42	9d. pink (Die C) (8.71)	£250	£130
F43	1s. pink (Die E) (8.71)	£190	£120
F44	1s. pink (Die F) (8.71)	£170	90·00
F45	2s. 6d. pink (Die O) (8.71)	£100	55·00

1874 (Nov). *Types as before embossed on white paper. Underprint Type F* **16**, *in green. W* **47** (*Small Anchor*). *P* 12½.

F46	2d. pink (Die A)	—	£160
F47	9d. pink (Die C)		
F48	1s. pink (Die F)	£170	95·00
F49	2s. 6d. pink (Die O)	—	£140

1875 (Nov)–**80.** *As last but colour changed and on white or bluish paper.*

F50	2d. vermilion (Die A) (1880)	£250	90·00
F51	9d. vermilion (Die C) (1876)	£250	£130
F52	1s. vermilion (Die E)	£150	60·00
F53	1s. vermilion (Die F)	£150	60·00
F54	2s. 6d. vermilion (Die O) (1878)	£190	90·00

1882 (Oct). *As last but W* **48** (*Orbs*).

F55	2d. vermilion (Die A)		
F56	9d. vermilion (Die C)		
F57	1s. vermilion (Die E)		
F58	2s. 6d. vermilion (Die O)	£400	£200

The sale of Inland Revenue stamps up to the 2s. value ceased from 30 December 1882 and stocks were called in and destroyed. The 2s. 6d. value remained on sale until 2 July 1883 when it was replaced by the 2s. 6d. "Postage & Revenue" stamps. Inland Revenue stamps still in the hands of the public continued to be accepted for revenue and postal purposes.

POSTMASTER AND U.P.U. SPECIMEN OVERPRINTS

At various times since 1847 the British Post Office, or its printers, has applied "SPECIMEN" or "CANCELLED" overprints to certain stamp issues.

Many of these overprints were purely intended for internal record purposes, but some had a wider use connected to the postal service. Between 1847 and 1873 the G.P.O. circulated examples of new stamps overprinted "SPECIMEN" to its postmasters and from 1879 similar overprints were applied to samples forwarded to the Universal Postal Union for distribution to member administrations. After 1892 such U.P.U. overprints were restricted to stamps with a face value of 1 shilling or above and they were discontinued altogether after March 1948.

In the listings below Types P **1** to P **6** are postmaster specimens and the remainder for the U.P.U.

For a complete listing of all other "SPECIMEN" overprints see the *Great Britain Specialised Catalogue.*

SPECIMEN

P 1

SPECIMEN

P 3

SPECIMEN

P 4

SPECIMEN

P 5

SPECIMEN

P 6

SPECIMEN

P 9

SPECIMEN

P 16

SPECIMEN

P 23

SPECIMEN

P 26

SPECIMEN

P 32

1847–54. *Embossed issues.*

No.	Type No.	*Specimen*	*Unused Price*
SP1	P **1**	1s. pale green (No. 54) (red opt)	£325
		a. Black opt	£450
SP2		10d. brown (No. 57)	£275
SP3		6d. mauve (No. 58)	£550

Specimen Overprints

1855–57. *Surface-printed issues. No corner letters.*

No.	Type No.	Specimen	Unused Price
SP4	P **3**	4d. carmine/*blued* (No. 62)	£160
SP5	P **4**	4d. rose/*white* (No. 65)	
SP6		6d. dp lilac/*white* (No. 69)	£100
		a. On azure paper	£140
SP7		1s. dp green (No. 71)	£100

1858–70. *Line-engraved issues.*

No.	Type No.	Specimen	Unused Price
SP 8	P **9**	½d. rose-red (pl 10) (No. 48)	£100
SP 9		1d. rose-red (pl 146) (No. 43)	£100
SP10		1½d. rose-red (pl 3) (No. 51)	£110
SP11		2d. blue (pl 15) (No. 46)	£150

1862–64. *Surface-printed issue. Small uncoloured corner letters.*

No.	Type No.	Specimen	Unused Price
SP12	P **5**	3d. dp carmine-rose (No. 75)	80·00
SP13		4d. brt red (No. 79)	60·00
SP14	P **6**	9d. bistre (No. 86)	£100

1867–80. *Large uncoloured corner letters. Wmk Spray of Rose.*

No.	Type No.	Specimen	Unused Price
SP15	P **5**	10d. red-brown (No. 112)	80·00
SP16		2s. dull blue (pl 1) (No. 118)	70·00
SP17	P **9**	2s. dull blue (pl 1) (No. 118)	70·00
SP18		2s. brown (No. 121)	£500

1867–83. *Wmk Maltese Cross or Anchor (£5).*

No.	Type No.	Specimen	Unused Price
SP19	P **6**	5s. rose (pl 1) (No. 126)	£225
SP20	P **9**	5s. pale rose (pl 2) (No. 127)	£250
SP21		10s. greenish grey (No. 128)	£550
SP22		£1 brown-lilac (No. 129)	£900
SP23		£5 orange/*blued* (No. 133)	£700

1872–73. *Uncoloured letters in corner. Wmk Spray of Rose.*

No.	Type No.	Specimen	Unused Price
SP24	P **6**	6d. chestnut (pl 11) (No. 123)	60·00
SP25		6d. grey (pl 12) (No. 125)	70·00

1873–80. *Large coloured corner letters.*

No.	Type No.	Specimen	Unused Price
SP26	P **9**	2½d. rosy-mauve (pl 6) (No. 141)	50·00
SP27		2½d. blue (pl 17) (No. 142)	45·00
SP28		3d. rose (pl 18) (No. 143)	60·00
SP29		4d. sage-green (pl 15) (No. 153)	70·00
SP30		4d. grey-brown (pl 17) (No. 154)	£120
SP31		6d. grey (pl 16) (No. 147)	60·00
SP32		8d. orange (pl 1) (No. 156)	60·00
SP33		1s. green (pl 12) (No. 150)	60·00
SP34		1s. orange-brown (pl 13) (No. 151)	£100

1880–83. *Wmk Imperial Crown.*

No.	Type No.	Specimen	Unused Price
SP35	P **9**	3d. on 3d. lilac (No. 159)	90·00
SP36		6d. on 6d. lilac (No. 162)	90·00

1880–81. *Wmk Imperial Crown.*

No.	Type No.	Specimen	Unused Price
SP37	P **9**	½d. dp green (No. 164)	20·00
SP38		1d. Venetian red (No. 166)	20·00
SP39		1½d. Venetian red (No. 167)	20·00
SP40		2d. pale rose (No. 168)	30·00
SP41		5d. indigo (No. 169)	30·00

1881. *Wmk Imperial Crown.*

No.	Type No.	Specimen	Unused Price
SP42	P **9**	1d. lilac (14 dots) (No. 170)	25·00
SP43		1d. lilac (16 dots) (No. 172)	20·00

1883–84. *Wmk Anchor or Three Imperial Crowns (£1).*

No.	Type No.	Specimen	Unused Price
SP44	P **9**	2s. 6d. lilac/*blued* (No. 175)	£175
SP45		5s. crimson (No. 181)	£175
SP46		10s. ultramarine (No. 183)	£175
SP47		£1 brown-lilac (No. 185)	£350

1883–84. *Wmk Imperial Crown.*

No.	Type No.	Specimen	Unused Price
SP48	P **9**	½d. slate-blue (No. 187)	20·00
SP49		1½d. lilac (No. 188)	45·00
SP50		2d. lilac (No. 189)	45·00
SP51	P **9**	2½d. lilac (No. 190)	45·00
SP52		3d. lilac (No. 191)	45·00
SP53		4d. dull green (No. 192)	70·00
SP54		5d. dull green (No. 193)	70·00
SP55		6d. dull green (No. 194)	£130
SP56		9d. dull green (No. 195)	70·00
SP57		1s. dull green (No. 196)	70·00

1887–91. *"Jubilee" issue.*

No.	Type No.	Specimen	Unused Price
SP58	P **9**	½d. vermilion (No. 197)	22·00
SP59		1½d. dull purple & pale green (No. 198)	35·00
SP60		2d. green & scarlet (No. 199)	35·00
SP61		2½d. purple/*blue* (No. 201)	40·00
SP62		3d. purple/*yellow* (No. 202)	30·00
SP63		4d. green & purple-brown (No. 205)	30·00
SP64		5d. dull purple & blue (Die I) (No. 207)	30·00
SP65		6d. purple/*rose-red* (No. 208)	20·00
SP66		9d. dull purple & blue (No. 209)	30·00
SP67		10d. dull purple & carmine (No. 210)	55·00
SP68		1s. dull green (No. 211)	30·00

1902–10. *King Edward VII. De La Rue printings.*

No.	Type No.	Specimen	Unused Price
SP69	P **16**	2s. 6d. lilac (No. 260)	£120
SP70		5s. brt carmine (No. 263)	£130
SP71		10s. ultramarine (No. 265)	£200
SP72		£1 dull blue-green (No. 266)	£400

1913. *King George V. Wmk Royal Cypher.*

No.	Type No.	Specimen	Unused Price
SP73	P **26**	1s. bistre-brown (No. 395)	£120

1913. *"Seahorse" high values. Printed by Waterlow.*

No.	Type No.	Specimen	Unused Price
SP74	P **26**	2s. 6d. dp sepia-brown (No. 399)	£200
SP75		5s. rose-carmine (No. 401)	£175
SP76		10s. indigo-blue (No. 402)	£400
SP77		£1 green (No. 403)	£1000

1929. *Ninth U. P. U. Congress.*

No.	Type No.	Specimen	Unused Price
SP78	P **32**	£1 black (No. 438) (opt in red)	£750

1936. *Photogravure.*

No.	Type No.	Specimen	Unused Price
SP79	P **32**	1s. bistre-brown (No. 449)	40·00

1939. *King George VI.*

No.	Type No.	Specimen	Unused Price
SP80	P **23**	1s. bistre-brown (No. 475)	28·00
SP81		2s. 6d. brown (No. 476)	£200
SP82		2s. 6d. yellow-green (No. 476a)	£200
SP83		5s. red (No. 477)	£200
SP84		10s. dark blue (No. 478)	£350
SP85		10s. ultramarine (No. 478a)	£300

POSTAGE DUE STAMPS

1915. *Wmk Simple Cypher.*

No.	Type No.	Specimen	Unused Price
SP86	P **23**	1s. brt blue (No. D8)	25·00

1924. *Wmk Block Cypher.*

No.	Type No.	Specimen	Unused Price
SP87	P **23**	2s. 6d. purple/*yellow* (No. D18)	

OFFICIAL STAMPS

1887–91. *Optd "GOVT PARCELS".*

No.	Type No.	Specimen	Unused Price
SP88	P **9**	1½d. dull purple & pale green (No. O65)	65·00
SP89		2d. grey-green & carmine (No. O70)	50·00
SP90		6d. purple/*rose-red* (No. O66)	65·00
SP91		9d. dull purple & blue (No. O67)	50·00
SP92		1s. dull green (No. O68)	65·00

POST OFFICE STAMP BOOKLETS

The following listing covers all booklets sold by post offices from 1904 until early 1995.

All major variations of contents and cover are included, but minor changes to the covers and differences on the interleaves have been ignored.

From 1913 each booklet carried an edition number, linked to an internal Post Office system of identification which divided the various booklets into series. In 1943 these edition numbers were replaced by edition dates. No attempt has been made to list separate edition numbers for booklets prior to 1943, although notes giving their extent are provided for each booklet. Edition dates from August 1943 are listed separately and exist for all £.s.d. and most Decimal Stitched booklets (except for the 1s. booklets, the 2s. booklets (N1/3), the 5s. "Philympia" booklets (No. HP34), the £1 "Stamps for Cooks" booklet (No. ZP1) and the Decimal Sponsored booklets). They are those found printed upon the booklets, either on the outer back cover or on the white leaves.

ERRORS OF MAKE-UP of booklets exist but we do not list them here. More detailed listings can be found in the 2nd, 3rd and 4th volumes of the *Great Britain Specialised Catalogue*.

ILLUSTRATIONS. The illustrations of the covers are $\frac{3}{4}$ size except where otherwise stated.

PRICES quoted are for complete booklets containing stamps with "average" perforations (i.e. full perforations on two edges of the pane only). Booklets containing panes with complete perforations are worth more.

KING EDWARD VII

2s. Booklets

Type BA1

1904 (Mar). *Red cover printed in black as Type BA1. Pages of six stamps: 24 × 1d. Wmk Imperial Crown (No. 219).*
BA1 .... £130

HAVE YOU READ THE NOTES AT THE BEGINNING OF THIS CATALOGUE?
These often provide answers to the enquiries we receive.

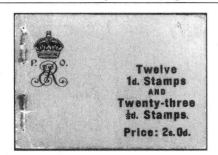

Type BA2

1906 (June). *Red cover printed in black as Type BA2. As before but make-up changed to include 12 × 1d. and 23 × $\frac{1}{2}$d. and label showing one green cross (Nos. 217 and 219).*
BA2 .... £400

1907 (Aug). *Red cover printed in black as Type BA2. Make-up changed to include 18 × 1d. and 11 × $\frac{1}{2}$d. and label showing one green cross (Nos. 217 and 219).*
BA3 .... £500

1911 (June). *Red cover printed in black as Type BA2 but showing a larger Post Office cypher on cover. As before, but containing stamps by Harrison & Sons (Nos. 267 and 272).*
BA6 .... £500

KING GEORGE V

2s. Booklets

1911 (Aug). *Red cover printed in black as Type BA2 showing King George V cypher. Pages of six stamps: 18 × 1d. and 12 × $\frac{1}{2}$d. Wmk Crown (Nos. 325, 329) Die 1B.*
BB1 .... £275

Type BB2

1912 (April). *As before, but red cover printed in black as Type BB2.*
BB2 .... £400

1912 (Sept). *As before, but wmk Simple Cypher (Nos. 334, 336) Die 1B.*
BB3 .... £450

Type BB5

1913 (Jan).   *As before, but red cover printed in black as Type BB5.*
BB5   No Edition number or 8 or 9 .... £450

1913 (April).   *As before, but 1912–22 Wmk Simple Cypher (Nos. 351, 357).*
BB6   Edition numbers 10 to 45 .... £150

1916 (July).   *As before, but orange cover printed in black as Type BB5.*
BB9   Edition numbers 46 to 64 .... £175

Type BB10

1917 (Sept).   *As before, but orange cover printed in black as Type BB10.*
BB10   Edition numbers 65 to 81 .... £200

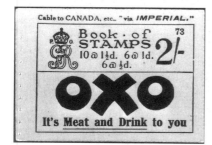

Type BB11

1924 (Feb).   *Blue cover printed in black as Type BB11. Pages of six stamps: 10 × 1½d. (first completed by two perforated labels), 6 × 1d. and 6 × ½d. 1912–22 Wmk Simple Cypher (Nos. 351, 357, 362).*
BB11   Edition numbers 1 or 2 .... £550

1933 (Oct).   *As before, but 1924–26 Wmk Block Cypher (Nos. 418/20).*
BB12   Edition numbers 3 to 102 & 108 to 254 .... £150

Type BB13

1929 (May).   *Postal Union Congress issue. Cover of special design as Type BB13 printed in blue on buff as before but containing stamps of the P.U.C. issue (Nos. 434/6).*
BB13   Edition numbers 103 to 107 .... £275

1934 (Feb).   *Blue cover printed in black as Type BB11, but containing stamps with Block Cypher wmk printed by Harrison & Sons (Nos. 418/20).*
BB14   Edition numbers 255 to 287 .... £190

1935 (Jan).   *As before, but containing stamps of the photogravure issue with the se-tenant advertisements printed in brown (Nos. 439/41).*
BB15   Edition numbers 288 to 297 .... £400

Type BB16

1935 (May).   *Silver Jubilee issue. Larger size cover printed in blue on buff as Type BB16 and containing pages of four stamps with no se-tenant advertisements: 12 × 1½d., 4 × 1d. and 4 × ½d. (Nos. 453/5).*
BB16   Edition numbers 298 to 304 .... 45·00

1935 (July).   *As No. BB15, but containing stamps of the photogravure issue with se-tenant advertisements printed in black (Nos. 439/41).*
BB17   Edition numbers 305 to 353 .... 80·00

3s. Booklets

Type BB18

1918 (Oct). *Orange cover printed in black as Type BB18. Pages of six stamps: 12 × 1½d., 12 × 1d. and 12 × ½d. 1912–22 Wmk Simple Cypher* (Nos. 351, 357, 362).
BB18　Edition numbers 1 to 11 . . . . £225

1919 (July). *As before, but make-up altered to contain 18 × 1½d., 6 × 1d. and 6 × ½d.*
BB19　Edition numbers 12 to 26 . . . . £225

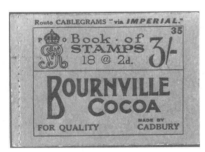

Type BB20

1921 (April). *Experimental booklet bound in blue covers as Type BB20, containing pages of six stamps: 18 × 2d. (Die I) (No. 368).*
BB20　Edition numbers 35 and part 37 . . . . £300

1921 (Dec). *As before, but containing 2d. (Die II) (No. 370).*
BB21　Edition numbers 12, 13 and part 37 . . . . £250

Type BB22

1922 (May). *Scarlet cover printed in black as Type BB22. Pages of six stamps: 18 × 1½d., 6 × 1d. and 6 × ½d. (Nos. 351, 357, 362).*
BB22　Edition numbers 19, 20, 22, 23 and 25 to 54 . . . . £225

1922 (June). *Experimental booklet as Edition numbers 12 and 13 bound in blue covers as Type BB22, containing pages of six stamps: 24 × 1½d.* (No. 362).
BB23　Edition numbers 21 or 24 . . . . £275

1924 (Feb). *Scarlet cover printed in black as Type BB22, but containing stamps with Block Cypher wmk, printed by Waterlow & Sons (Nos. 418/20).*
BB24　Edition numbers 55 to 167 & 173 to 273 . . . . 75·00

1929 (May). *Postal Union Congress issue. Cover of special design as Type BB13 printed in red on buff as before but containing stamps of the P.U.C. issue (Nos. 434/6).*
BB25　Edition numbers 168 to 172 . . . . £225

1934 (Mar). *Scarlet cover printed in black as Type BB22, but containing stamps with the Block Cypher wmk printed by Harrison & Sons (Nos. 418/20).*
BB26　Edition numbers 274 to 288 . . . . £125

1935 (May). *Silver Jubilee issue. Larger size cover printed in red on buff as Type BB16 and containing pages of four stamps: 20 × 1½d., 4 × 1d. and 4 × ½d. (Nos. 453/5).*
BB28　Edition numbers 294 to 297 . . . . 45·00

1935 (July). *As No. BB26, but containing stamps of the photogravure issue (Nos. 439/41).*
BB29　Edition numbers 289 to 293 & 298 to 319 . . . . £100

3s. 6d. Booklets

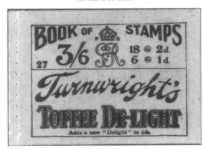

Type BB30

1920 (July). *Orange cover printed in black as Type BB30, containing pages of six stamps: 18 × 2d. and 6 × 1d. (Nos. 357, 368).*
BB30　Edition numbers 27 to 32 . . . . £300

Type BB31

1921 (Jan). *Orange-red cover printed in black as Type BB31, as before but make-up changed to include stamps of 1912–22 issue with the Simple Cypher wmk: 12 × 2d., 6 × 1½d., 6 × 1d. and 6 × ½d. (Nos. 351, 357, 362, 368 or 370).*
BB31   Edition numbers 1 to 11, 14 to 18, 33, 34, 36 & 38 .... £275

5s. Booklets

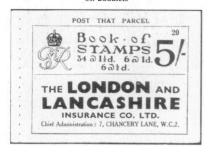

Type BB33

1931 (Aug). *Green cover printed in black as Type BB33. Pages of six stamps: 34 × 1½d., 6 × 1d. and 6 × ½d. The first 1½d. pane completed by two se-tenant advertisments. Printed by Waterlow & Sons on paper with Block Cypher wmk (Nos. 418/20).*
BB33   Edition number 1 .... £1100

1932 (June). *As before, but buff cover printed in black.*
BB34   Edition numbers 2 to 6 .... £350

1934 (July). *As before, but containing stamps with Block Cypher wmk printed by Harrison & Sons (Nos. 418/20).*
BB35   Edition numbers 7 or 8 .... £325

1935 (Feb). *As before, but containing stamps of the photogravure issue with se-tenant advertisments printed in brown (Nos. 439/41).*
BB36   Edition number 9 .... £800

1935 (July). *As before, but containing stamps of the photogravure issue with se-tenant advertisments printed in black (Nos. 439/41).*
BB37   Edition numbers 10 to 15 .... £100

KING EDWARD VIII

6d. Booklet

1936. *Buff unglazed cover without inscription containing 4 × 1½d. stamps, in panes of two (No. 459).*
BC1 .... 30·00

2s. Booklet

1936 (Oct). *As No. BB17. except for the K.E.VIII cypher on the cover and containing Nos. 457/9.*
BC2   Edition numbers 354 to 385 .... 50·00

3s. Booklet

1936 (Nov). *As No. BB29, except for the K.E.VIII cypher on the cover but without "P" and "O" on either side of the crown, and containing Nos. 457/9.*
BC3   Edition numbers 320 to 332 .... 40·00

5s. Booklet

1937 (Mar). *As No. BB37, but with the K.E.VIII cypher on the cover and containing Nos. 457/9.*
BC4   Edition numbers 16 or 17 .... £100

KING GEORGE VI

6d. Booklets

1938 (Jan). *As No. BC1, but containing stamps in the original dark colours. Buff cover without inscription (No. 464).*
BD1 .... 18·00

1938 (Feb). *As before, but pink unprinted cover and make-up changed to contain 2 × 1½d., 2 × 1d. and 2 × ½d. in the original dark colours (Nos. 462/4).*
BD2 .... 90·00

1940 (June). *Pale green unprinted cover and make-up changed to include two panes of four stamps with wmk sideways. Stamps in original dark colours with binding margin either at the top or bottom of the pane: 4 × 1d., 4 × ½d. (Nos. 462a/3a).*
BD3 .... 60·00

1s. Booklets

1947 (Dec). *Cream cover, unglazed and without inscription containing panes of two stamps in pale shades, all with wmk normal. Panes of two stamps: 4 × ½d., 4 × 1d. and 4 × 1½d. (Nos. 485/7).*
BD4 .... 12·00

1951 (May). *As before, but containing stamps in changed colours (Nos. 503/5).*
BD5 .... 10·00

1948. *Cream cover as before, but make-up changed to contain 4 × 1½d., 4 × 1d. and 4 × ½d. in panes of four of the pale shades with wmk normal (Nos. 485/7).*
BD6 .... £2500

1951 (May). *As before, but stamps in new colours all wmk normal, margins at either top or at the bottom. (Nos. 503/5).*
BD7 .... 10·00

Type BD8

1952 (Dec). *Cream cover printed in black as Type BD8. Make-up as before but with wmk either upright or inverted and margins only at the top (Nos. 503/5).*
BD8 .... 10·00

Type BD10

1954. *As before but cover showing GPO emblem with St. Edward's crown and oval frame as Type BD10 (Nos. 503/5).*
BD10 .... 14·00

2s. Booklets

1937 (Aug). *Blue cover printed in black as Type BB11, but with K.G.VI cypher on the cover and containing stamps in the original dark colours. Panes of six stamps: 10 × 1½d., 6 × 1d. and 6 × ½d. The first 1½d. pane completed by two se-tenant advertisements. (Nos. 462/4).*
BD11 Edition numbers 386 to 412 .... £175

Type BD12

1938 (April). *Blue cover printed in black as Type BD12 (Nos. 462/4).*
BD12 Edition numbers 413 to 508 .... £175

2s. 6d. Booklets

Type BD13

1940 (June). *Scarlet cover printed in black as Type BD13, containing panes of six stamps in original dark colours: 6 × 2½d., 6 × 2d. and 6 × ½d. (Nos. 462, 465/6).*
BD13 Edition numbers 1 to 7 .... £400

1940 (Sept). *As before, but blue cover printed in black as Type BD13.*
BD14 Edition numbers 8 to 13 .... £400

Type BD15

1940 (Oct). *As before, but with green cover printed in black as Type BD15 (Nos. 462, 465/6).*
BD15 Edition numbers 14 to 94 .... £175

1942 (Mar). *As before, but containing stamps in pale shades (Nos. 485, 488/9).*
BD16 Edition numbers 95 to 214 .... £225

Type A
Circular GPO Cypher

1943 (Aug). *As before, but green cover printed in black as Type A, with different contents details (Nos. 485, 488/9).*
BD18   Edition dates August 1943 to February 1951 .... 25·00

(1) AUG 1943 .... 30·00	(46) MAY 1947 .... 40·00
(2) SEPT 1943 .... 40·00	(47) JUNE 1947 .... 40·00
(3) OCT 1943 .... 40·00	(48) JULY 1947 .... 40·00
(4) NOV 1943 .... 40·00	(49) AUG 1947 .... 40·00
(5) DEC 1943 .... 40·00	(50) SEPT 1947 .... 40·00
(6) JAN 1944 .... 40·00	(51) OCT 1947 .... 40·00
(7) FEB 1944 .... 40·00	(52) NOV 1947 .... 40·00
(8) MAR 1944 .... 40·00	(53) DEC 1947 .... 40·00
(9) APR 1944 .... 40·00	(54) JAN 1948 .... 35·00
(10) MAY 1944 .... 40·00	(55) FEB 1948 .... 35·00
(11) JUNE 1944 .... 40·00	(56) MAR 1948 .... 35·00
(12) JULY 1944 .... 40·00	(57) APR 1948 .... 35·00
(13) AUG 1944 .... 40·00	(58) MAY 1948 .... 35·00
(14) SEPT 1944 .... 40·00	(59) JUNE 1948 .... 35·00
(15) OCT 1944 .... 40·00	(60) JULY 1948 .... 35·00
(16) NOV 1944 .... 40·00	(61) AUG 1948 .... 35·00
(17) DEC 1944 .... 40·00	(62) SEPT 1948 .... 35·00
(18) JAN 1945 .... 40·00	(63) OCT 1948 .... 35·00
(19) FEB 1945 .... 40·00	(64) NOV 1948 .... 35·00
(20) MAR 1945 .... 40·00	(65) DEC 1948 .... 35·00
(21) APR 1945 .... 40·00	(66) JAN 1949 .... 35·00
(22) MAY 1945 .... 40·00	(67) FEB 1949 .... 35·00
(23) JUNE 1945 .... 40·00	(68) MAR 1949 .... 35·00
(24) JULY 1945 .... 40·00	(69) APR 1949 .... 35·00
(25) AUG 1945 .... 40·00	(70) MAY 1949 .... 35·00
(26) SEPT 1945 .... 40·00	(71) JUNE 1949 .... 35·00
(27) OCT 1945 .... 40·00	(72) JULY 1949 .... 35·00
(28) NOV 1945 .... 40·00	(73) AUG 1949 .... 35·00
(29) DEC 1945 .... 40·00	(74) OCT 1949 .... 35·00
(30) JAN 1946 .... 40·00	(75) NOV 1949 .... 35·00
(31) FEB 1946 .... 40·00	(76) DEC 1949 .... 35·00
(32) MAR 1946 .... 40·00	(77) JAN 1950 .... 25·00
(33) APR 1946 .... 40·00	(78) FEB 1950 .... 25·00
(34) MAY 1946 .... 40·00	(79) MAR 1950 .... 25·00
(35) JUNE 1946 .... 40·00	(80) APR 1950 .... 25·00
(36) JULY 1946 .... 40·00	(81) MAY 1950 .... 25·00
(37) AUG 1946 .... 40·00	(82) JUNE 1950 .... 25·00
(38) SEPT 1946 .... 40·00	(83) JULY 1950 .... 25·00
(39) OCT 1946 .... 40·00	(84) AUG 1950 .... 25·00
(40) NOV 1946 .... 40·00	(85) SEPT 1950 .... 25·00
(41) DEC 1946 .... 40·00	(86) OCT 1950 .... 25·00
(42) JAN 1947 .... 40·00	(87) NOV 1950 .... 25·00
(43) FEB 1947 .... 40·00	(88) DEC 1950 .... 25·00
(44) MAR 1947 .... 40·00	(89) JAN 1951 .... 25·00
(45) APR 1947 .... 40·00	(90) FEB 1951 .... 25·00

1951 (May). *As before, but containing stamps in the new colours (Nos. 503, 506/7).*
BD19   Edition dates May 1951 to February 1952 .... 17·00

(1) MAY 1951 .... 17·00	(6) OCT 1951 .... 17·00
(2) JUNE 1951 .... 18·00	(7) NOV 1951 .... 17·00
(3) JULY 1951 .... 17·00	(8) DEC 1951 .... 17·00
(4) AUG 1951 .... 18·00	(9) JAN 1952 .... 17·00
(5) SEPT 1951 .... 17·00	(10) FEB 1952 .... 17·00

1952 (March). *As before, but make-up changed to contain: 6 × 2½d., 6 × 1½d., 3 × 1d. and 6 × ½d. The 1d. pane was completed by three perforated labels in the lower row inscribed "MINIMUM INLAND PRINTED PAPER RATE 1½d." (Nos. 503/5, 507).*
BD20   Edition dates March 1952 to May 1953 .... 17·00

(1) MAR 1952 .... 17·00	(9) NOV 1952 .... 17·00
(2) APR 1952 .... 18·00	(10) DEC 1952 .... 17·00
(3) MAY 1952 .... 17·00	(11) JAN 1953 .... 17·00
(4) JUNE 1952 .... 18·00	(12) FEB 1953 .... 17·00
(5) JULY 1952 .... 17·00	(13) MAR 1953 .... 17·00
(6) AUG 1952 .... 17·00	(14) APR 1953 .... 17·00
(7) SEPT 1952 .... 17·00	(15) MAY 1953 .... 18·00
(8) OCT 1952 .... 17·00		

3s. Booklets

1937 (Aug). *Scarlet cover printed in black as Type BB22 (without "P" and "O" except for K.G.VI cypher on the cover and containing stamps in the original dark colours (Nos. 462/4).*
BD21   Edition numbers 333 to 343 .... £275

1938 (April). *As before, but scarlet cover printed in black as Type BD12 (Nos. 462/4).*
BD22   Edition numbers 344 to 377 .... £275

5s. Booklets

1937 (Aug). *Buff cover printed in black as Type BB33, containing stamps of the new reign in the original dark colours. Pages of six stamps: 34 × 1½d., 6 × 1d. and 6 × ½d. The first 1½d. pane completed by two se-tenant advertisements. (Nos. 462/4).*
BD23   Edition numbers 18 to 20 .... £325

Type BD24

1938 (May). *As before, but with redesigned front cover showing GPO emblem as Type BD24 instead of royal cypher.*
BD24   Edition numbers 21 to 29 .... £275

1940 (July).   *As before, but make-up changed to contain:* $18 \times 2\frac{1}{2}d.$, $6 \times 2d.$ *and* $6 \times \frac{1}{2}d.$ *in the original dark colours (Nos. 462, 465/6).*
BD25   Edition numbers 1 to 16 (part) £300

1942 (Mar).   *As before, but containing stamps in pale shades (Nos. 485, 488/9).*
BD26   Edition numbers 16 (part) to 36 .... £300

1943 (Sept).   *As before, but buff cover printed in black as Type A (see No. BD18, 2s. 6d.) (Nos. 485, 488/9).*
BD28   Edition dates September 1943 to December 1950 ..... 50·00

(1) SEPT 1943 .... 60·00		(26) JUNE 1947 .... 60·00
(2) OCT 1943 .... 60·00		(27) AUG 1947 .... 60·00
(3) NOV 1943 .... 60·00		(28) OCT 1947 .... 60·00
(4) DEC 1943 .... 60·00		(29) DEC 1947 .... 60·00
(5) FEB 1944 .... 60·00		(30) FEB 1948 .... 60·00
(6) MAR 1944 .... 60·00		(31) APR 1948 .... 60·00
(7) AUG 1944 .... 60·00		(32) JUNE 1948 .... 60·00
(8) OCT 1944 .... 60·00		(33) JULY 1948 .... 60·00
(9) NOV 1944 .... 60·00		(34) AUG 1948 .... 60·00
(10) JAN 1945 .... 60·00		(35) OCT 1948 .... 60·00
(11) FEB 1945 .... 60·00		(36) DEC 1948 .... 60·00
(12) APR 1945 .... 60·00		(37) FEB 1949 .... 60·00
(13) JUNE 1945 .... 60·00		(38) APR 1949 .... 60·00
(14) AUG 1945 .... 60·00		(39) JUNE 1949 .... 60·00
(15) OCT 1945 .... 60·00		(40) AUG 1949 .... 60·00
(16) DEC 1945 .... 60·00		(41) SEPT 1949 .... 60·00
(17) JAN 1946 .... 60·00		(42) OCT 1949 .... 60·00
(18) MAR 1946 .... 60·00		(43) DEC 1949 .... 60·00
(19) MAY 1946 .... 60·00		(44) FEB 1950 .... 50·00
(20) JUNE 1946 .... 60·00		(45) APR 1950 .... 50·00
(21) AUG 1946 .... 60·00		(46) JUNE 1950 .... 50·00
(22) OCT 1946 .... 60·00		(47) AUG 1950 .... 50·00
(23) DEC 1946 .... 60·00		(48) OCT 1950 .... 50·00
(24) FEB 1947 .... 60·00		(49) DEC 1950 .... 50·00
(25) APR 1947 .... 60·00		

Type BD29

1944 (Apr).   *As before, but buff cover printed in black as Type BD29 (Nos. 485, 488/9).*
BD29   Edition dates April or June 1944 .... £375

(1) APR 1944 .... £375   (2) JUNE 1944 .... £375

1951 (May).   *As before, but buff cover changed back to Type A (see No. BD18, 2s. 6d.) and containing stamps in the new colours (Nos. 503, 506/7).*
BD30   Edition dates May 1951 to January 1952 .... 17·00

(1) MAY 1951 .... 17·00   (4) NOV 1951 .... 17·00
(2) JULY 1951 .... 17·00   (5) JAN 1952 .... 17·00
(3) SEPT 1951 .... 17·00

1952 (Mar).   *As before, make-up changed to contain:* $18 \times 2\frac{1}{2}d.$, $6 \times 1\frac{1}{2}d.$, $3 \times 1d.$ *and* $6 \times \frac{1}{2}d.$ *The 1d. pane was completed by three perforated labels in the lower row inscribed* "MINIMUM INLAND PRINTED PAPER RATE $1\frac{1}{2}d.$" *(Nos. 503/5, 507).*
BD31   Edition dates March to November 1952 .... 17·00

(1) MAR 1952 .... 17·00   (4) SEPT 1952 .... 17·00
(2) MAY 1952 .... 17·00   (5) NOV 1952 .... 17·00
(3) JULY 1952 .... 17·00

1953 (Jan).   *As before, but make-up changed again to include the 2d. value and containing:* $12 \times 2\frac{1}{2}d.$, $6 \times 2d.$, $6 \times 1\frac{1}{2}d.$, $6 \times 1d.$ *and* $6 \times \frac{1}{2}d.$ *(Nos. 503/7).*
BD32   Edition dates January or March 1953 .... 27·00

(1) JAN 1953 .... 27·00   (2) MAR 1953 .... 27·00

QUEEN ELIZABETH II

I. £.s.d. Booklets, 1953–70.

TYPES OF BOOKLET COVER WITH GPO CYPHER

Type A
Circular GPO Cypher
(See illustration above No. BD18)

Type B
Oval Type GPO Cypher

Type C
New GPO Cypher (small)

Type D
New GPO Cypher (large)

1s. Booklets

1953 (2 Sept)–**59**. *I. White unprinted cover. Pages of two stamps:*
4 × 1½d., 4 × 1d., 4 × ½d. For use in experimental "D" machines.

A. *Wmk Tudor Crown (Nos. 515/17)*

E1   No date .... 2·25

B. *Wmk St. Edward's Crown (Nos. 540/2)*

E2   No date (11.57) .... 5·00

II. White printed cover as Type B. Pages of four stamps: 4 × 1½d., 4 × 1d.,
4 × ½d. For use in "E" machines.

A. *Wmk Tudor Crown (Nos. 515/17)*

K1   No date (22.7.54) .... 3·50

B. *Wmk St. Edward's Crown (Nos. 540/2)*

K2   No date (5.7.56) .... 2·50

C. *Wmk Crowns (Nos. 570/2)*

K3   No date (13.8.59) .... 2·50

2s. Booklets

1959 (22 Apr)–**65**.   *Pages of four stamps: 4 × 3d., 4 × 1½d., 4 × 1d.,*
4 × ½d.

I. Salmon cover as Type B. Wmk. St. Edward's Crown (Nos. 540/2 and
545).

N1   No date .... 3·50

II. Salmon cover as Type C. Wmk Crowns (Nos. 570/2 and 575).

N2   No date (2.11.60) .... 3·50

III. Lemon cover as Type C. Wmk Crowns (Nos. 570/2 and 575).

N3   No date (2.61) .... 3·50

IV. Lemon cover as Type C. Wmk Crowns (sideways) (Nos. 570a, 571a,
572b, 575a) or phosphor (Nos. 610a, 611a, 612a, 615b).

N 4	APR 1961	15·00
	p. With phosphor bands	40·00
N 5	SEPT 1961	24·00
N 6	JAN 1962	24·00
N 7	APR 1962	24·00
N 8	JULY 1962	24·00
	p. With phosphor bands	55·00
N 9	NOV 1962	24·00
	p. With phosphor bands	40·00
N10	JAN 1963	24·00
	p. With phosphor bands	60·00
N11	MAR 1963	24·00

N12	JUNE 1963	24·00
	p. With phosphor bands	40·00
N13	AUG 1963	24·00
	p. With phosphor bands	40·00
N14	OCT 1963	24·00
	p. With phosphor bands	65·00
N15	FEB 1964	24·00
	p. With phosphor bands	38·00
N16	JUNE 1964	24·00
	p. With phosphor bands	55·00
N17	AUG 1964	24·00
	p. With phosphor bands	55·00
N18	OCT 1964	26·00
	p. With phosphor bands	40·00
N19	DEC 1964	26·00
	p. With phosphor bands	40·00
N20	APR 1965	22·00
	p. With phosphor bands	38·00

1965 (16 Aug)–**67**.   *New Composition. Pages of four stamps: 4 × 4d. and*
pane of 2 × 1d. and 2 × 3d. arranged se-tenant horiz.

Orange-yellow cover as Type C printed in black. Wmk Crowns
(sideways) (Nos. 571a, 575a and 576ab) or phosphor (Nos. 611a,
615d (one side phosphor band) and 616ab).

N21	JULY 1965	1·50
	p. With phosphor bands	14·00
N22	OCT 1965	1·50
	p. With phosphor bands	8·50
N23	JAN 1966	2·50
	p. With phosphor bands	12·00
N24	APR 1966	2·50
	p. With phosphor bands	6·00
N25	JULY 1966	2·50
	p. With phosphor bands	30·00
N26	OCT 1966	2·10
	p. With phosphor bands	6·00
N27	JAN 1967	2·25
	p. With phosphor bands	5·00
N28p	APR 1967. With phosphor bands	5·00
N29p	JULY 1967. With phosphor bands	4·00
N30p	OCT 1967. With phosphor bands	4·00

In the *se-tenant* pane the 3d. appears at left or right to facilitate the
application of phosphor bands.

The following illustration shows how the *se-tenant* stamps with one
phosphor band on 3d. were printed and the arrows indicate where the
guillotine fell. The result gives 1d. stamps with two bands and the 3d.
stamps with one band either at left or right.

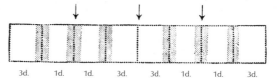

3d.   1d.   1d.   3d.   3d.   1d.   1d.   3d.

1967 (Nov)–**68**.   *Composition and cover as Nos. N21/30. Wmk Crowns*
(sideways) (Nos. 611a, 615b (two phosphor bands) and 616ab).

N31p	JAN 1968	2·25
N32p	MAR 1968	2·25

2s. Booklets with Machin type stamps

1968 (6 Apr–Aug).   *Orange-yellow cover as Type C. Pages of four*
stamps: 4 × 4d. and pane of 2 × 1d. and 2 × 3d. arranged se-tenant
horiz. PVA gum (Nos. 724, 730, 731Ev).

NP27	MAY 1968	70
NP28	JULY 1968	70
NP29	AUG 1968	2·00

1968 (16 Sept)–**70**. *Grey cover as Type C. New Composition. 4d. stamps only comprising page of 4 × 4d. with two phosphor bands (No. 731Ev) and page of 2 × 4d. with one centre phosphor band (No. 732) se-tenant with two printed labels.*

NP30	SEPT 1968	55
NP31	JAN 1969	£100

Same composition but all six 4d. stamps have one centre phosphor band (No. 732).

NP31a	SEPT 1968	£325
NP32	NOV 1968	55
NP33	JAN 1969	55

Same composition but change to 4d. bright vermilion with one centre phosphor band (No. 733).

NP34	MAR 1969	90
NP35	MAY 1969	1·10
NP36	JULY 1969	1·40
NP37	SEPT 1969	1·25
NP38	NOV 1969	1·25
NP39	JAN 1970	1·25
NP40	MAR 1970	1·25
NP41	MAY 1970	1·25
NP42	JULY 1970	1·25
NP43	AUG 1970	1·25
NP44	OCT 1970	1·25
NP45	DEC 1970	1·25

2s. Booklets for Holiday Resorts

1963 (15 July)–**64**. *I. Lemon cover as Type C printed in red. New composition. Pages of four stamps: two of 4 × 2½d. and one of 3 × ½d. and 1 × 2½d. arranged se-tenant. Chalky paper. Wmk Crowns (Nos. 570k and 574k).*

NR1	No date, black stitching	2·50
	a. White stitching (3.9.63)	3·00

II. Lemon cover as Type C printed in red. Composition changed again. Pages of four stamps 2 × ½d. and 2 × 2½d. arranged sideways, vertically se-tenant. Wmk Crowns (sideways) (No. 570m × 4).

NR2	1964 (1.7.64)	1·10

2s. Booklet for Christmas Cards

1965 (6 Dec). *Orange-yellow cover as Type C printed in red. Two panes of 4 × 3d. arranged sideways. Wmk Crowns (sideways) (No. 575a).*

NX1	1965	55

2s. 6d. Booklets

Green cover. Pages of six stamps: 6 × 2½d., 6 × 1½d., 3 × 1d. (page completed by three perforated labels), 6 × ½d.

LABELS. The wording printed on the labels differs as follows:

"PPR" = "MINIMUM INLAND PRINTED PAPER RATE 1½d." Two types exist:
A. Printed in photogravure, 17 mm high.
B. Typographed, 15 mm high.
"Shorthand" = "SHORTHAND IN 1 WEEK" (covering all three labels).
"Post Early" = "PLEASE POST EARLY IN THE DAY".
"PAP" = "PACK YOUR PARCELS SECURELY" (1st label) "ADDRESS YOUR LETTERS CORRECTLY" (2nd label), "AND POST EARLY IN THE DAY" (3rd label).

1953–54. *Composite booklets containing stamps of King George VI and Queen Elizabeth II.*

A. *K.G.VI ½d. and 1d. (Nos. 503/4) and Q.E.II 1½d. and 2½d. (Nos. 517 and 519b). Cover as Type A. No interleaving pages.*

F 1	MAY 1953 (PPR 17 mm)	11·00
F 2	JUNE 1953 (PPR 17 mm)	12·00
F 3	JULY 1953 (PPR 17 mm)	15·00
F 4	AUG 1953 (PPR 17 mm)	13·00

B. *Same composition but with addition of two interleaving pages, one at each end. Cover as Type A.*

F 5	SEPT 1953 (PPR 17 mm)	75·00
F 6	SEPT 1953 (PPR 15 mm)	14·00

C. *Same composition and with interleaving pages but with cover as Type B.*

F 7	OCT 1953 (PPR 17 mm)	15·00
F 8	OCT 1953 (PPR 15 mm)	18·00
F 9	NOV 1953 (PPR 17 mm)	15·00
F10	NOV 1953 (PPR 15 mm)	70·00
F11	DEC 1953 (PPR 17 mm)	15·00
F12	JAN 1954 (Shorthand)	20·00
F13	FEB 1954 (Shorthand)	15·00

D. *New composition: K.G.VI 1d. (No. 504) and Q.E.II ½d., 1½d. and 2½d. (Nos. 515, 517 and 519b).*

F14	MAR 1954 (PPR 17 mm)	£350

1954–57. *Booklets containing only Queen Elizabeth II stamps. All covers as Type B.*

A. *Wmk Tudor Crown (Nos. 515/17 and 519b).*

F15	MAR 1954 (PPR 15 mm)	£150
F16	APR 1954 (Post Early)	15·00
F17	MAY 1954 (Post Early)	15·00
F18	JUNE 1954 (Post Early)	15·00
F19	JULY 1954 (Post Early)	16·00
F20	AUG 1954 (Post Early)	18·00
F21	SEPT 1954 (Post Early)	15·00
F22	OCT 1954 (Post Early)	15·00
F23	NOV 1954 (Post Early)	15·00
F24	DEC 1954 (Post Early)	15·00

B. *Same composition but with interleaving pages between each pane of stamps.*

F25	JAN 1955 (Post Early)	18·00
F26	JAN 1955 (PAP)	45·00
F27	FEB 1955 (PAP)	16·00
F28	MAR 1955 (PAP)	15·00
F29	APR 1955 (PAP)	17·00
F30	MAY 1955 (PAP)	17·00
F31	JUNE 1955 (PAP)	16·00
F32	JULY 1955 (PAP)	17·00
F33	AUG 1955 (PAP)	16·00

C. *Mixed watermarks. Wmk Tudor Crown (Nos. 515/17 and 519b) and wmk St. Edward's Crown (Nos. 540/2 and 544b) in various combinations.*

F34	SEPT 1955 (PAP)	*From* 15·00

2s. 6d. booklets dated AUGUST, OCTOBER, NOVEMBER and DECEMBER 1955, JANUARY, MAY and JUNE 1956 exist both as listed and with the two watermarks mixed. There are so many different combinations that we do not list them separately, but when in stock selections can be submitted. The SEPTEMBER 1955 booklet (No. F34) only exists in composite form.

D. *Wmk St. Edward's Crown (Nos. 540/2 and 544b).*

F35	OCT 1955 (PAP)	15·00
F36	NOV 1955 (PAP)	15·00
F37	DEC 1955 (PAP)	15·00

F38	JAN 1956 (PAP)	12·00
F39	FEB 1956 (PAP)	15·00
F40	MAR 1956 (PAP)	15·00
F41	APR 1956 (PAP)	15·00
F42	MAY 1956 (PAP)	15·00
F43	JUNE 1956 (PAP)	15·00
F44	JULY 1956 (PAP)	15·00
F45	AUG 1956 (PAP)	15·00
F46	SEPT 1956 (PAP)	15·00
F47	OCT 1956 (PAP)	15·00
F48	NOV 1956 (PAP)	14·00
F49	DEC 1956 (PAP)	14·00
F50	JAN 1957 (PAP)	16·00
F51	FEB 1957 (PAP)	15·00
F52	MAR 1957 (PAP)	12·00

E. Same wmk but new composition. Pages of six stamps: 6 × 2½d. (No. 544b), 6 × 2d. (No. 543b) and 6 × ½d. (No. 540).

F53	APR 1957	13·00
F54	MAY 1957	15·00
F55	JUNE 1957	13·00
F56	JULY 1957	13·00
F57	AUG 1957	11·00
F58	SEPT 1957	12·00
F59	OCT 1957	11·00
F60	NOV 1957	10·00
F61	DEC 1957	13·00

3s. Booklets

1958–65. *Pages of six stamps: 6 × 3d., 6 × 1½d., 6 × 1d., 6 × ½d.*

I. Red cover as Type B.
A. Wmk St. Edward's Crown (Nos. 540/2 and 545).

M1	JAN 1958	10·00
M2	FEB 1958	10·00
M3	MAR 1958	10·00
M4	APR 1958	10·00
M5	MAY 1958	10·00
M6	JUNE 1958	10·00
M7	JULY 1958	10·00
M8	AUG 1958	10·00
M9	NOV 1958	10·00

The 3s. booklets dated NOVEMBER 1958, DECEMBER 1958 and JANUARY 1959 exist both as listed and with mixed St. Edward's Crown and Crowns wmks.

B. Wmk Crowns (Nos. 570/2 and 575) or graphite lines (Nos. 587/9 and 592).

M10	DEC 1958	14·00
M11	JAN 1959	13·00
M12	FEB 1959	13·00
M13	AUG 1959	13·00
	g. With graphite lines	£120
M14	SEPT 1959	13·00
	g. With graphite lines	£140

II. Brick-red cover as Type C. Wmk Crowns (Nos. 570/2 and 575), graphite lines (Nos. 587/9 and 592) or phosphor (Nos. 610/12 and 615).

M15	OCT 1959	13·00
	g. With graphite lines	£120
M16	NOV 1959	13·00
M17	DEC 1959	13·00
M18	JAN 1960	13·00
M19	FEB 1960	14·00
	g. With graphite lines	£140
M20	MAR 1960	13·00
	g. With graphite lines	£150
M21	APR 1960	14·00
	g. With graphite lines	£140
M22	MAY 1960	14·00

M23	JUNE 1960	14·00
M24	JULY 1960	14·00
M25	AUG 1960	14·00
	p. With phosphor bands	30·00
M26	SEPT 1960	14·00
M27	OCT 1960	14·00
M28	NOV 1960	14·00
	p. With phosphor bands	32·00

III. Brick-red cover as Type D. Wmk Crowns (Nos. 570/2 and 575) or phosphor (Nos. 610/12 and 615).

M29	DEC 1940	14·00
	p. With phosphor bands	35·00
M30	JAN 1961	14·00
M31	FEB 1961	14·00
M32	MAR 1961	14·00
M33	APR 1961	14·00
	p. With phosphor bands	25·00
M34	MAY 1961	14·00
M35	JUNE 1961	14·00
M36	JULY 1961	14·00
	p. With phosphor bands	25·00
M37	AUG 1961	14·00
	p. With phosphor bands	25·00
M38	SEPT 1961	14·00
	p. With phosphor bands	30·00
M39	OCT 1961	14·00
	p. With phosphor bands	25·00
M40	NOV 1961	14·00
M41	DEC 1961	14·00
M42	JAN 1962	14·00
M43	FEB 1962	14·00
	p. With phosphor bands	25·00
M44	MAR 1962	14·00
	p. With phosphor bands	25·00
M45	APR 1962	14·00
	p. With phosphor bands	25·00
M46	MAY 1962	14·00
	p. With phosphor bands	25·00
M47	JUNE 1962	16·00
	p. With phosphor bands	25·00
M48	JULY 1962	14·00
M49	AUG 1962	14·00
	p. With phosphor bands	25·00
M50	SEPT 1962	14·00
	p. With phosphor bands	25·00
M51	OCT 1962	14·00
	p. With phosphor bands	25·00
M52	NOV 1962	14·00
	p. With phosphor bands	25·00
M53	DEC 1962	14·00
	p. With phosphor bands	25·00
M54	JAN 1963	16·00
M55	FEB 1963	14·00
	p. With phosphor bands	25·00
M56	MAR 1963	14·00
	p. With phosphor bands	25·00
M57	APR 1963	14·00
	p. With phosphor bands	25·00
M58	MAY 1963	14·00
	p. With phosphor bands	80·00
M59	JUNE 1963	14·00
	p. With phosphor bands	23·00
M60	JULY 1963	14·00
	p. With phosphor bands	25·00
M61	AUG 1963	14·00
	p. With phosphor bands	25·00
M62	SEPT 1963	14·00
M63	OCT 1963	14·00
M64	NOV 1963	14·00
	p. With phosphor bands	23·00

M65	DEC 1963	14·00
	p. With phosphor bands	45·00
M66	JAN 1964	16·00
	p. With phosphor bands	25·00
M67	MAR 1964	14·00
	p. With phosphor bands	25·00
M68	MAY 1964	14·00
	p. With phosphor bands	35·00
M69	JULY 1964	14·00
	p. With phosphor bands	25·00
M70	SEPT 1964	14·00
	p. With phosphor bands	25·00
M71	NOV 1964	14·00
	p. With phosphor bands	23·00
M72	JAN 1965	14·00
	p. With phosphor bands	23·00
M73	MAR 1965	10·00
	p. With phosphor bands	23·00
M74	MAY 1965	10·00
	p. With phosphor bands	25·00

3s. 9d. Booklets

1953–57. *Red cover as Type B. Pages of six stamps: $18 \times 2\frac{1}{2}d$.*
A. *Wmk Tudor Crown (No. 519b)*

G 1	NOV 1953	14·00
G 2	JAN 1954	15·00
G 3	MAR 1954	14·00
G 4	DEC 1954	14·00
G 5	FEB 1955	14·00
G 6	APR 1955	15·00
G 7	JUNE 1955	15·00
G 8	AUG 1955	15·00
G 9	OCT 1955	14·00
G10	DEC 1955	16·00

3s. 9d. booklets dated OCTOBER and DECEMBER 1955 exist both as listed and with the two wkms mixed.

B. *Wmk St. Edward's Crown (No. 544b). Same composition but with interleaving pages between each pane of stamps.*

G12	FEB 1956	8·00
G13	APR 1956	8·00
G14	JUNE 1956	8·00
G15	AUG 1956	8·00
G16	OCT 1956	8·00
G17	DEC 1956	8·00
G18	FEB 1957	8·00
G19	APR 1957	8·00
G20	JUNE 1957	6·00
G21	AUG 1957	14·00

4s. 6d. Booklets

1957–65. *Pages of six stamps: $18 \times 3d$.*

I. *Purple cover as Type B.*
A. *Wmk St. Edward's Crown (No. 545).*

L1	OCT 1957	8·00
L2	DEC 1957	8·00
L3	FEB 1958	10·00
L4	APR 1958	8·00
L5	JUNE 1958	10·00
L6	OCT 1958	10·00
L7	DEC 1958	10·00

B. *Wmk Crowns (No. 575).*

L8	DEC 1958	32·00

II. *Purple cover as Type C. Wmk Crowns (No. 575) or graphite lines (No. 592).*

L 9	FEB 1959	11·00
L10	JUNE 1959	11·00
L11	AUG 1959	11·00
	g. With graphite lines	10·00
L12	OCT 1959	11·00
L13	DEC 1959	11·00

III. *Violet cover as Type C. Wmk Crowns (No. 575), graphite lines (No. 592) or phosphor (No. 615).*

L14	FEB 1959	12·00
L15	APR 1959	11·00
	g. With graphite lines	10·00
L16	JUNE 1959	11·00
	g. With graphite lines	10·00
L17	DEC 1959	10·00
L18	FEB 1960	12·50
	g. With graphite lines	11·00
L19	APR 1960	12·50
	g. With graphite lines	11·00
L20	JUNE 1960	12·50
L21	AUG 1960	13·00
	p. With phosphor bands	24·00
L22	OCT 1960	14·00

IV. *Violet cover as Type D. Wmk Crowns (No. 575) or phosphor (No. 615).*

L23	DEC 1960	15·00
L24	FEB 1961	16·00
	p. With phosphor bands	18·00
L25	APR 1961	14·00
	p. With phosphor bands	18·00
L26	JUNE 1961	14·00
L27	AUG 1961	14·00
	p. With phosphor bands	18·00
L28	OCT 1961	14·00
	p. With phosphor bands	18·00
L29	DEC 1961	14·00
L30	FEB 1962	14·00
	p. With phosphor bands	18·00
L31	APR 1962	15·00
	p. With phosphor bands	18·00
L32	JUNE 1962	15·00
	p. With phosphor bands	26·00
L33	AUG 1962	15·00
	p. With phosphor bands	26·00
L34	OCT 1962	15·00
	p. With phosphor bands	90·00
L35	DEC 1962	15·00
	p. With phosphor bands	18·00
L36	FEB 1963	15·00
	p. With phosphor bands	18·00
L37	APR 1963	15·00
	p. With phosphor bands	18·00
L38	JUNE 1963	15·00
	p. With phosphor bands	20·00
L39	AUG 1963	15·00
	p. With phosphor bands	18·00
L40	OCT 1963	15·00
	p. With phosphor bands	18·00
L41	NOV 1963	15·00
	p. With phosphor bands	18·00
L42	DEC 1963	16·00
	p. With phosphor bands	80·00
L43	JAN 1964	15·00
L44	FEB 1964	15·00
	p. With phosphor bands	20·00
L45	MAR 1964	15·00
	p. With phosphor bands	40·00

L46	APR 1964	20·00
	p. With phosphor bands	18·00
L47	MAY 1964	15·00
	p. With phosphor bands	18·00
L48	JUNE 1964	15·00
	p. With phosphor bands	18·00
L49	JULY 1964	15·00
	p. With phosphor bands	18·00
L50	AUG 1964	20·00
	p. With phosphor bands	18·00
L51	SEPT 1964	15·00
	p. With phosphor bands	18·00
L52	OCT 1964	15·00
	p. With phosphor bands	20·00
L53	NOV 1964	15·00
	p. With phosphor bands	18·00
L54	DEC 1964	12·00
	p. With phosphor bands	18·00
L55	JAN 1965	12·00
	p. With phosphor bands	18·00
L56	FEB 1965	12·00
	p. With phosphor bands	18·00
L57	MAR 1965	12·00
	p. With phosphor bands	£175
L58	APR 1965	8·00

1965 (26 July)–**67.** *New composition. Pages of six stamps:* 12 × 4d.,
6 × 1d. *Slate-blue cover as Type D. Wmk Crowns (Nos. 571 and 576a)
or phosphor (Nos. 611 and 616a).*

L59	JULY 1965	8·00
	p. With phosphor bands	15·00
L60	SEPT 1965	8·00
	p. With phosphor bands	15·00
L61	NOV 1965	7·50
	p. With phosphor bands	15·00
L62	JAN 1966	8·00
	p. With phosphor bands	15·00
L63	MAR 1966	8·00
	p. With phosphor bands	7·00
L64	JAN 1967	7·50
	p. With phosphor bands	7·00
L65	MAR 1967	15·00
	p. With phosphor bands	8·00
L66p	MAY 1967. With phosphor bands	7·00
L67p	JULY 1967. With phosphor bands	7·00
L68p	SEPT 1967. With phosphor bands	6·00
L69p	NOV 1967. With phosphor bands	5·50
L70p	JAN 1968. With phosphor bands	5·50
L71p	MAR 1968. With phosphor bands	5·50

4s. 6d. Booklets with Machin type stamps

1968–70. *Slate-blue cover as Type D. Pages of six stamps:* 12 × 4d.,
6 × 1d. *PVA gum (Nos 724, 731Ev).*

LP45	MAY 1968	5·00

Type LP46
Ships Series with GPO Cypher

(Des S. Rose)

Blue cover as Type LP46. Ships Series. Composition as last.

LP46	JULY 1968 (*Cutty Sark*)	1·25

*Same composition but changed to 4d. with one centre phosphor band
(No. 732).*

LP47	SEPT 1968 (*Golden Hind*)	1·25
LP48	NOV 1968 (*Discovery*)	1·25

*Same composition but changed to 4d. bright vermilion with one centre
phosphor band (No. 733).*

LP49	JAN 1969 (*Queen Elizabeth 2*)	1·25
LP50	MAR 1969 (*Sirius*)	1·25
LP51	MAY 1969 (*Sirius*)	1·60
LP52	JULY 1969 (*Dreadnought*)	2·25
LP53	SEPT 1969 (*Dreadnought*)	3·25
LP54	NOV 1969 (*Mauretania*)	2·50
LP55	JAN 1970 (*Mauretania*)	2·50
LP56	MAR 1970 (*Victory*)	2·50
LP57	MAY 1970 (*Victory*)	5·00

Type LP58
Ships Series with Post Office
Corporation Crown Symbol

(Des S. Rose)

As last but cover changed to Type LP58.

LP58	AUG 1970 (*Sovereign of the Seas*)	3·00
LP59	OCT 1970 (*Sovereign of the Seas*)	4·75

5s. Booklets

1953–57. *Buff cover. Pages of six stamps.* 12 × 2½d., 6 × 2d., 6 × 1½d.,
6 × 1d., 6 × ½d.

*I. Composite booklets containing stamps of King George VI and Queen
Elizabeth II.*
A. K.G.VI ½d., 1d. and 2d. (Nos 503/4 and 506) and Q.E.II 1½d. and 2½d.
(Nos. 517 and 519b). *Cover as Type A. No interleaving pages.*

H1	MAY 1953	17·00
H2	JULY 1953	17·00

B. *Same composition but with addition of two interleaving pages, one at
each end. Cover as Type A.*

H3	SEPT 1953	18·00

C. Same composition and with interleaving pages but cover as Type B.

H4	NOV 1953	18·00
H5	JAN 1954	19·00

D. New composition: K.G.VI 1d. and 2d. (Nos. 504 and 506) and Q.E.II $\frac{1}{2}$d., 1$\frac{1}{2}$d. and 2$\frac{1}{2}$d. (Nos. 515, 517 and 519b).

H6	MAR 1954	£140

E. New composition: K.G.VI 2d. (No. 506) and Q.E.II $\frac{1}{2}$d., 1d., 1$\frac{1}{2}$d. and 2$\frac{1}{2}$d. (Nos. 515/17 and 519b).

H7	MAR 1954	65·00

II. Booklets containing only Queen Elizabeth II stamps. Buff cover as Type B. Two interleaving pages as before.
A. Wmk Tudor Crown (Nos. 515/18 and 519b).

H 8	MAR 1954	55·00
H 9	MAY 1954	18·00
H10	JULY 1954	27·00
H11	SEPT 1954	20·00
H12	NOV 1954	20·00

B. Same composition but with interleaving pages between each pane of stamps.

H13	JAN 1955	20·00
H14	MAR 1955	20·00
H15	MAY 1955	20·00
H16	JULY 1955	20·00

C. Wmk St. Edward's Crown (Nos. 540/3 and 544b).

H17	SEPT 1955	14·00
H18	NOV 1955	17·00
H19	JAN 1956	17·00
H20	MAR 1956	18·00
H21	MAY 1956	17·00
H22	JULY 1956	17·00
H23	SEPT 1956	17·00
H24	NOV 1956	20·00
H25	JAN 1957	22·00

5s. booklets dated SEPTEMBER and NOVEMBER 1955 and JANUARY 1956 exist both as listed and with the two watermarks mixed. There are so many different combinations that we do not list them separately, but when in stock selections can be submitted.

D. Same watermark. Introduction of 2d. light red-brown (No. 543b) in place of No. 543.

H26	JAN 1957	18·00
H27	MAR 1957	18·00
H28	MAY 1957	16·00
H29	JULY 1957	16·00
H30	SEPT 1957	16·00
H31	NOV 1957	16·00

1958–65. *E. New composition. Pages of six stamps: 12 × 3d. (No. 545), 6 × 2$\frac{1}{2}$d. (No. 544b), 6 × 1d. (No. 541), 6 × $\frac{1}{2}$d. (No. 540). Wmk St. Edward's Crown.*

H32	JAN 1958	16·00
H33	MAR 1958	16·00
H34	MAY 1958	14·00
H35	JULY 1958 (11.58)	12·00
H36	NOV 1958	12·00

5s. booklets dated JULY 1958, NOVEMBER 1958 AND JANUARY 1959 exist with mixed watermarks.

F. Blue cover as Type C. Wmk Crowns (Nos. 570/1, 574/5), graphite lines (Nos. 587/8 and 591/2) or phosphor (Nos. 610/11, 614 and 615).

H37	JAN 1959	14·00
H38	MAR 1959	16·00

H39	JULY 1959	16·00
	g. With graphite lines	60·00
H40	SEPT 1959	16·00
H41	NOV 1959	16·00
H42	JAN 1960	16·00
H43	MAR 1960	16·00
	g. With graphite lines	70·00
H44	MAY 1960	16·00
H45	JULY 1960	18·00
H46	SEPT 1960	18·00
	g. With graphite lines	70·00
	p. With phosphor bands	38·00
H47	NOV 1960	18·00

G. As last but blue cover as Type D. Same composition.
I. Phosphor has two bands on 2$\frac{1}{2}$d (No. 614).

H48	JAN 1961	19·00
H49	MAR 1961	19·00
	p. With phosphor bands	45·00
H50	MAY 1961	18·00
H51	JULY 1961	18·00
	p. With phosphor bands	45·00
H52	SEPT 1961	19·00
	p. With phosphor bands	45·00
H53	NOV 1961	18·00
H54	JAN 1962	18·00
	p. With phosphor bands	45·00

II. As last but phosphor has one band on 2$\frac{1}{2}$d (No. 614a).

H55	MAR 1962	18·00
	p. With phosphor bands	55·00
H56	MAY 1962	18·00
	p. With phosphor bands	45·00
H57	JULY 1962	18·00
	p. With phosphor bands	45·00
H58	SEPT 1962	18·00
	p. With phosphor bands	45·00
H59	NOV 1962	18·00
	p. With phosphor bands	45·00
H60	JAN 1963	18·00
	p. With phosphor bands	£250
H61	MAR 1963	18·00
	p. With phosphor bands	50·00
H62	MAY 1963	18·00
	p. With phosphor bands	45·00
H63	JULY 1963	18·00
	p. With phosphor bands	45·00
H64	SEPT 1963	18·00
	p. With phosphor bands	50·00
H65	NOV 1963	18·00
	p. With phosphor bands	45·00
H66	JAN 1964	18·00
	p. With phosphor bands	45·00
H67	MAR 1964	18·00
	p. With phosphor bands	45·00
H68	MAY 1964	18·00
	p. With phosphor bands	50·00
H69	JULY 1964	18·00
	p. With phosphor bands	45·00
H70	SEPT 1964	18·00
	p. With phosphor bands	45·00
H71	NOV 1964	19·00
	p. With phosphor bands	45·00
H72	JAN 1965	18·00
	p. With phosphor bands	38·00
H73	MAR 1965	18·00
	p. With phosphor bands	45·00
H74	MAY 1965	18·00
	p. With phosphor bands	45·00

5s. Booklets with Machin type stamps

Type HP26
English Homes Series
with GPO Cypher

(Des S. Rose)

1968 (27 Nov)–**70**. *Cinnamon cover as Type HP26 (English Homes Series). Pages of six stamps:* 12 × 5d. *(No. 735).*
HP26	DEC 1968 (Ightham Mote)	1·10
HP27	FEB 1969 (Little Moreton Hall)	1·10
HP28	APR 1969 (Long Melford Hall)	1·10
HP29	JUNE 1969 (Long Melford Hall)	1·50
HP30	AUG 1969 (Long Melford Hall)	1·50

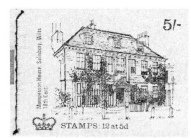

Type HP31
English Homes Series with Post
Office Corporation Crown Symbol

(Des S. Rose)

As last but cover changed to Type HP31.
HP31	OCT 1969 (Mompesson House)	1·50
HP32	DEC 1969 (Mompesson House)	2·40
HP33	FEB 1970 (Cumberland Terrace)	2·00

GIBBONS STAMP MONTHLY
– finest and most informative magazine for all
collectors. Obtainable from your newsagent or by
postal subscription – details on request.

Type HP34

(Des P. Gauld)

As last but cover changed to Type HP34 (special edition to advertise "Philympia" International Philatelic Exhibition, London, September 1970).
HP34	(no date) (3.3.70)	1·00

As last but cover changed to Type HP31.
HP35	JUNE 1970 (The Vineyard, Saffron Walden)	2·00
HP36	AUG 1970 (The Vineyard, Saffron Walden)	2·00
HP37	OCT 1970 (Mereworth Castle)	2·25
HP38	DEC 1970 (Mereworth Castle)	2·50

6s. Booklets

1965 (21 June)–**67**. *Claret cover as Type D. Wmk Crowns (No. 576a) or phosphor (No. 616a). Pages of six stamps:* 18 × 4d.
Q 1	JUNE 1965	15·00
	p. With phosphor bands	15·00
Q 2	JULY 1965	15·00
	p. With phosphor bands	15·00
Q 3	AUG 1965	15·00
	p. With phosphor bands	18·00
Q 4	SEPT 1965	15·00
	p. With phosphor bands	18·00
Q 5	OCT 1965	15·00
	p. With phosphor bands	18·00
Q 6	NOV 1965	15·00
	p. With phosphor bands	18·00
Q 7	DEC 1965	15·00
	p. With phosphor bands	18·00
Q 8	JAN 1966	15·00
	p. With phosphor bands	18·00
Q 9	FEB 1966	15·00
	p. With phosphor bands	18·00
Q10	MAR 1966	15·00
	p. With phosphor bands	18·00
Q11	APR 1966	15·00
	p. With phosphor bands	35·00
Q12	MAY 1966	15·00
	p. With phosphor bands	18·00
Q13	JUNE 1966	15·00
	p. With phosphor bands	17·00
Q14	JULY 1966	15·00
	p. With phosphor bands	22·00
Q15	AUG 1966	15·00
	p. With phosphor bands	65·00
Q16	SEPT 1966	15·00
	p. With phosphor bands	15·00
Q17	OCT 1966	15·00
	p. With phosphor bands	30·00

Q18	NOV 1966	15·00
	p. With phosphor bands	15·00
Q19	DEC 1966	15·00
	p. With phosphor bands	15·00
Q20	JAN 1967	18·00
	p. With phosphor bands	18·00
Q21	FEB 1967	18·00
	p. With phosphor bands	15·00
Q22	MAR 1967	15·00
	p. With phosphor bands	15·00
Q23	APR 1967	15·00
	p. With phosphor bands	15·00
Q24p	MAY 1967. With phosphor bands	15·00
Q25p	JUNE 1967. With phosphor bands	15·00
Q26p	JULY 1967. With phosphor bands	15·00
Q27p	AUG 1967. With phosphor bands	18·00

6s. Booklets with Machin type stamps

1967–70. *Claret cover as Type D. Pages of six stamps: 18 × 4d. Two phosphor bands. Gum arabic (No. 731).*

QP28	SEPT 1967	26·00
QP29	OCT 1967	28·00
QP30	NOV 1967	30·00
QP31	DEC 1967	32·00
QP32	JAN 1968	32·00
QP33	FEB 1968 (No. 731Ea)	32·00
QP34	MAR 1968 (No. 731Ea)	26·00
QP35	APR 1968 (No. 731Ea)	24·00
QP36	MAY 1968 (No. 731Ea)	13·00

Change to PVA gum (No. 731Ev).

QP37	MAY 1968	£200

Type QP51
Birds Series with Post Office
Corporation Crown Symbol

(Des S. Rose)

As last but cover changed to Type QP51.

QP51	NOV 1969 (Cormorant)	2·25
QP52	JAN 1970 (Cormorant)	2·25
QP53	APR 1970 (Wren)	2·25
QP54	AUG 1970 (Golden Eagle)	2·50
QP55	OCT 1970 (Golden Eagle)	2·50

QP47	MAR 1969 (Jay)	1·75
QP48	MAY 1969 (Jay)	2·00
QP49	JULY 1969 (Puffin)	2·00
QP50	SEPT 1969 (Puffin)	2·25

10s. Booklets

1961 (10 Apr–Oct). *Green cover as Type D. Pages of six stamps: 30 × 3d., 6 × 1½d., 6 × 1d., 6 × ½d. Wmk Crowns (Nos. 570/3 and 575).*

X1	No date	65·00
X2	OCT 1961	65·00

1962–64. *New Composition. Pages of six stamps: 30 × 3d., 6 × 2½d., 6 × 1½d., 6 × 1d. (Nos. 571/2 and 574/5).*

X3	APR 1962	50·00
X4	AUG 1962	65·00
X5	MAR 1963	50·00
X6	JULY 1963	50·00
X7	DEC 1963	50·00
X8	JULY 1964	40·00
X9	DEC 1964	90·00

1965 (23 Aug)–**66.** *Ochre cover as Type D. Pages of six stamps: 24 × 4d., 6 × 3d., 6 × 1d. Wmk Crowns (Nos. 571, 575, 576a).*

X10	AUG 1965	16·00
X11	DEC 1965	18·00
X12	FEB 1966	18·00
X13	AUG 1966	14·00
X14	NOV 1966	12·00

1967–68. *Ochre cover as Type D. Pages of six phosphor stamps: 24 × 4d., 6 × 3d., 6 × 1d. Wmk Crowns (Nos. 611, 615c (one side phosphor band), 616a).*

X15p	FEB 1967	5·00

Composition as No. X15p. Wmk Crowns (Nos. 611, 615e (one centre phosphor band), 616a).

X16p	AUG 1967	6·00
X17p	FEB 1968	5·00

Type QP38
Birds Series with GPO Cypher

(Des S. Rose)

Orange-red cover as Type QP38 (Birds Series). Same composition. Two phosphor bands. PVA gum (No. 731Ev).

QP38	JUNE 1968 (Kingfisher) (4.6.68)	1·25
QP39	JULY 1968 (Kingfisher)	5·50
QP40	AUG 1968 (Peregrine Falcon)	1·25

Change to one centre phosphor band (No. 732).

QP41	SEPT 1968 (Peregrine Falcon) (16.9.68)	1·25
QP42	OCT 1968 (Pied Woodpecker)	1·50
QP43	NOV 1968 (Pied Woodpecker)	1·75
QP44	DEC 1968 (Great Crested Grebe)	1·75
QP45	JAN 1969 (Barn Owl)	1·75

Change to 4d. bright vermilion with one centre phosphor band (No. 733).

QP46	FEB 1969 (Barn Owl) (20.2.69)	1·75

10s. Booklets with Machin type stamps

Type XP4
Explorers Series with GPO Cypher

(Des S. Rose)

1968 (25 Mar–Aug). *Bright purple cover as Type XP4 (Explorers Series). Pages of six stamps: 24 × 4d., 6 × 3d., 6 × 1d. PVA gum (Nos. 724, 729Ev, 731Ev).*
XP4   MAY 1968 (Livingstone) .... 3·50
XP5   AUG 1968 (Livingstone) .... 3·50

1968 (16 Sept)–**70**. *Yellow-green covers as Type XP4 (Explorers Series) New composition. Pages of six stamps: 12 × 5d. (with two phosphor bands), 12 × 4d. (with one centre phosphor band) and pane comprising 4 × 1d. se-tenant with vert pair of 4d. (each with one centre phosphor band). PVA gum (Nos. 725, 732 and 735).*
XP6   SEPT 1968 (Scott) .... 3·50

Change to 4d. bright vermilion (one centre band) but se-tenant pane comprises 1d. with two phosphor bands and 4d. with one left side phosphor band (Nos. 724 and 733/4).
XP 7   FEB 1969 (Mary Kingsley) (6.1.69) .... 2·25
XP 8   MAY 1969 (Mary Kingsley) .... 3·00
XP 9   AUG 1969 (Shackleton) .... 2·25
XP10   NOV 1969 (Shackleton) .... 5·00

Type XP11
Explorers Series with Post Office
Corporation Crown Symbol

(Des S. Rose)

As last but cover change to Type XP11.
XP11   FEB 1970 (Frobisher) .... 5·00
XP12   NOV 1970 (Captain Cook) .... 5·00

£1 Booklet with Machin type stamps

Type ZP1

1969 (1 Dec). *"Stamps for Cooks". Type ZP1 (150 × 72 mm) with full colour pictorial cover showing "Baked, Stuffed Haddock". Contains 12 recipes on interleaving pages and on se-tenant labels attached to booklet panes. PVA gum. Stapled.*
ZP1   £1 containing panes of fifteen stamps (5 × 3): 15 × 5d. (No. 735), 30 × 4d. (No. 733) and pane comprising 6 × 4d. (three each of Nos. 734 and 734Eb) se-tenant with 6 × 1d. (No. 724) and 3 × 5d. (No. 735) .... 75·00
ZP1a   As last but booklet is sewn with thread instead of being stapled .... 10·00

II. Decimal Booklets, 1971 onwards.

A. Stitched Booklets.

The 25p., 30p., 35p., 45p. and 50p. booklets have pictorial covers (except for the 35p. and 45p.) without the design inscription.
This was no longer necessary as the designs and background information were given on the inside of the front cover. Each series was numbered.

10p. Booklets

Type DN46
British Pillar Box Series

(Des R. Maddox)

1971 (15 Feb–1 June). *British Pillar Box Series. Orange-yellow cover as Type DN46. Pages of four stamps: 2 × 2p. se-tenant vertically with 2 × ½p. and 2 × 1p. se-tenant vertically with 2 × 1½p. (Nos. X841l and X844l).*
DN46   FEB 1971 (No. 1 1855 type) .... 1·25
DN47   APR 1971 (No. 1 1855 type) (19.3.71) .... 1·50
DN48   JUNE 1971 (No. 2 1856 type) (1.6.71) .... 1·25

1971 (14 July)–**74**.   *British Pillar Box Series continued. Orange-yellow cover as Type DN46. Contents unchanged but panes are se-tenant horizontally (Nos. X841l/a and X844m).*

DN49	AUG 1971 (No. 2 1856 type) (14.7.71)	2·00
DN50	OCT 1971 (No. 3 1857–9 type) (27/8/71)	2·00
DN51	DEC 1971 (No. 3 1857–9 type) (6.10.71)	2·00
DN52	FEB 1972 (No. 4 1866–79 type) (8.12.71)	2·00
DN53	APR 1972 (No. 4 1866–79 type) (24.2.72)	2·00
DN54	JUNE 1972 (No. 5 1899 type) (12.4.72)	2·00
DN55	AUG 1972 (No. 5 1899 type) (8.6.72)	2·00
DN56	OCT 1972 (No. 6 1968 type) (2.8.72)	2·00
DN57	DEC 1972 (No. 6 1968 type) (30.10.72)	2·00
DN58	FEB 1973 (No. 7 1936 type) (5.1.73)	2·00
DN59	APR 1973 (No. 7 1936 type) (2.4.73)	3·50
DN60	JUNE 1973 (No. 8 1952 type) (18.4.73)	2·00
DN61	AUG 1973 (No. 8 1952 type) (4.7.73)	10·00
DN62	OCT 1973 (No. 9 1973 type) (16.8.73)	2·00
DN63	DEC 1973 (No. 9 1973 type) (12.11.73)	2·00
DN64	FEB 1974 (No. 9 1973 type) (17.12.73)	2·00
DN65	APR 1974 (No. 10 1974 type) (22.2.74)	1·50
DN66	JUNE 1974 (No. 10 1974 type) (23.4.74)	1·50

In No. DN47 the pillar box is slightly reduced in size.

Type DN67
Postal Uniforms Series

(Des C. Abbott)

1974 (23 July)–**76**.   *Postal Uniforms Series. Orange-yellow cover as Type DN67. Contents unchanged.*

DN67	AUG 1974 (No. 1 1793 type)	1·50
DN68	OCT 1974 (No. 1 1793 type) (27.8.74)	1·50
DN69	DEC 1974 (No. 2 1837 type) (25.10.74)	1·50
DN70	FEB 1975 (No. 2 1837 type) (12.12.74)	1·50
DN71	APR 1975 (No. 3 1855 type) (26.3.75)	1·50
DN72	JUNE 1975 (No. 3 1855 type) (21.5.75)	1·50
DN73	AUG 1975 (No. 3 1855 type) (27.6.75)	1·00
DN74	OCT 1975 (No. 3 1855 type) (3.10.75)	75
DN75	JAN 1976 (No. 3 1855 type) (16.3.76)	75

25p. Booklets

Type DH39
Veteran Transport Series

(Des D. Gentleman)

1971 (15 Feb).   *Veteran Transport Series. Dull purple cover as Type DH39. Pages of six stamps: 5 × 2½p. with one printed label, 4 × 2½p. with two printed labels, 5 × ½p. with one printed label (Nos. X841m and X851l/m).*

DH39	FEB 1971 (No. 1 Knife-board omnibus)	3·00

Type DH40

1971 (19 Mar).   *Issued to publicise the National Postal Museum Exhibition of 80 Years of British Stamp Booklets. Dull purple cover as Type DH40.*

DH40	APR 1971	5·00

1971 (11 May)–**73**.   *Dull purple cover as Type DH39. Veteran Transport Series continued.*

DH41	JUNE 1971 (No. 2 B-type omnibus)	5·00
DH42	AUG 1971 (No. 2 B-type omnibus) (17.9.71)	7·00
DH43	OCT 1971 (No. 3 Showman's Engine) (22.11.71)	7·00
DH44	FEB 1972 (No. 4 Mail Van) (23.12.71)	5·50
DH45	APR 1972 (No. 4 Mail Van) (13.3.72)	7·00
DH46	JUNE 1972 (No. 5 Motor Wagonette) (24.4.72)	6·00
DH47	AUG 1972 (No. 5 Motor Wagonette) (14.6.72)	6·00
DH48	OCT 1972 (No. 6 Taxi Cab) (17.7.72)	6·00
DH49	DEC 1972 (No. 6 Taxi Cab) (19.10.72)	5·50
DH50	DEC 1972 "Issues S" (No. 6 Taxi Cab) (6.11.72)	6·00
DH51	FEB 1973 (No. 7 Electric Tramcar) (26.2.73)	8·00

Nos. DH42/51 contain panes showing the perforations omitted between the label and the binding margin.

Type DH52

1973 (7 June). *Dull mauve cover as Type DH52.*
DH52   JUNE 1973 . . . .   8·00
No. DH52 contains panes showing the perforations omitted between the label and the binding margin.

30p. Booklets

Type DQ56
British Birds Series

(Des H. Titcombe)

1971 (15 Feb). *British Birds Series. Bright purple cover as Type DQ56. Pages of six stamps: 2 panes of 5 × 3p. with one printed label (No. X855l).*
DQ56   FEB 1971 (No. 1 Curlew) . . . .   4·00

1971 (19 Mar). *Bright purple cover as Type DH40.*
DQ57   APR 1971 . . . .   3·50

1971 (26 May)–**73**. *Bright purple cover as Type DQ56. British Birds Series continued.*
DQ58   JUNE 1971 (No. 2 Lapwing) . . . .   3·50
DQ59   AUG 1971 (No. 2 Lapwing) (23.7.71) . . . .   4·00
DQ60   OCT 1971 (No. 3 Robin) (1.10.71) . . . .   4·00
DQ61   DEC 1971 (No. 3 Robin) (10.11.71) . . . .   4·00
DQ62   FEB 1972 (No. 4 Pied Wagtail) (21.12.71) . . . .   4·00
DQ63   APR 1972 (No. 4 Pied Wagtail) (9.2.72) . . . .   4·00
DQ64   JUNE 1972 (No. 5 Kestrel) (12.4.72) . . . .   4·00
DQ65   AUG 1972 (No. 5 Kestrel) (8.6.72) . . . .   5·00
DQ66   OCT 1972 (No. 6 Black Grouse) (31.7.72) . . . .   4·00
DQ67   DEC 1972 (No. 6 Black Grouse) (30.10.72) . . . .   4·00
DQ68   DEC 1972 "Issue S" (No. 6 Black Grouse) (6.12.72) . . . .   4·00
DQ69   FEB 1973 (No. 7 Skylark) (29.1.73) . . . .   4·00
DQ70   APR 1973 (No. 7 Skylark) (2.4.73) . . . .   5·00
DQ71   JUNE 1973 (No. 8 Oyster-catcher) (8.5.73) . . . .   4·50
DQ72   AUG 1973 (No. 8 Oyster-catcher) (7.6.73) . . . .   5·00
DQ72a   As DQ72 but buff cover (10.8.73)* . . . .   5·00
Nos. DQ59/72a contain panes showing the perforations omitted between the label and the binding margin.
*No. DQ72a was printed with a buff cover because of a shortage of the original purple-coloured card.

1974 (30 Jan). *Red cover similar to Type DH52. Make-up as before but with blank label.*
DQ73   SPRING 1974 . . . .   3·75

1974 (2 June). *Red cover similar to Type DT9. Make-up as before.*
DQ74   JUNE 1974 . . . .   3·75

35p. Booklets

Type DP1
British Coins Series

(Des P Gauld)

1973 (12 Dec)–**74**. *British Coins Series. Blue cover as Type DP1. Pages of six stamps: 2 pages of 5 × 3½p. with one blank label (No. X858Eb).*
DP1   AUTUMN 1973 (No. 1 Cuthred's Penny) . . . .   2·50
DP2   APR 1974 (No. 1 Cuthred's Penny) (10.4.74) . . . .   4·50
DP3   JUNE 1974 (No. 2 Silver Groat) (4.7.74) . . . .   2·50

1974 (23 Oct). *Blue cover as Type DT9. Make-up as before but with No. X859.*
DP4   SEPT 1974 . . . .   2·50

45p. Booklets

1974 (9 Oct–26 Nov). *British Coins Series continued. Yellow-brown cover as Type DP1. Pages of six stamps: 2 pages of 5 × 4½p. (No. X865) with one blank label.*
DS1   SEPT 1974 (No. 3 Elizabeth Gold Crown) . . . .   4·00
DS2   DEC 1974 (No. 3 Elizabeth Gold Crown) (1.11.74) . . . .   4·50
DS2a   As DS2 but orange-brown cover (26.11.74)* . . . .   7·50
*No. DS2a was printed with an orange-brown cover because of a shortage of the original yellow-brown card.

50p. Booklets

Type DT1

(Des Rosalie Southall)

1971 (15 Feb)–**72**. *British Flowers Series. Turquoise-green cover as Type DT1. Pages of six stamps: 6 × 3p., 4 × 3p. se-tenant horizontally with 2 × 2½p. (side band), 5 × 2½p. (centre band) with one printed label and 5 × ½p. with one printed label (Nos. X841m, X851l, X852l and X855 × 6).*

DT1	FEB 1971 (No. 1 Large Bindweed)	8·00
DT2	MAY 1971 (No. 2 Primrose) (24.3.71)	7·00
DT3	AUG 1971 (No. 3 Honeysuckle) (28.6.71)	7·00
DT4	NOV 1971 (No. 4 Hop) (17.9.71)	8·00
DT5	FEB 1972 (No. 5 Common Violet) (23.12.71)*	8·00
DT6	MAY 1972 (No. 6 Lords-and-Ladies) (13.3.72)	7·00
DT7	AUG 1972 (No. 7 Wood Anemone) (31.5.72)	7·00
DT8	NOV 1972 (No. 8 Deadly Nightshade) (15.9.72)	7·00

Nos. DT4/8 contain panes showing the perforations omitted between the label and the binding margin.

* Although generally released on 24 December, this booklet was put on sale at the London E.C.1 Philatelic Counter and also at one other Philatelic Counter on 23 December.

Type DT9

1973 (19 Jan–June). *Turquoise-green cover as Type DT9.*

DT 9	FEB 1973	7·00
DT10	APR 1973 (26.2.73)	9·00
DT11	MAY 1973 (2.4.73)	9·00
DT12	AUG 1973 (14.6.73)	12·00

1973 (14 Nov)–**74**. *Moss-green cover similar to Type DT9. Pages of six stamps: 2 pages of 5 × 3½p. with one blank label (No. X858Eb) and 1 page of 5 × 3p. (centre band) and one blank label (No. X856).*

DT13	AUTUMN 1973	6·00
DT14	MAR 1974 (18.2.74)	4·00

85p. Booklet

1974 (13 Nov). *Purple cover similar to Type DT9.*

DW1   Containing 3 pages of 5 × 4½p. (No. X865) with one blank label and 1 page of 5 × 3½p. (No. X859) with one blank label .... 6·00

Sponsored Booklets

Type DX1

(Des J. Wallis)

1972 (24 May). *"The Story of Wedgwood". Full colour pictorial cover, Type DX1 (150 × 72 mm). Containing information and illustrations on interleaving panes and on se-tenant label attached to booklet panes.*

DX1   £1 containing 12 × 3p. (No. X855) and booklet panes X851n, X841o and X841p .... 75·00

Price quoted for No. DX1 is for examples showing the ½p. 1 side band, No. X842, (in pane No. X841p) with full perforations. Examples of the booklet with this ½p. value showing trimmed perforations are priced at £25.

Type DX2

(Des J. Wallis)

1980 (16 Apr). *"The Story of Wedgwood". Multicoloured cover, Type DX2 (163 × 97 mm) showing painting "Josiah Wedgwood and his Family" by George Stubbs. Booklet contains text and illustrations on the labels attached to panes and on interleaving pages.*

DX2   £3 containing booklet panes Nos. X849n, X849o, X888l and X895l .... 7·50

No. DX2 is inscribed "January 1980".

Type DX3

(Des B. Dedman)

1982 (19 May). *"Story of Stanley Gibbons". Multicoloured cover, Type DX3 (163 × 97 mm) showing early envelope design on front and stamp album with text on back. Booklet contains text and illustrations on labels attached to panes and on interleaving pages.*

DX3   £4 containing booklet panes Nos. X849p, X899m and X907l/m .... 11·00

No. DX3 is inscribed "February 1982".

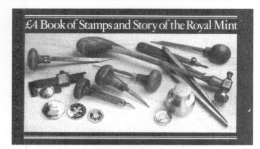

Type DX4

(Des B. West)

1983 (14 Sept). *"Story of the Royal Mint". Multicoloured cover, Type DX4 (163 × 97 mm) showing current coins, die and tools. Booklet contains text and illustrations on labels attached to panes and on interleaving pages.*
DX4 £4 containing booklet panes Nos. X899m × 2, X930b and X949l .... 11·00

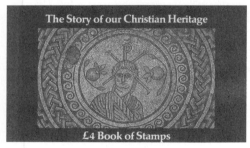

Type DX5

(Des P. Miles)

1984 (4 Sept). *"The Story of our Christian Heritage". Multicoloured cover, Type DX5 (163 × 97 mm) showing mosaic of Christ from Hinton St. Mary Roman villa. Booklet contains text and illustrations on labels attached to panes and on interleaving pages.*
DX5 £4 containing booklet panes Nos. X886bl, X901m × 2 and X952l .... 20·00

Type DX6

(Des D. Driver)

1985 (8 Jan). *"Story of The Times" (newspaper). Multicoloured cover, Type DX6 (163 × 95 mm) showing "Waiting for The Times" (painting by Haydon). Booklet contains text and illustrations on labels attached to panes and on interleaving pages.*
DX6 £5 containing booklet panes Nos. X846l, X900l, X952l and X952m .... 20·00

Type DX7

(Des Trickett and Webb Ltd)

1986 (18 Mar). *"The Story of British Rail". Multicoloured cover, Type DX7 (162 × 95 mm) showing diesel locomotive. Booklet contains text and illustrations on labels attached to panes and on interleaving pages.*
DX7 £5 containing booklet panes Nos. X896l, X897m, X952l and X952m .... 20·00

Type DX8

(Des Aitken Blakeley Designers)

1987 (3 Mar). *"The Story of P & O". Multicoloured cover, Type DX8 (162 × 95 mm) showing the "William Fawcett". Booklet contains text and illustrations on labels attached to panes and on interleaving pages.*
DX8 £5 containing booklet panes Nos. X847m, X900l, X900m and X955l .... 20·00

Type DX9

(Des The Partners)

1988 (9 Feb). *"The Story of the Financial Times" (newspaper). Multicoloured cover, Type DX9 (162 × 97 mm). Booklet contains text and illustrations on labels attached to the panes and on interleaving pages.*
DX9   £5 containing booklet panes Nos. X1005l, X1006l, X1009l
      and X1009m .... 23·00

Type DX10

(Des Tayburn)

1989 (21 Mar). *"The Scots Connection". Multicoloured cover, Type DX10 (162 × 97 mm). Booklet contains text and illustrations on labels attached to the panes and on interleaving pages.*
DX10   £5 containing booklet panes Nos. S54l, S55l, S61l and
       S61m .... 16·00

Type DX11

(Des D. Driver)

1990 (20 Mar). *"London Life". Multicoloured cover, Type DX11 (162 × 97 mm). Booklet contains text and illustrations on labels attached to the panes and on interleaving pages.*
DX11   £5 containing booklet panes Nos. X906m, 1469n × 2
       and 1493a .... 20·00

Type DX12

(Des Trickett and Webb Ltd)

1991 (19 Mar). *"Alias Agatha Christie". Multicoloured cover, Type DX12 (162 × 97 mm). Booklet contains text and illustrations on labels attached to the panes and on interleaving pages.*
DX12   £6 containing booklet panes Nos. X1008l × 2, X1016l
       and X1016m .... 19·00

Type DX13

(Des G. Evernden and J. Gibbs)

1992 (25 Feb). *"Cymru–Wales". Multicoloured cover, Type DX13 (162 × 97 mm). Booklet contains text and illustrations on labels attached to the panes and on interleaving pages.*
DX13   £6 Containing booklet panes Nos. 1591a, W48a, W49a
       and W59a. .... 17·00

Type DX14

(Des The Partners)

1992 (27 Oct). *Birth Centenary of J. R. R. Tolkien (author). Multicoloured cover, Type DX14 (162 × 97 mm). Booklet contains text and illustrations on labels attached to the panes and on interleaving pages.*
DX14   £6 containing booklet panes Nos. X1011l, X1012l and
    X1017l × 2 . . . .   14·00

Type DX15

(Des The Partners)

1993 (10 Aug). *"The Story of Beatrix Potter". Multicoloured cover, Type DX15 (162 × 97 mm). Booklet contains text and illustrations on labels attached to the panes and on interleaving pages.*
DX15   £5.64, containing booklet panes Nos. X1012m, 1451al,
    1649a and NI48l . . . .   18·00
    Although inscribed "£6.00" No. DX15 was sold at the face value of
its contents, £5.64.

Type DX16

(Des Carroll, Dempsey and Thirkell Ltd)

1994 (26 July). *"Northern Ireland". Multicoloured cover, Type DX16 (162 × 97 mm). Booklet contains text and illustrations on labels attached to the panes and on interleaving pages.*
DX16   £6.04, containing booklet panes Nos. Y1748a, 1812a and
    NI70l/m, together with a 35p. postal stationery air card   9·00

B. Folded Booklets.

NOTE: All panes are attached to the covers by the selvedge.

10p. Booklets

Type FA1

(Des Post Office artist)

1976 (10 Mar)–**77**. *Cover as Type FA1 printed in dull rose on very pale lavender. Containing booklet pane No. X841r.*
FA1 NOV 1975 70
FA2 MAR 1976 (9.6.76) 80
FA3 JUNE 1977 (13.6.77) 70

Type FA4

(Des N. Battershill)

1978 (8 Feb)–**79**. *Farm Buildings Series. Bistre-brown and turquoise-blue covers as Type FA4, containing booklet pane No. X843m.*
FA4 Design No. 1, Oast Houses 75
FA5 Design No. 2, Buildings in Ulster (3.5.78) 75
FA6 Design No. 3, Buildings in Yorkshire (9.8.78) 75
FA7 Design No. 4, Buildings in Wales (25.10.78) 75
FA8 Design No. 5, Buildings in Scotland (10.1.79) 75
FA9 Design No. 6, Buildings in Sussex (4.4.79) 75
Nos. FA4/5 are inscribed "January 1978", FA6 "July 1978", FA7 "October 1978", FA8 "December 1978" and FA9 "March 1979".

Type FA10

(Des Hamper and Purssell)

1979 (17 Oct)–**80**. *"London 1980" International Stamp Exhibition. Red and blue cover as Type FA10 showing Post Office exhibition stand and containing No. X845l.*
FA10 Inscr "August 1979" 50
FA11 Inscr "January 1980" (12.1.80) 60

50p. Booklets

All booklets were sold at the cover price of 50p. although some contain stamps to a greater value.

Type FB1

1977 (26 Jan). *Cover as Type FB1 printed in maroon and pale blue.*
FB1A Containing booklet pane X841s .... 2·50
FB1B Containing booklet pane X841sa .... 2·50

1977 (13 June). *Cover as Type FB1. Printed in chestnut and stone.*
FB2A Containing booklet pane X844n .... 4·00
FB2B Containing booklet pane X844na .... 2·50

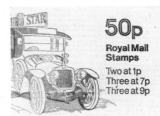

Type FB3

(Des J. Ireland)

1978 (8 Feb)–**79**. *Commercial Vehicles Series. Olive-yellow and grey covers as Type FB3. A. Containing booklet pane No. X844n. B. Containing booklet pane No. X844na.*

		A	B
FB3	Design No. 1, Clement Talbot van	4·00	3·00
FB4	Design No. 2, Austin taxi (3.5.78)	4·00	2·50
FB5	Design No. 3, Morris Royal Mail van (9.8.78)	4·50	2·50
FB6	Design No. 4, Guy Electric dustcart (25.10.78)	4·00	3·00
FB7	Design No. 5, Albion van (10.1.79)	5·00	2·50
FB8	Design No. 6, Leyland fire engine (4.4.79)	4·00	2·50

Nos. FB3/4 are inscribed "January 1978", FB5 "July 1978", FB6 "October 1978", FB7 "December 1978" and FB8 "March 1979".

1979 (28 Aug). *Contents changed. A. Containing booklet pane No. X849l. B. Containing booklet pane No. X849la.*

		A	B
FB9	Design No. 6, Leyland fire engine	2·00	2·00

Type FB10

(Des B. Smith)

1979 (3 Oct)–**81**. *Veteran Cars Series. Orange-red and reddish lilac covers as Type FB10. A. Containing booklet pane No. X849l. B. Containing booklet pane No. X849la.*

		A	B
FB10	Design No. 1, 1907 Rolls-Royce Silver Ghost	2·50	2·50

No. FB10 is inscribed "August 1979".

Contents changed. A. Containing booklet pane No. X849m. B. Containing booklet pane No. X849ma.

		A	B
FB11	Design No. 2, 1908 Grand Prix Austin (4.2.80) ...	2·50	2·00
FB12	Design No. 3, 1903–5 Vauxhall (25.6.80)	2·50	2·00
FB13	Design No. 4, 1897–1900 Daimler (24.9.80)	2·50	2·00

No. FB11 is inscribed "January 1980", No. FB12 "May 1980" and No. FB13 "July 1980".

Contents changed. A. Containing No. X841t. B. Containing No. X841ta.

		A	B
FB14	Design No. 5, 1896 Lanchester (26.1.81)	2·25	2·25
FB15	Design No. 6, 1913 Bull-nose Morris (18.3.81) ...	2·25	2·25

Nos. FB14/15 are inscribed "January 1981".

Type FB16

(Des R. Downer)

1981 (6 May)–**82**. *Follies Series. Brown and orange-brown covers as Type FB16. A. Containing No. X841t. B. Containing No. X841ta.*

		A	B
FB16	Design No. 1, Mugdock Castle, Stirlingshire	2·00	2·00

No. FB16 is inscribed "January 1981".

Contents changed. A. Containing No. X854l. B. Containing No. X854la.

		A	B
FB17	Design No. 1, Mugdock Castle, Stirlingshire (26.8.81)	5·00	9·00
FB18	Design No. 2, Mow Cop Castle, Cheshire-Staffs border (30.9.81)	4·00	7·00

Nos. FB17/18 are inscribed "January 1981".

Contents changed. A. Containing No. X841u. B. Containing No. X841ua.

		A	B
FB19	Design No. 3, Paxton's Tower, Llanarthney, Dyfed (1.2.82)	2·50	2·50
FB20	Design No. 4, Temple of the Winds, Mount Stewart, Northern Ireland (6.5.82)	2·50	2·50
FB21	Design No. 5, Temple of the Sun, Stourhead, Wilts (11.8.82)	2·50	2·50
FB22	Design No. 6, Water Garden, Cliveden, Bucks (6.10.82)	2·50	2·50

Nos. FB19/22 are inscribed "February 1982".

Type FB23

(Des H. Titcombe)

1983 (16 Feb–26 Oct). *Rare Farm Animals Series. Bright green and black covers as Type FB23. A. Containing booklet pane No. X841u. B. Containing booklet pane No. X841ua.*

		A	B
FB23	Design No. 1, Bagot Goat	2·50	2·50

Contents changed. Containing No. X845n.

FB24	Design No. 2, Gloucester Old Spot Pig (5.4.83)	5·00
	b. Corrected rate	10·00
FB25	Design No. 3, Toulouse Goose (27.7.83)	5·00
FB26	Design No. 4, Orkney Sheep (26.10.83)	5·00

No. FB23 is inscribed "February 1982" and Nos. FB24/6 "April 1983". The corrected rate reads, "36p. for 200g" instead of "37p. for 200g".

Type FB27

(Des P. Morter)

1984 (3 Sept)–**85**. *Orchids Series. Yellow-green and lilac covers as Type FB27. Containing booklet pane No. X845p.*

FB27	Design No. 1, *Dendrobium nobile* and *Miltonia* hybrid .	3·50
FB28	Design No. 2, *Cypripedium calceolus* and *Ophrys apifera* (15.1.85)	3·50
FB29	Design No. 3, *Bifrenaria* and *Vanda tricolor* (23.4.85)	3·50
FB30	Design No. 4, *Cymbidium* and *Arpophyllum* (23.7.85) ..	3·50

Nos. FB27/30 are inscribed "September 1984".

Type FB31

(Des M. Thierens Design)

1985 (4 Nov). *Cover as Type FB31 printed in black and bright scarlet. Containing booklet pane No. X909l.*
FB31 Pillar box design .... 3·00
No. FB31 is inscribed "November 1985".

Type FB32

(Des P. Morter)

1986 (20 May–12 Aug). *Pond Life Series. Dull blue and emerald covers as Type FB32. Containing booklet pane No. X909l.*
FB32 Design No. 1, Emperor Dragonfly, Four-spotted Libellula and Yellow Flag .... 2·75
FB33 Design No. 2, Common Frog, Fennel-leaved Pondweed and Long-stalked Pondweed (29.7.86) .... 3·50
    a. Containing booklet pane No. X909Ela (12.8.86) ... 3·75
Nos. FB32/33a are inscribed "November 1985".

Type FB34

(Des N. Battershill)

1986 (29 July). *Roman Britain Series. Brown-ochre and Indian red cover as Type FB34. Containing booklet pane No. X845q.*
FB34 Design No. 1, Hadrian's Wall .... 8·00
No. FB34 is inscribed "November 1985".

1986 (20 Oct)–**87**. *Pond Life Series continued. Dull blue and emerald covers as Type FB32. Containing booklet pane No. X845s.*
FB35 Design No. 3, Moorhen and Little Grebe .... 4·00
FB36 Design No. 4, Giant Pond and Great Ramshorn Snails (27.1.87) .... 4·00
No. FB36 is inscribed "October 1986".

1986 (20 Oct)–**87**. *Roman Britain Series continued. Brown-ochre and Indian red covers as Type FB34. Containing booklet pane No. X847l.*
FB37 Design No. 2, Roman Theatre of Verulamium, St. Albans 3·00
FB38 Design No. 3, Portchester Castle, Hampshire (27.1.87) .. 3·00
No. FB38 is inscribed "October 1986".

Type FB39

(Des Patricia Howes)

1987 (14 Apr)–**88**. *Bicentenary of Marylebone Cricket Club Series. Brown and dull ultramarine covers as Type FB39. Containing booklet pane No. X847l.*
FB39 Design No. 1, Father Time weather vane .... 3·00
FB40 Design No. 2, Ashes urn and embroidered velvet bag (14.7.87) .... 3·00
FB41 Design No. 3, Lord's Pavilion and wrought iron decoration on roof (29.9.87) .... 3·00
FB42 Design No. 4, England team badge and new stand at Lord's (26.1.88) .... 3·00
Nos. FB39/42 are inscribed "October 1986".

Type FB43

(Des G. Evernden)

1987 (14 Apr)–**88**. *Botanical Gardens Series. Covers as Type FB43. Containing booklet panes No. X845s (FB43/4) or X845sa (FB45/6).*
FB43 Design No. 1 (cover in ultramarine and rose-red), Rhododendron "Elizabeth", Bodnant .... 3·25
FB44 Design No. 2 (cover in deep ultramarine and cobalt), Gentiana sino-ornata, Edinburgh (14.7.87) .... 3·25
FB45 Design No. 3 (cover in dull ultramarine and orange-yellow), Lilium auratum and "Mount Stuart" (incorrect inscr) (29.9.87) .... 3·25
    a. With corrected spelling "Mount Stewart" (30.10.87) .... 3·25
FB46 Design No. 4 (cover in dull ultramarine and yellow-orange), Strelitzia reginae, Kew (26.1.88) .... 3·00
Nos. FB43/6 are inscribed "October 1986".
The panes from Nos. FB45/6 have imperforate vertical sides.

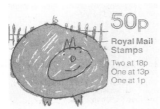

Type FB47

1988 (12 Apr–5 July).   *London Zoo. Children's Drawings Series. Covers as Type* FB47.

FB47   Pigs design (cover in black and rose) containing booklet pane No. X847l .... 3·00

FB48   Birds design (cover in black and yellow) containing booklet pane No. X845sa .... 3·25

FB49   Elephants design (cover in black and grey) containing booklet pane No. X847l (5.7.88) .... 3·00

Nos. FB47/9 are inscribed "October 1986". The pane from No. FB48 has imperforate vertical sides.

Type FB50

(Des P. Morter)

1988 (5 July).   *Marine Life Series. Blue and orange-brown cover as Type* FB50. *Containing booklet pane No.* X845sa.

FB50   Design No. 1, Parasitic Anemone on Common Whelk Shell and Umbrella Jellyfish .... 3·00

No. FB50 is inscribed "October 1986" and has the vertical sides of the pane imperforate.

Type FB51

(Des Lynda Gray)

1988 (5 Sept)–**89**.   *Gilbert and Sullivan Operas Series. Black and red covers as Type* FB51. *Containing booklet pane No.* X904l.

FB51   Design No. 1, *The Yeomen of the Guard* .... 3·00

FB52   Design No. 2, *The Pirates of Penzance* (24.1.89) .... 3·00

FB53   Design No. 3, *The Mikado* (25.4.89) .... 3·00

1989 (18 July).   *Marine Life Series continued. Blue and orange-brown cover as Type* FB50. *Containing booklet pane No.* X904l.

FB54   Design No. 2, Common Hermit Crab, Bladder Wrack and Laver Spire Shell .... 4·00

For Design No. 3, see £1 Booklet No. FH17.

Type FB55

(Des P. Hutton)

1989 (2 Oct)–**90**.   *Aircraft Series. Turquoise-green and light brown covers as Type* FB55. *Containing booklet pane No.* X906l.

FB55   Design No. 1, HP42, Armstrong Whitworth Atalanta and De Havilland Dragon Rapide .... 5·00

No. FB55 was incorrectly inscribed "Atlanta".

As before, but containing Penny Black Anniversary booklet pane No. 1468l.

FB56   Design No. 2, Vickers Viscount 806 and De Havilland Comet 4 (30.1.90) .... 5·00

1990 (4 Sept)–**91**.   *Aircraft Series continued. Turquoise-green and light brown covers as Type* FB55. *Containing booklet pane No.* X911l.

FB57   Design No. 3, BAC 1-11 and VC10 .... 3·00

FB58   Design No. 4, BAe ATP, BAe 146 and Aérospatiale–BAC Concorde (25.6.91) .... 3·00

Type FB59

(Des A. Drummond)

1991 (10 Sept)–**92**.   *Archaeology Series. Covers as Type* FB59. *Containing booklet pane No.* X925m.

FB59   Design No. 1 (cover in bright blue and lake-brown), Sir Arthur Evans at Knossos, Crete .... 2·00

a. Corrected rate (10.91) .... 3·00

FB60   Design No. 2 (cover in bright blue and yellow), Howard Carter in the Tomb of Tutankhamen (21.1.92) .... 2·50

FB61   Design No. 3 (cover in bright blue and yellow), Sir Austen Layard at Assyrian site (28.4.92) .... 2·50

FB62   Design No. 4 (cover in new blue and yellow), Sir Flinders Petrie surveying the Pyramids and temples of Giza (28.7.92) .... 2·50

On the inside front cover of No. FB59 the inland letter rates are shown as 1st class 24, 35, 43, 51p. and 2nd class 18, 28, 33, 39p. These were corrected on No. FB59a to read: 1st class 24, 36, 45, 54p. and 2nd class 18, 28, 34, 41p.

Type FB63

(Des J. Matthews)

1992 (22 Sept). 1000*th Anniv of Appointment of Sheriffs. Dull blue and scarlet cover as Type* FB63. *Containing booklet pane No.* X925m.
FB63 Design showing Crest, with Helm and Mantling, and Badge of The Shrievalty Association .... 2·00

Type FB64

(Des M. Newton)

1993 (9 Feb–6 July). *Postal History Series. Covers as Type* FB64. *Containing booklet pane No.* X925m.
FB64 Design No. 1 (cover in grey-green and grey-black), Airmail postmarks .... 1·50
FB65 Design No. 2 (cover in dull orange and black), Ship mail postmarks (6.4.93) .... 1·50
FB66 Design No. 3 (cover in blue and grey-black), Registered mail postmarks (6.7.93) 75

1993 (1 Nov). *Postal History Series continued. Rose-red and grey-black cover as Type* FB64 *containing booklet pane No.* Y1701a.
FB67 Design No. 4, "Paid" postmarks 75

Type FB68

(Des A. Davidson)

1994 (25 Jan–6 Sept). *Coaching Inns Series. Covers as Type* FB68. *Containing booklet pane No.* Y1701a.
FB68 Design No. 1 (cover in myrtle-green and pale myrtle-green), "Swan with Two Necks" 75
FB69 Design No. 2 (cover in sepia and buff), "Bull and Mouth" (26.4.94) 75
FB70 Design No. 3 (cover in reddish brown and cinnamon), "Golden Cross" (6.6.94) 75
FB71 Design No. 4 (cover in black and slate-blue), "Pheasant Inn, Wiltshire" (6.9.94) 75

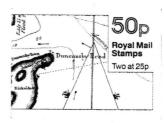

Type FB72

(Des D. Davis)

1995 (7 Feb). *Sea Charts Series. Rosine and black cover as Type* FB72, *containing booklet pane No.* Y1701a.
FB72 Design No. 1, John o' Groats, 1800 75

65p. Booklet

1976 (14 July). *Cover as Type FB1, but larger (90 × 49 mm). Printed in turquoise-blue and pale buff. A. Selvedge at left. B. Selvedge at right.*

		A	B
FC1	Containing ten 6½p. (No. X872)	8·00	6·00

70p. Booklets

1977 (13 June). *Cover as Type FB1, but larger (90 × 49 mm). Printed in purple-brown and dull rose. A. Selvedge at left. B. Selvedge at right.*

		A	B
FD1	Containing ten 7p. (No. X875)	5·00	5·00

Type FD2

(Des E. Stemp)

1978 (8 Feb)–**79**. *Country Crafts Series. Grey-green and red-brown covers as Type FD2 (90 × 49 mm). Containing ten 7p. (No. X875). A. Selvedge at left. B. Selvedge at right.*

		A	B
FD2	Design No. 1, Horse-shoeing	11·00	4·00
FD3	Design No. 2, Thatching (3.5.78)	40·00	4·00
FD4	Design No. 3, Dry-stone-walling (9.8.78)	£120	4·00
FD5	Design No. 4, Wheel-making (25.10.78)	7·00	4·50
FD6	Design No. 5, Wattle fence-making (10.1.79)	14·00	5·00

Nos. FD2/3 are inscribed "January 1978", FD4 "July 1978", FD5 "October 1978" and FD6 "December 1978".

Type FD7

(Des F. Wegner)

1979 (5 Feb). *Official opening of Derby Mechanised Letter Office. Pale yellow-green and lilac covers as Type FD7 (90 × 49 mm). Containing ten 7p. (No. X875). A. Selvedge at left. B. Selvedge at right.*

		A	B
FD7	Kedleston Hall	7·00	7·00

No. FD7 is inscribed "December 1978".

On sale only in the Derby Head Post Office area to promote postcode publicity and also at the Philatelic Bureau and philatelic sales counters.

1979 (4 Apr). *Country Crafts Series continued. Grey-green and red-brown covers as Type FD2 (90 × 49 mm). A. Selvedge at left. B. Selvedge at right.*

		A	B
FD8	Design No. 6, Basket-making	6·00	4·00

No. FD8 is inscribed "March 1979".

80p. Booklet

Type FE1

(Des P. Hutton)

1979 (3 Oct). *Military Aircraft Series. Blue and grey cover as Type FE1 (90 × 49 mm). Containing ten 8p. (No. X879) attached by the selvedge. A. Selvedge at left. B. Selvedge at right.*

		A	B
FE1	Design No. 1, BE2B, 1914, & Vickers Gun Bus, 1915	3·00	3·00

No. FE1 is inscribed "August 1979".

85p. Booklet

1976 (14 July). *Cover as Type FB1 but larger (90 × 49 mm). Printed in light yellow-olive and brownish grey. A. Selvedge at left. B. Selvedge at right.*

		A	B
FF1	Containing ten 8½p. (No. X881)	5·50	5·50

90p. Booklets

1977 (13 June). *Cover as Type FB1, but larger (90 × 49 mm). Printed in deep grey-blue and cobalt. A. Selvedge at left. B. Selvedge at right.*

		A	B
FG1	Containing ten 9p. (No. X883)	4·50	5·00

Type FG2

(Des R. Maddox)

1978 (8 Feb)–**79**. *British Canals Series. Yellow-olive and new blue covers as Type FG2 (90 × 49 mm). Containing ten 9p. (No. X883). A. Selvedge at left. B. Selvedge at right.*

		A	B
FG2	Design No. 1, Grand Union	18·00	6·00
FG3	Design No. 2, Llangollen (3.5.78)	5·00	£250
FG4	Design No. 3, Kennet & Avon (9.8.78) ..	12·00	8·00
FG5	Design No. 4, Caledonian (25.10.78) ...	4·50	6·00
FG6	Design No. 5, Regents (10.1.79)	15·00	7·00

Nos. FG2/3 are inscribed "January 1978", FG4 "July 1978", FG5 "October 1978" and FG6 "December 1978".

(Des F. Wegner)

1979 (5 Feb). *Official Opening of Derby Mechanised Letter Office. Violet-blue and rose cover as Type FD7 (90 × 49 mm). Containing ten 9p. (No. X883). A. Selvedge at left. B. Selvedge at right.*

		A	B
FG7	Tramway Museum, Crich	8·00	8·00

No. FG7 is inscribed "December 1978".
On sale only in the Derby Head Post Office area to promote postcode publicity and also at the Philatelic Bureau and philatelic sales counters.

1979 (4 Apr). *British Canals Series continued. Yellow-olive and new blue cover as Type FG2. A. Selvedge at left. B. Selvedge at right.*

		A	B
FG8	Design No. 6, Leeds & Liverpool	4·00	4·00

No. FG8 is inscribed "March 1979".

£1 Booklets

All booklets were sold at the cover price of £1 although some contain stamps to a greater value.

Type FH1

(Des N. Battershill)

1979 (3 Oct). *Industrial Archaeology Series. Red and green cover as Type FH1 (90 × 49 mm). Containing ten 10p. (No. X887). A. Selvedge at left. B. Selvedge at right.*

		A	B
FH1	Design No. 1, Ironbridge, Telford, Salop	4·00	3·75

No. FH1 is inscribed "August 1979".

1980 (4 Feb–24 Sept). *Military Aircraft Series continued. Blue and grey covers as Type FE1 (90 × 49 mm). Containing ten 10p. (No. X888). A. Selvedge at left. B. Selvedge at right.*

		A	B
FH2	Design No. 2, Sopwith Camel & Vickers Vimy ..	3·25	3·25
FH3	Design No. 3, Hawker Hart* & Handley Page Heyford (25.6.80)	4·00	4·00

FH4	Design No. 4, Hurricane & Wellington (24.9.80) ..	4·00	4·00

No FH2 is inscribed "January 1980", No. FH3 "May 1980" and No. FH4 "July 1980".
*On the booklet cover the aircraft is wrongly identified as a Hawker Fury.

Type FH5

(Des M. Newton and S. Paine)

1986 (29 July)–**87**. *Musical Instruments Series. Scarlet and black covers as Type FH5. Containing six 17p. (X952).*

FH5	Design No 1, Violin		5·00

No. FH5 is inscribed "November 1985".

Contents changed. Containing No. X901n.

FH6	Design No. 2, French horn (20.10.86)		5·00
FH7	Design No. 3, Bass clarinet (27.1.87)		5·00

No. FH7 is inscribed "October 1986".

Type FH8

(Des A. Davidson)

1987 (14 Apr)–**88**. *Sherlock Holmes Series. Bright scarlet and grey-black covers as Type FH8. Containing booklet pane No. X901n (FH8/9) or X901na (FH10/11).*

FH 8	Design No. 1, *A Study in Scarlet*		5·00
FH 9	Design No. 2, *The Hound of the Baskervilles* (14.7.87)		5·00
FH10	Design No. 3, *The Adventure of the Speckled Band* (29.9.87)		5·00
FH11	Design No. 4, *The Final Problem* (26.1.88)		5·00

Nos. FH8/11 are inscribed "October 1986".
The panes from Nos. FH10/11 have imperforate vertical sides.

1988 (12 Apr). *London Zoo. Children's Drawings Series. Cover as Type FB47 in black and brown. Containing booklet pane No. X901na.*

FH12	Bears design		5·00

No. FH12 is inscribed "October 1986" and has the vertical sides of the pane imperforate.

For full information on all future British issues, collectors should write to the British Post Office Philatelic Bureau, 20 Brandon Street, Edinburgh EH3 5TT

Type FH13

(Des Liz Moyes)

1988 (5 July)—**89**. *Charles Dickens Series. Orange-red and maroon covers as Type FH13.*

FH13   Designs No. 1, *Oliver Twist,* containing booklet pane No. X901na .... 6·00

FH14   Design No. 2, *Nicholas Nickleby,* containing booklet pane No. X904m (5.9.88) .... 6·00

FH15   Design No. 3, *David Copperfield,* containing booklet pane No. X904m (24.1.89) .... 6·00

FH16   Design No. 4, *Great Expectations,* containing booklet pane No. X1051l (25.4.89) .... 6·00

No. FH13 is inscribed "October 1986" and No. FH16 "September 1988", Nos. FH13/16 have the vertical sides of the pane imperforate.

1989 (18 July). *Marine Life Series continued. Cover as Type FB50 in turquoise-green and scarlet. Containing booklet pane No. X904m.*

FH17   Design No. 3, Edible Sea Urchin, Common Starfish and Common Shore Crab .... 6·00

No. FH17 has the vertical edges of the pane imperforate.

Type FH18

(Des J. Sancha)

1989 (2 Oct)—**90**. *Mills Series. Grey-black and grey-green matt card cover as Type FH18.*

FH18   Design No. 1, Wicken Fen, Ely containing booklet pane No. X960l .... 7·00

As Type FH18 *but glossy card cover containing Penny Black Anniversary booklet pane No. 1476l printed in litho by Walsall.*

FH19   Design No. 1 (cover in bottle-green and pale green), Wicken Fen, Ely (30.1.90) .... 7·00

No. FH19 was an experimental printing to test a new cover material. This appears glossy when compared with Nos. FH18 and FH20.

As Type FH18 *but changed to matt card cover containing Penny Black Anniversary booklet pane No. 1469l printed in photo by Harrison.*

FH20   Design No. 2 (cover in grey-black and bright green), Click Mill, Dounby, Orkney (30.1.90) .... 7·00

1990 (4 Sept)—**91**. *Mills Series continued. Covers as Type FH18. Containing booklet pane No. X911m.*

FH21   Design No. 3, (cover printed in light blue and buff) Jack and Jill Mills, Clayton, Sussex .... 4·00

FH22   Design No. 4, (cover printed in dull blue and bright yellow-green). Howell Mill, Llanddeusant, Anglesey (25.6.91) .... 4·00

Nos. FH18/22 have the vertical edges of the pane imperforate.

Type FH23

(Des J. Gibbs)

1991 (10 Sept)—**92**. *150th Anniv of Punch Magazine. Magenta and grey-black covers as Type FH23 containing booklet pane No. X927l.*

FH23   Design No. 1, Illustrations by Richard Doyle and Hoffnung .... 4·00

 a. Corrected rate (10.91) .... 5·00

FH24   Design No. 2, Illustrations by Sir John Tenniel and Eric Burgin (21.1.92) .... 4·00

FH25   Design No. 3, Illustrations by Sir John Tenniel and Anton (28.4.92) .... 4·00

FH26   Design No. 4, Illustrations by Sir John Tenniel and Hewison (28.7.92) .... 3·75

Nos. FH23/6 have the vertical edges of the pane imperforate. No. FH23a has corrected letter rates as No. FB59a.

(Des J. Matthews)

1992 (22 Sept). *1000th Anniv of Appointment of Sheriffs. Scarlet and dull blue cover as Type FB63 containing booklet pane No. X927l.*

FH27   Design as Type FB63 but elements in reverse order ... 3·75

Type FH28

(Des J. Lawrence)

1993 (9 Feb–6 July). *Educational Institutions Series. Covers as Type FH28 containing booklet pane No. X1050l printed in litho by Walsall.*

FH28   Design No. 1 (cover in lake-brown and light blue), University of Wales .... 2·50

FH29   Design No. 2 (cover in deep dull green and lemon), St. Hilda's College, Oxford (6.4.93) .... 2·50

FH30   Design No. 3 (cover in purple-brown and flesh), Marlborough College, Wiltshire (6.7.93) .... 1·50

1993 (1 Nov). *Educational Institutions Series continued. Deep bluish green and lilac cover as Type FH28 containing four 25p. (No. Y1750) printed in litho by Walsall.*
FH31 Design No. 4, Free Church of Scotland College,
Edinburgh .... 1·50

Type FH32

(Des H. Brockway)

1994 (25 Jan). *20th-century Prime Ministers Series. Brown and pale brown cover as Type FH32 containing four 25p. (No. Y1750) printed in litho by Walsall.*
FH32 Design No. 1, Herbert Asquith .... 1·50

(Des H. Brockway)

1994 (26 Apr–6 Sept). *20th-century Prime Ministers Series continued. Covers as Type FH32. Containing four 25p. (No. Y1701) printed in photo by Harrison.*
FH33 Design No. 2, (cover in sepia and buff) David Lloyd-
George .... 1·50
FH34 Design No. 3 (cover in greenish blue and pale blue),
Winston Churchill (6.6.94) .... 1·50
FH35 Design No. 4 (cover in black and yellow-olive), Clement
Attlee (6.9.94) .... 1·50

Type FH36

(Des L. Thomas)

1995 (7 Feb). *50th Anniv of End of Second World War. Brown-olive and brownish black cover as Type FH36 containing four 25p. (No. Y1701) printed in photo by Harrison.*
FH36 Design No. 1, Violette Szabo (S.O.E. agent) .... 1·50

1981 (26 Jan–18 Mar). *Military Aircraft Series continued. Blue and grey covers as Type FE1 (90 × 49 mm). Containing ten 11½p. (No. X893). A. Selvedge at left. B. Selvedge at right.*

	A	B
FI1 Design No. 5, Spitfire & Lancaster	4·00	4·00
FI2 Design No. 6, Lightning & Vulcan (18.3.81)	4·00	4·00

Nos. FI1/2 are inscribed "January 1981".

Type FI3

(Des R. Maddox)

1981 (6 May–30 Sept). *Museums Series. Blue and turquoise-green covers as Type FI3 (90 × 49 mm). Containing ten 11½p. (No. X893). A. Selvedge at left. B. Selvedge at right.*

	A	B
FI3 Design No. 1, Natural History Museum (British Museum), London	4·00	4·00
FI4 Design No. 2, National Museum of Antiquities of Scotland (30.9.81)	4·00	4·00

Nos. FI3/4 are inscribed "January 1981".

1980 (4 Feb–24 Sept). *Industrial Archaeology Series continued. Red and green covers as Type FH1 (90 × 49 mm). Containing ten 12p. (No. X943). A. Selvedge at left. B. Selvedge at right.*

	A	B
FJ1 Design No. 2, Beetle Mill, Ireland	4·00	4·00
FJ2 Design No. 3, Tin Mines, Cornwall (25.6.80)	4·00	5·00
FJ3 Design No. 4, Bottle Kilns, Gladstone, Stoke-on-Trent (24.9.80)	4·00	4·00

No. FJ1 is inscribed "January 1980", No. FJ2 "May 1980" and No. FJ3 "July 1980".

1986 (14 Jan). *Pillar box "Write Now" cover as Type FB31 (90 × 49 mm), printed in yellow-green and pale red. Containing ten 12p. (No. X896). A. Selvedge at left. B. Selvedge at right.*

	A	B
FJ4 "Write Now" (Pillar box design) (no imprint date)	5·00	5·00

Type FJ5

(Des R. Maddox)

1986 (29 Apr). *National Gallery cover as Type FJ5 (90 × 49 mm), printed in magenta and blue-green. Containing ten 12p. (No. X896). A. Selvedge at left. B. Selvedge at right.*

		A	B
FJ5	National Gallery design	5·00	5·00

No. FJ5 is inscribed "November 1985".

Type FJ6

(Des Trickett and Webb Ltd)

1986 (29 July). *Handwriting cover as Type FJ6 (90 × 49 mm), printed in bright orange and bright blue. Containing ten 12p. (No. X896). A. Selvedge at left. B. Selvedge at right.*

		A	B
FJ6	"Maybe"	5·00	5·00

No. FJ6 is inscribed "November 1985".

£1.25 Booklets

1982 (1 Feb–6 Oct). *Museums Series continued. Blue and turquoise-green covers as Type FJ3 (90 × 49 mm). Containing ten 12½p. (No. X898) A. Selvedge at left. B. Selvedge at right.*

		A	B
FK1	Design No. 3, Ashmolean Museum, Oxford	4·00	4·00
FK2	Design No. 4, National Museum of Wales, Cardiff (6.5.82)	4·00	4·00
FK3	Design No. 5, Ulster Museum, Belfast (11.8.82)	4·00	4·00
FK4	Design No. 6, Castle Museum, York (6.10.82)	4·00	4·00

Nos. FK1/4 are inscribed "February 1982".

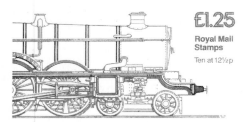

Type FK5

(Des S. Paine)

1983 (16 Feb–26 Oct). *Railway Engines Series. Red and blue-green covers as Type FK5 (90 × 49 mm). Containing ten 12½p. (No. X898). A. Selvedge at left. B. Selvedge at right.*

		A	B
FK5	Design No. 1, GWR *Isambard Kingdom Brunel*	6·00	6·00
FK6	Design No. 2, LMS Class 4P Passenger Tank Engine (5.4.83)	8·00	8·00
	a. Corrected rate	30·00	30·00

		A	B
FK7	Design No. 3, LNER *Mallard* (27.7.83)	6·00	6·00
FK8	Design No. 4, SR/BR *Clan Line* (26.10.83)	6·00	6·00

No. FK5 is inscribed "February 1982". The corrected rate reads, "36p. for 200g" instead of "37p. for 200g".

£1.30 Booklets

Type FL1

(Des J. Gibbs)

1981 (6 May–30 Sept). *Postal History Series. Covers as Type FL1 (90 × 49 mm). Containing No. X894l. A. Selvedge at left. B. Selvedge at right.*

		A	B
FL1	Design No. 1, Penny Black (red & black cover)	5·00	4·00
FL2	Design No. 2, The Downey Head, 1911 (red & green cover) (20.9.81)	7·00	19·00

No. FL1 is inscribed "April 1981" and No. FL2 "September 1981".

Type FL3

(Des J. Thirsk)

1984 (3 Sept)–**85**. *Trams Series. Yellow-orange and purple covers as Type FL3 (90 × 49 mm). Containing ten 13p. (No. X900). A. Selvedge at left. B. Selvedge at right.*

		A	B
FL3	Design No. 1, Swansea/Mumbles Railway Car No. 3	5·00	5·00
FL4	Design No. 2, Glasgow Car No. 927 & Car No. 1194 (15.1.85)	5·00	5·00
FL5	Design No. 3, Car No. 717, Blackpool (23.4.85)	5·00	5·00
FL6	Design No. 4, Car No. 120 & "D" Class Car, London (23.7.85)	5·00	5·00

Nos. FL3/6 are inscribed "September 1984".

Type FL7

(Des Anne Morrow)

1986 (20 Oct). *Books for Children. Cover as Type* FL7 *(90 × 49 mm) printed in rose-red and lemon. Containing ten 13p. (No. X900). A. Selvedge at left. B. Selvedge at right.*

	A	B
FL7 Teddy bears design	5·00	5·00

Type FL8

(Des Trickett and Webb Ltd)

1987 (27 Jan). *"Keep in Touch" cover as Type* FL8 *(90 × 49 mm), printed in light green and bright blue. Containing ten 13p. (No. X900). A. Selvedge at left. B. Selvedge at right.*

	A	B
FL8 Handclasp and envelope design	5·00	5·00

No. FL8 is inscribed "October 1986".

Type FL9

(Des Hannah Firmin)

1987 (14 Apr). *"Ideas for your Garden". Cover as Type* FL9 *(90 × 49 mm) printed in bistre and orange-brown. Containing ten 13p. stamps (No. X900). A. Selvedge at left. B. Selvedge at right.*

	A	B
FL9 Conservatory design	5·00	5·00

No. FL9 is inscribed "October 1986".

Type FL10

(Des Trickett and Webb Ltd)

1987 (4 July). *"Brighter Writer". Cover as Type* FL10 *(90 × 49 mm) printed in orange and bright reddish violet. Containing ten 13p. stamps (No. X900). A. Selvedge at left. B. Selvedge at right.*

	A	B
FL10 Flower design	5·00	5·00

No. FL10 is inscribed "October 1986".

Type FL11

(Des E. Stemp)

1987 (29 Sept). *"Jolly Postman". Cover as Type* FL11 *(90 × 49 mm) printed in pale blue and deep blue. Containing ten 13p. stamps (No. X900). A. Selvedge at left. B. Selvedge at right.*

	A	B
FL11 Boy drawing design	5·00	5·00

No. FL11 is inscribed "October 1986".

Type FL12

(Des E. Hughes)

1988 (26 Jan). *Bicentenary of Linnean Society. Cover as Type FL12 (90 × 49 mm) printed in blue and claret. Containing ten 13p. stamps (No. X900). A. Selvedge at left. B. Selvedge at right.*

	A	B
FL12 Mermaid, fish and insect (from "Hortus Saniba- tis", 1497)	5·00	5·00

No. FL12 is inscribed "October 1986".

Type FL13

(Des Hannah Firmin)

1988 (12 Apr). *Recipe Cards. Cover as Type FL13 (90 × 49 mm) printed in brown and green. Containing ten 13p. stamps (No. X900). A. Selvedge at left. B. Selvedge at right.*

	A	B
FL13 Vegetables design	5·00	5·00

No. FL13 is inscribed "October 1986".

Type FL14

(Des Trickett and Webb Ltd)

1988 (5 July). *"Children's Parties". Cover as Type FL14 (90 × 49 mm) printed in blue-green and bright purple. Containing ten 13p. stamps (No. X900). A. Selvedge at left. B. Selvedge at right.*

	A	B
FL14 Balloons and streamers design	5·00	5·00

No. FL14 is inscribed "October 1986".

£1.40 Booklets

1981 (26 Jan–18 Mar). *Industrial Archaeology Series continued. Red and green covers as Type FH1 (90 × 49 mm). Containing ten 14p. (No. X946). A. Selvedge at left. B. Selvedge at right.*

	A	B
FM1 Design No. 5, Preston Mill, Scotland	5·00	5·00
FM2 Design No. 6, Talyllyn Railway, Tywyn (18.3.81)	5·00	5·00

Nos. FM1/2 are inscribed "January 1981".

Type FM3

(Des E. Stemp)

1981 (6 May–30 Sept). *19th-century Women's Costume Series. Claret and blue covers as Type FM3 (90 × 49 mm). Containing ten 14p. (No. X946). A. Selvedge at left. B. Selvedge at right.*

	A	B
FM3 Design No. 1, Costume, 1800-15	5·00	5·00
FM4 Design No. 2, Costume, 1815–30 (30.9.81)	5·00	5·00

Nos. FM3/4 are inscribed "January 1981".

Type FM5

(Des A. Drummond)

1988 (5 Sept). *"Pocket Planner". Cover as Type FM5 (90 × 49 mm) printed in grey-black and yellow. Containing ten 14p. stamps (No. X903). A. Selvedge at left. B. Selvedge at right.*

	A	B
FM5 "Legal Charge" design	5·00	5·00

Type FM6

(Des Debbie Cook)

1989 (24 Jan). *150th Anniv. of Fox Talbot's Report on the Photographic Process to Royal Society. Cover as Type FM6 (90 × 49 mm) printed in reddish orange and black. Containing ten 14p. stamps (No. X903). A. Selvedge at left. B. Selvedge at right.*

	A	B
FM6 Photographs and darkroom equipment	5·00	5·00

No. FM6 is inscribed "September 1988".

£1.43 Booklets

1982 (1 Feb–6 May). *Postal History Series continued. Covers as Type FL1 (90 × 49 mm). Containing No. X899l. A. Selvedge at left. B. Selvedge at right.*

		A	B
FN1	Design No. 3, James Chalmers (postal reformer) (orange & turquoise-blue cover)	5·00	5·00
FN2	Design No. 4, Edmund Dulac (stamp designer) (brown & red cover) (6.5.82)	5·00	5·00

£1.43

The Holiday Postcard Stamp Book

Royal Mail Stamps
6 at 15½p
First Class
4 at 12½p
Second class

Type FN3

(Des J. Gardner)

1982 (12 July). *"Holiday Postcard Stamp Book". Purple and turquoise-blue cover as Type FN3 (90 × 49 mm). Containing No. X899l. A. Selvedge at left. B. Selvedge at right.*

		A	B
FN3	*Golden Hinde* on front, postcard voucher on back	5·50	5·50

1982 (21 July)–**83**. *Postal History Series continued. Covers as Type FL1 (90 × 49 mm). Containing No. X899l. A. Selvedge at left. B. Selvedge at right.*

		A	B
FN4	Design No. 5, "Forces Postal Service" (grey & violet cover)	5·50	5·50
FN5	Design No. 6, The £5 Orange (orange & black cover) (6.10.82)	5·50	5·50
FN6	Design No. 7, Postmark History (brt scarlet & dp dull blue cover) (16.2.83)	5·50	5·50

No. FN1 is inscribed "February 1982". FN2/3 "May 1982", FN4 "July 1982", FN5 "October 1982", FN6 "November 1982".

For booklet No. FS2 with cover price of £1.45, see £1.60 booklets.

£1.46 Booklets

1983 (5 Apr–26 Oct). *Postal History Series continued. Covers as Type FL1 (90 × 49 mm). A. Containing No. X899n. B. Containing No. X899na.*

		A	B
FO1	Design No. 8, Seahorse High Values (blue & green cover)	8·00	8·00
	a. Corrected rate	16·00	12·00
FO2	Design No. 9, Parcel Post Centenary (turquoise-blue & carmine cover) (27.7.83)	8·00	8·00
FO3	Design No. 10, Silver Jubilee of Regional Stamps (dull green & reddish violet cover) (26.10.83) .	8·00	8·00

No. FO1 is inscribed "March 1983", No. FO2 "May 1983" and No. FO3 "June 1983".

The corrected rate reads, "36p. for 200g" instead of "37p. for 200g".

£1.50 Booklets

1986 (14 Jan). *Pillar box "Write Now" cover as Type FB31 (90 × 49 mm), printed in ultramarine and red. A. Containing No. X897l. B. Containing No. X897la.*

		A	B
FP1	"Write Now" (Pillar box design)	6·00	6·00

No. FP1 shows no imprint date.

1986 (29 Apr). *National Gallery cover as Type FJ5 (90 × 49 mm), printed in violet and vermilion. A. Containing No. X897l. B. Containing No. X897la.*

		A	B
FP2	National Gallery design	6·00	6·00

No. FP2 is inscribed "November 1985".

1986 (29 July). *Handwriting cover as Type FJ6 (90 × 49 mm), printed in blue-green and bright blue. A. Containing No. X897l. B. Containing No. X897la.*

		A	B
FP3	"No"	6·00	6·00

No. FP3 is inscribed "November 1985".

£1.54 Booklets

1984 (3 Sept)–**85**. *Postal History Series continued. Covers as Type FL1 (90 × 49 mm). A. Containing No. X901l. B. Containing No. X901la.*

		A	B
FQ1	Design No. 11, Old & new Postage Dues (reddish purple and pale blue cover)	7·00	7·00
FQ2	Design No. 12, Queen Victoria embossed stamps (yellow-green & blue-cover) (15.1.85)	7·00	7·00
FQ3	Design No. 13, Queen Victoria surface-printed stamps (blue-green & carmine cover) (23.4.85)	7·00	7·00
FQ4	Design No. 14, 17th-century mounted & foot messengers (dp brown & orange-red cover) (23.7.85)	7·00	7·00

No. FQ1 is inscribed "July 1984" and Nos. FQ2/4 are inscribed "September 1984".

£1.55 Booklets

1982 (1 Feb–6 Oct). *19th-century Women's Costume Series continued. Claret and blue covers as Type FM3 (90 × 49 mm). Containing ten 15½p. (No. X948). A. Selvedge at left. B. Selvedge at right.*

		A	B
FR1	Design No. 3, Costume, 1830–50	5·00	5·00
FR2	Design No. 4, Costume, 1850–60 (6.5.82)	5·00	5·00
FR3	Design No. 5, Costume, 1860–80 (11.8.82)	5·00	5·00
FR4	Design No. 6, Costume, 1880–1900 (6.10.82)	5·00	5·00

Nos. FR1/4 are inscribed "February 1982".

£1.60 Booklets

£1.60

Royal Mail Stamps
Ten at 16p

FREE Birthday Box
see inside back cover for details

Type FS1

(Des Carol Walklin)

1983 (5 Apr). *"Birthday Box" Design. Magenta and red-orange cover as Type FS1 (90 × 49 mm). Depicting birthday cake and associated items. A. Selvedge at left. B. Selvedge at right.*

		A	B
FS1	Containing ten 16p. stamps (No. X949) (no imprint date)	6·00	6·00
	a. Rates altered and "February 1983" imprint date	16·00	30·00

Type FS2

(Des R. Maddox)

1983 (10 Aug). *British Countryside Series. Special Discount Booklet (sold at £1.45). Greenish blue and ultramarine cover as Type FS2 (90 × 49 mm). Containing ten 16p. stamps (No. X949Eu). A. Selvedge at left. B. Selvedge at right.*

	A	B
FS2 Design No. 1, Lyme Regis, Dorset	6·75	6·75

Stamps from No. FS2 show a double-lined "D" printed in blue on the reverse over the gum.

No. FS2 is inscribed "April 1983".

1983 (21 Sept). *British Countryside Series continued. Dull green on violet cover as Type FS2 (90 × 49 mm). Containing ten 16p. stamps (No. X949). A. Selvedge at left. B. Selvedge at right.*

	A	B
FS3 Design No. 2, Arlington Row, Bibury, Gloucestershire	6·00	6·00

No. FS3 is inscribed "April 1983".

Type FS4

(Des M. Newton)

1984 (14 Feb). *"Write it" Design. Vermilion and ultramarine cover as Type FS4 (90 × 49 mm). Containing ten 16p. stamps (No. X949). A. Selvedge at left. B. Selvedge at right.*

	A	B
FS4 Fountain pen	6·00	6·00

No. FS4 is inscribed "April 1983".

GIBBONS STAMP MONTHLY
– finest and most informative magazine for all collectors. Obtainable from your newsagent or by postal subscription – details on request.

£1.70 Booklets

Type FT1

(Des G. Hardie)

1984 (3 Sept). *Social Letter Writing Series. Rose and deep claret cover as Type FT1 (90 × 49 mm). Containing ten 17p. (No. X952). A. Selvedge at left. B. Selvedge at right.*

	A	B
FT1 Design No. 1, "Love Letters"	6·50	6·50

No. FT1 is inscribed "September 1984".

1985 (5 Mar). *Social Letter Writing Series continued. Special Discount Booklet (sold at £1.55). Turquoise-blue and deep claret cover as Type FT1 (90 × 49 mm). Containing ten 17p. (No. X952Eu). A. Selvedge at left. B. Selvedge at right.*

	A	B
FT2 Design No. 2, "Letters abroad"	7·00	7·00

Stamps from No. FT2 show a double-lined "D" printed in blue on the reverse over the gum.

No. FT2 is inscribed "September 1984".

1985 (9 Apr). *Social Writing Series continued. Bright blue and deep claret cover as Type FT1 (90 × 49 mm). Containing ten 17p. (No. X952). A. Selvedge at left. B. Selvedge at right.*

	A	B
FT3 Design No. 3, "Fan letters"	6·50	6·50

No. FT3 is inscribed "September 1984".

Type FT4

(Des B. Smith)

1985 (30 July). *350 Years of Royal Mail Public Postal Service. Special Discount Booklet (sold at £1.53). Cover Type FS4 (90 × 60 mm), printed in rosine and bright blue. Containing ten 17p. (No. 1290Eu) with selvedge at top.*

FT4 Datapost Service design	7·00

The stamps from this booklet show double-lined letters "D" printed on the reverse over the gum.

No. FT4 is inscribed "September 1984".

1985 (8 Oct)–**86**. *Social Letter Writing Series continued. Black and bright scarlet cover as Type FT1 (90 × 49 mm). Containing ten 17p. (No. X952). A. Selvedge at left. B. Selvedge at right.*

		A	B
FT5	Design No. 4, "Write Now" (Pillar box)	6·50	6·50
	a. Revised rates (2nd class (60g) 12p.) (1.86) ...	12·00	10·00

1986 (29 Apr). *National Gallery cover as Type FJ5 (90 × 49 mm), printed in blue-green and blue. Containing ten 17p. (No. X952). A. Selvedge at left. B. Selvedge at right.*

		A	B
FT6	National Gallery design	6·50	6·50

No. FT6 is inscribed "November 1985".

1986 (29 July). *Handwriting cover as Type FJ6 (90 × 49 mm) printed in red and bright blue. Containing ten 17p. (No. X952). A. Selvedge at left. B. Selvedge at right.*

		A	B
FT7	"Yes"	6·50	6·50

No. FT7 is inscribed "November 1985".

£1.80 Booklets

1986 (20 Oct). *Books for Children. New blue and orange-brown cover as Type FL7. Containing ten 18p. (No. X955). A. Selvedge at left. B. Selvedge at right.*

		A	B
FU1	Rabbits design	7·00	7·00

1987 (27 Jan). *"Keep in Touch" cover as Type FL8 printed in magenta and bright blue. Containing ten 18p. (No. X955). A. Selvedge at left. B. Selvedge at right.*

		A	B
FU2	Handclasp and envelope design	7·00	7·00

No. FU2 is inscribed "October 1986".

1987 (14 Apr). *"Ideas for your Garden". Claret and brown-olive cover as Type FL9 (90 × 49 mm). Containing ten 18p. stamps (No. X955). A. Selvedge at left. B. Selvedge at right.*

		A	B
FU3	Garden path design	7·00	7·00

No. FU3 is inscribed "October 1986".

1987 (14 July). *"Brighter Writer". Turquoise-green and reddish orange cover as Type FL10 (90 × 49 mm). Containing ten 18p. stamps (No. X955). A. Selvedge at left. B. Selvedge at right.*

		A	B
FU4	Berries and leaves design	7·00	7·00

No. FU4 is inscribed "October 1986".

1987 (29 Sept). *"Jolly Postman". Cover as Type FL11 (90 × 49 mm) printed in deep blue and claret. Containing ten 18p. stamps (No. X955). A. Selvedge at left. B. Selvedge at right.*

		A	B
FU5	Girl drawing design	7·00	7·00

No. FU5 is inscribed "October 1986".

1988 (26 Jan). *Bicentenary of Linnean Society. Cover as Type FL12 (90 × 49 mm) printed in dull yellow-green and dull claret. Containing ten 18p. stamps (No. X955). A. Selvedge at left. B. Selvedge at right.*

		A	B
FU6	Wolf and birds (from "Hortus Sanitatis", 1497) ..	7·00	7·00

1988 (12 Apr). *Recipe Cards. Cover as Type FL13 (90 × 49 mm) printed in claret and Indian red. Containing ten 18p. stamps (No. X955). A. Selvedge at left. B. Selvedge at right.*

		A	B
FU7	Fruits, pudding and jam design	7·00	7·00

No. FU7 is inscribed "October 1986".

1988 (5 July). *"Children's Parties". Cover as Type FL14 (90 × 49 mm) printed in violet and rosine. Containing ten 18p. stamps (No. X955). A. Selvedge at left. B. Selvedge at right.*

		A	B
FU8	Balloons and party hats design	7·00	7·00

No. FU8 is inscribed "October 1986".

£1.90 Booklets

1988 (5 Sept). *"Pocket Planner". Cover as Type FM5 (90 × 49 mm) printed in yellow-green and magenta. Containing ten 19p. stamps (No. X956). A. Selvedge at left. B. Selvedge at right.*

		A	B
FV1	"Marriage Act" design	7·00	7·00

1989 (24 Jan). *150th Anniv. of Fox Talbot's Report on the Photographic Process to Royal Society. Cover as Type FM6 (90 × 49 mm) printed in emerald and black. Containing ten 19p. stamps (No. X956). A. Selvedge at left. B. Selvedge at right.*

		A	B
FV2	Fox Talbot with camera and Lacock Abbey	7·00	7·00

No. FV2 is inscribed "September 1988".

£2 Booklets

Type FW1

(Des Debbie Cook)

1993 (1 Nov)–**94**. *Postal Vehicles Series. Covers as Type FW1. Containing eight 25p. (No. Y1701).*

FW1	Design No. 1 (cover in dull vermilion and deep blue), Motorised cycle-carrier	3·00
FW2	Design No. 2 (cover in green and deep violet-blue), Experimental motor-mail van (26.4.94)	3·00
FW3	Design No. 3 (cover in red and black), Experimental electric mail van, 1932 (6.9.94)	3·00

Type FW3

(Des The Four Hundred)

1995 (7 Feb) *Birth Bicentenary of Sir Rowland Hill. Purple and new blue cover as Type FW3 containing eight 25p. (No. Y1701).*
FW4 Design No. 1, Rowland Hill as director of London and
    Brighton Railway Company .... 3·00

Christmas Booklets

Type FX1

(Des J. Matthews)

1978 (15 Nov). *"Christmas Greetings". Cover Type FX1 (90 × 49 mm). Printed in rose-red and sage-green.*
FX1 £1.60, containing booklet pane No. X875l .... 4·50
    No. FX1 is inscribed "August 1978".

Type FX2

(Des P. Sharland)

1979 (4 Nov). *"Christmas Greetings". Red and green cover as Type FX2 (90 × 49 mm), showing Christmas cracker.*
FX2 £1.80, containing booklet pane No. X879l .... 5·00
    No. FX2 is inscribed "October 1979".

Type FX3

(Des E. Fraser)

1980 (12 Nov). *Christmas. Red and blue cover as Type FX3 (90 × 49 mm), showing Nativity scene.*
FX3 £2.20, containing booklet pane No. X888m .... 6·00
    No. FX3 is inscribed "September 1980".

Type FX4

(Des W. Sanderson)

1981 (11 Nov).   *Christmas. Red and blue cover as Type FX4, (90 × 49 mm), showing skating scene.*
FX4   £2.55, containing booklet pane No. X893l . . . .   7·00
No. FX4 is inscribed "January 1981".

Type FX5

(Des A. Davidson)

1982 (10 Nov).   *Christmas. Red and green cover as Type FX5 (90 × 49 mm), showing Christmas Mummers.*
FX5   £2.50, containing booklet pane No. X898l . . . .   9·00
No. FX5 is inscribed "February 1982" and was sold at a discount of 30p. off the face value of the stamps.
Each stamp in the pane has a blue star printed on the reverse over the gum.

Type FX6

(Des Barbara Brown)

1983 (9 Nov).   *Christmas. Brown-lilac and yellow cover as Type FX6 (90 × 49 mm), showing pantomime scenes.*
FX6   £2.20, containing twenty 12½p. (No. X898Eua) . . . .   8·00
No. FX6 is inscribed "April 1983" and was sold at a discount of 30p. off the face value of the stamps.
Each stamp in the pane has a double-lined blue star printed on the reverse over the gum.

Type FX7

(Des Yvonne Gilbert)

1984 (20 Nov).   *Christmas. Light brown and red-orange cover as Type FX7 (90 × 60 mm), showing Nativity scene.*
FX7   £2.30, containing twenty 13p. (No. 1267Eu) . . . .   9·00
No. FX7 is inscribed "September 1984" and was sold at a discount of 30p. off the face value of the stamps.
The stamps from this booklet show double-lined blue stars printed on the reverse over the gum.

Type FX8

(Des A. George)

1985 (19 Nov).   *Christmas. Bright blue and rose cover as Type FX8 (90 × 60 mm), showing The Pantomime.*
FX8   £2.40, containing twenty 12p. (No. 1303Eu) . . . .   8·00
The stamps from this booklet show double-lined blue stars printed on the reverse over the gum.

Type FX9

(Des Lynda Gray)

1986 (2 Dec). *Christmas. Red and dull blue-green cover as Type* FX9 *(90 × 49 mm), showing Shetland Yule cakes. A. Selvedge at left. B. Selvedge at right.*

	A	B
FX9 £1.30, containing ten 13p. (No. X900Eu)	9·00	9·00

No. FX9 is inscribed "October 1986" and was sold at a discount of 10p. off the face value of the stamps.

Each stamps in the pane has a blue star printed on the reverse over the gum.

For 1990 and later Christmas stamps, see Barcode Booklets Section G.

Greetings Booklet

£1.90 Booklet

Type FX10

(Des L. Moberly)

1989 (31 Jan). *Greetings Stamps. Multicoloured cover as Type* FX10 *(89 × 60 mm). Containing booklet pane No.* 1423a, *including twelve special greetings labels in a block (3 × 4) at right, attached by the selvedge.*

FX10 Greetings design .... 28·00

No. FX10 is inscribed "September 1988".

The cover of No. FX10 shows an overall pattern of elements taken from the stamp designs. Due to the method of production the position of these elements varies from cover to cover.

For Greetings stamps in Barcode booklets, see Barcode Booklets Section F..

Barcode Booklets

These booklets are listed in five sections.

SECTION C.   G numbers containing Machin stamps

SECTION D.   H numbers containing Machin NVI stamps

SECTION E.   J numbers containing Machin Penny Black
Anniversary stamps

SECTION F.   K numbers containing Greetings stamps

SECTION G.   L numbers containing Christmas stamps

C. Barcode Booklets containing Machin stamps with values shown as
Type **367**.

These are produced for sale in both post offices and commercial
outlets.

COVERS. These are all printed in scarlet, lemon and black with the
barcode on the reverse. Type GA1 has a clear "window" to view the
contents. Type GB3 is shorter and has a stamp illustration printed on
the cover to replace the "window". These illustrations show an oblique
white line across the bottom right-hand corner of the "stamp". Unless
otherwise stated all covers were printed by Harrison.

NOTE: All panes are attached to the covers by the selvedge.

Barcode booklet covers are illustrated at two-thirds linear size
unless otherwise stated.

52p. Booklet

Type GA1

1987 (4 Aug).   *Laminated cover Type GA1 (75 × 60 mm)*.
GA1   Containing booklet pane No. X900n . . . .   3·00
No. GA1 is inscribed "20 October 1986".

56p. Booklets

1988 (23 Aug).   *Laminated cover as Type GA1 (75 × 56 mm)*.
GB1   Containing booklet pane No. X903l . . . .   5·00

1988 (11 Oct).   *Laminated cover as Type GA1 (75 × 56 mm) printed by
Walsall.*
GB2   Containing booklet pane No. X903l . . . .   5·00

Type GB3
Large Crown

1988 (11 Oct).   *Laminated cover as Type GB3 (75 × 48 mm) with stamp
printed on the cover in deep blue.*
GB3   Containing booklet pane No. X903n . . . .   6·00
No. GB3 is inscribed "5 September 1988" and has the horizontal
edges of the pane imperforate.

1989 (24 Jan).   *Laminated cover as Type GB3 (75 × 48 mm) with stamp
printed on the cover in deep blue by Walsall.*
GB4   Containing booklet pane No. X903q . . . .   16·00
No. GB4 is inscribed "5 September 1988" and has the three edges of
the pane imperforate.

72p. Booklet

1987 (4 Aug).   *Laminated cover as Type GA1 (75 × 60 mm)*.
GC1   Containing booklet pane No. X955m . . . .   3·00
No. GC1 is inscribed "20 October 1986".

76p. Booklets

1988 (23 Aug).   *Laminated cover as Type GA1 (75 × 56 mm)*.
GD1   Containing booklet pane No. X956l . . . .   6·00

1988 (11 Oct).   *Laminated cover as Type GA1 (75 × 56 mm) printed by
Walsall.*
GD2   Containing booklet pane No. X956l . . . .   6·00

1988 (11 Oct).   *Laminated cover as Type GB3 (75 × 48 mm) with stamp
printed on the cover in bright orange-red.*
GD3   Containing booklet pane No. X956n . . . .   6·00
No. GD3 is inscribed "5 September 1988" and has the horizontal
edges of the pane imperforate.

1989 (24 Jan).   *Laminated cover as Type GB3 (75 × 48 mm) with stamp
printed on the cover in bright orange-red by Walsall.*
GD4   Containing booklet pane No. X956q . . . .   16·00
No. GD4 is inscribed "5 September 1988" and has the three edges of
the pane imperforate.

NEW INFORMATION

The editor is always interested to correspond with people
who have new information that will improve or
correct the Catalogue.

78p. Booklet

GD4a (As Type GL1 but, without "4")

1992 (28 July). *Multicoloured laminated cover as Type GD4a (75 × 49 mm) with stamp printed on cover in bright mauve by Walsall.*
GD4a   Containing two 39p. stamps (No. X1058) (pane No. X1058l with right-hand vert pair removed) and pane of 4 air mail labels ....   1·75
    Stamps in No. GD4a have top or bottom edge imperforate.
    Booklet No. GD4a was produced in connection with a Kellogg's Bran Flakes promotion.

£1.04 Booklet

1987 (4 Aug). *Laminated cover as Type GA1 (75 × 60 mm).*
GE1   Containing booklet pane No. X971al ....   14·00
    No. GE1 is inscribed "20 October 1986".

£1.08 Booklets

1988 (23 Aug). *Laminated cover as Type GA1 (75 × 56 mm).*
GF1   Containing booklet pane No. X973l ....   7·00

1988 (11 Oct). *Laminated cover as Type GB3 (75 × 48 mm) with stamp printed on the cover in chestnut.*
GF2   Containing booklet pane No. X973m ....   22·00
    No. GF2 is inscribed "5 September 1988" and has the horizontal edges of the pane imperforate.

£1.16 Booklets

Type GG1
Redrawn Crown

1989 (2 Oct). *Laminated cover as Type GG1 (75 × 48 mm) with stamp printed on the cover in deep mauve by Walsall.*
GG1   Containing booklet pane No. X1054l ....   12·00
    No. GG1 has three edges of the pane imperforate.

1990 (17 Apr). *Laminated cover as Type GG1 (75 × 48 mm) with stamp printed on the cover in deep mauve by Walsall.*
GG2   Containing booklet pane No. X1055l ....   20·00
    No. GG2 has three edges of the pane imperforate.

£1.24 Booklet

Type GH1
Crown on White

1990 (17 Sept). *Multicoloured laminated cover as Type GH1 (75 × 49 mm) with stamp printed on the cover in ultramarine by Walsall.*
GH1   Containing booklet pane No. X1056l ....   5·50
    No. GH1 has the horizontal edges of the pane imperforate.

£1.30 Booklet

1987 (4 Aug). *Laminated cover as Type GA1 (98 × 60 mm).*
GI1   Containing booklet pane No. X900o ....   6·00
    No. GI1 is inscribed "20 October 1986".

£1.32 Booklet

Type GJ1

1991 (16 Sept). *Multicoloured laminated cover as Type GJ1 (75 × 49 mm) with stamp printed on the cover in light emerald by Walsall.*
GJ1   Containing booklet pane No. X1057l and a pane of 4 air mail labels ....   3·50
    No. GJ1 has the horizontal edges of the pane imperforate.

£1.40 Booklets

1988 (23 Aug). *Laminated cover as Type GA1 (97 × 56 mm).*
GK1   Containing booklet pane No. X903m ....   8·00

1988 (11 Oct). *Laminated cover as Type GA1 (97 × 56 mm) printed by Questa.*
GK2   Containing ten 14p. (No. X1007) ....   12·00

1988 (11 Oct). *Laminated cover as Type GB3 (75 × 48 mm) with stamp printed on the cover in deep blue.*
GK3   Containing booklet pane No. X903p ....   8·00
    No. GK3 is inscribed "5 September 1988" and has horizontal edges of the pane imperforate.

1988 (11 Oct). *Laminated cover as Type GB3 (75 × 48 mm) with stamp printed on the cover in deep blue by Questa.*
GK4   Containing ten 14p. (No. X1007) ....   12·00

1993 (1 Nov). *Laminated cover as Type GJ1 (76 × 50 mm) with stamp printed on the cover in yellow by Walsall.*
GK5   Containing four 35p. (No. Y1751) and a pane of 4 air mail
       labels . . . .   2·10

£1.56 Booklet

Type GL1

1991 (16 Sept). *Multicoloured laminated cover as Type GL1 (75 × 49 mm) with stamp printed on cover in bright mauve by Walsall.*
GL1   Containing booklet pane No. X1058l and a pane of 4 air
       mail labels . . . .   3·50
No. GL1 has the horizontal edges of the pane imperforate.

£1.64 Booklet

1993 (1 Nov). *Laminated cover as Type GL1 (76 × 50 mm) with stamp printed on cover in drab by Walsall.*
GM1   Containing four 41p. (No. Y1752) and a pane of 4 air mail
       labels . . . .   2·40

£1.80 Booklet

1987 (4 Aug). *Laminated cover as Type GA1 (98 × 60 mm).*
GN1   Containing booklet pane No. X955n . . . .   6·50
No. GN1 is inscribed "20 October 1986".

£1.90 Booklets

1988 (23 Aug). *Laminated cover as Type GA1 (97 × 56 mm).*
GO1   Containing booklet pane No. X956m . . . .   10·00

1988 (11 Oct). *Laminated cover as Type GA1 (97 × 56 mm) printed by Questa.*
GO2   Containing ten 19p. (No. X1013) . . . .   14·00

1988 (11 Oct). *Laminated cover as Type GB3 (75 × 48 mm) with stamp printed on the cover in bright orange-red.*
GO3   Containing booklet pane No. X956o . . . .   12·00
No. GO3 is inscribed "5 September 1988" and has the horizontal edges of the pane imperforate.

1988 (11 Oct). *Laminated cover as Type GB3 (75 × 48 mm) with stamp printed on the cover in bright orange-red by Questa.*
GO4   Containing ten 19p. (No. X1013) . . . .   14·00

£2.40 Booklets

1994 (9 Aug). *Laminated cover as Type GL1 (75 × 49 mm) with stamp printed on cover in dull blue-grey by Walsall.*
GP1   Containing four 60p. (No. Y1753) and a pane of 4 air mail
       labels . . . .   3·50

Type GP2

1994 (4 Oct). *Laminated cover as Type GP2 (75 × 49 mm) with stamp printed on cover in dull blue-grey by Walsall.*
GP2   Containing four 60p. (No. Y1753) and a pane of 4 air mail
       plus 4 "Seasons Greetings" labels . . . .   3·50

D. Barcode Booklets containing No Value Indicated stamps with barcodes on the reverse.

Panes of 4 2nd Class stamps

Type HA1
Redrawn Crown (small)

1989 (22 Aug).   *Laminated cover as Type HA1 (75 × 48 mm) with stamp printed on the cover in bright blue by Walsall.*
HA1   Containing booklet pane No. 1449b . . . .   3·50
No. HA1 has three edges of the pane imperforate.
No. HA1 was initially sold at 56p., which was increased to 60p. from 2.10.89.

1989 (28 Nov).   *Laminated cover as Type HA1 (75 × 48 mm) with stamp printed on the cover in bright blue by Walsall containing stamps printed in photo by Harrison.*
HA2   Containing booklet pane No. 1445b . . . .   3·50
No. HA2 has three edges of the pane imperforate and was sold at 60p.

Type HA3
Crown on white

1990 (7 Aug).   *Multicoloured laminated cover as Type HA3 (75 × 48 mm) with stamp printed on the cover in deep blue by Walsall.*
HA3   Containing booklet pane No. 1515a . . . .   3·00
No. HA3 has the horizontal edges of the pane imperforate.
No. HA3 was initially sold at 60p., which was increased to 68p. from 17.9.90.

1991 (6 Aug).   *Multicoloured laminated cover as Type HA3 (75 × 48 mm) with stamp printed on the cover in bright blue by Walsall.*
HA4   Containing booklet pane No. 1449c . . . .   1·50
No. HA4 has the horizontal edges of the pane imperforate.
No. HA4 was initially sold at 68p., which was increased to 72p. from 16.9.91.

Type HA5
Olympic Symbols

1992 (21 Jan).   *Multicoloured laminated cover as Type HA5 (75 × 48 mm) with stamp printed on the cover in bright blue by Walsall.*
HA5   Containing booklet pane No. 1449b . . . .   1·50
No. HA5 has the horizontal edges of the pane imperforate and was sold at 72p.

PERFORATIONS. Booklets from No. HA6 show perforations on all edges of the pane.

1993 (6 Apr).   *Multicoloured laminated cover as Type HA3 (75 × 48 mm) with stamp printed on the cover in bright blue by Walsall.*
HA6   Containing four 2nd Class stamps (No. 1665) . . . .   1·10
No. HA6 was initially sold at 72p., which was increased to 76p. from 1.11.93.
No. HA6 was re-issued on 6 December 1994 showing the inscriptions on the inside of the cover re-arranged.

1993 (7 Sept).   *Multicoloured laminated cover as Type HA3 (75 × 48 mm) with stamp printed on the cover in bright blue by Harrison.*
HA7   Containing four 2nd Class stamps (No. 1663a) . . . .   1·10
No. HA7 was initially sold at 72p., which was increased to 76p. from 1.11.93.

Type HA8

1995 (10 Jan).   *Multicoloured laminated cover as Type HA8 (75 × 48 mm) with stamps printed on the cover in bright blue by Harrison.*
HA8   Containing four 2nd Class stamps (No. 1663a) . . . .   1·10
No. HA8 was sold at 76p.

Panes of 4 1st Class stamps

1989 (22 Aug). *Laminated cover as Type HA1 (75 × 48 mm) with stamp printed on the cover in brownish black by Walsall.*
HB1   Containing booklet pane No. 1450a ....   7·50
    No. HB1 has three edges of the pane imperforate.
    No. HB1 was initially sold at 76p., which was increased to 80p. from 2.10.89.

1989 (5 Dec). *Laminated cover as Type HA1 (75 × 48 mm) with stamp printed on the cover in brownish black by Walsall containing stamps printed in photo by Harrison.*
HB2   Containing booklet pane No. 1447b ....   9·00
    No. HB2 has three edges of the pane imperforate and was sold at 80p.

1990 (7 Aug). *Multicoloured laminated cover as Type HA3 (75 × 48 mm) with stamp printed on the cover in bright orange-red by Walsall.*
HB3   Containing booklet pane No. 1516a ....   2·00
    a. Containing pane No. 1516ca ....   8·00
    No. HB3 has the horizontal edges of the pane imperforate.
    No. HB3 was initially sold at 80p., which was increased to 88p. from 17.9.90 and to 96p. from 16.9.91.

1992 (21 Jan). *Multicoloured laminated cover as Type HA5 (75 × 48 mm) with stamp printed on the cover in bright orange-red by Walsall.*
HB4   Containing booklet pane No. 1516a ....   2·50
    No. HB4 has the horizontal edges of the pane imperforate and was initially sold at 96p., which was increased to £1 from 1.11.93.

PERFORATIONS. Booklets from No. HB5 show perforations on all edges of the pane.

1993 (6 Apr). *Multicoloured laminated cover as Type HA3 (75 × 48 mm) with stamp printed on the cover in bright orange-red by Harrison*
HB5   Containing four 1st Class stamps (No. 1664) ....   1·50
    No. HB5 was initially sold at 96p., which was increased to £1 from 1.11.93.

1993 (17 Aug). *Multicoloured laminated cover as Type HA3 (76 × 50 mm) with stamp printed on the cover in bright orange-red by Walsall.*
HB6   Containing four 1st Class stamps (No. 1666) ....   1·50
    No. HB6 was initially sold at 96p., which was increased to £1 from 1.11.93.

1994 (27 July). *Multicoloured laminated cover as Type HA3 (76 × 50 mm) with stamp printed on the cover in bright orange-red by Questa.*
HB7   Containing booklet pane No. 1666a which includes a label commemorating the 300th anniv of the Bank of England ....   1·50
    No. HB7 was sold at £1.

1995 (10 Jan). *Multicoloured laminated cover as Type HA8 (75 × 48 mm) with stamps printed on the cover in bright orange-red by Walsall.*
HB8   Containing four 1st Class stamps (No. 1666) ....   1·50
    No. HB8 was sold at £1.

Panes of 10 2nd Class stamps

1989 (22 Aug–2 Oct). *Laminated cover as Type HA1 (75 × 48 mm) with stamp printed on the cover in bright blue by Harrison.*
HC1   Containing booklet pane No. 1445a ....   6·00
    a. Inside cover with new rates (2 Oct) ....   6·00
    Nos. HC1/a have the horizontal edges of the pane imperforate. No. HC1 was initially sold at £1.40, which was increased to £1.50 from 2.10.89. No. HC1a was sold at £1.50.

1989 (19 Sept). *Laminated cover as Type HA1 (75 × 48 mm) with stamp printed on the cover in bright blue by Questa.*
HC2   Containing ten 2nd Class stamps (No. 1451) ....   7·00
    No. HC2 has perforations on all edges of the pane and was initially sold at £1.40, which was increased to £1.50 from 2.10.89.

1990 (7 Aug). *Multicoloured laminated cover as Type HA3 (75 × 48 mm) with stamp printed on the cover in deep blue by Harrison.*
HC3   Containing booklet pane No. 1511a ....   6·00
    No. HC3 has the horizontal edges of the pane imperforate.
    No. HC3 was initially sold at £1.50, which was increased to £1.70 from 17.9.90.

1990 (7 Aug). *Multicoloured laminated cover as Type HA3 (75 × 48 mm) with stamp printed on the cover in deep blue by Questa.*
HC4   Containing ten 2nd Class stamps (No. 1513) ....   7·50
    No. HC4 has perforations on all edges of the pane and was initially sold at £1.50, which was increased to £1.70 from 17.9.90.

1990 (7 Aug). *Multicoloured laminated cover as Type HA3 (75 × 48 mm) with stamp printed on the cover in deep blue by Walsall.*
HC5   Containing booklet pane No. 1515b ....   6·00
    No. HC5 has the horizontal edges of the pane imperforate.
    No. HC5 was initially sold at £1.50, which was increased to £1.70 from 17.9.90.

1991 (6 Aug). *Multicoloured laminated cover as Type HA3 (75 × 48 mm) with stamp printed on the cover in bright blue by Questa.*
HC6   Containing ten 2nd Class stamps (No. 1451) ....   3·75
    No. HC6 has perforations on all edges of the pane and was initially sold at £1.70, which was increased to £1.80 from 16.9.91.

1991 (6 Aug). *Multicoloured laminated cover as Type HA3 (75 × 48 mm) with stamp printed on the cover in bright blue by Walsall.*
HC7   Containing booklet pane No. 1449d ....   4·00
    No. HC7 has the horizontal edges of the pane imperforate.
    No. HC7 was initially sold at £1.70, which was increased to £1.80 from 16.9.91.

1992 (21 Jan). *Multicoloured laminated cover as Type HA5 (75 × 48 mm) with stamp printed on the cover in bright blue by Walsall.*
HC8   Containing booklet pane No. 1449d ....   4·25
    No HC8 has the horizontal edges of the pane imperforate and was initially sold at £1.80, which was increased to £1.84 from 1.11.93.

1992 (31 Mar). *Multicoloured laminated cover as Type HA5 (75 × 48 mm) with stamp printed on the cover in bright blue by Questa.*
HC9   Containing ten 2nd Class stamps (No. 1451) ....   2·75
    No. HC9 has perforations on all edges of the pane and was sold at £1.80.

1992 (22 Sept). *Multicoloured laminated cover as Type HA3 (75 × 48 mm) with stamp printed on the cover in bright blue by Harrison.*
HC10   Containing booklet pane No. 1445a ....   2·75
    No. HC10 has the horizontal edges of the pane imperforate and was sold at £1.80.

PERFORATIONS. Booklets from No. HC11 show perforations on all edges of the pane.

1993 (6 Apr). *Multicoloured laminated cover as Type HA3 (75 × 48 mm) with stamp printed on the cover in bright blue by Questa.*

HC11   Containing ten 2nd Class stamps (No. 1665) ....   2·75

No. HC11 was initially sold at £1.80, which was increased to £1.90 from 1.11.93.

No. HC11 was re-issued on 17 August 1993 showing changes to the text on the inside of the cover and again on 6 September 1994 showing further changes.

1993 (1 Nov). *Multicoloured laminated cover as Type HA3 (75 × 48 mm) with stamp printed on the cover in bright blue by Walsall.*

HC12   Containing ten 2nd Class stamps (No. 1665) ....   2·75

No. HC12 was sold at £1.90.

1995 (10 Jan). *Multicoloured laminated cover as Type HA8 (75 × 48 mm) with stamps printed on the cover in bright blue by Questa.*

HC13   Containing ten 2nd Class stamps (No. 1665) ....   2·75

No. HC13 was sold at £1.90.

Panes of 10 1st Class stamps

1989 (22 Aug–2 Oct). *Laminated cover as Type HA1 (75 × 48 mm) with stamp printed on the cover in brownish black by Harrison.*

HD1   Containing booklet pane No. 1447a ....   8·00

    a. Inside cover with new rates (2 Oct) ....   8·00

Nos. HD1/a have the horizontal edges of the pane imperforate.

No. HD1 was initially sold at £1.90 which was increased to £2 from 2.10.89. No. HD1a was sold at £2.

1989 (19 Sept). *Laminated cover as Type HA1 (75 × 48 mm) with stamp printed on the cover in brownish black by Questa.*

HD2   Containing ten 1st Class stamps (No. 1452) ....   10·00

No. HD2 has perforations on all edges of the pane and was initially sold at £1.90, which was increased to £2 from 2.10.89.

1990 (7 Aug). *Multicoloured laminated cover as Type HA3 (75 × 48 mm) with stamp printed on the cover in bright orange-red by Harrison.*

HD3   Containing booklet pane No. 1512a ....   4·50

No. HD3 has the horizontal edges of the pane imperforate.

No. HD3 was initially sold at £2, which was increased to £2.20 from 17.9.90 and to £2.40 from 16.9.91.

1990 (7 Aug). *Multicoloured laminated cover as Type HA3 (75 × 48 mm) with stamp printed on the cover in bright orange-red by Questa.*

HD4   Containing ten 1st Class stamps (No. 1514) ....   4·25

No. HD4 has perforations on all edges of the pane and was initially sold at £2, which was increased to £2.20 from 17.9.90 and to £2.40 from 16.9.91.

1990 (7 Aug). *Multicoloured laminated cover as Type HA3 (75 × 48 mm) with stamp printed on the cover in bright orange-red by Walsall.*

HD5   Containing booklet pane No. 1516b ....   4·00

No. HD5 has the horizontal edges of the pane imperforate and intially sold at £2, which was increased to £2.20 from 17.9.90 and to £2.40 from 16.9.91.

1992 (21 Jan). *Multicoloured laminated cover as Type HA5 (75 × 48 mm) with stamp printed on the cover in bright orange-red by Harrison.*

HD6   Containing booklet pane No. 1512a. ....   5·50

No. HD6 has the horizontal edges of the pane imperforate and was sold at £2.40.

1992 (21 Jan). *Multicoloured laminated cover as Type HA5 (75 × 48 mm) with stamp printed on the cover in bright orange-red by Walsall.*

HD7   Containing booklet pane No. 1516b. ....   5·50

No. HD7 has the horizontal edges of the pane imperforate and was sold at £2.40.

1993 (9 Feb). *Multicoloured laminated cover as Type HA3 (77 × 44 mm) with advertisement for Greetings Booklet on reverse showing Rupert Bear as in Type KX5. Stamp printed on the cover in bright orange-red by Walsall.*

HD8   Containing booklet pane No. 1516b ....   4·00

No. HD8 has the horiziontal edges of the pane imperforate and was sold at £2.40.

PERFORATIONS. Booklets from No. HD9 show perforations on all edges of the pane.

1993 (6 Apr). *Multicoloured laminated cover as Type HA3 (75 × 48 mm) with stamp printed on the cover in bright orange-red by Harrison.*

HD9   Containing ten 1st Class stamps (No. 1664) .....,.....   3·50

No. HD9 was initially sold at £2.40., which was increased to £2.50 from 1.11.93.

No. HD9 was re-issued on 17 August 1993 showing changes to the text on the inside of the covers.

1993 (6 Apr). *Multicoloured laminated cover as Type HA3 (75 × 48 mm) with stamp printed on the cover in bright orange-red by Walsall.*

HD10   Containing ten 1st Class stamps (No. 1666) ....   3·50

No. HD10 was initially sold at £2.40., which was increased to £2.50 from 1.11.93.

No. HD10 was re-issued on 17 August 1993 showing changes to the text on the inside of the covers.

1993 (1 Nov). *Laminated cover as Type HA3 (75 × 50 mm) with stamp printed on the cover in bright orange-red by Questa.*
HD11 Containing ten 1st Class stamps (No. 1666) .... 3·75
No. HD11 was sold at £2.50.

No. HD11 was re-issued on 6 September 1994 showing changes to the text on the inside of the cover.

1993 (1 Nov). *Laminated cover as Type HA3 (75 × 50 mm) with advertisement for Greetings Booklet on reverse showing Rupert Bear as in Type KX5. Stamp printed on the cover in bright orange-red by Walsall.*
HD12 Containing ten 1st Class stamps (No. 1666) .... 3·75

1994 (22 Feb). *Multicoloured laminated cover as Type HA3 (75 × 48 mm) with stamp printed on the cover in bright orange-red by Walsall. Inscribed "FREE POSTCARDS" on yellow tab at right.*
HD13 Containing ten 1st Class stamps (No. 1666) and additional page giving details of Greetings Stamps postcard offer .... 3·75
No. HD13 was sold at £2.50.

1994 (1 July). *Multicoloured laminated covers as Type HA3 (76 × 50 mm) with advertisement for Greetings Booklet on reverse showing Rupert Bear as in Type KX5. Stamp printed on the cover in bright orange-red by Walsall. Inscribed "OPEN NOW Chance to win a kite" on yellow tab at right.*
HD14 Containing ten 1st Class stamps (No. 1666) with "Better luck next time." etc on inside back cover .... 3·75
HD15 Containing ten 1st Class stamps (No. 1666) with "You've Won!" etc on inside back cover .... 3·75
Nos. HD14/15 sold at £2.50 each and were initially only available from branches of W.H. Smith and Son. They were issued in connection with a competition in which the prizes were Paddington Bear kites. The booklets were not available from Royal Mail philatelic outlets until 4 October 1994.

1995 (10 Jan). *Multicoloured laminated cover as Type HA8 (75 × 48 mm) with stamps printed on the cover in bright orange-red by Harrison.*
HD20 Containing ten 1st Class stamps (No. 1664) .... 3·75

1995 (10 Jan). *Multicoloured laminated cover as Type HA8 (75 × 48 mm) with stamps printed on the cover in bright orange-red by Questa.*
HD21 Containing ten 1st Class stamps (No. 1666) .... 3·75

1995 (10 Jan). *Multicoloured laminated cover as Type HA8 (75 × 48 mm) with stamps printed on the cover in bright orange-red by Walsall.*
HD22 Containing ten 1st Class stamps (No. 1666) .... 3·75
Nos. HD20/2 were sold at £2.50 each.

Type HD23

1995 (14 Feb). *Multicoloured laminated cover as Type HD23 (76 × 50 mm) showing card, Thorntons chocolates and box, printed by Walsall. Inscribed "DETAILS INSIDE" on yellow tab at right.*
HD23 Containing ten 1st Class stamps (No. 1666) .... 3·75
No. HD23 was sold at £2.50.

Type HD16

1994 (20 Sept). *Multicoloured laminated covers as Type HD16 (76 × 50 mm) printed by Walsall. Inscribed "ORDER YOURS INSIDE" on yellow tab at right.*
HD16 Containing ten 1st Class stamps (No. 1666) with "DO NOT OPEN UNTIL....." on front cover .... 3·75
HD17 Containing ten 1st Class stamps (No. 1666) with "KEEP IN TOUCH" on front cover .... 3·75
HD18 Containing ten 1st Class stamps (No. 1666) with "HAPPY BIRTHDAY" on front cover .... 3·75
HD19 Containing ten 1st Class stamps (No. 1666) with "What's Happenin'?" on front cover .... 3·75
Nos. HD16/19 were sold at £2.50 each.

Panes of 20 1st Class Stamps

Type HE1

1993 (19 Oct).   *Multicoloured cover as Type* HE1 (91 × 77 *mm*).
HE1   Containing booklet pane No. 1789a .... 7·25
    No. HE1 contains self-adhesive stamps and was initially sold at
£4.80., which was increased to £5 from 1.11.93.

E. Barcode Booklets containing Penny Black Anniversary stamps with barcodes on reverse.

60p. Booklet

Type JA1

1990 (30 Jan). *Laminated cover as Type JA1 (75 × 48 mm) showing Penny Black Anniversary stamp in bright blue. Containing booklet pane. No. 1475l, printed in litho by Walsall.*
JA1 Containing booklet pane No. 1475l .... 5·00
No. JA1 has three edges of the pane imperforate.

80p. Booklets

1990 (30 Jan). *Laminated cover as Type JA1 (75 × 48 mm) showing Penny Black Anniversary stamp in brownish black and cream. Containing booklet pane No. 1476m, printed in litho by Walsall.*
JB1 Containing booklet pane No. 1476m .... 5·00
No. JB1 has three edges of the pane imperforate.

1990 (17 Apr). *Laminated cover as Type JA1 (75 × 48 mm) showing Penny Black Anniversary stamp printed on the cover in brownish black by Walsall containing stamps printed in photo by Harrison.*
JB2 Containing booklet pane No. 1469r .... 4·50
No. JB2 has three edges of the pane imperforate.

£1.50 Booklets

1990 (30 Jan). *Laminated cover as Type JA1 (75 × 48 mm) showing Penny Black Anniversary stamp in bright blue. Containing booklet pane No. 1467l printed by photo by Harrison.*
JC1 Containing booklet pane No. 1467l .... 5·00
No. JC1 hs the horizontal edges of the pane imperforate.

1990 (17 Apr). *Laminated cover as Type JA1 (75 × 48 mm) showing Penny Black Anniversary stamp printed on the cover in bright blue by Questa.*
JC2 Containing ten 15p. (No. 1477) .... 8·00

1990 (12 June). *Laminated cover as Type JA1 (75 × 48 mm) showing Penny Black Anniversary stamp in bright blue. Containing booklet pane No. 1475m, printed in litho by Walsall.*
JC3 Containing booklet pane No. 1475m .... 6·00
No. JC3 has three edges of the pane imperforate.

£2 Booklets

1990 (30 Jan). *Laminated cover as Type JA1 (75 × 48 mm) showing Penny Black Anniversary stamp in brownish black and cream. Containing booklet pane. No. 1469m, printed in photo by Harrison.*
JD1 Containing booklet pane No. 1469m .... 7·00
No. JD1 has the horizontal edges of the pane imperforate.

1990 (17 Apr). *Laminated cover as Type JA1 (75 × 48 mm) showing Penny Black Anniversary stamp printed on the cover in brownish black by Questa.*
JD2 Containing ten 20p. (No. 1478) .... 10·00

1990 (12 June). *Laminated cover as Type JA1 (75 × 48 mm) showing Penny Black Anniversary stamp in brownish black and cream. Containing booklet pane No. 1476n, printed in litho by Walsall.*
JD3 Containing booklet pane No. 1476n .... 8·00
No. JD3 has three edges of the pane imperforate.

F. Barcode Booklets containing Greetings stamps with barcodes on the reverse.

£2 Greetings Booklet

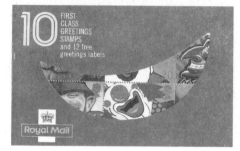

Type KX1
(Illustration reduced. Actual size 135 × 85 mm)

(Des Michael Peters and Partners)

1990 (6 Feb). *Greetings Stamps. Cover printed in scarlet, lemon and black as Type KX1 (135 × 85 mm). Containing booklet pane No. 1483a, and a separate sheet of 12 greetings labels.*
KX1 "Smile" design cut-out showing stamps inside .... 16·00

Greetings Booklets containing No Value Indicated stamps

Type KX2

(Des T. Meeuwissen)

1991 (5 Feb). *Greetings Stamps. Multicoloured laminated cover as Type KX2 (95 × 69 mm). Containing booklet pane No. 1536a, including twelve special greetings labels in a block (3 × 4) at right, attached by the selvedge.*
KX2 "Good Luck" charms design .... 9·00
No. KX2 was initially sold at £2.20, which was increased to £2.40 from 16.9.91.

Type KX3

(Des Michael Peters and Partners)

1991 (26 Mar). *Greetings Stamps. Multicoloured laminated cover as Type KX3 (95 × 69 mm). Containing booklet pane No. 1550a, including twelve special greetings labels in a block (3 × 4) at right, attached by the selvedge.*

KX3   Laughing pillar box design . . . .   3·25
   No. KX3 was initially sold at £2.20, which was increased to £2.40 from 16.9.91 and to £2.50 from 1.11.93.

Type KX4

(Des Trickett and Webb)

1992 (28 Jan). *Greetings Stamps. Multicoloured laminated cover as Type KX4 (95 × 69 mm). Containing booklet pane No. 1592a, including twelve special greetings labels in a block (3 × 4) at right, attached by selvedge.*

KX4   Pressed Flowers design . . . .   3·50
   No. KX4 was initially sold at £2.40, which was increased to £2.50 from 1.11.93.

Type KX5

(Des Newell and Sorell)

1993 (2 Feb). *Greetings Stamps. Multicoloured laminated cover as Type KX5 (96 × 60 mm). Containing booklet pane No. 1644a and pane of twenty special greetings labels in a block (5 × 4), both panes attached by a common gutter margin.*

KX5   Children's Characters design . . . .   3·50
   No. KX5 was initially sold at £2.40, which was increased to £2.50 from 1.11.93.

Type KX6

(Des Newell and Sorell)

1994 (1 Feb). *Greetings Stamps. Multicoloured cover as Type KX6 (96 × 60 mm). Containing booklet pane No. 1800a and pane of twenty special greetings labels in a block (5 × 4), both panes attached by a common gutter margin.*

KX6   Children's Characters design . . . .   3·50
   No. KX6 was sold at £2.50.

G. Barcode Booklets containing Christmas stamps with barcode on the reverse.

Type LX1

(Des A. Davidson)

1990 (13 Nov). *Christmas. Multicoloured laminated cover as Type LX1 (95 × 60 mm). Containing booklet pane No. 1526a, attached by the selvedge.*
LX1   £3.40, Snowman design ....   9·00

1991 (12 Nov). *Multicoloured laminated cover as Type LX1, but 95 × 70 mm. Containing booklet pane No. 1582b attached by the selvedge.*
LX2   £3.60, Holly design ....   8·25

Type LX6

(Des Yvonne Gilbert)

1994 (1 Nov). *Multicoloured laminated covers as Type LX6 (95 × 60 mm), showing different Nativity Play props. Panes attached by selvedge.*
LX6   £2.50, containing ten 25p. stamps (No. 1844) ....   3·75
LX7   £3.80, containing twenty 19p. stamps (No. 1843) ....   5·75

Type LX3

(Des Karen Murray)

1992 (10 Nov). *Multicoloured laminated cover as Type LX3 (95 × 70 mm). Containing booklet pane No. 1634a attached by the selvedge.*
LX3   £3.60, Santa Claus and Reindeer design ....   7·50

1993 (9 Nov). *Multicoloured laminated covers as Type LX3, but 95 × 60 mm, each showing Santa Claus and Reindeer. Panes attached by selvedge.*
LX4   £2.50, containing ten 25p. stamps (No. 1791) ....   5·00
LX5   £3.80, containing twenty 19p. stamps (No. 1790) ....   7·50
    No. LX4 was only available from Post Offices in the Central T.V. area and from philatelic outlets.

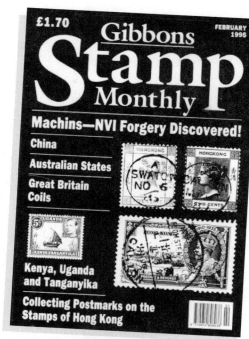

A Catalogue For Every Collection

Whether you collect by country, reign or by theme, Stanley Gibbons have a wide range of highly acclaimed guides to assist you. Compiled by our team of international experts all catalogues contain numerous illustrations, accurate descriptions and postal histories and up to the minute market prices, to provide maximum assistance in building your collection.

BRITISH COMMONWEALTH 'PART 1'

The definitive British Commonwealth guide published in August in two casebound volumes and widely acclaimed as the 'industry standard' for collectors and dealers alike. The latest editions include extra pages of illustrations, descriptions and postal history, new issues, post office booklets and an exclusive philatelic directory.

GREAT BRITAIN SPECIALISED SERIES

The winner of many international awards, this detailed authoritive work is split into five volumes from Queen Victoria to Elizabeth II, each clearly laid out with thousands of illustrations and explanatory notes to cover everything the GB specialist could need.

COLLECT BRITISH STAMPS

A simple colour and checklist of British stamps from 1840 to the present day. Published annually in November Collect British Stamps is a must for all enthusiasts from beginners to experts.

FREE 32 PAGE BROCHURE
TEL: 01425 472363

STANLEY GIBBONS

• THE COLLECTOR'S CHOICE •

VISIT OUR SHOWROOM 399 STRAND, LONDON Open 6 days a week

IMPORTANT MESSAGE TO GREAT BRITAIN CONCISE COLLECTORS!

You know how important it is to have the very latest edition of the Great Britain Catalogue to refer to. If you would like us to notify you as to when the next edition will be published (entirely without obligation!), just fill in the form below and send it to the Stanley Gibbons Advance Information Service. If there are any other Stanley Gibbons Catalogues in which you are interested, these may also be included on the form.

To: The Advance Information Service,
      Stanley Gibbons Publications,
      5 Parkside, Christchurch Road,
      Ringwood, Hampshire BH24 3SH

Please notify me of publication dates of new editions

of ....

Name: ....

Address: ....

             ....

             ....